SEVEN CENTURIES
OF SERVICE

Margaret Bolton

SEVEN CENTURIES OF SERVICE

The Lives of the Dukes of York
1385 to today

Margaret Bolton

CheckPoint
Press

SEVEN CENTURIES OF SERVICE

The Lives of the Dukes of York, 1385 to Today

ISBN-13: 978-1-906628-49-9

Published by CheckPoint Press

www.checkpointpress.com

CONTENTS

ACKNOWLEDGEMENTS

This volume would have been impossible without the excellent research facilities supplied by the Wellcome Institute in London and the University of Kent at Canterbury. I am also grateful to staff at the National Library of Australia and the British Library and at the London Library for their assistance in finding materials.

I would like to thank HRH The Duke of York for his encouragement of this project. I hope that he will be pleased with the result and that the work will be successful in raising funds for the On Course Foundation (Registered Charity Number 1136618) of which he is Patron.

INTRODUCTION

It has been said that the first duty of a Queen or Princess of Wales is to produce "an heir and a spare." In ordinary circumstances the heir goes on to become king; but what happens to 'the spare'?

In his youth, 'the spare' is feted and cherished as a potential future leader. As a young man, he may have more freedom than his older brother, resulting in the development of a more popular personality and attracting a certain glamour-interest from the wider community. But as the years go by and the king has his own sons and even grandsons, that situation can change dramatically. Instead of being the honoured second in line, 'the spare' gradually moves down the list of royal influence, leading people to question his existence, even accusing him of being a 'hanger on' or 'a parasite' on the public purse.

Being Duke of York is a difficult role and it is not one for which anyone ever applies. It is a gift of the sovereign and stems from being born into the royal family. If the title holder does nothing but go hunting and visit the theatre, he is seen as indolent, yet the occupations open to him are few. If he attempts a career in business or the creative arts he is accused of exploiting his position. If he engages in diplomacy, he is seen as interfering in politics. If he goes into the armed services, he risks being killed. If he spends his time in charitable work, he gets criticised for not having a 'proper job.' In short, he cannot win.

This volume seeks to explore how the fourteen holders of the title have each tried to redefine the role in line with their own circumstances. It considers the unique perspective on history that their position affords them, being at the very heart of power and yet not exercising it.

*　*　*

The first Duke of York was Edmund, born in 1341, brother of the Black Prince and one of the earliest Garter Knights. He served his country in various wars and acted as a counsellor to the young Richard II. Edmund's son Edward, the second Duke, was the archetypal medieval prince being a successful soldier, an able diplomat and a poet. In 1399, deciding that Richard's reign had descended into intolerable tyranny, both father and son played a crucial role in the accession of Henry IV. Their decision to support Henry would change the course of history.

The third Duke, Richard, born 1411, was one of the most important political leaders of his day, being the instigator of the Wars of the Roses. His son, the fourth Duke, was the first title holder to succeed to the throne. Edward spent just nine weeks as Duke of York before becoming King Edward IV.

The fifth Duke, another Richard, was one of the Princes in the Tower. Being murdered as a child he made no contribution in his own right to the country, but his death in 1483 was highly instrumental in the accession of the Tudor dynasty.

Henry VIII became the sixth Duke in 1494 and his colourful character was evident even in childhood. He was the only Duke of York to face a serious pretender to the title, namely Perkin Warbeck.

The arrival of the Stuarts from Scotland in 1603 resulted in the union of the titles of Duke of York and Duke of Albany, the traditional names given to the second sons of the kings in each country; England and Scotland respectively. Charles I was the first holder of that combined title and his frequent bouts of ill health meant that many of his contemporaries doubted he would ever grow up. His son James was the most controversial Duke of York in history. In his youth he was a national hero, winning battles at sea and on land, as well as fighting the Great Fire of London of 1666 and rebuilding the royal navy. Yet he also carried on a treasonable correspondence with the French king, accepting money to try to subvert the laws and dispense with parliament.

In 1716, the title was bestowed on Ernest of Hanover, the only time it has been given to the brother of the reigning monarch and to a prince who did not live in England. He did, however, serve with British forces earning the admiration of the Duke of Marlborough for his bravery. He was also a keen music lover and on holiday one year met a keyboard player whom he thought showed some promise – George Friedrich Handel.

His successor was Edward, the engaging younger brother of George III. Edward's naval career was cut short when the government decided his life was too valuable to risk and so he became a roving ambassador. He was the first royal to do the Grand Tour and the best travelled for several generations. He died in 1767 at the age of just twenty-eight, leaving, it was said, hundreds of women to mourn and weep.

The eleventh Duke was Frederick, born 1763, uncle of Queen Victoria and brother to the Prince Regent. He was a man who was no stranger to scandals but he was a serious man too. His reforms of the army were essential to the victories gained in the Napoleonic War and his interest in medical research had a significant impact on the defeat of smallpox and improved understanding of mental health.

The most recent Dukes have experienced a different political world to their predecessors. They have not been expected to get involved in politics or to lead national armies, although both Prince Albert and Prince Andrew have served in war. In fact, their immediate predecessor George, who served as Duke of York during 1892-1901, remains the only Duke to survive to adulthood who never fought in battle. The lives of these latter three Dukes have revolved around charity work and in encouraging

British business. Prince Albert for example, was very active in the Industrial Welfare Society from 1919 which did so much to promote better working conditions, and Prince Andrew has laboured hard for International Trade and Investment. All three Dukes have travelled extensively and taken a keen interest in the Commonwealth. With more than five hundred engagements in a typical year, the current Duke is one of the busiest members of the royal family and the Community Initiative he founded in 1997 continues to do valuable work in the north of England.

*   *   *

For almost seven hundred years, these fourteen men have done their best to serve their country according to the requirements of the world about them. Some have achieved more than others but all have tried to live up to the responsibilities placed on them as princes.

In 1774, the eleventh Duke, who was only ten years old, speculated on the need for him to "labour hard" to render the hopes of all about him "effectual" and to care for the people who depended on him. He wrote "I hope I shall gain both the love and esteem of the public which are my most ardent wishes."

Some Dukes have succeeded in that more than others. This is the story of their triumphs and disasters through good times and ill.

NOTES AND ABBREVIATIONS

CCR	Calendar of Close Rolls
CGPW	Correspondence of George, Prince of Wales
CPR	Calendar of Patent Rolls
CSPD	Calendar of State Papers, Domestic
CSPS	Calendar of State Papers, Spain
CSPV	Calendar of State Papers Relating to English Affairs in the Archives of Venice
HMC	Royal Commission on Historical Manuscripts
L&P	Calendar of State Papers of King Henry VIII
LCKG	Later Correspondence of King George III
PROME	Parliamentary Rolls of Medieval England

Dates throughout are shown using the modern calendar. Thus, the year begins on January 1st. Dates on letters or for historical events are given according to the calendar in use at the time and place in question. (Gregorian or Julian calendars).

Footnotes generally provide full details of the source except for certain documents which exist in numerous editions. References to the diary of Samuel Pepys, for example, do not apply to any particular published copy but simply refer to the diary entry date. Similarly with the diary of John Evelyn and the letters of Horace Walpole. This is deliberate to enable interested readers to follow up references more easily.

Where readily available English translations exist, these have been used. Otherwise, the translations from original documents in French and Latin are my own. I am indebted to assistance from Julia Wells and Fiona Harvey for their help with German and the advanced Latin. Original spelling and punctuation throughout has been modernized.

At various points in the text, reference is made to modern equivalents of money. This is a very complex area and readers are advised to consult www.measuringworth.com which was the source of these figures.

THE MEDIEVAL DUKES

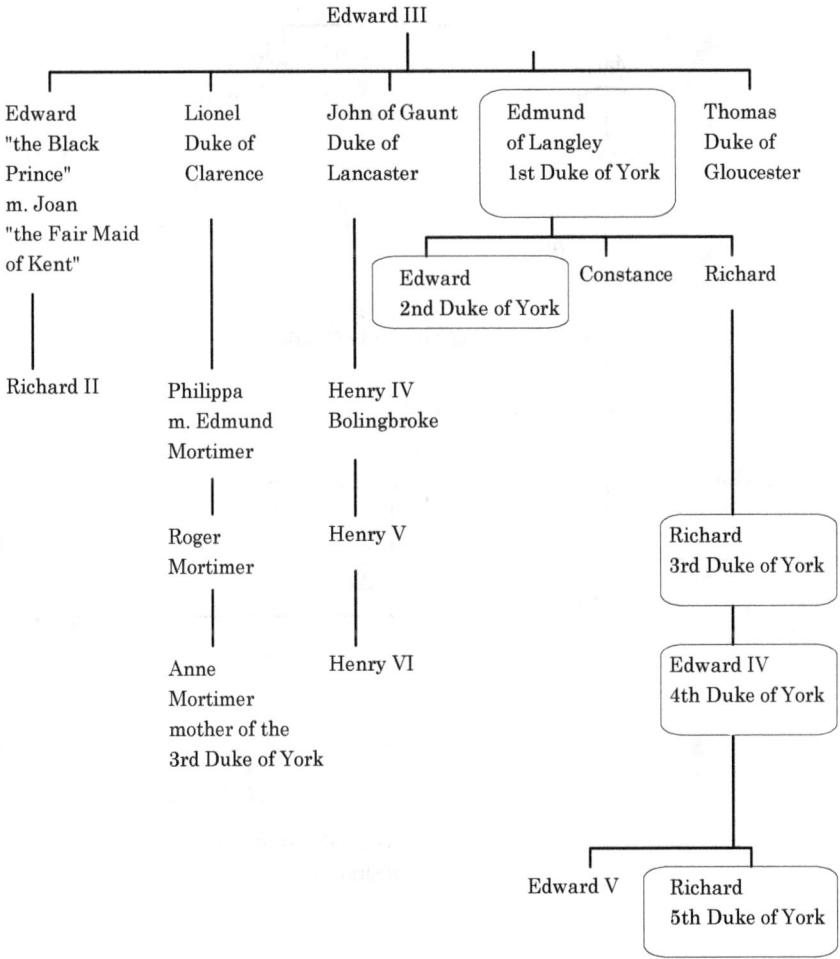

Edward III

| Edward "the Black Prince" m. Joan "the Fair Maid of Kent" | Lionel Duke of Clarence | John of Gaunt Duke of Lancaster | Edmund of Langley 1st Duke of York | Thomas Duke of Gloucester |

Edward 2nd Duke of York   Constance   Richard

Richard II

Philippa m. Edmund Mortimer

Henry IV Bolingbroke

Roger Mortimer

Henry V

Richard 3rd Duke of York

Anne Mortimer mother of the 3rd Duke of York

Henry VI

Edward IV 4th Duke of York

Edward V   Richard 5th Duke of York

The "princes in the Tower"

THE EARLY MODERN DUKES

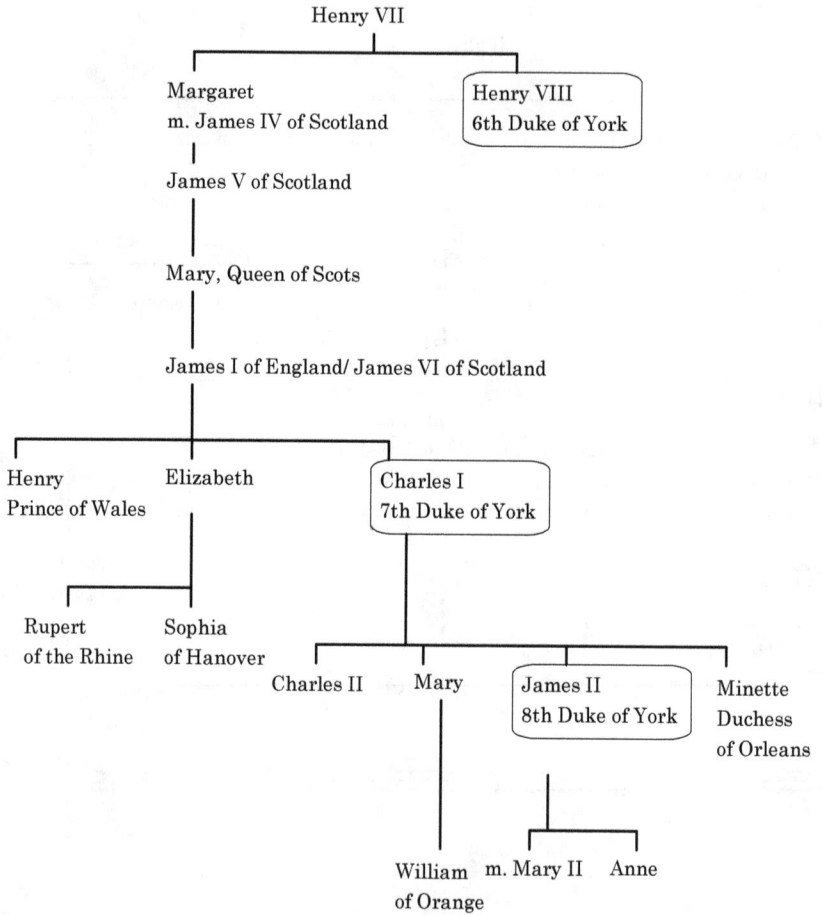

Henry VII
- Margaret
  m. James IV of Scotland
- Henry VIII
  6th Duke of York

James V of Scotland

Mary, Queen of Scots

James I of England/ James VI of Scotland
- Henry
  Prince of Wales
- Elizabeth
- Charles I
  7th Duke of York

- Rupert
  of the Rhine
- Sophia
  of Hanover

Charles II   Mary   James II
8th Duke of York   Minette
Duchess
of Orleans

William m. Mary II   Anne
of Orange

THE HANOVERIAN DUKES

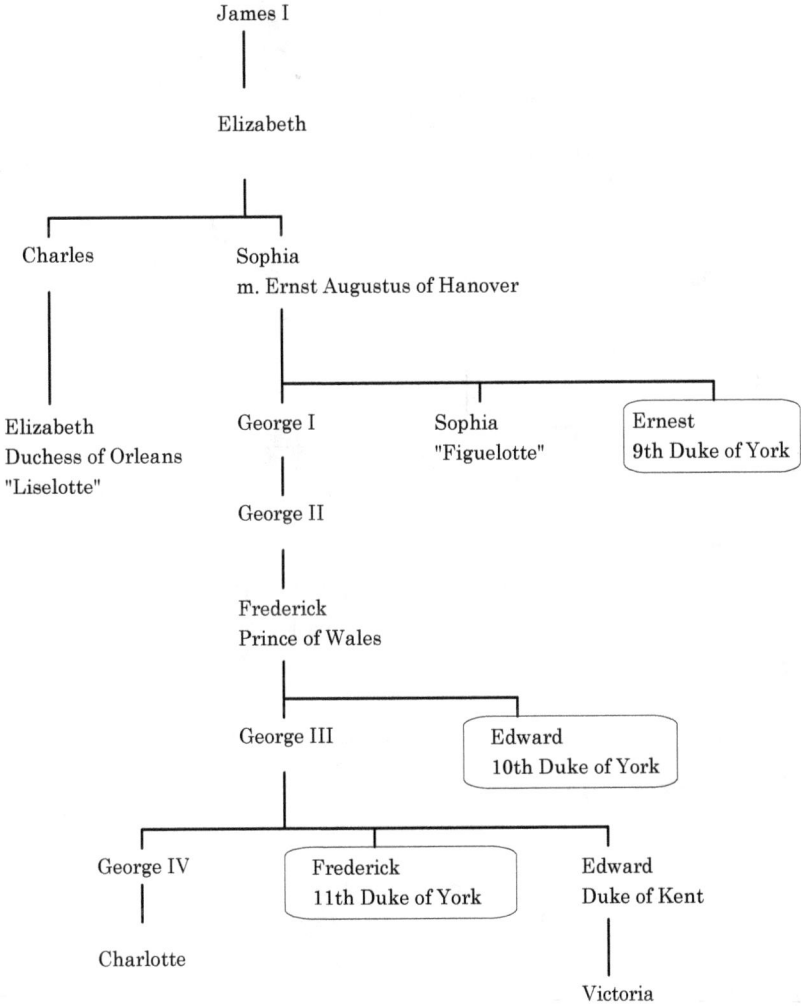

James I
|
Elizabeth
|

Charles   Sophia
m. Ernst Augustus of Hanover

Elizabeth   George I   Sophia   Ernest
Duchess of Orleans   "Figuelotte"   9th Duke of York
"Liselotte"
|
George II
|
Frederick
Prince of Wales

George III   Edward
10th Duke of York

George IV   Frederick   Edward
11th Duke of York   Duke of Kent
|
Charlotte   Victoria

THE MODERN
DUKES

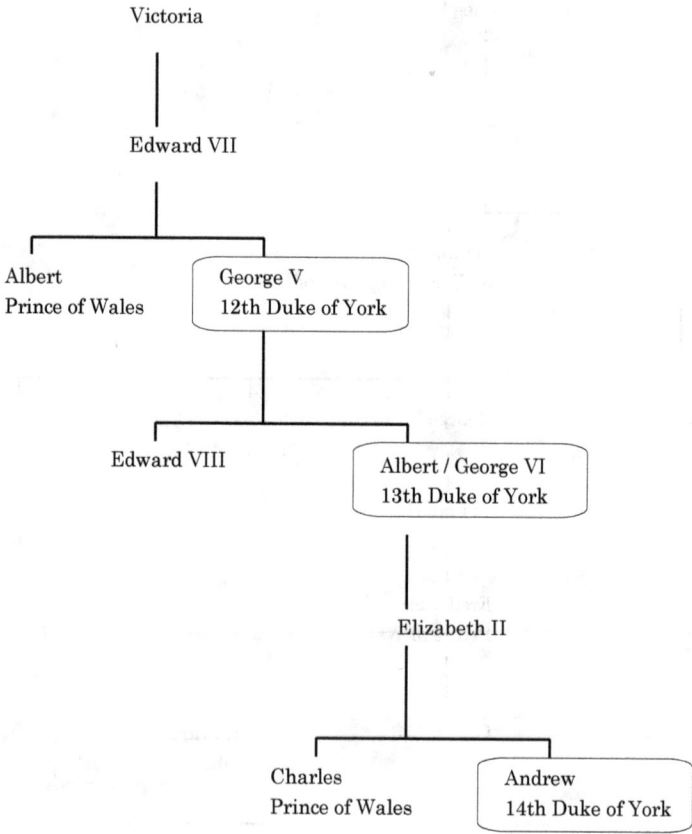

Victoria

Edward VII

Albert
Prince of Wales

George V
12th Duke of York

Edward VIII

Albert / George VI
13th Duke of York

Elizabeth II

Charles
Prince of Wales

Andrew
14th Duke of York

The principal office of history I take to be this:
to prevent virtuous actions from being forgotten,
and that evil words and deeds should fear
an infamous reputation with posterity

Tacitus

Edmund

1341-1402

Duke of York 1385-1402

Had a heart courageous as a lion[1]

When Ian Mortimer wrote his biography of Edward III, he entitled it *The Perfect King*. To contemporaries, Edward was the ideal medieval king. He was a brilliant military strategist and brave leader who led his men through a variety of battles to enhance the wealth and reputation of England. He was a chivalrous prince with a virtuous and beautiful wife to whom he was devoted. He produced five legitimate sons who survived to adulthood which safeguarded the monarchy. He loved justice and raised the status of Parliament, showing himself willing to listen to the desires of his people. He was also a builder, a patron of the arts and a man who understood the importance of public relations. For his son Edmund it was bound to be a hard act to follow.

Edmund was born at King's Langley on 5th June 1341.[2] His father appears to have been there at the time and stayed with his wife for a week afterwards. The new prince was baptised by the Abbot of St Albans who stood godfather along with the Earls of Surrey and Arundel. Edward III ordered great celebrations including a joust for which he had a new

---

[1] Chandos Herald, *The Life and Feats of Edward the Black Prince* translated by Francisque Michel (London, 1883) p.267

[2] H. T. Riley (ed.), *Ypodigma Neustriae a Thomas Walsingham* (London, 1876) p.253

breastplate made and more than a dozen shields in gold and silver leaf.[3]

The next few years of Edmund's life were spent in the royal nursery in the care of Joan of Oxenford, Agnes Markaunt and Matilda Plumpton, who had previously served his eldest brother.[4] Closest to him in age was John of Gaunt who was sixteen months his senior. Those two brothers remained close all their life. Three years older was Lionel. The eldest son was Edward, known to history as the Black Prince, who was just days away from his eleventh birthday when Edmund was born. There were also two sisters, Isabella who was almost nine and Joan who was six. Five more children were to follow Edmund, two who died in infancy, two sisters who died of plague in 1361 and a further son Thomas who was fourteen years his junior. It is likely that the elder brothers, including Edmund, hardly knew Thomas for they were grown up and left home before he could even walk.

The first recorded public appearance of Edmund is at a tournament held in Windsor in June 1348 to celebrate the birth of his brother William, a child who only survived a few weeks.[5] Attending with his brother John in matching purple velvet outfits, the spectacle must have been very exciting for the seven year old Edmund and seems to have inspired a lifelong interest in such events.[6] He inherited this from his father who loved pageantry and did his best to promote the chivalric ideal. It was Edward III who had announced in 1344 his intention of establishing a Round Table in honour of King Arthur and who had built an enormous home for said structure at Windsor.[7] Although this project was never completed, it is virtually certain that the royal children used the building for their own games, playing the parts of heroic knights and damsels in distress. Just a few years later, Edward III founded the Order of the Garter which was also based at Windsor.

Another early reference to Edmund is in the Anonimalle Chronicle which records a visit made by him and his brothers John and Lionel to St Mary's Abbey, York on 11th June 1349.[8] The chronicle was written by a monk at the said abbey who noted that the plague was raging in the city at the time. Across England, the Black Death was said to have killed between a third and half of the population and it is curious that Edward III sent three of his

---

[3] Ian Mortimer, *The Perfect King,* (London, 2006) p.467

[4] CPR 1358-61 p.168

[5] He had appeared as a babe in arms at banquets, ref W M Ormrod 'The royal Nursery' in *English Historical Review* (2005) vol CXX no 486 p.411

[6] Mortimer op.cit. p.259. King David of Scotland, then a prisoner of Edward III, was also there.

[7] See Julian Munby et al., *Edward III's Round Table at Windsor* (London, 2007) for full details including results of an archaeological dig on the site.

[8] V H Galbraith (ed.), *The Anonimalle Chronicle* (Manchester, 1927) p.30

four sons living at the time into such a dangerous environment. Their sister Joan had already died of the plague and the royal surgeon perished a month before.[9] Perhaps, unaware of the situation in York, he believed the north would be safer. Whatever the motive, the boys requested permission to join the monks for prayers and this was granted so that they might all pray for deliverance from the pestilence together.

In September 1354, Edmund was removed from his mother's care. It is unknown where he went. His older brother John had been placed in the household of Edward, the Black Prince, but there is no evidence that Edmund joined him there. As a mark of this event, Edward III appointed a steward and a receiver to manage the households and property of Edmund and his brother John. They were to keep the properties in good repair, ensure that rents were properly collected and to purchase necessary food and clothing for the young princes.[10] Later, they were appointed their guardians.[11]

Whilst Edmund studied to be a knight, his father continued his campaigns in France and Scotland. In 1356, as the King planned another invasion, the Black Prince went into battle at Poitiers earning not only a spectacular victory but capturing the King of France whom he subsequently brought back to England as a prisoner. It is likely that the teenage Edmund felt he was missing out on the action. His brother, admired for his exploits at Crécy when he was just sixteen, was now lionised as the ultimate hero. Every boy wanted to be like the Black Prince, Edmund included, but he remained living apart as he pursued his studies.

He may have been overseas in the winter of 1357-58 since he is the only member of the royal family who was not recorded as visiting his ailing grandmother in this period.[12] He was certainly home in May 1359 when his brother John married the heiress Blanche of Lancaster and his thirteen year old sister Margaret married the similarly aged Earl of Pembroke. Ten days later, a celebration tournament was held at Smithfield. It was an event which demonstrated a great deal about the personality of Edward III and his relationship with his sons. The chronicler John of Reading described how people were invited to see the Mayor and Aldermen of London take on all comers in a variety of feats of horsemanship and knightly combat. To the audience's surprise, the Mayor and Aldermen did extremely well, defeating

---

[9] Philip Zeigler, *The Black Death* (London, 1969) p.159

[10] CPR 1354-58, p.137, 154

[11] CPR 1354-58 p.458

[12] Edward Bond 'Notices of the Last Days of Isabella, Queen of Edward the Second' in *Archaeologia* vol 38 (1854) pp.453-69

all who came against them. At the end of the three day tournament, the victorious London team removed their helmets and were revealed to be the King and his four eldest sons, Edward, Lionel, John and Edmund.[13] No doubt the audience cheered and the princes revelled in the joke and the chance to display their prowess alongside their famous father.

Toward the end of 1359, the eighteen year old Edmund had his first experience of war when his father decided to invade France again in pursuit of his claim to the throne which he had through his mother.[14] On 28th October 1359, the King and the same four sons departed from Sandwich and Dover in Kent, for Calais.[15] Froissart said it was one of the largest armies ever to leave England with over five thousand men-at-arms and even more archers. He added that the baggage train contained over six thousand carts each of which were drawn by four horses. Edward had gone prepared with tents, ovens, grinding wheels, forges and even small boats so that men could go fishing. He had also taken thirty falconers and over a hundred greyhounds and hunting dogs. [16] After a brief rest, the army prepared to march through Artois and into Cambrésis, Edmund and John travelling as part of the Black Prince's own battalion. On the early part of their journey, they found little succour due to famine so they moved into Picardy which was more fertile and replenished their supplies. Since this was an invasion, the English naturally simply took what they wanted, burning homes and farms and generally laying waste wherever they went. They continued on toward Rheims where the Black Prince set up his court at St Thierry. One of their party carried out a raid on Achery where three thousand butts of wine were found which were promptly delivered for the consumption of the royal family and other lords.

The siege of Rheims continued for a couple of months. Rheims was too well-defended to attack and the French declined to be drawn into open battle with the English. In the end, the King decided that it would be more politic to move on toward Paris. The army travelled via Tonnere which they attacked, taking the town together with its large wine stores but not the castle. A number of assaults were made on Paris and the outlying villages but despite the English wreaking considerable destruction they failed to take Paris. They moved south west with the intention of travelling slowly toward Brittany where they would stay for the harvest before returning for

---

[13] J. Tait (ed.), *Chronica Johannis de Reading*, (Manchester, 1914) p.132

[14] Edward III's mother, Isabella, was daughter of Philip IV of France and should have become Queen in 1328 but, as French law prohibited a female ruler, her uncle was chosen instead. Edward argued that this was wrong and he was rightful King of France.

[15] *Anonimalle* op.cit p.44

[16] John Froissart, *Chronicles of England, France, Spain and the adjoining countries*, trans Thomas Johnes (London, 1839) volume 1 p.279

another attack on Paris. However, the French approached with an offer of a peace treaty. According to Froissart, Edward III was opposed to any such idea and only agreed to it following an incident called by chroniclers, "Black Monday." On this day, April 13th 1360, there was "such a storm and violent tempest of thunder and hail which fell on the English army that it seemed as if the world was come to an end. The hailstones were so large as to kill men and beasts and the boldest were frightened."[17] It is unlikely that the English were cowed by a storm even if some of them saw it as God's judgment on them, but the terms offered were good and Edward III decided to accept.

Edmund, now nineteen, was recorded as a witness to the peace treaty agreed at Brétigny on 8th May and at its ratification in Calais on 24th October of the same year.[18] The peace was seen as a great triumph by the English who came home rejoicing for a full two weeks of feasts and celebrations. Six months later, alongside his brothers Lionel and John, Edmund was created a Knight of the Garter, the thirty-seventh such man to join the order. The Black Prince had been the very first member.[19] As a mark of his new status as a warrior-prince and junior diplomat, plans were made to give Edmund his own household as would befit his rank. On 24th November 1361, Edmund's receiver William de Ford was ordered to "hire tailors, broiderers, sadlers, carpenters, masons, hewers of stone, tilers and other workmen for his works in London and elsewhere."[20]

Another reason for Edmund's promotion in status was that the King had decided it was time for him to marry. Princes were rarely allowed a choice of bride. They were expected to make dynastic alliances to strengthen the country's defences or to bring wealth or trade to the country. An exception had been made a year before for the Black Prince whose choice of Joan Holland seems to have been a love match. Edmund, however, was not to be so fortunate. The bride selected for him was Margaret of Flanders.[21] Margaret was then aged twelve, already a widow, and heiress to the wealthy territories of Holland and Brabant. Not only was the intention to provide Edmund with an independent income, it would ensure that England had a loyal base which it could use in any future invasion of France and a potential source of further soldiers for its European campaigns. Edmund's

---

[17] Froissart, op.cit. p.283. Walsingham says the storm was of unusual severity but adds that the harsh winter also took its toll on men and horses. see *Ypodigma Neustriae* op.cit. p.259

[18] *Anonimalle* op.cit p.48

[19] Peter Begent and Hubert Chesshyre *The Most Noble Order of the Garter – 650 Years* (London, 1999) p.309

[20] CPR 1361-64 p. 121

[21] CPR 1361-64 p.167. The commission to negotiate the marriage was appointed on 8th February 1362.

brother John was entrusted with leading the negotiations.

1362 was declared a year of jubilee by Edward III and on 13th November, he gave three of his sons new titles. Lionel became Duke of Clarence, John became Duke of Lancaster and Edmund became Earl of Cambridge.[22] The chronicler Thomas Walsingham records that Edmund's rise followed a petition of the Commons which was made in the English language, clearly regarded as unusual at the time when the majority of documents were in Latin or Norman-French.[23] Edmund was by then twenty-one. It is unclear how he was spending his time at this period. The Black Prince was in Aquitaine, Lionel in Ireland and John was dividing his time between his new wife and family and carrying out official business. Edmund had properties in Yorkshire and Lincolnshire to tend and he was reported to be keen on hunting. The chronicler John Hardyng later said: "When all the lords to council and parliament went, he would to hunt and also to hawking."[24] Hardyng is not a reliable guide and almost certainly never met his subject but Edmund was made keeper of the royal hawks almost forty years later and his son wrote a book on hunting which suggests that his enjoyment of the sport was true.[25] He also enjoyed music and tournaments for official records show payments made to him for his services in hiring minstrels for such events.[26] Nonetheless, it is evident that Edmund was under-employed during these years. He had been brought up to be a soldier and the peace with France must have been rather frustrating.

Also unsettling for him was the situation with regard his marriage. Negotiations had not gone as smoothly as had been hoped. Margaret's grandfather had been a first cousin of his father, both being grandchildren of Edward I, and there were allegations that since that meant she and Edmund were second cousins once removed, they were too closely related to wed.[27] Such obstacles could normally be circumvented by the payment of certain monies to papal officials, but Edmund had a problem here. The Pope was French and France was naturally opposed to the idea of England controlling the lands on their northern border. Nonetheless, on 24th September 1364, John and Edmund travelled to Flanders to meet with

---

[22] *Calendar of Charter Rolls, 1341-1417* (HMSO 1916) p.174

[23] Ypodigma Neustriae op.cit p.307

[24] Henry Ellis, *The Chronicle of John Hardyng* (London, 1812) p.340

[25] Edmund received the appointment on October 10th 1399 from Henry IV, see CPR 1399-1401 p. 31

[26] *Issue Roll of Thomas de Brantingham* (London, 1835) p. xxxix which relates to a tournament held in the summer of 1362 at Smithfield.

[27] Margaret's first husband had been her second cousin, Philip of Burgundy, which was a closer relationship but that had caused no concern. Joan Holland was the first cousin of the Black Prince's father.

Margaret's father, Count Louis, and to bring him back to Dover where their father was waiting.[28] Arriving on 12th October, a marriage agreement was signed a week later declaring that Edmund and Margaret would marry in Bruges in February 1365 and that Edmund would inherit and later rule Flanders, Brabant, Holland, Zealand and Friesland.[29] In return, Edward would send troops, no doubt under the command of John and Edmund, to assist Louis in his efforts to regain Burgundy. In the end, no troops were sent, the pope did not grant the dispensation and the wedding was postponed ever further back. At the start of 1366, Edmund and the Bishop of Ely went to Flanders again to try to resolve the situation but they were not allowed to see or speak to Margaret.[30] The plans to give Edmund a major fiefdom of his own were abandoned.

1366 did, however, see the resumption of Edmund's military career when he and John were sent to join the Black Prince's latest campaign which was in Spain.[31] The Spanish campaign had its origin in the treaty agreed between Castile and England in 1363 to which Edmund had been a witness.[32] Since that date, King Pedro had been deposed by his illegitimate brother Henry of Trastamara. Pedro decided to ask his ally for assistance and the Black Prince agreed to lead an army with the goal of restoring him. John and Edmund sailed to France just after Christmas 1366 and went to join the Black Prince in Gascony, stopping only en route to pay their respects to the Princess of Wales and her new born son who was later to rule as Richard II. In February, the army passed through the Pyrenees and across Navarre to Vittoria where the first action occurred. The English under Gaunt held the high ground but were defeated by a larger body of Castilian forces. The army moved on toward Navaretta where a major battle took place on 3rd April. The Spanish unseated English knights with the stones from their slings but then the English archers began to respond with

---

[28] Hardyng op.cit. p.331 says Edmund was at the Battle of Auray on the 8th October 1364 where he fought alongside his brother John, describing the scene thus:

Were never two better knights then they in deeds

That better fought upon a field afore

It was but grace that they escaped there

They put themselves so far forth in the throng

That wounded were they both full sore, no less

This account is clearly impossible and demonstrates the caution needed regarding Hardyng as a source.

[29] Anthony Goodman, *John of Gaunt*, (London, 1992) p.44

[30] F. S. Haydon (ed.), *Eulogium (historiarum sive temporis)* (London, 1860) vol 3 p.237

[31] *Eulogium op.cit* p.333. It might be noted that neither Froissart nor Chandos Herald mention Edmund being on this expedition though Froissart listed many other lords and Chandos Herald was present. There is, however, no record of Edmund being in England during this period.

[32] CPR 1361-64 p.299.

such force that it caused panic in the Spanish ranks. As the Black Prince cried out "advance banners in the name of God and St George" hand to hand combat followed with short swords, daggers and two handed spears. The English were victorious and the Black Prince led the triumphant procession into Burgos where he and King Pedro celebrated Easter two weeks later. In thanksgiving, Pedro gave the Black Prince a huge ruby or spinel which today adorns the front of Britain's Imperial State Crown.

Edmund returned to England that summer and stayed there for almost two years, mostly resident in London. He was experiencing problems. His northern estates in Yorkshire were becoming subject to regular attacks. Not only were men poaching his deer and pheasants, they were attacking his staff and refusing to pay rent. When Edmund's staff impounded livestock in return for non-payment of dues, the locals were releasing them and imprisoning his staff in their place. Tenants who did pay were being threatened by their neighbours so that a number were abandoning their land altogether leaving Edmund further without income. Unsurprisingly, new tenants did not want to move in and the estates were collapsing in a state of lawlessness. With staff being regularly wounded to the point where they were unable to work again, action was needed. Edmund appointed a new receiver for his properties on the generous salary of £10 per annum with added benefits of clothing, fuel, transport and hay for his horses as well as a promise of one per cent of every pound which he safely delivered to Edmund in London. Nonetheless, Edmund was forced to borrow £1320 from his father and to surrender the deeds on all his lands in Yorkshire and Lincolnshire until he had returned every penny, something which appears to have taken him about four years.[33]

His financial concerns made him keen to return to military life. Although a lord faced the expense of raising and equipping a group of men-at-arms and archers, one of the reasons for war was the prospect of monetary gain either through new territory or loot or through ransoms. Figures for the Rheims campaign show how a substantial profit could be made just on horses.[34] In the summer of 1369, Edmund departed England with his brother in law John Hastings, Earl of Pembroke, to join the Black Prince in Aquitaine taking a force with them of four hundred men-at-arms and four hundred archers. Chandos Herald reports that the Black Prince had

---

[33] CPR 1367-70 pp.51, 141, 210. CPR 1370-74 p.3. CCR 1369-74 p.77 Edmund surrendered his lands on 6th March 1369. The sum borrowed would be worth around £270,000 today.

[34] Andrew Ayton *Knights and Warhorses* (London, 1999) p.265 shows that Lionel for example, took 126 horses valued at £8 7s each, lost 6 but returned with 164. The Black Prince took 1369 at a value of £8 10s each, lost 395, but returned with 2114. Edmund, as the poor younger brother, took only around a hundred horses and they were valued at £6 12s 6d but came back with 145.

requested aid from Edward III and he had chosen to send Edmund "who had a heart courageous as a lion."[35] By this time, the Black Prince was ill, almost certainly with recurrent dysentery and fevers which he had contracted shortly after leaving Spain.[36]

The Black Prince gave Edmund and Pembroke three objectives, the first of which was to destroy Périgord and lay siege to Bourdeilles. For two months, their army of three thousand men remained encamped around the town. There were daily skirmishes but Bourdeilles remained well defended. Then someone, possibly Edmund, had an idea. On the next occasion when the French sent men out to fight in the fields, the English would make a good show but then retire as if defeated. Whilst the French followed them to where the main army would be waiting, the cavalry would move up to cut off the possibility of a French retreat. The manoeuvre was completed successfully and following a two hour battle, all the French soldiers were killed or captured. Edmund rode in behind his banner and accepted the town's surrender. Leaving a new governor and detachment of archers to defend it, Edmund then returned to Angoulême to await new orders. [37]

His next target was Roche-sur-Yon which was held on behalf of the Duke of Anjou. The castle was well defended with a good store of provisions. The governor saw no reason to fight so Edmund and his army surrounded it and settled down to wait. Each day, food and supplies were brought to the English from Poitiers. Those inside the castle realised that they had no chance of escape. The English were well armed, with cannons and siege engines, and there were thousands of them. An agreement was therefore made that if the French did not come to the relief of the castle within a month and thus provide battle for the English, the governor would surrender it. The English even agreed to pay him for the supplies if he left them behind in good condition. The French did not come and so the governor surrendered and he and his men were allowed to depart in peace. Edmund returned to the Black Prince to report he had gained his strategic objective, had additionally boosted supplies, and all this with scarcely any loss of life.[38]

The third assignment was to relieve the castle of Belle Perche which the Duke de Bourbon was besieging with a large body of men and heavy artillery. Edmund and his army camped nearby and waited for two weeks.

---

[35] Chandos Herald, *The Life and Feats of Edward the Black Prince*, translated by Francisque Michel (London, 1883) p.267

[36] ibid. pp260-62 where the Black Prince is stated to be bedridden and unable to help himself.

[37] Froissart, vol 1, op.cit., pp 416-417

[38] ibid. p.420

The Duke made no move so Edmund sent Chandos Herald to offer the Duke battle in any location which he should choose. The Duke refused to fight or be distracted from his siege. Edmund hereupon decided it would be better to surrender the castle and withdraw his men than face the costs of succouring it for months. On a given signal, he led his army and the garrison from within Belle Perche away behind banners and music, and took them back to his brother whose reaction is not recorded.[39]

The final action which Edmund saw in that campaign was at Limoges, a town traditionally held by the English but which had recently fallen to the French. The Black Prince not only wished to regain the town, but to punish the inhabitants who had given in, he felt, too easily. For this campaign, John of Gaunt joined the army with his men and the Black Prince travelled too, although he had to be carried in a litter. What happened next is not totally clear. Froissart describes a massacre of more than three thousand men, women and children but there is no other contemporary evidence of slaughter on this scale. Had there been, it might be supposed that the French would have proclaimed it as an example of English brutality for generations. Chandos Herald says "all were slain or taken" but he almost certainly meant the armed men rather than the inhabitants.[40] Whatever the exact numbers of dead, it was a bloody battle and Edmund was in the thick of it engaging in hand to hand combat with the knight, Sir Hugo de la Roche. At the end, everything of value was looted and the town destroyed by fire. The Black Prince and his army returned to Angoulême where he learnt that his eldest son had died. By now increasingly ill, the Black Prince agreed to be taken back to England with his wife and only surviving son Richard. John of Gaunt was left in charge whilst Edmund escorted his brother and family home. Given the hero worship in which he had held his older brother, it must have been very difficult for him.

Edmund was now thirty years old and unmarried. His elder brother Lionel had died as had his two younger sisters and his mother. The King decided it was time that Edmund settle down and chose for his bride Isabella, the youngest daughter of King Pedro of Castile. Despite the English restoration of her father, Pedro had subsequently lost his throne and his life to Henry of Trastamara. Pedro had left no sons just three daughters, one of which was in a nunnery. Edmund's brother, John, had already married the elder sister Constance and he was claiming to be the rightful King of Castile through her. By marrying the youngest, Edmund was supporting the English royal family's desire to maintain influence in Spain which it regarded as strategically important both to safeguard the

---

[39] ibid. pp 440-442

[40] See Froissart vol 1, op.cit., pp 453-454 and Chandos Herald op.cit p276

trading routes to the Mediterranean and to prevent it being used as a base to attack English territories in southern France. The marriage took place at Wallingford on 11th July 1372. Just a month later, Edmund joined his father and brothers at Sandwich in Kent ready for another invasion of France. Bad weather prevented them reaching their goal and the expedition was abandoned in October enabling Edmund to return home to his new wife.

Some nine months after the wedding, Edmund's first son was born. The date is unknown but his father gave him the valuable lordship of Tyndale in April 1373 and his brother John gave him a silver cup in the same month.[41] The child was named Edward after the King and the Black Prince. Two further children were to be born. Constance who seems to have been born in 1376[42] and Richard who was named after Edmund's nephew, by then King of England.

Those early years of marriage were a busy time for Edmund. In 1374, he was sent to Brittany as King's Lieutenant where he was to remain until a truce was signed with France in the summer of 1375. [43] He returned to England only briefly but was back in France a few weeks later for diplomatic negotiations. His campaign, although short, seems to have been quite successful. He took St Pol de Léon, Brest and laid seige to Quimperlé which he probably would have taken but for the truce.[44] On 12th June 1376, Edmund was made Constable of Dover Castle and Warden of the Cinque Ports, a position of both responsibility and honour which he was to hold until 1st February 1381. Five months later, Edward III gave him an allowance of £667 per year. Perhaps these marks of favour from the king toward the end of his life were a sign that he thought Edmund had finally matured. Previously, his attention had been very much focussed on the Black Prince and John of Gaunt.

On 21st June 1377, Edward III died. He had ruled England and much of France for fifty years. The Black Prince had died a year before so the new

---

[41] *CPR* 1370-1374, p.289. See also Sydney Armitage-Smith (ed.), *John of Gaunt's Register* vol 2 (London, 1911) p.191. This proposed date fits also with Edward's stated age when his father died.

[42] Two factors argue against a birth in 1375 which some have suggested. Firstly, Edmund was overseas and secondly, there is no evidence of any gift from John of Gaunt whose accounts end in December 1375. Given the child was named after Gaunt's wife, it is certain there would have been a gift.

[43] Thomas Hardy, *Syllabus of the Documents relating to England and other Kingdoms contained in the collection Known as "Rymer's Foedera"* (London, 1869) vol 1 p.470. The appointment was dated 24th November 1374.

[44] *Ypodigma Neustriae* op.cit p.321. Walsingham states that Edmund took the Castle of Auray at this time which could account for the confusion of Hardyng who had suggested Edmund fought there in 1364.

King was his son Richard, aged just ten. Although not appointed formally as a guardian or counsellor, Edmund was expected to play his part in guiding the young boy in his new role. His first concern, however was defence of the realm for the French had decided that the death of Edward III and accession of a child was too good an opportunity to miss. The truce had expired and so they sent their men to harry the southern coast. Winchelsea, Rye and Hastings were all attacked and burnt, a direct assault on Edmund for all of these places were connected with the Cinque Ports. The *Vita Ricardi* describes how after the Isle of Wight was attacked, the French continued to attack the coast for three months: "They burnt many places and killed, especially in the southern areas, all the people they could find. As they met with little resistance, they carried off animals and other goods as well as several prisoners. It is believed that at this time, more evils were perpetrated than had been caused by enemy attacks on England during the previous forty years."[45] Edmund's role put him in the front line. Richard had been King for just nine days when he issued his first orders to his uncle "to take order for the safety and defence of the coast of Kent against the French who have landed in great force and to compel all of that county to resist them."[46] He was presumably pleased by his service for Edmund started to get more regular grants and favours than he had from his father.

In 1378, Edmund was sent to France again with his brother John for an offensive in Brittany. The English laid seige to St Malo but despite their heavy artillery and policy of destroying all the land in the vicinity, the inhabitants remained firm and succeeded in killing many of the attackers. The French sent their own army to break the siege and Froissart tells the story of how the English and French were camped on opposite sides of the river. Each day, both armies would come out in battle array and yell insults at one another and posture their bravery. After some days of this with the French refusing to cross and fight, Edmund lost his temper. Fully armed and mounted, he shouted "Let them who love me follow me for I am going to engage!" upon which point he rode into the river brandishing his sword. It is unknown how many men followed him for the sudden turn of the river meant that Edmund had to beat a hasty retreat under covering fire of the English archers. John of Gaunt was said to have commented proudly: "See how my brother ventures. He shows the French by his example his willingness for the combat but they have no such inclination."[47] Froissart was not there but it sounds the sort of memorable event which would have been discussed and laughed about for some time afterwards and it fits into

---

[45] Thomas Hearne (ed.) *Vita Ricardi* (London, 1729) p.2. The same chronicler noted how one Frenchman had said that they would not have dared make such raids had John of Gaunt been made king. p.3

[46] CPR 1377-81 p.7.

[47] Froissart, op.cit. p.548

what is known of Edmund's rather hasty temper. Edmund might have been approaching forty but he lacked his brother's judgment.

Edmund's own skills as a military commander were to be put to the test in 1381 when he was appointed to lead an army to Portugal which was under threat from Castile. Portugal had asked for English help and it was agreed to provide this in return for Portugal supporting John of Gaunt's claim to the Castilian throne and for Edmund's eight year old son being married to the King of Portugal's heir. As John was busy in Scotland, Edmund was to be sent ahead with a small force and John would follow with a larger one as soon as practical.

Edmund left England in July 1381. Froissart later claimed that news of the peasants' uprising had reached them at Plymouth and they took to sea despite bad weather in order to secure their safety. Together with his wife and son, Edmund arrived in Lisbon on 19th July. King Fernando greeted them with open arms and expensive gifts of jewels and silks. The agreement had been that the Portuguese would supply the English with horses because it had been impossible to take animals on such a long sea journey, and it was reported that Edmund had been given the biggest and best black horse in the country. Ordering the English not to attack without his consent, Fernando then sent the English into their quarters to await instructions. It was then that the problems began. At first, the English were content to wait but as the weeks passed by, the soldiers grew restless. Not only were they not being allowed to fight but they were not being paid. A number of the men started to take things into their own hands. The Portuguese chronicler Don Fernando Lopes recorded: "They began to behave not as men who had come to defend the country but as if they had been called in to destroy it and to visit upon its inhabitants as much suffering and dishonour as possible. They started to stray out and around the city and its districts killing, robbing and raping and treating everyone with such haughtiness and contempt as if they were their mortal enemy whom it was necessary to dominate." The same chronicler added that Edmund's response was to demand that each householder buy a pennant with a red background and white falcon and display it in their garden. If they did not, his soldiers would rob them.[48] Even the English chronicler Thomas Walsingham admitted that the English had not behaved well. He denied that they had plundered their hosts but said they had raped so many wives and daughters that they were universally detested.[49]

---

[48] Derek Lomax and R J Oakley trans. *The English in Portugal* (Warminster 1988) pp75-77. The falcon was Edmund's own emblem.
[49] H. T. Riley, *Chronica Monasterii S. Albani* vol.II (Rolls Series, London, 1863) p.83

Relations between the English and Portuguese soured rapidly. A few soldiers decided to carry out some raids of their own hoping that their prowess might strengthen the resolve of King Fernando for the fight. However, Fernando just became more nervous. There was no sign of John or his army and the Portuguese were heavily outnumbered. English numbers had been decimated by disease and the Portuguese remained unhappy that the English had only sent a fraction of the men they had requested. Two hundred extra men had actually been sent but they had been captured by the Castilians.[50] A concerned Edmund sent the constable of his army back to England to obtain news of the promised reinforcements.[51]

In June 1382, eleven months after their arrival, the English finally came face to face with the Castilian army at Caia. Fernando had his army assembled and estimated there were four times as many of the enemy. He decided to go behind Edmund's back and sue for peace. When Edmund found out, he was apoplectic with rage and his fury at what he regarded as Fernando's betrayal lasted for years. He felt humiliated and said that if he still had the number of men which he had with him on arrival, he would have led the English against Castile on his own, notwithstanding the odds.[52] Without John's army, however, an attack would have been suicidal.[53] Edmund withdrew his army and his family and sailed for home arriving back late in the autumn of 1382. A series of prosecutions for mutiny followed which ran for two years, those involved being told they had "behaved so rebelliously that he could not accomplish the object of the expedition".[54]

The failure of the expedition to Portugal seems to have had some wider implications for Edmund. When John of Gaunt died in 1399, he included in his will a statement that his executors were not to make any payments toward the cost of the 1381 exhibition. Clearly there remained financial tension over the event although it appears that John, like Walsingham, blamed Parliament for not supporting Edmund with arms and money rather than Edmund himself. In Froissart, Edmund is described as stating that his goal had only ever been reconnaissance and that his brother agreed that withdrawal had been the only option given the Portuguese refusal to fight and lack of additional men. Edmund said: ""Happen what may, I have done

---

[50] P. Russell, *English Intervention in Spain and Portugal* (London, 1955) p.327

[51] L. C. Hector and Barbara Harvey (ed.), *The Westminster Chronicle* (Oxford 1982) p.31.

[52] Lopes, op.cit. p.149. The reduction of the army can be seen by the fact that it took just over forty ships to send them out but barely twelve to get them home, see Russell op.cit p.343

[53] *Chronica Monasterii S. Albani* vol I op.cit. p.453. The *Westminster Chronicle* says that the Castilians were themselves unwilling to fight a son of the illustrious Edward III, op.cit. p.31

[54] CPR 1381-85 p.256, 349, 494

nothing that I repent of."[55]

It appears also to have damaged Edmund's relationship with his wife. Their final child, Richard, was probably conceived while they were abroad and when Isabella died, she left financial care of him to his godfather, Richard II rather than Edmund.[56] Thomas Walsingham described Isabella as a sensual, lustful, self indulgent and worldly woman who had greatly enjoyed life before her repentance late in the day.[57] Shirley commented on a copy of Chaucer's *Complaint of Venus* that many believed she had enjoyed an affair with the notorious John Holland, infamous for murdering Stafford and for impregnating Gaunt's own daughter and that this poem was about it.[58] If such was the case, the poem certainly left little to the imagination. Venus or Isabella was described as the "well of beauty, lust, freedom and gentleness" and the "causer of pleasure." Of her meetings with Mars, it said:

The great joy that was betwixt them two
When they met, there may no tongue tell
There is no more but unto bed they go

Isabella's will, made in 1392, included valuable gifts to John Holland. Her son Edward also referred to presents he had received from Holland in his own will of 1415.[59]

The next few years were relatively quiet for Edmund. He was not involved in military action until 1385 when, together with his brothers John and Thomas, he accompanied Richard II on his invasion of Scotland.[60] It was a short summer campaign only notable for one event. On 6th August, just as they were about to cross the border, Richard chose to raise Edmund and Thomas to the status of dukes. The grant was formally ratified by Parliament in October when the King, duly seated on his throne, presented Edmund with a copy of the charter together with his ducal cap, sword and

---

[55] Froissart, op.cit. pp.686, 694. Froissart knew Edmund so may have discussed the event with him.

[56] Prob 11/1 ref 295/25226 at the National Archives, Kew. By implication, Richard was a child when his mother made her will late in 1392 so he must have been several years younger than his siblings. Supporting this is the fact that payments were not to commence until 1395, see CPR 1391-96 p.245. Also, he played no part in the events of 1397-1399 which would suggest he was still a minor. Isabella's decision to make the King his guardian may indicate Edmund was not Richard's father or reflect her concern over Edmund's ability with money.

[57] Chronica Monasterii S. Albani vol II op.cit. p.215

[58] John Scattergood 'Chaucer's complaint of Venus' in *Essays in Criticism* July 1994 vol 44 issue 3 p.174.

[59] Prob 11/1 ref 295/25226. Holland was the King's half brother.

[60] The *Westminster Chronicle* notes that John led the vanguard with Thomas whilst Edmund led the main army with the militarily inexperienced Richard. op.cit p.125

gold coronet. The charter declared:

> A country resplendent with noblemen who excel not only in mature counsel but in vigour of arms is certain to be happy....Considering which, in our royal deliberation, we directed our thoughts to consider the person of our magnificent and most beloved uncle Edmund Earl of Cambridge whom we have sought to raise to the height of honour since the very beginning of our reign for the eminence of his merits and especially his accomplishments in arms and the wisdom of his counsel...and therefore when recently we entered the kingdom of Scotland and displayed our conquering standards against the enemy, we raised our aforementioned uncle to the rank of duke to reward his outstanding merits and former services, assigning to him the title and name of Duke of York.[61]

To enable him to live in a manner befitting his new status, Richard gave Edmund an annuity of £1000 and Isabella one of £100.[62] By comparison with his brothers who had both gained huge incomes through their wives, Edmund remained the least wealthy of the brothers[63] but he did seem to have become the King's favourite uncle. In June 1385, just before they departed to Scotland, Richard gave Edmund a further maintenance allowance for his family which suggests that they were mainly resident at court.[64] Richard probably wanted a family. His own father had been an invalid for most of his childhood and had died when he was just nine. He had no surviving brothers or sisters and his mother was shortly to die. The opportunity to spend time with an uncle who shared his interest in hunting and jousts,[65] a warm hearted aunt and their children who were like surrogate siblings was probably quite attractive.

Of immediate concern the following year was the prospect of a French invasion. Edmund was sent to raise a thousand archers from Chester and bring them to the King in London, a far greater number than any other lord was asked to provide.[66] In the event, there was no invasion but the costs of

---

[61] PROME, October 1385 item 14. The *Westminster Chronicle* p.127 says that Edmund was initially created Duke of Canterbury not York but this probably reflects a transcription error. Edmund's previous title was Earl of Cambridge which in Latin is Cantubrigie.

[62] CPR 1385-89 p.38, 62. In modern money, an income just under half a million pounds.

[63] As an example of this, the size of the retinues taken to Scotland that year can be compared. John brought 4000 men, Thomas 1600 and Edmund 800. See N. B. Lewis 'The Last Medieval Summons of the English Feudal Levy 13 June 1385' in *English Historical Review* vol CCLXXXVI (January 1958) pp.17-18

[64] CPR 1381-85 p.574

[65] James Gillespie, 'Richard II's knights' in *Journal of Medieval History* vol 13 no 2 June 1987 pp.143-60

[66] CPR 1385-89 p.217

the defence strategy together with those of the last ten years had resulted in a lot of discontent. In 1386, chiefly at the encouragement of Edmund's brother Thomas, Parliament demanded that a commission be set up to investigate royal expenditure. They were granted virtual carte blanche to go everywhere and to demand to see any documents they wished.[67] Both Edmund and Thomas were appointed to the commission together with men such as the Archbishops of Canterbury and York, the Earl of Arundel, William Wykeham and Lord Cobham. John of Gaunt was excluded because he was overseas having left for Spain in July of that year.

The Commission was to play a crucial role in the reign of Richard II. At the time, the King was almost twenty and he was in debt. His crown had been given in pledge to the City of London from whom he had borrowed £4000.[68] Nonetheless, he and his favourites resented the appointment of a group of investigators to pry into his private affairs. The commission was not simply to consider how monies voted by Parliament had been spent but to review every grant of money or land or employment which the King had made since he came to the throne, to verify the whereabouts of each of the royal jewels and to look at the income being generated by each acre of royal land. Richard was legally a minor and powerless to prevent its appointment but there is evidence that his favourites did all they could to hinder its progress. Documents and witnesses were moved to less accessible areas and a range of other sudden emergencies meant that officials did not have time to answer all the commissioners' questions.

Although it is clear that Thomas was the leader of those seeking a commission, it is not certain exactly what role Edmund played in proceedings. As uncle of the king, Parliament was bound to appoint him as the most senior member of the Lords. Was Edmund active in trying to promote its business or did he find excuses to avoid meetings? Did he try to protect Richard's interests or was he supporting his brother?

In 1387, Richard took legal advice on whether Parliament had any right to appoint a commission with such powers. This worried Thomas and Arundel who had threatened Richard with deposition if he would not agree to the appointment of the commission.[69] The judges declared that the commission was derogatory to the rights of the King and that those who served on it were traitors and within a few weeks, the country stood on the brink of civil war. At this point, it became obvious that Edmund was on the King's side. When Thomas, Arundel and the Earl of Warwick appeared on

---

[67] ibid. p.244
[68] ibid. p.246
[69] G. H. Martin (ed.) *Knighton's Chronicle* (Oxford 1995) p.361

the outskirts of London with a large army[70] Richard sent Edmund to try and negotiate with them. Edmund said they should leave their armed men behind and talk to the King. Thomas agreed on condition that those whom he accused of treason should be arrested and charged and that he himself should be allowed to return to his men. Meantime, Richard and his other advisors hatched a plot to ambush the three lords. Although this plan was not carried out, the situation continued to deteriorate.

Richard decided to spend Christmas in the Tower of London which was then a regular royal palace. Thomas, now joined by the retinues of Mowbray and Bolingbroke, entered London "accoutred for war" and received a welcome from the city. Edmund continued his role of go-between. The chronicler of Westminster Abbey said of Edmund and the Archbishop of Canterbury: "day in and day out they painstakingly conducted negotiations between the parties to secure peace and harmony."[71] Thomas, however, would not be placated. The five lords entered the Tower fully armed and with hundreds of soldiers in their wake. As Thomas later admitted, for two or three days, his plan was to depose the King and the only reason that it failed was because his party could not agree on an alternative.[72] Instead, they forced Richard to agree to their demands in fear of his life.

Early 1388 saw the start of the Parliament which would be known to history as the Merciless Parliament. Thomas was in the ascendancy and he and his cronies accused many of the King's closest friends and supporters of being traitors to the country and an evil influence on Richard. In accordance with the process of the time, they appealed to the King in Parliament to hear their argument, which meant they became known as the Lords Appellant. It was an extremely bitter struggle.

Edmund's loyalty to the King was shown particularly in the case regarding Simon Burley whom the Lords Appellant charged with multiple counts of treason. Amongst the accusations were that he had intervened to prevent the commission doing its work and discouraged the King from accepting the advice of Parliament. Richard II was very attached to Burley, who had been his tutor and had carried him on his shoulders at his own coronation.[73] Burley had a long history of service with the Black Prince and he had fought alongside both Edmund and John in a number of campaigns. He had been one of those entrusted by Richard's mother with overseeing her affairs following her death. He was not popular with the people because he

---

[70] ibid. p.403

[71] Westminster Chronicle op.cit. p.225-227

[72] PROME September 1397 item 14

[73] Westminster Chronicle op.cit 417

was considered to be vain and trying to act in a manner above his station, but neither Richard nor Edmund considered he was guilty of treason. Even Parliament, which spent almost two months discussing his case and which was packed with Thomas' supporters, failed to convict him on fifteen of the sixteen charges. The Westminster Chronicle tells of how the argument became personal on 27th April as Edmund, increasingly angry with the whole affair, rose in full Parliament and stated that Burley had always been totally loyal to the King and country and added that he would be prepared to take on anyone who wished to dispute this in personal combat. Such a declaration from a senior member of the royal family, must have caused a sensation. Thomas promptly rose from his seat and offered to take his brother on saying that Burley was indeed a traitor. Edmund called Thomas a liar and prepared to commence an assault, but as the two men squared up to one another ready to fight, the King himself intervened and forced them to sit down again.[74]

Eventually, Burley was convicted on just the eighth charge that he had conspired the destruction of those who sought to establish the commission and he was executed on May 5th 1388. It was said that Queen Anne had spent three hours on her knees begging Thomas to amend the sentence. Edmund and Lord Cobham had also tried making a further appeal to the Commons but to no avail.[75] Thomas later admitted that he had threatened Richard with loss of his crown if he refused to let the execution go ahead.[76]

Richard II never forgave his uncle Thomas for this act. Four years later, he built Burley a new tomb. John of Gaunt, who had remained overseas and missed the events of the Merciless Parliament, contributed toward this same tomb suggesting that he shared Richard's faith in the man.[77] It is likely that Edmund also contributed though his accounts have not survived. For his efforts to save Burley, Richard made two grants to Edmund of land in Rutland, just a week after the exchange in Parliament. The King appreciated Edmund's support.[78]

Edmund's role in the Merciless Parliament was unique and complex. For many of the sessions, he sat as the King's representative in the Lords. Blake, Usk, Beauchamp, Salisbury and Berners were all tried and condemned to death by him. He clearly, therefore, shared Thomas' views

---

[74] ibid. p.329

[75] ibid. p. 331

[76] Revealed in Thomas' confession, see PROME September 1397 item 7.

[77] Anthony Goodman, *John of Gaunt*, (London, 1992) p.150

[78] CPR 1385-89 p.434,451

about some of the men accused.[79] Edmund was not, however, overawed by Thomas as his defence of Burley showed. When it came to the judgment on Brembre, he again argued that no crime had been committed which was worthy of death.[80] It was a mark of Edmund's evident independence that when the Appellants appointed their team to oversee Richard in future, he was not one of those selected.

In the aftermath of all the executions and turmoil, Richard retreated to spend the summer hawking with Edmund and his son Edward. In May 1389, following Easter spent at Langley with Edmund and his family, Richard declared himself of age and removed Thomas and Warwick from his council.[81] Records show that Edmund remained his most regular advisor over the next four years, though it is impossible to know how far Richard took his advice or the nature of his counsel.[82] Marks of favour were extended to his son such as the grant of the Earldom of Rutland in 1390. Family tensions with Thomas remained until John of Gaunt returned. John may not have been Richard's favourite uncle but he was a very experienced leader and his presence tended to keep Thomas in check. John's efforts to try and restore family relations included a hunting break for the King and Queen, and both his brothers in August 1390 at his estate in Leicester.[83]

An example of the family working together came in the summer of 1392 when Richard decided to take steps against London which he felt had supported Thomas and the Appellants in the 1386-88 crisis. Withdrawing himself from the city and setting up court in Edmund's estate of Stamford, he appointed Edmund and Thomas to investigate "notorious defaults in the government of the city of London."[84] Richard ordered the arrest of certain officers and Edmund arranged hearings to be held at Aylesbury with himself in the chair.[85] Further hearings followed through July before the commission made their decision that the city was guilty. Richard demanded the surrender of their liberties, a report on the city's money, and set a fine of £100,000.[86] London decided that the best way to win Richard's favour back was to make a lavish show of loyalty to him and to his uncles. John of Gaunt received £400 and Edmund and Thomas both £200. The King thought that

---

[79] *Westminster Chronicle* op.cit. p.285, 293

[80] ibid p. 311

[81] Chronica Monasterii S. Albani vol II op.cit. pp.181-182

[82] Chris Given-Wilson, *The Royal Household and the King's affinity*, (Yale, 1986) p.184

[83] Knighton op.cit p.535

[84] CPR 1391-96 p.166

[85] CCR 1391-96 p.9

[86] For a full account of this dispute see F. R. H. Du Boulay, *An Age of Ambition*, (London, 1970) pp.173-199. There is a contemporary letter describing how the gifts were made to the uncles in M.D. Legge *Anglo-Norman Letters and Petitions* (Oxford 1967) pp.185-186

he might feel forgiving for £10,000. As money and gifts changed hands, Richard did indeed pardon the city and the fines were reduced or cancelled, but the incident demonstrated the way he worked.

The same year also saw Edmund getting involved in one of the policies closest to Richard's heart – peace with France. Richard was not a warrior king in the way that his father and grandfather had been. He saw war as expensive and disruptive. Many of his subjects, especially Thomas, disagreed and found the idea of making peace with England's long standing enemy distasteful. Richard was, however, determined and he sent John to France to negotiate, together with both Edmund and his son. Edward may have proved naturally talented in this field for he served on a large number of international diplomatic expeditions over the years. Froissart gave an account of the meeting at Amiens, of how the English arrived with an enormous train of horses, were sumptuously dressed and feted magnificently. The talks failed because the English refused to surrender Calais but the peace process went on.

Two days before Christmas 1392, Edmund was widowed. Isabella, around thirty-seven, was buried at Langley where she most likely had died.[87] Isabella had made her will only a couple of weeks before so it is reasonable to imagine she died after a short illness. She left seven books which was a sign of wealth at the time and also indicative of an interest in learning. They included two Bibles, two prayer books or primers, a volume full of tales highlighting vices and virtues and a story book about Sir Lancelot of the Round Table.[88] She also left various items of jewellery and precious stones including a tablet of jasper from King Leo of Armenia who had spent a lot of time at the English court.[89] The crown which she had from her days in Castile, she left to her eldest son, Edward. A devotional image was left to Thomas' wife.

A mystery surrounds Isabella's tomb. As Enoch Powell noted in 1965, the heraldry on the tomb shows it was built for Richard II. His arms are on the end flanked by those of St Edward the Confessor and St Edmund, the same two saints who appear with him on the Wilton Diptych. At the other end are the arms of two of his half brothers whilst down one long side are the arms

---

[87] She was not buried until 14th January according to Walsingham. A three week delay for a funeral would be unusual if the death occurred in the same place but it is likely that they waited until the Christmas feast was over so that the King, who had been at Eltham that year, could attend. Richard had spent Christmas 1391 with Edmund at Langley, see *Westminster Chronicle* op.cit pp.485, 515

[88] K B McFarlane *The Nobility of Later Medieval England* (OUP 1973) p.236-237. The original will is at the National Archives, see Prob 11/1 ref 295/25226

[89] He was in England in 1385, 1389 and 1392.

of his father in law in Bohemia and then four of Edward III's sons. The shields are carved in order so that after Edward the Black Prince come the arms of Lionel, then Edmund and Thomas. John of Gaunt's arms are missing and have been replaced by Isabella's, thereby making her arms and Edmund's central on the panel.[90] The tomb cannot have been carved before 1385 as Edmund and Thomas are shown as dukes and it must have been made before 1397 as it shows Henry Bolingbroke as Earl of Derby not Duke of Hereford. Richard's wife, Queen Anne, died in 1394 and records of payments show her tomb took from 1395 to 1399 to build. Assuming Richard ordered his own tomb at the same time so they could be buried together, Isabella must have been laid to rest in a different tomb originally. It seems unlikely that Edmund would have chosen to have John's arms removed rather than used to replace those of Bohemia. It is possible that following Richard's deposition, the tomb was redundant and Edmund claimed it but it is more likely that the switch was made by Edward. Richard was buried originally at Langley, quite probably in this tomb, but he was moved in 1414 to Westminster. Edward at this date was responsible for supervising building works at Westminster Abbey.[91] It would appear that he took the opportunity of moving his parents and sister in law[92] into what he thought was a better tomb than his father had provided.

It is unknown when Edmund remarried but it was almost certainly within the year. His choice of bride was indicative of the close links which he had with the King for he married Richard's niece, Joan Holland, a lady young enough to be his daughter. Richard's mother had been married before she wed the Black Prince and four of the children of that prior union had survived into maturity. Joan was the daughter of Richard's eldest half brother and sister of Eleanor, wife of Roger Mortimer.

In 1394, Richard decided to lead an expedition to Ireland taking Edmund's son Edward with him. Traditionally, when the king left the country, a regent or Guardian of the Realm was appointed to take his place until he returned. Most commonly, the duty devolved on the heir to the throne regardless of age, or the most senior member of the royal family left in England. In 1394, with John of Gaunt en route to Gascony and Thomas due to travel to Ireland with the King, Edmund was the only one of Edward III's sons left. Richard could have chosen John's son, Henry Bolingbroke or Roger Mortimer who was Lionel's grandson, but he deliberately chose

---

[90] Enoch Powell, 'A King's Tomb' in *History Today,* October 1965, pp.713-716

[91] J.H. Wylie, *The Reign of Henry the Fifth,* volume 2 (London, 1968) p.205

[92] When Edmund's tomb was opened, it was found to contain three sets of bones, his and Isabella's plus another young woman thought to be Anne Mortimer, first wife of his son Richard. See John Evans, 'On Edmund of Langley and His Tomb', *Archaeologia* vol XLVI pp. 297-328 (1881)

Edmund. Did Richard select him because he thought he was a safe pair of hands? Did he see Edmund as his heir? Or was it because Edmund was no longer fit enough to go on expedition? Whatever his motivation, Richard appointed Edmund as Guardian on September 29th 1394.[93] Edmund remained in the role until the following summer, summoning a parliament and handling all matters of state. Richard was clearly happy with the way he had performed his duties for not only did he grant him an addition to his income when he returned but he appointed him to the role again.[94]

It is hard to determine the nature of a person's character across the centuries, particularly when there are no personal papers or financial records and very few eye witness accounts. The most often quoted comment about Edmund is Hardyng's that he was "full of gentleness."[95] This can be misleading for two reasons. Firstly, gentleness in the medieval period meant full of gentlemanly qualities, not meek and mild. Secondly, as has been mentioned, Hardyng almost certainly never met Edmund and if he had, he would have been a child not a confidante. Hardyng was also writing for the York family which meant he was sure to be flattering. This does not mean that what he said was untrue but that it needs to be considered in light of other evidence. The other person who wrote about Edmund was Jean Froissart and he did know him. Froissart was connected with the English court through the 1360s when Edmund was a young man and he met him again when he came on an extended visit in 1395. He notes that Edmund came out to meet him and spoke with him on several occasions.[96] Froissart was keen to get material for his history and to interview people but it is impossible to know what subjects he discussed with Edmund. He does, however, say, that Edmund "interfered little in public affairs and was without malice or guile wishing only to live in quiet: he had beside just married a young and beautiful wife, daughter to the earl of Kent, with whom he spent most of his time." Edmund by now was in his mid-fifties which was old by medieval standards. He may have been hoping to retire to his estates after a lifetime of public service, though this pleasure was not to be permitted to him. Indeed, when Froissart met him in 1395, it was immediately after Edmund's nine month period as Guardian of the Realm.

Froissart goes on to give an account of Thomas' character whom he also knew well. He says: "The duke of Gloucester was cunning and malicious and continually soliciting favours from his nephew Richard, pleading poverty,

---

[93] CPR 1391-96 p.501. For a fuller discussion of the inheritance question, see the chapter on Edward.

[94] ibid. p.656. Edmund was appointed Guardian again in 1396, see CPR 1396-99 p.21, and again in 1399.

[95] Hardyng, op.cit p.329

[96] Froissart vol 2 p. 595

though he abounded in wealth…and he would not exert himself in any way to serve his king or country if he were not well paid for it."[97] He added that Thomas was very keen to see John of Gaunt stay in Aquitaine "for he felt he was too powerful when in England and too nearly allied to the King." That Thomas may have felt that way is something which any amateur psychologist could have guessed. John had been Edward III's right hand man after the Black Prince's health failed and he had consistently held senior roles under Richard. Edmund had grown up with John, served in wars with him, and was very close to him. Thomas was a lot younger and he had missed out on their campaigning years. He had scarcely been a toddler when the Black Prince won the Battle of Poitiers and captured the King of France. His rebellion in 1386-88 may have been inspired by a genuine concern for the kingdom but more likely reflected his need to make his own mark on history and his desire to be taken seriously as a leading member of the royal family, rather than just the young brother. Thomas, whose experience of warfare was limited, was diametrically opposed in his opinions to Richard. The King wanted peace and Thomas did not. As he explained to Froissart, "the people of this country want battle because it is a source of wealth and bold adventure." The King, Thomas continued, "all he wants is to drink, to eat, to sleep, to dance and to skip about with the ladies."[98]

Thomas' dismissive view was remarkably ill informed. If people had thought that they had seen signs of Richard's vindictive streak in his treatment of London in 1392, the events of 1397 were to leave no doubt about his feelings about Thomas and the nature of royalty. Alleging that Thomas, Arundel and Warwick had been plotting against his life – though he offered no evidence in support of this – Richard arranged for all three to be arrested and tried. To ensure that Parliament brought in guilty verdicts on the three, Richard not only ensured that a number of the members elected were loyal to him, but he had Westminster surrounded with thousands of his own Cheshire archers, a highly feared band.[99] To add to the pressure, he ordered his uncles John and Edmund to bring their own armed retinues to London. Thus, Edmund arrived in London with one hundred men-at-arms and two hundred archers "for the comfort of the King."[100]

As in 1388, the process of trial was that a group of senior lords appealed to the King in Parliament against the three lords they said were traitors.

---

[97] ibid p.596

[98] Kervyn de Lettenhove(ed.)*Oeuvres de Froissart*, vol. 16 ed. (Osnabrück 1967) p.3

[99] see PROME, September 1397. At least two chroniclers put Richard's armed guard at four thousand or more, see E. M. Thompson (ed.) *Chronicon de Adam de Usk* (London, 1904) p.154 and *Eulogium* op.cit. p.373

[100] SC 8/221/11038. John's retinue was three times the size of Edmund's. They had also provided men for the meeting at Nottingham in August, CPR 1396-99 p.192

For this action, they became known as the Counter-Appellants. The difference was that on this occasion, the lords were not acting on their own behalf but the King's. As they were to testify afterwards, they had been called into meetings at Nottingham during the summer and simply asked to sign the appeal.[101] The Counter Appellants were led by Edmund's eldest son and included his son-in-law Thomas Despenser as well as Richard's half brother John Holland. John of Gaunt himself was to try the case.

It did not take Parliament long to bring in guilty verdicts on Thomas, Arundel and Warwick and given that the charges related to 1387 when they had raised an army and marched on the King, there was no doubt that they had committed treason. Richard had pardoned them at the time but he now rescinded that. He further declared that all who had been involved in the commission of 1386 were to be considered traitors. Edmund had been part of this but Richard said that he was excusing him "of the execution and exercise of the said commission and all the evil purpose and intent of the same."[102] The Parliament ended with Richard rewarding the Counter Appellants with new titles, which meant Edmund's son became a duke and his son in law an earl.

For Richard, the parliament had been a triumph and his policy of ruling by fear was set to continue. For Edmund, however, it must have been a worrying time. The King may have pardoned him for being part of the 1386 Commission, but he had rescinded other pardons so this was not a long term guarantee. Richard had also spoken of fifty traitors whom he would later name and charge but had declined to name them. Could he be on that list? Thomas had been convicted and only escaped execution because he had died in captivity in Calais. The common word was that he had been murdered. If that was the case, it meant that Edmund's brother had been killed by his nephew. Rumours said that Edward was involved in the death and if he had been, it is certain that Edmund must have known more about this than almost anyone else in England. That put him in a very vulnerable position. Edmund knew too much and Richard had already shown that he had no compunction about removing senior members of the royal family. His son may have been Richard's current favourite but that was unlikely to last forever. Although Edmund remained loyal and close to the King[103], there

---

[101] PROME October 1399 Part 2 items 2, 4, 6 and 8

[102] Adam of Usk, who was present, said that Edmund was so grateful for this favour that he fell on his knees in tears to give thanks to the king, see *Chronicon* op.cit p.156. Edmund's colleague Lord Cobham was, however, arrested and sentenced to death.

[103] Edmund witnessed every royal charter from 1396 to 1398 and almost three quarters of those in the first half of 1399; proof that he remained physically at Court throughout this period. Suggestions later made by people such as Froissart that he had departed to the country were simply not true. See Chris Given-Wilson, 'Royal Charter Witness Lists' in *Medieval Prosopography* (1991) vol 12 part 2 p.68.

must have been a certain unease and tension in the relationship following the 1397 parliament.

Nor was Edmund the only man to be worried. John's son, Henry Bolingbroke, testified to the King's committee in January 1398 that Mowbray had told him in December that Richard was plotting with the earls of Surrey, Wiltshire, Salisbury and Gloucester to destroy Henry and his father and Mowbray himself.[104] Henry naturally told the King that he did not believe that he would ever be party to such an underhand deed and instead accused Mowbray of treason for having told the story, something Mowbray denied. The council, including Edmund and his son, were in a difficult situation. The four earls were members of the council. Gloucester was married to Edmund's daughter. They could not find truth in the story without implicating the King. In the end, they decided to let the issue be settled by combat. Mowbray and Bolingbroke were ordered to make themselves ready for a fight to be held at Coventry on 16th September. God, it was felt, could then decide by ensuring that the innocent party was victorious. The two parties attended in battle array but Richard decided to end the fight before a blow could be landed. Arguing that it was bad for the kingdom to have two such senior members of the nobility in open conflict, and aware that the two refused to be reconciled, he called together his committee and had their agreement for his verdict, exile for both Mowbray and Bolingbroke.

It cannot have been easy for John to vote to see his son exiled. Richard may have promised him that it would only be for a short time but even that was to be too long. John died in February 1399. Richard did not bother to inform Henry but instead opted to declare his inheritance forfeit to the crown. Officially, the decision not to allow Henry to inherit was made by the committee at Westminster on 18th March 1399. The minutes do not record who was in attendance that day but seven of the eight lords were present.[105] It is therefore almost certain that Edmund was one of the signatories to this decision which was to have such disastrous consequences. Very possibly, he did not feel that he had any choice. Richard was reigning as a despot by now. There were stories of him demanding people sign blank charters so that he could fill in an amount for them to pay as a fine. He was still travelling in the company of his Cheshire archers. Men were being arrested and punished for criticising the King. Justice was left in the hands of people

---

[104] This committee had been set up ostensibly to handle matters which had not been concluded at the time the 1397 parliament ended. For an account of its meetings and composition, see J. G. Edwards "The Parliamentary Committee of 1398" in EHR vol 40 (1925) pp321-333

[105] Ten lords had been appointed to the committee. Two had died – Gaunt and Mortimer. The eight available to attend were Edmund, his son Edward, the Dukes of Surrey and Exeter, the Marquis of Dorset, and the Earls of Salisbury, Northumberland and Gloucester.

the King selected. Edmund still appeared to have Richard's trust for he was once again appointed Guardian of the Realm when the King went to Ireland soon after, yet he was probably extremely wary of him. He did not doubt Richard had killed his brother Thomas and he knew that he had plotted to have both John and Thomas murdered previously.[106] Richard was certainly not the same sort of ruler as his father had been.

Henry's response to the disinheritance was simple. He waited until Richard was overseas, then raised an army and invaded England. This action set Edmund at the centre of the greatest political crisis since the deposition of Edward II over seventy years before for he was responsible for defending the country. His first problem was to identify where Henry would land. His ships were seen off the coast but there was clearly a lot of miles of English coastline for Edmund to see defended. He sent orders out to officials in various counties ordering them to be ready. On 3rd July, the one to the Sheriff of Sussex advised that "on information that certain enemies of the King in no small number, armed and unarmed, have assembled in parts beyond the sea to invade the realm during his absence in Ireland and that others have landed and taken the castle of Pevensey, Sussex, and hold it as in War" he was "to besiege the said castle with all the posse comitatus and take order for its recovery as well as guard the coasts against invasion." [107] Orders were sent to officials inland ordering them to prepare also and to send him armed men. The constable of Windsor, for example, was instructed to make sure he had sufficient supplies and men to hold it "when peril shall threaten."[108] Within London, orders were issued that no arms or armour should be sold, hired or given to anyone except for the purposes of defending Richard II.[109] Edmund further arranged for emergency payments to be made to raise and equip soldiers, and to strengthen city walls and castle defences. He even got money to Richard.[110] Meantime, as news of Henry's actual landing reached Edmund, a messenger was sent to Richard in Ireland.[111]

Edmund raised an army and set off to St Albans and then Ware where he had ordered armed men to meet him on 12th July. Judging by payments

---

[106] Westminster Chronicle, op.cit p.213 and Chronica Monasterii S. Albani vol II op.cit. p.161

[107] CPR 1396-99 p.596

[108] CCR 1396-99 p. 508

[109] ibid. p.509

[110] Dorothy Johnston, 'Richard II's departure from Ireland' in *English Historical Review* (1983) vol. XCVIII p.795. The payment was made two days after Edmund met Henry at Berkeley.

[111] ibid. p.792. On the 4th July, Edmund ordered armed men to be sent to his aid and he sent despatches to Richard. On 12th July, the day on which a messenger was paid for informing the council that Henry had landed, Edmund wrote to him again and he also despatched men to report on Henry's location, size of army and plans.

made, he should have had an army of around three thousand by then[112] but as Walsingham noted, many men took money to fight for Richard but then went and joined Henry.[113] Another chronicler put it even more bleakly: "The Duke of York that was lieutenant of Engand would have gone against him but no man would follow him; and Sir William Scrope, Treasurer of England, offered men wondrous large wages but he could no man have, for no money."[114] Even those who did join Edmund, started to defect so that by 20th July, he was losing men faster than he was gaining them. Two men were sent on a reconnaissance mission to find out the strength and position of Henry and his army.[115] Although the reports were possibly exaggerated in the panic, it was clear that Henry's force was several times the size of Edmund's. The main English army which was about ten thousand strong, remained with Richard in Ireland and although they were on their way back, Edmund was left in an unenviable position. The northern lords, including no doubt subjects from his own territories in Yorkshire and Lincolnshire, had joined Henry.[116] The loyalty of London was doubtful. If he was to raise a substantial army, it would have to be from the south and that meant the counties which Richard had accused of treason only a year before and decided to charge a heavy fee to pardon.[117] It was abundantly clear to Edmund that the people really did not want Richard II as king.

Edmund's own feelings were also torn at this point. The brother he had so admired, Edward the Black Prince, had expressed the opinion when he agreed to restore Pedro of Castile that notwithstanding the fact that Pedro was a bad man and a bad king, he was the rightful king and a prince had a duty to uphold the law and ensure that true kings kept their throne. Richard was Edward's son and was undoubtedly the rightful King of England. Yet, Henry was the son of his brother John. Henry was a dutiful man who had won great fame as a crusader and for his knightly skills. Edmund probably liked Henry more as a person and saw in him the sort of qualities which he associated with regality. He definitely believed that

---

[112] Douglas Biggs 'To aid the custodian and council: Edmund of Langley and the Defense of the Realm, 1399' in *Journal of Medieval Military History* vol 1, 2003 p.135

[113] Henry Riley (ed.) *Annales Ricardi Secundi et Henrici Quarti* (Rolls series 1866) p.245

[114] Silvester Davies, *An English Chronicle*, (Camden Society, 1856) p.15

[115] Douglas Biggs, 'A wrong whom conscience and kindred bid me right' in *Albion* vol 26 1994 issue 2 p.60

[116] Doncaster where Henry met the Percies and other northern lords had been in Edmund's hands since 1347. Richard had granted Edmund some of Henry's Suffolk inheritance in May 1399 and his son Edward had received Pontefract and other castles in March 1399 but these were too recent grants to have aroused a change of loyalty on the part of the inhabitants, see *Calendar of Fine Rolls* 1391-99 pp.297, 303.

[117] Caroline Barron, 'The Tyranny of Richard II' in *Bulletin of the Institute of Historical Research* (1968) volume 41 issue 103 pp.1-18. See John Silvester David (ed.) *An English Chronicle* (Camden Society 1856) p.12

Henry should have been allowed to inherit his father's estates and he said so publicly and even addressed him as Duke of Lancaster.[118]

On 27th July, in the church next Berkeley Castle, Edmund met Henry.[119] According to the *Vita Ricardi*, he was accompanied by the Bishop of Norwich and the lords Berkeley and Seymour. Henry arrived with a bigger contingent including Archbishop Arundel and the Percies. Although the details of the negotiations remained private, what was certain was that Edmund agreed to join Henry. Perhaps he felt he had no choice. Maybe he thought that if he fought on, there would be a civil war which would be deeply destructive and benefit nobody. Edmund knew his son had gone to Ireland with Richard and it is possible that he did a deal with Henry that he would stand down his army in return for Henry sparing Edward's life. Or perhaps Henry lied to him and told Edmund that he was only in England to claim his inheritance and that he meant Richard no harm.[120] Maybe, after the murder of Thomas and Richard's increasingly wayward behaviour, Edmund simply thought it was time to remove him from the throne, before he had a chance to have a son to carry on the line. He may also have been concerned that his own lieutenant in control of the army was none other than Henry's half brother, John Beaufort. On whose side would his loyalties lie in a battle? Most likely, it was a combination of all these factors which played on Edmund's mind. Given that he knew he would face certain death if Richard did return and defeat Henry in battle, it was undoubtedly a brave decision on his part.

According to the *Vita Ricardi* and Gregory's Chronicle, Edmund went with Henry to Bristol where they captured and executed Scrope, Bushey and Green, three of Richard's most hated advisers.[121] He stayed there a few days before going to Wallingford where Richard's young wife was staying. Isabel of France was only ten years old.

On 2nd September 1399, Richard was brought to London. Although not in chains, it was clear that he was Henry's prisoner. Whilst in the Tower, Richard allegedly abdicated the throne cheerfully and of his own free will. It is unlikely that any of the men summoned to the Parliament which opened the same month believed this.[122] With the throne vacant, the first question

---

[118] *Annales Ricardi Secundi* op.cit. p.244. Edmund's orders on 12th July to the two men on the reconnaissance mission were to report on the Duke of Lancaster.

[119] *Vita Ricardi* op.cit p.152

[120] The Percies were to claim that Henry had sworn this on the body of Christ at Doncaster. See Henry Ellis, *The Chronicle of John Hardyng* (London, 1812) p.350

[121] *Vita Ricardi* op.cit p.153 Adam of Usk who was present in Bristol for the executions does not mention Edmund's presence.

[122] Some French accounts say that Edmund and his son both went to visit Richard in the Tower

of the day was who should succeed to the throne. Unsurprisingly, Henry was chosen. Richard may have hoped it would be Edmund but as he himself had hinted in his own will, he feared Edmund would have refused it anyway.[123] Instead, Edmund gave Henry his hand as he led him to the throne.[124] The new regime now had the public blessing of the old and all had been effected without loss of blood, something due very largely to Edmund himself.

The first Parliament of Henry's reign turned out to be a turbulent event as men sought to blame one another for events of recent years, particularly the death of Thomas. At one point, Edmund's son Edward, was sent to the Tower, but ultimately he was punished only by a loss of title. The divisions in society were not so quickly resolved and just three months after his accession, Henry faced the first plot to kill him. The French chroniclers, who blamed Edward for Richard's failure to return in time to save his throne, claimed that he was involved in it and told a fanciful story of how Edmund had uncovered the truth over dinner one day. According to them, Edmund had spotted a roll of paper in Edward's hands and had asked what it was. Edward had not told him so Edmund simply read it anyway and thus discovered the details of the plot. At this point, Edmund rushed from the room to saddle his horse to go and warn the king whilst Edward decided to do likewise, arriving before his father.[125] The tale shows Edmund in a very heroic light but is improbable. There is no reason to suppose that the Duke of York invited chroniclers to his home for dinner with his son so they would be on hand to record such conversations and it would have been a very foolish group of plotters who committed the details of their plans to paper complete with signatures. There certainly was a plot and Edward was involved in its suppression, but there is no evidence that Edmund played any part in this.

---

and that Richard turned on them saying: "they are not fit to speak to me...thou traitor of Rutland thou art neither good nor worthy enough to speak to me nor to bear the name of duke, earl or knight; thou and the villain thy faher have both of you foully betrayed me...by your false counsel was my uncle of Gloucester put to death." M Gaillard, 'A relation of the Death of Richard II' in *Accounts and Extracts of the Manuscripts in the Library of the King of France* (London, 1889) p.226. No English account, official or independent, corroborates this and it is utterly improbable.

[123] J. Nichols, *A Collection of all the Wills Now Known to be extant of the Kings and Queens of England* (London, 1780) pp.191-202. Richard's tomb which was used for Isabella showed Henry's arms rather than the Mortimers or Edward of York which may indicate that he was undecided about the issue of the succession. Since he expected to have children with his second wife, he may not have thought it especially important.

[124] Ian Mortimer, *The Fears of Henry IV* (London 2008) p.191

[125] Benjamin Williams *Chronique de la Traison et Mort* (London, 1846) pp.233-234. The story also appears in M Gaillard, 'A relation of the Death of Richard II' in Accounts and Extracts of the Manuscripts in the Library of the King of France (London, 1889) vol 2, p.229 , John de Waurin *A collection of the Chronicles* ed. William and Edward Hardy (London, 1887) pp.24-25, and in John Webb 'Translation of a French Metrical History' in *Archaeologia* vol 20 (1824) p.211

A month later, in February 1400, Richard II died at Pontefract Castle. In Shakespeare's play, Richard died heroically fighting off those sent by Henry IV to murder him. English contemporary sources agree that Richard died of starvation, though some believe that Henry denied him food whilst others say that Richard chose to stop eating. When Richard's body was examined in 1871, there were no signs of injury on the body which would accord with this story.[126] He was buried at Langley close to his brother. Neither Edmund nor Edward nor any members of the nobility, attended the funeral, though it may be supposed that they were able to pay their respects to him afterwards for it was their own family church. The French author of the *Traison* says Edmund had petitioned Henry to execute Richard just a month before but that Henry had said he would only do so if there was an uprising in his favour.[127] This appears to be just a literary device so that the chronicler can blame Henry and further blacken the York family. The French were deeply upset by the deposition because Richard's wife was French, hence all their sources portray Richard as a saintly victim and everyone else as totally evil. Edmund may have thought Richard was unsuitable to reign but it does not follow that he wished him ill. Given the vast amount of time that he and his family had spent with Richard over the years and the value of the gifts exchanged,[128] there must have been some feeling between them.

Edmund continued to spend the bulk of his time at court as his almost ubiquitous signature on royal charters proves. Henry not only put him in charge of his hawks but he tried to ensure that Edmund obtained some of the money he was owed by the Exchequer[129]. Edmund had been given various allowances by his father and by Richard but a document saying he was entitled to the money was no guarantee that he was going to get it. As early as 1380, Richard had been forced to find other sources of ready revenue for Edmund because he had not been paid and "in consideration of the great expense he has incurred in suing at the exchequer for payment of the said sum"[130] At the time Henry IV ascended the throne in 1399, money was still owing to Edmund from the reign of his father who died in 1377.

On 1st August 1402, Edmund died. It is probable that his death occurred suddenly. He died in Lincolnshire, possibly at Edenham which was near his Stamford estates. The vicar of the parish where he died wrote to the Bishop of Lincoln to complain that Edmund's retainers had rushed to take his body

---

[126] Arthur Stanley 'On an Examination of the tombs of Richard II and Henry III in Westminster Abbey' in *Archaeologia* vol xlv (1880) pp. 309-327

[127] Benjamin Williams (ed) *Chronique de la Traison et Mort* op.cit p.230 (London, 1846)

[128] E101/411/9

[129] Biggs 'A Wrong' op.cit pp263-270

[130] CPR 1377-1381 p.440

back to Langley for burial even before a funeral mass could be said.[131] Edward was in France at the time. An analysis of Edmund's remains carried out in 1877 revealed that Edmund had been suffering from a severe form of arthritis for some time, something which would have left him in crippling pain. This would have been particularly sad for him because he had been so physically strong and active in the past.[132]

History has not been kind to Edmund. He has been accused of being an ineffective, weak nonentity, largely because of his failures to defend the country against Bolingbroke in 1399 and to capture Castile in 1381. Certainly he does not stride across the history of the fourteenth century as colourfully as his brothers, John of Gaunt, Thomas of Gloucester and the Black Prince. There is no evidence that he ever plotted to murder anyone nor that anyone had any serious designs on his life. He was a plain-speaking man, personally brave and totally dedicated to his family and country. In an age where war was the norm and politics often descended into violence, Edmund tried to be a voice of reason. He attempted to make peace between England and France and between his brother and nephew. That he did not always succeed does not alter the fact that he was a man of integrity in an age where that was in short supply. As the first holder of the title, he set a standard of behaviour for future Dukes of York, one that some were to fail to meet.

---

[131] Legge op.cit p.35. The parish of death is uncertain because the vicar only identified himself and his church by initials.

[132] John Evans, 'On Edmund of Langley and His Tomb', *Archaeologia* vol XLVI pp. 297-328 (1881) The same investigation found Edmund was slightly above average height and had greying red hair at the time of his death, aged sixty one. It also found evidence of wounds gained either in battle or tournaments.

Edward

1373-1415

Duke of York 1402-1415

He is a loyal and valiant knight in all that he does.[1]

There is no doubt that Edward has received the worst press of any Duke of York. At various times he has been called false, incompetent, treacherous, a murderer and traitor. Most of those accounts were written by people who barely knew him or were composed after his death. Other people who knew him well thought of him as a brave and able soldier, a loyal advisor and a man of culture. Which was he? Or, was he the archetypal 'Jekyll and Hyde' – a man of many masks?

Edward was the eldest son of Edmund, Earl of Cambridge and his wife Isabella of Castile. He was named after his grandfather, Edward III who was still alive at the time he was born. Edmund's brother, the Black Prince, had had a son of the same name who had died just a year or two before. Edward was thus the only one of the great king's grandchildren to bear his name and survive. Exactly when he was born is unknown but it was probably in the early part of 1373.[2] A substantial grant of the Tyndale

---

[1] View of the future Henry V when Prince of Wales in 1407, see PROME October 1407 item 24.

[2] At the inquisitions held when Edmund died in August 1402, Edward was described as being at least twenty-nine years of age. In some counties, his age was put at thirty but that would have meant he was conceived before his parents married. See J L Kirby (ed.) *Calendar of*

estate was given to Edmund on 24th April 1373 which may have been in celebration of the new arrival.[3] Edmund's brother John also bought him a silver cup in the same month.[4]

Edward spent much of his young childhood at Langley with his mother and sister, Constance, who was born a couple of years later.[5] His father was away for much of the time being involved with the war in France so it is unlikely that Edward knew him well. In 1381, that changed when his father took his wife and son to Portugal. The family spent over a year together with long sea journeys at either end. The trip had been planned the summer before when the Portuguese had asked the help of the English in their war with Castile. Edmund, with a wealth of military experience, was selected to lead the army and his reward was to be a crown for his son. Despite being just eight years old, Edward was going to marry Princess Beatrice, the only child of King Ferdinand of Portugal, who was a few months older than him.

The family set sail from Plymouth in the summer of 1381 just as the Peasants' Revolt was about to break out. They arrived in Portugal on 19th July to a tumultuous welcome. For Edward as a child, it must have been incredibly exciting. The weather was warmer than anything he had known in England. The court was rich and the English were showered with gifts of jewels, silken clothes, horses and fine food. He met his bride to be and that too seemed to go well with the children soon being seen holding hands together. The couple were duly married and laid symbolically in the same bed. A specially made embroidered coverlet depicted them in pearls as king and queen surrounded by representations of the Portuguese nobility.[6] Great feasts were held to celebrate the union which went on for eight days. Finally, Edmund bade his son farewell and went with the army to Estremoz. Edward was left with his young bride and his father in law, King Ferdinand. He might be a child but he needed to be taught the ways of his new countrymen and how to rule them.

Meanwhile, Edmund's military expedition turned out to be a disaster, though this was scarcely his fault. The Portuguese had asked England for a large force and they got a relatively small one with the promise of more men to follow under John of Gaunt. The reinforcements never arrived and

---

Inquisitions Post Mortem vol xviii (HMSO) 1987 p.206

[3] CPR 1370-1374, p.289

[4] Sydney Armitage-Smith (ed.), *John of Gaunt's Register* vol 2 (London, 1911) p.191

[5] Constance was probably born in 1376. The register of John of Gaunt ends in December 1375 and includes no gifts in celebration of the new arrival which would have happened since the child was his niece and named after his wife. Indeed, his wife was quite possibly her godmother.

[6] Derek Lomax and R J Oakley trans. *The English in Portugal* (Warminster 1988) p.71

Edmund's army dwindled, thanks largely to disease. The Portuguese royal family were warring between themselves and the English troops were bored, unpaid and mutinous. When finally there seemed the chance of some action, King Ferdinand went behind the backs of the English and negotiated a peace treaty with Castile. The English were left having spent a lot of money to equip an army which was never to fight a battle and which could not even boast having gained enough loot to recoup their costs.

As a child, Edward probably had little understanding of what was going on but he must have been aware of lots of rows and shouting. His father was livid. His Castilian mother was in a difficult situation. She did not recognise the Castilian ruler but the enemy army was composed of her countrymen. King Ferdinand, who a few months earlier had welcomed Edward into his home with smiles and gifts, now wanted him out of the way. He could no longer play with Beatrice. He was not required to meet Portuguese nobles. It must have been bewildering to the boy that, through no fault of his own, he was being told to pack his things and leave in a hastily located boat. He was not going to be king after all.

With the English duly departed, Ferdinand had Beatrice's marriage to Edward annulled on grounds of their age and in the spring of 1383, he married her to King Juan of Castile. As Edmund had predicted, the marriage was deeply unpopular in Portugal and civil war broke out. Froissart claimed that Beatrice had been asked by her father whom she would prefer to have as a husband, Edward or Juan. She had said that she would prefer Edward as he was the more handsome.[7] Princesses, however, did not have a choice in the matter and Edward was never to see Beatrice again.

Edward appears to have spent much of his adolescence at court. Richard II, whose own father had died when he was a child and who lost his mother in 1385, seemed especially fond of his parents and regularly spent time with them. The King may have viewed Edward—who was six years his junior—in terms of a younger brother, because certain official documents such as patent rolls, quite often describe Edward as the King's brother when in fact he was his cousin.[8] In September 1384, Richard granted the property of a draper in Shoreditch to Edmund and Isabella, and their son.[9] This was highly unusual for in medieval society, grants were generally made to the

---

[7] John Froissart, *Chronicles of England, France, Spain and the adjoining countries,* translated by Thomas Johnes (London, 1839) vol 2 p.151

[8] For example, see CPR 1396-1399 pp.118, 191. These references appear from early 1397 to 1399.

[9] CPR 1381-1385 p.462

husband only. Richard also granted Isabella her own income and later took steps to ensure that provision was made for both Edward's sister and brother, the latter of whom Edmund had chosen to name after the King.[10] In December 1387, just seven months after being invested a Knight of the Garter, Edward got his first grant of land in his own right though the property was taken away from him just three months later when it was discovered that the original owner, who had been reported dead, was in fact alive and well.[11]

Being closely connected with the court meant that Edward would have learnt to enjoy the better things in life. He would have been witness to some things which would normally have been hidden from a teenage boy. He was inevitably a close spectator to the turmoil of the 1388-89 crisis which tore both the country and the royal family apart. The impact of seeing his uncle, Thomas, Duke of Gloucester, attack his father and the King as well as many other members of the court whom Edward would have known well, must have been profound at such a formative age. It must have appeared to him that every day someone he knew was being taken away and executed. For a long while, the King seemed powerless against Gloucester but eventually he was able to regain control. It was an extreme political education. Edward learnt the need to dissemble and to play the waiting game. He also learnt that even close family were not to be trusted, although Gloucester maintained he was acting on behalf of the King whom he claimed was incapable of selecting his own advisors. He saw Richard II, who was his friend and companion, pushed almost to breaking point and yet rising again, and Edward must have been filled with sympathy, and then with much admiration for him. Surviving the troubles drew them closer and created attitudes which were to colour the next decade of Richard's reign. They must have felt that their security depended on a strong monarchy and a weakened Gloucester.

From January 1390, the grants of land and honours started to appear on a regular basis. Edward was granted the Stewardship of Bury[12] and then, on 25th February 1390, the title of Earl of Rutland.[13] He was given Oakham in May and when it was discovered that much of the income from the estate was tied up in previously agreed annuities, Richard decided that the Exchequer would have to help out.[14] In 1391, when just eighteen, Edward

---

[10] CPR 1396-1399 p.219. Isabella left her jewels to the king asking that he would use them to settle an annuity on her youngest son who was probably only about ten at the time. Prob 11/1 ref 295/25226

[11] CPR p.379,412

[12] CPR 1389-1392 p.176

[13] Calendar of Charter Rolls 1341-1417 (HMSO, 1916) p.318

[14] CPR 1389-1392 pp.255, 354

was sent to investigate treasons, felonies and acts of rebellion in Norfolk and Suffolk.[15] This was a job which showed the trust which Richard had in him and this sentiment was to be confirmed in 1392 when Richard not only appointed Edward to his Council but said that he was to take over as Constable of the Tower of London when the Earl of Kent died.[16] The Tower was home to the most politically dangerous prisoners and controlling it represented a significant responsibility. From 1389, Edward was to be seen exercising that right of princes to intercede directly with the King to ask for mercy to be shown to certain convicted prisoners whose cases had been brought to their attention.[17] He also witnessed many royal charters and letters, for example the one which Richard sent to the pope in May 1390. In this, Richard complained about foreign bishops being appointed to English benefices, men who exercised no pastoral care over their people and did not even speak the language. He suggested that the pope's policy was: "he who leaps highest may pay most abundantly" and commented that the men appointed did not have "their vocation of God like Aaron" but were "inflamed with ambition with Simon Magus." It ended with a reminder to the pope that he was the "successor of the chief of the apostles, who took upon him the command of Christ to feed his sheep and not to shear them, to comfort his brethren and not to oppress them."[18] King Richard was a man of strong opinions.

Late in February 1392[19] when he was just nineteen, Edward was sent on his first diplomatic mission. The leader of the expedition was his uncle John of Gaunt, a highly experienced negotiator and diplomat. There was nobody more able for Edward to learn from. Edward's father was also in the party. The goal was to arrange a peace with England's traditional enemy, France. A truce had existed since 1389 but Richard was keen to see a more permanent peace. Sending such senior members of the royal family was a sign of how seriously Richard was taking the policy, although he effectively prevented an agreement being made by refusing to allow Gaunt to agree to anything which Richard had not previously authorised. Chroniclers of the time agreed that the meetings at Amiens were splendid, with the French King welcoming Gaunt as if he were a king himself. Knighton described the grandeur of the scene saying that Edward appeared with a thousand knights all of whom were marvellously dressed[20] and Froissart spoke of the

---

[15] ibid. p. 527

[16] CPR 1391-1395 p.16. The Earl of Kent died in 1397.

[17] See for example, CPR 1389-1392 p. 32, 1391-1395 p. 223

[18] CCR 1389-1392 p.141. The letter is also interesting for it shows Edward as the first witness, and therefore highest ranking member of the royal family, after the king's uncles. The Earl of March, whom some were to claim was rightful heir to the throne, followed Edward.

[19] D. M. Legge, *Anglo-Norman letters and petitions*, (London, 1967) p. 182

[20] Henry Knighton, *Chronica de eventibus Angliae*, (OUP 1995) p. 545. Lewis Clifford, who

two hundred horses which the English lords had taken with them for their retinue.[21]

International affairs of a different nature harnessed Edward's attention in 1394. Richard II was concerned about the loss of revenue which stemmed from an increasing number of Irish rebels and about the situation in Leinster, the province in the east of Ireland. As he had asserted his authority in England, so Richard wished to do the same in Ireland. His army of thirty thousand archers and four thousand men-at-arms was quite substantial but there was a lack of experienced leaders. Richard's older half brother, John Holland was the only one of the leaders who was not still in his twenties. Gaunt was in Aquitaine and Edmund was left home as regent or Guardian of the Realm. With his two hundred men, Edward could not claim to have one of the principal retinues but he was close to the King. Richard granted Edward the title of Earl of Cork. It seems to have been an empty title in that no lands were granted with it, but Edward was to retain the title until his death more than twenty years later.[22]

The army landed at Waterford on 2nd October 1394. As Admiral, Edward had been given the important task of obtaining sufficient ships and men to carry them across two months earlier.[23] He may also have been sent on a reconnaissance mission in the spring for in June, Richard issued a permit to allow one of Edward's servants to travel abroad with various boxes of bows and arrows for him.[24] Joined a month later by Thomas of Gloucester, uncle to Edward and the King, the army moved on toward a confrontation with MacMuragh, Lord of Desmond. They found him camped in the woods near Garrowkill from which the English, led by Mowbray, drove him out. Richard wrote an excited letter back to Edmund at home detailing the battle and paying tribute to Edward's hard work and valour. He was particularly impressed at the way Edward had used his initiative to create a bridge from

---

served as executor to Edward's mother who died at the end of 1392, was part of the same expedition.

[21] John Froissart, *Chronicles of England, France, Spain and the adjoining countries*, trans Thomas Johnes (London, 1839) volume 2, pp.516-20

[22] Legge, op.cit p.207 quotes from a 1394 letter of Richard referring to Edward as Earl of Rutland and Cork. In Jean Froissart, *Oeuvres*, vol. 18 ed. Kervyn de Lettenhove (Osnabrück 1967) p.570 there is a letter signed by "Edward of York, Earl of Rutland and of Cork" which is attributed to 1392 on grounds that the Bishop of St David's referenced in the letter was at Amiens. However, the said Bishop was with Edward in 1395 and the letter indicates that Edward was taking a major role in negotiations at time of writing which he did not in 1392. Also, the letter was written at Leeds Castle on a date when the king was in residence there.

[23] CPR 1391-1396 p.520

[24] CCR 1392-1396 p.212. The permit only says that Edward was overseas and not where he was exactly. He could have been with his uncles in France for the peace negotiations at Leulighen but there is no reason why he would then have required arms.

some casks, logs and rope and had used that to get across the water to attack MacMuragh's men from the rear. Richard reported that Edward had not only slaughtered a great number of the enemy troops but he had come back with immense plunder, especially in the form of livestock.[25]

The English stayed in Ireland throughout the winter. Richard demonstrated his political sense by adopting the arms of Edward the Confessor, an English king who was highly revered by the Irish due to his wife's Irish kin. His goal, as he explained to Edmund, was to win the loyalty of the Irish rebels by negotiation. His plan was that in return for allowing them full rights over lands they claimed to be traditionally theirs, they would remove themselves from Leinster, thereby effectively dividing Ireland with the eastern part being English and the western Irish.[26] A number of the chieftains agreed to this. In January, Thomas was sent back to England to report on progress to date and to obtain some additional men. Meantime, Edward was busy touring the country and receiving the submissions of the Irish chieftains.[27] Not all agreed to co-operate. Tadhg MacCarthy of Desmond wrote to Richard saying that he would only do homage if Richard came to him and not the other way round. Richard sent Edward to Munster with some men-at-arms and archers to change Tadhg's mind. Edward defeated Tadhg in battle and on April 6th, Tadhg did homage to Richard.[28]

It was while they were in Ireland that Richard developed his plan to find Edward a wife. Richard had determined that he wished to marry Isabella, daughter of the King of France as part of a peace treaty and he wrote to the said king saying that he would be sending Edward to France to negotiate this later in the year and recommending at the same time that the King select a cousin who would be a suitable match for Edward. Richard explained that he thought marriages between the blood royal of France and England would strengthen the links between the two countries. He described Edward as his "very dear cousin" and went on to say he was not only one of his greatest nobles, but a marvellous man "in whom all virtues abound."[29]

Richard celebrated Easter in Dublin with what he believed were now his

---

[25] Legge op.cit.p.207

[26] Edmund Curtis, *A History of Ireland* (London, 1950) p.126

[27] Edmund Curtis, *History of Medieval Ireland* (London, 1923) p.327

[28] ibid p.332.

[29] Legge, op.cit pp.158-160. An alternative proposal was received from Milan at this time that Edward be given Lucia Visconti as a bride in return for English assistance in their war against the French, but Richard ignored this as it conflicted with his policy of peace. It does, however, show Edward's international standing at the time. See F. R. H. Du Boulay, *An Age of Ambition*, (London, 1970) p.101

loyal Irish subjects. From the English viewpoint, it had been a great success and Richard returned home triumphant. For Edward, whose reputation had been enhanced, there was to be little relief from travel. Following meetings of the royal council at Leeds Castle in Kent, he and Mowbray, and four others were sent to France to open negotiations in July 1395. The Archbishop of Dublin was to accompany them to negotiate the marriage of Edward with the King of France's younger daughter, Jeanne.[30] The talks continued for some months and involved a fair number of journeys to and from France, not an easy or pleasant task in the conditions of the middle ages. There was considerable debate about the size of dowry which Isabella would bring with her. Ultimately, Richard was forced to reduce his financial demands but he did so in return for a very interesting condition which was that the king of France would offer him military support in event of any uprising by any of his subjects.[31] Clearly Richard had not forgotten the events of 1386-1388 and he distrusted his uncle Thomas who was known to be deeply opposed to the peace process.

On 8th March 1396, agreement was finally reached. Richard would marry Isabella of France and the truce between the two countries would be renewed. Edward's seal was appended to this document and it shows the arms of Edward the Confessor. This use of the arms could only have been authorised by the King and it shows how close Edward was to Richard at this time.[32] The marriage was celebrated in Paris on 12th March with Mowbray representing Richard. Later that year, Richard went to France himself to escort his young bride back to England. He was accompanied by Edward and Gaunt and a dazzling retinue who were laden with sumptuous gifts.[33] The plan to marry Edward to Jeanne had not materialised which meant he may have found the atmosphere a little difficult.

Aside from a deep-seated mistrust of France which was endemic amongst the English nobility, the other chief grounds for concern at the marriage was Isabella's age. She was just six years old. Richard had previously been married to Anne of Bohemia and that union had not produced any children. Medieval life was dangerous and medical knowledge relatively primitive. At best, Isabella would not be able to have children for some ten years, and it would be even longer before any such children would be old enough to rule.

---

[30] Thomas Duffus Hardy, *Syllabus of the Documents relating to England*, (London, 1873) vol ii p. 528

[31] T.F. Tout, *Chapters in the administrative history of mediaeval England*, (London, 1920) vol 4 pp.2-3

[32] Rodney Dennys, *Heraldry and the Heralds*, (London, 1982) p.106

[33] Thomas Walsingham, *Annales Ricardi Secundi et Henrici Quarti* pp.189-94 as published in H. T. Riley (ed) *Johannes de Trokelowe* (Rolls Series, London 1866), hereinafter cited as *Annales*.

What would happen if Richard died? Who would inherit the throne? Edward III had produced five sons who reached adulthood. The eldest, the Black Prince, was Richard's father. The second son was Lionel who had died quite young but he had produced a daughter. She had married Edmund Mortimer and her son Roger was now in his early twenties. Monarchies generally passed through sons so was Roger a true heir? The alternative candidate was Edward III's third son John of Gaunt, now approaching sixty, and his son Henry Bolingbroke. Gaunt was highly respected if not loved and his son was very popular as a crusader.

For Richard, it did not seem too great an issue. He was healthy and he anticipated having children. He wrote in a letter to Albert of Bavaria in 1397 that "my son when he rules will be deadly when angered." [34] He had allegedly said that he favoured Mortimer's claim in 1386, though only one chronicler records any such statement, but he seems to have disliked the prospect of both Mortimer and Bolingbroke as his successors. [35] The person Richard trusted most was the man he had left to govern during his absence in Ireland, his uncle Edmund. If Edmund were to succeed, then he would be followed by Richard's favourite, Edward. In July 1398, Richard reportedly had a conversation with Bagot in which he said that he would most like Edward to follow him because he thought him the wisest and most able man in the kingdom. [36] Whether this conversation ever took place is uncertain. Bagot remembered it at a very convenient time when Richard was in no position to dispute it and when he probably hoped to save his own skin by turning Bolingbroke against Edward. However, the sentiment fits in with what we know of Richard's relationship with Edmund and Edward and what was said in his will. It also explains why Richard was keen to see Edward married to a French princess. What Edward thought about it is unknown. Most likely, he assumed that Richard would have children of his own in due course and the issue would not arise.

Following the successful marriage negotiations, Edward returned to Ireland. It is unknown why, or for how long he stayed, but clearly it was for a short while. [37] Richard planned to send Edward next to Italy to help the French in their war against Milan but Parliament refused to vote the money

---

[34] E Scott and L Gilliodts-van-Severen (ed) *Le Cotton Manuscripts Galba* (Brussells 1896) pp.78-79

[35] Ian Mortimer, 'Richard II and the Succession to the Crown' in *History* (2006), vol 91 p.321. The chronicle which recorded the statement was the Eulogium, see Frank Scott Haydon (ed.) *Eulogium Historiarum sive Temporis* vol III, (Rolls Series, London, 1863) p.361 Edward III had favoured the Gaunt line over Mortimer.

[36] PROME, October 1399 Appendix 1

[37] CPR 1396-1399 p.2. Edward was in France at the end of October 1396, returning with the king in November.

so the expedition was abandoned.[38] Instead, in February 1397, Edward was sent to Germany. Richard's brother in law, Wenceslaus of Bohemia was King of the Romans but deeply unpopular and since that was an elected monarchy, Richard decided that he would like to have that title to boost his European stature. As a result, Edward and Mowbray were sent to try and secure the votes of the electors. Bribes of a thousand pounds a year, the normal grant for a royal duke, were offered to the Count Palatine and Frederick Archbishop of Cologne and smaller amounts to other lords.[39] Sadly for Richard, the German princes had no interest in an Englishman and they chose Rupert of the Palatine instead.

Edward returned in the summer of 1397 and married the widow Philippa Golafre[40]. Born de Mohun, she had been married twice before. Her first husband had been Walter Fitzwalter, a widower with a son who was five years older than Edward. Walter was a contemporary of Edmund and had been a witness to his creation as Duke of York in 1385. Following Walter's death in 1386, Philippa married John Golafre, a close friend of Richard II who had served as a soldier as well as diplomat and been Keeper of the King's Jewels. When John died in 1396, Richard decided that instead of being buried in his parish church John should be laid to rest in Westminster Abbey in the plot next to that reserved for him and beside the tomb of Edward the Confessor.[41] It was an extraordinary mark of honour. Philippa's close links with the royal court may explain how she came to Edward's attention though she had family links too. Her cousin Elizabeth was mother of Thomas Despenser, Edward's brother in law. She was also linked to John of Gaunt through his last wife.[42] Philippa was not a major heiress so it is likely that Edmund regarded his son's marriage with some disappointment. After all, Edward's previous prospective brides had all been princesses who would have brought money, honour and territory into the family. Over the centuries, there has been much speculation about Philippa's age with many sources estimating that she was old enough to be his mother. However, at

---

[38] Tout op.cit p.15

[39] Hardy, op.cit p. 530

[40] The exact date is unknown. They were married by 1398 for the Papal register records them as such, see W. H. Bliss and J. A. Twemlow (ed) *Calendar of Papal Registers Relating to Great Britain and Ireland* vol 5 (1904) p. 135. However, in July 1397, Richard II granted Edward the lands of Richard Le Strange during his minority. Le Strange was Philippa's nephew and heir so the grant suggests that Edward and Philippa were either married at this date or betrothed. See *Calendar of Fine Rolls* 1391-1399 p. 222. On 4th June 1397, Edward had been granted the Isle of Wight which had previously been held by the recently deceased William Montacute, Philippa's brother in law. See CPR 1396-1399 p.150

[41] Derek Pearsall, 'Chaucer's Tomb: The Politics of Reburial' in *Medium Aevum* (Spring 1995) p.53 The tomb was in the St Nicholas Chapel.

[42] John of Gaunt married Katherine Swinford née Roet. Her sister, Philippa married John Burghersh (great uncle of Philippa de Mohun) and then the poet Geoffrey Chaucer.

the time her mother died in 1404, she was said to be between twenty-six and twenty-eight which would mean a birth of around 1377 making her slightly younger than Edward.[43] Philippa had not had any children with her previous husbands and she was to have none with Edward despite the fact that she was now of child bearing age. It is possible that the marriage was Richard's idea, for Edward had barely spent four months in England in the last three years – so his opportunities for courtship were extremely limited.

That summer also saw one of the turning points in Richard's reign. Buoyed up by his experience in Ireland and with the security of the French alliance, Richard decided it was time to take revenge on Thomas of Gloucester and the Earls of Arundel and Warwick, the Lords Appellant who had so discomforted him in 1388. Announcing that the said lords were plotting against him, Richard ordered their arrest.[44] He went in person to capture his uncle whilst Edward was sent to take Arundel. [45] The arrests were not popular. People suspected that Richard wanted to punish the lords for their actions a decade earlier and they felt this was not right. Richard had pardoned the men for that and since his coronation oath bound him to uphold justice and the law, they thought it would be wrong to effectively rescind their pardons and try them now. So great was the outcry that Richard was forced to take the unusual step of justifying himself, saying that the arrests had been made on the basis of new extortions; details of which would be revealed at the next parliament.[46] He also issued a proclamation that nobody should muster armed men without express permission from himself or his advisors, a group of eight men headed by Edward, promising that anyone criticising the said arrests was to be

---

[43] The theory that Philippa was much older stems from the fact that her sister Elizabeth married William Montacute whose son married in 1378 when he was at least in his 'teens. If Elizabeth was the mother of the child, she must have been born in the 1340s. Elizabeth and Philippa's father had been permitted to marry his guardian's niece in 1341 but it is likely both were children at the time so the actual wedding took place years later. At the time of her mother's death in 1404, Elizabeth was stated to be in her thirties which clearly proves that William Montacute's son came from a previous marriage. See J L Kirby (ed.) *Calendar of Inquisitions Post Mortem* vol xviii (HMSO 1987) p.386.

It is also possible that Philippa was cousin to Guy de Mohun who was made Bishop of St David's in 1397 and Treasurer of England in January 1398. The names of the children of her uncle William Mohun are not all known and another cousin had married Guy de Bryan in 1330 after whom he was probably named.

[44] The anonymous author of the *Traison* says Richard told the council that Thomas was planning to imprison him, Gaunt and Edmund and execute the rest of the council. They promptly advised the king to arrest Thomas and his accomplices. See Benjamin Williams *Chronique de la Traison et Mort* (London, 1846) p.126-127.

[45] ibid. p.132. Walsingham says that Edward went with the king to arrest Gloucester, see *Annales Ricardi* p. 203

[46] CCR 1396-1399 p.198. The proclamation was also discussed by Thomas Walsingham in his *Ypodigma Neustriae* (London, 1876) p.375, .

regarded as a traitor.[47] According to Edward's later testimony, he was at Nottingham at the start of August 1397 when he was called in and told that he was to appeal, or, denounce the three lords for treason. He said that he had told his father and his uncle "that he was commanded to do that day a thing the doing of which made him sadder than he ever had been." He added he did not dare oppose the King "for fear of his life."[48]

The Parliament held in September 1397 was a carefully stage-managed affair by Richard. Many of the members were loyal to him and those who were not were likely to be intimidated by the thousands of armed men which were stationed outside the tent where parliament was meeting.[49] Richard's troops were augmented by those of his uncles John of Gaunt and Edmund, Duke of York and those of Bolingbroke.[50] Adam of Usk, who was present, described how the Speaker of the Commons, Bushy, requested the impeachment of the three lords. Richard added to the atmosphere of terror by saying that he had the names of fifty traitors in mind but that anyone who asked for details was themselves a traitor and deserving of death. Dressed in matching outfits of red silk edged with white and embroidered in gold, Edward and his fellow Counter-Appellants then made their accusations of treason against Thomas, Arundel and Warwick.[51] The charges all related to the commission of 1386, the rising of 1387 and the merciless parliament of 1388. Unsurprisingly, all were found guilty. Arundel was sentenced to execution, Warwick to exile on the Isle of Man and Thomas was condemned posthumously, an announcement having been made that Thomas had died in prison in Calais so could not be tried.

Richard's victory in the Parliament was absolute. He regarded Edward as one of his right hand men which is why at the end of the sitting he created him Duke of Albermarle, or Aumale as he was generally known. The other Counter-Appellants were given titles too which resulted in Walsingham, angry at what he regarded as the cheapening of the honour, dismissively referring to them as the duketti.[52] Richard's confidence grew

---

[47] The group included Mowbray, Edward's brother in law Thomas Despenser, the king's half brothers John and Thomas Holland, Gaunt's son John Beaufort, the Earl of Salisbury and William LeScrope. See CCR 1396-1399 p.196. It is worth noting that neither Gaunt nor Edmund were on the list nor Gaunt's heir, Henry Bolingbroke.

[48] PROME, October 1399 Part 2 item 2

[49] Westminster Hall was still under construction. E. M. Thompson (ed.) *Chronicon de Adam de Usk* (London, 1904) p.154 *Eulogium* op.cit p.373

[50] CPR 1396-1399 p.192

[51] *Chronicon* op.cit p. 157. Adam of Usk was an eye witness to events within the parliament. The fact that they wore such outfits was indicative of Richard's involvement since it is hardly likely that each man would have designed and purchased such a costly outfit of their own accord.

[52] Annales Ricardi op.cit p.223

but his behaviour raised eyebrows. One chronicler described how Richard next set up a throne in his chamber and ordered anyone whom he looked at to kneel, no matter what their station.[53] Walsingham noted Richard's pleasure when people addressed him as if he were a god.[54] The Monk of Evesham said Richard was: "abrupt and stammering in his speech, capricious in his manners, and too apt to prefer and to follow the recommendations of the young to the advice of the elder nobles. He was prodigal in his gifts, extravagantly splendid in his entertainments and dress... arrogant, rapacious and too much devoted to luxury; remaining sometimes till midnight and sometimes till morning in drinking and other excesses that are not to be named."[55]

An idea of what was in Richard's own mind at the time can be seen through the letter he wrote to Albert of Bavaria. In this, Richard reiterated that Thomas had again been plotting "to illegally gain our crown" and recalled that Thomas in the merciless parliament had attacked so many of the royal household that "scarcely any of us beyond the royal name remain." Claiming God was on the side of kings, he said it was his duty to ensure that rebels were "hammered back into confusion" adding "we make their punishment everlasting."[56]

To the Emperor of Constantinople, Richard wrote of how certain magnates had sought to take power but "when we could no longer endure their rebellion and wantonness, we collected the might of our prowess and stretched forth our arm against our enemies; and at length by the aid of God's grace, we have by our own valour trodden on the necks of the proud and haughty, and with a strong hand have ground them down, not to the bark only, but even to the root; and have restored to our subjects peace."[57]

This then was the man whom Edward and his father served. It is small wonder that people were afraid. Mowbray apparently voiced his fears to Henry Bolingbroke who promptly reported them to the King. Henry told Parliament when it reconvened in the new year that Mowbray had said that he and Edward with two other earls had agreed not to destroy any more lords without a just and reasonable cause, a comment suggesting they thought the recent accusations had been unwarranted. Probably even more alarming to Edward was Mowbray's claim that Richard, notwithstanding

---

[53] John Silvester Davies, *An English Chronicle*, (Camden Society, 1856) p.12

[54] Annales p.212

[55] Taken from the *Vita Ricardi*. This translation appears as an appendix to *Traison* op.cit p.294. The *Eulogium* op.cit p.384 includes similar acusations.

[56] E Scott and L Gilliodts-van-Severen op.cit pp.78-79

[57] A.R. Myers, *English Historical Documents* (London, 1969) vol 4 p.175

his loyal service, was considering destroying him.[58]

Publicly, Richard decided to show his support for Edward by making him Warden of the West March of Scotland. As such he was to treat for peace and to extend royal power in the north. A month later, together with Richard's nephew Thomas, he was given the vague but considerable task: "to follow and arrest all traitors found within the realm of England and after they have informed themselves of their treasons and convicted them by their acknowledgment or otherwise, chastise them at discretion according to their deserts."[59] Richard evidently had no time for courts of law and preferred to let those he trusted handle such matters with no questions asked. The following day, Richard issued orders that no letters were to be allowed into the country from abroad for anyone unless they had first been presented to the royal council for inspection.[60] In so far as the medieval system of government permitted it, Richard was trying to be an autocrat and Edward was one of his chief supporters.

The dispute between Bolingbroke and Mowbray dragged on and it was decided by Richard that the two men should fight it out in combat at Coventry on 16th September 1398. As Constable of England, Edward was closely involved with the arrangements. He had to swear in the combatants and check their equipment. At the last moment, Richard cancelled the contest and exiled both parties.[61]

For Richard, there was a more urgent issue to consider. Roger Mortimer whom he had sent to govern Ireland had been killed in battle in June 1398. Regardless of where exactly Roger was believed to fit in the succession, he was a member of the royal family and his death had to be avenged. Richard therefore planned a new invasion of Ireland. He departed with the main army at the end of May 1399. Edward was still in Scotland where he had been negotiating a truce so he arrived some three weeks later when the King was already in Dublin. A few days later, news arrived that Henry Bolingbroke had returned from exile and invaded England. Richard naturally had to abandon his plans for Ireland and return to fight for his throne. Jean Creton, a Frenchman who was a junior member of the expedition, claimed that Edward "slyly resolved upon a trick." He said that Edward told the King to take his time arguing that they lacked sufficient boats to get everybody back. He suggested that the Earl of Salisbury should go back first to fight Henry and that meantime, Richard should go to

---

[58] PROME, September 1397 Part 2 item 11

[59] CPR 1396-1399 p.365

[60] CCR 1396-1399 p. 288

[61] See *Traison* op.cit pp. 150-156

Waterford where he could summon the necessary boats. "You shall soon see your enemies captive, dead or discomforted: of the whole of this be well assured."[62]

Creton's view has been frequently quoted over the years as evidence that Edward was disloyal to his king or even that he was already committed to Bolingbroke. This is unlikely. Edward's advice was sound. The vessels which had taken the army to Ireland had already been sent back. Either the whole army would have to wait for boats or a contingent could be returned to counter the invaders. It would not have been supposed that Bolingbroke could have had a great army and both Wales and Chester, the areas closest to Ireland, had traditionally been loyal to Richard. Creton also comments that the advice was given to Richard secretly and there is no way that Creton as a lowly French servant would have been invited to attend a top level council of war between Richard and his advisors. Creton further said of Edward that "anything that he pleased he might have asked of the king for I solemnly declare there was no man alive, brother nor uncle, cousin young nor old, whom he loved better."[63] Historians living over six hundred years later should be careful before they disagree with an eye-witness account, but it is possible that this was not the case in the summer of 1399. In February 1398, Edward lost his position as Lord Warden of the Cinque Ports[64] and three months later he lost his position as Admiral.[65] In the same year, Edward decided to give Richard all the income from the lands which he had received from Queen Anne, either a gesture of great friendship or a sign of fear.[66] His recommendations of July 1398 for re-organisation of the Scottish marches had been ignored.[67] Even allowing for his travelling, it is notable that Edward was witnessing significantly less charters than he had been.[68] There was also Mowbray's story that Richard planned to destroy Edward.[69] All this, combined with Edward's own testimony, suggests that the relationship might not have been as warm as it had been in the past, though Edward remained loyal to his king.

---

[62] John Webb, 'Translation of a French Metrical History' in *Archaeologia* vol 20 (1824), p.45. Hereinafter cited as Creton.

[63] Ibid. p.45.

[64] CPR 1396-1399 p.289

[65] CPR 1396-1399 p.334

[66] CPR 1396-1399 p.518. Edward had been granted the lands in 1395 along with Archbishop Arundel but held them alone since the banishment of the Archbishop in 1397, see CCR 1396-1399 p.33

[67] Joseph Bain, *Calendar of Documents relating to Scotland* (Edinburgh 1888) p.106

[68] Chris Given-Wilson, 'Royal Charter Witness Lists 1327-1399' in *Medieval Prosopography* Autumn 1991 volume 12 number 2 p.77. From June 1394-June 1397, Edward signed three quarters of charters. In the last two years of Richard's reign, it was a quarter.

[69] PROME September 1397 Part 2 item 11

Whatever prompted his decision, Richard did indeed send Salisbury back first with at least some men.[70] He then returned some days later with Edward and the greater part of the army. It was a hastily arranged evacuation. Exchequer records show that more than 500 bows, 3000 sheaves of arrows, 30 gross cords for bows, 300 lances, 8 guns, 200lb gunpowder and 300 shields together with most of the money and horses were left behind. [71] Moreover, those returning from Ireland landed at a variety of different ports which must have added to the confusion. Edward's proposal, as outlined by Creton, had not been fully followed for the few ships which they had were required to make several trips to and from Ireland.

Exactly what happened next is not clear. Henry Bolingbroke continued to advance across England whilst Richard pondered. Rumours of the size of his army were spreading and although Edward's father was trying to defend the country, he was facing a losing battle. As the Monk of Evesham commented, nobody wanted to fight Henry.[72] On the 27th July, Edmund decided to join Bolingbroke himself. When Richard and Edward learnt of this is uncertain. Creton claimed they heard the news when they were in Ireland but this is impossible for Richard was back in England at this date. Faced with the general loss of his own troops, all sources agree that Richard's response to the situation was to run. He left what remained of his army by fleeing in disguise one night with a dozen or so of his most trusted retainers.[73] Significantly, Edward was not amongst them. Had they argued about tactics or was this further evidence that Edward was not as close to Richard as Creton had suggested? Perhaps Edward was left behind deliberately so that he could scout for information or maybe one of his father's retainers had already reached him and counselled him not to go. Edmund's official actions as Guardian were a matter of record but it is likely that as a father he sought to communicate with his son in what was an extremely dangerous and volatile situation.[74]

The impact of Richard's departure was a predictable loss of faith in the

---

[70] The number of men sent back at this time is unknown. Creton travelled with them so his account of what happened afterward in Ireland is based on conjecture.

[71] Dorothy Johnston, 'Richard II's departure from Ireland, July 1399' in *English Historical Review* (1983) vol. XCVIII pp.796-800. Edward did not get his horses back until February 1400.

[72] Vita p.152

[73] These included Edward's brother in law Thomas Despenser, and Bishop Guy de Mohun who was probably a cousin of his wife.

[74] Two manuscripts held in the French royal library claimed Edward was seen reading a letter prior to Richard's departure – MS 635 and MS 10212. Ever keen to put a bad interpretation on Edward's actions, the authors concluded that the letter must have been sent from Bolingbroke. If any such document existed, the letter could equally have been from his father. However, since the eye witness for this was said to be a squire who probably could not read, the document may have been something as mundane as a list of equipment.

King. In the middle ages, people wanted and respected a strong ruler. Contemporaries knew that the Black Prince would never have behaved in this manner nor the mighty Edward III. Edward told those left "Let us be gone; since my lord is so careful to secure himself, we are all lost."[75]

There is no evidence that Edward went to join his father at Bristol. He may not have known he was there. At the time of his flight, Richard probably did not know that Edmund had joined Bolingbroke so there is no reason to suppose that Edward did.[76] Edward himself went north opting to join Bolingbroke at Chester.[77] He subsequently went on his behalf to see Richard at Flint. Creton, who was in the room, noted that Edward "said nothing to the King but kept at as great a distance as he could from him, just as though he had been ashamed to see himself in his presence."[78] Another witness claims Edward whispered to Richard's half brother: "Dear cousin don't be angry; if it please God, things will go well."[79] From that point onwards, events moved fast. Bolingbroke rode against Richard who was forced to face the reality that nobody wanted him as king. Bolingbroke lured Richard out with promises that he had only come to claim his inheritance and then ambushed him and took him prisoner. The official record states that Richard, aware of his limitations, cheerfully surrendered the role of king to Henry as a man he recognised to be more suited to it than himself. It is an improbable interpretation but the world was changing very fast. For Edward, it must have been a very difficult time. He had grown up with Richard and, even though he may not have approved of everything which he did, he probably liked him. He owed him his fortune and his career. Records kept by Richard's staff indicate that over the years, Edward had spent a lot of money on gifts and that he had taken great trouble in commissioning works to please Richard, something he need not have done.[80] He must have been very nervous as he wondered what was going to happen next.

---

[75] Creton op.cit p. 99. He was not present to hear what Edward said but it is likely that it was something on these lines. Walsingham, the Monk of Evesham and the Dieulacres Chronicle all report that Worcester, who had been left behind with Edward, symbolically broke his staff of office and announced that the king would no longer keep household and that consequently everyone should depart and do the best they could to save themselves. see *Annales* op.cit. p.249, *Eulogium* op.cit p.381

[76] See *Vita* op.cit p.149 and M. V. Clarke and V. H. Galbraith, 'The Deposition of Richard II' in *Bulletin of John Rylands Library* (1930) vol XIV pp.172-173

[77] Thomas Hearne (ed), *Vita Ricardi* (London, 1729) p.154

[78] Creton op.cit. pp.158-159

[79] M Gaillard, 'A relation of the Death of Richard II' in *Accounts and Extracts of the Manuscripts in the Library of the King of France* (London, 1889) p.218

[80] E101/411/9. The gifts were valued by the royal staff so it is possible to see that Edward spent almost thirty times more on gifts for Richard than Henry Bolingbroke did, though both were cousins of the king. In return, Richard spent more on gifts for Edward than he did his other relatives, see Frederick Devon, *Issues of the Exchequer* (London, 1837) p.265.

In September, Parliament met to consider the situation. Faced with Richard's apparent abdication, they had no choice but to recognise the conquering Bolingbroke. Having established Henry as king, Parliament turned its attention to those men whom it believed were most responsible for Richard's bad government. Tradition generally said that the monarch must be good so that any faults – and in Richard they had found many – must be due to evil advisors. Walsingham, supported by the parliament roll itself, describes quite astonishing scenes. Lord Fitzwalter accused Edward of being to blame for the death of Thomas, Duke of Gloucester, saying openly: "You are the principal cause of his death."[81] Edward denied it and said that he would be happy to prove his innocence in single combat, a means of determining cases not unusual amongst the nobility at that date. Bagot also accused Edward of the same thing. Shouting broke out and the scene descended into chaos. In the end, Edward was arrested and sent to Windsor Castle to await trial.[82]

What is interesting in this is that the accuser was the stepson of Edward's wife. This cannot be coincidental. Had she passed him information gained from Edward himself or was he trying to get revenge for some mistreatment he thought Edward had given her? We do not know. Edward denied any involvement in his uncle's death and the evidence produced against him was questionable. On Bagot's recommendation, one of Mowbray's servants named John Hall was arrested, and Hall signed a confession saying that he had been one of nine men who had gone to Thomas' quarters in Calais in September 1397 where they had smothered him with a feather bed. In his confession, he claimed that he had recognised two of Edward's servants being part of the group, though he was unable to provide full names for either of them.[83] None of the other men who were supposedly part of the group were questioned so there is no corroboration of Hall's story. That Thomas was murdered is almost certain and that Hall was part of it is clear too, for no man would confess to a crime of that nature if he were innocent; knowing it would result in an extremely painful death. However, Hall was not brought into Parliament for interrogation. It is quite possible that he was tortured and he may have been encouraged to generate

---

[81] *Annales Henrici Quarti* p.303. Walsingham was clearly opposed to Edward for he describes him giving a confused a long winded speech in response in which he blamed Mowbray. Walsingham also says that Hall said that Richard and Edward had ordered the death, though Hall's signed confession to Parliament says only the king ordered it.

[82] CCR 1399-1400 p.28. Edward's arrest was ordered on the 20th October. Other advisors of Richard including Salisbury, Exeter and Edward's brother in law were arrested at the same time. Orders to produce them for trial at Parliament were issued on 28th October but none was issued for Edward suggesting that he may have been bailed. No orders were issued relating to the Marquis of Dorset either. The *Traison* op.cit p.233 suggests that Edmund pledged his own life and property on his son's good behaviour.

[83] Hall's confession appears in PROME October 1399 part 2 items 11 to 15

names in return for some small favour, such as a slightly faster execution. The English chroniclers of the period preferred to put the blame on Richard II and Mowbray.[84] Even the French, who blamed Edward for Richard's deposition, did not seek to accuse Edward of Thomas' murder. In Creton's account, the blame is given to Salisbury, Surrey and Exeter.[85]

There is evidence, however, that Edward was aware of events in Calais before most other people. He petitioned Richard that the title of Constable of England, which he had been granted on 12th September 1397, be backdated to 9th September, six days *before* Thomas had died – according to official records.[86] In truth though, the moment Thomas was arrested the remaining royal family would have known what would happen. Thomas was too dangerous to let live and a public execution would have been politically unwise. When Edmund and Gaunt—whose men stood guard outside Parliament—called to give judgment on their brother, they almost certainly knew he was dead. Edmund, with a father's love, just might have forgiven Edward if he thought he was involved, but Gaunt's son Henry—now king of England—had no such scruples. If he had believed Edward was guilty, he would have sacrificed him and the people would probably have rejoiced that a great lord had paid the price for Thomas' death.[87] As it was, he simply announced he was stripping Edward of his dukedom and some lands, before taking him back on to the Privy Council.[88] As a further mark of support, he then confirmed much of Edward's landholdings including the strategically important Channel Islands.[89] The mystery of Thomas' death was not mentioned again and Edward resumed his career at the centre of power.

Things, however, remained unsettled. Henry might have been crowned but Richard still lived and that gave hope to some of his supporters. A plot was devised to lure Henry to attend a tournament at Windsor at which

---

[84] Walsingham, for example, blamed Richard and Mowbray, see *Annales* op.cit p.223

[85] Creton op.cit p.134

[86] SC 8/45/2202. Richard's half brother, John Holland, testified to Parliament that Richard had told him that Thomas would be killed before trial so it is not impossible that he told Edward too, see PROME October 1399 Part 2 item 5. The date of 15th September appears in CPR 1396-1399 p.323 though instructions were issued on 7th September to escheators in ten counties plus London to seize the property of the "late duke" and to value it as it was "during his lifetime," see Calendar of Fine Rolls 1396-1399 p.224. Both the murderer Hall and Rickhill, who had been sent to receive Thomas' confession, both told Parliament that they were surprised by their orders because they thought he was already dead.

[87] Walsingham noted that the people were unhappy that all of Richard's advisers were released. See *Annales* op.cit p.320

[88] His condemnation was for his role in appealing Thomas, Warwick and Arundel in 1397 not his uncle's murder. Edward lost his dukedom on 3rd November. He was present at the first recorded meeting of the Privy Council on 4th December, see Harris Nicolas (ed.), *Proceedings and Ordinances of the Privy Council of England* (HMSO, 1834) p.100

[89] CPR 1399-1401 p.106

those involved would rise up and slaughter him and his family. They would then release and restore Richard. The French chroniclers claimed that Edward was one of the plotters. English sources such as Adam of Usk, Thomas Walsingham and the Monk of Evesham do not indicate him being involved. According to the *Traison*, Edward not only united with the plotters but he was daft enough to attach his seal to a document outlining the plans. When his father caught him, Edward changed sides and rushed to tell Henry all about it. If this was not dastardly enough, the author then has Edward ride off in pursuit of the plotters whom he meets and gives false information about the size of Henry's following army. Edward, in this account, rushes back to Henry so he can take part in the bloodbath that follows. The author describes Edward being present at the execution of Blount who allegedly turns round, having been disembowelled, to call him a "false traitor" and says that by him "the noble knighthood of England is destroyed." The author even goes so far as to say that Edward chased his brother in law to Bristol and then returned to London behind a fanfare of trumpets with said brother in law's head on a pole.[90] It is a tale where Edward is seen as having a character as evil as anyone in a comic book. Yet, the story has been repeated in a host of books without question and has done much to damage Edward's reputation.

The known facts are that there was a plot and that the principal men involved were the three earls of Salisbury, Huntingdon and Kent plus Thomas Despenser, husband of Edward's sister Constance. These four had all been recently charged alongside Edward in Parliament with encouraging Richard to do evil. Kent, Huntingdon and Despenser had been amongst the small party who fled at night with Richard when he returned from Ireland whilst Salisbury had returned early to raise resistance to Henry. They had a reputation of being close to him to the end, though Despenser had spectacularly changed sides and served on the commission which deposed him a few weeks later. It would have been reasonable for such men to have supposed that Edward might be interested in joining them and it is possible that they invited him to do so. He may even have pretended to go along with it in order to obtain information. Edward was later to work as a spy and the Dieulacres Chronicle did give him the credit for revealing the details to Henry and thus saving not just his life but those of his children.[91] Whether he was involved in its discovery or not, he was certainly active in its suppression as exchequer records confirm.[92] He did not, however, execute

---

[90] *Traison* op.cit. pp.233-257

[91] Clarke and Galbraith, op.cit. p.174. Edward is also credited with the revelation in *An English Chronicle*, op.cit. p.20 which is slightly later but based on an earlier source. For Edward's later work as an informer, see *Privy Council* op.cit. p.182

[92] Devon op.cit. p.278

his brother in law because that was done by the mob at Bristol.[93] Edward was rewarded for his loyalty shortly afterwards by being pardoned for all debts.[94]

The next few years saw Edward being given some unenviable jobs. Despite the great popular support which Henry had received when he took the throne, he was not finding it easy to reign. The Welsh rose up against him, the Scots and the French threatened. To add to this, he was short of money, not least because he had been foolish enough to promise not to levy unnecessary taxes when he came to the throne and Parliament had decided that this was one manifesto pledge they planned on helping him keep. He needed the support of experienced men. His uncle Edmund was on hand to advise but he was crippled with arthritis so not fit enough to lead armies any more. Edward, however, was still under thirty, fit and he had experience of both diplomacy and warfare, including in Ireland where guerrilla tactics prevailed. For Henry, therefore, Edward was an ideal choice for any role which appeared difficult. His trust in Edward is shown by the fact that he entrusted the military education and care of his eldest son to him. When Henry led an army into Scotland in the summer of 1400, he returned to London after only a few weeks but Edward remained at Roxburgh for three months with Henry junior, the future Henry V.[95]

1401 began with the King trying to make peace between Edward and Lord Fitzwalter. Philippa's stepson remained angry that Edward had not been convicted of Gloucester's murder and continued to try to foment trouble. Henry told him to stop.[96] He then appointed Edward as Lieutenant of Aquitaine with the task of demanding redress from the French for their infractions of the truce.[97] He was to be paid £16,750 for each of the three years he was there, a vast sum but it was meant to cover not just his wages but all his men, all the support personnel such as fletchers and smiths and cooks, and military equipment.[98] Edward departed in August but was clearly concerned about his safety for he made his will before he departed.[99] He was probably right to be wary for within his new lordship was Bordeaux, where Richard II had been born, and whose loyalty to the new regime was in doubt. The area was alleged to be lawless and in need of good government. The Archbishop of Bayeaux had specifically asked Henry to send Edward

---

[93] Chronicon op.cit p.198, Annales Henrici Quarti op.cit p.329

[94] CPR 1399-1401 p.249

[95] J. H. Wylie, *The History of England under Henry The Fourth*, (London, 1884) vol. 4 p. 249

[96] PROME, January 1401 item 32. Fitzwalter then went on pilgrimage to Rome where he met Usk, see *Chronicon* op.cit.p.248

[97] Hardy op.cit p.543

[98] Devon, op.cit p.446

[99] CPR 1399-1401 p.531

because he felt that he alone would have the maturity and strength to provide that.[100]

Edward's time in Aquitaine was cut short by the sudden death of his father in August 1402. He returned home and did not resume his lieutenancy. He may have been disinclined to go for he had received very little money for his time in France. In May 1403, he was still owed £8000.[101] He was also a wanted man in France. At the end of 1402, Creton had confirmed the death of Richard II and called on the Duke of Burgundy to "avenge and punish the death of that good Catholic, King Richard, whose noble blood has been shed in so villainous and traitorous a manner."[102] Richard's brother in law, the Count de St Pol, promptly ordered that an effigy of Edward be made and hung upside down on a gibbet opposite the gates of Calais [103] It was a sign that trouble was brewing.

At home too, things were not peaceful for Henry. The Percies rose in the north and on 21st July 1403, the battle of Shrewsbury took place. It was one of the bloodiest encounters in English history and the Prince of Wales himself was badly wounded. As Duke of York, Edward was at Henry's side. Curiously, when parliament met in February 1404, it was noted that there had been rumours that Edward had secretly sided with the Percies. No less than the Earl of Northumberland, father of the Harry Percy alias Hotspur who had led the rebellion, stood up to say that Edward had played no part in it and was totally loyal to the King.[104]

Meantime, Edward's next mission was in another war zone, this time in Wales where Owain Glyn Dŵr had been heading a rebellion since 1400. In November 1403, Edward was appointed Lieutenant of South Wales with the responsibility of holding the area for the English. In this role, he was again working with Henry's eldest son, the Prince of Wales and his opponents were not just the Welsh rebels but the French who had decided to support them and were raiding the coast. His job was to regain some of the castles which had recently fallen such as Caermarthen, Newcastle Emlyn and Brecon as well as to hold those that remained. To aid him he had 250 men-

---

[100] Malcolm Graham Allan Vale, *English Gascony, 1399-1453* (Oxford University Press 1970) p.43

[101] CPR 1402-1405 p.235

[102] P W Dillon,'Remarks on the manner of the death of King Richard the Second' in *Archaeologia* vol 28 (1840) p.82

[103] Thomas Johnes (trans) *The Chronicles of Enguerrand de Monstrelet* (London, 1867) p.23. Despite Henry having Richard's body put on public display when he died in 1400, the French had hoped that the body was that of an imposter and that Richard had in fact escaped and was awaiting restoration.

[104] PROME, February 1404 item 14.

at-arms and 780 archers.[105] He clearly made a good start in his new job for Henry wrote in October 1403 of his pleasure in hearing the good news about Edward's latest "exploit", details of which were not given.[106] Once again, however, he lacked money and he was forced to resort to pawning his own household goods in order to raise money to pay the troops. The situation was a disgrace and in Parliament a year later, the Commons went to the King to remind him of all the good work which Edward had done on behalf of the kingdom in France and now in Wales and to reproach him for not paying him. They suggested that for a peer to be left in this position was unacceptable and said that Henry as a man of honour should keep his promises and pay his debts.[107]

It is possible that financial concerns were a factor in the bizarre events of February 1405. That month, the two young sons of Roger Mortimer, who were being housed at Windsor Castle, were abducted. The boys were in some people's mind the true heirs to the English throne due to their descent from Edward III's second son Lionel. The alarm was raised and the boys were caught quite quickly. They were in the company of Constance Despenser who claimed to be taking them to her brother in Wales. Constance was Edward's sister and she put on a great show for the council, saying it was all his idea and she would be happy to defend her allegations with her life if she were a man, promising to throw herself in the flames if she spoke a lie. She even claimed that he had obtained a ladder and had planned to scale the walls of Eltham at Christmas to murder the King. Most of the tale was quite preposterous but once again Edward found himself arrested. He admitted that he had known of the scheme but added that he had been the one to assist the King in thwarting it saying he would have done so sooner had he been able.[108]

Edward was sent to Pevensey Castle and the King confiscated all his properties on grounds he was a traitor. It was all very strange. Had Henry seriously thought that Edward planned to murder him or release an alternative claimant to the throne, he would have had him executed. Instead, he left him in rather comfortable captivity in a castle which was known not be secure and allowed him to maintain lawyers to continue a legal action he was pursuing.[109] Most of the chroniclers of the day did not even mention the incident which suggests it was not taken very seriously even by contemporaries. Perhaps they suspected that Constance was lying

[105] J. H. Wylie op.cit vol 1 p. 378

[106] J. L. Kirby (ed.), Calendar of Signet Letters of Henry the Fourth (HMSO 1978) p.52

[107] PROME October 1404 item 12

[108] Eulogium p.402, Annales Henrici Quarti op.cit. p.398

[109] Signet Letters op.cit. p.86, Privy Council op.cit. p.261

about Edward as revenge for him allowing her husband to be beheaded in 1400. The question arises then why Henry even bothered to put Edward away. He owed Edward a lot of money so he might have thought that jailing him and confiscating his estates was a convenient way out. He may have wanted to warn Edward against too close an association with his wayward sister who was having an affair with the under-age Earl of Kent whose marriage Henry was trying to negotiate.[110] Another factor which was not revealed at the time but which may have influenced the decision was that Edward had taken a mistress while he was in Wales.[111] She was Elizabeth Charlton, wife of Walter, kinsman of Edward Charlton, the Lord of Powys and very important defender of English interests in Wales. Edward Charlton was married to the mother of the Mortimer boys. A chance to cool his ardour from this potentially unwise liason may have been deemed advisable.

Whatever the truth of the matter, Edward was released within a few weeks so that he could continue his defence work in South Wales.[112] By the end of the year he was back on the Privy Council as if nothing had ever happened and his property had all been restored together with all the incomes back to the day of the arrest.[113] His closeness to the King was evidenced by the fact that in 1405-6, he witnessed eighty-eight per cent of royal charters and that rose to one hundred per cent for each of the next three years.[114]

Some sources say that it was whilst Edward was in jail in Pevensey that he wrote *The Master of Game*. This seems unlikely for two reasons. Firstly, he would have lacked time and secondly, he says in the preface that he is Master of the King's Game and he only obtained that position in 1406. A

---

[110] Constance had a bastard daughter by the teenaged Kent. Henry had her daughters taken from her in December 1404 ref Devon op.cit. p.300 which may have provoked her abduction plot.

[111] Jacobus Nasmith (ed.) *Itineraria Symonis Symeonis et Willelmi de Worcestre*, (London, 1775) p.161. Walter Charlton was serving in South Wales at this time, see CPR 1405-1408 p.31. Interestingly, an order was issued for his immediate arrest as part of the Southampton Plot in 1415 though he survived and went on to fight at Agincourt. Elizabeth Charlton died in 1412.

[112] At the end of May, Edward is described as guarding South Wales, see Signet Letters op.cit. p.90. Edward wrote to the Privy Council on 20th June about his recent trip to Somerset and referencing a previous exchange of letters which have not survived but presumably were made there. See Privy Council op.cit. pp.270-273. He advised he had made arrangements for rental money from his own northern estates to be brought south, promising them that he would not accept a penny himself until they had been paid in full "on my truth and as I am true gentleman."

[113] CCR 1405-1408 p.14ff. 8th Dec 1405

[114] Douglas Biggs, 'Royal Charter Witness Lists for the Reign of Henry IV, 1399-1413' in *English Historical Review* (2004) 119(481) pp.421-423. From 1405 onwards, Edward was termed "our dearest kinsman" a phrase not used before.

more probable date is 1409-1410. The volume is important for several reasons. It is the first book written by a Duke of York and it is in English rather than Latin. Richard II and John of Gaunt had both done their best to encourage the language but this was a very public recommendation of it, enhanced by it being dedicated to Edward's friend the Prince of Wales whom he had undoubtedly taken on hunting expeditions. Also, it is the earliest native work on hunting. A large part of the book is a translation of Gaston de Foix's *Livre de Chasse* but Edward added five chapters of his own, a new prologue, and made various additions throughout the text. For example, he suggested that the hunter would drink good English ale at the end of the day rather than French wine. He cut sections which he felt were inappropriate to England such as that on reindeer. Many people today would find distasteful the graphic descriptions of how animals are to be chased and then beaten to death, but there are interesting sections on how to care for the dogs or the manner in which the royal hunt was organised. Throughout is Edward's belief that hunting is not only a manly art and good preparation for war but a means of maintaining physical and spiritual well being: "since hunters eat little and sweat always, they should live long and in health. Men desire in this world to live long in health and in joy, and after death the health of the soul. And hunters have all these things."[115]

Edward had inherited books from his mother when she died and he is known to have spent considerable money buying books from France, particularly histories.[116] With each copy having to be hand written on individually prepared sheets of vellum, books were then a luxury item. He was also a patron of writers. Thomas Hoccleve dedicated one of his editions of *The Regiment of Princes* to Edward, a further sign of his interest in promoting the English language. He clearly liked to read but he tried his hand at poetry too. Whether this was a serious endeavour is uncertain. Only one example survives. Some have suggested it was addressed to Queen Joan for it begins with a reference to his "sovereign lady" but that could have just been a poetic allusion like "queen of my heart." It goes on:

Your womanly beauty delicious
Hath me all bent unto its chain,
But grant to me your love gracious
My heart will melt as snow in rain
If ye but understood my life and knew
Of all the pains that I for you feel
I wish ye would upon me rue
Although your heart were made of steel.[117]

---

[115] W Baillie-Grohman and F. Baillie-Grohman (ed), *Master of Game* (London, 1909) pp.11-12

[116] James Wylie, *The Reign of Henry the Fifth* (London, 1968), vol 2, p.272

[117] Agnes Strickland, *Lives of the Queens of England* (Philadelphia 1852) vol 3 p.64. The word

For now, however, Edward lacked time for such pleasures. The war continued with Owain Glyn Dŵr and the King was short of money. Notwithstanding all that he was already owed, Edward lent him a further sum and he went to five counties trying to encourage others to feel similarly generous. Where people did not, Edward was empowered to launch investigations into the value of property. When the King explained that he lacked money to send his daughter Philippa to Denmark to be with her new husband, Edward contributed the necessary money.[118] Edward was further given the task of visiting Southampton to prepare the area "for defence against the King's enemies of France and others who intend shortly to invade the realm."[119]

He remained active in South Wales where he was the Prince of Wales' right hand man. Henry praised him for his excellent and humble service, his administrative skills and loyal advice, and his assistance in the sorties against the rebels.[120] In 1407, he was at Aberystwyth where the situation was extremely challenging. The castle was in the hands of Glyn Dŵr's men. The English had brought a gun from the Tower but that had exploded. The King ordered all men who held land of the crown to send armed men to meet him at Evesham so they might go to assist Edward and the Prince of Wales claiming this was necessary "in consideration of the good to be obtained by the conquest of the castle by which the whole rebellion of the Welsh is like to finish."[121]

After the siege of Abersytwyth, the Prince paid a glowing tribute to Edward in the presence of the King and all Parliament. He said that had it not been for his "good advice and counsel" both himself and those in his company "would have suffered great loss and peril." He added that Edward had "served and laboured in such a way as to support and embolden all the other members of the aforesaid company, as if he had been the poorest gentleman in the realm wishing to serve him in order to win honour and renown." He concluded his speech by saying "he is a loyal and valiant knight in all that he does."[122]

Edward's favour was not restricted to the Prince of Wales. He was still a member of the Privy Council and Constable of the Tower of London. He

---

"rue" here meant to take pity.

[118] CPR 1405-1408 p.215. Edward's loan of £536 would be worth around £200,000 today. It covered the full cost of the ship which was £166 13s 4d, see David Loades, 'The King's Ships' in *Medieval History*, vol.1 no 1 (1991) p.95 plus the cost of supplies and crew.

[119] CPR 1405-1408 pp.153, 199, 231.

[120] Legge op.cit. p.356

[121] CPR 1405-1408 p.361

[122] Said on 2nd December 1407, see PROME October 1407 item 24

continued to be given a variety of jobs, including investigating a murder in Southampton.[123] He was a witness to the King's will.[124] Henry IV was ill for considerable periods from 1406 onwards and he selected Edward to represent him in Parliament.[125] Edward served on the council established to govern during the King's incapacity and continued to be a trier of petitions. He witnessed almost ninety per cent of royal charters from 1405-1413 which proves that despite his duties in Wales, he was still in regular meetings with the King.[126]

Something else which did not change was the fact that he was owed money. In 1408, he was still awaiting £1100 payment for the time he had spent in Aquitaine, seven years before. The King recognised the "danger in which he is acknowledged to stand to his people and divers other creditors of his" but the cash was not forthcoming.

In 1409, Edward moved his base from Cardiff to Hanley. His accounts for that year survive and show him purchasing various items from strawberries and apples to larks. He built new kitchens, cattle stalls and a brewhouse and grew a variety of vegetables in the gardens including onions. There remained insufficient room for everything and he had to rent storage for his grain and also a laundry. His household at this point numbered almost a hundred people and it cost just over 8d per day to feed each one.[127]

Shortly before Christmas 1411, Edward was involved in the foundation of a college for priests at Fotheringay. It was a joint foundation with the King who had purchased the six acres on which it was to be built from Edward. Henry's charter tells how he was "inflamed by the fervour of charity and devotion" and that it was his wish that Edward "participate with us in the aforesaid pious enterprise." [128] Undoubtedly, he wanted Edward to assist with the funding. Four years later, Edward was permitted to raise a loan on his properties following his expenses in building the college.[129] Fotheringhay Castle had been held by the Dukes of York since 1347 and was to remain

---

[123] CPR 1408-1413 p.111

[124] J. Nichols, *A Collection of all the Wills now known to be extant of the Kings and Queens of England*, (London, 1780) p.205. Edward had also been executor of Richard II's will, ibid. p.196

[125] For example, April 1406.

[126] Douglas Biggs, 'Royal Charter Witness Lists for the Reign of Henry IV' in *English Historical Review* vol 119 issue 481 (2004) p.412

[127] Chris Woolgar, *The Great Household* (Yale, 1999) pp.12, 16, 83, 114, 117, 131. C. C. Dyer reviewing his accounts in 'Gardens and Garden Produce in the Later Middle Ages' in Chris Woolgar (ed) *Food in Medieval England* (Oxford, 2006) pp. 27-41 notes that Edward's household consumed more fruit and vegetables than was average for a noble household.

[128] PROME, November 1411 item 18

[129] CPR 1413-1416 p.349

their principal seat throughout the middle ages.

A sign that Edward had not forgotten his youth in southern Europe came in 1412 when Ferdinand of Castile became King of Aragon. He possessed a ten year old daughter, Eleanor, whom Edward thought would be a good match for his year old nephew Richard.[130] His uncle John of Gaunt had married the elder daughter of King Pedro of Castile but they had no son only a daughter Catherine. John had agreed to drop his claim to the crown in return for a marriage between Catherine and Ferdinand's brother but Edmund had not agreed to this.[131] Edward believed that as the son of Pedro's younger daughter, he had a better claim than Catherine, a male taking precedence over a female in royal succession. He was realistic enough to know that it might be too late for him to claim the crown but perhaps his nephew could. After all, Edward's finances gave him little chance of providing him with a respectable inheritance. Sadly for Edward, Ferdinand rejected the idea. His own nephew, after all, was ruling as King Juan II of Castile and he saw no reason to depose him.

During the same year, Edward returned to international conflict. France was in a state of civil war and Henry decided to send an army to assist the Armagnacs. Control of the army was vested in Henry's son, Thomas, but he was young and with very little battle experience. Edward's role was to exercise some guidance on him as he had done before with the Prince of Wales. The army sent was 6,500 strong and with support personnel numbered well over seven thousand. However, in a similar manner to the ill fated Portuguese campaign of his father, this expedition was to see little action other than some raiding.[132] As the English were on their way to assist them, the Armagnacs decided to sue for peace. Thomas was furious, partly at the wasted resources but also no doubt because he felt he had lost face and was not going to see action. He demanded compensation for himself and his men. Edward put a claim in for 36,150 crowns. He received 5,430 and a gold cross studded with emeralds, pearls, sapphires and rubies – no doubt a beautiful object but not of much practical use in paying wages and feeding horses.[133]

In 1413, Henry IV died. The new king, Henry V, remembering his friendship with Edward, proceeded to restore him to his title of Duke of

---

[130] Anthony Goodman and David Morgan, 'The Yorkist claim to the throne of Castile' in *Journal of Medieval History* vol 11 (1985) p.63

[131] SC 8/103/5145

[132] Ernest Jacob, *The Fifteenth Century*, (Oxford 1961) p.114. Edward had contributed 1060 men to the army.

[133] J. H. Wylie op.cit vol 4 p.83

Aumale and formally pronounced the judgment of 1399 invalid.[134] He tried to find Edward lands from which he could draw an income in part recompense of the £8000 still owed to him from his time in Aquitaine thirteen years before.[135] Anxious to employ Edward, a man whom he clearly trusted implicitly and deeply admired, on the first day of his reign, he chose Edward to sort out an affair of financial mismanagement. [136] He also invited him to resume his diplomatic career giving him responsibility in 1414 for negotiating a truce with the Scots and in 1413 sending him to Paris to open discussions about the possibility of him marrying Catherine de Valois. He additionally gave him the job of superintending building work at Westminster Abbey.[137] It seemed there was little limit to the range of skills which Edward was believed to possess.

The most famous event of Henry V's reign was the Battle of Agincourt and Edward was in the forefront of this from planning to the conflict itself. As early as May 1414 Edward was being forced "to borrow great sums from divers persons for his service to the kingdom in the King's proposed voyage beyond the sea."[138] The King did promise to repay him but past experience would have made Edward doubtful of this. As a pledge of good faith, he was given a gold alms dish made like a ship standing on a bear and studded with pearls worth £332.[139]

Before the army departed, Edward suffered embarrassment when his brother was revealed to be leading a plot to assassinate Henry V and replace him with the Mortimer heir. Also involved was Henry LeScrope who had married his stepmother.[140] Both men were executed, the King kindly excusing Edward from sitting in judgment on them.

The events of the Agincourt campaign have been indelibly left on the English mind thanks to the Shakespeare play which is broadly accurate. The siege of Harfleur occupied the first part of the campaign. Edward wrote his will when he was there leaving his best sword and dagger to the King.[141]

---

[134] PROME, April 1414 item 9

[135] CPR 1413-1416 p.192

[136] CPR 1413-1416 p.23

[137] CPR 1413-1416 p. 145. The money for the work was to be handled by Richard Whittington, the "Dick" of pantomime fame. It is likely that the task would have been almost impossible for at the time Edward was appointed, the building fund contained just £3. See James Wylie, op.cit vol 1 p.205

[138] CPR 1413-1416 p.401

[139] Harris Nicolas, *History of the Battle of Agincourt*, (London, 1832) Appendix III p.16. The crown was not able to find the money to redeem the alms dish until 1430.

[140] Edmund's widow Joan – Edward's stepmother - had married Lescrope in 1410.

[141] Testamenta Vetusta op.cit vol 1 pp.186-189

Twenty four of his men died at Harfleur. After a five week siege, the town fell and the army began its march to Calais. Henry V said: "If my enemies attempt to prevent me, it will be at their peril. I shall not seek them but the fear of them will not induce me to deviate from my route nor will the sight of them cause me to quicken my pace."[142] The French deliberately blocked his route and the two sides came together in a field near Agincourt on the 25th October, 1415. Estimates vary but it is generally believed that the French outnumbered the English around five to one.

There are a number of accounts of the battle but they do differ. This is not too surprising. The witnesses were in different places and trying to follow events amidst the noise, carnage and mud. Even Henry V was said at the end not to know who had won. There is universal agreement that Edward requested and was granted the honour of leading the vanguard on the day. There is also no doubt that he was killed, but there the stories differ. Monstrelet, who interviewed survivors just after the event, said:

> During the battle, the Duke of Alençon most valiantly broke through the English line and advanced, fighting near to the King – insomuch that he wounded and struck down the Duke of York. King Henry seeing this stepped forth to his aid and as he was leaning down to raise him, the Duke of Alençon gave him a blow on the helmet that struck off part of his crown. The king's guards on this surrounded him.[143]

Thomas of Elmham tells the same story but says the King was going to the aid of the Duke of Gloucester whilst St Remy says it was a group of knights who damaged the crown and not Alençon. The Kingsford Chronicle says that Edward was killed when his head was split in two by a French man at arms. Thomas of Elmham, writing within a couple of years of the event, said "The Duke of York was overcome by the whirlwind of war. The King washed his body for burial with royal care."[144] Titius Livius, a member of the household of the Duke of Gloucester, simply said that Edward was killed "in the first fight." Not one of the sources gives any real details of how he met his end. Certainly his retinue was in the worst of the fighting for a quarter of them were killed and there were heavy casualties amongst his horses too.[145]

---

[142] Nicolas *Agincourt* op.cit p.98

[143] Thomas Johnes (trans), *The Chronicles of Enguerrand de Monstrelet* vol 1 (London, 1840) p.346

[144] Anne Curry, *The Battle of Agincourt*, (New York, 2000) p.47

[145] ibid. p.432. The names of many of those who fought alongside Edward can be found in the

The author of the *Gesta Henrici Quinti*, a priest serving with the English and who watched the entire battle from the baggage train, said that Edward had the idea of getting the archers to make sharpened stakes and place them in the ground in front of them. These deterred the French horses which safeguarded the archers and enabled them to fire more easily. Elmham said: "The warlike bands of archers with their strong and numerous volleys darkened the air, shedding as a cloud laden with a shower, an intolerable multitude of piercing arrows."[146] The *Gesta* says the archers then moved out and using axes, swords, the stakes and stray spear heads that were lying on the battle field, they began to butcher the French. Describing the enemy as confused and unmanly, the writer noted how "the living fell over the dead and others also falling on the living were slain" until the stacks of bodies "increased higher than a man."[147] A French writer of the time said: "Never, since God was born, did anyone, Saracens or any others, do such destruction in France."[148]

Although Edward died, he would have been delighted to see his prodigy win such a spectacular victory against enormous odds. The fact that the French did not help themselves in their choice of location or outfits should not detract from what was achieved. English losses were probably around five hundred if all ranks are considered, of which less than thirty were knights or gentlemen. Henry V must have been especially sad to learn of Edward's death. He had spent a lot of time with him in both peace and war and he valued him greatly as an advisor, a cousin and a friend. It was the end of an era.

Over a century after the battle, the antiquary John Leland wrote of Edward that "being a fat man, he was smouldered to death." Evidently, Leland did not know him and nor could he have met anyone who knew him. His comment reflected pure political bias. Edward was great-uncle of Richard III and any employee of the Tudors – and Leland was writing for Henry VIII – understood that no praise was to be given to anyone connected with him. Just as developed the image of the utterly evil, hunchbacked king who murdered his nephews in the Tower, so developed the myth of Edward, Duke of York as a fat and incompetent knight who fell off his horse in the midst of a great battle. No contemporary would have recognised the

---

National Archives in rolls E 101/45/2 and E 101/45/19. These show Edward's retinue clearly contained a large number of men from his northern estates for it included people with surnames such as Louth, Sheffield, Rotherham, Haukeswell, Donington and Leeds as well as John of Fotheringhay, Watkin of St Albans, Henry of Langley and a number presumed to come from Wales, such as Davy ap Yvan

[146] Nicolas *Agincourt* op.cit p. 263

[147] ibid. p.272

[148] Janet Shirley, *A Parisian Journal* , (Oxford, 196) p.96

description at all. [149] A more representative chronicle put it: "The Duke of York held the tide of war that day, fighting against the enemy hosts valiantly, and he was slain honourably, a man who in our time might truly be called the Second Solomon".[150]

Edward's bones were returned to England for a state funeral at St Paul's. The King and his three brothers, the dukes of Clarence, Bedford and Gloucester, all kept vigil overnight before the solemn requiem mass. His remains were then carried to Fotheringhay for burial in the choir. Edward had specified that he did not want a magnificent tomb for himself, just a plain stone. He thought the money would be better spent on feeding the poor and he directed his executors accordingly.

Edward's wife survived him by sixteen years. She died at Carisbrooke Castle in 1431. She had not remarried but her will suggests that she had not regarded the marriage as a success. She did not ask to be buried with him or request masses to be said for his soul, as was usual at the time. People named in her will included the grandson of her first husband, Lord Walter Fitzwalter and her cousin Thomas Chaucer. [151] Philippa was buried with her second husband, John Golafre, which meant that she was lain in a place of honour in Westminster Abbey, whilst Edward, hero of Agincourt, was at Fotheringhay.

His inheritance in history has been a host of negative press but Edward was clearly an extremely able man. He held positions of great responsibility under three kings and he carried out his duties well. He was one of the most experienced soldiers of the day and so well respected that in a crisis, people asked for him. He was a cultured man, but perhaps one whose private life was not entirely happy. He would have regretted not having children. His younger life was spent as favourite at a court which Froissart believed was the wealthiest and most splendid in Europe. His later life was spent trying to maintain law and order in various places. He was a warrior, a scholar, a diplomat and a deeply pious man, really the quintessential medieval knight. The adaptability which some of his contemporaries saw as being an indication of treachery was simply a sign that unlike many of them, he was prepared to put the good of England before his own dynasty. Richard II was probably quite right when he suggested that Edward would have proved an extremely able king.

---

[149] John Leland, *The Itinerary of John Leland the Antiquary* vol. 1 (Oxford 1770) p.6

[150] G. L. and M A Harriss (ed), 'John Benet's Chronicle' in *Camden Miscellany* vol. 24 (1972)

[151] Nicholas Nicolas, *Testamenta Vetusta* vol.2 (London, 1826) p.218. Her other heir was her nephew Richard LeStrange.

Richard

1411-1460

Duke of York 1415-1460

He governed the whole realm of England well and nobly

and wonderfully pacified all rebels and malefactors

with justice and without great severity[1]

The most unpopular king in English history is, arguably, the usurper Richard III who spread stories alleging his mother was a whore to justify his claim to the throne. Despite efforts of his admirers, he remains associated with the murder of the princes in the tower and suspected of killing his wife so he could marry his nubile young niece. He has also been accused of involvement in the deaths of his brother and King Henry VI. His brother Edward IV was a glutton and a libertine with a reputation for avarice. His brother Clarence had a history of joining plots and was totally untrustworthy, a trait shared with his sister Margaret who financed a handsome young fortune hunter to try and kill her niece's husband. If a man can be judged by the calibre of his offspring, the character of Richard, Duke of York, father of this colourful brood, must be considered suspect.

---

[1] G. L. and M.A. Harriss, 'John Benet's Chronicle' in *Camden Miscellany* vol 24 (London, 1972) p.212

Richard was born on September 22nd 1411, the second child of the Earl of Cambridge and his wife Anne. It appears that his mother may have died as a result of the birth for within the year, his father had remarried Maud Clifford. Although Richard never knew his mother, she was to have a profound impact on his life for she was Anne Mortimer, the great grand-daughter of Edward III's short lived second son.

Richard's father was a rather obscure character of seemingly limited intelligence. The youngest son of Edmund, Duke of York, he had not been favoured with landed estates or significant political appointments in the way that his elder brother had. The only jobs which he seemed to be given came from his brother suggesting that his talents were not obvious to his contemporaries. In the first decade of the 1400s he was serving in South Wales where his brother was Lieutenant and responsible for trying to quell the rebellion of Owain Glyn Dŵr. It was there that Cambridge, then in his early twenties, met the teenage Anne Mortimer. Although it is possible that it was a love match, it is more likely that his brother arranged the union. Since their father's death in 1402, Edward had become head of the family and he would have been acutely aware of the dynastic importance of his brother marrying well. Edward's own marriage had not been successful so he knew that he was unlikely to have a son to succeed him as Duke of York. As Edward also had a claim to the throne of Castile and Leon through their mother, Cambridge seemed destined to inherit both an English dukedom and possibly an overseas throne.[2] It was important therefore that a suitable bride be found, someone of the right background and who would bear healthy sons. However, despite his prospects, Cambridge currently had no wealth to attract an overseas noblewoman and his status was insufficient to attract a princess. A marriage within the royal family seemed the only solution and Anne as his first cousin twice removed and his step-mother's niece seemed ideal.[3] Having two brothers and a younger sister meant she was not a great heiress in her own right but she had good connections.

Edward knew about the Mortimers only too well. Early in 1405, his sister had planned to seize Anne's brothers and use them to claim the throne arguing that as descendents from Edward III's second son they had a better claim than the King who was descended from the third son. Edward had avoided involvement in the scheme and remained a highly trusted and respected member of the Court, very close to both the King and the Prince of Wales. It is inconceivable that Edward would not have discussed the proposed match with the King before allowing it to go ahead, even though

---

[2] Cambridge used the arms of Leon indicating he believed the claim was valid, see Anthony Goodman and David Morgan, 'The Yorkist claim to the throne of Castile' in *Journal of Medieval History*, Vol 11 (1985) p.63

[3] Edmund, Duke of York, had married Joan Holland whose sister Eleanor was Anne's mother.

there was no law requiring him to do so. A formal union of York and Mortimer just three years after a plot to depose the King involving the same two families, would have been political suicide without the King's approval and possibly cost all of them their lives. Presumably following said assent, the marriage of Cambridge and Anne took place in 1408.[4]

When Richard was four, his father decided to organise a plot against the King. It was an ill thought out endeavour concocted with his stepmother's husband and it failed abysmally. Cambridge proposed to hire a man to pretend to be the previous ruler, namely Richard II who had died fifteen years before, who would not only announce his evident resurrection but declare Cambridge's brother in law to be his heir. The actor would no doubt soon have met a bloody end and Cambridge would then have been left in a position of power and able to accrue great wealth. Quite aside from being an improbable plan, Cambridge failed to take into account the fact that his brother in law was loyal to the King and had no desire to be thrust upon the throne. Indeed, it was his brother in law who exposed the plot. Despite Cambridge's sycophantic supplication for mercy, the King promptly had him executed.[5]

The orphan Richard might have expected to be passed into the care of his uncle Edward, but his death just two months later at the Battle of Agincourt meant Richard was left at the age of four as a royal ward. He was now Duke of York but his lands were in the hands of others until he reached twenty-one.[6] There is no evidence of Richard being left in the care of his stepmother but rather he seems to have been placed with Robert Waterton, Constable of Pontefract Castle who received £100 a year for him.[7] Waterton was responsible for a number of prisoners brought back from Agincourt and for other high status prisoners and it is questionable how much time he had to spend with Richard. Evidence from his later life, indicates that Richard was well educated but when this process began is unknown. It is likely that Richard had a rather strange childhood, bereft of friends of his own age but hearing a lot about military exploits.

---

[4] It appears that the couple celebrated their union before they had official consent for the dispensation granted by the Pope in May 1408 required them to separate and marry again, see T. B. Pugh, *Henry V and the Southampton Plot*, (Gloucester, 1988) p.94

[5] For Cambridge's confession see Appendix IV of Harris Nicolas, *History of the Battle of Agincourt*, (London, 1832)

[6] The release of the lands was actually made a few months before his twenty-first birthday, see *CCR*, 1429-35, p.260

[7] Thomas Hardy (ed.), *Syllabus of the Documents relating to England and other Kingdoms contained in the Collection known as Rymer's Foedera*, vol. 2, (London, 1873) p.589. This sum would be worth around £40,000 today.

When Richard was twelve, his wardship was sold to Ralph Neville for three thousand marks, or about eighty thousand pounds in today's money. Henry V had died in 1422 leaving a baby son as the new king. The regency council were keen to save on the cost of Richard's keep and the sum offered was the equivalent of twenty years' keep. Neville was willing to pay the money because he knew that Richard would become one of the country's leading landowners in the next ten years. As Duke of York, Richard had considerable property in the north, which was the seat of Neville power. He also knew that Richard was the King's cousin so would be bound to take a role in government one day. His motivation, therefore in taking Richard into his home was an investment. He planned to marry Richard to his daughter Cecily and this event probably happened almost immediately although the couple would not have lived together as husband and wife until some years later. He had previously betrothed Richard's sister Isabel to his grandson.[8] It was a plan which worked out even better than Ralph might have anticipated for just a few months later, Richard's uncle died suddenly leaving him as heir to the Mortimer estates and titles. This meant that as an adult, Richard would be the wealthiest landowner in the country saving the King himself, and also that he was now heir to the Mortimer claim to the throne, the cause which had cost his father his head.

The next few years saw Richard starting to take his place in the wider world. At Whitsun 1426, he was knighted at Leicester.[9] In 1428, he took up residence at court as part of the royal household. Being eleven years older than the King, it was no doubt hoped that he would be able to provide a role model to him as well as being a fit companion. In 1429, he attended the coronation of Henry VI at Westminster. A few months later, Richard travelled with Henry to his coronation as King of France in Paris, becoming temporary Constable of England in the same year.[10] On April 22nd 1433, he was elected a Knight of the Most Noble Order of the Garter.

Richard was clearly conscious of his heritage and he was keen for others to be aware of it too. Almost as soon as he came into his inheritance at twenty-one he commenced a programme of church building and improvement. At Cirencester, he built a chapel to the Holy Trinity with windows to commemorate himself, his two great-grandfathers King Pedro of Castile and Thomas Holland, his uncle and predecessor as Earl of March, and another Mortimer relation, Peter Geneville. At St Laurence, Ludlow, he became involved in the rebuilding of the quire and had the traditional

---

[8] Isabel was betrothed to Thomas Grey who was the son of Alice Neville, elder half sister of Cecily. The plans were made when both were infants and never materialised.

[9] Charles Kingsford, *Chronicles of London,* (Oxford, 1905)

[10] Hardy op.cit. p.648

Yorkist emblems of a falcon and fetterlock carved on a misericord.[11] At Fotheringhay, just two days after his twenty-third birthday, Richard made an agreement with master mason William Horwood to build a nave and eighty feet high tower. Richard undertook to provide "stone, lime, sand, ropes, bolts, ladders, timber, scaffold, engines and all manner of stuff that belong to the said work" and to pay Horwood three hundred pounds to cover his own wages and those of the men. The same agreement also sought to protect Richard with its proviso: "If it so be that the said William Horwood make not full end of the said work within time reasonable...then he shall yield his body to prison at my lord's will and all his moveable goods and heritages at my said lord's disposition and ordinance."[12] Faced with this prospect, Horwood duly completed the work on time.

The death of the King's uncle, John, Duke of Bedford, in 1435 created a vacancy for the prestigious role of Regent or Lieutenant of France. It was not likely to be an easy job for anyone. The French were in a militant mood having been inspired six years before by Joan of Arc to reclaim the country from the English. At the time, they were preparing an assault on Paris. England was still under the control of a regency council for Henry VI was only thirteen. The position normally went to a senior member of the royal family but there was a shortage of candidates. Richard was only twenty-four and had no military experience whatsoever but he was part of the royal family and he was willing to go. He was appointed on 8th May 1436 but the Council decided to give him much more limited powers than Bedford and to leave the army under the control of Lord Talbot. On 24th May, the Exchequer advanced the money to send across the Channel 2,200 archers and 490 men-at-arms together with Richard who was to get 13s 4d for each day he was in France.[13] Two weeks later he departed and made his way to Rouen where he was to remain for just over a year. Whilst Lords Talbot and Camoys led armies against the French, Richard remained there except for one excursion to lay siege to the Abbey of Ffescham. Having taken that, he returned to Rouen "and did not more in all his time" according to one chronicler of the time.[14]

It seems to have been after his return from France that Richard started living with his wife who was then twenty-two. The couple were to have twelve children between 1439 and 1455, four girls and eight boys. Of these, three girls and four boys survived infancy. Despite it being an arranged

---

[11] Ann Darracott, *The Rebuilding of the Quire of Great Malvern Priory in the Fifteenth Century*, (Maidenhead, 2005) pp.28-29

[12] L. F. Salzman, *Building in England down to 1540*, (Oxford, 1952) pp.508-509

[13] Frederick Devon, *Issues of the Exchequer: being a collection of payments made out of His Majesty's revenue, from King Henry III to King Henry VI inclusive*, (London, 1837) pp.428-429

[14] Kingsford op.cit. p.141

marriage, it seems to have been very happy and unlike many other nobleman's wives, Cecily followed her husband almost everywhere.

June 1441 saw Richard return to France together with his wife and daughter Ann who was almost two. A son had died a few weeks before. He had accepted the position of Lieutenant of France almost a year before, this time with enhanced powers and a salary of twenty thousand a year. The way in which Richard negotiated terms before he departed demonstrated his growing confidence. He stipulated the number of guns, arrows, carts, bows and spears that he required. He wanted guarantees that he would get the money and that it would not be diverted to other government projects warning that if any part of the agreement "be broken and not fulfilled nor performed in any point and the King and the lords of his Council certified and notified thereof, that then in such case my said lord of York may be at his freedom and liberty to depart thus and to return again into this realm of England...without that any impeachment, charge, or blame may be laid upon him."[15]

The political situation for Richard's second term as Lieutenant was different because the King was now of age and wishing to impose his own policies. Henry VI was a peace loving man and devout Christian who was appalled at the idea of war and the horrific impact it had on people's lives. On paper he was King of both France and England because he was the son of Henry V of England and Catherine of France, but in practice, England did not control France and her share was diminishing every year. The King wanted to pursue an honourable peace but his uncle, the Duke of Gloucester, vehemently opposed this and urged a campaign of re-conquest. Gloucester felt that the King should take more pride in his father's achievements and seek to extend them, not sacrifice them. Opinion on the Council was divided as some nobles yearned for military glory with the prospect of rich financial prizes which came with victory, whilst others considered the costs and the logistics of England trying to find and equip sufficient men to hold the whole of France and concluded it was impossible. Richard's selection as Lieutenant reflected the fact that he was not closely associated with either party but was a senior member of the royal family who would thus have the influence required to work with the various parties involved.

At the time of Richard's arrival, war was still being waged and France remained on the offensive. Indeed, France had used the year in which

---

[15] Joseph Stevenson, *Letters and Papers illustrative of the Wars of the English in France*, vol 2 pt 2 (London, 1864) p.589. A similar clause about the right to return was in his predecessor's agreement, ibid. p.lxx

Richard had kept Normandy waiting for him to their advantage. Talbot remained effectively in charge of the English army, and Richard was happy to confirm him in this role. Richard joined Talbot to save Pontoise for a time but other towns were lost including Beaumont-le-Roger and Creil. French sources made fun of Richard's reputation for tardiness by telling how Talbot had developed a plan to capture the French King but Richard had arrived late and found the bed still warm.[16] Whilst Richard retreated to Rouen, the French continued to attack English shipping in the Channel. His performance and general disinclination to go out and harry the enemy failed to impress the Council back in England who resorted to sending him instructions which should not have been necessary, such as one to send more artillery and men to the ports.[17] The Treasurer told the Council on 6th February 1443 that considerable money and resources had been invested with Richard in France and he had no idea why they had failed to produce better results and who was responsible for this.[18] It is likely that he was simply being polite and mindful of the fact that Richard was the King's cousin. The Council, however, remained concerned and on 5th April, the King sent Garter King of Arms to advise Richard that the Duke of Somerset was being sent to France with a new "great and mighty" army. Unlike Richard, Somerset was an experienced soldier with a successful record in France having relieved Avranches and captured Harfleur in 1440. Quite deliberately, Somerset was not placed under Richard's command.

The King suspected that Richard would be upset by the move. He had known Richard all his life and must have been aware of his pride. The letter sent explained that Somerset was going to be Richard's "shield", standing between him and the King's enemy, namely Charles VII. Saying that "it is seemed full behoveful and necessary that the manner and conduct of the war be changed" the letter advised that Somerset was to wage an offensive war going into the heart of enemy country to "seek the King's said adversary with all his diligence and do his best to meet with him, wherever he may be, and in the King's right to fight with him... and there use most cruel and mortal war that he can...to resist and withstand his malice." The King urged Richard to give Somerset his full support adding that it was not his intention "do anything that might prejudice or hurt in any way the power that his cousin of York has" but stressing that necessity gave him no choice. Detailed instructions followed regarding the defence of Rouen and other places in Normandy including the need to obtain stores so that towns could

---

[16] T. B. Pugh, 'Richard Plantagenet, Duke of York, as the King's Lieutenant in France and Ireland' in J G Rowe (ed.) *Aspects of Late Medieval Government and Society,* (Toronto 1986) p.118
[17] Harris Nicolas, *Proceedings and Ordinances of the Privy Council of England,* vol V (London, 1835) p.160
[18] ibid. p. 223

withstand sieges, the requirement to hold regular searches for potential traitors and the importance of maintaining constant watch. The letter ended with the comment that whilst the King would do what he could to help Richard, he must recognise "the great charge that the setting forth of his said cousin of Somerset with the army has" and for this reason Richard would have to wait for his money.[19]

Richard's reaction to this move which he interpreted as effectively a vote of no confidence in his efforts was immediate. Only a few weeks after the King's letter, the Council felt it necessary to assure Richard that they had spoken to Somerset themselves to make sure he understood the honour and deference he owed to Richard and promising that there was no intention to injure his "wealth, worship and profit."[20] They also sent him a further thousand men for the siege of Dieppe.[21] Richard was not mollified but in 1444 two events happened to change the picture. Somerset died at the end of May and a truce was signed with France. Richard could now excuse his inactivity on grounds little was expected of him but to maintain the peace and administer justice which he seemed to enjoy. With time on his hands, he started to make plans for the future. In 1445, he began planning marriages for his three year old son and six year old daughter. He determined that Anne should marry his sister's nephew, Henry Holland, heir of the Duke of Exeter and agreed to provide a dowry of three thousand pounds, though in the event he never paid this.[22] In July 1447, Holland was made Richard's ward as well as his son-in-law.[23]

For his son, he decided that only royalty would do and that meant a princess. He approached King Charles VII of France who had three unattached daughters and proposed a match. It must be supposed that he did this with the consent of Henry VI for the boy seems to have been granted the title of Earl of March about this time. In May 1444, the truce of Tours had been signed together with an agreement for Henry VI to marry the niece of Charles VII's queen. Richard may have thought that a double wedding would be a good idea although there was no reference to a marriage for his son at either Tours or in the Parliamentary debate which discussed the agreement.

In February 1445 Richard received a letter from Charles VII advising

---

[19] ibid. pp.259-263

[20] ibid. p.289

[21] Devon op.cit. p.446. Dieppe fell on 14th August.

[22] T. B. Pugh, 'The Estates, Finances and Regal Aspirations of Richard Plantagenet, Duke of York' in Michael Hicks (ed.), *Revolution and Consumption in Late Medieval England*, (London, 2001) p.77

[23] CPR 1446-52 p.86

that he was willing to entertain the proposal and inviting him to send his ambassadors for talks. These took place in May and Richard wrote to the said king afterwards claiming he was "perfectly rejoiced...for I am well aware that my said eldest son could not be placed in and appointed to a more lofty position and connection." Yet, he was not entirely content because Charles VII had proposed his daughter Magdalena. Richard wrote "considering her very tender age and that naturally and as speedily as age will permit I desire that issue should proceed of my said eldest son" he would prefer Joanne. He continued: "My eldest son is of an age better adapted and suitable for madam Joanne...I have settled and fixed upon her, if it be the good pleasure of your highness to give heed thereto."[24]

It was soon made evident to Richard that Charles VII not only disagreed with him but that he did not appreciate being questioned by a mere duke. The French king's daughters were aged eleven, nine and eighteen months and Richard's son was three, so he felt that his youngest daughter, Magdalena, was the most suitable. He seems to have found Richard's plan to send his son out to stud as soon as practical with whichever daughter he could rather perturbing. Richard rapidly sent back a letter expressing his delight in the prospect of Princess Magdalena as a daughter in law and accepting that Charles VII had intended this all along. It was as close as Richard ever came in his life to issuing an apology. Yet his hopes were to be frustrated and by the time of Richard's death, his son was eighteen and still unmarried.

At the same time as he was trying to secure a French match, Richard was also investigating the possibility of pursuing his claim to the throne of Castile. King Pedro of Castile had been deposed and killed in 1369 leaving three daughters as his heirs. One had entered a nunnery but the other two had married sons of Edward III. John of Gaunt, the great-grandfather of the current King of England, had married the elder daughter Constance in 1371, whilst Richard's own grandfather, Edmund. had married the younger, Isabella, in 1372. Despite some efforts by England to restore Constance, the Spaniards showed no interest in having her as Queen or Gaunt as King. Eventually, in 1387, Gaunt had agreed to surrender his own claim on condition that his daughter – the only child of his union with Constance – marry the heir to the reigning Castilian monarch. That had happened and Gaunt's daughter had married the future Henry III of Castile. By the time that Richard started to take an interest in the subject, her son Juan had been on the throne for almost forty years. It seemed unlikely that the Castilians would depose him in Richard's favour.

---

[24] Stevenson op.cit. vol. 1 pp.83-86.

Richard's argument was twofold. Firstly, Gaunt had made the agreement without consulting his brother and this made it unlawful. Legally this was untrue though there is evidence that Edmund had been angry at the time about it. Secondly, Gaunt and Constance had only produced a single daughter whereas Edmund and Isabella had produced two sons and a daughter. In the martial world of medieval monarchy, male heirs were always preferred. Richard's theory was that as men took precedence in the succession, he was rightful heir. He still faced the problem that he was descended from Pedro's younger daughter but his solution to that was the myth that Gaunt and Edmund had agreed that the first son born of either couple should be heir. Richard even had this story perpetrated in print through Harding's chronicle, a document written for and dedicated to him.[25] In making his claim, Richard was following family tradition. His father's arms had included the crown of Castile and lions of Leon[26] and his uncle Edward had sought to arrange a marriage for him with Leonora of Aragon when he was just an infant, a project which was ended by Edward's early death.[27] Although Richard was unable to enforce his claim to Castile, his investigation of it at the same time as he was trying to marry his son to a French princess, indicates his ambition. The King of England was then in his early twenties and Richard expected him to marry and sire a brood of sons. If this happened, Richard would cease to be a senior royal and instead become just a princely cousin, relegated to jobs which involved a show of status but no actual power. Believing his prospects in England to be limited, Richard was keen to look elsewhere and he must have been disappointed to find that they were no better abroad.

At the end of 1445, Richard returned to England to attend Parliament and to discuss the proposed peace. His five years as Lieutenant of France had ended but he clearly anticipated being appointed for a second term and there is documentary evidence that plans were being made to send him back the following year. The King had recently granted Richard a major landed estate in Normandy which suggested that he too saw Richard's future as being in France.[28] However, all of this changed when the Keeper of the Privy Seal, Adam Moleyns, denounced Richard for corruption. Richard was undoubtedly furious, not least because the allegations had been made behind his back. He demanded that Moleyns present his case in Parliament

---

[25] Henry Ellis, *The Chronicle of John Hardyng* (London 1812) p.21. Richard never saw the finished volume because he died during its production.

[26] Francis Sandford, *A Genealogical History of the Kings and Queens of England* (London, 1707) p.384

[27] Anthony Goodman and David Morgan, 'The Yorkist claim to the throne of Castile' in *Journal of Medieval History*, Vol 11 (1985) p.63. Leonora was grand-daughter of John I of Castile.

[28] Michael Jones, 'Somerset, York and the Wars of the Roses' in *English Historical Review*, vol 104 (1989) p.290

so that Richard could answer it publicly and so clear his name.[29] Yet he cannot have been surprised for in Richard's subsequent written response, he noted that he was aware of rumours about financial mismanagement circulating even when he was in France which was why he had brought the account books back with him.[30]

Moleyns accused Richard of paying pensions to his friends and councillors whilst leaving the regular soldiers unpaid. Richard responded that the pensions had been established by his predecessor and accused Moleyns of offering money to soldiers in order to persuade them to come to England to say they had not been paid. Richard went on to accuse Moleyns not just of bribery but of slander on grounds that Moleyns had suggested that Richard was "the cause of loss and destruction in Normandy." Having opened his ledgers to prove the soldiers had been paid, he demanded that the King punish Moleyns.

Moleyns responded that it was not him who had started the rumours about Richard's mismanagement because "they were here long before that." He denied bribery, slander and blaming Richard for the loss of Normandy, arguing that he did not yet consider it lost. He too appealed for the matter to be discussed in Parliament and said that otherwise he may be forced to take direct legal action against Richard for slander.

In the event, the matter was not discussed, the King probably feeling that it was better to avoid the publicity or divide his council further. Richard was not convicted of mismanagement but neither was he reappointed.[31] Instead, on Christmas Eve 1446, Edmund, Duke of Somerset − brother of the man who had been sent out to lead an offensive war in 1443 and his lieutenant in that campaign - was given the job. Chroniclers of the time in England and France agreed that this engendered a deep seated jealousy in Richard which was to have fateful consequences.[32]

Richard spent the next few months in England planning new building projects and claiming his share of the assets of the Duke of Gloucester who had died in circumstances contemporaries found suspicious. His next

---

[29] PRO SC 8/336/15877

[30] The allegations and responses appear as Appendix 3 of PROME, 1445.

[31] J M W Bean, 'The Financial Position of Richard Duke of York ' in J. Gillingham and J. C. Holt (ed.), *War and Government in the Middle Ages* (Cambridge 1984) p.190 has reviewed the data and suggests that there may have been some truth in Moleyns allegations of embezzlement.

[32] For example see Henry Riley (ed.), *Registrum Abbatiae Johannis Whethamstede* vol. 1 (London, 1872) p.160

appointment came a year later when he was made Lieutenant of Ireland.[33] It is possible that he was not keen on the role for it took him nineteen months to depart England. His mother's father and brother, Roger and Edmund Mortimer respectively, had both been Lieutenant of Ireland and had both died there. Roger had been killed by rebels in 1398 and Edmund had died of the plague in 1425. Since through his Mortimer inheritance Richard was not only a landowner in the country but he bore the title of Earl of Ulster, he seemed an obvious choice. For the Council, it had an added advantage in that it kept him as far as possible from France and the Duke of Somerset.

For his service, Richard was to receive four thousand marks in the first year and two thousand pounds in subsequent years.[34] The first half year's money was to be paid in advance and it may have been that Richard delayed his departure whilst he awaited the cash. His powers in Ireland were to be those of his predecessors which meant that he could raise armies and summon Parliaments. His duties were to keep the peace and ensure the loyalty of Ireland to the English Crown. With only about a third of the country in English hands, this was not going to be easy. Richard was also given the right to appoint a deputy to govern in his absence.

Richard arrived at Howth in July 1449 and went directly to Dublin. After a few days rest he went on to Trim, an ancestral property of the Mortimers. He may have visited the church there for he gave orders to restore the building later that year. He then moved north under his banner of Earl of Ulster, an astute political decision for it was likely that the Irish would be more welcoming to him as that than as Duke of York. In the King's name, he summoned the people to attend him and do homage. Thousands arrived and he received gifts of hundreds of cows. Wild promises were made by chieftains from a vow to learn English to one to hand over the proceeds of every wreck to the English Crown. Whether Richard actually believed them or merely pretended to do so in order to keep the peace is unknown. Either way, after a few days he returned to Dublin where he had left his wife to await the birth of their next child. George, future "false fleeting perjured Clarence"[35] was born on 21st October.

Richard was to spend just over a year in Ireland during which time he opened two parliaments. The success of his personal relationships with the Irish was shown in the second at Drogheda which voted a tax on his behalf on grounds he "has had no payment from our said Lord the King for the

---

[33] CPR 1446-52 p. 185
[34] Stevenson op.cit. vol. 1 pp.487-8
[35] William Shakespeare, *Richard III*, Act 1 Scene 4 Line 56

protection of this his said land and he is likely to bear great charges and costs in resistance of the Irish who, according to appearances mean to go to war."[36] Richard had clearly been complaining to the King about the same matter for on the 17th May 1450, Henry VI demanded his Treasurer pay Richard the 4,700 marks owing on grounds the non-payment had caused him "right great hindering and grievous damage...as he say" and forced him to pawn goods to raise cash. The King ordered the debt to be settled "in all goodly haste...and to make him ready payment hereafter of his wages."[37] Meantime Richard wrote to his brother in law, the Earl of Salisbury, warning that without money "my power cannot stretch to keep this land in obedience and very necessity will compel me to come unto England to live there upon my poor livelihood, for I had rather be dead than...Ireland was lost by my negligence."[38]

Yet it was not to be a lack of money which caused Richard to hurry home in September 1450. It was events in England itself. The early summer had seen a rebellion against the government led by a man who claimed to be a Mortimer and Richard's cousin.[39] The revolt had failed but not without bloodshed and the murder of the Lord High Treasurer. The rebels demands had included one that the King "take about him a noble person the true blood of the realm that is to say the high and mighty prince the Duke of York late exiled from our sovereign lords presence by the false traitor Duke of Suffolk."[40] Despite it being shown that the rebel leader was named Cade not Mortimer, suspicions existed within the court that Richard was somehow involved in the rebellion. Just a few weeks before the revolt, an enquiry had been launched in Ipswich into a plot to depose Henry VI in favour of Richard.[41] This plot was masterminded by William Oldhall, Richard's own treasurer.

Discontent at home and concern over the deteriorating situation in France where war had been declared in 1449 had resulted in the fall of Suffolk, the King's leading minister. Henry VI had stepped in to announce that he would be his judge rather than Parliament and this enabled him to sentence Suffolk to exile rather than death. Others disapproved and the

---

[36] Edmund Curtis, 'Richard, Duke of York as Viceroy of Ireland 1447-1460' in *The Journal of the Royal Society of Antiquaries of Ireland,* vol. 2 no 2 (December 1932) p.174

[37] Harris Nicolas, *Proceedings and Ordinances of the Privy Council of England,* vol 6 (London, 1837) p.93. Richard was also owed six thousand pounds in annuities as Duke of York as the King acknowledged.

[38] Curtis op.cit. p.174

[39] Kingsford op.cit. p.159

[40] R A Griffiths, 'Duke Richard of York's intentions' in *Journal of Medieval History,* vol 1 no 3 (1975) p.206

[41] Ralph Griffiths, *The Reign of Henry VI,* (Stroud, 2004) p.685

vessel taking Suffolk abroad was intercepted and Suffolk taken and killed. It was a gross affront to the King.

The atmosphere in England was tense. Staff in the royal household were issued with weapons to enable them to better defend their King and the public were banned from carrying weapons in the streets.[42] It should have been no surprise to Richard therefore that his arrival at Beaumaris was met by obstructive royal officials whom, he later complained, sought to prevent him obtaining supplies for his men or horses on grounds "I come against your intent as your traitor."[43] The King responded saying that it was natural that his staff should act defensively when Richard returned to the country without leave but promising that he would take action if anyone actually lied about him.[44] An evidently still disgruntled Richard then observed that justice was not being carried out which meant criminals had no fear of the law. He offered his services to go and punish all offenders for the tranquillity of the Kingdom and to take the role of chief minister. Henry thanked him for the proposal but said that he did not believe it was "accustomed nor expedient" to be advised by one man only but he looked forward to allowing Richard a seat on his Council.[45]

The most significant thing about Richard's letters to the King was the fact that he deliberately made them public. William Wayte wrote to John Paston about the exchange reporting that "all the King's household was and is afraid, right sore."[46] Bales Chronicle commented: "people stood in great dread and doubt."[47] The only reason that Richard would have done this was if he was trying to obtain support for something. He had not been accused of any misdemeanours in Ireland and he could not be blamed for the failures in France. Though some were suspicious, there was no evidence to link him to Cade's recent rebellion. Richard's motivation was contained in his second letter where he demanded the arrest of all traitors "of what estate, degree or condition so ever they be" and their commitment to the Tower "there to abide without bail or mainprice to the time that they be utterly tried." In Richard's eyes, Somerset was responsible for the loss of Normandy which made him a traitor. That other people were involved and the causes of defeat were complex, was not important to Richard. He was still angry about Somerset being given what he regarded as his job and he wanted to

---

[42] C. Cl. R. 1447-54 pp.194-195, Griffiths, 'York's Intentions' op.cit. p.182

[43] Michael Hicks, 'From Megaphone to Microscope' in *Journal of Medieval History*, vol. 25 no 3 (1999) p.252

[44] Ralph A Griffiths, 'Richard, Duke of York and the Royal Household in Wales, 1449-50' in *Welsh History Review*, vol. 8. (1977) p.19

[45] Griffiths, 'Intentions' op.cit. p.205

[46] James Gairdner, *The Paston Letters*, (London, 1904) vol.2 p.174

[47] Ralph Flenley, *Six Town Chronicles*, (Oxford, 1911) p.136

destroy him and saw the disturbances as his opportunity to do this. The extent of his personal vendetta against Somerset can be further seen in the way his retainers attacked Somerset's property in Sudbury and Corfe, stealing his property and assaulting his servants.[48] On 1st December 1450, Richard and his nephew, the Duke of Norfolk, sent a "great multitude... ..strongly armed" to Blackfriars to attack Somerset in person, or at the very least arrest him. Somerset escaped to the Tower where he was to remain in protective custody for a few days until things calmed down.[49]

Richard had arrived in London to attend Parliament but he had come with three thousand men and entered the city with his sword carried before him in state.[50] His supporters erected his arms and his badge of the falcon and fetterlock alongside the King's arms. It was provocative behaviour and if Richard did not directly order his men to do these things, he was still their master so responsible for them. The King sought peace and urged Richard to ride through the streets with him to restore order and so that matters could be addressed in a proper manner in Parliament. One eye witness said: "The King with all the lords came through the city all in harness and the Citizens standing upon every side of the street in harness which was the gloriousest sight that ever man in those days saw."[51] Yet, it would take more than a show of unity in the streets to settle Richard's ambitions. In the Commons, where the Speaker was Richard's chamberlain, William Oldhall, the MP for Bristol proposed that since the King had been married for five years and not produced a child, Richard should be declared heir. The MP in question, Thomas Young, happened to also be employed by Richard, in this case as his attorney. Whilst it cannot be proved that Richard was behind Young's action, it seems unlikely that he was unaware of it or disapproving since he rewarded Young with the manor of Eason in Gordano the same year.[52] The King promptly had Young sent to the Tower together with other officers of Richard's household and dissolved Parliament.[53]

For Richard, the situation must have seemed bleak. His enemy Somerset was high in the King's favour and he was not. He could have returned to Ireland as he was still officially Lieutenant there but he chose not to do so. Instead, he made his way to Taunton where the Earl of Devon was besieging his own uncle, Lord Bonville. Richard's excuse was that he was keen to

---

[48] William and Edward Hardy (ed.), *Recueil des Croniques et Anchiennes istories par Jehan de Waurin* (London, 1891) p. 265. See also Jones op.cit p.288

[49] The pro-Yorkist chronicler Benet claims Richard sent men under the Earl of Devon to save Somerset and not arrest him, see Harriss op.cit. p.203

[50] Flenley op.cit. p.137

[51] Kingsford op.cit. p.162

[52] Bean op.cit p.192

[53] P. A. Johnson, *Duke Richard of York, 1411-1460*, (Oxford, 1988) pp.98-99

bring peace within the family, Bonville and Devon being both his cousins.[54] The King and his Council disbelieved this. Peacemakers rarely travelled with two thousand armed men and Devon had been involved in the affray at Blackfriars less than a year before. Most significantly, the dispute was taking place in Somerset. They thought that at best, Richard was acting to protect his ally Devon, or more likely he was interfering in the affairs of his enemy again.[55] Furious at his lords behaving in such a manner, the King summoned all those involved to his presence whereupon they received clear indications of the royal displeasure and a fine.[56] Richard and Devon decided to ignore the summons. Instead Richard departed to his castle at Ludlow from where he sent a letter to the King declaring his loyalty and demanded the Bishop of Hereford attend to witness him repeating his oath of allegiance on the sacrament. A month later, on 9th February 1452, Richard sent a letter to the people of Shrewsbury which spoke of the loss of trade and national dishonour occasioned by the loss of France which he claimed was due to the Duke of Somerset. Predicting that the French were about to invade, it continued..

> I, as the King's true liege man and servant (and so I shall be to my life's end), for my true acquittal ...advertised his royal majesty of certain articles concerning the weal and safeguard as well of his most royal person as the tranquillity and conservation of all this his realm. the which ...were laid apart and to be of no effect through the envy, malice and untruth of the said Duke of Somerset; which ... labours continually about the King's highness for my undoing, and to corrupt my blood and to dishonour me and mine heirs and such persons as be about me, without any desert or cause done or attempted on my part of theirs....Seeing that the said Duke ever prevails and rules about the King's person and that by his means the land is likely to be destroyed, I am fully concluded to proceed in all haste against him with the help of my kinsmen and friends.

To this end, Richard asked them to "fortify, enforce and assist me and to come to me with all diligence wheresoever I shall be or draw with as many goodly and able men as you may make to execute the intent abovesaid." Ever mindful of his image in the eyes of the public, he added a footnote that the men they sent were to be told to "do no offence nor robbery nor oppression unto the people."[57]

---

[54] Richard's aunt Eleanor Mortimer had married the Earl of Devon whose grandson now bore the title. Her daughter had married Lord Bonville.

[55] Johnson op.cit. notes that Berkeley who was also present was involved in a dispute with the family of Somerset's wife, p.103

[56] Harriss op.cit.p.205

[57] *Theatrical Inquisitor*, vol 11, November 1817 pp.348-349

Three weeks later, Richard, together with the Earl of Devon, encamped his newly gathered army at Blackheath where he was joined by the King whose forces were said to number fifteen thousand.[58] Richard was outnumbered and realised he had miscalculated. Neither the men of London nor Kent would support him. There might not be a great love for Somerset but taking up arms against the King was treason and that was a different prospect to most people.

Anxious to avoid a bloodbath, the King sent emissaries to Richard to treat for peace amongst them the Earls of Warwick and Salisbury and Bishop Bourchier, all of whom were related to the Duke of York.[59] It was reported that Richard was tricked into sending home his army in return for a promise that Somerset would be despatched to prison to await trial. Although it may have suited Richard to promulgate this version of events in order to exonerate himself and further blacken the reputations of those about the King, it is improbable. The King was in a strong position and only a fool would have believed that he had suddenly become convinced that Richard was right in his judgment and all the Council were wrong. It is more likely that Richard realised that he had little choice but to submit and as he knelt before the King he saw Somerset standing beside the throne. To increase his humiliation, Richard was forced to enter London riding before the King "like a prisoner."[60] After two week's house arrest at Baynard's Castle, Richard was forced to swear a public oath of loyalty at St Paul's in front of the King, senior churchmen and most of the nobility, including Somerset. It was commented that there had never been so many people in the church to witness Richard say:

> I, Richard, Duke of York, confess and acknowledge that I am and ought to be the humble subject and liegeman to you my sovereign lord King Henry VI....I shall come at your command whenever I am called by the same, in a humble and obedient manner, unless I am prevented by sickness or by bodily weakness, or by such other causes as shall be thought reasonable by you, my sovereign lord. I shall never hereafter presume to gather a body of men or assemble your people without your command or licence... nor shall I take action against any of your subjects, of whatever estate, degree or condition they be; but whenever I feel myself wronged or aggrieved, I shall sue humbly for remedy to your highness, and proceed according to your laws, and in no other way... I shall in all the things abovesaid, and in others,

---

[58] John Silvester Davies, *An English Chronicle*, (Camden Society, 1861)p.70

[59] Salisbury was his brother in law and Warwick was Salisbury's son. Bourchier was the brother of his sister's husband.

[60] Kinsgford op.cit. p.163

conduct myself towards your highness as a humble and true subject ought to conduct himself towards his sovereign lord.[61]

It was the nadir of Richard's fortunes. He was sent home to Ludlow in disgrace.

Just over a year later, in the summer of 1453 an event was to take place which was to change Richard's life: the King had a breakdown. Bales Chronicle reported that Henry VI "suddenly was taken and smitten with a frenzy and his wit and reason withdrawn."[62] When members of the Council visited they found him unable to walk without support and seemingly incapable of comprehending anything they said.[63] When his wife, who was pregnant at the time of his collapse, presented to him his new son, he showed not a flicker of emotion or recognition.[64] These verdicts were confirmed by Abbot Whethamstede who knew the King well.[65] It was clearly an extremely serious situation and as each week went by without any sign of improvement in the King's health, it became more so. Yet, the Council was reluctant to act. When Parliament met in November 1453, the Chancellor simply advised that the King was unable to attend due to fears of plague and promptly prorogued it until February. By that point, something had to be done. Rumours about the King's health were circulating and it was said that the Queen wanted to be given "the whole rule of this land."[66]

For Richard, the King's illness represented an opportunity and he lost no time in making his way to London for a Council meeting where his nephew, the Duke of Norfolk, presented a list of complaints against the Duke of Somerset. Fearing that Richard might once again seek to take the law into his own hands and raise another army, Somerset was promptly removed to the Tower for his own protection, where he was to stay for over a year.[67] Yet even without Somerset and the King being able to exercise power, Richard was still unable to progress his ambitions very far. He was given authority by the Council to open Parliament in the King's name on grounds he was the senior royal prince but he had no special role. Richard was able to thwart the Commons choice of Speaker whom he knew to be loyal to

---

[61] PROME, November 1459, item 9

[62] Flenley op.cit. p.140

[63] PROME, March 1453, item 32

[64] Gairdner, *The Paston Letters*, vol 2 op.cit. p.295

[65] Riley, *Whethamstede*, op.cit p.163

[66] Gairdner, *The Paston Letters*, vol 2 op.cit. p.297

[67] Somerset himself confirmed that he was placed in the Tower for his own protection, see Hardy, *Syllabus*, op.cit. p.685

Somerset[68] and he may have had some influence over the acquittal of the Earl of Devon for his part in the rising at Blackheath. Richard argued that the suggestion that the rising was treasonable was false and libellous and he offered to fight anyone who disagreed. Richard's motives had been pure, he claimed, and therefore so were Devon's. Although the Lords publicly accepted this statement, they chose to create the King's infant son as Prince of Wales the next day, a clear sign of their loyalty to Henry VI and a warning to Richard not to over-reach himself.[69]

The situation may have continued with the Council doing its best to rule collectively with the help of Parliament but for a disaster which struck a week later when Chancellor Kemp died. He had been the lynch pin of the government and his death left a vacuum. Council members were sent to advise the King and ask his will but they returned to Parliament to report that the King remained so ill that he was unable to respond in any way. Faced with a political crisis, the decision was made two days later that Richard be appointed Protector. It was not a prospect which many regarded with any enthusiasm. More than half the members of the Lords absented themselves and those which accepted the appointment took care to ensure that strict limits were placed on Richard.[70] He was told that they had chosen "a name different from other councillors, not the name of tutor, lieutenant, governor nor of regent, nor no name that shall imply authority or government of the land, but the said name of Protector and Defender, the which implies a personal duty of attendance to the actual defence of this land as well against the enemies outward, if required, as against rebels inward."[71] It was hardly the ringing endorsement which Richard craved. It reflected the desperation of the position. The King had been ill for eight months and seemed unlikely to recover. His son was barely three months old and would inevitably be unable to rule for another twenty years. The Queen was French which guaranteed her unpopularity, and besides there was no precedent for a woman ruling.[72] The King's three uncles, the brothers of Henry V, were all dead. The King himself was an only child. Richard was his nearest relative of the blood royal and so, notwithstanding his behaviour of the past three years, he was chosen.

Richard naturally accepted the offer with alacrity, and a speech where he declared his unworthiness for the honour. His appointment was to continue

---

[68] Richard had Thorpe arrested in the late autumn of 1453 in connection with an alleged theft.

[69] PROME, March 1453, items 48 and 49

[70] J. S. Roskell, 'The Problem of the Attendance of the Lords in Medieval Parliaments' in *Bulletin of the Institute of Historical Research*, vol 29 (1956) p.191

[71] PROME, March 1453, item 36

[72] The last time a woman had sought to rule England there had been a civil war.

until the Prince of Wales came of age. Since Richard was forty-one at the time, this meant that he might expect to remain Protector for the rest of his life. His first concern was how much he would be paid. He wanted "a notable sum of money" to be paid on time. He told Parliament that his service in France and Ireland "drove and compelled me for lack of payment of my wages to sell a great substance of my livelihood, to pledge all my great jewels and the most part of my plate not yet redeemed and therefore like to be lost and forfeited and over that to endanger myself with all my friends by borrowing."[73] The Treasurer promised to see what could be done and Richard demanded that this answer be recorded on the Parliament Roll. Meanwhile, he faced the problem of finding lords who were willing to serve on his council. Five bishops and seven lords, amongst them his relatives the Duke of Norfolk and the Earl of Warwick, all declined on grounds that included being suddenly too ill, too inexperienced or simply too busy.[74]

During Richard's time as Protector, he faced a rebellion from his son in law, the Duke of Exeter, and problems in Calais where the garrison had mutinied. Richard's rapid movement against Exeter and his efforts to broker a settlement in Calais earned him some respect. Yet he did not have much opportunity to enjoy his successes for within nine months of his appointment, the King suddenly recovered. Almost overnight, York was out of a job and his enemy Somerset was released. Richard's response to what he regarded as a threat to his honour was to do as he had three years before: he raised an army and marched against the King, again claiming that his quarrel was not with him but his evil advisors, namely the Duke of Somerset. This time, however, he had greater force on his side for his brother in law, Salisbury had decided to join him in protest at Somerset's release, and he brought with him his energetic son, Warwick. Once more, Richard decided to make his case to the public, a deliberate attempt to involve them in what could and should have been a courtly dispute. In this document, Richard argued that his "enemies of proved existence such as abide and keep themselves under the wing of your Majesty Royal" had "right studiously and right fraudulently" spread stories that he was not loyal which he maintained was not true. As a result, the three of them – together with their armed retainers - were coming to tell the King not to "give trust or confidence unto the sinister, malicious and fraudulent labours and reports of our said enemies."[75]

On May 22nd 1455 the two sides came together in battle at St Albans. In

---

[73] PROME, March 1453, item 54

[74] Ralph A. Griffiths, 'The King's Council and the first Protectorate of the Duke of York' in *English Historical Review* vol. 94 (1984) p.75

[75] Gairdner, *The Paston Letters,* vol. 3 op.cit. pp23-24

one account, Richard demanded that the King "deliver such as we would accuse" vowing that they would accept "no promise, surety nor other till we have them which have deserved death, or else we die." The King refused saying that it was inappropriate for any subject to take up arms in this way or make demands of his sovereign. Richard then gave the orders to attack saying "better it is for us to die in the field that cowardly to be put to a great rebuke and shameful death."[76] Abbot Whethamstede described the carnage which followed with corpses strewn across the streets, men lying with their throats cut or their brains dashed out, people slowly bleeding to death.[77] The King himself chose not to fight. Unlike his warrior father, he was a pacifist by conviction and he was also keenly aware that his coronation oath bound him to rule all his people, not just one section. Instead, he stood and watched the horror unfold before him, becoming more upset as it went on. Being still amid a storm of arrows, he was hit by one in his neck and this forced him to flee to a neighbouring house for shelter.[78] It did not appear a life threatening wound but it was shocking that the King had been hurt at all.[79] The battle ended when Warwick's men succeeded in killing the Duke of Somerset. Richard promptly ordered his men to stop the attack and went to pay his respects to the King.

Had Richard wished, he could have killed the King at this point, but he did not. His opposition, as he had said all along, was to Somerset. Instead, he carried the King back to London like a trophy. The King was not a prisoner but he was not returned to his palace of Westminster; rather he was sent to stay with the Bishop of London. Henry VI had been deeply affected by the trauma of the battle which was not surprising given that he had been witnessed some of his closest friends and servants cut down in cold blood. He was suspicious of Richard and his followers and he went to Westminster to make arrangements for his own funeral monument. At Whitsun, the first Sunday after the battle, when the King traditionally wore his crown to lead his people in prayer, he left Richard to place the crown on his head, a symbolic reminder of who was in the ascendant. With little option, the King approved the grant of offices to Richard and his allies. As Gregory's Chronicle noted: "it was no season to treat of peace." [80] Warwick, to whose strategy the victory at St Albans had been attributed, did best becoming Captain of Calais as well as receiving land grants in Wales.[81] A

---

[76] ibid. p.26-27

[77] Riley, *Whethamstede*, op.cit. p.168

[78] ibid. p.169

[79] Gairdner, *The Paston Letters,* vol 3 op.cit. p.43. The King was still receiving treatment almost two months later, see Johnson op.cit. p.167

[80] James Gairdner, *The Historical Collections of a Citizen of London in the Fifteenth Century,* (London, 1876) p.198

[81] Gairdner, *The Paston Letters,* vol 3 op.cit. p.28.

week later, the King departed to Windsor.

There has been some speculation over recent years regarding the state of Henry's health and its contribution to the political crises of the 1450s. There is no doubt that he suffered a breakdown in 1453 which was probably stress related. The loss of France and rebellions at home, together with Richard's ongoing hostility which had expressed itself so forcefully at Blackheath, must all have taken their toll. Previous to that date, the King seems to have been as fit and healthy and mentally sound as any of his subjects. Indeed, he was arguably more balanced than Richard whose vendetta against Somerset and hypersensitivity to imagined slights bore the hallmarks of paranoia. There had been instances of people in the past calling the King a fool but they were expressions of political frustration made by people who had never met him. Henry's sudden descent into a state of stupor was unexpected and was difficult for contemporaries to understand. Since the first clinical account of catatonia was not to be published until 1874 this is not surprising.[82] Poisoning was suspected, and this may have been the case since poison is recognised as a cause of catatonia.[83]

A more general belief was that it was an affliction sent by God and this may have encouraged a disinclination to interfere. The King was taken ill in July or August 1453 but the first notice of doctors being appointed to care for him is from the 6th April 1454, shortly after the visit of the Councillors and Richard's appointment as Protector. The doctors then were to employ laxatives, blisters and ointments of their devising and authorised to shave his head and bathe him.[84] In this, their treatment was to be almost the same as that meted out to George III three centuries later. Carole Rawcliffe has suggested that the doctors would also have followed other elements of Gaddesden's recommendations including trying to shock the King from his stupor by making loud noises beside him, setting off bad smells, physically assaulting him and forcing things down his throat to make him sick.[85] Kahlbaum's pioneering 1874 study of catatonia said that these were precisely the things which should be avoided. He described how the illness often followed anaemia and a seizure and how it could last for months. He noted how patients could recover quite suddenly and completely after a long period and that when they did so, they would often explain that they knew they had been ill but they had been unable to respond to anyone during this

---

[82] Karl Ludwig Kahlbaum, *Catatonia,* (Baltimore, 1973) translated by Y. Levij and T. Pridan. The original *Die Katatonie oder das Spannungsirresein* was published in Berlin, 1874

[83] Alan Gelensberg, 'The Catatonic Syndrome' in *The Lancet,* 19th June 1976 p.1340

[84] Thomas Rymer, *Foedera conventiones, literae et cujuscunque generis Acta Publica,* vol. 5 (The Hague, 1741) p.55

[85] Carole Rawcliffe, *Medicine and Society in Later Medieval England,* (Stroud, 1995) p.64

time because they could not hear or fully comprehend what was going on.[86] Karl Jaspers said: "the patient is like a dead camera. He sees everything, hears everything, understands everything and yet is capable of no reaction, of no affective display and of no action. Even though fully conscious he is mentally paralysed."[87] Henry VI, when he recovered said that when ill he had not known where he was or been able to understand what was happening about him.[88]

In cases where there was no cure, Kahlbaum noted that there could be a gradual descent into dementia which might prove fatal. Kraepelin, in 1893, argued that catatonia was not an illness in its own right but simply a form of schizophrenia, and this has led to claims that Henry VI was schizophrenic. In this view, the King never properly recovered from his illness of 1453 but instead deteriorated to the point where he was incapable of ruling which meant Richard was forced to take action. In such a scenario, Richard is the hero saving the realm from catastrophe and Henry the disabled victim. The alternative view denies that Henry VI was so ill and sees Richard as an overwhelmingly proud man whose sense of ambition caused him to become a traitor.

Inevitably, it is impossible to make a clear diagnosis of Henry VI's condition more than half a millennium later. He may have had physiological abnormalities in his brain or a metabolic disorder. What is certain is that he never had any subsequent attack of catatonia and there is no record of anyone in his family, either ancestor or descendent, doing so. The fact that the battle of St Albans occurred just five months after his recovery is a complicating factor. Henry did initially show signs of passivity after this, of withdrawal and he was said to be sleeping a lot.[89] This may be indicative of depression or post traumatic stress disorder. Henry's withdrawal allowed both Richard and the Queen to vie for power and it was to be 1456 before the King reasserted himself fully. From thereafter, and most clearly in 1458, Henry was transacting business and creating policy. This capability, together with the fact that he maintained normal relationships with those about him, and gave no evidence of mood swings or delusions suggest he was not schizophrenic.[90] Yet, in the immediate aftermath of St Albans, the

---

[86] Kahlbaum op.cit. pp.46, 90, 95

[87] Max Fink, Ed Shorter and Michael Taylor, 'Catatonia is not Schizophrenia' in *Schizophrenia Bulletin* vol. 36, part 2 (2010) pp.314-320

[88] Gairdner, *The Paston Letters*, vol. 3 op.cit. p.13

[89] Johnson op.cit. p.167

[90] After Henry's death, it was claimed that he had seen visions of Jesus and the Blessed Virgin during the Mass but these were hearsay presented as part of a report to have him canonised. If he did have such, they should be understood within the confines of mystical experience, Henry VI being a very pious man, see M. R. James (ed.), *John Blacman's Memoir of Henry the Sixth,*

King was weak both politically and emotionally and Richard was able to exploit this. In November 1455 Richard was appointed Protector once again.

Richard's first term of duty as Protector had lasted nine months. His second lasted three. During his time in office he had to handle the ongoing dispute between Bonville and Devon which was creating considerable disorder in the west country and the continued problems in Calais. Once more, he did a reasonable job but he failed to secure the support of the nobility. In February, he resigned his position and retreated back to his estates. The King granted him the gold and silver mines of Devon and Cornwall in thanks for his service.[91]

The next couple of years saw the King re-establishing his position, ably assisted by his Queen whom one correspondent described as "a great and strong laboured woman."[92] Margaret had originally been content to keep out of politics and had been careful to show no partiality to either Richard or Somerset but her attitude had changed since St Albans.[93] She was a more forceful personality than the King and she was deeply defensive of him and their son. Although the King did not seem adverse to using Richard for various tasks such as handling the threatened invasion of the Scots, the Queen did not want Richard anywhere near the court.[94] As a result, Richard saw his influence decline.

Across England as a whole, troubles remained. The King had decided to establish himself in Coventry which seemed safer than London and this created problems of disorder in the capital and across the south east. On 28th August 1457 an event took place which shocked England to the core as is demonstrated by the amount of attention given to it by every chronicler of the times. One wrote:

> In the end of this year came the French men and other enemies and spoiled and robbed the good port of Sandwich and slew much people for they came suddenly to Sandwich in the morning when men were a bed and searched every house and all the plate, riches, gold, silver and other merchandise and goods of value they shipped it into their ships and went smartly away with all.[95]

(Cambridge, 1919) p.44

[91] CPR 1452-1461 p.291

[92] Gairdner, *The Paston Letters*, vol. 3 op.cit. p.75

[93] Helen Maurer, *Margaret of Anjou* (Woodbridge, 2003) p.85

[94] Griffiths, *The Reign of King Henry VI*, op.cit. p.772

[95] J. G. Nichols (ed.), *Chronicle of the Grey Friars of London,* (Camden Society, 1852) p.20

Another said: "The Frenchmen robbed and spoiled the town of Sandwich in Kent abiding therein a whole day."[96] Bales said the town had been "robbed and despoiled by enemies without rebuke or damage done to them."[97] The author of the Short English Chronicle reported that three thousand Frenchmen had landed and "and slew divers persons and took many prisoners."[98] If national pride had been dented by the loss of France, the fact that the enemy had actually landed and injured English citizens in their own homes, created widespread questioning. The fundamental duty of the King and his government was to protect his people. If they could not do that, many reasoned, there must be something very wrong.

The King did his best. Having no navy, he appointed Warwick to hire ships to protect the English Channel and trade. This he did with aplomb rapidly becoming a national hero for his attacks on foreign ships. Bales wrote: "No lord of the land took the jeopardy nor laboured for the honour and profit of the King and the land but only he, for the which manhood and his great policy and deeds of worship in fortifying of Calais and other feats of arms, all the commons of this land had him in great laud…and so repute and take for as famous a knight as was living."[99] Some of Warwick's actions created a severe embarrassment for the government because he attacked vessels which belonged to England's allies, but the general population did not mind. A great wave of xenophobia was sweeping the country and making itself manifest in numerous attacks on foreigners, especially bankers and merchants. Aware that they had inadvertently created an even bigger problem, the government later sought to remove Warwick from Calais but he refused to leave and they had no power to force him.

Toward the end of 1457, the King made a direct intervention into what appeared a deteriorating situation. Conscious that Richard and his allies felt disenfranchised and threatened by the growing influence of new faces at court, and knowing the likely repercussions of such divisions, he summoned a council for 27th January advising his lords, spiritual and temporal, that he would accept no excuses whatsoever for non-attendance. The task for the council was to "set apart such variances as be betwixt divers lords of this our realm" and on 14th February, the King noted the great "diligence" being given to the work and expressed his hopes for a "fruitful conclusion" very

---

[96] Davies op.cit. p.74

[97] Flenley op.cit. p.145

[98] James Gairdner (ed.), *Three Fifteenth Century Chronicles*, (Camden Society, 1843) pp.70-71. If this number was correct rather than an exaggeration for effect, the French would have outnumbered the resident population two to one, see Karen Jones, *Gender and Petty Crime in Late Medieval England*, (Woodbridge, 2006) p.16

[99] Flenley op.cit. p.147

soon.[100] The need for a settlement was very real for Richard had duly arrived for the council only to be set upon by his son-in-law Exeter on his way to the meeting.[101] On 9th March, another attempted ambush took place, this time on Warwick. In such a volatile atmosphere, the Mayor of London, Geoffrey Boleyn, took to patrolling the streets daily with five thousand armed men.[102]

The King was angry and returned to London to oversee the negotiation process himself. On 23rd March, a settlement was agreed. Richard, Warwick and Salisbury would pay compensation to the families of those whose deaths they had caused at St Albans and they would fund the erection of a permanent memorial to the slain, all this in return for peace keeping bonds.[103] To celebrate the settlement, on Lady Day which was the start of the new year in the Justinian calendar,[104] the King led the nobility to St Paul's for a service of thanksgiving. As a mark of humility, they walked to the church and to publicly demonstrate their new accord, they walked in pairs, Richard taking the Queen's hand. The event was proclaimed as a Loveday, a term used at the time for disputes which were settled by arbitration rather than force. The Loveday made a great impression on those present. Gough's Chronicle said: "the King and each took other by the hand and so came forth together arm in arm as friends ...and all the lords went on procession at Paul's solemnly thanking God...and there was seen that day one of the greatest multitude of people that ever was seen in Paul's."[105] Bales, a keen Yorkist, described it as "a great gladness and comfort to the people."[106] A ballad written by the poet John Lydgate claimed:

There was between them lovely countenance
Which was great joy to all that were there
That long time had been in variance,
As friends for ever that had been in fear
They went together and made good cheer.[107]

Although later historians with the benefit of hindsight have tended to dismiss the event, it was a significant triumph for the King. Without him,

---

[100] Nicolas op.cit. pp.291, 293

[101] Johnson op.cit. p.181. With Exeter were Clifford (his stepmother's great nephew) and Egremont (his wife's nephew).

[102] Kingsford op.cit. p.168. Boleyn was the great-grandfather of Queen Anne Boleyn.

[103] C. Cl. R. 1454-1461 p.292

[104] In use in England until 1752. The belief was that the year began at the time of Christ's conception which it was reasoned took place on March 25th, nine months before Christmas.

[105] Flenley op.cit. p.160

[106] ibid. p.145

[107] H. Nicolas, *A Chronicle of London*, (London, 1827) p.253

there would have been no settlement. The Loveday negotiations showed Henry VI was still capable of leading from the front and implementing policy. It was only unfortunate that his confidence in those involved being fundamentally men of honour was misplaced. Richard, due to pay the greatest sum on grounds he was most to blame, never paid a penny in compensation.[108] As a preacher at the time had commented, making an agreement between Richard and his enemies was like Judas greeting Jesus with a kiss.[109]

At first, things went well for Richard. He received some of the money owed to him and the King decided to involve him in his new European peace plan. Henry VI wanted to cement ties between England, France and Burgundy by arranging a series of marriages which would unite three European princesses to three English lords, namely the Prince of Wales, Richard's eldest son and the son of the new Duke of Somerset.[110] The decision to involve Richard in this policy was a mark of favour and Charles VII did not seem adverse to the idea. There had been talks about marrying Richard's son, Edward, to Princess Magdalena in 1445. By the end of 1458, Edward was sixteen and Magdalena fifteen so the marriage could have gone ahead quite quickly. Unfortunately for Richard, the talks broke down due to wider political problems.[111]

The situation deteriorated rapidly in 1459, due largely to Warwick's activities in Calais. Not only was he attacking the shipping of England's allies but he was believed to be negotiating directly with Burgundy on Richard's behalf. Indicative of the changing mood, at the Garter meeting that year, Richard's son was not elected. Tension mounted with the government purchasing large amounts of weapons for its defence and requiring men to attend the King with armed retainers equipped for two months.[112] In the summer, a Council meeting was scheduled to be held at Coventry, home of the royal family, and neither Richard nor his allies, Warwick or Salisbury, were invited. Past experience taught that a lack of invitation usually meant that the Council wished to discuss someone behind their back and that generally meant that treason charges would follow. Feeling directly threatened, Richard did what he had done before, and he mobilised his forces. He met with Warwick and Salisbury at Worcester where they swore an oath of loyalty to the King on the sacrament and vowed

---

[108] Johnson op.cit. p.184

[109] Gairdner, *Historical Collections*, op.cit. p.203

[110] Griffiths, *The Reign of King Henry VI*, op.cit p.816

[111] Richard's daughter Margaret later married the ruler of Burgundy, Charles the Bold, but this was after her father's death.

[112] R. L. Storey, *The End of the House of Lancaster*, (Stroud, 1999) p.186

that they would attend the King in person to tell him how:

> We be proclaimed and defamed in our name unrightfully... it accords neither with your said intent nor with your will or pleasure that we should be otherwise taken or reputed...Our lordships and tenants have been of high violence robbed and spoiled against your peace and laws and all righteousness. ...Persons intend of extreme malice to proceed under the shadow of your high might and presence to our destruction - for such inordinate covetousness whereof God is not pleased.[113]

They then sent their declaration to Henry and set up camp at Ludlow to await a response.

The fact that Richard had chosen to appeal over the Council's head to the King was a sign that he maintained confidence in him. The problem was that people generally were losing faith. The author of the English Chronicle, admittedly one of Richard's supporters, wrote:

> In this same time the realm of England was out of all good governance as it had been many days before for the King was simple and led by covetous counsel and owed more than he was worth. His debts increased daily but payment was there none; all the possessions and lordship that pertained to the crown the King had given away, some to lords and some to other simple persons so that he had almost nought to live on...For these misgovernances and for many others the hearts of the people were turned away from them that had the land in governance and their blessing was turned into cursing....The Queen with such as were of her affinity ruled the realm as she liked gathering riches innumerable.[114]

The government sought to prevent trouble by sending men to intercept Salisbury en route to join Richard with more men. The two retinues met at Blore Heath on 23rd September where some two thousand men were killed and two of Salisbury's sons were captured. The prospects of peace seemed further away than ever. Yet still, the King tried. He offered Richard a pardon if he would disband his men but Richard refused on grounds he distrusted the Queen and wanted to clear his name. He left the government no choice but to mobilise against him. The two sides faced one another at Ludford Bridge on 12th October when Richard's side fired their guns. They were outnumbered and they knew that to fight on would be suicidal. Even

---

[113] Davies op.cit. p.82

[114] ibid. p.79. The word simple means innocent or trusting. The same appellation was given to Cade by his supporters, see Gairdner, *Historical Collections* op.cit. p.192

though they had some support, it was far from universal. The men whom Warwick had brought from Calais had baulked at actually taking the field against the King. They would fight his enemies or for justice but not their King. That was treason and the penalty for that was death and the loss of all property, which meant penury for their wives and families. Richard made the decision to abandon the field and England itself. He placed his eldest son into the care of Warwick and Salisbury and he fled to Ireland taking his second son, Edmund, with him.

The Irish were delighted to have Richard back. He was still their Lieutenant and the loyalists had been petitioning him for several years to actually return to his duties and restore order. Those who were less keen on English rule were also happy to see him because they hoped that his dissatisfaction with Henry VI's government could be used to their own advantage. This proved to be the case. Richard promptly summoned a Parliament to Drogheda and approved a series of laws which at once safeguarded himself and effectively gave Ireland independence. These included introducing a native coinage, declaring that nobody could be extradited to England for treason, denying the force of English law without consent, making the act of threatening Richard or his family in any way an act of treason and requiring all landowners to maintain an armed man on permanent alert ready to defend Ireland or Richard himself. To further strengthen his position, Richard made his son Edmund, then aged sixteen, Chancellor.[115]

His caution was understandable for while he was away, Parliament in England had passed an act of attainder against him, his two eldest sons, and against his allies Warwick and Salisbury for treason. The indictment reminded those present that Richard had spent much of his youth at court and had been well favoured with appointments which should have ensured his gratitude and loyalty. Instead he had used "false and traitorous imaginations, conspiracies, feats and diligent labours born up with colourable lies" in his campaign to destroy the King. He had joined with Warwick and Salisbury in "premeditated malice and damnable opinions... most diabolical inhumanity and wretched envy and their most unreasonable craving for an estate that by right ought not to be desired or had by any of them." To this end, Richard had waged war against the King at Blackheath, St Albans and Ludford Bridge. He had written letters to various towns urging them to join him in his disobedience. He had refused to attend Councils when invited which was his duty as a senior lord. The indictment also claimed he had entered the King's palace "with a great multitude of people equipped and arrayed for war, and there they broke down the screens

---

[115] Curtis op.cit. pp.181-182

and walls."[116] Since there was absolutely no dispute that he had done those things and they constituted treason, it was no surprise that he was convicted. Whether his motive was malicious as the indictment said, or noble as he claimed, was irrelevant. Taking up arms against the King was treason. His behaviour in the reign of any other medieval monarch would have seen him beheaded long ago. He was fortunate that Henry VI was both a keen believer in forgiveness and also gullible.

Although his situation in Ireland was comfortable, Richard was aware it was not a permanent solution. His wife remained in England with their younger children where she received an allowance from the King. His eldest son was in France. Richard himself had lost all his lands so had no income at all saving that which Ireland chose to give him. As a royal duke, he was not accustomed to being homeless and penniless and he needed to take action to restore his fortunes and to ensure that he could pass on his lands and titles to his son.

In March 1460, Warwick sailed to Ireland to meet with Richard to discuss their next move. Together they drafted a manifesto which shows signs of being principally Richard's work. He was always keen to try to appeal to the people because he knew his support amongst the lords was rather tenuous. He may also have been concerned about the lack of understanding of his cause, with even men as well connected and educated as William Gregory, sometime Mayor of London, wondering "where was or is the fault I know not...what wrong there was, no man dared say."[117] The document contained another declaration of loyalty to the King himself before reiterating how the fall of France and the decline of law and order at home were due to the evil counsellors whom they said must be removed. Yet the manifesto implied, for the first time, some criticism of the King himself for being unable to control his advisors.[118] A strategy was then agreed. Warwick, together with Edward and Salisbury, would invade England from the south and assess the response they received. When they judged it safe, Richard would join them for a final confrontation with the King. This time, they would need to either prove their loyalty and have the treason verdicts overturned or they would face death.

That summer, Warwick, Edward and Salisbury duly entered England and they fought a battle with the King's forces at Northampton. They not only won the fight but they captured the King himself, although as at St Albans, Henry chose not to take part in the battle itself. Richard received

---

[116] PROME, November 1459, items 7 to 18
[117] Gairdner, *Historical Collections,* op.cit. pp.196, 198
[118] Davies op.cit. pp.86-90

the news with joy and made his way back, timing his arrival in London for the start of the new Parliament. What he did next caused consternation amongst all those present and the country as a whole. He appeared with his sword carried upright before him as if he were a king. The banner in front of him showed not his coat of arms but the arms of England. He entered the Parliament chamber and placed his hand on the throne as if about to sit down. Amidst the gasps of astonishment at this behaviour, the Archbishop of Canterbury bravely went up to him and asked if he had come to see the King. Richard retorted that if there were to be any visits made, the King should come to him. At that point, he turned and marched into the royal palace of Westminster and took up residence where "he kept King Harry there by force and strength." [119] Less than a week later, Richard formally submitted his claim to the throne of England to Parliament. The chronicler reported "all the lords were sore dismayed."[120]

Why did Richard choose to claim the crown at this point? It is possible that the King's health had declined for in Lent 1460, during a visit to Croyland, an eyewitness wrote: "in consequence of a malady that had been for many years increasing upon him he had fallen into a weak state of mind and had for a length of time remained in a state of imbecility and held the government of the realm in name only."[121] Yet this statement appears on the same page as one highlighting Edward's kingly qualities so it may not be totally impartial or true. Similarly, Warwick's accusation that the King was "a dolt and a fool who is ruled instead of ruling" or his brother's comment that Henry was but a "puppet" should be seen in context.[122] They were attempting to justify their position. There is no evidence that at the time, anybody suggested deposing the King on grounds he was mad or not fit to rule, though almost everyone thought he was led too much by his wife.

Richard may also have wanted revenge on those he felt had slighted him. Richard's entire career is indicative of a man with a severe chip on his shoulder. This could stem from his childhood. He had never known his mother. His stepmother seems to have rejected him.[123] His father was

---

[119] Kingsford op.cit. p.171, Riley, *Whethamstede,* op.cit. pp.376-377, Gairdner, *Historical Collections*, op.cit. p.208

[120] Kingsford op.cit. p171

[121] Henry Riley (ed.) *Ingulph's Chronicle of the Abbey of Croyland*, (London, 1908) p.424

[122] Quoted in Nigel Bark, 'Did schizophrenia change the course of English History? The mental illness of Henry VI' in *Medical Hypotheses*, vol. 59, issue 4, (2002) pp.416-421

[123] Richard did sometimes use a white rose as part of his badge and this was the emblem of the Clifford family so there may have been some link. It was more commonly used by his son. See Henry Ellis, 'Enumeration and Explanation of the Devices formerly borne as Badges of Cognizance by the House of York' in *Archaeologia*, vol 17 (1814) pp.226-227, Sandford op.cit. p.386

executed for treason when he was four, something that would have been deeply shameful to him and may have occasioned some bullying. He would not have forgotten that his father had been executed by the King's father. Now he had been accused of the same crimes and had lost his name and livelihood, he may have wanted to get his own back on all those who had punished him.

Another possible reason for Richard's decision was financial pressure. Richard had complained to Parliament in 1454 that he had not been fully paid for his service in France or Ireland and nor had he received all the annuities he was due as Duke of York. At the time he was owed over twenty four thousand pounds, which was the equivalent of around four years income.[124] During his first term as Protector, he had been successful in getting some of this money, including five years back payments from London, but he was still owed money.[125] In this, he was not unique. The wars with France had been expensive and the treasury was exhausted so there were many people who had not been paid. The Duke of Buckingham was owed almost twenty thousand pounds too.[126] One of the principal reasons that the Crown appointed high ranking nobles to senior positions was that it was assumed they would have the resources to make up the shortfall. Richard was recognised to be the richest man in England after the King with an income which today would be worth over three million pounds. He should not, therefore, have experienced difficulties although there is evidence that he had a wife with very expensive tastes.[127] Despite this, he does seem to have had financial problems. He had pawned jewels in 1452 but was unable to redeem them. He failed to pay the dowries for either of his daughters. He also sold a number of properties from the late 1440s onwards, a period of high inflation.[128] Yet, his difficulties were not all the fault of the King or even his wife. Raising private armies was expensive and Richard had to borrow money to pay them. The extent of his financial plight is evident that when he died just two months after making his claim, his executors were unable to process his will because he lacked assets to meet his bequests.[129] He may have thought that becoming king would solve his money problems.

Richard may also have been motivated by a sense of desperation. On three occasions in the last ten years, he had taken up arms. He had killed

---

[124] Bean op.cit. p.189

[125] ibid. p. 185

[126] Pugh, 'Richard Plantagenet, Duke of York as the King's Lieutenant' op.cit. p.126

[127] ibid. p.112. Her dress to welcome the new Queen cost a tenth of Richard's annual income.

[128] T. B. Pugh, 'The Estates, Finances and Regal Aspirations of Richard Plantagenet' op.cit. pp.79-80

[129] Bean op.cit. p.197

his enemy Somerset but had not become the King's chief councillor in his place. He and his allies had killed other prominent royal advisors such as Buckingham but that had not earned him a place of trust either. It must have seemed that whenever he rid the King of one "evil" councillor, another emerged to take their place. With the Queen's known animosity to him, he may have reasoned that the only way forward was to become king himself and select his own advisors.

A detail which suggests that Richard was motivated by a desire for status is to be seen in the fact that in the claim, he referred to himself as Richard Plantagenet, the first known use of the name on an official document.[130] The royal family did not traditionally use a surname because they had titles instead. Richard was known as the Duke of York or Richard of York. In 1605, William Camden suggested the name came from Geoffrey of Anjou who had lived in the twelfth century and married Matilda, granddaughter of William the Conqueror. Camden said that Geoffrey was known as Plante Genest because he wore a sprig of broom in his hat, the derivation being the Latin name of the flower.[131] The assumption has been made since that Richard was identifying himself with Geoffrey but there is no evidence that he felt any special link to an obscure ancestor who died more than three centuries before and who had never even set foot in England.[132] No other member of the royal family in the succeeding years had either used the name or taken broom as a symbol. There is no evidence that Richard himself ever wore broom, used it in his shield or seal or banners or as decoration. In the ancestry which he presented to parliament, Richard did not even include Geoffrey. The more likely explanation is that Richard was seeking to remind people that he was descended from more than one European royal house. The prefix planta in both Latin and Welsh signifies an offshoot. Genet was a breed of Spanish horse, famous at this time. Richard was the great grandson of King Pedro of Castile and he believed he had a claim to the Spanish throne as well as the English. Richard, like his father, used the arms of Spain on his shield and his son Edward, when he became King of England, maintained his claim to be King of Spain until 1467.[133] The reason that none of the royal family since Geoffrey had used the name Plantagenet until Richard was because they were not claiming descent from him and nor were they descendants of a Spanish princess. Whether Richard knew of Geoffrey's nickname is unknown but there is

---

[130] The name appears against an entry for 1448 in Gregory's Chronicle but this was most likely the addition of a later copyist, see Gairdner, *Historical Collections*, op.cit. p.189

[131] William Camden, Remaines of a greater worke, concerning Britaine, the inhabitants thereof, their languages, names, surnames, empreses, wise speeches, poësies, and epitaphes (London, 1605) p.90

[132] Geoffrey was Richard's great-great-great-great-great-great-great-grandfather

[133] Goodman and Morgan op.cit. p.63

nothing to suggest that his use of the surname at this important stage in life, when he was making a claim for the throne, was anything other than a reflection of his own immediate personal ancestry.[134]

In order to understand Richard's claim to the throne it is necessary to consider the situation in 1377 when Edward III died. He had produced five sons who had reached adulthood, the first two of whom had died before him. His eldest son, the Black Prince, had left a son Richard who succeeded Edward III without controversy. Despite marrying twice, Richard did not produce any children which raised questions about the succession. Edward III had said that Richard should be followed by the next male heir in such a case but Richard argued that as king, he was not bound by any decision made by his predecessor.[135] During his reign, there were rumours that he had chosen either Mortimer or his cousin Edward as heir, but these were just evidence of political games. Richard expected to have a son. The situation changed when Henry, eldest son of Edward III's third son, deposed Richard. There was no lineal justification for this whatsoever. It was simply a case of conquest and Henry IV, as he became, was followed by his son and then his grandson, Henry VI. For sixty years, the situation had not been questioned by anyone, including Richard. As the Lords reminded him, he took his title from his grandfather, Edmund, Duke of York, the fourth son of Edward III and a fourth son naturally came after a third. Yet Richard, was also descended from the second son, Lionel whose only daughter was his great-grandmother. The question was whether a claim made through a woman was valid. Richard's claim to Castile was made through his grandmother and the English claim to France was through a woman too.[136] In an ordinary landed estate, a woman could inherit but was the Crown like this? Did there need to be different rules to prevent England being divided or passed into the hands of a foreign prince? These were the issues which Parliament and the judges were compelled to decide in 1460 as a result of Richard's claim and they did not find it easy.

After more than two weeks deliberation, an Accord was reached. Henry would remain king for the rest of his life but Richard would be his successor. This solution was based on that applied in the Treaty of Winchester three hundred years before when King Stephen had faced a challenge from Matilda, daughter of his predecessor. Her claim was stronger by blood but

---

[134] In his claim, Richard only used the surname for himself and his father, not for any of his other forebears. This again suggests that he was implying inheritance from his Spanish grandmother.

[135] Michael Bennett 'Edward III's entail and the succession to the Crown, 1376-1471' in *English Historical Review*, vol 113 (1998) p.583

[136] The English claimed France through Isabella, daughter of Philip IV, who was mother of Edward III.

hardly anybody believed she was fit to rule, not least because of her gender. Despite Stephen having two adult sons, it was agreed that his heir would be Matilda's son. The Treaty of Winchester had ended a civil war then and it was hoped that the Accord would now. Henry had ruled since 1422 and few people had known any other monarch. They had all sworn allegiance to him and he had been consecrated at his coronation which meant he was chosen by God. It was undoubtedly true that his grandfather had taken the throne but Parliament at the time had been very pleased to accept this. The idea of over-turning more than sixty years of history and declaring that all laws passed, all land transactions, all judgments made since 1399 were null and void, was simply unworkable. Besides, there is evidence that most people liked and trusted Henry VI, even if they did not admire him in the way they had his father. They did not like or trust Richard. Since Henry was more than ten years younger than Richard and in good health, it is likely that some of those who agreed to the Accord did so in the hope that the King would outlive Richard and the problem would somehow go away. Some would also have feared that failing to agree would have subjected the realm to a bitter civil war which nobody wanted. In order to further sweeten the Accord for Richard, he was voted a large annuity so that he and his two eldest sons could live in a manner befitting their status as royal princes and heirs to the throne.[137]

The major weakness in the Accord was that it disinherited the King's son. Richard's supporters had been spreading rumours for the last three or four years that the Prince of Wales was actually just the Queen's son, the inference being that the father was Somerset. The stories were so widespread that they were reported in France with the Milanese ambassador sending home the story which someone had told him that the King himself had said that the Prince must have been born of the Holy Spirit because he had never touched his wife.[138] There is no reason to believe these were anything but malicious stories designed to discredit the Prince and to strengthen Richard's claim to the throne. Henry and his wife appear to have been completely devoted to one another and had a happy and faithful marriage. The fact that the King signed the Accord gave some credence to the stories and has caused some later historians to assume that he must have been mentally incapacitated at this stage. One contemporary claimed Henry acted "for fear of death" having been held effectively as Richard's prisoner all this time.[139] It is possible that Henry accepted the Accord as a temporary expedient, assuming that the situation would have changed by the time his seven year old son matured. Although Henry was to

---

[137] PROME, October 1460 item 30

[138] Allen Hinds, *Calendar of State Papers and Manuscripts In the Archives and Collections of Milan*, (London, 1912) p.58

[139] Gairdner, *Historical Collections*, op.cit. p.208

claim a decade later: "For this kingdom which is transitory and of the earth I do not greatly care" he was very aware of his inheritance and wanted to pass it on to his son.[140]

The Queen, however, was not prepared to wait and see what happened. She had hated Richard for waging war against the King at St Albans and claimed his behaviour now was motivated by "pure malice."[141] She raised an army to defend the rights of the Prince of Wales and to free the King from his dreadful position. On 30th December 1460, barely two months after the Accord was signed, her troops attacked Richard in his castle at Sandal. Exactly what happened is unclear. Some say that Richard had sent out foraging parties and left himself unprotected, others that a truce had been agreed for the Christmas period which the Queen's army breached. Richard was supposed to have declared that "he had never kept castle in France even when the Dauphin came to besiege him and he would not be caged like a bird by a scolding woman."[142] For whatever reason, he went outside and he was killed. His son Edmund died in the same battle. Salisbury was captured and taken to Wakefield for execution. The Queen had all three heads placed on the gates of York, Richard's wearing a paper crown.[143]

The story of Richard, Duke of York, is that of a troubled man. Politically, he was never satisfied and he refused to accept that the King had a right to choose his own advisors. That some of the ministers did a poor job is incontrovertible but it is far less certain whether their failures justified his actions. Richard himself had not been a resounding success in either France or Ireland and his record as a military leader was poor. It is clear that Richard was not loved in his lifetime, except by his wife and those who had never met him. Those who knew him or worked with him tended to find him pompous, untrustworthy and possessed of a confidence in his abilities they found impossible to justify. His decision to wage war on his anointed king in defiance of his oaths of allegiance was to cost the lives of thousands of his fellow subjects. Estimates of dead vary but it is likely that around one in ten adult men were killed and many more were injured.[144] Richard's pride was directly responsible for that. As the historian Pugh once wrote: "Seldom has a mediocre man had more influence on the course of English history."[145]

---

[140] James op.cit. pp.44-45. Henry was speaking after years of imprisonment in the Tower.

[141] George Goodwin, *Fatal Colours*, (London, 2011)p.107

[142] Joel Rosenthal, 'Richard, Duke of York: A Fifteenth Century Layman and the Church' in *Catholic Historical Review*, vol 50 part 2 (July, 1964) p.175

[143] Stevenson op.cit. vol.2 part 2 p.775

[144] For evidence of the barbarity, see reports by the Towton Battlefield Archaeological Survey Project. Estimates of dead vary from 50,000 to 200,000. The adult male population at the time was around 600,000, see Andrew Hinde, *England's Population*, (London, 2003) p.64

[145] T. B. Pugh, 'The Estates, Finances and Regal Aspirations of Richard Plantagenet' op.cit. p.84

Edward

1442-1483

Duke of York 1460-1461

A goodly man of personage, of stature high, of countenance and beauty comely, of sight quick, broad breasted and well set...Against his adversaries fierce and terrible, to his friends liberal and bounteous.[1]

Of all the men who have held the title of Duke of York, Edward bore it for the shortest time, just sixty-three days from 31st December 1460 to 4th March 1461. Yet in the space of these nine weeks he achieved something which none of his predecessors had done – he became King of England, France, and Ireland.[2]

Edward was born on the 28th April 1442 at Rouen in Normandy where his father Richard, Duke of York, was serving as Lieutenant. His mother Cecily was twenty-seven and she had already given birth to two children: Anne was two and a half years old but the boy had already died. Six more brothers and three sisters were to follow, though four of these died in infancy. The fact that seven of the twelve children survived was testament to the care lavished on them and their strong genetic inheritance.

---

[1] Henry Ellis (ed.), *The Chronicle of John Hardyng,* (London, 1812) p.467
[2] He also claimed to be King of Castile and Leon.

As the eldest surviving son and heir to his father's titles and estates, Edward was given the best of everything. He had a French nurse named Anne de Caux who probably stayed with him until he was seven, the age at which a boy of his station in life would generally be removed from the care of women and transferred to "the rules and teachings of men wise and strenuous, to understand the acts and manners of a man."[3] Anne may have nursed the younger children too because Edward clearly maintained contact with her. When he was King, he granted her an annuity of twenty pounds a year.[4]

Closest in age to Edward was his brother Edmund, thirteen months his junior. Sisters followed who would have been educated separately as would his other two surviving brothers who were seven and ten years younger respectively.[5] Details of their upbringing are not known but they would have led a very structured life. The timetable which Edward was to lay down for his own sons was probably based on his own experiences. The day began with prayers before breakfast and then came lessons in a room set aside for the purpose. After a meal at which uplifting and heroic stories were read to the children came more lessons and some exercise. Edward and his brother would have learnt to ride at an early age and received training in the arts of war and how to handle weapons. Then it would have been back to the chapel for evensong which was followed by supper and a brief period of recreation before bedtime.[6] Although many children of noble families were sent away for their education, it appears that Edward spent most of his young life with his parents. His first three years were spent with them in Normandy, the next four years in England and then just over a year in Ireland. Following the family return in the autumn of 1450, Edward and his brother lived initially at Fotheringhay with their parents but at some date they were moved to their father's estate of Ludlow Castle.[7] There they continued their training as knights, learnt languages, read, practised the social arts of polite conversation and dancing and studied estate management. Edward expected to inherit lands scattered across England, Wales and France and such a diverse group of properties required organisation and staff to maintain them and ensure they yielded the income expected.[8]

---

[3] CPR 1452-1461 p.567

[4] CPR 1467-1477 p.439

[5] The future Duke of Clarence and Richard III

[6] J. A Giles (ed.), *The Chronicles of the White Rose of York*, (London, 1843) pp.153-154

[7] Richard's rebellion of 1452 meant he needed to ensure the safety of his heir. The King was at Ludlow in the late summer of 1452 and the children would not have been moved there until he had left. Richard thereafter was mainly based at Fotheringhay in Northamptonshire and Baynard's Castle in London.

[8] It is unknown when Edward was knighted. He was the only Duke of York not to be invited to

When Edward was eleven, his father became Protector of England owing to the illness of the King. This position naturally took his father away from home a great deal but he exchanged letters with his son on a regular basis and there is evidence that Edward visited him in London. In January 1453, John Stokeley had reported that Richard was coming to London with Edward and that Edward was sending his household men ahead together with their helmets, jackets and weapons.[9] This showed the separation of their households and that Edward already had his own armed men, even though he was presumably too young to control them. In April, Edward was present when his father became Protector. [10]

Two of Edward's letters to his father have survived. The first was written on the 20th April 1454, a week before Edward's twelfth birthday and just over two weeks after his father became Protector. Signed by himself and his younger brother, it shows the formality which existed in the relationship and also Edward's interest in politics:

We recommend us unto your noble grace humbly beseeching your noble and worthy fatherhood daily to give us your hearty blessing through which we trust much the rather to increase and grow to virtue and to speed the better in all matters and things that we shall use, occupy and exercise. Right high and right mighty prince our full redoubted lord and father we thank our blessed Lord not only of your honourable conduct and good speed in all your matters and business and of your gracious prevail against the intent and malice of your evil willers

Richard's appointment as Protector had not been without issue and it was known that there were others amongst the nobility who disapproved. Edward would have known of this and his father's dispute with the Duke of Somerset plus the problems in Calais. Yet he remained a boy and the letter continues showing his interest in clothes and his confidence that his father will not only be ready to supply his exact requirements but that he will resolve a situation which Edward found intolerable, the apparent bullying behaviour of the Croft brothers who were presumably sharing his lessons:

We thank your noble and good fatherhood of our green gowns now late sent unto us to our great comfort, beseech your good lordship to

---

be elected to the Garter.

[9] James Gairdner, *The Paston Letters,* (London, 1904) vol.2 pp.297-298

[10] Carole Rawcliffe, 'Richard, Duke of York, the King's obeisant liegeman' in *Historical Research* vol. LX, (1987) pp.238-239. Although the letter quoted was more likely to Richard's son in law than his son, it does show that there had been a family gathering in London at the time he became Protector.

remember our prayer books and that we might have some fine bonnets sent unto us by the next sure messenger for necessity so requires. Over this right noble lord and father please it your highness to know that we have charged your servant William Smith bearer of this to declare to your nobility certain things on our behalf namely concerning and touching the odious rule and demeaning of Richard Croft and of his brother. Wherefore we beseech your gracious lordship and full noble fatherhood to hear him in exposition of the same and to his relation give full faith and credence.[11]

Edward's second surviving letter was written a month later on 3rd June and began:

If it please your highness to know of our welfare at the making of this letter, we were in good health of bodies, thanks be to God, beseeching your good and gracious fatherhood of our daily blessing. And where you command us by your letters to attend specially to our learning in our young age that should cause us to grow to honour and worship in our old age, please it your highness to know that we have attended our learning since we came hither and shall hereafter by the which we trust to God your gracious lordship and good fatherhood shall be pleased.

Edward referred to his father's journey to quell the rebellion of the Duke of Exeter saying: "We conceive your worshipful and victorious speed against your enemies to their great shame and to us the most comfortable tidings that we desired to hear." In fact, his father had not yet defeated Exeter but he had evidently told his son that he had achieved this. The letter ended with a request that his father send him a particular member of staff from his kitchen. Edward was to be known throughout his adult life as a man who was very keen on food and the request was almost certainly a veiled criticism of the food being provided at Ludlow.[12]

It is very difficult to assess Edward's relationship with his parents. As a prince growing up with an interest in the arts of war, he would have drawn close to his father. He certainly inherited from him a love of books. Richard is known to have possessed at least six volumes including a copy of the very ornate *Grandes Chroniques de France*, a history of that country which had been purchased originally by his own uncle.[13] The volume is today held in

[11] James Halliwell-Phillipps, *Letters of the Kings of England*, vol.1 (London, 1848) pp.121-122

[12] Samuel Bentley, *Excerpta Historica*, (London, 1833) p.9

[13] Livia Visser-Fuchs, 'Richard of York: Books and the Man' in Julia Boffey and Virginia Davis (ed.) *Recording Medieval Lives*, (Donnington, 2009) p.266. The price paid would be worth

the British Library.[14] As an adult, Edward was to become the founder of the royal library and to purchase some of the most sumptuous works ever created, a testament to his taste and wealth. He bought books in a number of languages and it would appear that he inherited his gift for linguistics from his father who was said to have "great intelligence" and be confident in Latin.[15]

The British Library also holds a volume purchased by Edward during his teenage years which provides an insight into his preoccupations at this time. The book is a collection of eight separate texts bound together and appears to have Edward's own inscription inside: "iste liber constat Edwardo comiti Marchie primogenitus filius ducis Eboraci." The first is a treatise on blood-letting and the second a manual on how to treat wounds through cauterisation, something which would have been relevant to a young soldier. The fifth is an illustrated work on the anatomy of the pig, taken from Cophon. It was believed at the time that the internal organs of the pig were particularly similar to human beings. With the restriction on human dissection, studying the pig was the most common way for physicians to learn their trade. The fourth and sixth tracts date from the thirteenth century. One describes the five senses and considers which is the most important. Deciding that sight, touch, hearing and smell are just external, the author concludes that taste is the chief sense because it involves the person changing the nature of the food or medicine by consumption. It then explains how best to taste, something Edward clearly took seriously with his passion for food. The other tract continued the same theme to look at how medicinal qualities can be divined from the colour of something. This linked in with the prevailing understanding of treatment as being based on the four humours of blood, phlegm, yellow and black bile. The third tract is an interesting choice for a book owned by a man because it concerned cosmetics and advice on the appearance and was a work written for women and allegedly by a woman, it was the *Trotula Minor*. Edward would have learnt from this that in order to have white teeth he should chew fennel and rinse his mouth with wine. To brighten his hair, he should wash it in a concoction of boiled cabbage stalks and powdered ivory. The seventh tract in the collection was a variation of the *Secretum Secretorum* with a tenth century paper within by the physician Rhazes about the complexion and how to cure skin disorders. This was an important work because, like the *Trotula*, it was based on empirical observation and not just Aristotelian theories of matter. The fact that Edward had two tracts on

---

around twenty-five thousand pounds in modern money which highlights the enormous amount of work involved in producing such a volume with each page being copied by hand and illuminated.

[14] Royal MS 20 C vii

[15] Livia Visser-Fuchs op.cit. p.265

skincare may indicate that like many other teenage boys, he suffered from acne. The eighth tract was a copy of the *Centiloquium* by Ptolemy, one of the most important astrological works of all time. It presented one hundred guidelines on how to interpret a horoscope and discussed different techniques such as synastry, which compares charts to understand a relationship, horary work which seeks to answer specific questions and electional astrology which attempts to predict the most fortuitous time for a particular plan to be effected. The hand written notes against the text and the scribbled calculations of moon positions show that Edward took the subject seriously. It is probable based on evidence from this volume that he developed the habit of having the heavens analysed before making decisions.[16]

Edward would have spent less time with his mother but his treatment of her when she was a widow was good suggesting that they got along well. Like most women of her day, she was not educated. Hardyng observed that she barely understood any Latin and had "little intellect."[17] She was a lady who took a keen interest in her appearance, at one time spending six hundred pounds on a single outfit, a crimson velvet dress encrusted with more than three hundred pearls.[18] Yet she was also very religious, becoming a member of the Palmer's Guild in Ludlow alongside her husband to signify her belief in the spiritual efficacy of pilgrimages.[19] After she was widowed, she chose to live the life of a semi-religious. She rose early for prayers, then breakfasted before attending Mass. Over dinner she listened to devotional readings from volumes such as Bonaventure's *Meditationes Vitae Christi*. She would then take an afternoon nap before more prayers and then spend the evening with her family.[20] There is no evidence that Edward shared her piety but he did enjoy spending time with his younger brothers and sisters, visiting them daily whenever he could.[21]

Aside from these two letters, there is no certainty about how or where Edward spent his young life and it follows that it is uncertain how much he knew about what was going on in the wider world. He was only ten when his

---

[16] Royal MS 12 E xv

[17] Henry Ellis, *The Chronicle of John Hardyng*, (London 1812) p.23

[18] T. B. Pugh, 'Richard Plantagenet, Duke of York, as the King's Lieutenant in France and Ireland' in J G Rowe (ed.) *Aspects of Late Medieval Government and Society*, (Toronto 1986) p.111

[19] Ann Darracott, *The Rebuilding of the Quire of Great Malvern Priory in the Fifteenth Century*, (Maidenhead, 2005) p.29

[20] C. A. J. Armstrong, 'The piety of Cicely Duchess of York, a study in late medieval culture' in *England, France and Burgundy in the Fifteenth Century* (London 1983) pp.138-156, Mary Dzon, 'Cecily Neville and the apocryphal Infantia Salvatoris' in *Medieval Studies*, vol. 71(2009) pp.235-300

[21] James Gairdner, *The Paston Letters*, (London, 1904) vol.3 p.233

father first raised an army to protest against the behaviour of certain advisors about the King, and thirteen at the time of the Battle of St Albans when his father fought against the royal army and killed the Duke of Somerset. Richard maintained that he was loyal and simply wished to rid the King of his evil counsellors, but there were many who disbelieved him and when he started raising an army for the third time in 1459, it was felt in government that a stand had to be taken.

By this stage, Edward was seventeen and old enough to get involved in his own right. Together with his brother Edmund, he joined his father and the Earls of Warwick and Salisbury in their camp at Ludford Bridge. Salisbury was his mother's brother and Warwick was his son and hence Edward's cousin, so he would have known them well. What Edward thought of the politics is unknown but as a loyal son he naturally took his father's part although he did not sign the letter sent by his father, Warwick and Salisbury to the King just before the conflict.[22] He was probably both excited and a little nervous about the prospect of taking part in his first battle, but in the event no real fighting took place despite it being reported that Richard had fired his guns.[23] The Earl of Warwick had brought with him a large number of men from the garrison at Calais who were led by Andrew Trollope. When Trollope realised that he was required to fight against the King and not just his evil counsellors, he decided to take his men over to the King's side. His departure left Richard and his allies seriously outnumbered and as a result, the decision was taken to flee "for fear of death that they said was imagined by the King and his lords."[24] Richard went to Ireland with Edward's younger brother, Edmund. Edward was placed in the care of the two earls and they headed south west toward Devon. Richard's decision to split the family was an attempt to try and safeguard the family fortunes. The King's troops would inevitably attempt to follow them and requiring them to go in several directions meant that there was more chance of him and his sons getting away safely. Edward's mother, meantime, with her three youngest children, was left behind and consequently captured. Ever kindly to his enemies, the King placed them in quite honourable confinement at the home of her sister, the Duchess of Buckingham and offered them financial support.

Warwick, Salisbury and Edward headed toward Nutwell near Newton Abbot where Joanna Dinham, a widow, gave them shelter.[25] As they hid in

---

[22] John Silvester Davies, *An English Chronicle,* (Camden Society, 1861) pp.81-82

[23] PROME, November 1459, item 18.

[24] James Gairdner, *The Historical Collections of a Citizen of London in the Fifteenth Century,* (London, 1876) p.205

[25] CPR 1461-1467 p.75

her home, her son John hired a boat for them together with a crew.[26] They set sail for Guernsey which had long been a Yorkist stronghold. After pausing for supplies and refreshment, they travelled to Calais arriving there on 2nd November 1459. Warwick had been Captain of Calais before the recent conflict and he remained held in high esteem there. When the King sent the Duke of Somerset to remove Warwick, he failed to find any support. Calais was a very safe place for Edward to be.

The three men spent the winter and spring in France. While they were away, Parliament in England passed an act of attainder on each of them declaring them traitors. This meant that their lands and titles were forfeit to the crown and that they would face death should they be captured. Edward at this stage had little in his own right to lose. He had no great lands and would not have expected to receive any until he married. However, he was the Earl of March, a title he had held since childhood[27] and he was heir to the dukedom of York which was the wealthiest lordship in the country. For this reason it was important to clear his name and restore his inheritance.

For Edward, it was impossible to accept the situation as it stood but the extent of his own political involvement in what happened next is unclear. When it was decided that there should be talks with Richard in Ireland about what to do next, it was Warwick alone who attended the meeting. Edward was left in Calais with Salisbury. Whether he was considered too young for the talks or an unnecessary security risk, cannot be confirmed. Salisbury was then almost sixty and Edward was a teenager, someone who did not feature in the public eye and who was probably more interested in hawking and girls than politics. Warwick meantime was widely regarded as a hero in England for the way he had attacked foreign shipping in the English Channel. Whether the vessels were a risk to England or not had no effect on public opinion. National confidence had been dented by the loss of France so news of Spaniards or Germans being defeated by the English at sea was extremely welcome. A verse published at Canterbury described Warwick as "that noble knight and flower of manhood...shield of our defence."[28] Warwick also had flair. When the King sent Lord Rivers and his son to assist Somerset in removing the three earls from Calais, Warwick sent his own men under Dinham across to Sandwich where Rivers was preparing his fleet and captured him in his bed. Almost every chronicle of the period told the story of how Rivers and his son were literally caught

---

[26] Kingsford op.cit. p.170

[27] There is no record of when Edward was created Earl of March but it is likely that it was around 1455 during mariage negotiations for a French princess.

[28] Davies op.cit. p.93

napping and unceremoniously bundled off to Calais to be berated by Warwick, Salisbury and Edward.[29]

Warwick must have returned from his visit to Richard with a scheme. The grand plan involved Warwick, Salisbury and Edward invading England while Richard sat in Ireland and waited to see what success they had. If he felt secure, he would join them. If not, he would stay there and hope his son and allies were able to escape with their lives. To assist them in gauging the mood of people in England, a manifesto was created, almost certainly by Richard during Warwick's visit of March 1460. This was issued by the Earls from Calais and contained twelve articles.[30] It began with a declaration of loyalty to the King whom it described as being "as noble, as virtuous, as righteous and blessed of disposition as any prince earthly." It proceeded to catalogue the ills of society including the "great oppression, extortion, robbery, murder and other violence done to God's church and to his ministers" and the general lawlessness: "All righteousness and justice is exiled of the said land and no man dreads to offend against the laws." The loss of France was condemned and blamed on those avaricious and evil counsellors about the King who had not only cost him his landed inheritance but his income at home which meant that he was unable to live like a true king and his people were being oppressed with taxes. Thus far the mainfesto was largely a summary of common opinion. A poem from more than a decade before had criticised advisors who left the King so poor "that now he begs from door to door" and which said: "Truth and poor men be oppressed and mischief is not redressed - The King knows not all."[31]

The later clauses of the manifesto were much more controversial and confrontational. They accused those about the King of causing him to write letters and give orders which threatened national security. The ban on aid to Calais was said to put this last stronghold of the English in France at risk whilst the encouragement to rebels in Ireland was thought to promote attacks on the rights of English landlords. It added that the French king was mobilising in response to these signs of weakness. The manifesto rather sensationally, and without offering evidence, claimed that the Duke of Gloucester had been murdered and went on to say that plots had been laid against Richard and Edward:

It has been laboured studied and conspired to have destroyed and murdered the said Duke of York and the issue that it has pleased God

---

[29] Davies op.cit. p.85, James Gairdner (ed.), *Three Fifteenth Century Chronicles*, (Camden Society, 1843) p.72, James Gairdner, *The Paston Letters*, (London, 1904) vol.3 pp.203-204.
[30] Davies op.cit. pp.86-90
[31] Thomas Wright (ed.), *Political Poems and Songs*, vol. 2. (London, 1861) p.230

to send me of the royal blood; and also of us the said Earls of Warwick and Salisbury for none other cause but for the true heart that God knows we ever have borne and bear to the profit of the King's estate, to the common weal of the said realm and defence thereof.

The document ended by suggesting that the King was just a puppet of their "mortal enemies" who were named as the Earls of Wiltshire and Shrewbury and Viscount Beaumont. The King was shown to be a man who was unable to make a decision or to control his lords and who was totally out of touch with reality. Although the document ended by saying the King was "neither assenting nor knowing" of all the evils they had listed and stressed their loyalty, readers and listeners cannot have been left in any doubt that Richard, Edward, Warwick and Salisbury had no respect for their monarch. It is doubtful that any king would have felt reassured by such a manifesto, even if the senders had come alone and without several hundred armed men.

On 26th June 1460, Warwick, Salisbury and Edward landed at Sandwich in Kent where they were met by the Archbishop of Canterbury, brother in law of Richard's sister. They were greeted warmly and they made their way up to London, arriving there on July 2nd. Their journey had shown they were in favour and London allowed them a triumphal entry. Warwick made a number of speeches which were on the lines of the manifesto and Salisbury was then left to hold the city whilst Edward and Warwick went north to Northampton where they hoped to see the King.

The English Chronicle gives the fullest account of events on Thursday 10th July, 1460, and once again, it is Warwick who is shown to be the hero. With sixty thousand men apparently in their train, Warwick sent a group of bishops to beg an audience of the King. He had no time to reply for the Duke of Buckingham stepped in to say that the bishops clearly did not come in peace for they came with an armed escort. The bishops agreed that they did but said that they felt the need to do this because "they that be about the King be not our friends." Buckingham retorted: "the Earl of Warwick shall not come to the King's presence and if he come he shall die."[32] The bishops left and reported the exchange to Warwick who then sent a herald to the King saying that he was prepared to come unarmed into the King's presence if only the King would agree to an exchange of hostages as surety for his safety. The herald could obtain no hearing. Undaunted and keen to maintain the image of himself as a man of peace, Warwick tried again and said that if the King would not see him, battle would commence at two

---

[32] Davies op.cit. p.96. The number of men involved as quoted by the chronicler may not be accurate.

o'clock. Predictably, there was no response and as a result, the two armies met in the field that afternoon. At this point, Edward appears for the first time in the story. The Chronicler says that he and Warwick went around the field to tell their men not to harm the King or the common people – hurting either of whom would destroy their credibility and popularity – but that they could and should kill all the lords, knights and squires. The trumpets were then blown and "many were slain and many fled and were drowned in the river." Amongst those killed were Buckingham, Shrewsbury and Beaumont who were cut down in the King's tent as they tried to defend him. The King himself was taken apparently without a fight.

For Warwick and Edward, it was a huge success. They now controlled the King and after a suitable show of bending the knee before him and swearing loyalty, they took him back to London as a trophy. They had complained before that he was weak willed but now that inadequacy played into their own hands as they were able to use him to control patronage and policy. News of their victory was quickly spread and for the first time, Edward began to figure in popular verse of the time. In a poem about the battle of Northampton and written just afterwards, Edward was referenced as the Bearward, indicating a follower of the Bear who was Warwick, so known because of the bear image he bore. Using imagery of the hunt, the poet imagined Edward and Warwick going in pursuit of the King's allies whom he labelled dogs. The King, however, was seen as the Hunt and not the direct enemy:

The Bearward and the Bear
they did the dogs chase
And put them to flight
to great confusion...
The Bearward asked no questions why
But on the dogs he set full round
...But the Hunt he saved from harm that day
He thought never other in all his mind
The Hunt said then "I want you here
You be right welcome, both to me
Always I pray you to stand me near
You be my friends, I may well see. [33]

---

[33] Frederick Madden, 'Political Poems of the Reign of Henry VI and Edward IV' in *Archaeologia* vol 29 (1842) pp.335-336

Although this poem paints Edward in an heroic light, he is still cast as a minor player. The poem ends with a prayer for the real master of the hunt to come home, namely Edward's father, Richard.

The noble prince, Richard, by name
Whom treason nor falsehood never did shame
But ever obedient to his sovereign
Falsehood evermore put him in blame
And lay awaiting him to have slain. [34]

Richard returned from Ireland that autumn and made his appearance in London just after Parliament voted to repeal the attainders passed a year before on him and his allies. Edward was now a free man, in favour with the King and able to look forward to much improved prospects. The goals of the allies had largely been met. The so called evil counsellors had been removed and replaced by themselves. The country was still in debt and France remained both lost and threatening, but these were issues which the triumphant Yorkists presumably planned to handle, although their manifesto had notably failed to offer any solution. It was, therefore, a total shock to everyone when Richard arrived and, notwithstanding, many years of taking oaths of loyalty to the King, calmly claimed the throne. His behaviour horrified everyone and created a huge constitutional crisis. Waurin says that Edward himself was sent to see his father to tell him that he had gone too far.[35] Although it is likely that Warwick had discussed the claim with York before, it is uncertain whether the question had been debated with Edward. Even if he had known, he could not but be aware that his father had misjudged public opinion to a huge degree. Edward's future was on a knife edge. The favour which he had could be taken away and he would be indicted for treason again and executed or, if his father won, he could become heir to the throne.

The compromise produced by Parliament was the Act of Accord which accepted that Richard had a just claim but said that it could not depose the King who had held the title for almost forty years and to whom everyone had sworn an oath of allegiance. Instead, Parliament would change the succession so that after the King's death, Richard would inherit the throne rather than the King's own son. Edward would then follow his father. Thus overnight, by act of parliament, Edward became second in line to the Crown. On 31st October,1460, Edward swore the following oath:

---

[34] ibid. p.239

[35] William and Edward Hardy (ed.), *Recueil des Croniques et Anchiennes istories par Jehan de Waurin* (London, 1891) pp.315-317

In the name of God, Amen. I, Edward, Earl of March, promise and swear by the faith and truth that I owe to Almighty God, that I shall never do, consent, procure or stir, directly or indirectly, in private or openly, ...anything that may be or lead to the abridgement of the natural life of King Henry the sixth, or to the hurt ...of his reign or dignity royal, by violence or any other ways, against his freedom and liberty: but that if any person or persons would do or presume anything to the contrary, I shall with all my power and might withstand it, and make it to be withstood as far as my power will stretch thereunto; so help me God and the Holy Evangelists.[36]

In return for this declaration of loyalty and in recognition of his new role in the succession, an allowance of 3,500 marks was granted to him, in modern values worth just over £120,000. The Act also confirmed that any future attack on Edward or his father was to be regarded as treason, the same as an attack on the King.

Unsurprisingly, despite Parliament's efforts to create a workable peace settlement and to secure the loyalty of Richard and Edward and their allies, the agreement failed. King Henry VI had a healthy son who was then seven years old and his mother, Queen Margaret, had absolutely no intention of letting her son be disinherited. As a result, she raised an army and her forces did battle with Richard at Wakefield shortly after Christmas 1460. Richard was ignominiously defeated and killed. Edward lost his brother Edmund in the same battle and also his cousin Edward Bourchier, son of his aunt Isabel. Edward was not present having decided to spend the festive season on his estates to the west.[37]

To his credit, Edward, now Duke of York, did not react instantly. He paused not just to mourn but to consider his position. He had three options. He could flee the country before the Queen caught up with him and had him executed. An honourable exile overseas might not be unpleasant and, given low levels of life expectancy, there was always the chance that he would outlive the Queen's son. His second option was to claim the throne directly in his own name. Reaction to his father doing that suggested this would be unwise. Or he could fight on as his oath demanded to defend the Act of Accord which made him heir to the throne.

Edward chose not to flee but to raise men to fight the Queen. Early in February 1461, he led his men against the forces of the King's half brother, Jasper Tudor, Earl of Pembroke and against the Earl of Wiltshire. The

---

[36] PROME, October 1460, item 21
[37] He had been appointed Constable of Bristol on 14th November, see CPR 1452-1461 p.632

battle was fought at Mortimer's Cross and was the first occasion on which Edward had experienced sole command. Contemporary accounts provide little information about the encounter saving the essential fact that Edward won a great victory. The most famous detail is that before battle began, three suns were seen in the sky. This sight created concern amongst the men but Edward rode out and told them: "Be thee of good comfort and dread not; this is a good sign for these three suns betoken the Father, the Son and the Holy Ghost and therefore let us have a good heart and, in the name of Almighty God, go we against our enemies."[38] Ever after, Edward adopted the sun as one of his symbols linking it most often with the white rose which he used. At this time, Edward was most commonly known as the Rose of Rouen. [39]

Happy with his victory, Edward turned toward London but his plans were interrupted by some unwelcome news. Whilst he had been fighting in Wales, Warwick had led his own forces against the Queen's army at St Albans. In the battle there on 16th February, Warwick had not only been outnumbered and forced to flee for his life but he had lost charge of the King. Whether Henry VI had been captured by the Queen's men or had gone of his own free will, was a matter for debate. Pro Yorkist contemporaries tended to regard it as the latter. Gregory's Chronicle reported: "in the midst of the battle King Harry went unto his Queen and forsook all his lords and trusted better to her party than unto his own lords."[40] The Short English Chronicle claimed: "King Henry broke his oath and agreement made between him and his true lords and so wickedly forsworn went to the contrary part of the north and dis-served his true lords that stood in great jeopardy for his sake."[41] The English Chronicle said: "when the King saw his people dispersed and the field broke, he went to his Queen."[42] Only Vitellius disagreed noting: "the King was taken and brought to the Queen."[43] Warwick's brother in a letter to the Papal Legate claimed that Warwick fled so fast that he had not time to take the King and that the "puppet" was simply left behind for the Queen's forces to take home.[44]

The question of whether Henry left of his own free will or was captured was a crucial one. Edward had sworn an oath of loyalty to the King and it followed that if the King had been taken away against his will then Edward

---

[38] Davies op.cit. p.110

[39] Madden op.cit. pp.332, 335, 341, 343-4, 347. The white rose was the symbol of Clifford, Maud Clifford having been his father's stepmother.

[40] James Gairdner, *Historical Collections* op.cit. p.212

[41] James Gairdner (ed.), *Three Fifteenth Century Chronicles*, (Camden Society, 1843) p.76

[42] Davies op.cit. p.108.

[43] Kingsford op.cit. p.173

[44] CSPV vol. 1 p.99

should go to his rescue. However, if the King had voluntarily left Warwick, then it was a demonstration of support for the Queen and her party, the people responsible for killing Edward's father and brother. The terms of the Act of Accord bound Edward to obey the King only as long as the King himself kept the agreement. If the King were to breach it – and permitting his wife to wage war on Richard and Edward did contravene it – then it followed that Henry was no longer fit to rule and Edward was rightful King of England.

Richard's claim to the throne had been based on the fact that he was the descendent of Edward III through his second son whilst Henry VI was his descendent through his third son. Details of genealogy were fine in theory but Edward had to face the fact that Henry had ruled for almost forty years and was the son of the revered Henry V, victor of Agincourt. People retained a loyalty to him. The Queen's army had won significant victories at St Albans and Wakefield, far more important that Edward's own at Mortimer's Cross, and the prospects for Edward at another battle seemed uncertain, particularly if the opposition included the King himself. A week or so after St Albans, Edward met up with Warwick to discuss the future. Meantime London closed its gates for fear of the rampaging army of Queen Margaret entering to spoil the city. Whether true or not, contemporaries in the south were convinced that Margaret was leading men from the north intent on their destruction, like an ancient viking horde. A letter written at the time declared: "The people in the north rob and steal and be appointed to spoil all this country and give away men's goods and livelihoods in the south."[45] This fear played into the hands of Edward and Warwick. It was something they could exploit together with the image of a King abandoning his faithful people, especially in favour of a Queen who was French, a nationality instinctively distrusted. Government required a king and if the King had left, then Edward, Warwick argued, must step into his shoes. Warwick's intention was to take power and it made little difference to him through which king he worked.

Warwick and Edward arrived in London on 27th February where they were welcomed with open arms. A campaign immediately began to blacken the King's name. On Sunday 2nd March, crowds were treated to an explanation of how the King had left them:

Then it was demanded of the people whether the said Henry were worthy to reign still and the people cried "Nay! Nay!! And then they asked if they would have the Earl of March to be their king and they said "Yea! Yea!" And then certain captains were sent to the Earl of

---

[45] Gairdner, *The Paston Letters* vol.3 op. cit. p.250

March's place at Baynards Castle and told the earl that the people had chosen him king whereof he thanked God and them and by the advice of the bishops of Canterbury and of Exeter and of the Earl of Warwick with others he took it upon him.[46]

Two days later, at Westminster, Edward sat in the King's seat, sceptre in his hand and accepted the homage of the lords. The reign of Edward IV had begun, even though at this stage, only a minority of the population supported him.

Edward was only Duke of York for nine weeks, such a short period that there is only one known official document which refers to him by that title.[47] People generally continued to call him the Earl of March. Whether his claim to the throne was legitimate or not is a matter that divided people at the time and has divided historians since. Ultimately, most of Henry VI's supporters gave up because Edward seemed so much more fitting to be a king. Unlike Henry, he was active in government, a promoter of law and order, a strong military leader, and he was also young and handsome and charming with a gift for popular words. His speech after taking the throne promised: "I shall be unto you, with the grace of Almighty God, as good and gracious a sovereign lord as ever was any of my noble progenitors....If I had any better goods to reward you with than my body, you should have it, the which shall always be ready for your defence."[48] One eyewitness commented: "I am unable to declare how well the commons love and adore him as if he were their god."[49] Henry meanwhile was recognised by friend and foe alike to be, by this stage, incapable of strong leadership as the fighting of the past ten years proved.[50] Those who elected Edward, Duke of York, as King hoped that the future would be more peaceful. The chronicler at Croyland Abbey described Edward at this time as being "in the flower of his age, tall of stature, elegant in person, of unblemished character, valiant in arms...and well fitted to endure the conflict of battle while, at the same time, he was fully equal to the management of the affairs of state."[51]

---

[46] Kingsford op.cit. p.174. The Bishop of Salisbury acclaimed him as Duke of York not Earl of March, see CSPV vol. 1 p.100

[47] Thomas Hardy (ed.), *Syllabus of the Documents relating to England and other Kingdoms contained in the Collection known as Rymer's Foedera*, vol. 2, (London, 1873) p.691. It is a commission dated 12th February asking him to raise men to defeat the rebellious forces of the Queen.

[48] PROME, December 1461, item 38

[49] CSPV vol. 1 p.112

[50] The three medieval kings with the greatest military reputation were Edward I, Edward III and Henry V. The successors of all three were deposed on grounds of alleged inadequacies in comparison.

[51] Henry Riley (ed.) *Ingulph's Chronicle of the Abbey of Croyland*, (London, 1908) pp.424-425

In the event, deposing Henry VI was not to prove quite so easy and Edward's reign was to see a number of bloody battles. Henry VI and his son would both be murdered. Yet his reign would see great developments in literature, architecture and the arts. For a teenage boy rather suddenly thrust upon the throne without any of the training in government which a prince might normally expect, he did a very fair job.

Richard

1473-1483

Duke of York 1475-1483

Very joyful and witty, quick with dances and frolics.[1]

R ichard is unique amongst the Dukes of York in that his chief claim to fame lies in the alleged circumstances of his death rather than in what he achieved during his life. He is best known as one of the Princes in the Tower whom tradition records were murdered by their uncle Richard III.

A manuscript in the British Museum from c.1482 states that Richard was born on the 17th August 1472 in Shrewsbury.[2] The town chronicle contains an entry in the year from Michaelmas 1472 to 1473 which states: "this year the Duke of York was born in the Black Friars within the town of Shrewsbury, the which friars stand under St Mary's church in the said town eastwards." [3] This would make his date of birth August 1473. Further support is given to this date by the fact that the King was then at Lichfield which was not far away[4] whereas in the summer of 1472, he was in London.

---

[1] J. A. Buchon (ed.), *Chroniques de Jean Molinet*, (Paris 1827) p.402

[2] Additional MSS 6113 quoted in *Gentleman's Magazine* volume CI part 1 (1831) pp.24-25. The document is undated but the references to his sisters as Dauphiness of France and Princess of Scotland indicate it was written before these two projected marriages were abandoned.

[3] Laurence Tanner and William Wright 'Recent Investigations regarding the fate of the Princes in the Tower" in *Archaeologia* vol lxxxiv (1935) p.4

[4] CPR 1467-1477 pp.399, 405, 408. Richard's aunt was buried at the Black Friars in

Richard's parents were Edward IV and his wife Elizabeth Woodville. They had been married nine years and already had a son and three daughters. Richard's sisters were Elizabeth aged seven, Mary aged six and Cecily aged four. His brother Edward was approaching his third birthday and had travelled west with his parents that August for he was to be left at Ludlow where he was to commence his education as Prince of Wales. Aside from trips home each summer and at Christmas, brother Edward was to remain at Ludlow until he became king which meant that Richard cannot have known him very well.[5] In addition he had two half brothers named Thomas and Richard Grey who came from his mother's first marriage. They were in their later 'teens so they would not have been part of the nursery group although Richard would have got to know them well as frequent visitors. A further three daughters and a boy were to follow Richard's birth.

Edward IV was a larger than life character who dominated his court totally and provided the strong rule which the country so badly needed after the turmoil associated with the collapse of Henry VI's government. He was a womaniser who enjoyed the good things in life. As a young man, he was extremely handsome with an athletic figure, but over indulgence in food and drink led to him becoming extremely fat. A contemporary who knew him said that he wore "a great variety of most costly garments...lined within with most costly furs...He being a person of most elegant appearance and remarkable beyond all others for the attractions of his person." [6] Edward IV was extremely keen on building carrying on major works at Windsor, Eltham and Westminster and lesser works across England. Most notably, he was well over six feet tall.[7] He was, in many ways, like his famous grandson, Henry VIII.

Richard's mother was one of the most famous beauties of her day. Although some contemporaries resented her family for obtaining honours they wanted to secure for themselves, there is no record of any scandal ever being attached to her name as queen. She was considered devoted to her husband, a strong woman who managed her affairs well but who knew her place. Unlike her predecessor, she did not seek to rule. Judging by her possessions, she enjoyed literature and this love of books is something she tried to pass down to her children. The Prince of Wales was described as

---

Shrewsbury just two weeks after his birth. It is likely that his mother had gone there in support of her brother and his family.

[5] Michael Hicks, *Edward V* (Stroud, 2003) pp.65-66

[6] N. Pronay & J. Cox (ed) *The Crowland Chronicle Continuations 1459-86* (London 1986) p.149

[7] Henry Emlyn 'The vault, body and monument of Edward IV' in *Vetusta Monumenta* vol. 3 (1799) p1. Edward was around 6'4" in his stockinged feet and the tallest king in English history.

being very well read by Mancini[8] and her daughter Elizabeth owned books and later taught her own children to read and write.[9]

Richard's early life would have been spent in the royal nursery under the care of a team of staff including a wet nurse and rocker. Although all their children were precious to the King and Queen, princes were undoubtedly more favoured. Infant mortality was high in all classes and it would not have taken much for an infection or chill to take the life of the Prince of Wales and leave Richard as heir. His importance to the succession, combined with the high proportion of females in the household, probably meant that he was cossetted. Unlike his elder brother, he was not sent away from home in infancy so he spent his entire life with his mother and sisters. His father was present for much of the time too, although his duties as king inevitably meant he was away on occasion.

Few details exist of Richard's childhood. He would have seen the building of St George's Chapel at Windsor which was commenced when he was two. He almost certainly attended the first service to be held there. He would also have seen the erection of the Great Hall at Eltham when he was around seven. Since this was the royal family's favourite home, Richard probably spent time exploring the works and may have tried his hand at helping the builders, if he had been able to escape his tutors. A huge building site with lots of craftsmen and scaffolding would have been an exciting playground for any young boy including a prince.

It was at Eltham on 11th November 1480 that Richard took his place at the baptism of his youngest sister, Bridget. The procession to the chapel began in the Queen's Chamber with knights bearing unlit torches. Behind them came Richard's uncle, Lord Maltravers bearing a bowl and towel and then the Earl of Lincoln with an ornate container of salt. During the service, a few grains of salt would be placed in the baby's mouth to signify the word of God which permeated and enriched the world. After the Earl came a canopy, probably of scarlet cloth with gold trim to denote the child of a king. Richard's aunt, Lady Maltravers followed with the oil used to anoint the baby as a token of the Holy Spirit, and a white cloth to wrap about her to represent purity and innocence. Behind her was the Countess of Richmond who carried the new princess.[10]

The procession reached the font where Richard's grandmother, the Dowager Duchess of York, was waiting with his eldest sister, Elizabeth.

---

[8] C. A. J. Armstrong (ed), *The Usurpation of Richard III by Dominic Mancini* (Oxford 1969) p.83
[9] David Starkey, *Virtuous Prince*, (London, 2008) p.120
[10] The Countess of Richmond was the mother of Henry Tudor.

They were to be the godmothers. The Bishop of Chichester performed the ceremony and the torches were lit to represent the triumph of Christ, the light of the world, over darkness. As the senior male representative of the royal family, Richard himself was stood directly beside the font to see both the baptism and confirmation.[11] He watched the ceremonies, joined in the prayers, and then followed the procession to the high altar where Princess Bridget was formally blessed. They then moved on to the nursery where gifts were presented to the baby by the godparents and wine was shared. In accordance with tradition of the time, the parents were not present.[12]

In the same year, Richard was involved in the state visit of his aunt, the widowed Margaret of Burgundy, sister of Edward IV. Considerable sums were spent on preparations for the visit which lasted between a month and six weeks. Richard's chamberlain took delivery of five yards each of black satin, purple velvet and green satin plus smaller amounts of lining fabric to make gowns for the "right high and mighty Prince Richard Duke of York."[13] More money was spent on decorating barges and arranging special entertainments for her. The nine year old Prince of Wales was brought back from Ludlow for the occasion. It was an opportunity not just for high level diplomatic negotiations but for the King to show off his family. Edward wanted to show that he was secure on his throne, that he was wealthy and cultured and that he had healthy sons available to succeed him. This was important to his standing at home but also to his reputation in Europe, and by extension people's attitudes to England.

By the time he was seven, Richard already had a string of titles. He had been created Duke of York when he was just nine months old. A year later, together with his elder brother, he became a Knight of the Most Noble Order of the Garter.[14] He did not get his robes for this until his seventh birthday when the royal wardrobe accounts show that he was to receive from the King "a mantle of blue velvet lined with white damask garnished with a garter of ruddeur and a lase of blue silk with buttons of gold."[15] On 12th June 1476, aged two, he became Earl of Nottingham.[16] On 7th February 1477, aged three, he became Duke of Norfolk and Earl of Warenne.[17] In January 1478, the King told Parliament that he had done this because "the great surety, defence, honour and the politic governance of this noble realm

---

[11] It was usual at this time to carry out both ceremonies together.

[12] *Gentleman's Magazine* volume CI part 1 (1831) p.25

[13] Nicholas Nicolas, *Privy Purse Expenses of Elizabeth of York* (London 1830) p.156

[14] Peter Begent and Hubert Chesshyre *The Most Noble Order of the Garter – 650 Years* (London 1999) p.313

[15] ibid.p.161

[16] CCR 1476-1485 p.4

[17] CPR 1476-1485 p.15

stands and ought to be in the noble persons born of high blood and exalted to high estate and power and the more near they be of the king's blood the more they ought of right to be honoured and enhanced to might and power."[18] In May 1479, he was appointed Lord Lieutenant of Ireland and promised all the income of that role "provided that he do not meddle with the disposition of vacant archbishoprics, bishoprics, abbeys and priories of the king's patronage or put lands acquired to other uses than the defence of that land", something that as a five year old he was unlikely to do.[19]

The title Duke of York was a family title. His father Edward had inherited it from his father who had inherited it from his uncle. The grant to Richard was the first time a king had given the title to his son and it was to become the traditional title of the second son over the following centuries in the same way that the eldest son became the Prince of Wales. As Edward's will made in 1475 showed, Richard was to have both the name and the lands including Fotheringhay, Stamford, Grantham as well as other estates in Lincolnshire and Rutland, some when his grandmother died, others when he reached sixteen.[20]

The other titles such as Duke of Norfolk were not traditionally associated either with the Yorks or the royal family. Richard was granted those following the death of John Mowbray in January 1476.[21] His heir was a three year old daughter Anne who thus became a royal ward. The King announced that "by the advice and assent of the noble lords of his blood and other lords of his council" he intended to marry Richard to Anne. He admitted that he might have enriched himself by keeping her valuable inheritance for himself but claimed that he wanted his son to have it so that the "estate and honour of his said entirely beloved son might by the same marriage the better be sustained" and his subjects would not be "charged nor impoverished" with the costs of keeping Richard. Parliament warmly approved this and was happy to agree that even if Anne were to die without issue, Richard should keep the Norfolk lands and income for "term of his life."[22]

The marriage took place on Thursday 15th January 1478 at St Stephen's Chapel at Westminster. Four year old Richard waited beside the door for his five year old red haired bride who arrived escorted by the Queen's brother,

---

[18] PROME 16th January 1478
[19] CPR 1476-1485 pp.153, 210
[20] Samuel Bentley, *Excerpta Historica*, (London 1833) p.371
[21] James Gairdner, *The Paston Letters* vol. 5 (London 1904) p.245
[22] PROME 16th January 1478.

Anthony, Earl Rivers and the King's nephew, the Earl of Lincoln.[23] In accordance with medieval tradition, the service began at the door, signifying the transition from a purely worldly state to that of holy matrimony. The Bishop of Norwich asked if there were any objections to the marriage and Dr Cooke formally said that since the couple were related, they could not marry. This was the cue for Dr Gunthorpe to present the dispensation received from Pope Sixtus IV.[24] This having been read, the couple proceeded toward the choir. The chapel had been hung with azure tapestries on which were embroidered gold fleur-de-lis. The King and Queen, together with the Prince of Wales, the King's mother and their three eldest daughters, were sat under a gold canopy of state. The King stepped down to welcome the bride and when the Bishop asked who gave her away to be married, he replied that he did. The vows were then exchanged and Richard gave Anne a ring. As their first walk together as husband and wife, they approached the high altar for a nuptial mass. After this, Richard's uncle, the Duke of Gloucester, took golden basins filled with coins, and scattered this sign of the King's largesse amongst the poor. He and Buckingham escorted the bride to the King's Great Chamber where a great feast had been provided with minstrels and the finest delicacies that money could buy. One eyewitness wrote: "The press was so great that I might not see to write the names of them that served; the abundance of the noble people were so innumerable."[25]

A week later, in the Sanctuary at Westminster, a joust was held to celebrate the marriage. There were to be three events with six knights representing the King taking on all comers. The proclamation issuing the challenge had been made by heralds in various parts of London on 10th December, stating that it was "the laudable and noble custom of this martial and triumphant realm" to celebrate "high days of honour" with demonstrations of "the necessary discipline of arms" and "chivalry by the which our mother Church is defended, Kings and Princes served, realms and countries kept and maintained in justice and peace."[26] For Richard as a young child, it would have been an exciting, colourful and noisy spectacle.

---

[23] Anne's body was discovered in 1964 and evidence of her red hair remained on the skull. See Alex Werner, *London Bodies*, (London 1998) p.69.

[24] J. A. Twemlow (ed.), *Calendar of Papal Registers Relating to Great Britain and Ireland*, vol 13, (London 1955) p.236. The dispensation is dated 12th May 1477 and incorrectly says that Richard is five and Anne four. It further states that the scope was to enable the "infants" to "contract espousals forthwith, and, as soon as they reach the lawful age, to contract marriage." The King decided to have the couple married rather than espoused so that Richard would receive Anne's lands immediately, though naturally both were much below the age at which the union could be consummated. Anne and Richard were third cousins once removed, both being descended from Ralph Neville.

[25] W. H. Black (ed.), *Illustrations of Ancient State and Chivalry* (London 1840) p.31

[26] ibid. p. viii

Richard's eldest half brother the Marquis of Dorset entered the arena first with the Duke of Buckingham holding his helmet. He was accompanied by knights and esquires in embroidered coats and five coursers covered in crimson velvet and cloth of gold with the initial "A" for Anne embroidered in gold. His brother followed with a similar entourage. Next came Richard's maternal uncle, Earl Rivers who emerged from a black velvet tent with artificial windows in the white garb of a hermit. This was a play on his name of Anthony, remembering St Anthony of the desert. His brother Sir Edward Woodville came next in full war dress with his horse dressed in crimson velvet and cloth of gold and his servants in blue and tawny. Sir James Tyrell appeared in similar garb but with his horses in red and green diaper cloth, the different fabric reflecting his lower rank. Finally came the men who were to fight in the tourney event who rode in behind two swords borne in state. Their outfits included embroidered bells, tigers, and silver or white roses in suns of gold.

The three events were the joust royal, the tourney and the tilt. In the joust royal, two combatants, one representing the King and the other a challenger, rode against each other across a demarcated area separated by a wooden board. They carried blunted spears or lances and the objective was to hit the opponent on the breastplate or helmet or to knock him from his horse. Richard's two half brothers both took part in the joust, but despite breaking six lances against their opponents, Thomas Fines was declared the winner on behalf of the challengers. The tourney saw Dorset and Tyrell each take on a number of challengers in mounted one to one combat in a relatively small enclosed arena using swords. This proved a particularly exciting event with one competitor losing his sword "so furious was their assembling, enforcing their weapons, desirous either to disarm other." In the battle between Rivers and Hansard, when the tournament official called time, Rivers returned to his corner but Hansard "rudely let fly a spring between the shoulder and the helmet of the said Earl. Then the said Earl furiously returned upon him and so accomplished six strokes between them." The reaction of the crowd to this display of most unchivalrous behaviour can be imagined. The third event was the tilting which involved knights in heavy war armour mounted on horses who were similarly protected, riding against a series of rings with their lance. It was a test of fitness, co-ordination, and dexterity. The Queen's brother had his horse injured in the first run so was unable to complete his competition until later in the afternoon. Again the challengers won.

After a superb afternoon of entertainment before the entire royal family and overseas ambassadors, there was a feast in the King's Great Chamber followed by dancing. There is no evidence of Richard attending that. Most likely, he was tired and had been sent to bed.[27]

Although we know very little of Richard's education, we can be sure that it would have involved instruction in the skills which were seen as necessary for princes. He was taught to ride for he was given when he was five, crimson velvet and gold cloth to go with his saddle and his horse's harness.[28] He was taught Latin grammar so that he could read prayers and would be able to read official documents. A payment was made to his tutor for this in May 1476 when he was just two though it may be doubted if he had actually commenced his studies quite this young. He was said to have the same tutor as his brother but since his brother was in Ludlow and Richard was in London, the supposition must be that Master Giles was already teaching the Prince of Wales and would move back to teach the Duke of York a year or two later. Richard would also have been taught French from infancy for that remained the international language of diplomacy. Edward IV and his wife did both communicate in English on occasion but French remained in common usage. He may have learnt Spanish too as his sister was reported to have done.[29] It is certain that he was taught archery for in January 1483, John Howard spent 2s 6d on buying him a bow and one of the last sightings of him that summer was in the garden at the Tower shooting arrows.[30]

The regulations drawn up for the royal household in 1478 indicate that by then Richard had his own schoolroom and bedroom for they show him being allowed four containers of coal, twenty bundles of chopped wood and eight bundles of faggots to warm his rooms. He was the only person with a coal allowance which could indicate that he was susceptible to chills as a child or just that his parents were taking no chances with the second in line to the throne. He was also unique in being given no candles which was no doubt because he was generally in bed by the time it became dark. Although his food was not separately listed, as the son of the King, he was entitled to bread and meat daily served by an usher who bore a towel. If he ate with the King and Queen, he was to receive two courses. [31] The overall objective of his education was that he be "virtuously, cunningly and knightly brought up to serve Almighty God Christianly and devoutly as accords to his duty and to live and proceed in the world honourably after his estate and dignity."[32] In 1481, one of the earliest books to be printed in England was

---

[27] ibid. pp.32-39

[28] Nicolas op.cit. p.155. The grant was dated 28th April 1480.

[29] Thomas Heywood, *The Most Pleasant Song of Lady Bessy*, (London, 1829) p.12

[30] J. Payne Collier (ed.) *Household Books of John Duke of Norfolk*, (London 1844) p.348. A. D. Thomas and I. D. Thornley, *The Great Chronicle of London*, (London, 1938) p.234

[31] A. R. Myers, *The Household of Edward IV*, (Manchester, 1959) pp.223, 93-94.

[32] Hicks op.cit. p.71.

dedicated to him by William Caxton, whose press had been established just five years before next to Westminster Palace. It was a life of Godfrey of Bouillon, one of the Nine Worthies and Caxton said that he hoped Richard would have "leisure and pleasure to see and hear this simple book" which he was confident would be edifying to him and encourage him in behaviour which would "deserve laud and honour."[33] Godfrey was said by Caxton to have been the greatest hero since King Arthur. Born around the time of the Norman Conquest, Godfrey had played a leading role in the first crusade becoming the first King of Jerusalem in 1099. Caxton hoped that Richard or his brother might lead another crusade and so become the Tenth Worthy.[34]

For the most part, Richard was kept within the confines of the royal family and rarely seen by the wider world. He did, however, sometimes get to meet overseas ambassadors. In 1482, de Souza came from Spain and spent some time at the court. Years later, de Souza was to recall those days saying: "He was a very noble little boy." He said that he had seen him singing with his mother and one of his sisters and that he sang very well and he was "the most beautiful creature" he had ever seen. He also recalled seeing him playing very well at sticks and with a two handed sword.[35]

As with any medieval child of whatever social rank, Richard had to face the loss of people who were close to him. His sister Mary, six years older than him, died when he was nine. A younger brother George died as a toddler when he was six. His aunts Jacquetta and Mary both died when he was eight. His wife Anne died in November 1481 less than a month from her eleventh birthday. Yet the most significant loss by far for him was the death of his father on April 9th 1483. Richard was then four months short of his tenth birthday and still resident in the royal nursery, though plans probably existed for him to be moved out in the not too distant future. Fifteenth century men believed that a boy left too long in the hands of women would become soft and unsuited for war, which was a primary occupation of many men but especially princes. The King's death was not expected and followed a very short illness. Contemporaries speculated that it could have been the result of over indulgence or a chill caught when out fishing but the exact cause remains unknown.[36] Edward IV was just fifty years old.

On April 14th, Richard's elder brother learnt the news that he had

---

[33] William Caxton, *Here begynneth the boke intituled Eracles, and also of Godefrey of Boloyne the whiche speketh of the conquest of the holy londe of Iherusalem* (London 1481)

[34] Constantinople had fallen in 1453 and the desire to reclaim it for Christianity was popular in this period.

[35] Anne Wroe, *Perkin*, (London, 2004) p.525

[36] Armstrong op.cit. p.59

become king. He was twelve and a half. Advised that his coronation was scheduled for May 4th, he departed Ludlow with his uncle and guardian Earl Rivers and his half brother Richard Grey on April 24th. They started their journey to London where Richard and his mother and sisters were waiting at Westminster Palace, no doubt making plans for his reception. Five days later, the new King and his party were met by his father's brother, the Duke of Gloucester, who arrested Rivers and Grey and advised Edward that they were not to be trusted. The young King responded that "he had seen nothing evil in them and wished to keep them unless otherwise proved to be evil" reminding his uncle that his counsellors were the choice of his father the King and that he trusted in his father's prudence. He added that he had confidence in the Queen at which point the Duke of Buckingham, who was with Gloucester, said "if he cherished any confidence in her, he had better relinquish it."[37]

News of the arrests and the way Gloucester had gained control of the King, reached London and caused panic. The Queen, seeing her brother and second son now taken, decided that her safest option was to remove herself and her remaining children into the Sanctuary at Westminster Abbey. Thomas More, who wrote his account in 1513 and who clearly therefore was not present at the time though he may have interviewed those who were, described the scene at Westminster Palace where the Archbishop of York found the Queen amid "much heaviness, rumble, haste and business, carriage and conveyance of her stuff into Sanctuary, chests, coffers, packs, fardelles, trusses, all on men's backs, no man unoccupied, some loading, some going, some discharging, some coming for more, some breaking down the walls to bring in the next way.... The Queen herself sat alone low on the rushes all alone and dismayed."[38]

Whether Richard was woken when the news came or allowed to sleep through one final night at the palace in peace is unknown. Certainly, he would have been aware by morning of the bustle everywhere, of his possessions being gathered up and of there being a sudden need to move out of his home. Most likely he would have sensed that there was something seriously wrong even if at just nine he was too young to understand it. He may have been happy initially that he was going to miss his lessons for a day but the sight of his mother in tears would have concerned him. The disintegration of his world which had been privileged and protected had begun.

Gloucester, Buckingham and Edward arrived in the city on May 4th,

---

[37] ibid. p.77
[38] Thomas More, *The History of King Richard the Third*, (London 1821) p.30

conveniently too late for the coronation which was rescheduled to June 22nd. In Gloucester's train were a number of carts which he claimed were full of Woodville arms which he said the Queen's family had been hiding in preparation for a coup of their own. Other observers commented that they were simply arms which had been collected for the war against Scotland.[39] On May 8th, Gloucester persuaded the Council to appoint him as Protector until the coronation. Some tried to argue that it was only natural for him as Edward IV's brother to be given this role and that it was unimportant since it would only be for a short time anyway. Edward would soon grow up. As the author of the Crowland Chronicle said "everyone hoped for and awaited peace and prosperity in the kingdom" and they believed that Edward V "promised best" for the future.[40] The Queen, however, remained mistrustful of Gloucester and stayed in Sanctuary.

In June, Gloucester made his move. He wrote letters to his supporters in the north asking them to send him armed men so he could defend himself against the Queen. Two days later, on the 13th, he had Lord Hastings removed from the council and executed without trial. He also ordered the arrest of the Archbishop of York and Bishop of Ely, this last being the man in whose household Thomas More spent part of his youth and who was undoubtedly the source for much of the history he later wrote of this period.[41] John Forster, one of the Queen's officials, was arrested and sent to the Tower the next day. Meantime, the young king Edward V who had not been required to sign any official documents since the 8th, had all his regular attendants taken from him and new ones appointed. A letter dated June 9th from Simon Stallworth who was in the household of the Lord Chancellor recently appointed by Gloucester reported that the King had already been moved to the Tower.[42]

Throughout this period, Richard remained in Sanctuary with his mother. She probably tried to maintain some semblance of normal life for her children but it must have been extremely difficult. Her eldest brother and second son from her first marriage remained in custody and a warrant had been issued for the capture of another brother. She had not seen Edward since Christmas so had not been able to talk to him about his father's death or about the responsibilities of his new role. Gloucester's men were surrounding the Sanctuary, both on the River Thames and on land. Her son Dorset's properties were being confiscated. It was in this atmosphere that

---

[39] Armstrong op.cit. p.83

[40] Pronay & Cox op.cit. pp.157-159

[41] More joined Morton around 1490, Thomas Stapleton, *The Life of Thomas More*, (London, 1966) p.2

[42] Samuel Bentley, *Excerpta Historica*, (London 1833) p.16

Gloucester decided that it was necessary for Richard to join his brother in the Tower. He argued that Edward needed the support and companionship of his younger brother as he prepared for his coronation and suggested to the council that the Queen was being a cruel mother by keeping him with her instead. Mancini reported that Gloucester told the Council that Richard, "on account of his nearness of kin and his station ought to play an important part in the ceremony."[43] However, Wardrobe accounts show that although various garments had been ordered for Edward's coronation, none were ever ordered for Richard indicating that there never was any plan that he do this,[44] something which made the claim he needed to move to the Tower to prepare open to doubt.

It was decided to send the Archbishop of Canterbury, Cardinal Thomas Bourchier, to see the Queen at Westminster. He was the uncle of her first husband and well known to her not just because of his position – he had crowned both her and Edward IV – but because her eldest brother and her sister had married his niece and nephew respectively. Bourchier was by then around eighty. Mancini said that Gloucester chose him because he suspected "no guile" and he knew that Bourchier was afraid that if he refused, Gloucester would send his troops direct into the Abbey, thus violating the house of God. The Crowland chronicler said that Gloucester had the sanctuary surrounded by "a great crowd with swords and clubs" and that these armed men were in "terrifying numbers" such as nobody had ever seen or heard about before.[45] Mancini wrote: "When the Queen saw herself besieged and preparation for violence she surrendered her son, trusting in the word of the Cardinal of Canterbury that the boy should be restored after the coronation."[46] Stallworth, in London at the time, claimed that Gloucester and Buckingham had twenty thousand men in the city "to what intent I know not." He described how Richard was taken in a letter written just five days after the event: "On Monday last was at Westminster great plenty of harnessed men. There was the deliverance of the Duke of York to my Lord Cardinal, my Lord Chancellor and other many lords temporal." He said that Buckingham received Richard in Westminster Hall and that Gloucester greeted him with "many loving words" at the door of the Star Chamber. Richard was then taken by Cardinal Bourchier to the Tower. Stallworth's testimony is interesting because he worked for the Lord Chancellor and so had inside information. It was clear that Stallworth was concerned for he took care to tell his correspondent that he had asked about Richard since and was relieved to say he was supposed to be "merry" or healthy. He

---

[43] Armstrong op.cit. p.89

[44] Dr Milles, 'Observations on the Wardrobe accounts for the Year 1483' in *Archaeologia* vol 1 (1770) pp. 361-383

[45] Pronay op.cit. pp.158-159

[46] Armstrong op.cit. p.89

nonetheless said "I hold you happy that you are out of the press for with us is much trouble and every man doubts other."[47]

Richard's reaction to the move is unrecorded. More suggested that the Queen said: "farewell my own sweet son. God send you good keeping. Let me kiss you once yet before you go for God knows when we shall kiss together again." She then blessed him "turned her back and wept and went her way leaving her child weeping as fast."[48] Although not an eyewitness account, it is quite likely that this was what happened. The Queen would have kissed her son good-bye and tried to hide her fears but Richard would have sensed them and been aware of the unusual number of soldiers to be seen everywhere. He probably cried when he was led away and almost certainly did so later that night when he found himself in the Tower. Despite having his brother, he must have felt very alone, being now bereft of both parents and all the servants and family members who were familiar to him.

On the following day, June 17th, an announcement was made that the coronation was being postponed until November. Gloucester cast off his mourning clothes and donned purple, a highly significant and symbolic gesture for only kings were entitled to wear purple.[49] On June 22nd, sermons were preached in London alleging that Richard and his brother were bastards because his parents had not been lawfully married. The Crowland chronicler described this as pure "sedition and infamy" and it is doubtful that anyone believed it.[50] On June 25th, Earl Rivers and Richard Grey were executed at Pontefract, The next day, Gloucester was declared King Richard III.

It is unclear whether Richard or his brother knew of these events. Initially the boys had been seen together in the gardens with bows and arrows, but Mancini, who left England in July 1483, reported that: "he and his brother were withdrawn into the inner apartments of the Tower proper and day by day began to be seen more rarely behind the bars and windows till at length they ceased to appear altogether." He said that he had been told by Dr Argentine, the last of Edward's attendants, that the young King had feared the worst and daily prayed that he would meet his death bravely,

---

[47] Bentley op.cit. pp.16-17

[48] More op.cit. p.62

[49] Anne Sutton & P. W. Hammond, *The Coronation of Richard III* (Gloucester 1983) p.22

[50] Armstrong op.cit. p.161. Gloucester was so keen to invalidate the claim of his nephew that he not only alleged that Edward IV's marriage to Elizabeth Woodville was invalid due to a precontract with a woman long dead who could not comment, but because Elizabeth and her mother were witches. He further alleged that Edward IV himself was a bastard because he did not look like his father, a claim which cannot have pleased Gloucester's mother who was still alive.

hardly normal behaviour for a twelve year-old boy.[51] The Mayor of Bristol wrote in his journal that during the summer "the two sons of King Edward were put to silence in the Tower of London."[52] The Anlaby Cartulary gives the date of death as June 22nd, a date confirmed in several early Tudor chronicles, including one produced by a man with links to Archbishop Morton.[53]

On June 28th, twelve days after being sent to the Tower, Richard's titles of Duke of Norfolk and Earl Marshal were given to John Howard, and his title of Earl of Nottingham was given to William Berkeley. Even had the bastardy allegations been true, they would not have affected Richard's right to hold these titles or the lands which went with them. Unlike his title of Duke of York which was inherited, Richard had been made Duke of Norfolk and Earl of Nottingham by his father. He was entitled to the lands through his marriage, a fact which could not be nullified by a declaration of bastardy. The grants had been confirmed by Parliament and the terms were clear. Richard would hold the titles and the lands until he died. Either the new king was unlawfully suspending an act of parliament or he was declaring his nephew dead. Contemporaries believed it was the latter and this view is supported by the fact that there is no record of any payments being made which relate to Richard or Edward from this date onward, excepting a final payment of arrears to attendants on July 18th. [54] Had the boys remained in the Tower, they would have needed food and clothes and people to look after them. The lack of any such provision indicates they were no longer there. They had disappeared. Richard at the time was a few weeks from his tenth birthday.

Sixty years later, Thomas More's history of King Richard III was published as the final part of the Hardyng Chronicle. The history had been written thirty years before but remained a manuscript privately held by the family. Given the volume of More's writings which were published in his lifetime, the decision not to make it public was clearly deliberate. Whether his decision was influenced at all by Henry VIII is unknown and later

---

[51] Armstrong op.cit. p.93. A H Thomas & I D Thornley (ed.), *The Great Chronicle of London,* (London 1938) p.234

[52] Lucy Toulmin Smith (ed.) *The Maire of Bristowe is Kalendar* (Camden Society, 1872) p.46

[53] Colin Richmond, 'The death of Edward V' in *Northern History* vol 25 (1989) pp 278-80. See also S J Gunn, 'Early Tudor dates for the death of Edward V' in *Northern History* vol 28 (1992) pp 213-216. The chronicler John Rous writing in 1489 also stated that Edward and Richard died before Gloucester took the throne. See Thomas Hearne (ed.), *Joannis Rossi, Historia Regum Angliae* (Oxford 1745) p.214. The Colchester Oath Roll further confirms that Edward was dead by the end of September, see John Ashdown-Hill, 'The Deathof Edward V' in *Essex Archaeology and History Transactions,* series 3 vol 35 (2004) p.228

[54] Rosemary Horrox and P.W. Hammond (ed.) *BL Harleian Manuscript 433* vol 2 p.2 (Gloucester, 1980)

historians can only speculate on his motives. In his history, More claims that James Tyrell had confessed to sending two men to kill the young princes on the orders of Richard III. The men entered the bedroom of the princes around midnight and "suddenly lapped them up among the clothes, so bewrapped them and entangled them, keeping down by force the feather bed and pillows hard unto their mouths that within a while smothered and stifled, their breath failing, they gave up to God their innocent souls into the joys of heaven, leaving to the tormentors their bodies dead in the bed. After that the wretches perceived first by the struggling with the pains of death and after long lying still to be thoroughly dead they laid their bodies naked out upon the bed and fetched Sir James to see them."[55]

The confession does not exist in any other source and over the years, people have questioned its veracity, not least because Tyrell continued in favour under Henry VII for some years. A letter of John Flamank from 1503 comments that it had been years before the King and his Council "would believe anything of untruth to be in Sir James Tyrell."[56]

In 1674, the story seemed to be confirmed when a wooden box was found containing the skeletons of two children, one thrown on top of the other. An eyewitness to the actual discovery added that there were "pieces of rag and velvet about them."[57] These bones were examined in 1933 and found to be those of two children aged around ten and twelve respectively. The cause of death could not be identified.[58] Although the gender of bones of such young children could not be confirmed, it was assumed that they were the remains of Edward V and Richard, Duke of York. The presence of velvet suggested they were of high status individuals and must have dated from no earlier than the fifteenth century.

When Anne Mowbray's body was found and examined in 1964 a comparison was made with the 1674 bones, although the experts could only work from photographs of the latter. Theya Molleson agreed that the 1674 bones were of the age previously stated and were almost certainly male due to dental development. She found three areas of similarities between the 1674 remains and Anne Mowbray's which suggested that there was a familial relationship between them. Anne had been a cousin of the princes.

---

[55] The Middleham King Roll says the princes were "submerged" which could mean drowned or stifled, see Philip Morgan, 'The Death of Edward V and the Rebellion of 1483' in *Historical Research* vol.68 issue 166, June 1995, p.229

[56] James Gairdner (ed.), *Letters and Papers Illustrative of the Reigns of Richard III and Henry VII*, (London, 1861) vol. 1 p.235

[57] Richard Davey, *The Tower of London* (New York, 1910) pp.22-23.

[58] Laurence Tanner and William Wright 'Recent Investigations regarding the fate of the Princes in the Tower" in *Archaeologia* vol lxxxiv (1935) pp.1-25

Given the inter-marriage between the nobility at the time, these findings did not preclude the 1674 bones being those of other relations who died around the same time in the Tower but it was noted that there was no record of anyone else who fitted the bill other than the princes.[59] If the bones are genuine, they indicate that Richard had inherited his father's stature and was already tall for his age.

For some people, the idea that the princes had been murdered was too much to comprehend. Mancini spoke of seeing "many men burst forth into tears and lamentations" at the mere mention of their names.[60] When something horrific happens or an event seems beyond belief, there are those who refuse to accept it because they want it to be untrue. Thus, the modern era has seen Holocaust deniers and people who maintain Elvis Presley is alive and well and living incognito somewhere. A parallel might be drawn to the case of the Russian Imperial family who were killed by the Bolsheviks in 1918. In the years which followed, almost two hundred people came forth claiming to be a survivor of the massacre. The most famous was Anna Anderson who claimed to be the Grand Duchess Anastasia. A number of people accepted her and even when DNA evidence in 1995 showed she was in fact of Polish working class descent, they claimed the tests were flawed. In 2007 the remains of Anastasia were found in Ekaterinburg but still some people dispute that these are genuine and consider it all a conspiracy to defraud Anna Anderson.

Similarly, there have been those who have denied that Richard met his death in 1483. Jack Leslau published a number of articles from the 1970s expressing his theory that Richard took the name of John Clement and lived in the household of Sir Thomas More who wrote the account of the princes being murdered simply to cover up Richard's survival. To further put anyone off the scent, Leslau argues that More had Holbein paint John Clement at half his age and that More referred to Clement as a boy in his 1516 Utopia when – if he were Richard – he would have been forty-three.

In 1978, Audrey Williamson reported a verbal tradition in the Tyrell family that far from murdering the princes, he had offered a home to them and their mother.[61] Thirty years later, David Baldwin argued that a bricklayer in Eastwell, Kent who had claimed around 1542 to be the bastard son of Richard III was in fact Richard, Duke of York who had been taken

---

[59] Theya Molleson, 'Anne Mowbray and the Princes in the Tower: A study in identity' in *London Archaeologist* vol 6 (1987) pp258-262

[60] Armstrong op.cit. p.93

[61] Audrey Williamson, *The Mystery of the Princes*, (Guernsey, 1981) p.122

from the Tower.[62]

In the 1490s, a young man appeared in Ireland who was said to be Richard. For eight years, he travelled around Europe, mostly supported by Margaret of Burgundy who was Richard's aunt but who had only met him once when he was seven. The young man was about twenty and the less respectful suggested her determination to see him on the throne of England indicated he was either her lover or illegitimate son.[63] Other countries who had a dispute with England accepted him as Richard, Duke of York and gave him money but he later admitted to being Perkin Warbeck of Tournai, a fact his father there confirmed.[64] Perkin had once been in the household of Edward Brampton, a Portuguese Jew who had converted to Christianity and been accepted as an English subject. Brampton had led naval forces on behalf of England and had lent Edward IV money and was familiar with the court so was in a position to furnish the young man with knowledge for his stories.[65] Perkin attempted to invade England to enforce his claim, perhaps significantly choosing to do this after the death of Elizabeth Woodville, a woman who would undoubtedly have been able to identify her own son.[66] The English, however, were unimpressed by him and he was executed by Henry VII in 1499 after writing a long and detailed confession describing his early life and how he came to play the role of Richard, Duke of York.[67]

Richard was formally stated to be dead on November 27th 1489. No date was given but it was said to have occurred before 7th November 1485.[68] A court poem of 1486 said the same.[69] The exact details of his demise are uncertain for murderers do not leave paper trails for later generations. What is certain is that Richard disappeared when he was in the care of his uncle and that Richard III therefore had the ultimate responsibility. That would be the case even in the unlikely scenario of a total stranger or madman breaking into the heavily fortified and guarded Tower of London to murder or abduct the princes. As uncle, Protector and King, Gloucester had

---

[62] David Baldwin, *The Lost Prince*, (Stroud 2008) p.87

[63] Allen B. Hinds (ed.), *Calendar of State Papers and Manuscripts in the Archives and Collections of Milan*, (London, 1912) p.292

[64] Wroe op.cit. p.528

[65] CPR 1467-1477 pp.340, 357, CPR 1476-1486 pp.248, 318 . A Richard Brampton, who may have been a brother, was employed in the household of Elizabeth Woodville as a pointmaker. See CCR 1476-1485 p.157. Edward Brampton was a cloth merchant.

[66] Elizabeth died in 1492. Her will makes no reference to Richard indicating that she did not believe he was alive. See J. Nichols, *A Collection of all the Wills now known to be extant of the Kings and Queens of England*, (London, 1780) pp.350-351.

[67] Pretenders generally claimed to be Richard rather than Edward because he was less well known which reduced the risk of someone disproving his identity.

[68] CPR 1485-1494 p.308

[69] James Gairdner, *Historia Regis Henrici Septimi*, (London, 1858) p.lvii

a duty of care to Richard. Instead, he bastardised him, unlawfully took his property, and removed his right to a safe childhood with his loving mother. Since rumours abounded that Richard was dead within weeks of his disappearance, the King could have brought him out in public to show all was well if he was alive. If someone unauthorised had killed him, the King could have presented the body and vowed vengeance on the murderer. He did nothing which explained why his contemporaries believed him guilty. In January 1484, the French Chancellor openly accused Richard III of being responsible, telling the Parliament at Tours: "look what has happened since the death of King Edward: how his children already big and courageous have been put to death with impunity and the royal crown transferred to their murderer."[70]

Whatever actually happened to Richard, Duke of York, it is clear that he did not grow up to enjoy the life which his parents had planned for him or which his birth had led him to expect. As the author of a ballad about his sister wrote, he had "neither justice nor right but had great wrong."[71]

---

[70] J. Masselin, *Journal des Etats-généraux e France tenus à Tours en 1484* (Paris, 1835) p.38

[71] Heywood op.cit. p3

Henry

1491-1547

Duke of York 1494-1502

My mind shall be virtue to use and vice to refuse.[1]

enry Tudor was born on 28th June 1491 at the palace of Greenwich, the second son of Henry VII and his wife Elizabeth of York. His grandmother was the redoubtable Lady Margaret Beaufort, Countess of Richmond, who laid down a detailed set of instructions for the birth and how Henry was to be tended. From these we know that his nursery was to have three rooms and to be staffed by a team of nurses and rockers. He was to have two cradles, a large state one with the royal coat of arms carved upon it which sat under a luxurious canopy and a smaller wooden one with silver and gilt fittings. Her instructions also covered the christening which took place in the church of the Observant Franciscans:

---

[1] Part of the lyric of 'Pass time with good company', a song written by Henry VIII c.1509 quoted in John Stevens, *Music and Poetry in the Early Tudor Court*, (London, 1961) p.345

Now the whole church where the child shall be christened must be hanged with rich arras or cloth of gold in the best manner and in like sort shall the altar be arrayed also, and well carpeted throughout the whole chancel under foot; also there must be long and large carpets laid under foot at the church door and the porch must be hanged with rich cloth of gold of arras work....Then must the font of silver that is at Canterbury be sent for...The font must be set of a great height that the people may see the christening without pressing too nigh the font, and the same shall be hanged all about with cloth of gold. Over the font there must be hanged a great and large canopy of damask....

When the child goes to church to be christened, a duchess must bear the child and a duchess must bear the chrism before it upon her shoulder...An earl shall bear the train of the mantle which must be of rich cloth of gold with a long train furred throughout with ermine....There must be borne before it to the church two hundred torches of which twenty-four shall be borne about the child...The baptizer must be an Archbishop or Bishop...As soon as the christening is done all the aforesaid torches shall be lighted and the child's taper which the child shall bear up to the high altar in his hand.[2]

The fact that these directions came from the King's mother rather than the King or Queen is indicative of who had the greatest say about the court. That the King left such affairs to a woman is perhaps not so surprising but it is easy to understand why the Spanish ambassador reported that Queen Elizabeth needed "a little love" because she was kept "in subjection" by her mother in law, whom he felt was more influential than any politician.[3]

As a young child, Henry would not have sensed any tension and indeed for the most part, Elizabeth seemed willing to acquiesce in everything the King required. Expenditure records indicate that the royal couple spent much of their time together and that they regularly exchanged gifts. The same records show that Henry grew up in an environment which was luxurious and cultured. There were more payments for books than for any other item and the King spent the equivalent in modern terms of almost £44,000 on them in thirteen years.[4] He also spent large sums on musicians and instruments and singers. He bought lutes for his children and also owned flutes, recorders and a clavichord. Money was paid to various tumblers, dancers, actors and fools and to those who organised the more

---

[2] Thomas Hearne (ed.) *Leland's Collectanea,* vol IV (London, 1770) pp.180-182. Henry was baptised by Richard Fox, Bishop of Exeter, ref. L&P vol.4 p.2588

[3] CSPS vol.1. p.17

[4] Samuel Bentley, *Excerpta Historica,* (London, 1823) pp.85-133.

formal entertainments. Sports were encouraged and there were payments for costs associated with archery, tennis, hunting and swimming. When the weather was bad, chess and backgammon were played and a number of dice and card games. The expenses show sixty-six shillings given to Henry when he was ten to play at dice. The King took an interest in wildlife too, buying a lion and a leopard for the Tower of London zoo as well as "wild cats and popinjays" from the recently discovered Newfoundland. Payments for bird cages show that some exotic birds were kept as pets in the palace. For a young child, it would have been a very colourful and exciting world. Large sums were spent on clothes and incredible amounts on jewels. The King spent on average almost £7,500 per annum on jewels which in modern money is approaching four million. He did this because he believed it was important for a ruler to physically demonstrate his status, a lesson his son was to take to heart. Created some forty years later, the bejewelled image of Henry VIII standing legs astride in the Holbein portrait remains one of the most easily recognised and quintessential images of kingship. The displays of conspicuous consumption, evident in the lifestyle, the quality of the homes and in little things like having money to place valuable carpets on the ground for people to walk upon, all went to show that the Tudors were a successful family, one in which Henry was fortunate to be born.

It was not until 1494 that Henry was created Duke of York. He was three at the time although he may have been well developed for his age since onlookers thought he was at least four.[5] The ceremonies lasted three days and were followed by three days of jousts. Proceedings began on the afternoon of 29th October when Henry was brought from his nursery at Eltham and required to ride a courser in procession through the streets of London to a reception by the Mayor and aldermen at Westminster. Following this he was reunited with his parents at the palace. The next evening, saw a formal state banquet and Henry was required to demonstrate his obedience to the King by waiting on his father at table. Given his age, he was given the job of washing his father's hands and drying them with a towel, an act traditionally carried out at various stages of the meal. His instructions began:

> Fold the two ends of the towel to the outer edge of the cloth and so hold the three ends together then fold them all so that there is a pleat at about a foot's distance, and lay it fair and smooth for your lord to wash after meat...Carry a towel about your neck: when serving your lord, bow to him...Go for water, some pour upon his hands...Hold the towel for him until he has done and leave not until ye have heard grace said. Stand as still as a stone unless he

---

[5] C. Lethbridge Kingsford, *Chronicles of London*, (Stroud, 1977) p.201

speak....When your lord has washed you must take up the surnape with your two arms and carry it back to the ewery yourself.[6]

The idea of service was significant because that same night, Henry was to commence preparation for being made a knight. The chivalric ideal required knights to be heroic and brave, virtuous and loyal, but also good Christians. Just as Jesus washed the feet of his apostles at the Last Supper, so Henry would wash the hands of his father at the banquet.

The order of knighthood into which Henry was to be instituted was that of the Bath. Thus, after the dinner, baths were prepared for Henry and the twenty others who were to be given the honour. Henry's was set up in the King's Closet at Westminster Palace and at the appointed time, his father came in and took some of the water and used it to make the sign of the cross on his shoulder. He then kissed the same spot and gave his son his blessing. Telling him:

Be ye strong in the faith of Holy Church. Relieve widows and maidens oppressed as right commands. Give you to each his own. With all thy mind, above all things, love and dread God. And above all other earthly things, love the King thy sovereign Lord: him and his, defend unto thy power.[7]

Whilst the other would-be knights were expected to carry out an all night prayer vigil in rough robes to denote poverty, young Henry was tucked up in a "rich bed well empanelled." [8] The next morning, he was given a new shirt and taken to St Stephen's Chapel. After prayers, he went on to Star Chamber where he mounted his horse and rode across to where his father was sitting enthroned. There, the Duke of Buckingham fastened his right spur and the Marquess of Dorset his left. The King then dubbed him a knight and presented Henry with his own sword, no doubt a miniature version made specially for the event. Having buckled the sword about his waist, his proud father then lifted Henry up on to the table to show everyone. Sir William Sandys carried Henry back to the chapel so that he could formally offer up his sword on the altar as he promised to use it only in defence of right.

For Henry, the day was almost over. As he left the chapel, his spurs were

---

[6] Edith Rickert and L. J. Naylor (trans.), *The Babees' Book*, (Ontario, 2000) pp.2, 4, 29

[7] James Gairdner (ed.) *Three fifteenth century chronicles with historical memoranda by John Stowe* (London 1880) p.113

[8] The account of the celebrations appears in James Gairdner (ed.), *Letters and Papers Illustrative of the Reigns of Richard III and Henry VII*, (London, 1861) vol 1, pp.388-401

removed and he was allowed to return to the palace for a meal. Church tradition said that only fish could be eaten on a Friday but the King decided that on this special occasion, Henry could have meat. Possibly it was a cold day and he did not want to take any risks with his son's health. Meantime, the remaining new knights who went through the same ceremony, went to take their meal in the parliament chamber.

On Saturday 1st November, at Westminster Hall, Henry received his formal grant of title. He was carried in by the Earl of Shrewsbury to where his father sat enthroned amidst all the nobility, the bishops, the judges, and the abbots. It must have been an imposing sight even for a prince to be faced with such an array of robed dignitaries. Garter King-of-Arms carried the patent, the Earl of Suffolk the sword and the Earl of Derby the ermine edged cape and the ducal coronet. The procession stopped part way down the hall and Henry was set down. The Marquess of Dorset and Earl of Arundel then took him up to the throne itself where the Bishop of Exeter read the patent creating Henry Duke of York. The King then publicly confirmed the grant and announced that Henry would forthwith be entitled to an allowance of one thousand pounds per annum, around half a million pounds in today's money.[9] The cape was wrapped round Henry's shoulders and the coronet placed on his head. After this, the court departed to the chapel where the Archbishop of Canterbury celebrated mass. Again, Henry was carried by Shrewsbury, himself then in his mid twenties and godfather to Henry's elder sister. Shrewsbury had fought bravely at the Battle of Stoke and was considered a fine example of knighthood and nobility, just the sort of young man Henry should emulate.

The tournaments must have been a welcome chance to relax after the ceremonial. They were held on three separate days in November. As was customary, a challenge was issued to all comers to take on the royal representatives in the tourney and the joust. On the first day, the royal defenders wore the King's colours of green and white. On the second, they wore the colours of the Duke of York, blue and tawny. Quite aside from the excitement of the actual sport, the tournaments represented a remarkable spectacle. The horses were trimmed in black velvet with silver bells, Tudor roses and gold embroidery. The defenders each had their own pavilion, one topped by a golden lion, another by a silver falcon, a third with a red dragon and the fourth with a lion's head in ermine trapped with gold. There were ladies wearing white satin who rode about the arena on white palfreys, knights in polished armour with feathered crests, and just to make the young duke laugh, pretend knights in paper suits. One eyewitness said that no other tournaments were "equal to these" adding that they brought

---

[9] The rate of £1000 per annum for the Duke of York had been set for Edmund in 1385.

pleasure to the royal family and "great gladness to all the common people."[10]

Being Duke of York was just one of a number of titles which Henry was to receive. In April 1493, two months before his second birthday, he was made Lord Warden of the Cinque Ports and Constable of Dover Castle.[11] In September 1494, when three, he was made Lord Lieutenant of Ireland with responsibility for keeping the peace, upholding the laws and customs of Ireland, granting pardons, receiving homage of the King's tenants, conferring ecclesiastical benefices, ensuring necessary supplies for soldiers, summoning parliaments, calling all officers to account and enquiring into forfeited or concealed lands.[12] He was also made Earl Marshal of England and Warden of the Marches toward Scotland. By giving these appointments to his infant son, the King was following the practice started by Edward IV of keeping positions of power within the family. Since Henry was clearly too young to administer estates or defend land, other people had to be appointed to deputise for him, but these were then servants of the crown and it was relatively easy to dismiss a servant who failed to perform but much more difficult to do the same with a noble who might have several hundred armed retainers. The years of civil war had taught kings to exercise much greater caution in their appointments. Another advantage to maintaining key positions in the hands of his children was that the King could keep the income in the royal coffers.

Issues of government were vitally important to the King. Monarchy was regarded as a divine gift and a responsibility exercised directly under God. It was essential that it was taken seriously and for that reason, the education of his children was a matter close to the King's heart. His eldest son was Arthur, Prince of Wales, named after the legendary king to demonstrate how the arrival of the Tudors was the dawn of a new golden age. Next came a daughter called Margaret. Henry was the third child. After him came two daughters named Elizabeth and Mary. Two more children named Edmund and Katherine completed the family. Of these seven children, just four survived infancy and tutors were supplied for each of them. In Henry's case, he was taught by John Skelton, William Hone, John Holt and Giles D'Ewes. Although it was anticipated that Arthur would become king, life expectancy in Tudor England was low and Henry received an education designed to prepare him to rule. If he never became King of England, it was to be expected that he would be appointed to govern other parts of the country's dominions, possibly in France, or else be wed to an

---

[10] Kingsford op.cit. p.203. Prominent in the tournaments was Thomas Brandon, uncle of Charles who would be for many years Henry's closest friend and who became his brother in law when he married the Princess Mary.

[11] CPR 1485-1494 p. 423

[12] CPR 1494-1509 p.12

heiress who would naturally need him to rule her lands, women not being expected to govern alone in their own right.[13] Margaret and Mary's education was similarly focussed, the King's goal being to marry them to suitable heirs, something which was achieved with Margaret becoming Queen of Scotland and Mary, Queen of France.

Henry probably learnt his letters in infancy from his mother: David Starkey has highlighted the similarities in their handwriting.[14] From the age of four or five, he would have received a more formal education within the palace. Each school day would have begun early with attendance at Mass. He would then have had a brief meal before starting his lessons. After dinner, he would have been taught "to ride cleanly and surely" and to handle weapons. Following evensong and another meal, came the arts. Henry was to learn "harping, to pipe, sing and dance." Finally, came bedtime. Throughout the day he was to be surrounded by people of good character who would encourage him in princely behaviour. There were to be none who were a "swearer, brawler, backbiter, common hazarder, adventurer" or who used "words of ribaldry." They were to ensure that Henry's every minute was to be spent wisely and not "suffered in idleness or in unvirtuous occupation."[15]

Henry was particularly fortunate that the late fifteenth century was the era of the Renaissance, the time in which contemporaries felt they were being reborn and shaking off the middle ages. The concept of the New Learning with its concentration on the classics had been enthusiastically adopted by his father who employed overseas poets like Carmeliano and André and sculptors like Torregiano. The King's choice of Skelton as a tutor for Henry was praised by Desiderius Erasmus, the most celebrated scholar of the Renaissance. Erasmus said Skelton was: "the first to bring the Muses hither from the world of Rome. This man was the first to teach men refined and pure speech. Under your sway, Skelton, England need not fear to contend in song even with the poets of Rome."[16]

It was Skelton who was to teach Henry Latin, speech writing, classical history and the principles of government. It was barely thirty years since the introduction of printing which meant that none of Henry's tutors had easy access to textbooks and as a result, they were forced to write their own.

---

[13] There were some exceptions such as Isabella of Castile but ordinarily a consort would become effective ruler.

[14] David Starkey, *Virtuous Prince,* (London, 2008) p.120

[15] John Nichols, *A Collection of Ordinances and Regulations for the Government of the Royal Household* (London, 1790) pp.29,45. The regulations were originally laid down by Edward IV for the Queen's brothers.

[16] Clarence Miller (trans.), *The Collected Works of Erasmus,* vol.85 Poems (Toronto 1993) p.335

Skelton wrote volumes entitled *The Book to Speak Well, Dialogues of Imagination*, a *New Grammar in English, Of Sovereignty*, and the *Book of Honourable Estate* whilst Holt wrote *Lac Puerorom*, a Latin primer. Only one of Skelton's such works has survived and that is *Speculum Principe* or *A Mirror for Princes* written in August 1501. Full of classical and biblical allusions, the volume is in the style of the Book of Proverbs and other ancient wisdom literature. It includes a series of moral precepts which undoubtedly would have served as the basis for lessons with Henry being expected to illustrate the precepts by examples he had learnt from books. Some of those exhortations were:

If a man conquers many lands, if he lacks good character and neglects his soul, he is not worthy of the name.

Prosperity does not last forever.

Bad times need to be borne like the good.

Hate gluttony.

Be sober and cultivate moderation.

Outlaw drunkenness.

Do not indulge yourself.

Keep away from prostitutes

Do not marry recklessly.

Do not deflower virgins or violate widows.

Marry a woman of your own choice.

Do not forget goodness.

Do not believe everyone. Abhor flatterers. Listen to wise counsel.

Do not be parsimonious but be bountiful, lavish, kind and generous

Rebuke fools but honour philosophers, teachers and theologians.

Discuss problems for a long time with a few trusted men.

Think always about your reputation

Be strong in adversity, careful in prosperity.

Be merciful and humble always

Have compassion on the poor.

Learn from history about leadership and godliness.

Observe justice.[17]

---

[17] F.M. *Salter*, 'Skelton's *Speculum* Principis' in *Speculum, vol.* 9 (1934) pp.34-36

Erasmus' *Adages,* written for a similar purpose, indicate how such sayings would have been used in Henry's education with each phrase being interpreted in light of Christian ideals. Thus Terence's "Between friends all is common" was seen as a signifier of the relationship between Christ and his disciples while Theophrastus' "the year not the field produces the yield" was regarded as indicating that princes should encourage education for that would build character in the people and overcome any deficiencies in nature.[18]

Exactly which classical writers Henry read is unknown but his brother was said to have studied works by Terence, Virgil, Cicero, Homer, Ovid, Thucydides, Caesar, Quintilian and Tacitus. Most of these volumes had been imported by the King direct from Italy at a cost of hundreds of pounds so it is almost certain that they were used for Henry too.[19] He certainly had *La Chronique de Rains* with its stories of the crusades and the minstrel Blondel. The list is similar to that recommended by Erasmus in *De ratione studii* where he advocates studying Homer because it is easier to learn Latin from him than from reading the Psalms and a good classical understanding will assist in the comprehension of the Bible.[20]

Yet Henry's education was wider than Erasmus would have chosen and this by necessity. Henry was a prince. He needed the social graces such as music and dancing and it was important that he could communicate with ambassadors in a variety of foreign languages. Since it was likely that one day he would be leading an army, it was essential too that he learnt about war and weaponry. Erasmus was a pacifist and a monk, undoubtedly not keen on austerity but equally averse to exercise and non-cerebral entertainments. It would not have been appropriate for Henry to follow a strictly Erasmian schedule of study.

It was in the late summer of 1499 that Henry had the opportunity of meeting Erasmus. At that time, Erasmus had published very little, just some religious poems and a tribute to Robert Gaguin. The meeting was effected by William Blount, Lord Mountjoy, who had recently been taken on as a study companion for Henry. At twenty, Blount was more than twice Henry's age and his role was to assist Skelton by encouraging Henry in his letters and to broaden his knowledge of history. Blount had returned from

---

[18] Margaret Mann Phillips (trans.), *The Collected Works of Erasmus* vol 31 Adages (Toronto 1982) pp.15,95

[19] David Carlson, 'Royal Tutors in the reign of Henry VII' in *Sixteenth Century Journal* vol 22 no 2 (Summer 1991) p.257. For the cost of books see Bentley, op.cit. The first specific reference to a book being bought for Henry is on 2nd November 1495, see p.105.

[20] J K Sowards (ed.) *The Collected Works of Erasmus,* Vol.25 Literary and Educational Writings, (Toronto 1985) p.xv-xvi.

Paris a few months before where he had been a student of Erasmus and it was he who had invited him to England. Erasmus arrived with Thomas More, then a student at Lincoln's Inn and just twenty-one. He does not seem to have been warned about the visit for he complained some years later that More had arrived with a gift for Henry whereas he was not prepared. Erasmus described entering the great hall at Eltham and finding Henry standing in the middle of the dais "having already something of royalty in his demeanour in which there was a certain dignity combined with singular courtesy."[21] His sisters Margaret and Mary were on either side whilst the baby Edmund was in a nurse's arms. Henry received the visitors with a formality that defied his eight years and invited them to stay to dinner. During the meal, he sent Erasmus a note saying that so noted a poet should surely be able to produce a verse or two to entertain the gathering. Erasmus went back to his lodgings and three days later produced an ode *Prosopopoeia Britannie maioris* which paid tribute to the King as the "unparalleled wonder of these times, equally trained in the weapons of both Mars and Athena...a match for Caesar" whilst Henry was "the golden Phoebus."[22] In a covering letter to Henry, Erasmus promised that he would "bring richer offerings when virtuous manhood increasing with your years shall furnish me with richer themes for my verse." His letter ended with the hope: "May you illuminate good literature by your high distinction, protect it with your royal authority and encourage it by your generosity."[23]

Although this meeting was one of the most famous events of Henry's childhood, there were other memorable occasions. In February 1498, there was a fire at Westminster Palace[24] which came just two months after one at Sheen. Henry was woken in the middle of the night and watched with his parents as much of the palace there was destroyed together with jewels, clothes, beds and Christmas gifts.[25] Renamed Richmond, it was rebuilt within a couple of years complete with a set of apartments for the Duke of York.[26] 1497 saw Henry forced to flee to the Tower with his mother as thousands of rebels from Cornwall, angry over taxation demands, marched on London. The rebels were defeated at Blackheath and the King went in triumph to the Tower to reclaim his wife and son but it was a reminder of the fragility of power, most especially to the Queen who would have recalled how she had been forced to flee herself as a child and how her brothers had entered the Tower never to be seen again. Indeed, for the first eight years of

---

[21] Francis Morgan Nichols, *The Epistles of Erasmus* (London 1901) p.201

[22] Miller op.cit. p.33

[23] Nichols op.cit. p.202

[24] CSPV vol 1. p.267

[25] Kingsford op.cit. p.222

[26] Starkey op.cit. p.147

Henry's life, there existed a rival Duke of York in the form of the pretender Perkin Warbeck, who was "solicited, allured and provoked by that old venomous serpent the Duchess of Burgundy, ever being the sower of sedition and beginner of rebellion."[27] It is small wonder that as an adult, Henry was to be so obsessed with the need to secure his own succession and to put down revolts firmly.

Few of Henry's possessions from this period have survived, but one which has is a roll of prayers. This long document would have been carried with him wherever he went, both as an aid to devotion and in the belief that it offered protection to the bearer. Over ten feet long and about five inches wide, the roll consists of a number of religious images interspersed with prayers and spiritual exercises. Beside one image, Henry has written, "William Thomas, I pray you pray for me, your loving master Prince Henry."[28] The images fall into two categories, those relating to Christ's crucifixion and those relating to the saints. Some of the saints are well known, such as St Christopher, but others are less so, such as St Herasmus of Campania who is pictured being disembowelled. Saints Michael, George and Armoul all appear with dragons or monsters which they have defeated, and it is easy to understand why a boy would have liked those pictures. A comment on the roll reveals St Armoul was a saint to whom Henry's father was particularly attached and promises: "he that prays heartily to God and to St Armoul shall be delivered from all these sicknesses underwritten. That is to say of all gouts, aches, agues, fevers and poxes and many other infirmities." In an age of limited medical knowledge, the intercession of the saints was seen as being an important means of avoiding illness and the roll also contains images of saints Anthony and Pantaleon who were to be similarly invoked.

The first part of the roll contains instructions on how Henry is to pray each day. After attending Mass daily, he was to spend time in private devotion in his chapel. The roll provides an image of the crucifixion and says he should kneel down and ask for God's mercy and the forgiveness of his sins, remembering how Jesus on the cross offered paradise to the thief who shared his pain.[29] He should then recite Psalm 121 "I lift up my eyes to the hills", followed by the Gloria and an anthem. Next he should repeat the Lord's Prayer and say the Hail Mary. A time of meditation on each of Christ's wounds came next with a further recitation of the Lord's Prayer and

---

[27] Hall op.cit. p.495. Warbeck was executed in 1499.

[28] A full description exists in Edward Charlton, 'Roll of Prayers formerly belonging to Henry VIII when Prince' in *Archaeologia Aeliana*, new series vol 2 (1858) pp.41-45. The roll was exhibited at the British Library as part of the 2009 exhibition marking five hundred years since his accession.

[29] Luke 23:32-43

Hail Mary after each. Finally, Henry was to stand and say the Creed.

The roll includes two examples of the sort of papal promises which were to so offend the Protestants during Henry's own reign. The first promised a remission of 52,712 years and forty days from punishment in purgatory every time Henry was to gaze at a particular image and recite the Lord's Prayer and Hail Mary five times. The second promised on behalf of Pope Innocent that so long as he carried an image of the nails and recited a set pattern of prayers he would have seven blessings: "The first is he shall not die a sudden death. The second is he shall not be slain with sword nor knife. The third is he shall not be poisoned. The fourth is his enemies shall not overcome him. The fifth is he shall have sufficient goods to his life's end. The sixth is he shall not die without all the sacraments of holy church. The seventh is he shall be defended from all evil spirits, pestilences, fevers and all other infirmities on land and on water." This talismanic aspect of the prayer roll appears elsewhere with it being said that carrying the image of the blood soaked cloth of Christ would preserve Henry from thunder and lightning and from drowning. It further declared that if, when married, Henry placed it on the body of his wife when she was giving birth, then the life of mother and child would be secure.

With such wonderful blessings to be gained from simply carrying a roll of prayers and reciting them regularly, it is perhaps not surprising that the roll shows every sign of being well used. Around the edges were images of angels which were reverenced as being the messengers of God. In 1496, Erasmus had written a poem *In Laudem Angelorum* which Henry had probably read before he met him at Eltham which said:

When we get up you undertake to guard us faithfully, nor do you leave off till the daylight disappear. Always trusting in your guardianship we make light of the furious enemy... In life and finally in death we are safe through your service. You know how to give strength to the weak, to encourage the troubled and the grieving with words of good cheer...You fly continually back and forth between the heights of heaven and the lowly earth. From here you carry up our lamentations, but from there you bring back gifts...We beg that our prayers may always penetrate to the ears of our Father on high and that they may be validated by you, oh patrons and blessed guardians of the family of Christ."[30]

Throughout his life, Henry was to demonstrate a sincere faith in God. He was educated by humanists who sought to return the Church to what they

---

[30] Miller op.cit. pp.119,121. The poem originally appeared in *De Casa Natalitia Iesu*

regarded as its original purity. He read widely on religious issues and volumes in the British Library provide evidence of this through the annotations he wrote in the margins. As King, Henry was to authorise the publication of the Holy Bible in English, the greatest gift ever given by a monarch to his people. In time, he was to come to understand that the pope could no more guarantee freedom from pain than he could dispense with the requirements of the Holy Scriptures and he was to re-establish the church in a reformed state centred on the scriptures and increasingly bereft of superstition, corruption and bribery. Yet the prayer roll forms an essential part of understanding his childhood faith and the things which were most important to him.

In his beliefs, Henry was typical of his age. An assistant to the Venetian ambassador wrote an account of the country in 1500 for his master in which he spoke of the frequency with which the English went to pray. He described parish churches as treasure houses and abbeys as "more like baronial palaces than religious houses."[31] He was particularly impressed by the signs of luxury he saw everywhere with regard to homes, furnishings and clothes though he did not like the weather describing "the rain which falls almost every day during the months of June, July and August."[32] He noted the abundance of food but suggested that the English were rather more devoted to it than was good for them, claiming that in battle "when the war is raging most furiously they will seek for good eating and all their other comforts without thinking of what harm might befall them."[33] He thought the English generally well built, because they ate well, and handsome but complained that they were vain and insular: "The English are great lovers of themselves and of everything belonging to them; they think that there are no other men than themselves and no other world but England."[34] The ambassador complained about the crime rates, especially in London, arguing that it was not safe for a man to go out alone at night for "they never cease to rob and murder in the streets."[35] He thought the people feared the King but were not grateful to him for all that he had achieved and considered the belief that present sovereigns were not as good as their predecessors was a national characteristic.[36] Toward the end of his report,

---

[31] Charlotte Sneyd (trans.) *A Relation or Rather a true account of the Island of England* (London Camden 1847) p.29

[32] ibid. p.8

[33] ibid. p.23

[34] ibid. pp.20-21

[35] ibid. p.36. By contrast, another Venetian in 1506 contrasted the order and civility of London with Falmouth which he described as "a very wild place which no human being ever visits, in the midst of a most barborous race so different in language and customs from the Londoners and the rest of England that they are as unintelligible as these last to the Venetians." See CSPV vol.1 p.315

[36] ibid.pp.31,46

the ambassador provided data on what he believed to be the royal income suggesting that the King received around £180,000 each year and Henry as Duke of York £16,750.[37] In modern money, that would be around ninety-five million pounds for the King and over eight and a half million for the nine year old Henry. Of course, those sums were not simply a private income. The King was responsible for government so his income covered the wages of all officials just as Henry's paid the costs of those who managed and worked on his estates. As early as 1498, Henry had his own household headed by a Treasurer named John Reding who was responsible for purchasing supplies and managing expenses.[38]

In November 1501, aged ten, Henry was called upon to play his part in the wedding of his older brother Arthur to Catherine of Aragon. This was the first time he had been required to carry out such a large and public role. Events such as being made Duke of York or receiving the Garter took place primarily within the court but the royal wedding was the biggest spectacle since the coronation and arguably the most lavish royal wedding ever. Securing the hand of a princess from Spain, rich with the gold of the Americas, was a political coup for the King and he was determined to demonstrate not just to the Spanish visitors but his own people, just how much he valued the alliance.

Catherine arrived in England in October and following a rest, began her journey towards London. On Friday 12th November, she arrived at St George's Fields to be met by over fifty lords who were to escort her into London itself. The lords were led by Henry, Duke of York sumptuously dressed and keen to show he could behave in the manner of a true and courtly knight. Having greeted his new sister-in-law, the procession set off making its way through Southwark to London Bridge where the first of seven pageants took place. Each of them was designed to showcase the wealth, traditions and talents of England in a symbolic manner. Thus, each pageant included Tudor roses, the Beaufort portcullis, Welsh dragons, English lions rampant, French fleur-de-lis and the ostrich feathers of the Prince of Wales. There were singers, dancers and players reciting poems and welcome speeches. Since Catherine did not understand any English, it would have been rather bewildering for her so Henry had a key role to play in explaining things to her in French.[39] An eyewitness account of the

---

[37] ibid. pp.49-50

[38] CPR 1494-1500 p.126. By 1503, the names of some of those suppliers are given, such as Robert Lincoln (wheat and flour), John Proctor (fresh fish, swans, geese), Robert Cutter (faggots, rushes), William King (beef, mutton, salted fish), John Day (coal), John Passey (carriages and carts), John Buttill (poultry, eggs and butter), William Atkinson (pigs and lambs), John Cressey (hay, oats and necessaries for Henry's horses). pp.325-326

[39] CSPS vol 1 p.154. Five years later, Catherine still did not speak English as she admitted: "I

procession spoke of how Catherine wore a small hat like a cardinal with her auburn hair hanging loose about her shoulders and of the splendour of the clothes. Heralds in their richly embroidered surcoats went before the royal couple and there were over one hundred horses in the cavalcade.[40]

The wedding itself took place on Sunday 14th at St Paul's. Catherine had been staying at the home of the Bishop of London at which Henry arrived to take her to the church. The walls of the interior had been lined with costly tapestries depicting various heroic and virtuous deeds from history. That the King could do this was a sign of wealth for it would have taken a team of thirty or more weavers well over a year to prepare these tapestries and the wool would have had gold and silver thread interwoven to ensure that they shimmered.[41] A dais had been erected and covered in scarlet worsted for the wedding itself and to one side was a specially created chamber where the King and Queen sat with their other children so that they could watch the proceedings without detracting from the attention due to the bride and groom. Henry wore white velvet and Catherine a gown of white satin with large sleeves and a heavily pleated body which onlookers thought was "much like unto men's clothing." On her head was a white waist length silk veil bordered with pearls and precious stones. Her train was carried by the Queen's sister, Lady Cecily.[42]

Amidst a fanfare of trumpets, Henry took Catherine through the west door and into the body of the church where they were met by the Archbishop of Canterbury. They then processed to where Arthur was waiting, probably nervously for he was only fifteen. After the wedding itself, Henry stepped aside as bride and groom walked hand in hand up to the high altar for a nuptial mass. Following that, Arthur left the church so he could get to the reception which meant Henry had to escort the new Princess of Wales from the church. As they passed through the nave, minstrels played trumpets, sackbuts and shawms.[43] At the moment that they emerged into the sunlight, a specially created fountain beside the west door began "to rain diver sorts of good wines."[44]

The reception banquet continued until around five in the afternoon after which the young couple were put to bed publicly. No events were planned for

---

do not understand the English language nor know how to speak it." ref CSPS vol.1 p.385

[40] Gordon Kipling (ed.) *The Receyt of the Ladie Katheryne* (Oxford, 1990) p.32

[41] Thomas Campbell, 'How Medieval and Renaissance Tapestries were made' in *Helibrunn Timeline of Art History* (New York, 2000). The Abraham tapestries later bought by Henry VIII for Hampton Court cost more than two new battleships.

[42] Kipling op.cit. p.43

[43] Sackbuts were akin to trombones and shawms to oboes.

[44] James Gairdner (ed.), *Letters and Papers Illustrative* vol 1 op.cit. p.415

the next day deliberately, which may have been as well since several reported an exhausted Prince Arthur emerging late next morning from the bedchamber demanding a drink saying: "I have this night been in the midst of Spain, which is a hot region, and that journey maketh me so dry, and if thou haddest been under that hot climate, thou wouldest have been dryer than I."[45]

The celebrations continued later that week with a series of official dinners given in turn by the English and the Spanish and with three days of jousts. Henry attended every event and appears to have enjoyed himself thoroughly. Thursday was a case in point. The afternoon was spent at the joust and the evening at a banquet in Westminster Hall where the walls had been lined with tapestries and seven shelves of gold plate to dazzle and impress all who attended. After the royal family had taken their place on the platform, Henry being next to his father, the show began. A castle on wheels was drawn in by men costumed as lions. Within the castle were eight fair maidens whilst in the turrets were choirboys who sang "most sweetly and harmoniously." The castle was set to one side while a boat was wheeled in complete with mast, sails and sailors. That anchored near the castle and two figures emerged dressed as ambassadors, supposedly from the knights on the Mount of Love. They took their petition to the ladies in the castle who declined their suit. The ambassadors took the news back and next arrived eight knights bearing banners who waged war on the castle until they captured the hearts of the ladies. The show ended with the eight knights and eight ladies putting on a dancing display. After that the floor was cleared and Prince Arthur led the rest of the family out on the floor. Henry danced with his older sister Margaret. After two dances, one of the King's household staff reported: "he perceiving himself to be encumbered with his clothes suddenly cast off his gown and danced in his jacket with the said Lady Margaret in so goodly and pleasant a manner that it was to the King and Queen great and singular pleasure."[46]

The marriage was to be one of the last occasions Henry would see his elder sister for two months later, aged twelve, she was married to King James of Scotland. Henry was in attendance at the ceremony which took place at Richmond with the Earl of Bothwell standing in for King James. Again, there were jousts, pageants and banquets in celebration, with a new

---

[45] L&P vol. 4 part 3 pp. 2577, 2580, 2581. Prince Arthur made the comment to at least seven different people. The question of the consummation of the marriage was to be examined in some detail in 1529 and details of the various testimonies given can be found in Henry Ansgar Kelly, *The Matrimonial Trials of Henry VIII* (Stanford 1976) or at the National Archives. Catherine's parents confirmed the consummation in a treaty of 20th June 1503, see CSPS vol.1 p.306

[46] Thomas Hearne (ed.) *John Leland's Collectanea* vol 5 (London 1774) pp.361-362

young star emerging at the first named Charles Brandon who was reported to have broken two spears and "right well jousted."[47] In time he was to become Henry's closest friend, Duke of Suffolk and his brother in law through his marriage in 1515 to Princess Mary.

Despite the joy of the weddings, just weeks later tragedy was to strike when Arthur died suddenly at Ludlow. Although there is no account of Henry's reaction, it may be imagined. The King was told by his confessor in the early hours of Tuesday 9th April and he then sent for the Queen and broke the news to her. Seeing his distress, she reminded him that England needed him to be strong and so did their surviving children. Recalling how God had preserved him through battles and challenges all his life, she said that they must take heart together and pray for all to be well. They still had two daughters and "a fair prince" and they were yet young enough to have more children. Eventually, having quietened the King, the Queen returned to her own chamber where she herself broke down, weeping with such passion and for so long that her attendants felt it necessary to summon the King to comfort her.[48]

The future of the dynasty now rested on Henry's ten year old shoulders and in the hope of learning more of what was in store, the King asked his astrologer William Parron, to provide a forecast. Just two copies of the volume exist today, one in Paris and the other in the British Library. The *Liber de optimo fato Henrici eboraci ducis* or *Book of the Destiny of Henry, Duke of York* is over one hundred pages long and interesting for a number of reasons, not least being the clues it gives concerning the time at which Henry was born.[49] Henry's grandmother, Lady Margaret Beaufort, had only recorded the date in her Book of Hours and there is no contemporary record of the actual time, an essential piece of information for an astrologer. In the year that Henry died, the celebrated astronomer and astrologer Cardano, published a chart showing the birth time as 10:40 a.m. which appears to have been the same as that used by Guarino, astrologer of the Medicis.[50] At least one modern source has argued that this is some two hours out and has

---

[47] ibid. vol 4 pp.258-264

[48] ibid. vol 5 pp.373-374

[49] Parron is also the only source of information regarding the time at which Henry VII was born and this must have been obtained from Lady Margaret Beaufort herself. The time was around 3.30 a.m.

[50] Hieronymi Cardano, *De Exemplis Centum Geniturarum*, (Nuremberg, 1547) Chart XLVI pp.148-149 Guarico does not give a time but states that Henry died when Saturn was in negative aspect, ref Anthony Grafton, *Cardano's Cosmos : the worlds and works of a Renaissance astrologer* (Harvard 1999) p.234. At time of death, Saturn was at 1 Capricorn which on the basis of a 10.40am birth would have been square to his ascendant, semi-sextile to saturn and opposite to jupiter.

been adjusted to make the planets fit later events.[51] Given that Parron obtained his information from Henry's own parents, an impeccable source, and he wrote before Henry became king or married, the significance of his work cannot be over estimated. Unfortunately, Parron does not include a chart or actually state the time, but he does list out the planetary positions which enables this to be calculated.

According to Parron, at the time Henry was born, Virgo was on the ascendent, the sun was in the eleventh house, mercury in the eleventh and the moon in the eighth. He added that mercury was sextile the midheaven and trine to the moon, and that mars was conjunct the ascendent. For an astrologer, the constellation on the ascendant was key because it shaped the character. Virgo was associated with a love of music and drama as well as a deep seated spirituality and sense of morality. Parron said that Henry would be a good son of the church and a just ruler.[52] The houses reflect the division of the sky at the time of birth with different houses being associated with different areas of life. The second, for example, indicates money, the seventh marriage, and the eleventh friends and non familial relationships. Although astrologers agree on the nature of the houses, the method of division varies. Cardano was a proponent of the equal house scheme which is the method most commonly used today. Parron clearly did not use that as is evidenced by his house positions and comments about the cusps[53] but to have jupiter conjunct the midheaven and mars conjunct the ascendant, he must have used a birth time of around 10.40am indicating that Cardano was correct.

To Parron's eyes, Henry had an extremely positive chart. Like most late medieval astrologers, he placed great store on the Arabic Part of Fortune which was conjunct jupiter and the midheaven.[54] That indicated wealth and success. He interpreted the trine between the moon and mercury as showing wisdom and a propensity for learning.[55] He thought the moon in eight would mean that he would inherit things easily, a prospect which must have delighted his father who had been forced to face so many alternative claimants for the throne.[56] The negative aspect of saturn being retrograde and in opposition to mercury, Parron glossed over, though he did comment that saturn was in its own house of aquarius which meant that the more unfortunate repercussions of this would be ameliorated. For Henry himself,

---

[51] Nicholas Campion, *Born to Rule*, (London, 1993) p.63

[52] William Parron, *Liber de optimo fato*, (1502) image 11. The manuscript is held by the British Library as Royal 12 B VI. References here are to the image numbers of the microfilm copy.

[53] ibid. image 26

[54] ibid. image 23

[55] ibid. image 34

[56] ibid. image 30

he predicted that he would be a popular and liberal king who would be fortunate in his choice of friends, selecting people who would be loyal and offer wise advice. He said he would be successful in battle, a veritable second Caesar. He said he would grow up to be charming, accomplished and manly.[57] With the seventh house being empty, Parron tried to avoid the issue of marriage, settling for just a general comment that Henry would be a successful king and since that was defined as one who was happily married and who produced sons, it must follow that Henry would be so blessed.

More than two months passed from Arthur's death before Henry was accorded the title of Prince of Wales. Its first use appears toward the end of June when he was granted the forest of Gaultres in York.[58] It could not be used earlier because people had to wait to see if Catherine was pregnant. Had she been carrying a child, it would have taken precedence over Henry in the succession. The formal grant of title took place at Westminster on 18th February 1503.[59] This must have been an extremely difficult time for Henry. He was now almost twelve. The loss of his brother probably affected him materially more than emotionally for he had been brought up separately from Arthur, but he would have been aware of the additional responsibilities and expectations that fell upon him as a result. It was a time of adjustment when he needed support but just a week before his creation, his mother, Queen Elizabeth, died on her thirty-seventh birthday, days after giving birth to a premature daughter. Princes are trained to rarely express their feelings but Henry was later to write to Erasmus describing "the death of my most dear mother" as "hateful intelligence" which created a deep "wound" within. He added, however, "it is right for mortals to submit to whatever pleases heaven.[60]

In January 1504, almost two years after Arthur's death, Henry was formally stripped of the title of Duke of York by Parliament and the incomes he had received as such reverted to the crown:

> Whereas it hath pleased Almighty God to call the king's dearest son Henry, Duke of York, to be now the king's heir apparent and Prince of Wales, Duke of Cornwall and Earl of Chester, by reason whereof he hath great and notable possessions; wherefore it is for him convenient to leave and be discharged of the said name of Duke of York... Be it therefore enacted, ordained and established by the advice and assent of the lords spiritual and temporal and the commons in this present

---

[57] ibid. image 11

[58] CPR 1494-1509 p.258.

[59] Edward Hall, *Hall's Chronicle*, (London, 1809) p.497

[60] Francis Morgan Nichols, *The Epistles of Erasmus*, (London, 1901) p.425

parliament assembled, and by authority of the same, that the ... annuity to him granted by the king our sovereign lord of, for and upon the same creation, and the lands, tenements, possessions, hereditaments, offices or other things, whatsoever they be, to him heretofore given and granted by the King's letters patents, act of parliament or otherwise, be from henceforth utterly void and of none effect.[61]

In 1509, Henry was to succeed as King Henry VIII, becoming known to contemporaries as Henry the Great. Five centuries later, he remains one of the most famous English monarchs and arguably the one who made the greatest impact on his country. In a paean of praise, Thomas More was to call him: "a young man who is the everlasting glory of our time...a king who is worthy not merely to govern a single people but singly to rule the whole world."[62] Having been only a child when Duke of York, he achieved nothing of note in that role, but his education at that period of his life prepared him for his future and shaped the man. Athlete, scholar, warrior, musician and theologian, Henry was the very model of the Renaissance prince. As his friend William Thomas said, he was "undoubtedly the rarest man that lived in his time."[63]

---

[61] PROME 25th January 1504

[62] Clarence Miller, Leicester Bradner, Charles Lynch and Revilo Oliver (ed.) *The Complete works of St Thomas More* vol 3 part 2 Latin Poems (Yale, 1984) p.101

[63] Quoted in Carolly Erickson, *Great Harry*, (London 1980) p.17

Charles

1600-1649

Duke of York 1605-1625

There was never in any prince of his race more religion, understanding and good nature, honesty and activeness.[1]

On Wednesday 19th November 1600, just after mid-day, Queen Anne of Scotland gave birth to her second son at Dunfermline. Her husband, King James VI, whom she had met eleven years to the day before,[2] rejoiced though his mind may have been elsewhere for on the same day at Edinburgh, the bodies of the Earl of Gowrie and Alexander Ruthven were being publicly dismembered. The two men had attempted to kill the King at Perth on 5th August but died in the attempt. It was a reminder of the dangerous world into which the new prince was born.

Baby Charles was baptised at Holyrood on 23rd December. He was given the title of Duke of Albany, in accordance with a Scottish tradition.[3] His elder brother Henry was six at the time and his sister Elizabeth was four. Another girl named Margaret had died in the spring.

---

[1] Anon, *The Copy of a Letter written by an honourable gentleman servant to His Highness to a lord of His Majesty's Privy Council*, (1623) p.4

[2] Edwin Beresford Chancellor, *The Life of Charles I*, (London, 1886) p.2

[3] Dukes of York were to continue to be created Duke of York and Albany for almost two hundred years, the last holder being Frederick.

On 24th March 1603, when Charles was just two years old, his father became King of England and on 5th April, James left for London closely followed by his wife and two older children. Charles was left behind at Dunfermline because he was considered too weak to make the journey. Lord Fyvie, who had responsibility for Charles' care, wrote to the King at the end of the same month:

> That precious jewel it pleaseth your highness to credit to my keeping, is (praised be God) for the present at better health far than he was, and to make Your Majesty more particular account, eats, drinks and uses all natural functions as would wish in any child of His Grace's age, except that his nights rest is not as yet as sound as we hope in God it shall be shortly. The great weakness of his body, after so long and heavy sickness, is much supplied by the might and strength of his spirit and mind. I will assure Your Majesty he looks all stately and bears all grace and majesty in his countenance as could be required of any prince albeit four times his age.[4]

A month later, Lord Fyvie reported to the King that Charles was:

> ..in good health, good courage and lofty mind. Although yet weak in body, is beginning to speak some words – far better as yet of his mind and tongue than of his body and feet. But I hope in God he shall be all well and princely, worthy of Your Majesty as His Grace is judged by all very like in lineaments to your royal person.[5]

Robert Carey, who visited Charles at Dunfermline later wrote in his memoirs that, "I found him a very weak child."[6]

Dr Henry Atkins was sent by James to assess Charles' health in the spring of 1604 and wrote a series of reports over the next three months.[7] He noted that Charles had scurvy, which was not unusual for anyone at that time of year, and had been suffering from diarrhoea for three weeks. He further reported that the "joints of his knees, hips and ankles being great and loose are not yet closed and knit together."[8] Two months later, he wrote: "he is recovering and is beginning to walk alone which he never did before." Soon after, he was to say he had seen Charles dance and "His Highness now

---

[4] George Seton, *Memoir of Alexander Seton*, (Edinburgh 1882) p.55

[5] ibid. p.56

[6] Robert Carey, *Memoirs of Robert Carey, Earl of Monmouth*, (Edinburgh 1808) p.137

[7] Frederick Devon, *Issues of the Exchequer*, (London, 1836) p.10

[8] J. Keevil, 'The illness of Charles Duke of Albany' in *Journal of the History of Medicine* vol 9 (October 1954) pp.408, 411

walks many times a day all over the length of the great chamber at Dunfermline like a gallant soldier all alone."[9]

With the weather now warmer, it was decided to bring Charles south to England. Lord Fyvie and Dr Atkins attended him and Sir Robert Carey was sent to meet them. The party left Scotland on July 13th 1604 reaching Leicester on 15th August. They stayed in the home of Sir William Skipworth where the corporation arranged a special banquet and presented gifts to Charles and his servants. Unfortunately, the visitors were not well behaved and the corporation was forced to pay compensation to Sir William for damaged dishes and filched linen. Charles' entourage had requested the provision of three hundred and fifty gallons of beer for the three day visit which may have contributed to the problems. Certainly, they could not be blamed on the three year old prince.[10]

Following a reunion with his parents in Northamptonshire, Charles was created a Knight of the Bath and then Duke of York on Twelfth Night 1605. Sir Dudley Carleton wrote to Ralph Winwood saying: "We have a Duke of York in title but not in substance." He described the masque or pageant which followed. Written by Ben Jonson and staged by Inigo Jones, it involved the Queen and her principal ladies dressing up as Africans:

There was a great engine at the lower end of the room which had motion and in it were the images of sea horses with other terrible fishes...At the further end was a great shell in form of a scallop wherein were four seats; on the lowest sat the Queen with my Lady Bedford...Instead of vizzards their faces and arms up to the elbows were painted black which was disguise sufficient for they were hard to be known.[11]

He commented in a letter to John Chamberlain that it was: "a very loathsome sight. I am sorry that strangers should see our court so strangely disguised."[12] A number of ladies missed the performance because there was so much confusion getting in that they were shut up in a passage for the duration. When they were finally released, they rushed in a blind panic into the Great Chamber where a banquet had been laid out for the King,

---

[9] M. Giuseppi (ed.) *Calendar of the MSS of the Most Honourable the Marquess of Salisbury*, Vol xvi (HMSO 1933) p.163

[10] Seton op.cit pp.59-60. The exact size of the entourage is unknown but they travelled in two coaches and requested twelve beds so the volume of beer provided would seem excessive to requirements.

[11] Edmund Sawyer (ed.), *Memorials of Affairs of State in the Reigns of Queen Elizabeth and King James I* (London, 1727) vol 2 pp.43-44

[12] SP14/12/6

accidentally overturning the tables so that all the food was destroyed before a morsel could be touched.

In February 1605, Charles was placed in the care of Lady Carey, wife of Sir Robert. In his memoirs, Sir Robert wrote that many ladies had planned to try to secure care of the young prince "but when they did see how weak a child he was and not likely to live, their hearts were down and none of them was desirous to take charge of him."[13] He continued that Charles was unable to walk "nor scant stand alone, he was so weak in his joints and especially his ankles insomuch as many feared they were out of joint." His account, written over twenty years later, conflicts with that of Lord Fyvie and the official record that Charles was handed over "in perfect health."[14] James had paid for Charles to have fencing lessons soon after his arrival in England which he would surely not have done had he observed his son to be so poorly.[15] Lord Cecil, who saw the prince often, wrote in May 1605 that Charles was "in perfect health."[16] It suggests that Sir Robert may have exaggerated in order to increase his financial recompense. Certainly, visiting ambassadors to the court who were notorious for their gossip and often keen to look at the royal children in case of a future matrimonial alliance or for evidence of a weakness which would affect the nation's stability, never made any report of Charles being deformed or unable to walk properly.

Nonetheless, Charles continued to have some difficulties. His older brother Henry was a model of health, vitality and athleticism which made the contrast even greater. James remained concerned, urging the use of iron boots to help strengthen his limbs.[17] Charles was duly given customised reinforced boots, a customised suit of armour[18] and it is possible he may have had a rocking horse too as compensation for not being able to ride freely.[19] In addition, Charles was inarticulate, something probably made worse by his desperate desire to emulate Henry who excelled in his communication skills. James recommended cutting the string under his tongue, an idea referenced in the Bible[20], but Lady Carey protested and it

---

[13] Carey op.cit. p.138

[14] SP38 14th February 1605

[15] Devon op.cit. p.17. Payments began in November 1604, three months before he was passed into the care of the Careys.

[16] Giuseppi op.cit vol xvii p.201

[17] Carey op.cit. p.141. Charles Carlton, *Charles I: the Personal Monarch*, (London, 1983) p.4

[18] The boots are held in the Museum of London, the armour in the Tower of London

[19] The Victoria and Albert Museum have one from around 1608 which may have come from Theobalds. If this is the case, then it would have been used by the royal children. As Henry and Elizabeth were too old, it would follow that it must have belonged to Charles.

[20] Mark 7:35

was never carried out.[21] Instead, Charles was encouraged to try to speak with pebbles in his mouth, a trick recommended by the ancient Greek orator Demosthenes, and applied to children generally in order to improve the clarity of their diction. Yet, the problem remained. In 1622, Girolamo Landi described Charles as "having some impediment through the length and size of his tongue which prevents him from expressing himself freely."[22] In an effort to be positive, L'Estrange said that Charles may have been secretly wise for "there was never, or very rarely, known a fool that stammered."[23]

The general opinion since has been that Charles had rickets, a disease normally caused by lack of vitamin D which is ordinarily absorbed via sunshine and diet.[24] Francis Glisson, writing fifty years later, noted that rickets was regarded by Europeans as being particular to this country which he attributed to the damp climate and he observed further that it was particularly common amongst the upper classes where babies were weaned earlier and then given a much richer diet. In particular he blamed salted meat and fish, warm bread, excessive cheese and strong wine taken on an empty stomach.[25] He also thought that hot baths were dangerous.[26]

Glisson's treatise is interesting as the first full medical account of the disease published in England and the nearest in date to Charles' case. His comments indicate how Charles' doctors might have thought. To Glisson, the indicators of rickets were an enlarged head, a general lack of energy, late development of teeth, short stature, a swollen liver, breathing problems, wind, a chest shaped like "the breast of a hen", swollen wrists, and muscles which are "daily more and more worn away." He wrote:

..the musculous flesh is less rigid and firm, the joints are easily flexible and many times unable to sustain the body... For the most part they speak before they walk which amongst us English men is vulgarly held to be a bad omen... They are ingenious not stupid... their countenances are much more composed and severe than their age requireth as if they were intent and ruminating upon some serious matter.[27]

---

[21] Carey op.cit. p. 141. James was reported by Anthony Weldon to have a similar problem with his speech, see Anthony Weldon, *Court and Character*, (London, 1650) p.165

[22] CSPV vol 17 p.452

[23] Hamon L'Estrange, *The Reign of King Charles* (London, 1655) p.1

[24] See J. Keevil, 'The illness of Charles Duke of Albany' in *Journal of the History of Medicine* vol 9 (October 1954) pp.402-419

[25] Francis Glisson, *A treatise of the rickets* translated by Philip Armin (London, 1651) p.170

[26] ibid p.168

[27] ibid. pp.232-238

To Glisson, it was a relatively new disease having emerged only in the last thirty or forty years. He recommended "a plentiful diet is altogether to be abandoned and a thin spare diet ought to be observed" and said that efforts should be made to encourage exercise. If a child could be made active, then by five he should be all right and grow up normally. If not, and at five he was still exhibiting the same signs, then the expectation was that life would be short and miserable due to pain and deformity.[28]

Archaeological evidence shows that rickets existed before the seventeenth century though it was on the increase at this time.[29] Dr Atkins had said that Charles' joints were loose but added: "as it happen to many in their tender years which afterwards, when years hath confirmed them, prove very strong and able persons."[30] Certainly Charles grew up to be a keen horseman though he remained short, albeit not dramatically so. His armour in the Tower of London suggests he reached 5'4" when the norm was 5' 7".[31]

Charles' enemies certainly believed he had rickets. Hamon L'Estrange in 1655 described him as having bowed legs – a classic sign of the disease – and being unable to exercise.[32] Another went further and claimed that up to the age of seven, Charles was crawling on all fours.[33] Although such descriptions have been quoted by later writers as evidence, it should be noted that neither writer was present during Charles' childhood and their testimony conflicts with facts. They were Cromwellians whose motive in writing was to blacken Charles' name. The latter author describes him as being wilful, ill natured and treacherous from infancy and said: "I admire God's justice that he, who unjustly made war upon unwarrantable grounds, should have war thus brought home to him so that now God hath given him the same measure he hath met to others even full, pressed down and running over." The attribution of abnormalities was common at this time

---

[28] ibid. pp.169, 253-256

[29] Charlotte Roberts and Margaret Cox, *Health and Disease in Britain* (London 2003) reported that 0.8% of Roman burials showed signs of rickets (p.143), 0.7% of late medieval (p.248), and 3.65% of post medieval (p.310). There was no evidence of rates being higher in Scotland than in southern England. Ann Stirland, *Raising the Dead* (Chichester, 2001), found that up to 5% of men on the Mary Rose which sank in 1545 showed signs of childhood rickets. R. Pinhasi, P. Shaw, B. White. A R Ogden 'Morbidity, rickets and long bone growth in post medieval Britain' in *Annals of Human Biology*, vol 33 no 3 (May-June 2006) p.379 found 20% of child burials 1569-1770 showed signs of rickets.

[30] Keevil op.cit p.408

[31] Roberts and Cox op.cit. p308

[32] L'Estrange op.cit. p.1. L'Estrange admitted in his introduction that he had not seen Charles himself.

[33] Osborne, 'Observations upon the King from his Childhood' in *Secret History of the Court of James the First* (Edinburgh 1811) p.61

because physical imperfections were seen as indicating wickedness. Just as the Tudors said Richard III was a hunchback and the Catholics said Anne Boleyn had six fingers, so the Cromwellians said Charles had rickets.

If he did, it may have been hypophosphatemic which affects more females than males but has a greater effect on males. Unlike certain other types of rickets, this reduces the risk of fractures and there is no indication of Charles ever having broken or fractured bones.[34] In this form, vitamin D levels might be entirely normal if the cause of the phosphate metabolism dysfunction is genetic.[35] Certainly, there seems to have been a family tradition of problems with five out of six generations affected. James' doctor, Theodore de Mayerne, described both his legs as atrophied though he did not report any deformity or shortness which might be expected with rickets. Weldon said "that weakness made him ever leaning on other men's shoulders, his walk was ever circular." adding that had been unable to walk until he was around five.[36] James' father, the Earl of Darnley, appears in his portraits to have extremely thin legs but with no sign of deformity. Amongst future generations, Charles' daughter Elizabeth and his great-grandson William of Gloucester, both had problems with walking. Elizabeth, alone of the five, had severe skeletal deformities which may have resulted from rickets.[37] William, was unable to stand, walk or mount stairs unaided even when he was eleven. Yet only James and Charles were reported to have speech problems which are not associated with any variant of rickets. This has led to suggestions that they could have had a form of cerebral palsy or bone dysplasia or some other neurological disease.[38] Although the diagnosis is uncertain, there is universal agreement that Charles was a weak child and remained so for many years. Even at seventeen, he was described as lacking in stamina by one observer who reported: "He has not yet much breath."[39]

Just fifteen months after his arrival in England, Charles became the focus of one of the most famous assassination schemes of all time, the

---

[34] Signe Beck-Wilson et al. 'Phenotype Presentation of Hypophosatemic Rickets in Adults' in *Calcified Tissue International* (August 2010) vol 87 number 2 pp.108-19

[35] S. K. Bhadada et.al. 'Hypophoshataemic rickets/ osteomalacia: A descriptive analysis' in *Indian Journal of Medical Research*, (March 2010), pp.399-404

[36] Anthony Weldon, *The Court and Character of King James*, (London, 1651) p.165. Although Weldon's general conclusion on James is positive, he did not know the king as a child because he was not born until 1583.

[37] T.E.C., 'Princess Elizabeth, Second daughter of King Charles I and rickets' in *Pediatrics* vol 64 no 2 (August 1979) p.241

[38] For more on this theory see Frederick Holmes, *The Sickly Stuarts*, (London 2003) pp. 78-80, 96-98, 215-216. At no point in his life did anyone suggest Charles was deformed and no portrait indicates this either, although artists may have been inclined to flatter.

[39] CSPV vol 15 p.114

Gunpowder Plot. Guy Fawkes and his fellow conspirators planned to blow up Parliament when the King came to open the new session. They believed that this would not only rid them of the King but his son Henry and the nobility of England plus the bishops. They thought they would then seize the Princess Elizabeth, declare her queen and re-impose Roman Catholicism. The fact that the vast majority of the English population were Protestant and had no desire whatsoever to return to Rome, did not deter them in the least. The idea of killing hundreds of people, including the women and children of the royal family, did not upset them either. Had they succeeded in their explosion, they would not have had the slightest chance of obtaining the necessary support of the people to enable them to achieve their goals. It was an ill conceived murderous scheme from the outset and the confusion is evident in their plans for Charles. At first, they wondered if he might attend Parliament with his father and brother, but he was not yet five. It seemed unlikely. So they sent Thomas Percy to the Carey's house to ask questions. Assuming they had killed James and Henry, they would need to capture the two younger children. As a girl, Elizabeth was presumed to be more easily led so they could use her. Charles, as a boy, was more problematic because he would have become the rightful heir, so they would have had no choice to murder him.[40]

Thomas Percy visited the house on 2nd November 1605. The Careys and Charles were all away so he spoke to the maid Agnes Fortun. She recognised him from the court because he was a servant to the King. A description of him was later issued saying he was: "a tall man with a great broad beard, a good face, the colour of his beard and head mingled with white hairs but the head more white than the beard, he stoopeth somewhat in the shoulders, well coloured in the face, long footed, small legged." [41] He asked Agnes a number of questions about Charles, in particular his routine and how many guards he had. He asked to see his apartments. All this made Agnes rather suspicious but it put her in a difficult position for she was but a maid alone in the house and the visitor was a courtier known to her master, and this in an era where men were not discouraged from using physical force on female servants in order to get their way. In the end, she offered to let Percy in saying that he could wait to "see the Duke and Sir Robert Carey both." At this point, Percy departed.[42]

In the event, the plot was discovered before any explosion could take place. Lord Harington, in whose care the Princess Elizabeth had been placed

---

[40] On 5th November, Fawkes testified that the plotters had no plans for a successor to James, but on the 8th, he said they had planned to make Elizabeth queen. See SP14/216/6 and SP14/216/49.

[41] SP14/73/115

[42] SP14/16/35

at Combe Abbey, said in a letter that he had been told by a messenger from the King that the whole Catholic community in England had been consulted about the scheme and that the pope was to pronounce a general absolution on those involved following its completion. He added: "His Majesty doth much meditate on this marvellous escape and blesses God for delivering his family and saving his kingdom from the triumphs of Satan and the rage of Babylon."[43]

The King had Charles returned to court in the aftermath of the plot and he brought him into an audience with overseas ambassadors saying: "This poor boy's innocence and that of the Prince and others has had more power with God than the perfidious malignity of men." [44]

Charles continued in the care of the Careys where, according to them, "he daily grew more and more in health and strength both of body and mind" to the amazement of many that knew his weakness when they first took charge of him.[45] He was certainly much stronger by the summer of 1610 when he played his part in the celebrations to mark his brother becoming Prince of Wales. On 5th June he took the role of the wind Zephyrus, in a spectacular masque at Whitehall. Queen Anne played Tethys, Queen of the ocean and wife of Neptune. Charles' costume was described by the author as "a short robe of green satin embroidered with golden flowers with a round wing made of lawn on wires and hung down in labels. Behind his shoulders two silver wings. On his head a garland of flowers consisting of all colours and on one arm which was out bare he wore a bracelet of gold set with rich stones." He was required to run about the stage accompanied by eight naiads attired in "light robes adorned with flowers, their hair hanging down and waving with garlands of water ornaments on their heads." As they danced together, two tritons in "skin coats to show the muscles of their bodies" with knee length fins and garlands of sedge on their heads, sang to an accompaniment of lutes. Perhaps significantly, Charles was not required to speak at any point in the performance for the role of the tritons was to speak on his behalf. [46]

Little is known about Charles' relationship with his mother. One letter of his to her survives. Undated, the wording suggests he was quite young for he wrote:

---

[43] John Harington, *Nugae Antiquae*, vol 1 (London, 1804) p.374

[44] CSPV, vol 10 p.296

[45] Carey op.cit p.141

[46] Samuel Daniel, *The Order and Solemnity of the Creation of the High and Mighty Prince Henry*, (London, 1610). The short costume shows his parents had no concern about Charles showing his legs, something they would not have done had they been deformed by rickets.

I wish from all my heart that I might help to find a remedy to your disease... But I must for many causes be sorry; and specially because it is troublesome to you and has deprived me of your most comfortable sight, and of many good dinners; the which I hope by God's grace, shortly to enjoy.[47]

He was certainly doted on by his father. The Venetian ambassador, Zorzi Giustinian in 1608 wrote "he is the joy of the King, the Queen and all the court," a sentiment repeated by his successor two years later.[48] Giustinian described how James delighted to laugh and joke with Charles and told of an incident in February 1607 when Charles was six:

While I was in the ante-chamber waiting to be introduced to the presence, the King sent out his second son, the little Duke of York with an harquebus on his shoulder. He came right up to me and said he was thus armed for the service of the Republic. I said that the Republic would be very proud of so big and brave a captain and that under his leadership she was sure to win a great and signal victory.[49]

Even when he was eighteen, an age when princes often found themselves in conflict with their fathers, it was reported that: "He is very dear to his father whom he imitates as much as possible."[50]

No letters exist from Charles' brother or sister to him but there are several from him to his brother. They demonstrate great love and an element of hero worship. In one, Charles wrote:

I will give anything that I have to you, both my horse and my books and my pieces and my crossbows or anything that you would have. Good brother love me and I shall ever love and serve you.[51]

In another dated 1609, he wrote:

Nothing can be more agreeable to me, dearest brother than your return to us; for to enjoy your company, to ride with you, will yield to me supreme pleasure. I am now reading the conversations of Erasmus from which I am sure I can learn both the purity of the Latin tongue

---

[47] James Halliwell (ed.), *Letters of the Kings of England*, (London, 1848) vol 2 p.118

[48] CSPV vol 11 op.cit. pp.96, 423

[49] ibid. vol 10 p. 471

[50] CSPV vol 15 p.421

[51] Ellis op.cit. p.92. The letter is undated and only the signature is in Charles' own handwriting

and elegance of behaviour. Farewell! [52]

The adulation of Henry was not unique to Charles for his sister Elizabeth clearly shared the same sentiments, writing in one of her letters to him: "I will ever endeavour to equal you, esteeming that time happiest when I enjoyed your company and desiring nothing more than the fruition of it again." [53]

Despite the fact that the three children were brought up separately in different households, James did his best to ensure that they maintained a sense of family. Stow gives an account of a family outing which took place in June 1609 to the Tower of London. At that time, the Tower was home to the Royal Menagerie, a collection of wild beasts.

> The King, the Queen, the Prince, the Lady Elizabeth and the Duke of York with divers great lords and many others came to the Tower to see a trial of the lion's single valour against a great fierce bear which had killed a child that was negligently left in the Bearhouse. This fierce bear was brought into the open yard behind the Lions Den which was the place for the fight. Then was the great lion put forth who gazed a while but never offered to assault or approach the bear. Then were two mastiff dogs put in who passed by the bear and boldly seized upon the lion.[54]

Much of Charles' time was inevitably spent in education. His father's directions to his tutor when he was five were to instruct "him in all kinds of good learning according to the capacity of his tender years but also in penning and framing his missive letters in divers languages directed either to ourself or foreign princes."[55] He was reported to be a good student, so much so that James threatened Henry, who was able but lazy, that if he did not try harder, he would make Charles his heir instead. Henry later told his tutor: "I know what becomes a prince. It is not necessary for me to be a professor but a soldier and a man of the world. If my brother is as learned as they say we'll make him Archbishop of Canterbury."[56] Charles studied the classics and theology and languages but he also learnt to play tennis, to ride and to fence and to play music.[57] He would have studied the works of his

---

[52] Halliwell op.cit p.114

[53] Ellis op.cit. p.90

[54] Quoted in Daniel Hahn, *The Tower Menagerie*, (London 2003) p.85

[55] James Halliwell-Phillipps, *Letters of the Kings of England*, (London, 1846) p.114

[56] CSPV vol 10 p. 511. At the time, Charles was six and Henry twelve.

[57] He began tennis lessons when he was nine, see Devon op.cit. p.116. His music and fencing lessons had begun when he was four, ibid. p.17

own father for James was an established and able writer who had written four volumes, one on witchcraft, another on tobacco, a book on the theory of kingship and a manual to prepare his son for the responsibilities of monarchy.

In *The True Law of Free Monarchies*, James listed the responsibilities of a king as being to administer justice, to advance the good and punish evil, to establish good laws and procure obedience to the same, to procure peace and to promote prosperity for himself and his people. In his eyes, a king was to be "a loving father and careful watchman caring more for them than for himself, knowing himself to be ordained for them and they not for him."[58] As a prince, Charles' role was to support the king and there is evidence of him trying to administer justice, such as his decision to intervene in a quarrel between vessels from Dunkirk and Holland in 1623.[59]

The instructions in *Basilikon Doron* were more practical than theoretical and included "marry one that were fully of your own religion"[60] and then be faithful to her and not allow her to meddle in politics. Moderation was recommended, especially in clothes, James urging his children to be "neither over superfluous like a debauched waster nor yet over base like a miserable wretch; not artificially trimmed like a courtesan... Specially eschew to be effeminate in your clothes, in perfuming, preening or such like...Make not such a fool of yourself in disguising or wearing long hair or nails which are but excrements of nature." Clothes were regarded as a mark of status and not to enhance physical attributes or draw attention to "natural parts ordained to be hid." They were not to "serve for baits to filthy lechery."[61] Exercises to preserve health were highly recommended such as ""running, leaping, wrestling, fencing, dancing and playing at the catch or tennis, archery, pall mall and such like other fair and pleasant field games." James went on to add "it becomes a prince best of any man to be a fair and good horseman...and specially use such games on horseback as may teach you to handle your arms thereon such as the tilt, the ring and low riding for handling of your sword."[62] These ideals were clearly used in Charles' education and he was to become a "master" of the tilt.[63] James did, however, warn that princes should beware becoming too passionate about sports "remembering that these games are but ordained for you in enabling you for

---

[58] Charles McIlwain (ed.), *The Political Works of James I*, (Cambridge 1918) p.55

[59] Andreas Almansa y Mendoza, *The Joyful Return of the most illustrious Prince Charles* (London, 1623) p.39

[60] Henry Morley (ed.) *A Miscellany*, (London, 1888) p.136

[61] ibid pp150-151

[62] ibid. p.155

[63] Anon, *The Copy of a Letter written by an honourable gentleman servant to His Highness to a lord of His Majesty's Privy Council* (1623) p.3

your office for the which you are ordained."

James was acutely aware that his family were in the public eye warning that even if a prince was to be a model of perfection in private, he would be judged by his outward behaviour and if that was poor, it would "breed contempt, the mother of rebellion and disorder." For this reason, a prince was to be extremely careful and to frame "your gesture according to your present actions: looking gravely and with majesty when you sit in judgment or give audience to ambassadors; homely when you are in private with your own servants, merrily when you are at any pastime or merry discourse: and let your countenance smell of courage and magnanimity when you are at war." Warning his son about being swayed by favourites rather than reason, he concluded: "above all, let the measure of your love to everyone be according to the measure of his virtue." [64]

The King also had an opinion on food, favouring plain food for himself and his family. In the *Basilikon* he wrote: "let all your food be simple without composition or sauces which are more like medicine than meat. The using of them was accounted amongst the ancient Romans a filthy vice because they serve only for pleasing of the taste and not for satisfying of the necessity of nature."[65] He counselled against dining privately lest it encourage gluttony and urged that during meals a prince should have "pleasant histories read to you for pleasure and profit." It is almost certain that this practice was followed in Charles' household. We know something about Charles' diet at this time for an account exists of the food served to him each day. In accordance with contemporary practice, days could be either flesh days or fish days, though the latter term was rather misleading since it simply meant a day without red meat. Thus, for example, for breakfast Charles would have been served bread, beer, milk, butter and two chickens. For dinner on a fish day, he would be served beer, wine, veal, cod, pike, carp, sole, gurnard, two partridges and a capon followed by tarts and custard. For supper on a flesh day, he would have bread, beer, more wine, plus mutton, mallards, partridges, larks, tongue, rabbits, capons and snytes. To end it all would be custard, tarts or fried swan's livers.[66] Although fruit and vegetables were not listed in the diet, this was because they were taken for granted and grown on palace property rather than purchased.

When he was eleven, Charles was removed from the Careys and given

---

[64] Morley op.cit. pp.147,153, 161

[65] Morley op.cit. p.148

[66] Edmund Turner, 'A declaration of the diet and particular fare of King Charles the First when Duke of York' in *Archaeologia* vol 15 (1806) pp.1-12

his own household.[67] As a further mark of maturity, he was invested as a Knight of the Garter the same year.[68] He was confirmed on Easter Sunday 1612. A year later, his world was rocked when his brother Henry died suddenly of typhoid fever.[69] This event was seen as disastrous by the whole country. Henry had been an extremely popular heir to throne and people had immense hopes of him. He was memorably called "the male stud of sovereignty."[70] The Venetian ambassador had observed as early as 1607 that James was unhappy about the adulation which his heir received and he was, to put it frankly, "growing jealous."[71] For Charles, it was an immense personal blow. He had idolised Henry and not only had he lost him, but he would have to try and step into his shoes. Charles was now heir to the throne, destined for a life of public speaking and responsibility. He must have felt overwhelmed and certainly his future subjects were rather dismayed at the prospect too. A paragon of princely virtue had been replaced by an insecure, shy youth with a speech impediment. Yet, the tragedy prompted some changes in Charles. Antonio Foscarini, the Venetian ambassador, reported six months later: "I have visited the prince who remains here alone. He is growing fair as a flower and in the few months since the death of Prince Henry he has developed greatly in body, far more than in many preceding months. His health is becoming sound, he advances in his studies and he has suavity of humour that renders him very popular....He is quite aware of his rise in importance as he is now the only son but all this only makes him more humane."[72]

It was not until 4th November 1616, just before his sixteenth birthday, that Charles was created Prince of Wales.[73] Perhaps it was the stress of the occasion or maybe another manifestation of a metabolic disorder, but Charles was reported to be suffering from "green sickness" at this time, or anaemia.[74] The actual ceremonial had been delayed that autumn due to Charles' weakness which one courtier observed "did not permit any public show."[75]

---

[67] Carey op.cit. p.142

[68] Peter Begent and Hubert Chesshyre *The Most Noble Order of the Garter – 650 Years* (London, 1999) p.317

[69] Holmes op.cit p.109

[70] L'estrange op.cit p.1

[71] CSPV, vol 11 p.511

[72] CSPV vol 12 p.524

[73] He had been made Duke of Cornwall in February 1613.

[74] SP14/89/35. Anaemia is sometimes associated with people who have hypophosphatemic rickets.

[75] Thomas Birch, *The Court and Times of James the First*, (London, 1848) p.434. Chamberlain uses the word "craziness" which at this date meant general debility rather than mental

Charles maintained his titles of Duke of Albany and Duke of York after his elevation.[76] His new role gave him further responsibilities but there is little sign of Charles taking these up. It is unclear if he was present at the meeting between the King and Pocahuntas which took place in January 1617[77] though the royal family had been together for Christmas and New Year. He took an interest in Parliament, attending sixty-three of the eighty-nine sessions in 1621[78] but he was generally devoid of dynamism. One account of Charles at this time describes him as being "entirely engrossed in the pleasures of the chase."[79] Another describes him as being virginal, innocent, remarkaby self controlled and grave:

> He moves like a planet in its sphere, so naturally and quietly that one does not remark it. In speech he shows good sense, his replies are prudent, he grasps things with quick judgment. ... He is methodical and most regular in his affairs and in the conduct of his household ...As a rule he dresses absolutely without jewels, more modestly than any gentleman soever...He excels at tilting and indulges in every other kind of horsemanship...In dancing he surpasses his condition. He delights in archery and in manipulating guns, the arquebus, the pike and sword. He loves old paintings...He has a school of arms which belonged to his brother and frequently works there upon out of the way mathemathics... being very interested in inventions.[80]

His father sought to encourage him into a greater public role by giving him a project. In 1622 he made Charles head of his council and said that he had long wanted to establish an academy for the better teaching of youth and the encouragement of art but until now he had lacked the money. Now he had set funds aside and wished Charles to found some such public work.[81] Instead, Charles went to Spain.

Despite his own comments about the advisability of selecting a wife who shared her husband's religion, James had agreed to seek the hand of the Spanish Infanta for Charles. James was desperately keen to preserve the balance of power in Europe. France was the traditional enemy of England as well as a long standing ally of Scotland. Spain had more recently been England's enemy but an alliance with her would prevent her allying with

---

instability
[76] Thomas Middleton, *Civitatis Amor*, (London, 1616)
[77] SP14/90/25
[78] Carlton op.cit p.30.
[79] CSPV vol 17 p.417
[80] ibid. pp.450-52
[81] SP14/131/25

France and therefore keep England's neighbour in check. The idea was not popular amongst his subjects who well remembered the Spanish Armada and who had heard much of the horrors of the Spanish Inquisition, but Charles was enthusiastic. Diplomatic negotiations took time and, Charles, young and impatient, was unhappy. The Earl of Clarendon, who knew Charles well, said that Buckingham, James' present favourite and Charles' friend, conceived the idea of going to Spain to speed the process up. Clarendon said the plan was "contrived wholly by the Duke...out of envy that the Earl of Bristol should have the sole management of so great an affair" as arranging the marriage of the heir to the throne. Clarendon added that Charles "whose nature was inclined to adventures" leapt at the idea and quickly became its greatest advocate.[82] Buckingham's biographer and the Venetian ambassador thought the idea was the King's, the latter attributing it to James mental impairment and blaming Charles for taking advantage of this. Certainly James at this time was suffering from a disorder which impaired his judgment, either vascular dementia[83] or porphyria.[84] The King, however, maintained the idea was Charles' own and said he did not wish to deny him.[85]

Charles' trip was meant to be a secret, though news got out. The idea of an heir to the throne – particularly one without brothers – leaving his homeland was unusual. The fact that the trip was being done without official backing or an invitation from the Spanish government, made it extraordinary. The Spanish ambassador to England said he had not been given an inkling of the plan.[86] Alvise Valoresso summed up the reaction in England and abroad when he described the trip as "a subject which is an abyss of marvels, a monster among decisions, a labyrinth without head or way out. No action more remote from all imagination and belief ever took place, or less founded in likelihood to say nothing of reason, utterly unknown to everyone and approved by nobody."[87]

The whole escapade was like something from a novel. Charles and Buckingham, with a single attendant, left Essex wearing false beards and calling themselves Thomas and John Smith. In royal tradition, they lacked any small change for the ferry at Gravesend so they offered the ferryman a

---

[82] Edward Hyde, Earl of Clarendon, *The History of the Rebellion and Civil Wars in England,* (Oxford 1843) vol 1 p.5

[83] Holmes op.cit p.77. Charles was also to have mental problems in later life, see ibid. pp.111-114.

[84] Ida MacAlpine et.al. 'Porphyria in the Royal Houses of Stuart, Hanover and Prussia' in *British Medical Journal* 9th January 1968 pp.7-18

[85] CSPV vol 17 p.583

[86] CSPV vol 17 p.575

[87] CSPV vol 17 p.582

unite,[88] probably about three weeks wages. Convinced this meant the men were up to no good, the ferryman reported them and a chase ensued across Kent. At Canterbury, the Mayor tried to arrest them as they changed horses. Eventually, they reached Dover where they met up with two more of Charles' servants and they set sail for France, arriving in Boulogne on 20th February, 1623.[89]

Filled with enthusiasm for their adventure, they rode to Paris where they purchased wigs and, thus disguised, crept into the palace where they spied on the King from the Gallery and went to watch the Queen and Henrietta Maria practising a masque. They then rode down to Bordeaux where they bought matching red riding jackets so they could appear "gentlemen of mean degree".[90] Two Germans who had recently seen Charles and Buckingham at Newmarket recognised them but Grehem told them they were mistaken which they accepted easily for "almost the impossibility to conceive so great a prince and favourite so suddenly metamorphosed into travellers with no greater train was enough to make any man living unbelieve his senses." At Bayonne, Charles decided that he was tired of the meat-free diet which accompanied Lent so the group, spotting a herd of goats, decided to take one back to the inn. Charles sat on his horse with his gun poised whilst Buckingham and servants ran about on foot trying to catch a goat. Eventually, they caught one and Charles shot it. To his credit, he insisted on paying the goatherd before settling down to eat.[91] By this time, rumours of the visitors had spread and James was forced to quickly send two representatives to the King of France to apologise for Charles' juvenile and totally undignified behaviour.[92] With some reluctance, the French king agreed to issue orders to his border guards to let Charles pass even though he lacked papers and was carrying goods which would ordinarily have ensured his arrest.

The group reached Madrid on 5th March, arriving unannounced one evening at the home of the English ambassador, the Earl of Bristol. The next day, Charles and Buckingham were introduced to the surprised King of Spain who promised them great hospitality. Charles immediately said that he wished to see the Infanta. A formal meeting was not thought appropriate since they were but unofficial visitors so it was arranged that Charles, Buckingham and Bristol would take a carriage ride in a certain park at the same time that the King and his family just happened to be doing the same.

---

[88] A coin, introduced in 1612 and valued at twenty two shillings
[89] Henry Wotton, *Life and Death of the Duke of Buckingham*, (London, 1651) p.81
[90] ibid. p.86
[91] ibid. p.88
[92] Henry Ellis (ed.), *Original Letters Illustrative of English History*, (London, 1824) pp.121,124

Charles and the Infanta were thereby allowed to see each other with Charles leaning out and duly doffing his hat as they slowly passed.[93] One of Charles' staff wrote: ""the famousest courtier or wooer in France would not have acted it more gallantly. He never did anything so well, not run at Tilt in which he is master."[94]

Rumours about the identity of the visitors spread and shortly afterward a formal welcome to the city was organised. Notwithstanding it being Lent and that the government had recently announced an austerity drive, all sorts of festivities were arranged. Pageants were put on in Charles' honour, plays performed, as well as bullfights and various sporting events. Charles stayed for six months so the cost must have been enormous. The King of Spain, who had released all the English galley slaves as a sign of good faith, gave him eighteen genets, six barbaries, six mares and twenty foals all covered with crimson velvet and gold lace and pearls, plus two stallions and mares, as well as a diamond encrusted pistol, sword and dagger.[95] The Queen gave him a gold basin, embroidered night gown, two trunks with gold locks which were lined with amber leather and filled with linen and perfume plus a rich desk in which every drawer was full of rarities.[96]

This magnificence presented Charles and Buckingham with something of a problem. Spain was famous for its gold thanks largely to its empire. England was not. How were they to respond? Buckingham wrote to James saying that he had been "so sparing" in jewels that he himself was forced to lend Charles some. He said this meant Charles did not appear a king's son which reflected badly on the country. He then proceeded to list out the jewels which he wanted James to send. As if the fact that he called the King "dad" was not sufficient indicator of Buckingham's privileged position, he ended his letter by listing out the fine horses and exotic animals he was sending him, including camels, rare birds and an elephant. He added: "but if you do not send your baby jewels enough, I'll stop all other presents. Therefore look to it." [97]

James had written to Charles at the start of April saying: "In earnest my baby, ye must be as sparing as ye can in your spending there for your officers are already put to the height with providing the five thousand pounds by exchange and now your tilting stuff - which they know not how to

---

[93] John Digby, Earl of Bristol, *A True Relation and Journal* (London, 1623) p.6

[94] Anon, *The Copy of a Letter written by an honourable gentleman servant to His Highness to a lord of His Majesty's Privy Council* (1623) p.3

[95] Mendoza op.cit. p.12, Bristol op.cit p.19

[96] Bristol op.cit pp.29-30

[97] Ellis op.cit pp.146-148

provide - will come to three more and God knows how my coffers are already drained."[98] However, faced with Buckingham's request, he arranged for a huge volume of precious items to be sent, including part of the Crown Jewels. Sir Joseph Meade estimated that the value was £600,000.[99]

Charles did his best to join in with events even though this upset his staff, many of whom had joined him by now. He met the Inquisitor General and was seen to kneel when the Host passed by on Corpus Christi.[100] He adopted Spanish clothes.[101] His staff were dismayed and distinctly unimpressed with the country. They complained about the weather, the climate, the people and the buildings. James Eliot actually told Charles that he had not believed in purgatory until he came to Spain which seemed to him a living purgatory.[102] Sir Richard Wynn described one property which had been used by the Spanish royal family as "so much decayed that we expected hourly it would fall upon us.... yet we wanted no air for there was not a foot of that royal room that wanted holes"[103] Of the women he wrote: "there was not one unpainted, and so visibly that one would think they rather wore vizards than their own faces." He added: "the most passable amongst them was the one that was descended from English parents."[104] Of Madrid, he wrote: "there were so many chamber pots and close stools emptied in the street that it did almost poison us."[105] Wynn also described a notable gaffe made by Charles in San Augustin. Two Spaniards had welcomed him saying they had been in England where they found the women very beautiful. Trying to be polite, Charles immediately said that the most beautiful woman he had ever seen in England was actually Spanish but "she had the most jealous cockscomb in the world to her husband, a very long eared ass, such a thing as deserved not to be master of such a beauty." The Spaniards were rather quiet and made their excuses to leave. One of them was the said husband.[106]

Despite the gifts and entertainments, Charles remained single. The Spanish would not allow the Infanta to marry a Protestant unless he

---

[98] ibid. p.139

[99] ibid.p.152. In modern terms, this would be around £95 million

[100] David Sanchez Cano, 'Entertainments in Madrid for the Prince of Wales' in Alexander Samson (ed.) *The Spanish Match* (Aldershot, 2006) p.71, Bristol op.cit. p.21

[101] Dr Mead, 'Sir Richard Wynn's Account of the Journey of Prince Charles's servants into Spain in the Year 1623' in Thomas Hearne, *Historia Vitae et Regni Ricardi II* (London, 1729) p.328

[102] Eliot op.cit. p.153

[103] Hearne op.cit. p.304

[104] ibid. pp.329, 301

[105] ibid. p.329

[106] ibid. p.325

converted. Charles decided to take over negotiations himself and, notwithstanding his future role as head of the Church of England or the fact that less than twenty years before the Catholics had sought to murder his father and brother, duly accepted articles which would have repealed all the anti-Catholic laws in England and allowed the foundation of a Jesuit college. Back home, the Privy Council and James were left in a very difficult situation but after much debate, they agreed they had to honour the terms lest Charles lose face. Since nobody dare criticise Charles, the blame was given to Buckingham. As Meade recorded "the nobility were so much incensed against the Marquess as to threaten but a bloody greeting if he ever returned again."[107]

Eventually Charles departed Spain. He reached Portsmouth on 5th October 1623. An eyewitness described how the bells rang drowning all speech and the bonfires were so plentiful that they made night appear as bright as day.[108] Charles was never as popular as he was that day. He had failed in his mission to bring back the Infanta and indeed the marriage was never to take place because he declined to convert, but the people were delighted. They had never wanted a Spanish queen. The last English monarch to marry a Spaniard had been Mary Tudor, infamous for burning hundreds of Protestants across the towns of England.

On 27th March 1625, Charles' father died and he became king. The history of his reign is well known though there has been much dispute over the centuries about the blame for what happened. He divided opinion to the extent that a civil war began which destroyed proportionately more than the First World War. He hired foreign mercenaries to try and kill his subjects and following accusations of supporting Catholicism, interfering with Parliament and manifold counts of duplicity, he was sentenced to death, facing execution in front of the Banqueting House in London on 30th January 1649. Whether he was a martyr or a tyrant is another subject, for in becoming king, he ceased to be Duke of York. His achievements as Duke had been slight as might be expected since he was only a child for the greater part of the time in which he held the title. He was renowned then for his scholarship, but had he spent more time studying the manual of kingship which his father had written and then tried to follow it, his end might have been very different.

---

[107] Ellis op.cit pp.150-156
[108] Mendoza op.cit. p.38

James

1633-1701

Duke of York 1633-1685

The worst subject, the most unkind brother, the most impolitic prince, and the maddest or the most monstrous man in the world.[1]

James Stuart remains probably the most famous Duke of York and one who has most sharply divided opinion. As a young man, he was lauded as "a Prince, the fame of whose transcendent virtues and unequalled valour has reached the utmost limits of the known world" but in later life he was the bloodthirsty traitor intent on destroying the British constitution.[2] His subsequent flight from England when King in 1688 lost him what remained of the respect he had in the view of most people but the facts of his disastrous reign should not detract from what he achieved as Duke of York, a title he held for over half a century, longer than anyone else before or since.

---

[1] Philanex Verax, *A letter to His Royal Highness the Duke of York touching his revolt from or return to the Protestant religion* (London, 1681) p.2

[2] Daniel Brown, *Some Historical Memoirs of the Life and Actions of HRH the Renowned and Most Illustrious Prince James Duke of York* (London, 1683) p.i

James was born on 14th October 1633 at St James' Palace in London His parents were Charles I, who had been King for eight years, and Henrietta Maria, a French princess by birth. He had an elder brother Charles who was three and a sister Mary who was two. Although there had been no formal grant of title, the Heralds asked Almighty God to "bless with long life in health, honour and all happiness the most high, mighty and excellent Prince James, Duke of York." [3] He was christened by the infamous Archbishop Laud who was assisted by the Archbishop of York and the Bishops of London and Norwich. Judge Hutton recorded in his diary that all the clergy wore very rich copes and that the choristers of the Chapel Royal sang "excellent anthems and music."[4]

Like all royal children, he was removed from his parents care. His first nurse was Mary Godbolt who remained his rocker until 1635. His wet nurse was Katherine Eliott, an enterprising lady who used her position to secure licences from the King to set up a silk stocking business and to reclaim land in Somerset.[5] By the time he was five, James had joined his brother Charles in the household of the Countess of Dorset who had been appointed their governess. A new bed and bedding was purchased for him in June 1638 for the truly princely sum of £530, the equivalent of about four years' wages for most of the working men in the country at the time.[6] In April of the same year, James was appointed Lord High Admiral of England "with all fees, emoluments and privileges pertaining to the same, to be held by him for life."[7]

James' childhood was not, however, to be as peaceful as that enjoyed by most princes. When he was seven, the Long Parliament began. Called by his father in order to raise money to send an army against the Scots, it was soon clear that relations between King and Parliament were being strained almost to breaking point. James would not have understood the reasons for the conflict. He would have been more interested in the marriage of his nine year old sister in March 1641 to William of Orange for whom he was part of the welcoming party, one of his earliest official royal duties.[8] In February 1642, following a continued deterioration in the political situation which was exacerbated by Charles going to Parliament to try to arrest five members, the royal family fled Windsor for Dover. There they bade farewell to James' mother, Queen Henrietta Maria, whose unpopularity caused the

---

[3] A. Lytton Sells (trans.), *The Memoirs of James II* (Indiana, 1962) p.2

[4] HMC *The manuscripts of the Duke of Beaufort* (London, 1891) p.127

[5] CSPD 1635-1636 p.430, 1637 p.219

[6] SP16/393/86. A labourer at this time would average seven shillings a week. In today's money, the value of the bed would be almost £68,000

[7] CSPD 1638 p.351

[8] Charles Carlton, *Charles I the personal monarch,* (London, 1983) p.221

King to think she would be safer overseas.

In April, after a few weeks in London, James was escorted north by the Marquess of Hertford. He was welcomed into York on the 16th by large crowds of royalists who lit bonfires in his honour. The next day he was knighted and on Monday 18th, he was elected as a Knight of the Most Noble Order of the Garter.[9] On the 22nd, Charles decided to take advantage of his son's apparent popularity by sending him to Hull. The town contained valuable ammunition stores and was suspected of being on the side of Parliament. Afraid that they would not let himself in, Charles thought he would send James over on an apparent social visit and then take the opportunity to go and call on him, it being thought much more difficult for Hull to refuse to allow a father to visit his son. James accordingly set off accompanied by his bodyguard and his cousin, the Elector Palatine.[10] Hull opened its gates and welcomed him, giving him a house to spend the night. The next morning, whilst dining with the governor Sir John Hotham, a messenger from the King announced he wished to visit too. Angry at what he saw as a plot, Hotham promptly ordered that James and his men be escorted back to their lodging and secured. The gates were then locked and soldiers posted so that when Charles arrived he was unable to enter. Two of James' servants escaped and tried to kill Hotham but they were caught.[11] Eventually, Hotham agreed to let James and his men go, though they were forced to depart singly in order to prevent them creating a disturbance. It must have been an eye-opening and humiliating experience to the eight year old prince.

In June 1642, James attended a fund raising rally of some seventy thousand people with his father and elder brother at Haworth. He was present in August 1642 when his father raised his standard at Nottingham signalling the start of the actual civil war and also at the Battle of Edgehill in October. James later described his pride in marching toward the battlefield behind the infantry alongside his father and brother. Following a charge by the enemy's horse which scattered his men, the King felt the need to move forward to try to rally his troops. He sent his sons back with Sir William Howard but they had barely got behind the line when they saw a brigade of enemy troops approaching. Howard hurriedly thrust his charges

---

[9] SP16/490/8. Owing to the Civil War, James was unable to take his oath and be installed until 1661, see Elias Ashmole, *The History of the Most Noble Order of the Garter*, (London, 1715) p.227

[10] The Elector Palatine, also named Charles, was the eldest son of the king's sister Elizabeth and then twenty-five. His two brothers, Princes Rupert and Maurice would also serve on the royalist side in the Civil War.

[11] James was later to suggest in his memoirs that his servants should have tried harder. See J. S. Clarke, *The Life of James II* vol 1. (London, 1816) p.5

behind a barn where the injured royalist soldiers were being treated. They hid beneath a hedge until the danger passed before withdrawing that evening to the top of the hill from which they were able to watch the end of the battle.[12] James was young enough to probably see the experience as part of a grand adventure. It was said that he revelled in the martial life, his own father advising him to "ply his book more and his gun less."[13] One early biographer wrote:

> ..bold and hardy he was, yet affable and courteous to all, desirous of learning those arts that best qualify princes for brave and grand designs; drums and trumpets were the only music that could charm his heroic soul, nor did the peals of cannons aught dismay him. [14]

As the war progressed, James got to know well some of his father's key supporters including Prince Rupert of the Rhine and Sir Edward Hyde, men who were to be very important to him as an adult. Yet for the most part, James was left in Oxford whilst his father and cousin Rupert went off to fight. At this point, the costs of his household were £653 per month[15] indicating that the royalists remained in good heart and well equipped. Unfortunately for James, despite a good start, the tide of the war soon turned against his father. As Parliament made increasing gains, Charles asked his wife if she thought James should be sent to Ireland for his own safety. [16] Henrietta Maria, who had briefly returned to England in 1643, was now based in Paris and Jermyn sent back her response to the King: "For the proposition concerning the Duke of York's going into Ireland, the Queen bids me tell you that she cannot yet, for any reason she can discern, approve of it."[17] So James, now twelve, remained in the heavily fortified city, even being required to attend Privy Council meetings in place of the King.[18]

Following defeat at Naseby and the fall of Bristol, Charles I left Oxford on 27th April 1646 for Newark, effectively surrendering himself into what he termed "honourable" captivity.[19] On 24th June 1646, Oxford surrendered to Parliament and James became a prisoner. He was taken to St James' Palace where his eleven year old sister Elizabeth and seven year old brother Henry

---

[12] Clarke op.cit. pp.12-15. It is often said that the two princes were in the care of the physician William Harvey at Edgehill but James makes no mention of him being there.

[13] Quoted in John Callow, *The Making of James II* (London, 2000) p.40

[14] Daniel Brown op.cit. p.8.

[15] SP16/498/8

[16] SP16/507/31,

[17] SP16/507/54

[18] SP16/510/126

[19] Carlton op.cit. p.308

were still living. His mother had fled the country two years before. Although James was forced to give up all his familiar servants and have new ones, he was not badly treated. Whilst his father was being held at Hampton Court from 24th August to 11th November 1647, James was allowed to go and visit him two or three times a week. After Charles escaped in November, James resolved to do likewise and his guardian, the Earl of Northumberland, did what he could to assist.[20]

James' first serious attempt in February 1648 was thwarted by his own stupidity. He put the details in a letter which the Parliamentary agents intercepted. At first, James denied all knowledge of it but given the letter was in his own handwriting, this was clearly beyond belief. Parliament appointed two members of the House of Lords and two of the House of Commons to visit the thirteen year old James and question him further. Eventually he admitted that it was his own work. The officials asked James to hand over the cipher which had been used to encode the message. James lied and said he had burnt it. They tried to get him to reveal the names of all those involved in the escape plan, but James refused to answer any questions, even though they threatened him with removal to the Tower of London. Eventually the decision was made that James should stay where he was but under tighter supervision.

James naturally had no wish to be bound. He regarded it as his duty to escape and to assist his father in regaining his throne. His next plan involved a Colonel Joseph Bamfield and George Howard who was brother-in-law to the Earl of Northumberland. James decided to become very keen on playing hide and seek with his brother and sister[21], even though at fourteen he might normally have been accounted a little old for this. On 20th April 1648, he went to hide but in fact slipped down the back stairs to a garden where Bamfield was waiting with a footman who handed James a wig and cloak. They then took a waiting hackney coach to Salisbury House. James and Bamfield alighted and went to the house of a Mrs Murray who helped James dress as a girl. Thus disguised, James went to Lyon Quay where he took a barge down the Thames. Again, James let the game away, this time by hitching up his skirts to adjust his stockings, a move which revealed to the master of the vessel that he was no girl. James was forced to admit his identity. Fortunately, the master agreed to keep silent, even extinguishing all lights on the barge so that they could sail unnoticed past the watch at Gravesend. Finally, James was able to transfer to a ship which took him to Flushing. There they spotted what was believed to be a

---

[20] Clarke op.cit. p.31

[21] It is interesting to see evidence of Elizabeth playing for she was badly disabled by rickets, see T.E.C., 'Princess Elizabeth, Second daughter of King Charles I and rickets' in *Pediatrics* vol 64 no 2 (August 1979)

parliamentary frigate and they made a rushed journey to Middleburg during which they were almost shipwrecked, the tide being too low. Eventually, James landed and he sent Bamfield to advise his sister Mary, now princess of Holland, that he was there and would really like to attend her court but could she first send him some male clothes.[22]

It was while he was in Holland that the disaffected Parliamentary navy arrived and announced that they wished to surrender to James as Lord High Admiral. He was delighted and hurried to get on board. He was still only fourteen. His brother Charles, who was then in France, decided that this was a potentially dangerous situation so sailed across to take command himself, no doubt much to James' annoyance. James remained in Holland until the new year of 1649 when he began his journey to Paris to be reunited with his mother. Shortly after his arrival, he learnt of the execution of his father in London. In his memoirs, James described the event in very simple terms using the deliberately impersonal third person: "what impression that made both upon the Queen and the Duke may be more easily imagined than expressed."[23]

The next few years were difficult for James and his brother Charles who was now a king without a kingdom. At first, they went to Jersey hoping to use that as a base for an invasion of Ireland but when they learnt there was little prospect of success there, Charles went on to Scotland whilst James returned to France where his brother declared him to be of age on his seventeenth birthday.[24] He argued with his mother and went back to Holland but money was extremely short. At one point, James had to pawn his Garter insignia for supplies.[25] Charles learnt of James' behaviour and ordered him to return to Paris telling him that he must obey his mother in all things except religion.[26] Reluctantly he did so. The summer of 1651 was spent awaiting news of Charles who had ventured again into England only to be defeated at Worcester. Following his return in October, James faced more months of poverty and inactivity. One visitor said that Charles, James and their seven year old sister Henrietta remained with their mother and they had but "one ill furnished table" between them. Charles, he said, was "very sad and sombre for the most part...he is very silent always." James was said to be more cheerful but "very childish."[27] In the end, in April 1652 when he was eighteen, James joined the French army of Louis XIV. He

---

[22] Clarke op.cit. pp.34-38

[23] Clarke op.cit. p.46

[24] SP18/11/53

[25] W. Dunn Macray (ed.), *Calendar of the Clarendon State Papers* (Oxford 1869) p.361

[26] HMC, *The manuscripts of the Earl of Carlisle*, (London, 1897) p.6, SP18/11/119

[27] SP18/16/84

reported that he had to borrow the money to equip himself with a horse and clothes from a Gascon named Gautier because "nothing was so rare as money."[28]

James was never happier than when he was in the army. He was to devote a considerable part of his later years to writing his memoirs and the greater part of these revolved around the years he spent serving in the continental wars. He revelled in camp life, the prospect of glory and the challenges of tactical planning. He served under Marshall de Turenne who was considered one of the greatest commanders of the era. Initially, James served as his scout for he reports that Turenne "saw not clearly at a distance" and therefore needed him to observe and report back on troop movements and entrenchments.[29] However, James soon moved on from this and his own accounts make it clear that he was sent into the frontline.

A clear example of this is contained in his account of the siege of Mousson which took place in the late summer of 1653. James described going to inspect a battery of half a dozen guns. Whilst he was there "a great shot came from the town which passed through three barrels of powder without firing them, which had it done, all who were in the battery had inevitably been blown up. But the danger came so suddenly and was so soon over that none of us had time to be concerned for it."[30] The French army advanced but was forced to retreat because "the enemy burnt us out by throwing down upon us such vast quantities of fireworks and combustible matter that they ruined our work." They then turned to mining but again the enemy rained down fire which burnt the first miner in his hole and suffocated the second with smoke. Meantime, the weather was foul with "perpetual rains and storms" which filled the trenches with water and mud and destroyed the defences they had erected. James noted that one day he was trying to make his way along one waterlogged defence which was such hard work that he failed to notice that he was in full view of the enemy. Eventually, one of the men with him mentioned this but James determined to go forward because "we were now so far forward the danger was equal in going forward or in returning." He duly did this and was surprised that the enemy made no attempt to shoot at him. Later, he was able to ask the opposing officer why and was told that he, "knowing me by my star had forbid his men to fire upon the company." However, as soon as James had passed, the enemy renewed its fire, killing several men who were in the same spot shortly afterwards.

---

[28] Sells op.cit. p.57
[29] Clarke op.cit. p.122
[30] ibid. James' account of the siege covers pp.179-186

Next, a well was opened and James and Turenne went to observe this. As they were in the lodgement above, a bomb landed in the well and they thought they would surely perish, but the bomb failed to explode with the anticipated level of force and merely filled the room with smoke for more than a quarter hour. The enemy "continually plied that place with hand grenades, fire and fireworks and, now and then, a bomb, none of which last happened to be so justly directed as the first, yet we carried on." One officer "had his head broken with a hand grenade" whilst another was hit "with a small shot which first came through the lodgement and then after glancing from his head passed through the leg of a pioneer and lastly through the toe of my boot without doing me any harm." Fortunately for all concerned, the mine worked and Mousson surrendered on 27th October. James reported that the encounter had lasted only seventeen days and had cost very few human lives although many horses had been lost due to the weather.

James clearly enjoyed his time in the army. In 1654 he was appointed Lieutenant General, the youngest to achieve that rank.[31] He continued to serve until November 1655 when France signed a peace treaty with Oliver Cromwell's republican government.[32] One of the clauses of the treaty was that France cease to employ James. Understandably, he was not happy because the army was his chosen career. He was an exile from his own country with no other means of income and no home of his own. James deliberately remained in the army as long as he could and he delayed his departure for Bruges until his brother ordered him to leave. Reports of a rift between the brothers continued to circulate until June 1657 when a reconciliation was said to have been effected by mediators concerned that the royalist prospects, already bleak, would be totally lost if there was division in the royal family itself. James agreed not to communicate with his mother or her advisors about public business in return for the command of Charles' forces, something Bamfield wrote: "all parties passionately desire...his reputation being very high amongst his subjects."[33]

For the present, however, James was required to serve in the army of the King of Spain who had promised his assistance to Charles' in his planned restoration. Spain was at war with France which meant that James was forced to fight against his mentor and friend, Turenne. James disliked the task and he was unhappy at being given a lower rank than he had enjoyed in the French army. He was also concerned that the Spanish might think he

---

[31] ibid. p.193

[32] James noted in his memoirs that owing to Turenne and other senior officers being absent at the negotiations, he was in charge of the French army at the time the peace was signed.

[33] Bamfield to Thurloe, 7th June 1657, CSPD 1657-1658 vol 155 p.8 Bamfield said that Charles' army at this stage consisted of six regiments of a thousand men.

was too "much a Frenchman."[34] Yet, he served two years in the Spanish army during which time he was universally critical of what he regarded as Spanish inefficiencies, slowness and tactical errors. At one point, James' men came across a party of French whom they could easily have taken but the Spanish officer in charge refused to attack on grounds he had not been ordered by Don John to do so. James offered to take responsibility but to no avail as the officer said that for him to do anything other than carry out orders would cost him his head.[35] Despairing, James took every opportunity to fraternise with the French officers which must have worried his Spanish colleagues. Had they known about how Tourville, a Frenchman serving with James, had taken the opportunity to advise the said French officers to fire next morning on the Spanish regiment rather than his own – and Tourville helpfully pointed out the location – they would have been even more unhappy. The Spanish lost a number of men and horses as a result.[36] In his memoirs, James acknowledged that he was told not to spend so much time speaking with the enemy but says that he declined to change his behaviour because they were his friends.[37]

The most famous encounter during James' service for Spain was the Battle of the Dunes which took place in June 1658. Dunkirk at the time was under siege by the French. The Spanish could not attack by sea because the English navy were guarding the entrance to the town and so they drew up their forces in the sand dunes to the east. James noted their position was totally exposed but the Spanish rejected his concerns. The next day, the French under Turenne, together with a number of Cromwell's troops, attacked. James was on the right where he was attacked by the English who he says "came on with great eagerness and courage."[38] Despite being "almost spent with climbing" they took the highest sand hill. They then regrouped and descended the hill where James charged them. He says "I was beaten off and all who were at the head of my own troop were either killed or wounded, of which number I had been one had not the goodness of my armour preserved me....Neither did the common men fare better, the loss falling so heavily amongst them that though I endeavoured all I could to rally them, it was not possible."

James departed and was able to find forty of his own guards to

---

[34] Clarke op.cit. p.287

[35] ibid. pp.306-307

[36] ibid p.309

[37] ibid. p.319

[38] James account of the battle appears in Clarke op.cit pp. 345-359. It is possible that this battle was the source of the famous nursery rhyme for the Spanish had their six thousand foot and four thousand horse ("The grand old Duke of York who had ten thousand men") and it was fought amidst hills.

accompany him back up the hill to try and find some more men, though most of those he found were either dead or dying. Taking those who were fit, he descended and then went up the next sand hill only to find the English marching up towards him. Together with his forty guards, James charged down "doing great execution upon them." He noted with some pride, that the English rebels with whom he was now fighting did not throw down their arms: "Every one defended himself to the last so that we ran as great danger by the butt end of their muskets as by the volley which they had given us. And one of them had infallibly knocked me off from my horse if I had not prevented him when he was just ready to have discharged his blow by a stroke I gave him with my sword over his face which laid him along upon the ground."

James' brother, Henry, Duke of Gloucester was alongside him at the time in what was his first battle. He had his sword knocked from his hand and an aide leapt from his horse to retrieve it, whilst Henry sat on guard, pistol in hand. As the aide handed Henry the sword and remounted, he was himself shot.

By now, the Spanish were in full retreat. The men whom James had left on top of the hill had been forced to flee with heavy casualties. Of his own Duke of York's regiment, only one man escaped the battle alive. By now, James only had twenty men with him and he was surrounded on all sides by the French. He attempted to move toward the left and was stopped by four or five enemy troopers. James called out to them in French and they, mistaking him for being of their own side, let him pass. Finding that the left flank had been defeated as badly as the right, he went down into Zudcote but found himself being pursued by the enemy. Accordingly, he parted from most of his men and took to the side roads to avoid being taken prisoner. He managed to reach Don John and the Prince of Condé and, following a brief final stand, they "set spurs again to our horses and did not stop till the enemy had left pursuing us."

Although the Battle of the Dunes was a clear defeat, James' personal bravery further enhanced his reputation. Biographies written of him during his lifetime are keen to describe the battle as evidence of his heroism. One patriotically notes how the French left Cromwell's English to do the fighting whilst the inadequate Spanish trusted not in their own officers but James, "the expertest captain under heaven." The Duke was said to have relished "fighting even in the mouth of slaughter, never seeming weary or discouraged." [39] Another said "with his sword he cut out a lasting name in characters of blood...like to Mars, he fought even in the face of slaughter

---

[39] Brown op.cit. p.28

whilst heaps of slain like ramparts hemmed him in."[40]

His efforts to frustrate the English republican government were not restricted to land. James remained Lord High Admiral and in January 1658, Charles authorised Captain Robert Holmes to buy or hire six frigates which could be used to interrupt trade and carry troops in event of a future invasion. It was also hoped that they might provide a small income since a share of the value of all ships taken was to be given to James.[41] State papers show a considerable number of encounters between English trading vessels and royalist ships whose captains carried a commission from James which read that they were authorised "to enter any port or river of His Majesty's dominions and seize as prize or destroy all such ships and vessels with their men, lading, goods and merchandise as belong to any place or person of His Majesty's subjects in actual rebellion, or not in present obedience to him."[42]

In September 1658, Oliver Cromwell died. Hopeful that this would mean the end of the republican regime, Charles and James tried to orchestrate an uprising in England for the summer of 1659. Charles duly went to Calais and James to Boulogne to await news. With France still being allied to England, James had to travel in disguise and to send his servant to procure a boat privily. Confused by hearing that only Cheshire had rebelled, James went to Calais but by this time Charles had gone to Dieppe and the authorities were watching for James. A French army officer recognised him and he was forced to go between houses hiding where he could in fear of his life. Early one morning he was woken by a loud hammering at the door and he rushed to dress ready to try and escape, only to discover that the soldiers outside were there not for him but to return the master of the house who had passed out in the street drunk. As a mark of respect for James, Turenne sent an offer of a regiment, ammunition, food to feed the troops for six weeks and even promised to pawn his plate to raise the money to hire the vessels necessary to take them to England. However, the failure of the uprising in England meant that Charles determined there was no point in setting out and the offer was rejected.

By October 1659, James was back in Brussels and his situation seemed worse than ever. He had resigned from the Spanish army so he would be ready to return to England but it seemed that England did not want him or Charles back. They were still in exile and having to rely on the generosity of friends and family for their keep. Ordinarily, a king and his heir would be attractive marriage prospects but this was not the case. In 1657, Bamfield

---

[40] Anon, *A Faithful Compendium of the Birth, Education, Heroic Exploits and Victories of HRH the illustrious Prince James, Duke of York*, (London, 1679) p.2

[41] CSPD 1657-1658 vol 179 p.269

[42] SP18/202/6

had thought James would marry one of the Princess Dowager's daughters whilst John Berkeley, had tried to negotiate a match for him with the French heiress, the daughter of the Duc de Longueville, an idea rejected by Louis XIV.[43] Shortly after his arrival in Brussels, James was advised of a plan for him to marry the "daughter of a general of power and good quality in England" which it was hoped would assist the restoration.[44] This scheme too failed to materialise which may account for why in November 1659, James got himself engaged to Anne Hyde, one of his sister's maids and the daughter of Edward Hyde, Charles' Chancellor in exile. As heir to the throne, James should have asked his brother's permission to do this, but instead he did it secretly, possibly because at this nadir in his fortunes, the chance of some affection seemed too good to miss.

Yet all was not lost. Without Oliver Cromwell, the republican government was on the verge of collapse. As England fell into anarchy, the moderate General Monck returned from Scotland and promised a new parliament. Reassured by Charles' promise of a pardon to all but the actual regicides, Parliament voted for the restoration of the monarchy. On May 9th 1660, orders went out to all parish clergy to institute public prayers for "our sovereign lord, Charles, by the grace of God, of England, Scotland, France and Ireland, King, Defender of the Faith and for the most illustrious Prince James, Duke of York."[45] On May 23rd, Charles, James and their brother Henry boarded three separate ships for England. They arrived at Dover on May 25th and made their triumphal entry into London on May 29th, Charles' thirtieth birthday.

The difficulties faced by the brothers should not be underestimated. The country had experienced seven years of bloody civil war followed by eleven years of division. Those who had hoped that the abolition of the monarchy would usher in an age of peace and plenty had been cruelly disappointed. Charles and James arrived to find the coffers bare and the people tired. It needed considerable diplomatic skill to unite the various groups and to start the rebuilding process. Those who met them agreed that Charles was charming and seemed anxious to make peace rather than reignite old arguments. James, meanwhile, was twenty-six and had a dashing reputation which impressed both the fighting men and ladies alike. Henry was only twenty and he failed to play any role in the new order for barely

---

[43] CSPD 1656-1657 p.362

[44] CSPD 1659-1660 p.247. This could not have been a daughter of Oliver Cromwell because his four daughters were already married, nor could it have referenced General Monck who had no daughters. It was probably Jemima, daughter of General Montagu who became Earl of Sandwich at the Restoration.

[45] *Journal of the House of Commons*: volume 8 - 1660-1667 (London, 1802) p.19

three months after his arrival in England, he died of smallpox. A few weeks later, their sister Mary, Princess of Orange who had supported them so strongly in exile, died of the same disease on Christmas Eve aged twenty-nine. James was required to serve as chief mourner for tradition did not allow the reigning monarch to attend funerals.

December 1660 was a difficult month for James in other ways too. Not expecting to have his fortunes restored, he had promised himself to Anne Hyde. At the restoration, she had returned with her father – and a baby on the way which she claimed was his. Her father declared her a strumpet and suggested that the King should have her thrown in the Tower and then beheaded. Charles rejected this idea and simply gave her father the enormous sum of £20,000, though whether this was for her keep or to encourage him to be quiet was less certain.

Anne, however, refused to be quiet and told everyone of how James had signed a paper vowing to marry her with his own blood, a document he had since stolen back according to her. She also said that James had actually married her on September 3rd and that this meant she was entitled to the rank of Duchess of York. James, aware of the displeasure of his mother and brother, denied doing this. Charles told James that he should do the decent thing and marry her – which was interesting advice given Charles' record for fathering bastards. The row continued and James tried to act as if nothing was amiss. On 14th October, Pepys reported: "the Duke of York and Mrs. Palmer did talk to one another very wantonly through the hangings that parts the King's closet and the closet where the ladies sit." A week later, Anne gave birth to a son whom she named after the King. With pressure mounting on James, his servants decided to launch a counter attack by spreading stories that Anne was a lady of easy virtue, that several of them had slept with her, and so the child could be anyone's. Whilst it is uncertain if James actually asked them to do this, the suspicion must be that he did for none of them lost their position. Eventually, in December, James was forced to admit that he was indeed legally married to Anne and on 1st January 1661, she was presented at court as Duchess of York.[46]

Despite this unpromising start, the marriage was not a complete disaster. They had eight children in eleven years, four boys and four girls. Just two girls survived to adulthood, the future queens Mary II and Anne. James' father in law wrote of his daughter:

---

[46] SP29/28/42 and Pepys diary, 21st December 1660. The man who spread most rumours about Anne was Charles Berkeley who, far from being censured, was raised to be Viscount Falmouth. When he died penniless five years later, James made provision for his dependents.

She had the happiness so well to behave herself toward the Duke that he was exceedingly pleased with her and lived towards her with an affection so remarkable and notorious that it grew to be the public discourse and commendation; and which made the liberties that were taken elsewhere the more spoken of and censured. It was very visible that he liked her company and conversation very well and was believed to communicate all his counsels and all he knew or thought without reserve to her.[47]

James himself recorded "Her want of birth was made up by endowments; and her carriage afterwards became her acquired dignity."[48] Nonetheless, not everyone was impressed. Five years later, Magalotti described her as "a woman obstinate, proud, vindictive, hot-tempered, deceitful, cruel, scornful and worshipping gluttony and amusements" and suggested that Charles had only agreed to the marriage out of a desire to revenge himself on his more popular brother. Bishop Burnet did not go so far but did say that "till his marriage lessened him, he really clouded the king" and said that Charles had warned James that "he must drink as he brewed" which was hardly an expression of confidence.[49]

A month after Anne's welcome at Court, there was a rising of the Fifth Monarchists in London. The King was away at the time and by the time James and Monck arrived on the scene, the rebels had been captured. Plans had been made to disband the existing troops the next day but given the situation, James called a meeting of the Privy Council and obtained their agreement to continuing their existence. Charles later approved the decision and as a result the foundations of the modern army were laid. Monck's regiment became the Coldstream Guards. The Blues and Royals were formed, royal denoting their support for the monarch and blue the colours worn under Cromwell. The Grenadiers and Life Guards also came into existence and new barracks were built for them on the old Tilt Yard, known thereafter as Horse Guards.[50] James had little involvement with the army despite his previous experience. His own regiment was brought back from Dunkirk and he was appointed Captain General of the Company of the Artillery Garden which was responsible for training the London militia. In 1664, he formed a Maritime Regiment of Foot which was to become the Royal Marines. To show they were his own troops, they wore his livery of yellow rather than the red associated with the King's troops.

---

[47] Edward Hyde, *The Life of Edward, Earl of Clarendon*, vol. 3 (Oxford 1827) p.66

[48] 'The Life of James the Second written by Himself' in James MacPherson, *Original Papers containing the Secret History of Great Britain*, (London, 1775) vol 1 p.16.

[49] William Middleton, *Lorenzo Magalotti at the Court of Charles II* (Waterloo, Canada, 1980) p.37, Gilbert Burnet, *Bishop Burnet's History of His Own Time*, (London, 1838) p.114

[50] Brian Harwood, *Chivalry and Command* (Oxford 2006) p.38

James' chief area of concern was the navy. Not only was he Lord High Admiral but he was apointed Lord Warden of the Cinque Ports in July 1660 which made him responsible for the safety of the English Channel. Within a month of the restoration, James was presenting to the Admiralty his plans for naval reform. He held a ceremonial burning of the figureheads which had been placed on ships during the republican era including the figure of Cromwell which had incongruously adorned the ship which brought Charles back to England at the Restoration.[51] In April 1665, James issued his first set of Fighting Instructions which incorporated material from the Cromwellian codes but added a distinction between leeward and windward attacks and a new signalling system. In the past, the commander had issued his instructions via flags but these were difficult to see in bad weather or during battle. James determined that as soon as a signal was raised, neighbouring vessels should confirm receipt of the instruction by raising the same signal. This in turn would be a sign to vessels nearer them and so the commands would be relayed quickly through the entire fleet greatly enhancing its manoeuvrability.[52]

It was important for James to exercise effective control over the navy for on March 4th 1665, war was declared against the Dutch. It had been discussed over a year before. Pepys recounted a conversation "of the good effects in some kind of a Dutch war and conquest which I did not consider before... the trade of the world is too little for us two, therefore one must down."[53] On June 3rd, the two fleets fought a battle off Lowestoft. Allen Apsley who was there, said the action began before dawn and lasted more than twelve hours. In a letter to his wife, he described the sight of Dutch sailors leaping into the sea and drowning as the English fireships went amongst them. He was particularly horrified by the actions of one fireship commander who, notwithstanding four Dutch vessels had declared their intention of surrendering, nonetheless went in and five hundred men died as a result. James later sought to court-martial the captain but he escaped. Apsley said it was "the greatest victory that ever the English won and our seamen say it is the most dreadful battle that ever was fought."[54]

In the battle, James commanded the red squadron, Prince Rupert the white and the Earl of Sandwich the blue. Again, he was in the thick of the danger. Pepys wrote in his diary on 8th June that "The Earl of Falmouth, Muskerry, and Mr. Richard Boyle killed on board the Duke's ship, the Royal

---

[51] The ship had neen called the Naseby but was renamed the Royal Charles.

[52] For a full discussion see Julian Corbett (ed.), *Fighting Instructions 1530-1816*, (Navy Records Society vol XXIX, 1905) pp.110-129

[53] 2nd February 1664

[54] HMC, *Report on the manuscripts of Earl Bathurst*, preserved at Circencester Park (London, 1923) p2

Charles, with one shot: their blood and brains flying in the Duke's face; and the head of Mr. Boyle striking down the Duke, as some say." As Pepys worked in the Navy Office, he was in a position to know the details and the same entry adds: "we having taken and sunk, as is believed, about 24 of their best ships; killed and taken near 8 or 10,000 men, and lost, we think, not above 700." James was particularly proud that it was the third gun from the lowest tier on his own flagship which hit the powder room of the vessel of Admiral Opdam, commander of the Dutch fleet, causing such a huge explosion that it destroyed the ship and led the rest of the enemy fleet to retreat. The Vice-Admiral of the same squadron did try to attack James but was defeated and captured. He was brought on board the Royal Charles where he died of his wounds, much to James' distress. Evidence of the severity of the fight was shown in the casualties of James' own ship which numbered two hundred men, about a third of the crew.[55]

It was an episode which gave rise to tremendous celebrations across England and quite a number of verses and songs in praise of James who was now a victorious naval commander as well as army expert. Edmund Waller composed one entitled *Instructions to a Painter* which included the lines:

Where burning ships the banished sun supply
And no light shines, but that by which men die,
There York appears, so prodigal is he
Of royal blood as ancient as the sea...
Our hero on the deck does stand
Exposed, the bulwark of his native land. ..
... a fatal volley we received
It missed the Duke but his great heart it grieved
Three worthy persons from his side it tore
And dyed his garment with their scattered gore. ...
The Dutch accustomed to the raging sea
And in black storms the frowns of heaven to see
Never met tempest which more urged their fears
Than that which in the young Prince's look appears
Fierce goodly young Mars he resembles when
Jove sends him down to scourge perfidious men...
The sea with spoils his angry bullets strow
Widows and orphans making as they go
Before his ship, fragments of vessels stir

---

[55] Hyde op.cit. vol 2 p.388. James' own brief report on the action is at SP29/123/40 with a fuller one at SP29/123/41. One of the officers on board the Royal Charles wrote his account published as, *A Second Narrative of the Signal Victory* (London, 1665)

Flags, arms and Belgian carcasses are borne...
What wonders may not English valour work
Led by the example of victorious York?

For weeks afterward, wherever James went in his coach he was mobbed by cheering crowds. Riding through Northampton, one man was so keen to see James that he literally pulled on his leg so hard that James was forced to dismount.[56] The Duke of York was undoubtedly the people's hero. A few critics within the government might have been unhappy that there was no effective chase of the Dutch which meant the remnants of their fleet escaped to fight another day, but they were in the minority. To almost everyone, James was a living super hero who could do no wrong. James, himself, answered his critics by claiming that he had gone below after the battle for a rest leaving clear instructions that the Captain was to watch the Dutch and be sure to follow them if they moved away. His aide Brouncker decided that his master needed a proper rest and so went and told the captain that they were to stay put. The Captain refused to accept a change of orders from anyone but the Duke so Brouncker waited until the captain went to bed and then told the Lieutenant that the order came from James. The Lieutenant believed him and so they let the Dutch get away. Next morning, James pursued them to the mouth of the Texel but a lack of fireships combined with low tide prevented an attack and he sailed home.[57] Charles, diplomatically, told his brother that his life was far too valuable to risk in this way again which did not please James but flattered his vanity and also appeased his critics.[58]

In the very early hours of Sunday 2nd September 1666, long before dawn, a fire broke out in a bakery in Pudding Lane. Fires were not unusual in an age of wooden houses and such engines as existed to extinguish them, were not always very successful. In this instance, Pudding Lane was too narrow for the engine to reach and so the fire spread quickly between the buildings. It had been an extremely dry summer and there was plenty of fuel for the fire. Across from the bakery were stables full of hay, whilst at the bottom of the road were the wharves with their supplies of oil, timber, tar, coal and spirits. Just beyond them was London Bridge, dense with housing. Samuel Pepys recorded in his diary going to the Tower to see the fire around eight in the morning and hearing that over three hundred properties had already been destroyed. He said: "the poor pigeons, I perceive, were loath to leave their houses, but hovered about the windows and balconies till ... some of

[56] SP29/128/1
[57] James' own account of the encounter is in MacPherson op.cit pp.29-35. Evelyn in his diary entry of 8th June 1665 said that the victory "might have been a complete one and at once ended the war had it been pursued but the cowardice of some, treachery, or both, frustrated that."
[58] HMC, *Report on the manuscripts of Allan George Finch* vol. 2 (London, 1914) p.395

them burned their wings, and fell down. Having stayed, and in an hour's time seen the fire rage every way, and nobody, to my sight, endeavouring to quench it, but to remove their goods, and leave all to the fire ... I to White Hall ... and did tell the King and Duke of York." The King said that efforts must be made to stop the fire by pulling down houses in its path and James offered troops for the work. Later that afternoon, Charles and James decided to go and see what was happening for themselves sailing in the royal barge from Whitehall toward the Tower. They met Pepys again who told them that the Lord Mayor had lost control. By now, the increasing wind was making the situation worse. Pepys described being on the river and going: "So near the fire as we could for smoke; and all over the Thames, with one's face in the wind, you were almost burned with a shower of firedrops." [59] The King decided that he needed to take action and so he put his brother in charge.

James said that he set to work that evening but that the strong north easterly wind left "tourbillons of smoke and flames" that prevented close access to the fire.[60] He divided up the city into distinct areas and set someone in charge of each. He ordered churches which had "great hooks for pulling down houses" to have them brought to Whitehall for distribution and ordered justices of neighbouring areas to provide as many workmen as they could complete with tools.[61] He spent the whole of Monday riding about the city with his guards trying to quell the rising panic and to keep order. The King also came out and together they sought to set an example by themselves "handling the water in buckets when they stood up to the ankles in water and playing the engine for many hours together."[62] James' father in law described how they "rode from one place to another and put themselves into great dangers among the burning and falling houses to give advice and direction what was to be done, underwent as much fatigue as the meanest and had as little sleep or rest."[63] It was important that they did give orders for city regulations stated that if anyone destroyed a property, they were legally bound to pay the costs of rebuilding it, which was why nobody else was prepared to issue instructions to pull down the houses which stood in the wake of the fire.

Yet despite their efforts, the fire continued to rage. The Reverend Thomas Vincent wrote:

---

[59] 2nd September 1666

[60] MacPherson op.cit. p. 36

[61] SP29/170/65

[62] *Notes and Queries,* series 11, December 1915 pp.234-235

[63] Hyde op.cit. vol 3 p.89

Some are at work to quench the fire with water, others endeavour to stop its course by pulling down of houses but all to no purpose. If it be a little allayed or beaten down or put to a stand in some places, it is but a very little while; it quickly recruits and recovers its force; it leaps and mounts and makes the more furious onset, drives back its opposers, snatches their weapons out of their hand, seizes upon the water houses and engines, burns them, spoils them and makes them unfit for service.[64]

He continued:

Rattle, rattle, rattle was the noise which the fire struck upon the ear round about as if there had been a thousand iron chariots beating upon the stones: and if you opened your eye...you might see in some places whole streets at once in flames that issued forth as if they...were united into one great flame throughout the whole street; and then you might see the houses tumble, tumble, tumble from one end of the street to the other with a great crash leaving the foundations open to the view of the heavens.[65]

In another vivid account, John Evelyn wrote:

The sky were of a fiery aspect like the top of a burning oven and the light seen above forty miles round about for many nights: God grant mine eyes may never behold the like who now saw above ten thousand houses all in one flame, the noise and crackling and thunder of the impetuous flames, the shrieking of women and children, the hurry of people, the fall of towers, houses and churches...the air all about so hot and inflamed that at the last one was not able to approach it....The clouds of smoke were dismal and reached upon computation near fifty miles in length... The ground under my feet so hot as made me not only sweat but even burnt the soles of my shoes.[66]

Wyndham Sandys served with James and expressed his admiration for his dedication. Between Sunday night and Wednesday evening, James took less than three hours sleep. He did not shirk going into the most dangerous areas. "The Duke on Tuesday about twelve o'clock was environed with fire...so the Duke was forced to fly for it and had almost been stifled with the heat." It was an attitude not shared by everyone. Pepys described how people were more keen to save their property than help fight the fire.

---

[64] Thomas Vincent, *God's Terrible Voice in the City* (London, 1667) p.60
[65] ibid. p.62
[66] 3rd September 1666

Sandys wrote: "The city for the first rank they minded only their own preservation, the middle sort so amazed and distracted they knew not what they did, the poorer they minded nothing but pilfering."[67] James resorted to having able-bodied people who refused to help, beaten and press ganged into teams of fire fighters. This was an emergency and no time for polite requests. Angry at the way people were trying to exploit the disaster by charging extortionate rates for the hire of carts, he constrained owners to hand them over so those at risk of losing their homes could evacuate their families and valuables.[68]

The fire raged all day Sunday, Monday, Tuesday and Wednesday. The Queen and the Duchess of York were evacuated to Hampton Court together with many of the King's valuables. The money in the treasury was boxed and sent to Nonsuch. Fears of the fire reaching the arsenal stored at the Tower of London caused that to be moved to Whitehall. On Tuesday, St Paul's caught fire when the wooden scaffolding outside was ignited. The diarist John Evelyn described stones falling like grenades and pavements so hot no man or horse could stand on them.[69] Vincent wrote: "the lead melts and runs down as if it had been snow before the sun and the great beams and massy stones with a great noise fall on the pavement."[70]

James was in the Strand at the time. Late into the night, he was ordering the demolition of homes from Somerset House down as far as Charing Cross to try to prevent the fire moving west toward Whitehall.[71] Sandys said that the soldiers were in a state of exhaustion but James continued his efforts, not only supervising his own section but answering the requests of messengers sent from other areas who sought engines, water, workers and advice.

By Wednesday night, it appeared that the worst was over. The wind had dropped and the fire seemed to be quenched in most areas saving Cripplegate. James returned to Whitehall for a much needed rest but had hardly sat down when news came that the Temple was on fire again. Immediately he went back where he found that an apparently dormant spark had indeed ignited a new blaze. The fire fighters were unable to access the area to do their work because the Temple guard was refusing to

---

[67] Sandys letter appears in *Gentleman's Magazine* 1st August 1831 pp. 6-9

[68] Atkyns said that some were charging £10 for a cart which was more than half a year's wages for an ordinary working man. Stephen Weston, 'Copy of a letter to Sir Robert Atkyns' in *Archaeologia* vol XIX (1821) p.106

[69] 4th September 1666

[70] Vincent op.cit. p.65

[71] One of those he ordered pulled down was the home of Lord Denham, whose wife was his mistress.

open the gates without the permission of a barrister. James was unimpressed. He said that the only way to save the Temple church was to blow up the Paper House nearby. He ordered the gunpowder to be brought in whilst the official continued to protest that this was simply not allowed on their premises. In the end, the Duke's Master of Horse got his cudgel out and simply battered the man into submission. Even Sandys thought that unnecessary violence was used but James was not prepared to risk what was left of the city for the sake of one man's adherence to legal regulations.

Finally, it was over, though the fire continued to smoulder in cellars and warehouses as late as Saturday when it rained for the first time in weeks.[72] Edward Atkyns wrote on that day to his brother: "It is impossible almost to conceive the total destruction...so you can hardly tell where such a parish or place was. I can say but this, that there is nothing but stones and rubbish and all exposed to the open air so you may see from one end of the city almost to the other. ...you can compare London, were it not for the rubbish, to nothing more than an empty field."[73]

It was estimated that almost ninety per cent of the city's inhabitants were homeless, many of them being camped out at Moorfields. Over thirteen thousand homes had been destroyed and eighty-seven parish churches. Important buildings such as the Royal Exchange which was the trading centre of the city had been lost. Shopping areas such as Cheapside had been decimated. Of particular concern was the loss of the city's grain store at Bridewell, especially full with the newly gathered harvest. There were huge losses of cloths and silks which had been brought to London for the Michaelmas Fair and it was estimated that £200,000 of books and stationery had been destroyed.[74] The fact that the fire had occurred when the country was at war had led to many accusations of plots and fears of foreign invasion, but the King reassured everyone that it was an act of God.

James himself was modest about his achievements devoting just a few lines to the fire in his memoirs. However, his behaviour had won universal praise. Daniel Brown said he was: "never being weary to succour and assist the distressed citizens by whose example and princely encouragement the people took heart."[75] The *London Gazette* spoke of his "indefatigable and personal pains" and told how he had watched all night in person "never

---

[72] Weston op.cit p.108

[73] Stephen Weston, 'Copy of a letter to Sir Robert Atkyns' in *Archaeologia* vol XIX (1821) p.106

[74] Hyde op.cit vol 3 p.99

[75] Brown op.cit p.86. This author also describes James being sent a few weeks after the Great Fire to take control of a fire which broke out in the Horse Guards and which threatened the royal palace of Whitehall. p.94. On that occasion, James saved the Banquetting House, see Lisa Jardine, *On a Grander Scale* (London, 2002) p.248

despairing or slackening his personal care."[76] John Evelyn described as "extraordinary" the way James had been "labouring in person and being present to command, order, reward and encourage workmen."[77] A letter from John Rushworth, written just three days after the scenes at the Temple, reported "the Duke of York hath won the hearts of the people with his continual and indefatigable pains day and night in helping to quench the fire."[78] Another witness was inspired to poetry claiming "princely York with sweat and dirt besmeared" had risen like Neptune with "thundering cannons" of water which he directed with the same power he had used at Lowestoft as he "baffled" the flames.[79]

A few years later, James' role came into question. The monument erected to the fire in 1668 had an inscription which claimed that it was "begun and carried on by the treachery and malice of the Popish faction. Popish frenzy which wrought such horrors is not yet quenched." The Chancellor noted that the belief that the papists had begun the fire was so firmly believed, even by many on the Privy Council, "that he who said the contrary was suspected for a conspirator or at best a favourer of them."[80] As James became increasingly identified with the Popish party, people wondered if he had been part of the plot to start the fire and suggestions were made that James had looked too cheerful throughout and that his guards had been more interested in helping catholic foreigners escape the mobs than extinguish the fire. Bishop Burnet, who knew James well, said that the stories were clearly untrue but came to be generally believed.[81]

Amongst the buildings lost in the fire was the Post Office in Threadneedle Street. Although this re-opened the next day which ensured deliveries continued to be made,[82] the greater loss was in the machinery that had been destroyed. Cromwell had installed equipment which enabled letters to be opened, read, copied and resealed and there had been a lengthy royal visit at the start of Charles' reign to see this in action. The machinery offered clear intelligence advantages which made its loss during a war especially unfortunate. It had been used to intercept and read the reports of foreign ambassadors as well as private citizens. In cases of messages which

---

[76] *London Gazette* 3rd to 10th September 1666

[77] 6th September 1666

[78] *Notes and Queries* series V, May 1876, p.307

[79] James Peller Malcolm, *Londinium Redivivum,* vol.IV, (London, 1807) p.88

[80] Hyde op.cit. vol 3 pp.85-86

[81] Gilbert Burnet, *Bishop Burnet's History of His Own Time,* (London, 1838) p.157. The King's illegitimate son, the Duke of Monmouth, made the same accusation when he invaded in 1685 in an attempt to secure support for himself in his effort to overthrow his uncle, James by then being king.

[82] SP29/170/61

seemed potentially treasonous, the government could either take immediate action or simply keep the original for future evidence and send the copy on so that the plotters could continue their work until it was deemed an appropriate time to intervene.[83] The fact that Charles gave control of this key surveillance tool to James was evidence of the high position of trust in which he was placed.

Two years after the fire, the Italian Lorenzo Magalotti visited England and wrote a detailed eye witness account of the court. He described James as being shorter than the King and rather fierce in appearance. He spoke of his square forehead, swollen blue eyes, large crooked nose, thick pale lips and pointed chin with a blond beard. He said that James walked quickly everywhere with a marked stoop. He thought he lacked dignity but claimed he was more popular than the King which he thought caused a certain strain between the brothers for Charles was jealous. He said James was very welcoming to foreigners and spoke several languages, though none well. Indeed, he noted that James had difficulty expressing himself. He described James as a martial man who was deeply motivated by hopes of glory and possessed of great faith in his ability to command on either land or sea. Yet, Magalotti did not like James.

> The Duke is impetuous and violent and consequently inconsiderate and unreasonable most of the time. He has not much penetration into political affairs because his rough and impatient spirit does not let him stop for long to examine things but makes him follow his first impulses blindly. Nevertheless he is very often influenced by people, and once he has chosen them it is not so easy for him to free himself from their sway. His mind is always like wax ready to receive and retain indelibly every slight impression of their ideas without considering whether these proceed from reason or from self interest or malignity or ambition.. To everyone except these people he is inflexible no matter if they come armed not only with reason but with evidence itself.[84]

Burnet, a man close to James, was later to express a very similar opinion. He said that whilst the King was more intellectually able and could have understood affairs had he only wished to take the trouble, James was keen to understand but incapable because, "he had no true judgment and was soon determined by those whom he trusted: he was obstinate against all other advices."[85] Clarendon, James' father in law, said that he disliked older

---

[83] HMC, *Report on the manuscripts of Marquis of Downshire*, (London, 1924) pp.594-595, 609

[84] Middleton op.cit. pp.35-36

[85] Burnet op.cit. p.114. Burnet said that James showed him the diary he kept of events which he used to try to help him follow events.

people "thinking age not only troublesome but impertinent" and agreed totally with Burnet and Magalotti.[86] The French ambassador recounted an exchange he had with James when James boasted that "being an Englishman is therefore stubbornness itself." The ambassador reminded him that he was French on his mother's side and James replied: "it is true. But know you that the English are obstinate when they are in the right; and when they are in the wrong then the French have all reason to be obstinate too. Do not, therefore expect anything from me." [87]

Magalotti was also critical of James' relationship with women saying, "he cares little for the more innocent preparations for tenderness and longs for the occasion for the release of a vicious brutality." Burnet said that James was "perpetually in one amour or other without being very nice in his choice, upon which the King said once he believed his brother had his mistresses given him by his priests for penance." Madame de Fiennes, who never became his mistress, commented on his company: "The Duke of York is courageous and fierce but perishingly dull and uninteresting in conversation."[88]

Pepys, who worked with James at the Navy Office, made a number of references to James' relationships in his diary. In June 1667, he described how a group of pimps would go and furnish the Duke's bed at Whitehall with a variety of women every night so that James could go along there for his entertainment after departing his wife's bed.[89] Nor did James keep his infidelities secret. A year earlier Pepys had written: "the Duke of York is wholly given up to his new mistress, my Lady Denham, going at noon-day with all his gentlemen with him to visit her in Scotland Yard; she declaring she will not be his mistress, as Mrs. Price, to go up and down the Privy-stairs, but will be owned publicly; and so she is."[90]

By 26th September, Pepys was noting that James was following her like a dog. The relationship did not last long however, for in November she was taken ill. Lady Denham claimed that she had been poisoned by a cup of chocolate and following her death a few weeks later, the Duchess of York was accused of being responsible. In 1667 Andrew Marvell said that the scorned Anne resorted to "forbidden arts" because she..

---

[86] Hyde op.cit. vol 3 pp.63-64. He describe James as obstinate, being averse to reasoned debate and easily swayed by people he liked.

[87] Jean Jusserand, *A French Ambassador at the Court of Charles the Second* (London, 1892) p.172

[88] Elizabeth of Orleans, *Life and letters of Charlotte Elizabeth*, (London, 1889) p.83

[89] 24th June 1667

[90] 10th June 1666

..nightly hears the hated guards, away
Gallopping with the Duke to other prey [91]

Rumours became so widespread that an autopsy was performed on Lady Denham's body which failed to find any trace of poison. The physicians advised she died of a blockage in the bowel.[92]

Another scandal was ignited by James' relationship with Lady Carnegie. At one point, he was said to have been at her house with his man Talbot on guard outside. Her husband returned and Talbot told him that since the Duke was busy within, he should depart. The husband was said to have attempted to get his revenge by going to a prostitute so he could catch the clap and thereby infect his wife and the Duke. Whether this was actually true is far from certain, but it was widely believed. Marvell wrote a poem about it, Pepys recorded it in his diary, Burnet told the story and the Count de Gramont who had been part of the Court since 1657 and was related to Lady Carnegie mentioned it as well in his memoirs.[93]

Partly James' behaviour was a reflection on his morals. Their father Charles I might have been a model of sobriety and faithfulness but Charles and James were total libertines. James was described as "the most unguarded ogler of his time."[94] Yet it was also indicative of the problems in James' marriage. Anne was, by now, extremely fat, and said by Gramont to be "the woman with the greatest appetite in England."[95] They had lost two of their sons in the space of less than a month in 1667. Owing to a political furore, Anne's father had been forced from office and into exile. In addition, they had severe financial problems. Pepys estimated that the Duke was spending £20,000 more per annum than he earned, something which he blamed on the Duchess describing her as "not only the proudest woman in the world, but the most expensefull."[96] Her own father had tried to advise them but had been ignored, James preferring the advice of his aides who told him that his problems were really the fault of the King and Parliament who had failed to make due provision for him.

James should have had sufficient income. At the Restoration, he had been granted a substantial share of the confiscated estates of the regicides

---

[91] *Last Instructions to a Painter*, 4th September 1667

[92] CSPD 1666-1667 pp.262-263

[93] Pepys diary 6th April 1668, Burnet op.cit. p.156, Anthony Hamilton (ed.), *Memoirs of the Count de Gramont* (London, 1889) vol 2 pp.14-15.

[94] Hamilton op.cit. p.20

[95] ibid. p.160

[96] 24th June 1667

in England and Ireland which generated considerable sums in rent. In February 1661, he was given a lifetime annuity of £20,000.[97] This was additional to the annual sum he received for being a Duke.[98] In 1663, an 'Act for Settling the Profits of the Post Office and Power of Granting wine licences on His Royal Highness the Duke of York' had granted him £21,500 per annum on the Post Office alone.[99] In 1670, another act had given the income of the wine licences back to the Crown and granted James £24,000 per annum in recompense. He also received £3000 a year for his children.[100] Together, they gave him an annual income which in today's money would be around eight and a half million. In 1665, James was rewarded for his efforts in the Dutch war with a one off payment of £120,902 15s 8d - around sixteen million pounds today.[101] He received various other gifts of money from the King including £10,000 in 1660 to establish himself, grants of £20,000 in 1662 and the same again in 1665, and one of £2,000 in 1664.[102] As Lord Admiral he continued to get a share of every prize taken which could generate a substantial income. His portion of one vessel in 1666 carrying gold and plate amounted to £5,000.[103] He had rent free apartments at Windsor, Hampton Court and Whitehall plus he was granted Richmond Palace and Holdenby House. He received £10,400 per annum toward his household costs and the maintenance on the buildings was paid from the public purse.[104] In the absence of a Prince of Wales, he also had St James' Palace where he was given £500 to build stables in 1661.[105] In addition to this, James had his business interests. Burnet estimated his annual income from all sources was normally around £100,000.[106]

James' involvement in trade had begun at the start of Charles' reign. Partly, it was from a genuine belief that Britain was great because it was a maritime nation whose economy depended on the sea. Yet it was chiefly because he saw it as an investment, a chance to increase his own income. James held shares in the East India Company and in the Hudson's Bay Company, though he was not particularly active in either. In April 1664, the Royal Fishing Company was founded with James as its first Governor. Its foundation charter noted the great plenty of fish around the coasts and

---

[97] SP29/31 *Docquet Book, p.* 87

[98] William Shaw (ed.), *Calendar of Treasury Books* 1660-1667 vol.1 (London, 1904) p.737

[99] James actually received just over £16,000 as this figure included salaries for the post office staff and costs, see SP29/43/44

[100] SP29/211/123

[101] John Raithby (ed), *Statutes of the Realm* vol.5 (London, 1819) p.706

[102] SP44/15 p.166, SP44/7 pp.82,242, SP44/16 p.289, SP44/22 p.217

[103] SP29/155/57

[104] SP29/79/82

[105] SP29/47/15

[106] Burnet op.cit. p.115. This would be about thirteen million today.

commented: "what an ease it will be to our kingdoms to have many of the lazy and idle people set on work and trained up in the fishing trade thereby to relieve themselves and improve the merchandise and traffic of our dominions" as well as for the "increase of strength unto our sea forces as well in times of war as peace." The Company was to be funded by a national lottery which James was to run as well as licensed collections in parish churches.[107] James' efforts to reorganise the trade were praised by Treasury officials some years later when they spoke of him overcoming "all the difficulties and discouragements" to achieve more than his predecessors.[108]

His greatest area of interest, and the one of which he spoke most proudly in his memoirs, was Africa. He was by far the greatest investor in the Company of Royal Adventurers Trading into Africa formed in December 1660, and which was re-launched as the Royal African Company in 1672. The purpose of the company was to send English vessels to the coast around modern Ghana laden with British goods which would return with African products such as gold, elephant's teeth and slaves. The last would be taken on to the West Indies for use on British plantations. In January 1662, James published a letter to potential investors saying:

The Royal Company being very sensible how necessary it is that the English plantations in America should have a competent and constant supply of negro servants for their own use of planting and that at a moderate rate have already sent abroad and shall within eight days despatch so many ships to the coast of Africa as shall by God's permission furnish the said plantations with at least 3000 negroes.[109]

The negroes were to be sold by lot for not less than £17 per head or 2400lb of well-cured muscovado sugar.

1675 to 1676 was a fairly typical year for the company and this showed over £36,000 of goods exported, over half being textiles, the remainder including pewter, brassware and metal bars. An unknown number of slaves were taken of whom 1,836 survived to be delivered to Barbados and sold at £15 5s per head, 1,188 arrived in Jamaica and were sold at £21 5s per head. The ships returned from the West Indies with over one thousand tons of sugar for the British market plus some tobacco. The amount of gold brought

---

[107] Cecil Carr, *Select Charters of Trading Companies 1530-1707* (New York, 1970)pp. 182-185. James involvement with fishing had begun in 1661 when the first lottery was launched, SP29/40/75.

[108] Shaw op.cit vol.6 pp.1-3

[109] Royal African Company, *The Several Declarations of the Company of Royal Adventurers*, (London, 1667) p.8

back each year varied but was melted down into coins which became known as guineas because that was the source of the gold. In 1677, enough gold was brought back to make 33,871 guineas.[110] For James, the trade of this one company alone earned him around twelve per cent per annum on his investment.[111] In terms of business, it employed over four hundred ships which themselves provided a considerable number of people with work as well as creating jobs in manufacturing and retail.[112]

To the modern mind, slave trading is an abomination but it is important not to judge James by standards of another age. Although the slaves were branded DY as in Duke of York, he encouraged owners to permit their slaves to be baptised which was a recognition that they were human beings with souls, something not all his contemporaries thought. In 1684, a tract was published called *The Negro's Complaint* which accepted that it was generally Africans who sold Africans into slavery but said that this did not mean that the Europeans had to buy: "Is this a fine employment think you for Christians to run to remotest regions to get their innocent fellow creatures and make slaves of them?... We expected another sort of treatment from the Christians who boast themselves the sons and favourites of the God of love and goodness, and who—we have been informed—are, or ought to be, endowed with the spirit of meekness, innocence and doing unto all as they would be done unto."[113]

It was the attack by the Dutch on the African forts and factories held by the Company in 1664 which led to the Dutch war of 1665-1667. James said that the Dutch had gambled on England not offering a response because the King and Chancellor Hyde were known to be opposed to conflict, but the House of Commons – which contained a number of merchants – was keen to fight. However, the war did not go well. A major outbreak of plague in 1665 reduced the numbers of available men whilst the costs of rebuilding London after the fire decimated financial resources. Much to James' fury, it was agreed to lay up the first and second rate naval vessels in an attempt to save costs and to switch from the offensive to the defensive. Reluctantly James ordered ships to be moored behind a chain in the Medway with a "competent" number of crew to act as guards.[114]

---

[110] K. G. Davies, *The Royal African Company* (London, 1957) pp.350-364

[111] Callow op.cit. p.252

[112] Royal African Company, *An Answer of the Company of Royal Adventurers of England*, (London, 1667) p.4. The trade may have employed directly and indirectly a quarter of a million people.

[113] Thomas Tryon, *Friendly Advice to the Gentlemen Planters of the East and West Indies*, (London, 1684) pp.83, 86

[114] SP29/195/15

On 10th June 1667, Pepys reported hearing the sound of guns from Sheerness as it tried to offer a defence to the Dutch fleet. It was unable to do so and as the Dutch advanced toward Chatham, drummers in London sounded the call to arms of the trained bands. General Monck, now Duke of Albemarle, reassured Pepys at Chatham "all is safe as to the great ships against any assault, the boom and chain being so fortified."[115] His confidence was misplaced for the same day, the Dutch broke through and set fire to the English navy. Having crippled their enemy, the Dutch chose to tow the Royal Charles, James' flagship, back to Holland as a trophy. It was the greatest defeat ever experienced by the navy. Pepys was particularly upset by the numbers of English sailors who had served on the Dutch vessels, openly saying that they were unwilling to risk their lives for their country any more because they were so long unpaid.[116] James observed in his journal that had his orders been followed, "the Dutch had not found so easy a work as they did."[117] Certainly, the episode demonstrated problems with actual defences ranging from an unfinished fort at Sheerness to a lack of ammunition on the Royal Charles.

Fears of invasion spread and James and Charles were active in trying to prepare the defences of London and to prevent panic. On the 13th, they were just beyond London Bridge ordering the sinking of old ships to prevent the Dutch being able to advance into London. They also mustered the city militia at Tower Hill where Charles gave them a rousing address. The Dutch fleet meantime stood off in the Thames effectively blockading London and all the ports along the north Kent coast as far as Margate. On the 28th June, Evelyn described this as "a dreadful spectacle as ever any Englishmen saw and a dishonour never to be wiped off." On the 19th June, James went to Chatham to see to its defence.[118] At the start of July, he went to Harwich ready to repel an attack there, though the Dutch who remained visible from the town never made any such attempt. It was said that "the Duke's presence much comforts the people."[119] For James, the Dutch attack came at a particularly difficult time. His only son who was almost four, had been ill since the spring. On 9th June, Pepys reported that the boy seemed to be responding to treatment but on the 20th, right in the midst of the crisis, he died.

The British had no option but to rapidly agree peace terms. As often happens when a national disaster occurs, it was felt necessary for someone

---

[115] 12th June 1667

[116] 14th June 1667

[117] MacPherson op.cit. p.38

[118] William Durrant Cooper (ed.), *Savile Correspondence* (Camden Society 1858) p.17

[119] SP29/208/82

to take the blame. In this case, the person chosen was the Chancellor, Edward Hyde. James was ill in the autumn with smallpox, a dangerous disease which had taken the lives of his brother Henry and sister Mary, but he did his best to support his father in law, particularly in the Lords. The opposition, however, was too great. As soon as James was out of danger, Charles visited him and told him to tell Hyde to depart the country quietly. He did so but the issue left a coldness between the brothers.[120]

There was one clause in the Treaty of Breda which ended the war which directly affected James and should have been of benefit to him though he proved unable to take advantage of it. Under the terms of the Treaty, the Dutch relinquished their claim to New Netherlands. The territory had originally been in English hands and was granted to the Earl of Stirling in 1635 but it later fell to the Dutch. James had purchased it from Stirling in 1663 for £3500 and promptly sent ships to claim his possession.[121] The expedition was successful and the chief town, New Amsterdam was renamed New York in James' honour. James' hope was that the land would prove an investment but this never happened. Against the advice of his man in New York, he gave away a large and very fertile portion of land to two of his supporters, Berkeley and Carteret, which became New Jersey. James kept for himself just the port and environs which he used for his African trading company. As ruler in America, James was unpopular. He imposed taxes without allowing the inhabitants any form of representative assembly and without contributing to the development of the area's economy or defences. When the area fell to the Dutch again in 1672, the inhabitants welcomed them back.

James was never entirely happy in peace time. Some years later he was to write that the Court "affords but little" interest for him given the absence of war.[122] He did have interests away from the armed services. He was extremely keen on hunting. He enjoyed attending plays and in November 1662 established his own company under Sir William Davenant with a theatre in Lincoln's Inn.[123] He played the guitar according to the Count de Gramont "tolerably well."[124] He possessed some interest in science, observing the conjunction of saturn and the moon with a telescope from the gardens at Whitehall and attending dissections with Pepys at the Royal

---

[120] Clarke op.cit. pp.429-434. The Venetian ambassador had claimed that James had smallpox in 1648 but this would have prevented him having it in 1667.

[121] In 1711, the executors of the Earl of Stirling complained to Queen Anne that James had never actually paid any money for the land and they demanded £9,600 in back payments. See HMC, *The manuscripts of His Grace the Duke of Portland*, vol 10 (London, 1896) p.459

[122] SP8/3/2 dated 29th April 1674

[123] CSPD 1661-1662 p.578. Davenant's company was the first to employ a woman on stage.

[124] Hamilton op.cit. p.21

Society.[125] He kept cockatoos at Windsor.[126] He also enjoyed sailing. One of his first acts after the restoration was to order a yacht and Evelyn records a race between James and the King from Greenwich to Gravesend which Charles won.[127] Competitive as well as athletic, James played tennis, skated and enjoyed curling.[128] In England, he enjoyed Pell Mell, a game which Pepys watched him play.[129] This was a game somewhat similar to the golf which he played when he was in Scotland.

Contemporaries were less interested in James' sporting pastimes than what was going on in his mind. Rumours about James' religious beliefs had existed for a long time. As early as February 1661, Pepys had commented that he hoped James would never succeed to the throne "he being a professed friend to the Catholics."[130] His first wife Anne had converted in the late 1660s. James had shown Burnet, the man whom he had asked to write his biography, a paper Anne had written explaining her reasons. This document was subsequently published and shows a pronounced lack of theological understanding. James suggested he was convinced by Anne though Burnet thought that Anne had developed her interest in Catholicism in an effort to win James back from his mistresses. Burnet said that James would never tell him exactly when he converted and that was probably because he did not know. Conversion is not necessarily the result of sudden revelation but can occur gradually over the years. By James' own admission, his doubts about Anglicanism had begun shortly before the Restoration[131] and he hid the truth from the world for some time: "I acknowledge to my own shame I did not do it so soon as I was thoroughly convinced of the truth of the religion I now profess."[132] Burnet was brave enough to ask James how a man of his clear convictions could behave in the way which he did toward women and James replied, without any trace of repentance or guilt: "must a man be of no religion unless he is a saint?"[133]

Suspicions also existed about Charles' commitment to Protestantism and documents found two centuries after his death seem to indicate they were

---

[125] Jardine op.cit p.142. Pepys diary 16th May 1664

[126] H. M. Colvin (ed.), *The History of the King's Works,* vol 5 (London, 1976) p. 330

[127] 1st October 1661. The vessel was launched in April 1661, ref SP29/332/46 though not without difficulties, the workmen having gone on strike because they were not paid, see SP29/33/48.

[128] Joseph Strutt, *The Sports and Pastimes of the People of England* (London, 1801) includes a print from 1641 of James playing tennis in 1641, probably at Whitehall. For his golfing activities, see p.99. and Callow op.cit. p.127 who describes his winter sport activities too.

[129] 2nd April 1661

[130] 18th February 1661

[131] Clarke op.cit. p.630

[132] Godfrey Davies (ed.) *The Papers of Devotion of James II* (Oxford, 1925) p.3

[133] Burnet op.cit. p.238

well founded. Lord Acton uncovered letters in the Jesuit library of Rome in which Charles spoke of one of his bastard sons who had become a Jesuit. This pleased the King because "we are therefore enabled to converse in all security with him and practice the rites of the Roman Catholic religion without exciting in our court the shadow of a doubt that we belong to that persuasion."[134]

By January 1669, both brothers appeared to have renounced privately the Protestant faith. On the 25th of that month, a meeting was held at James' house where the King asked advice on "the ways and methods fittest to be taken for the settling of the Catholic religion in his kingdoms." Charles spoke with tears in his eyes of the unhappiness he felt about not being able "to profess the faith he believed" and said that he thought they must act now while both of them were in their "full strength and able to undergo any fatigue" for he knew there would be many difficulties ahead. Charles said they must act "as wise men and good Catholics ought to do."[135] The debate went on for some hours and concluded that the only way to achieve this goal was to seek the assistance of Louis XIV, the Most Christian King of France and champion of the Counter-Reformation. What followed was a treaty which Russell described as "a monument of ingratitude, perjury and treason."[136] Even today, it is shocking.

The Treaty of Dover was brokered through Minette, sister of Charles and James and now Duchess of Orleans and sister-in-law of Louis XIV. France and England agreed to declare war together on the Netherlands and to divide it up after they had won. France would lead the land assault whilst England, under James, led the naval attack. France would pay England £800,000 per annum during the war and England would contribute six thousand infantry. Yet it was the first clause which was remarkable:

The King of Great Britain being convinced of the truth of the Catholic religion and resolved to declare himself a Catholic and be reconciled to the Church of Rome thinks the assistance of His Most Christian Majesty necessary to facilitate his design. It is therefore agreed and concluded upon that His Most Christian Majesty shall furnish to the King of England before the said declaration the sum of two hundred thousand pounds sterling...and farther that the said Lord, the Most Christian King, shall assist His Britannic Majesty with troops and money as often as there shall be need in case the subjects of the said

---

[134] Letter of Charles II dated 3rd August 1668 quoted in Walter Walsh, *The Jesuits in Great Britain*, (London, 1908) p.254.

[135] Clarke op.cit. p.442

[136] John Russell, *The Life of William, Lord Russell*, (London, 1820) p.47

Lord the King shall not acquiesce with the said declaration but rebel against his Britannic Majesty.[137]

For a monarch to accept money to renege on his coronation oath and to effectively invite a foreign power to invade his country to subdue his people "with all his forces" as it said in clause seven, was unheard of. It would have been like King George VI accepting money from Hitler to sit quietly in Windsor whilst the Nazis took over. Although James did not sign the treaty himself, he was involved in it from the outset and he was present during the negotiations.[138] By 10th June 1670, Louis XIV had confirmed his acceptance of the treaty and it was not long before Charles started to receive the promised funds. France made considerable financial gifts to other people involved in the secret deal and James himself benefited handsomely.[139] He commented that France always did its business by bribes and told the French ambassador that much money was necessary so that Charles could avoid calling Parliament. James said in July 1671: "a king and a parliament can exist no longer together" and that none should be called "till the war and the catholic faith had come to an happy issue and when they should be in a condition to obtain by force what they could not obtain by mildness."[140]

It is sometimes difficult for people today to understand the horror with which Protestants viewed Catholics in this period. The modern world sees Protestantism and Catholicism as simply two sects of Christianity of equal value. In the early modern period, they represented two different world views. Protestantism was associated with personal freedom and constitutional monarchy whilst Catholicism was associated with absolutism and persecution. A seventeenth century person who turned Catholic would have been regarded with the same level of mistrust and hatred as anyone in 1940 who joined the fascists. Every Protestant in the country knew about the atrocities committed by Roman Catholics. There had been the massacre in Paris on St Bartholomew's Day 1572 when the Duke de Sully said two hundred thousand Protestant men, women and children, had been dragged from their homes and killed in the streets. In Ireland, in 1641, thousands of Protestants had been murdered or turned from their homes. Within England, the memory of "Bloody Mary" who married a Catholic and had hundreds of ordinary men and women burnt at the stake, was very real. A particularly well known and oft repeated incident from John Foxe concerned Perrotine Massey in Guernsey. She was a pregnant woman who was burnt

---

[137] John Dalrymple, *Memoirs of Great Britain and Ireland* vol.2 (London, 1773) p.50

[138] SP29/275/185 is an eyewitness account of James' arrival at Dover on 26th May 1670. The Treaty was signed on the 1st June.

[139] Dalrymple op.cit. pp.81-82

[140] ibid. p.80. See also *British Biography* vol v (London, 1749) p.353

alongside her mother and sister following a trial at which none was allowed to defend themselves. Perrotine gave birth in the flames. By a miracle the child was alive and rescued only to be thrown back in the flames on grounds it was a Protestant and heretic child.[141] Later historians might dispute the actual numbers killed in each case or argue about the effectiveness of the Inquisition, but people at the time were genuinely fearful and the constant stream of Protestant refugees to the country – including many from France - with their tales of atrocities only added to the fear.

A few examples indicate the general reaction to James' conversion. Philanax Verax in 1681 equated popery with treason and said that to be a papist was "to follow the enchantments of a strumpet whose shameless adulteries have long since caused an utter divorce between her and the blessed Jesus." [142] Charles Blount asked people to imagine "troops of papists ravishing your wives and daughters, dashing your little children's brains out against the walls, plundering your houses and cutting your own throats...Casting your eyes towards Smithfield imagine you see your father or your mother or some of your nearest and dearest relations tied to a stake in the midst of flames...which was a frequent spectacle the last time popery reigned amongst us."[143] John Phillips said that the Pope saw James as "that second Moses who under the god like influence of Rome like a cloud by day and a pillar of fire by night should guide and lead them through all opposition and all dangers to their beloved Canann, a land that flows with milk and honey, Rome's old treasure house, that dear *puteus inexhaustus*, England."[144] Another writer, said that under a Catholic king, "no man is safe in his bed, none safe at all. They will adventure to murder people in their very houses for they hold it no more sin than to kill a dog."[145] Referencing the principles of the Inquisition, one person said that for James "its not only lawful and conscientious to kill us but a duty."[146] John Colt, M.P. for Leominster predicted that if James succeeded, it would be worse than it was in Bloody Mary's day "for we should have our children's limbs cut off and thrown in our faces."[147] Even Evelyn said that James' behaviour "gave exceeding grief and scandal to the whole nation. That the heir of it and the son of a martyr for the Protestant religion should apostatize. What

---

[141] John Foxe, *The First Volume of the Ecclesiastical History containing the Acts and Monuments* (London, 1570) book 11 p. 2128

[142] Verax op.cit. p.2

[143] Charles Blount, *Appeal from the Country to the City for the Preservation of His Majesty's Person, Liberty, Property and the Protestant Religion* (London, 1679) p.1

[144] John Phillips, *The Character of a Popish Successor* (London, 1681) p.12

[145] Anon. *Pereat Papa* (London, c1681) p.4

[146] Anon, *A Plea to the Duke's Answers,* (London, 1680) p.4

[147] SP29/420/4

the consequence of this will be God only knows and wise men dread." [148]

James' erstwhile chaplain, Thomas Jones, wrote with some concern to him saying "no prince in story was ever the darling of more English hearts than your Royal Highness" and telling him that he was being betrayed by Catholics whose support stemmed from their own political agenda rather than a genuine interest in his soul. Jones said "the nation, and city in general, design no hurt to the Duke, to a hair of his head or line of his picture, but have very strong desires to be effectually safe in their dearest concerns from the sworn enemies of their religion and country."[149] Again, James did not listen.

In accordance with the Treaty of Dover, in the spring of 1672, Louis XIV and Charles declared war on the Dutch. It was a war without any great victories or losses. The most famous incident took place on May 28th 1672, when the Battle of Southwold was fought. James commanded the entire allied fleet of English and French vessels, though it was widely reported that the French had left the real action to the English, something which did not go down well with the public. The fact that James had changed the battle plan without telling the French and gave them no new instructions was not publicised.[150] It was a bloody encounter which lasted from dawn to dusk. The English broke the Dutch line and decided to use the opportunity of proximity to indulge in some hand to hand action. This left them exposed, and the Dutch took full advantage, setting fire to the Royal James which killed the Earl of Sandwich. The Earl of Mulgrave, as an eyewitness wrote:

> The Duke of York had the noblest share in this day's action for when his ship was so maimed as to be made incapable of service, he made her lie by to refit and went on board another that was hotly engaged where he kept up his standard till she was disabled also, and then left her for a third in order to renew the fight.[151]

This is confirmed in James' own account. He says that within three hours of the battle commencing, his flagship The Prince had had her main top-mast shot off, her fore top-sail, starboard main shrouds, rigging and fighting sails all shot through and torn to pieces, and about two hundred of her men killed and wounded. He transferred to the St Michael but found himself

---

[148] 30th March 1673

[149] Jones published his letters in a volume called *Elymas the Sorcerer* (London, 1682). See pp.15, 21

[150] Callow op.cit. p.227

[151] John Sheffield, *The Works of John Sheffield Earl of Mulgrave* (London, 1723) p.14. James began on the Prince but ended on the St Michael, ref SP29/310/14

outnumbered with Dutch on either side. He noted: "the enemy and we were much mingled together." He witnessed the attack on the Royal James and sent boats to try and rescue as many of the drowning as they could. However, the St Michael was under heavy fire throughout and was taking in considerable amounts of water. This, together with the loss of men and damage to sails, made her impossible to control and likely to sink, so James transferred to the London where he remained until evening when the Dutch retreated.

Despite his efforts, England seemed likely to lose the war for want of money. Calculations made in 1670 showed that it cost over £250,000 per year to keep the navy afloat. At the time, it had around fifty ships and five thousand men, though this figure was naturally higher during wartime and lower in peace. It had debts of over half a million pounds, much of it unpaid wages and expenses for the wounded.[152] Money had been received from France but not enough. Pepys had speculated a year before the Treaty that if Charles entered into a financial alliance with France, it would be useless "for with this money the King shall wanton away his time in pleasures, and think nothing of the main till it be too late."[153] Unable to provide all that was necessary, Charles resorted to summoning Parliament. Since he had made the declaration of war when they were not sitting, the mood of the members was feisty. The terms of the secret treaty of Dover were unknown, but the debate showed the lack of faith in the King's integrity. Colonel Strangeways asked: "France has entangled us; the public articles are ill enough, what are the private articles?"[154] Charles replied on 7th January denying that there were any.

The fact that Charles had also decided to suspend the laws against Catholics and Dissenters was a further source of anger. What was the point of Parliament making laws if the King was to simply suspend them? If Charles was to get money for the war, he would have to accept what became known as the Test Act. This required all office holders to take the Oaths of Allegiance and Supremacy which had been specified in the aftermath of the Gunpowder Plot of 1605. The Oath of Allegiance specifically denied the right of the Pope to depose kings or to absolve Catholics of their loyalty to the crown. The Oath of Supremacy accepted the King as "the only supreme governor ...in all spiritual or ecclesiastical things or causes as temporal." In addition, office holders had to provide evidence that they had taken Holy Communion within the past year in their parish church and to make a

---

[152] SP29/284/22

[153] 28th April 1669

[154] Anchitell Grey, *Debates of the House of Commons* vol. 2 (London, 1769) p.200 31st October 1673

declaration against transubstantiation. This last was considered the test of faith for Catholics believed that at the consecration, the bread and wine became truly the body and blood of Christ whilst Protestants said that the presence was spiritual.[155] Desperate for funds, Charles agreed to all of Parliament's demands. He was voted enough to conclude a peace but not to continue the war.[156]

The Test Act forced James to make public his change of religion. His refusal to take Holy Communion at Easter had seemed quite pointed but he was still attending Anglican worship. On 15th June 1673, he went to the King to formally hand over his seals of office including those of Lord High Admiral and Lord Warden of the Cinque Ports. Phillips said it was indicative of his pride rather than his conscience, "a mark of his natural antipathy to parliaments...his disdain that such insolent earth and ashes should dare to give law to his divinity." [157] In a letter to Laurence Hyde, James denied this and said he would not take the test, "though I were sure it would restore me into the good opinion and esteem of the nation which I once had, and therefore I desire that neither you nor none of my friends will ever mention it to me or flatter themselves that I can ever be brought to it. What I did was never done hastily and I have expected many years and been prepared for what has happened to me and for the worst that can yet befall me."[158] The Venetian ambassador suggested that James may have felt less secure than he sounded telling the Doge that James was seeking to marry his daughters into the French royal family so that he might take advantage of Louis XIV's protection and also have somewhere that he could go to should the need arise.[159]

James' religion was important because he remained heir to the throne. Although the King had managed to father a number of bastards, he had been unable to have children by his wife and there was no expectation that this would change. The Queen was rumoured to have specific gynaecological problems which prevented it.[160]

---

[155] For full text of the oaths see John Raithby (ed.), *Statutes of the Realm* vol 4 (London, 1819)

[156] He also had to give up on his plans to declare himself a Catholic, if he had ever seriously planned to do so. He may have made the claim as a ruse to get money from France and to dupe James into using his connections to back the scheme.

[157] John Phillips, *The Character of a Popish Successor* (London, 1681) p.13 The Duke of Lauderdale went further and suggested that James actually wanted to be a catholic martyr himself, saying "his ambition is to shine in a red letter after he is dead." See Callow op.cit. p.153)

[158] Samuel Singer (ed.), *The Correspondence of Henry Hyde, Earl of Clarendon* vol.1 (London, 1828) p45

[159] CSPV vol 38 item 58 p.35

[160] John Reresby, *The Memoirs and Travels of Sir John Reresby, Bart,* (London, 1813) p.167

In spring 1671, James' wife Anne died followed a few weeks later by his only son. That left him three daughters, Mary aged nine, Anne aged six and baby Catherine who was just two months old. Aware of the importance of having a son to succeed him, James decided to seek a new bride. He considered a number of candidates, all of them Catholic. In the end he chose Mary of Modena whom he married by proxy in September 1673, deliberately choosing to make the match before Parliament sat because he anticipated their reaction.

On 31st October, the House of Commons did indeed present a petition to the King asking that he ensure the match remain consummated on grounds "if this marriage do proceed, it will be a means to disquiet the minds of your Protestant subjects at home and... for another age at least, this Kingdom will be under continual apprehensions of the growth of Popery, and the danger of the Protestant religion."[161] Parliament was particularly disturbed that Mary was the choice of Louis XIV and just fifteen, which meant there was every chance she would have children and they feared these would be brought up catholic.[162] Charles ignored the petition and in November, Mary arrived. There were some disturbances in London. Evelyn recorded that an effigy of the Pope had been processed through the city and burnt. [163] In order to let things quieten down, James decided to take Mary on a sightseeing tour of England as a honeymoon.[164]

The marriage seemed to be reasonably happy. Lady Chaworth described on Christmas Day 1676: "the Duchess is much delighted with making and throwing of snow balls and pelted the Duke soundly with one the other day and ran away quick into her closet and he after her but she durst not open the door."[165] Burnet said that Mary had an "innocent cheerfulness" and no interest in politics which made her popular.[166] Although less than half his age and forced to accept his routine unfaithfulness, Mary was not afraid of standing up for herself. She demonstrated her displeasure at his behaviour by openly boxing his ears, something which led the surprised Duchess of Orleans to wonder if he was not scared of her.[167]

Despite a miscarriage in 1674, Mary went on to prove that she was every bit as fertile as James' first wife had been. She had a daughter in 1675

---

[161] *Journal of the House of Commons* volume 9: 1667-1687 (1802), p.285
[162] Louis XIV paid the bride's dowry, see Callow op.cit. p.93
[163] 15th November 1673
[164] Brown op.cit. p.106
[165] HMC, *The manuscripts of His Grace the Duke of Rutland* vol. 2 (London, 1890) p.34
[166] Burnet op.cit. p.244
[167] Elizabeth of Orleans op.cit. p.43

followed by two more miscarriages, another girl in 1676 and then in 1677, the longed for son whom they named Charles after the King. Just five weeks later, the baby died. James wrote to his nephew William of Orange saying "I wish you may never have the like cause of trouble nor know what it is to lose a son."[168] Lady Chaworth wrote that "the Duchess is inconsolable but the Duke bears it like a great man."[169]

It was the fact that James continued to produce children which alarmed the country as a whole. His daughters had been brought up as Protestants but only because, as James said, he knew that if he did otherwise they would be taken from him.[170] When he became king, he would be able to bring up his children how he chose and that meant the spectre of not just a "popish successor" but an entire Catholic ruling dynasty. Various ideas were suggested to prevent this. One idea was that Charles could divorce his Queen and marry a Protestant lady who would hopefully have a son. The King vetoed that idea from the outset. Another idea was that he could legitimise his favourite bastard, the Duke of Monmouth. Again, the King refused to do that. The third option was based on James not having another son and proposed that his eldest daughter should be married to her cousin, William of Orange, the hero of European Protestants everywhere since his valiant stand against the French.[171] She would then hopefully produce similarly heroic Protestant heirs who would go on to rule Britain and build its empire. James was not at all keen, preferring a French match, but in August 1677, the wedding took place at the King's behest.[172]

The union with the Dutch altered the political situation. James spent the following year encouraging William in his war against France. He wrote to him almost weekly discussing troop movements and offering advice. James was deeply upset that Parliament would not vote the money for an army suggesting that this showed a want of patriotism, for if France attacked Flanders in the meantime, it would seriously affect English trade and he argued that their refusal was evidence of republican tendencies.[173] James was very keen to go across to fight. An exasperated Charles said: "Frankly my brother's talk pains me. We have not a penny for the raising of troops and he speaks as if we had an army. The idea of being a general has gone to

---

[168] SP8/3/13

[169] Rutland MSS op.cit. p.44. James is known to have fathered at least twenty-five children, eight by his first wife, seven plus four miscarraiges on his second and six by his principal mistresses Arabella Churchill (sister of his page John who went on to become Duke of Marlborough) and Catherine Sedley.

[170] Clarke op.cit. p.503

[171] SP29/360/112

[172] For James reaction see Rutland MSS op.cit. p.33, Burnet op.cit. p.272

[173] SP8/3/17, SP8/3/37

his head."[174] Yet James would not be discouraged. On August 20th 1678, he wrote to William about the dragoons, cavalry and infantry about to be sent to Flanders. He said: "Pray let me know when it may be proper for me to go over myself and then I shall bring some more troops with me."

James never got to lead his men to Flanders for that same month, news emerged of what was called the Popish Plot. The chief source of the revelations was a man named Titus Oates who was not held to be a totally credible witness. The King himself realised he was a liar when he said that he had met Don John and that he was a tall, thin man when the King knew Don John to be short and fat. Yet, Oates and his claims that the Catholics were planning an uprising which would destroy the Protestants was widely believed. As more and more people tried to get on the bandwagon with ever more outlandish stories, an element of doubt did creep in, but the majority remained convinced that there was a real plot. James expressed his opinion on the subject on October 18th writing: "I verily believe that, when this affair is thoroughly examined, it will be found nothing but malice against the poor Catholics in general and myself in particular."[175] Yet his confidence was misplaced for one of the first people to be implicated was one of his own servants.

Edward Colman had been employed by the Duke of York for some years, originally working directly for him and later for his wife. He was a Catholic and had been corresponding with Louis XIV's confessor, Monsieur Le Chaise as well as papal envoys and Jesuits. A search of his home found some of these letters, though Colman had destroyed many following a warning from James.[176] Some were in code, others had been written in lemon juice so the full contents were only visible when the paper was warmed beside a fire. One letter of 23rd October 1675 said:

> We have here a mighty work upon our hands, no less than the conversion of three kingdoms and by that perhaps the subduing of a pestilent heresy...There were never such hopes of success since the death of Queen Mary as now in our days when God has given us a prince who is become (may I say by a miracle) zealous of being the author and instrument of so glorious a work.

There was a reference to James receiving thousands of crowns from the King of France "towards gaining others to help him or at least not to oppose

---

[174] Quoted in Callow op.cit. p.108

[175] SP8/3/68

[176] In his memoirs, James admitted telling Colman to "look to himself" and saying that "if he had any papers that might hurt him to secure them immediately." See Clarke op.cit. p.534

him." This had been "of greater use than can be imagined." Moreover, a letter of James confirmed this gift and said that he regarded his interest and that of Louis XIV as "so clearly linked together that those that opposed the one should be looked upon as enemies to the other." Colman said that James was fully aware of the correspondence and had asked him to respond on his behalf, telling Louis in one letter that Parliament was not only "unuseful but very dangerous both to England and France." He boasted that Charles would be totally governed by him if only he could obtain sufficient revenue to enable him to reign without ever needing to call Parliament. Colman's understanding was that James was "unalterably addicted to the interest of his Most Christian Majesty."

To add to the embarassment, the letters contained a number of passages which were critical of the King. They said money was "the only way to gain the King" but complained that Charles "pretendeth to be effectually the Duke's friend but does nevertheless hold an intimate correspondence with his enemies." Revealing that Charles as well as James had sought to influence the Papal election of 1676, Colman confirmed that the King wanted to join the Catholics but said he thought it too dangerous. As a result "I dare put no confidence in the assistance of the King after so many demonstrations as he hath given us of his weakness as to that matter." Letters to himself from France and Rome showed a general distrust of Charles which was not too surprising given he had failed to announce his faith as promised in the Treaty of Dover. One from the Pope's representative did, however, vow that when James was King they would "employ at Rome both money and credit to assist him to restore the Catholic religion in England."[177]

The letters proposed several plans. One was to persuade Charles to put the management of the wealthy East India Company into James' hands "by which means he will have opportunity to enrich himself and all his Catholic associates." Another was to bribe sufficient MPs to petition Charles to give James his job back at the navy. Colman wrote "our prevailing in these things will give the greatest blow to the Protestant religion here that ever it received since its birth."

The letters, written between 1674 and 1677 and whose authenticity was never challenged by anyone, were political dynamite and published in full for everyone to read.[178] A Parliamentary committee later appointed to

---

[177] This letter is in Treby op.cit. p.121 but it was not fully deciphered until it appeared in Malcolm Hay, *Jesuits and the Popish Plot*, (London, 1934) p.206

[178] Edward Coleman, *Mr Coleman's Two Letters to Monsieur L'Chaise* (London, 1678) and George Treby, *A collection of letters and other writings related to the horrid Popish Plot*, (London, 1681). The passages quoted are from Treby pp. 3, 5, 7, 8, 13, 67, 92, 116-119.

investigate found in addition letters from James to the Pope which added further fuel to the anger, especially where James had apologised for letting his eldest daughter marry a "heretic" and raising the possibility of a match with the Catholic Medici for the younger.[179] They also showed James receiving gifts from the Pope and "very ample indulgences."[180] Colman was executed for treason and a lot of questions were asked about James' activities.[181]

In a further incident late in October 1678, Justice Edmund Godfrey, the judge to whom Oates had first told details of the plot was found dead near St Pancras. Burnet, who went to see the body, reported strangulation marks about the neck, a badly bruised chest, and a sword which had been run through the body clearly after death because there was no blood. A huge funeral was held with the judge's body lying in state before being processed through London followed by a crowd of thousands. James commented that it was clearly suicide and that the sword had been plunged in simply to discredit the Catholics, but the judge brought in a verdict of murder. Rumours abounded that James had been involved in arranging the death in an attempt to prevent the judge giving more details of the plot.

In this turbulent situation, the King believed that James would be safer overseas and accordingly wrote to him on 28th February 1679:

I expect you will satisfy me in this and that I wish it may be as soon as your conveniency will permit. You may easily believe that it is not without great deal of pain I write you this, being more touched with the constant friendship you have had for me than with anything else in the world; and I hope that you will do me the justice to believe for certain that neither absence nor anything will hinder me from being truly and with affection yours.[182]

Reluctantly, James departed on 3rd March for Flanders.[183] He had wanted to spend his exile in France but Louis XIV was still upset with him for allowing his daughter to marry his enemy, William of Orange. On 5th June, Henry Savile observed from Paris that all might not be lost, however, for "I will not doubt that when you have made him desperate in England

---

[179] John Reresby, *The Memoirs and Travels of Sir John Reresby, Bart,* (London, 1813) p.224 Treby op.cit. p. 95-96

[180] The Protestant reformation had begun with Luther's protest at the sale of indulgences by Tetzel so this was an extremely provocative act on James' part.

[181] Colman was beatified by the Pope in 1929

[182] Arthur Bryant, *The letters of King Charles II* (London, 1935) p.305

[183] As the centre for English Jesuits, it was not a politically astute choice.

upon the least application he will make here, he shall be received into favour as a proper instrument to hurt England with."[184]

Meantime the plot consumed the entire country. A Hereford weaver told of how his Catholic landlord had promised that following the death of the King, "all his Protestant subjects were to be massacred thereupon as far as the papists swords could reach and those whom the massacre reached nor weakened thereby were to be pursued and cut off by war and foreign assistance under the Duke of York's authority."[185] The main plot spurned others such as one known as the Meal Tub plot. According to this, James had paid Thomas Dangerfield to fabricate and plant evidence that the presbyterians had invented the popish plot. The matter was investigated at length by the House of Lords but Dangerfield proved an unsound witness so the case was dropped. James, ever keen on revenge, made it one of his first acts as King to prosecute Dangerfield for libel, safe in the knowledge that his close friend Judge Jeffreys would convict him.[186]

It was while James was abroad that Parliament voted to exclude James from the succession. His correspondence with France and the Pope had shown he was unwilling to abide by the laws of Great Britain which meant that he would not abide by the coronation oath. As the author of *Pereat Papa* claimed, it was "undoubtedly more pleasing to God to put one man by ...than expose millions of souls to damnation and the streets to flow with blood"[187]

James' own opinion on the exclusion bill was that it was "against law and destroys the very being of the monarchy."[188] Charles urged Parliament to consider limitation instead telling both houses:

> I am as ready to join with you in all the ways and means that may establish as firm a security of the Protestant religion as your own hearts can wish and this, not only during my time (of which I am sure you have no fear) but in all future ages even to the end of the world. And therefore am come to assure you that what reasonable bills you shall present to be passed into laws to make you safe in the reign of any successor (so as they tend not to impeach the right of succession nor the descent of the crown in the true line and so as they restrain

---

[184] Savile Correspondence op.cit. p.92

[185] Richard Greene, *The Popish Massacre*, (London, 1679) p.6

[186] James took similar action against Titus Oates.

[187] *Pereat Papa* op.cit, p.2

[188] His comments came in a letter to his son-in-law William of Orange dated 26th June 1679 quoted in Davies op.cit. p.xxiii

not the just right of any Protestant successor) shall find from me a ready concurrence.[189]

James' response to what he saw as a sign of support from his brother was:

I can never sufficiently acknowledge the sense of gratitude I have for your Majesty's goodness to me. I do assure you I can bear any misfortune with patience so long as you are so kind. I have but one life to lose and I shall always be ready to lay it down in your service, and at the rate the things now go, there is too great a probability an occasion may not long wanting. They will never be satisfied unless Your Majesty un-king yourself....Let not therefore knaves and mean spirited people flatter you into an opinion that you may be safe by yielding and temporising for nothing less than the destruction of your family and the monarchy itself will content them....I beg of Your Majesty to make use of those parts and courage God has given you and not rely upon concessions already made or to make any more; be pleased to use all possible diligence in providing your forts and garrisons. Certainly the speediest way of breaking their measures is to break the Parliament itself and proportion your way of living to your revenue.[190]

The summer of 1679 saw things get worse when Charles became seriously ill. Although he recovered, it made the pro-exclusion party even more determined to remove James from the picture. As the threats against him continued, Charles decided to send James to Scotland. It was far enough away from London to prevent any accusations that James was meddling in domestic affairs and was also further away from continental Catholics. At first, the Scots were glad, their Privy Council expressing pleasure that they were to have a royal visit after many years without. However, Scotland was a very Protestant part of the kingdom and they were concerned. James, aware of this, was determined to act responsibly. He and his wife did all they could to charm the local population. When the Scottish Parliament met in the summer of 1681, James accepted acts to safeguard the Protestant faith and the succession. Burnet, who was not in the country at the time but who wrote based on what friends there had told him, said that James tried to be merciful to those whom he felt were simply misguided. He offered a group of rebels who had declared that the only king they would own was Jesus, their lives if only they would say "God bless the King." They refused and seemed determined to be martyrs. After just over a

---

[189] Anon, *The Case Put Concerning the Succession of His Royal Highness the Duke of York* (London, 1679) p.9
[190] Clarke op.cit. pp.551-552

dozen had been executed, James called a halt to the proceedings and sentenced the remainder to hard labour. [191] Yet in cases where people had knowingly plotted treason, he was harsh. In the case of Spreul who had planned to blow him up, Burnet claimed James attended the torture saying: "he looked on all the while with an unmoved indifference and with an attention as if he had been to look on some curious experiment. This gave a terrible idea of him to all that observed it as of a man that had no bowels or humanity in him."[192]

Meanwhile in England, rumours of plots and efforts to exclude, banish or impeach James continued. In December 1680, Articles of High Treason were drawn up against him. These included accusations that he had confederated with the enemy French king to bring in absolutism, that he had used his position with the Post Office to destroy evidence and warn fellow traitors, that he had sought to undermine Parliament and the judicial system and that by his behaviour he had encouraged Catholics at home to plot against the King and led Catholics abroad to persecute Protestants, thereby causing loss of life.[193]

In reality, James had never had any designs on Charles' life and he had never attempted to create for himself a strong party with a view to seizing power. He had never needed to do so for he was secure in his brother's affections, even though they naturally had their disagreements. Nor were the Catholics capable of taking power for they amounted to barely one per cent of the population. Anglicans and Dissenters outnumbered Catholics by almost two hundred to one.[194] Yet genuine fears existed. Catholic France seemed all powerful in Europe. It was entirely possible that it would overrun Holland and use that as a base to attack England. Cherished traditions of liberty, enterprise and Christian faith were under threat. James refused to see it that way. To him, he was being persecuted for his faith by people intent on destroying the monarchy. [195] In fact, the opposition to him stemmed from the belief that Britain needed a strong and Protestant king to defend her. They did not want a republic and nor did they want someone pro-French on the throne. James might be absent but his men were still in control at the navy and in the army so to their mind the threat remained.

---

[191] The report appears in full in Brown op.cit. pp. 129-134

[192] Burnet op.cit. p.378. Some have cast doubt on this account

[193] SP29/414/176

[194] These figures are based on the Compton Census of 1676. Although Catholicism may have been under reported in some areas, it was undoubtedly not a significant proportion of the population.

[195] Clarke op.cit. p.594

A number of those about James urged him to recant his Catholicism and return to the Church of England. He refused. He seemed to take almost a perverse delight in his troubles claiming that he had gone from being "one of the happiest princes in Europe to that of the most unfortunate and abandoned man upon earth."[196] In a clear attempt to claim the moral high ground and distract people's attention from the number of laws he had broken and his relations with France, he wrote:

> Had I affected popularity or considered only my own well being in the world, I had not trodden the paths which I now am so entangled in. I could, without doing anything but what His Majesty himself pressed me to, have been above the malice of those false and mean spirited men who now seek my ruin, but I thank my God I have ever had a horror of those base methods of obtaining my ends and hope I shall still continue to make my duty to God and the King the only rule of my actions.[197]

His intransigence and total refusal to accept any blame for what had happened, made the situation impossible.

The dispute raged for two years with Charles continually sending Parliament away in an attempt to avoid the exclusion issue. He was evidently tired of the controversy for he admitted: "if it were not for my brother's folly, I would get out of all my difficulties."[198] Parliament itself was divided about what to do. Some argued Parliament had the right to alter the succession, others that the Crown was a gift of God so man should not interfere. Some said James should be entitled to defend himself in a proper trial, whilst others refused to contemplate him setting foot in the country again and were prepared to condemn him in his absence. For all those who feared that James' accession would lead to genocide on an unparalleled level, there were others who thought excluding him would bring a new civil war. Some people favoured limitations whilst others said that was a waste of time for James would only overturn those limits as soon as he became king. As one commentator wrote: "What could be more ridiculous then to expect that a prince should pass a bill for the deposal of himself."[199] Even if they did exclude him, who was to reign next? James' daughter Mary was the favoured choice but James was still having children and could have a son. If

---

[196] Clarke op.cit. p.540

[197] ibid. p.679

[198] Burnet op.cit. p.243

[199] Anon, *The Case Put Concerning the Succession of His Royal Highness the Duke of York* (London, 1679) p.25. All hope had been given up by this time of Charles having children by his Queen.

they disinherited James and his descendents, the next in line was Minette's daughter who was married to the King of Spain – and people remembered bitterly the last time a King of Spain had influence in England.[200]

The following resolutions which were passed by the House of Commons in January 1681 demonstrate the mood:

Resolved, there is no security or safety for the Protestant Religion, the King's life or the well constituted and established Government of this realm without passing a Bill for disabling James Duke of York to inherit the imperial crown

Resolved, that until a Bill be passed for excluding the Duke of York this House cannot give any supply to His Majesty

Resolved, that all persons who advised His Majesty ...against the Bill for excluding the Duke of York have given pernicious counsel to his Majesty and are promoters of popery and enemies to the King and Kingdom

Resolved, that whoever advised His Majesty to prorogue this Parliament... is a betrayer of the King, the Protestant religion, and of the Kingdom of England, a promoter of the French interest and a pensioner to France

Resolved, that it is the opinion of this house that the City of London was burnt in the year 1666 by the Papists designing thereby to introduce arbitrary power and popery into this kingdom. [201]

Finally, in spring 1681, Charles dissolved Parliament once and for all and made another secret treaty with France. This time there was no promise to declare himself a Catholic: Charles simply wanted money. James' memoirs state that the King gave him the job of negotiating the deal because he trusted in his good connections with the French court.[202] Had Parliament found out, they would probably have regarded this as further proof that their fears were well founded. James wrote to the French ambassador vowing: "Be persuaded that I will always do my duty for your master's service."[203] Louis XIV wrote to James: "Your counsels and firmness

---

[200] Phillip II of Spain was the husband of Bloody Mary and the man who sent the Armada.

[201] Grey op.cit. vol 8 pp.284-285

[202] Clarke op.cit. p.664

[203] Dalrymple op.cit. p.7

will henceforth be very necessary to strengthen the King of Great Britain in the resolution to avail himself of the means I have offered him to confirm the peace and render immoveable the ties of friendship to which you have so much contributed."[204]

Meantime, James continued to spend his time in Scotland and it was on his way there in May 1682 that he was involved in a serious incident when the Gloucester frigate on which he had been sailing ran aground off Yarmouth in a storm. The captain's report written a week after the accident, says that he tried to persuade James to depart in his barge but he refused hoping the ship could be saved. Eventually, when it became clear that all the pumping and bailing was not working, James agreed to go. Captain Berry wrote:

> Amidst all the disorder and confusion, the great duty and concern which the poor seamen had for His Royal Highness' preservation was most remarkable for when the barge was hoisted out and lowered down into the water, not one man so much as proffered to run into her

James, he said, took "all the persons of quality" he could and departed for the Mary yacht which was travelling with them. He ordered this and the Happy Return to send their boats back to try to pick up survivors. However, by this stage it was too late and around one hundred and fifty men died.

Sir James Dick, the Lord Provost of Edinburgh, who was also on the ship, confirmed that James left with less than a dozen people, excluding the rowers. The low number was due to the storm and the fact that they had just witnessed the first small boat to be let down capsize with the loss of all but two hands. The story thereafter changed with Dick observing that as the Duke's boat was lowered, some twenty seamen forced their way on. Another hundred or so tried to jump in too but were held off by swords. He said that the crew were "not at command every man studying his own safety." By this point, the barge was so full that Dick said "we had no room to stand." Getting the barge into the water proved difficult as the suction from the sinking Gloucester seemed likely to either draw it under the waves or smash it to pieces. Eventually, they got away:

> ..and when we came to row to the nearest yacht the waves were such, and we overloaded, that we every moment thought to have been drowned, and being about mid way to the yachts, there were a great many swimming for their lives who catched all a dead grip of our boat, holding up their heads above water crying "Help!" which hindrance

---

[204] ibid. p.45

was kept off and their hands loosed....When unexpectedly and wonderfully we came to the yacht's side we were like to be crushed in pieces by the yacht which by reason of the great seas was like to run us down till at length a rope was cast...and there every man clam for his life.

When Dick turned back, the Gloucester was gone with the loss of two hundred men.

The son of the Earl of Dartmouth also on the Gloucester, agreed that James had delayed his departure until the end and added that James had ordered his strong box be lowered into the barge "which besides being extremely weighty took up a good deal of time as well as room." Dartmouth, aware that men would die as a result of James' actions, queried if the box was absolutely essential and James replied that he would rather risk his life than lose it because it contained things of great importance to him and the King. Dartmouth admitted that he too had been forced to draw his sword to prevent men rushing the barge and overturning it.[205]

In the most famous account of the episode, Burnet suggested that James' chief concern had been for his dogs and a group of people assumed to have been his Catholic priests given his determination to get them to safety. The fact that this interpretation was widely believed, despite Burnet not being an eyewitness, indicated the continued distrust in which James was held.[206]

Yet, the next three years saw something of a renaissance in James' fortunes. His rule in Scotland had shown that Protestants could live safely under a Catholic. People were also reassured by the fact that all of his children by his second wife had died young. This led to a supposition that James, now in his fifties, would not have a healthy son which meant he would be followed as monarch by his Protestant daughter Mary. As rumours of plots and rebellions died down, even Charles was able to joke about the situation. James returned from hunting one day and saw the King walking across Hyde Park with just two companions. He rode up and remonstrated with him for not having a guard about him. Charles said he was in "no kind of danger, James, for I am sure no man in England will take away my life to make you King!"[207]

---

[205] The letters of Dartmouth and the Lord Provost appear in Dalrymple op.cit. pp.68-72. It would seem likely that the strong box contained details of the secret negotiations with France.

[206] Burnet op.cit. p.324.

[207] Told by Lord Cromarty who was walking with the King and recounted in *Gentleman's Magazine* vol xxxv (1851) p.505

Restored to favour, James became more dominant than ever. As it was clear that Charles could not live much longer, those seeking favours flocked round James whom they regarded as the coming man. The poet Waller quipped that because Parliament had been so set against James ruling after Charles, Charles had decided to let him rule during his reign.[208]

The end came in February 1685 when Charles suffered a stroke. James stayed with him to the end, being described as spending most of his time on his knees in prayers and tears. His last act of kindness as a brother was to obtain a Roman Catholic priest to perform the last rites for Charles.[209] Many doubts had been expressed during Charles' lifetime about his Protestant convictions and these were now confirmed.

James is a complex character and difficult to assess. As Duke of York, he served his country as bravely at sea as he had when fighting for France and Spain as a mercenary. He showed courage during the Great Fire and considerable dedication to rebuilding the navy.[210] Yet, his change of religion, sincere though it may have been, threatened his country with civil war and the fact that he was prepared to accept foreign aid to force his opinions on others and to dispense with Parliament indicates how far removed he was from the mind of the people. His father's final advice to him had been:

> If you never see my face again...I do require and entreat you as your Father and your King that you never suffer your heart to receive the least check against or disaffection from the true religion established in the Church of England. I tell you, I have tried it and after much search and many disputes, have concluded it to be the best in the world....Nor would I have you to entertain any aversion or dislike of Parliaments which in their right constitution with freedom and honour will never injure or diminish your greatness; but will rather be as interchangings of love, loyalty and confidence between a prince and his people.[211]

If James had followed that advice, his life would have been very different. He was fortunate that he was able to keep secret some of his dealings with overseas powers or he would have suffered the same fate as his father, public execution. Instead, he survived against the odds to become King but lost the throne after just three years, evicted by his subjects without a tear in what became known as the Glorious Revolution.

---

[208] Quoted by Burnet op.cit. p.378

[209] Clarke op.cit. pp.747-749. See also Evelyn's diary 4th February 1685.

[210] J. R. Tanner (ed.), *Samuel Pepys Naval Minutes* (London, 1926) pp.84,159

[211] Clarke op.cit. vol 2 pp.662-663

Ernest

1674-1728

Duke of York 1716-1728

He seems to be so very modest that I think you would like him.[1]

There is little doubt that Ernest is the most obscure of all the Dukes of York. He never set foot in England.[2] His life revolved around battlefields and the colourful European courts of people such as Louis XIV and Peter the Great. Yet the volume of letters which he left gives us a unique insight into his character and enables us to understand more of the man who could so easily have become Regent of Great Britain.

Ernest was born at Osnabrück on 17th September 1674, the sixth and youngest son of Ernst-August[3] of Brunswick-Lüneburg and his wife Sophia. His mother was the grand-daughter of James I of England and thus first

---

[1] Letter from the Duke of Marlborough dated 6th July 1702. See H L Snyder (ed.), *The Marlborough Godolphin Correspondence* volume 1 (London, 1975) p.85

[2] His cousin the Duchess of Orleans hinted he may have accompanied his brother George to England in November 1720 but there is no reference to this in the newspapers of the day nor in any of the courtiers diaries or political papers. The Duchess lived in Paris so it is possible that she was mistaken.

[3] In order to avoid confusion between father and son who shared the same name, references to the father are made as Ernst and the son as Ernest. Similarly, as mother and daughter shared the same name, the mother is always Sophia and the daughter is known by her family nickname of Figuelotte.

cousin to King Charles II and his brother James, Duke of York. Sophia's older brother, Prince Rupert of the Rhine, had achieved great fame for his military prowess in the English Civil War though she herself was not familiar with the country. At the time of Ernest's birth, it seemed highly unlikely that his mother would ever inherit the English crown but as the years passed and Charles II died without issue and James' children passed away, this became more of a possibility. At the time of his death, Ernest was fourth in line to the British throne.

On his father's side, Ernest had links to the Danish royal family, but his most famous ancestor was his great-great-grandfather, founder of the house of Brunswick who had studied under Martin Luther and was one of the first princes in Germany to espouse Protestantism.[4] These religious credentials, combined with Ernest's own religious beliefs, were to play a crucial role in his later career.

As the youngest child in a large family, Ernest had few prospects. Sophia had already given birth to nine children, three of whom were stillborn. Of the remainder, five were boys. Ernest was the last, born just before her forty-fourth birthday. In her memoirs, Sophia neglected to even mention his arrival though she recorded details of all the others. She wrote to her brother on 26th September 1674 saying that the birth had "nearly cost me my life but, thanks be to God, the danger is past and I brought a boy into the world, which I should not complain about, although I would have preferred a girl."[5] Two years later, she was to describe him as "the most easy going of all my children" and say that he would amuse himself for hours with his toys. His particular favourite was a doll named Hans which he carried everywhere. [6]

When Ernest was five, his father succeeded as Duke of Brunswick-Luneburg following the death of his elder brother. As a result, the family moved from Osnabrück to Hanover where his father was consecrated ruler on 12th October 1680. This was a significant move for the entire family representing a considerable increase in income and influence. Although Ernest would have been too young to appreciate the political ramifications of the move, he would have been aware that he now had bigger palaces in which to play and that his parents were more commonly away from home. His father was abroad for most of 1680 and 1681, and from 1685 to 1686. His mother was absent in 1679. Ernest's closest relationship within the

---

[4] Ernest I of Brunswick-Luneburg also known as Ernest the Confessor ruled 1520-46

[5] Erich Kielmansegg, *Briefe des Herzogs Ernst August ze Braunschweig-Luneburg an Johann Franz Diedrich von Wendt*, (Hannover, 1902) p.5

[6] ibid. p. 6

family was with his eldest brother George, fourteen years his senior. Even as an adult, his cousin would joke that he followed George round like a devoted spaniel.[7]

We know very little of Ernest's childhood. He studied languages because he was able to speak English as well as French, German, Italian and Latin.[8] He learnt to ride and received some military training. He also learnt music. His father was passionate about opera and built an opera house in the Leineschloss palace. Ernest's letters refer to him owning a violin as an adult so it is likely that he was taught to play the instrument when young.

In March 1687, the twelve year old Ernest was sent to France, together with his brother Christian who was two years older than him. The idea was to give them some polish and culture, just as later generations of girls were sent to "finishing schools." Sophia's niece was the famous Liselotte who had married the brother of King Louis XIV.[9] By sending the boys to live with her, they were able to spend two years at the court of the Sun King himself, enjoying the splendour of Versailles and Fontainebleau and St Cloud. Liselotte had a son of her own named Philip who was two months older than Ernest although she reported he was much smaller than his cousin. Liselotte wrote to Sophia in July:

> Prince Ernest is settling in well here. He is very amiable and is developing an engaging manner. Prince Christian, however, is very distracted. He has the misfortune that his younger brother is so lively because whenever he wants to say something and is thinking of the words, Prince Ernest has already grasped it and spoken it out loud.[10]

By September, Christian was said to have started to speak French and was even starting to understand some jokes. Liselotte attributed his advance to the need to keep up with his younger brother:

> Prince Ernest is making himself very popular here with everyone and he is considered extraordinarily impressive. He has convinced everyone of his intellect. The distinction which used to be made at the beginning between him and his brother has I think spurred on and

---

[7] Wilhelm Holland, *Briefe der Herzogin Elisabeth Charlotte von Orleans* vol. 2 (Stuttgart 1871) p.30

[8] It is generally stated that George I did not speak English but there seems no reason to suppose that Sophia would have only educated her younger sons in the language when their claim to the British throne was quite slight.

[9] Elizabeth Charlotte, Duchess of Orleans (1652-1722)

[10] Kielmansegg op.cit. p.6

encouraged Prince Christian.[11]

Whilst in France, the princes had the opportunity to attend the theatre seeing performances in both French and Italian. They also went to see the tennis matches at Fontainebleau and were invited to dine with a number of ladies. In the autumn of 1688, Liselotte reported that Ernest was the more talkative and vivacious but that both were very well mannered and good company. She said that despite being very cheerful, they had the maturity of adults. Ernest, in particular, was always keen to please and was "loved by everyone." [12]

Ernest was still in France when James II of England arrived at court. He had fled the country following the event known to history as the Glorious Revolution. Ernest undoubtedly met the man who had been Duke of York for over forty years before his accession because his guardian frequently entertained him. Liselotte described James as "an honest and worthy man but one of the silliest that I have ever seen."[13]

In March 1689, after almost two years in France, Ernest and his brother went on to Italy. They stayed for some weeks in Venice where their father maintained a house, a reflection both of his love of music and close links with the republic.[14] He returned to Hanover toward the end of that summer. The political situation had deteriorated sharply over the previous weeks and Hanover was now at war with France. To Ernest's annoyance, his parents decided that at fourteen he was too young to go so he remained at home for a year whilst his five older brothers, including Christian, all served in the army.[15]

The years 1690-1692 were not easy for the family. Two of Ernest's brothers were killed in battle, Karl in 1690 and Friedrich in 1691. Another son, Maximilian, was exiled the same year for his rebellion against his father. Ernst August wanted the status of his duchy to be elevated to an electorate, meaning that he would become one of the small number of German princes responsible for electing the Emperor. In order for this to happen, the royal family in Hanover had to adopt primogeniture. Previously, all the sons could hope to inherit a portion of the estate but now

---

[11] ibid. p.7

[12] ibid. p.8

[13] Elizabeth of Orleans, *Life and Letters of Charlotte Elizabeth*, (London 1889) p.53

[14] Osnabrück had supported Venice militarily in its war against the Turks and Ernest's father was a major patron of the arts in the city. For further details see the paper of Helen Watanabe-O'Kelly presented at the 2010 conference on Waterborne Pageants and Festivities in the Renaissance.

[15] Ernest was allowed to join the army in the Netherlands when he was fifteen.

only George as the eldest would get anything. The rest would be left without land and penniless. None of the younger sons was happy about this but Maximilian took his opposition too far and was jailed. He obtained release by surrendering all claims to Hanover but the estrangement from his family was total and permanent.

Ernest appears to have remained in Hanover for much of 1691 and 1692. In the summer of 1691, he travelled with Count Philip von Königsmarck to Brunswick where Philip developed malaria. Philip was more than a dozen years older than Ernest and a rather highly strung gentleman. At the time he professed himself in love with a mystery lady, writing to her: "my noble travelling companion could tell you of the state in which he sees me daily, though you may be sure that I hide from him the cause." Declaring, "I have never loved as I love you" he continued to write letters despite his illness, ending the next: "to convince you the better how I love you, how I worship you, I sign this with my blood." The letters refer to Ernest as "the Innocent" suggesting he was duped into sending Philip's letters back to Hanover together with his own, unaware that the lady in question was the wife of his elder brother.[16]

In the summer of 1693, the three remaining royal brothers took part in the bloody battle of Neerwinden. Unsurprisingly, their mother was distraught and she wrote that she had been three days without eating or sleeping as she wondered if her sons were alive or dead. Her state of mind was not put much at ease by hearing that her eldest son, George, had almost been killed when his horse was shot from him and that Ernest had been with him at the time.[17] The allies had been severely outnumbered and around a third were killed, wounded or taken prisoner. George himself, who led the Hanoverian contingent which represented a sixth of the force, came close to losing his life.[18] Ernest was amongst those forced to flee for their lives as the French broke through. It was said: "nothing but confusion could now be seen throughout the camp. Slaughter and flight prevailed everywhere."[19]

Shortly after the battle, George and Ernest were summoned home to Hanover. Their father's health was deteriorating and George was required to take an increasing role in government. By this stage, the relationship

---

[16] W. H. Wilkins, *The Love of an Uncrowned Queen*, (London, 1903) pp.143-146

[17] Kielmansegg op.cit. p.9. At this battle, which the French won, the Allies had twelve thousand men killed and two thousand taken prisoner.

[18] Wilhelm Havemann, *Geschichte der Lande Braunschwig und Luneburg* (Göttingen 1857) p.357

[19] James MacPherson, *The History of Great Britain*, (London, 1775) vol 2 p.42

between George's wife and Philip von Königsmarck had become physical and people were beginning to talk. In November 1693, Philip wrote to his mistress:

> Marshall Podeveils was the first to tell me to beware of my conduct because he knew on good authority that I was being watched....Prince Ernest has told me the same thing and he is not as guarded as the other for he admitted that the conversation I had from time to time with you might draw upon me very unpleasant and serious consequences.[20]

On 1st July 1694, Philip was assassinated within the palace itself. By that point, it was believed that George's wife had decided to leave him and run away with Philip. Ernst August, informed of this by his own mistress, Countess von Platen, decided to intervene. With George away in Dresden, one of his Italian courtiers, Nicolo Montalbano, was required to carry out the deed and he was paid the equivalent of seven hundred and fifty times his annual salary.[21] Ernest's reaction to the murder of his friend is not recorded.

Ernest's only sister, another Sophia who was known within the family as Figuelotte, had married Friedrich of Brandenburg in 1684. In 1697, she arrived with news which caused great excitement in Hanover. She was to be visited by Tsar Peter the Great. Since Ernst-August's health was too poor to enable him to host the Tsar, Sophia and her family travelled back with her to Koppenbrügge. It was to be Ernest's first meeting with Peter, a man he was to see on a number of occasions in the future. The Tsar was a colourful character. He had already horrified Figuelotte's husband during a visit to a prison by expressing his desire to see an execution. When advised there was nobody awaiting death, the Tsar first offered to sacrifice one of his servants and when Friedrich declined, suggested that they use one of his footmen instead.[22] Sophia wrote on 11th August that: "The Tsar is very tall, his features are beautiful and his figure very noble; he has much vivacity of mind, prompt and just repartee; but with all the advantages which nature has bestowed upon him, it is to be wished that his manners were a little less rough."[23] In the course of a four hour banquet, the Tsar himself served the wine and ordered his own attendants to entertain. Figuelotte noted: "The Tsar's fool also made his appearance: he is very stupid but it made us laugh to see his master take a great broom and begin to sweep him." Dancing

---

[20] Wilkins op.cit. p.322

[21] Ragnild Hatton, *George I Elector and King* (London, 1978) p.59

[22] K. Waliszewski, *Pierre le Grand,* (Paris, 1897) p.88

[23] Emma Atkinson, *Memoirs of the Queens of Prussia,* (London, 1858) p.70

followed the meal and the German ladies were most amused by the Tsar's confusion over their corsets. He commented to one of his aides that they had "fiendishly hard bones." Afterwards, the Tsar presented both Sophia and Figuelotte with a case of sables and Ernest with a cloak. Unfortunately for them, they were to discover the garments were infested with moth.[24]

In January 1698, Ernest's father died and his brother George became Elector of Hanover. His faithless wife remained in custody at Ahlden which meant that Sophia continued to be the first lady of the court. Although Ernst-August had been frequently and openly unfaithful to her, Sophia had loved her husband. In her *Memoirs* she often described the joy of being with him and the misery of being apart, saying: "life without his affection would be unsupportable."[25] Ernest returned home when he could to spend time with his mother but his role in the army meant he was away for long periods. He was with her and George in October of that year when they received a visit at their hunting lodge from King William III of England. William had no children so his heir was Anne, but her only child was sickly. Anne had just had her tenth miscarriage and this meant there was a real possibility of a Hanoverian succession. The meeting was to discuss that prospect and the European political situation.

As a reflection of the closer links between England and Hanover, on 9th July 1702, Ernest accepted a commission in the British army. Created Major-General, he served under Marlborough in the Netherlands where he was able to contribute his own valued experience of European conflict. He took part in the siege and capture of Venlo in September where Lord Cutts – known as the Salamander for his love of hot fire - masterminded a daring attack on Fort St Michael. Following one battalion taking the Ravelin next to the fort, many of the enemy were put to the sword but some escaped to the ramparts of the fort from which they sent down a barrage of great and small shot. One man who was there noted: "we had nothing for it but to take the fort or die."[26] Cutts gave the orders to the officers:

..to throw in their grenades and attack the fort sword in hand. This they did, charging and following the enemy so close that they had not time to break down the bridge though it was hotly disputed by fire and push of pike, specially by the enemy's grenadiers from the flank of one of their bastions. But the bravery of the English grenadiers surmounted all difficulties, by following the example of their officers and some brave English and other volunteers of distinction such as

[24] Maria Kroll, *Sophie, Electress of Hanover,* (London, 1973) p.218

[25] Forester op.cit. p.86

[26] Robert Parker, *Memoirs of the Most Remarkable Military Transactions,* (London, 1747) p.81

Prince Ernest Augustus....Some of them attacked the bridge, others climbed up the ramparts after having thrown in their grenades and forced their way into the fort. ...The enemy however continued to make a vigorous defence until the English poured in so fast upon them that they were no longer able to resist, which as soon as the Lord Cutts perceived, he checked the fury of the soldiers and put a stop to the slaughter.[27]

Prince Ernest in particular was singled out for behaving "with a great deal of gallantry."

From Venlo, they moved on to Liège which they also took following another bloody assault. Captain Parker wrote:

The attack was made about twelve o'clock and in less than an hour we carried it sword in hand with a very inconsiderable loss on our side. Our men gave no quarter for some time so that the greater part of the garrison was cut to pieces. They in the charter house being eyewitnesses to the fate of the Citadel surrendered next day.[28]

Marlborough wrote to George on 2nd November "I cannot sufficiently praise the conduct of Duke Ernest Augustus who has never failed to distinguish himself by exposing himself to dangers which are even beyond what we could wish." [29] Ernest had requested the right to lead the assault which Marlborough had been pleased to grant.

Following the campaign, the troops went into winter quarters. The higher ranking officers, including Ernest and Marlborough, travelled by yacht to the Hague. A party of hussars escorted them down the Maese but during bad weather one night, they became separated which left Marlborough and his men unprotected. The yacht moored near Venlo where the officers - who were unaware of the fact that the hussars had got lost - dined and went to bed. To their surprise, they were roughly woken by a party of Frenchmen who announced they were taking them prisoner. Fortunately for Ernest, the French did not recognise Marlborough and so they were able to bribe them in order to obtain free passage. As a result, they reached The Hague safely the next day from where Ernest was able to

---

[27] M. Dumont, *The Military History of HSH Prince Eugene of Savoy* translated by Paul Chamberlen (London, 1736) p.56

[28] Parker op.cit. p.88

[29] George Murray (ed.), *Letters and Dispatches of John Churchill* vol.1 (London, 1845) p.53

return home to Hanover. [30]

Late in July 1703, Ernest's brother Christian was shot through the head whilst crossing a river, and drowned, the third of Sophia's sons to die whilst on active service. A letter from Ernest dated 9th August notes that the camp in which he was staying was far less dangerous: "At least I am well assured of keeping my own life because everything is so slow here."[31] This was probably as well for in his next letter he reported that although they had cannons, they lacked powder, bullets and spades. [32] Notwithstanding that, by the end of the month, Ernest was involved in the attack on Fort Joseph describing the impact of the artillery and bombs as having a similar effect as it had on the citadel of Liège. Ernest's men came under heavy fire from the French muskets but they continued moving forward until the enemy surrendered.[33] The campaign that summer ended at Limburg which fell in September. Ernest had played a full part in the campaign, serving on Marlborough's war council and advising on military tactics.

Although we know that Ernest was a keen letter writer, it is only his letters to a fellow army officer, Johann Wendt, which have survived in any volume. Published in 1902, they cover the period from 1703 to 1726, although there are many years without any correspondence at all.[34] It is unknown when they met, though they fought together at Liège where Johann was shot through the arm.[35] However, he was from a long established family with links to Osnabrück and Hanover so it is entirely possible they were childhood friends. Johann had married in the spring of 1703 the daughter of Ernest's tutor, Major-General von Busch. His brother in law would subsequently marry the niece of George's mistress.[36] His own brother served Liselotte. He was, therefore, very well connected and Ernest's letters to him discuss members of the royal family with an air of familiarity which suggests that Johann knew them all. At this period, wars were fought from spring to autumn with armies generally retreating home for the winter and Johann clearly spent his winters with his wife and family in Hanover around the court. Judging by the letters – and we only have Ernest's to him and not those Johann sent – the men shared a love of music, good food, and horses, as well as their army experience.

---

[30] Parker op.cit. p.89

[31] Kielmansegg op.cit. p. 42

[32] ibid. p.44

[33] ibid. pp.47-48

[34] There are 11 letters for 1703, 20 for 1707, 44 for 1708, 18 for 1709, 26 for 1711, 31 for 1712, 22 for 1713, 1 for 1716, 1 for 1717, 2 for 1719 and 1 in 1726. There are no letters for 1704-1706, 1710, 1714-1715, 1718, 1720-25.

[35] Kielmansegg op.cit. pp.10, 20

[36] Ernst von Busch married Anna von Schulenburg, niece of Melusine, in 1708

Some later historians have seen in the letters evidence of a homosexual relationship but this seems unlikely. Writers of the day were inclined to express feelings of affection more openly than would be usual today and there are many references to people embracing one another at the Hanoverian court which consciously adopted the French styles.[37] Ernest's closing line on almost all letters saying that he looked forward to seeing him again and giving him a hug, was not therefore in any way unusual. It is true that he joked to Johann in April 1708 that after the war they might retire to a village and keep chickens so they could have fresh eggs for breakfast every day but nobody seriously expected a prince to do that and Johann would not have interpreted it as a literal proposal.[38] Ernest's letters are actually full of descriptions of ladies he has met or sought to meet. He did not marry because as the youngest son, he lacked resources. He did not get a home of his own until he was forty-one. Prior to that he was either in army camp or living with his family. In fact, of Sophia's six sons who survived to adulthood, only George did get married. His family, who evidently knew Ernest better than people writing three centuries later, simply saw him as somewhat shy and a bit of an idealist. His cousin Liselotte noted he was still a virgin at thirty-six and commented that he was the only man she knew who seemed to have no serious romantic interest in either sex, preferring instead to keep to his room with his books and music.[39] Perhaps her own cynicism about love had spread to him when he was in her care. Liselotte had said: "Generally when one marries for love, hate follows after a short time spent in each other's company"[40] and "among people of quality I do not know a single instance of reciprocal affection and fidelity."[41]

It is unknown what Ernest did in the years 1704 to 1706. He was almost certainly with the Hanoverians at the Battle of Blenheim and Marlborough visited Hanover not long after this for talks. However, by August 1707, he was describing himself as a "retired officer."[42] At this stage, he was only thirty-two and his country's troops were still very active in the War of the

---

[37] It is important to note that the verb "embrasser" which Ernest uses to end many of his letters to Johann which is today generally interpreted as to kiss, in this period merely meant to greet with a hug or put an arm about the shoulders. For a more detailed discussion on literary styles at this time see Ophelia Field, 'Queen Anne's Ladies' in *Gay and Lesbian Review* (May 2004). A visitor to Hanover in 1684 commented on how French it seemed, see Melville op.cit. p. 118. The open French style of greeting was commented upon by the exiled Queen Mary when she arrived at Louis XIV's court when she asked her husband if he wished her to adopt it in order to seem polite or to maintain the more reserved English style, see Mary Hopkirk, *Queen over the Water*, (London, 1953) p.166

[38] Kielmansegg op.cit. p.137

[39] ibid. p.9, 17

[40] Elizabeth of Orleans, *Life and letters of Charlotte Elizabeth*, (London 1889) p.206

[41] Hopkirk op.cit. p.168

[42] Kielmansegg op.cit. p.89

Spanish Succession. Since there is no known family reason to have compelled his return home, it may be conjectured that he had been wounded or taken ill. He was certainly in Hanover at the start of 1705 for the visit of his sister Figuelotte who was now Queen of Prussia. On the day of her arrival, she felt rather tired and unwell but found that a ball had been arranged in her honour. Her mother Sophia was too ill to attend so Figuelotte decided she must make the effort for the sake of the guests. The next day she felt worse and she took to her bed with a raging fever and abscess of the throat. She suffered for a full week. Ernest was in almost constant attendance doing all he could to comfort and to cheer her. In the early hours of the 1st February, the pastor was summoned as Figuelotte prepared for death. George visited her first and then Ernest. Her last words were to Ernest whose hand she held as she died, "Dear brother, I am suffocated."[43] Some years later, George's personal servant Mahomed, noted that after Figuelotte's death, George took to his room and refused to eat or sleep for five days. George just kept pacing up and down the room, crying and kicking the walls until his shoes fell apart. Mahomed went and found Ernest who immediately went in and took George in his arms and calmed him down and put him to bed.[44]

That same year saw Ernest become a British subject. Queen Anne's only child to survive infancy had died in 1700 which meant that Sophia was now heir to the throne. The British Parliament passed the *Act for the Naturalisation of the Most Excellent Princess Sophia, Electress and Duchess Dowager of Hanover and the Issue of her Body* late in 1705. This affected her two surviving Protestant sons, George and Ernest, who consequently took their place in the order of succession. It is unlikely that the subject excited Ernest greatly. His brother had a son and was likely to have grandchildren soon so the prospect of Ernest ever becoming king was slim. Nonetheless, with both George and his son still active in the war, it was not impossible. George came close to being killed at Oudenaarde in 1708. The prospect of succession meant an increasing stream of English visitors to Hanover. Having been much better than his brother at languages, Ernest found himself often having to entertain the various ambassadors. In his letters he expressed his apprehensions about this. It had been some time since he had needed to speak English regularly and he had forgotten some of it. Protocol meant that the visitors could not speak first and he confessed to finding it difficult to always maintain the flow of conversation himself. The international language of diplomacy was French but he found that a number of the English spoke that so badly that he was left wondering what they

---

[43] Atkinson op.cit. p.98

[44] Mary Cowper, *Diary of Mary Countess Cowper 1714-1720*, (London, 1844) p.150. Mahomed was one of two Turkish servants which George I employed. He brought them to England and they appear in the mural over the grand staircase at Kensington Palace.

meant just as they failed to understand him, however slowly he spoke.[45]

In the autumn of 1707, Ernest went to Verona, Vicenza and Venice. He particularly enjoyed Verona and commented that he had more fun in three days there than eight in Venice. He thought the women were more beautiful and far more interesting company than any of the men who seemed to him to be very dull conversationalists. Ernest seems to have been rather shy when it came to women. One lady pursued him into his rooms with clearly more than conversation on her mind and he reported that he "nobly resisted" the temptation by departing and leaving his servant to eject her. On another occasion, he found himself deeply attracted to a lady only to discover she was married to someone he knew. Fortunately, he made this discovery before things went too far. In another case, he persuaded someone to bring a woman he liked to a church so they could meet but after waiting some time, he gave up hope and left – only to find her in the box next to his at the opera the next evening. He was then able to speak with her but he found that despite her good looks, she was rather silly and incapable of intelligent conversation so he declined to pursue her further.[46]

He returned to Venice again in the winter of 1709 where he attended the premiere of the opera *Agrippina*. This was a performance which attracted rave reviews and had an unprecedented run. Mainwaring described the scene:

> The audience was so enchanted with the performance that a stranger who should have seen the manner in which they were affected would have imagined they had all been distracted. The theatre at almost every pause resounded with shouts and acclamations of "Long live the dear Saxon!" They were thunderstruck with the grandeur and sublimity of his style for never had they known till then all the powers of harmony and modulation so closed arranged and so forcibly combined.[47]

Ernest was so impressed with the young composer that he invited him back to Hanover. Handel took up the post of Kapellmeister in 1710. Sophia wrote that he "plays marvellously on the harpsichord."[48] It was the start of a

---

[45] Kielmansegg op.cit. p.285. Ernest's letters to Johann are in French just as George I's letters to his daughters were in French. Most of the diplomatic communications of the period kept at the National Archives are also in French.

[46] Kielmansegg op.cit. pp.95-102.

[47] John Mainwaring, *Memoirs of the life of the Late George Frederic Handel*, (London, 1760) pp.52-53

[48] Donald Burrows, *Handel*, (Oxford 1994) p.38

long career between Handel and the royal family.[49]

In October 1711, Peter the Great's son Alexei married Ernest's third cousin once removed, Charlotte of Brunswick-Wolfenbutel in Torgau. It was a strange wedding conducted in a mixture of Russian and Latin in a room that had been darkened by having all the windows covered over, then illuminated by hundreds of candles laid out in front of mirrors. The Tsar commented in a letter afterwards that the highlight of the event had been the watermelon which Prince Menshikov had sent and which took pride of place on the table attracting considerable attention from those present who had not seen one before.[50] Ernest did not mention the fruit in his letters. He was more astonished by the fact that the Tsarevich had blown his nose on the curtains.[51] His mother philosophically commented that if the King of France were to do that it would become the height of fashion.[52]

The next few years were spent in a continued round of events such as hunting, theatre trips and balls. These were punctuated by reviewing military operations elsewhere in the world, speculation on the proximity of the plague, and watching George's children and then grandchildren growing up. Occasionally, there was the excitement of a new lady appearing at court, generally followed by the disappointment that she was neither educated or virtuous. Otherwise, Ernest was left reading or playing backgammon. A plan to send him to England in preparation for the Hanoverian succession was dropped after Queen Anne let it be known that she did not want any representatives of her successor at her court for fear this would encourage division.[53] It would appear that not only did he find life rather dull, but Johann also said this, for Ernest comments in one letter that he is trying harder to make his letters interesting even though very little has happened.[54] An example of this appears in 1711 where the highlight of the summer turned out to be a dinner party which Ernest attended with his brother George at the home of Johann's mother-in-law. Ernest wrote:

A big bat was disturbing the company. Having recently read the wonderful Don Quixote with all the tales of his valour, I decided to use this terrible danger to my advantage. I asked my page for a sword

---

[49] Ernest may have been told of Handel's talent by his sister for Handel had performed for the Prussian court in 1698 when he was just thirteen.

[50] Eugene Schuyler, *Peter the Great* vol 2 (London, 1884) p.267

[51] Kielmansegg op.cit. p.284

[52] Kroll op.cit. p.280

[53] James MacPherson, *Original Papers containing the Secret History of Great Britain*, (London, 1775) vol. 2 p.498. Queen Anne's husband, George of Denmark, was first cousin to George and Ernest being the son of their father Ernst's sister.

[54] Kielmansegg op.cit. p.285

and, after the bat had made several laps around my head, I cut at her and made her fall to my feet.[55]

In 1714, two events happened which changed Ernest's life. In June, his mother died quite suddenly having collapsed whilst walking in the gardens of Herrenhausen. She was eighty-three. Six weeks later, Queen Anne died in England and his brother George became King. George departed for England in September taking his son with him. Ernest was left to rule Hanover as head of the regency council. The only other member of the royal family left was George's grandson, the seven year old Frederick. For a man who had spent almost his entire life with his mother and brother, these changes must have been extremely traumatic.

Just over a year later in December 1715, the Bishop of Osnabrück died. Under the 1648 Peace of Westphalia, this was a secular lordship which was ruled alternately by Catholics and Protestants. On 2nd March 1716, Ernest was elected Prince-Bishop. Finally, aged forty-one, he was to have a home of his own and a land to rule.[56] He packed his bags to move with some excitement. His life once more had a purpose.

Sadly for historians, Ernest's letters to Johann dwindled after he went to Osnabrück. He wrote to him soon after he arrived about the welcome he had received. Previous rulers had refused to live in the principality and only exploited it for its income. He described walking around the city ramparts and having the children run up to show him the sights. He was not impressed by his new residence describing it as being less attractive than he remembered and commenting that the gardens only contained cabbages and asparagus which made taking guests for an evening stroll rather embarrassing. He was especially upset that the lack of offices meant that he had to share the residence with all manner of officials and he had nowhere to store his papers. As a compensation though, he had met a number of interesting ladies, including one whom he felt had all the best qualities in the world. He confided that he had met with her on several occasions and was hopeful of spending more time with her.[57] For reasons unknown, nothing came of that relationship.

That same month, Ernest was created Duke of York, the only occasion on which a reigning monarch has given the title to his brother. The official announcement read:

---

[55] ibid. p.249

[56] The population was around 180,000.

[57] Kielmansegg op.cit. ibid. p. 341

His Majesty has been pleased to create His Royal Highness Prince Ernest Augustus, Duke of Brunswick-Lüneburg and Bishop of Osnabrück, His Majesty's brother, Duke of York and of Albany in Great Britain and Earl of Ulster in Ireland. [58]

Three days later came the news that Ernest and his great-nephew Frederick were elected as Knights of the Most Noble Order of the Garter. Unusually, the investment took place in Germany. The plan was that George would carry out the ceremony himself during his visit to Hanover that summer but there was a delay in getting the Herald out there. Another idea was for Ernest to come back to England with George and it was reported that apartments were being made ready for him at Kensington Palace. In the end however, Ernest remained in Germany and the investiture took place in Hanover just before Christmas, by which time the King was back in England.[59]

There was considerable speculation at the time about why George had chosen to bestow these honours on Ernest. The King had generally been very sparing in giving honours to his German relations or staff. Two main theories existed. Fanny Oglethorpe wrote to the Duke of Mar saying that George had quarrelled very badly with his son and had threatened to leave Ernest "successor to his new begotten throne and of the kingdom."[60] Such rumours had existed before. Liselotte had suggested in 1714 that the English would prefer Ernest as heir to the throne because George's son was quite mad.[61] What is clear is that George wanted to ensure that should anything happen to his own family, Ernest would be ready to take over as King or Regent because he insisted that regular reports on British affairs, parliamentary debates, new defence projects, state expenditure, foreign policy and such like be copied to his brother in Osnabrück. This practice continued into the reign of his son too.[62]

The other theory was that George wanted to increase Ernest's status so that he could use him as a marriage pawn. Great Britain was particularly concerned to maintain good terms with the Low Countries. Marie-Louise of

---

[58] *Daily Courant*, 2nd July 1716. It was only in England that Ernest was called His Royal Highness. In Hanover, he was His Serene Highness.

[59] *Weekly Journal* 6th October 1716, *Weekly Packet* 22nd December 1716, *London Gazette* 25th December 1716.

[60] Historical Manuscripts Commission, *Calendar of the Stuart Papers belonging to His Majesty the King: Preserved at Windsor Castle* vol 2 (HMSO 1905) p.490

[61] *Briefe der Prinzessin Elisabeth Charlotte von Orleans* op.cit p.180. The letter probably reflects Liselotte's dislike of George's wife more than British public opinion.

[62] Jeremy Black, *Parliament and Foreign Policy in the Eighteenth Century*, (Cambridge 2004) p.53. The newsletters are kept in the archives at Osnabrück.

Hesse-Kassel, the twenty-eight year old widow of John of Orange, was ruling on behalf of her infant son and the British mounted a strong campaign through the summer and autumn in order to persuade her to marry Ernest. The offer was politely refused. The Flemings said they appreciated the honour which was being shown them and had nothing against the prospective groom, but they believed they could manage their own affairs. They would be happy to remain good neighbours.[63]

Ernest was probably not too disappointed by this. He had set about improving Osnabrück with true reforming zeal. In his first year, he ordered a review of the pay of court officials whose income was still being paid largely in things such as chickens, pigs, wood or barley. He instituted a weekly market. He issued regulations on all sorts of subjects such as improving building safety by making houses less prone to fire, controlling the supply of arms, and banning the sale of "quack" medicines. He sought restrictions on the sale of alcohol and on begging. Over the next few years, he had new public offices built, new churches and bridges. He authorised the standardisation of weights and measures and tried to improve public order by introducing a new and corruption free police force. He aimed to improve the fairness of taxation and land registration and to reform the judiciary, though vested interests opposed some of these plans, particularly the Roman Catholic clergy who had previously sat in judgment on many worldly cases. He abolished legal fees so that the poor could obtain justice more easily and he set a maximum for interest payments of five per cent. He was deeply concerned about the poor and gave unceasingly to charity and maintained an open kitchen so that the hungry might be fed. He knew, however, that this was not a permanent solution and so he determined to create industry so that people could work their way out of poverty and develop pride in themselves. He had mulberry trees planted to develop a silk industry. He had mines at Hüggel brought back into operation. He founded a porcelain factory in Osnabrück and a glass factory in Borgloh. The porcelain factory became known for making large blue and white flower pots in the Delft style with handles in the form of masks.[64] He encouraged cottage industries such as cloth manufacture. He employed Johann Märcker to build four waterworks to ensure the people had clean water and to search for a salt spring. The salt works at Rothenfelde opened in 1725 and offered salt to the inhabitants at a fixed low price. He was frankly indefatigable and far ahead of his time in his ideas.

Moreover, since the income of the bishopric was insufficient for all his works, many of these activities – including all the industrial works - were

---

[63] *Stuart Papers* op.cit. vol 2. p.334, 345, 451, 503
[64] Emil Hannover, *Pottery and Porcelain*, vol.1 (London, 1925) p.396

funded from his own pocket. His mother had once commended Ernest for his ability to spend his money wisely and for his strict sense of honour which saw him always paying his bills, something quite unusual amongst princes of the time. His generosity to those less fortunate was noted and admired by those about him.[65] Now with a larger income plus a small annuity from England which went with being Duke of York, Ernest was genuinely able to do good. It would appear that having concluded he was not to be blessed with children himself, Ernest determined to devote his life to his people. Accounts of him at this time, and comments from his own letters, show that his days began with a time of reflection and Bible reading in his room followed by prayers for his household in the chapel. After a meal, he then spent his day going through papers and giving audiences. After his evening meal, he went for a walk. Even his enemies had to admit their respect for his dedication.

He continued to have the opportunity to see George who visited Hanover regularly throughout his reign. On such trips, the brothers would go hunting or to the theatre or share their love of music, books and gardens. On 20th June 1727 as he was en route to Osnabrück, George had a stroke.[66] He was blooded and given oil of cinnamon. Messengers were sent to the local doctor who unfortunately was away from home. George was still able to speak and he indicated that he wished to be taken to Osnabrück. He arrived just after ten o'clock at night when he was sufficiently conscious to doff his hat in recognition. Ernest's staff assisted in taking him upstairs where he was blooded again. That and other remedies were tried but to no avail. George fell into a coma. Ernest remained at his side desperately trying to think of something he could do. Sadly, there was nothing. Just before one in the morning, George died in Ernest's arms. After a few minutes alone, Ernest solemnly left the room and ordered that the body be taken to the vault. He directed that the royal apartments be sealed to prevent any disturbance of papers and sent a message to his nephew advising him that he was now king.[67]

Just over a year later in August 1728, Ernest himself was taken seriously ill with a fever. After a couple of days, he made his will but later that same evening remembered two of his staff to whom he wished to make special bequests. He asked his servant to be sure to remind him the next day but he died in the early hours. His last words were "Oh my God."[68] At

---

[65] Holland vol.2 op.cit. p.463-464

[66] SP35/64/143

[67] Wilhelm Havemann, *Geschichte der Lande Braunschwig und Lüneburg* (Göttingen 1857) p.513

[68] C. Stüve, 'Mittheilungen aus der Geschichte Ernst August's II. Aus Möser's Papieren' in *Osnabrücker Mitteilungen* - volume 1 (1848) p.24

the time of his death aged fifty-five, his new palace at Augustusburg was incomplete. His successor was to completely change the plans and turn it into the great baroque palace that remains today. He left 100,000 silver thaler (around £2.3 million in today's money) of which a quarter went to the poor of Osnabrück, another share was used to provide lifetime annuities to each of his servants, and the remainder was shared equally between his two nephews, George II of England and Frederick I of Prussia. Ernest was buried in the family vault in the Leineschloss castle alongside his brother George. Following damage to the property in the second world war, his remains were moved to a crypt in Herrenhausen in 1957.

Accounts of Ernest by people who met him were always favourable. One report in 1716 read:

> I have since been presented to the Duke of York who in his person somewhat resembles the King, though he appears much younger. He is a man of good sense improved with a great deal of learning, is of a steady even temper and great affability and deservedly enjoys the universal esteem of all who have the honour to know him.[69]

John Toland described him in 1705 as "a prince of a mild temper with very commendable dispositions."[70] In the same year, Liselotte wrote: "Duke Ernest Augustus is very popular everywhere and people feel more for him than for his brother the Elector."[71]

Later historians have been just as positive. One described him as being "of spotless character,, benevolent, active, insightful, he wanted to be the father of his people....The purest piety inspired his actions and every act was directed at the welfare of his subjects...Never did a prince possess a better heart or rule with more wisdom or justice."[72] Judging by his obituary, his contemporaries were just as appreciative: "his clemency, beneficent nature, charity and other moral and Christian virtues made him equally beloved by his Roman Catholic as well as Protestant subjects, so that he was universally lamented."[73]

As Duke of York, Ernest made no contribution whatsoever to British life though he had fought bravely in the allied army. However, his achievements as a ruler in his own dominions demonstrate a man who was deeply

---

[69] *Weekly Journal*, 6th October 1716

[70] John Toland, *An Account of the Courts of Prussia and Hannover*, (London, 1714) p.77

[71] Wolfgang Menzel, *Briefe der Prinzessin Elisabeth Charlotte von Orleans* (Stuttgart 1843) p.88

[72] Stüve op.cit p.1,8

[73] *The Historical Register*, vol XIII 1728 p.43

committed to the welfare of his people. He had once described himself as "always anxious for the happiness of others."[74] His belief that a prince should proactively seek to do good and promote industry, was new. The Hanoverians may not have been entirely popular when they arrived in England but they brought with them a sense of public service and private morality which was wholly different to the Stuarts. As one commentator put it: "The German Protestant was a cheaper and better and kinder king than the Catholic Stuart in whose chair he sat and so far loyal to England that he let England govern itself."[75] Had Ernest ever had to move to England, it is certain that he would have made his mark on the country in a very positive way.

---

[74] Kielmansegg op.cit. p.89
[75] *The Cornhill Magazine* July 1860 p.9

Edward

1739-1767

Duke of York 1760-1767

His affability, good nature, humanity and generosity endeared him to all ranks of people.[1]

On Wednesday 14th March 1739, around four o'clock in the afternoon, Augusta, Princess of Wales, gave birth to her third child at Norfolk House in St James' Square, London. The newspapers reported that all had gone well though it seems likely that the child was premature as his brother and sister had been. It had been just nine months and ten days since Prince George had been born. The new baby was named Edward Augustus and baptised by the Bishop of Oxford on the 11th April. His godparents were the King of Prussia (uncle to Frederick, Prince of Wales), the Duke of Brunswick Wolfenbuttel and the Duchess of Saxe Weissenfels (his mother's sister).[2]

The choice of names was significant. Augustus was traditional within the family being the middle name of George II, the child's grandfather, and also of Frederick's great-uncle with whom he had lived in Germany. Edward was unusual because there had been no prince of that name since the reign of Henry VIII two hundred years before. It was chosen because it appeared a

---

[1] *Annual Register* (London, 1767) p.210
[2] *London Evening Post*, 12th April 1739

very English name and the Prince of Wales wanted to demonstrate that his family were going to be British. Both George I and George II had been German by birth and they remained firmly attached to their homeland. The Prince of Wales may have grown up in Hanover but he knew that his future was going to be as King of Great Britain and his choice of names was a deliberate move to assure the public that his first loyalty would be to them.

Of Edward's early life, relatively little is known. Despite his parents' marriage being arranged, it seems to have been very successful with Frederick doting on his wife who was twelve years his junior. Frederick was a devoted father and enjoyed nothing more than playing with his children. He liked taking them out, taught them to play cricket, and shared his love of music with them. Frederick played the cello which was the instrument that Edward would later play. He was a patron of Handel who played for the family on a number of occasions. Frederick was a keen joker and on one occasion when Handel had been invited to perform at the house, he arranged for the instruments in the orchestra to have some tuning issues. Handel arrived and seated himself at the organ ready for the recital. The Prince of Wales and his family entered the room and took their seats. Handel rose and bowed then gave the signal to start. The musicians duly began to play but the result was a complete cacophony of sound. Handel was furious and leapt down from the organ, angrily overturning a double bass as he strode toward the drums. He then picked up a kettle drum and threw it at the leader of the orchestra, knocking his wig off. As the command performance seemed destined to descend into a brawl, the Prince of Wales stepped into the fray to try to calm Handel down and to assure him it had just been a joke.[3]

The Prince of Wales was also keen on amateur theatricals and wrote and helped produce little plays with his children. As they grew older, they started to perform in other works such as the Latin dramas of Terence. On 4th January 1749 when Edward was just nine, the royal children gave their first performance to those outside the family.[4] The play chosen was Joseph Addison's *Cato* in which Prince George played Portius and Prince Edward played Juba, the heroic and virtuous prince. Edward's role involved him winning a sword fight after declaring: "Better to die ten thousand deaths than wound my honour."[5] It is unlikely that a play involving suicide and fantasies of rape would be considered suitable for children today but at the time it was thought to be a highly moral play because it upheld the virtues of liberty against the evils of absolutism. It included lines such as:

---

[3] John Galt, *George III: His Court and Family* (1821) p.129
[4] ibid pp116-118
[5] Act 1 scene 4

A day, an hour, of virtuous liberty
Is worth a whole eternity in bondage [6]

and,

what pity is it that we can die but once to serve our country[7]

ending with..

let fierce contending nations know
what dire effects from civil discord flow [8]

The lesson for the princes was clear. It was ironic that the same play would one day be considered influential in the American fight for independence which took place during George's reign. For the royal performance a special epilogue was written where Edward promised to be faithful to his brother George as Juba had been to Cato, declaring:

In England born, my inclination
Like yours is wedded to the nation
Indeed I wish to serve this land
It is my father's strict command
and none he ever gave will be
more cheerfully obeyed by me. [9]

Frederick wrote to his children afterwards saying that he was "the proudest father."

The education of the princes was formal and centred around the skills which were thought necessary for them. They learnt French and German and Latin. They learnt to recite speeches as training for the memory and to develop their public speaking skills. In this they were instructed by James Quin, one of the finest actors of his day. They learnt to dance so they would be at home in society. Edward seems to have found all this much easier than George though he was rebuked by his teachers on occasion for lack of attention. One tutor said his Latin was excellent but he should spend more time on his German, a prospect Edward dismissed saying: "German

---

[6] Act 2 scene 1

[7] Act 4 Scene 4

[8] Act 5 scene 4

[9] Averyl Edwards, *Frederick Louis, Prince of Wales* (London, 1947) p.163

grammar! Why any dull child can learn that."[10] The princes were taught fencing and horsemanship by Domenico Angelo, thought to be the finest exponent of those skills in Europe at the time.[11] Their days were tightly structured to a strict timetable with lessons from eight in the morning to eight at night. In the winter they lived at Leicester House in Leicester Square, the home to which their parents had moved late in 1742, and the summers were spent at Cliveden or Kew.

In March 1751, the domestic idyll was suddenly brought to an end by the death of the Prince of Wales aged forty-four. As Dr Newton observed at the Prince's funeral:

> He was the most indulgent of parents...Such a calamity in any private family would be very affecting but it must needs affect us more sensibly as they are the children of the public and the hopes of the rising generation.[12]

For Edward, then a week past his twelfth birthday, it must have been especially difficult. He had always been the favourite son. Now, the brother with whom he had been brought up, was heir to the throne and that meant changes in lifestyle and responsibilities.

Just two months after the death, George was given his own establishment at Saville House.[13] It was only next door to Leicester House but it was a sign of separation. Two weeks later, Edward was appointed Colonel of the Royal Regiment of Horse Guards, something of which his father would have approved.[14] At the end of the year, George Knapton painted a portrait of the Princess Dowager in her widow's veil sitting beside a portrait of Frederick and with all her children about her, the new born baby Caroline on her lap. In that painting, George is showing a map of the fortifications at Portsmouth to Edward, a reminder of the life of service that he was to lead. To further encourage the two elder princes in what was

---

[10] Horace Walpole letter to George Montagu, 26th May 1748. In his *Memoirs of the Reign of King George the Second*, Walpole noted that Prince George was unable to read English at the age of eleven, see volume 1 p.80

[11] Henry Angelo, *Reminiscences of Henry Angelo with memoirs of his late Father* (London, 1830) p.9

[12] Galt op.cit. p.136

[13] *Whitehall Evening Post*, 23rd May 1751

[14] *London Evening Post*, 6th June 1751. Lord Egmont recorded a conversation which he had with Prince Frederick on 4th October 1750 where Frederick had said that he intended Edward to be given command of the senior guard regiment when he became king in order that he might rest assured of the loyalty of those soldiers closest to him. See Aubrey Newman 'Leicester House Politics' in *Camden Miscellany* (Fourth Series, 1969) p175

expected, they began regular visits to the King, their grandfather, a man they really did not know due to the ill blood which had existed between him and their father. It may be presumed that Edward grew to quite like the old man because he later told Bishop Newton that he wished someone would write a biography of George II because he would have found that interesting, unlike the volumes he had been given on ancient and medieval history.[15]

Edward's relationship with his mother was more difficult. Following Frederick's death, the Princess Dowager had grown very close to Lord Bute and there were widespread rumours that the relationship was not simply platonic. Whether that was the case – and it seems unlikely – Edward clearly resented the way he felt Bute was being allowed to take over his father's role. He became increasingly critical of Bute and made jokes about the "Scottish lord." When his mother asked him one day why he was so quiet, he calmly said: "I was thinking what I should feel if I had a son as unhappy as you make me." [16] It caused a rift in his relationship with George too because George was very docile and seemed almost as convinced of Lord Bute's perfections as his mother. The Princess Dowager, whose policy was to isolate George from everyone except herself and Bute, noted that Edward was upset at what he regarded as George's "want of spirit" in not fighting against this subjection.[17] She admitted that the only person that George seemed to care about was Edward which suggests there may have been some jealousy on her part.[18] Walpole was later to say of George that had she been able, the Princess would have "chained up his body as she fettered his mind."[19]

On the day before his thirteenth birthday, Edward was elected a Knight of the Most Noble Order of the Garter at St James' Palace. Edward was brought to where the King sat enthroned and knelt as the King knighted him with the sword of state. His brother George then fastened upon his left leg the garter and across his shoulder the ribbon and George.[20] Although Edward's life remained away from the public eye, it was shortly after this

---

[15] John Watkins, *Memoirs of Her Most Excellent Majesty, Sophia-Charlotte, Queen of Great Britain* (London, 1819) p.209

[16] Lewis Melville, *Farmer George* (London, 1907) p.52

[17] Henry Wyndham (ed.), *The Diary of the Late George Bubb Dodington* (London, 1809) p.228. Bubb Dodington had been one of Frederick's closest advisers and remained a friend of Edward's. The conversation with the Princess Dowager took place on 11th December 1755.

[18] John Carswell and Lewis Dralle (ed.) *The Political Journal of George Bubb Dodington*, (Oxford 1965) pp.178-179. Princess Augusta's comments were recorded in his diary entry for 13th October 1752.

[19] Horace Walpole, *Memoirs of the Reign of King George the Third*, vol 1 (London, 1845) p.63. Walpole adds that Edward was not "equally tractable" which accounted for the difficulties.

[20] *London Gazette*, 14th March 1752

that a song appeared called Prince Edward's Jig which was to feature in a number of books of country dances across the period making his name more familiar to the people.

Edward and George continued to have lessons together. One courtier recorded a conversation which took place one evening whilst the Princess was sitting with her sons supervising their homework. Edward was teasing his brother about how he would have to marry and be faithful when he grew up because he would be king, whereas he planned to just have a mistress or two. George urged his brother to be quiet or they would be in trouble. The Princess looked up and told them to get on with their studies and, in order to change the subject, demanded an explanation of the difference between a noun and a pronoun. Edward cheerfully replied: "a pronoun is to a noun what a mistress is to a wife, a substitute and a representative!"[21]

Edward's interest in the opposite sex began early and sometimes got him into trouble. One summer when he was fifteen, he fell for one of the milkmaids at Kew. She did her best to discourage him but he was most ardent in his suit. Eventually, she agreed to meet him in the dairy that night. Full of excitement, Edward made his way outside when it was dark and hid in the dairy. A little while later he heard the maid approaching. She called out to him and he came toward the door. Laughing, she quickly turned the key and ran off. Edward was found still locked inside the next morning. When his mother demanded an explanation, he said he was just keen on rural studies and wanted to learn how to churn![22]

The same source told of another occasion when Edward got himself into trouble and his mother ordered him to his room without dinner and forbade any of the family or staff from opening the doors to him. Later that night, after supper, the Princess Dowager and her children passed from the dining room into the music room where they found Edward sitting happily with the instruments. In a fury, she demanded to know who had let him out. Edward smiled and said that nobody had disobeyed her. He had simply climbed out of his bedroom window, gone to get the lamp lighter's ladder, and moved it round so he could climb in through the window of the music room. Adopting his most innocent expression, he asked if she would forgive him. Faced with the cheers and laughter of the other children, the Princess had no choice.

In 1756, when George turned eighteen, the King offered him a suite of

---

[21] Walpole, *Memoirs of the Reign of King George the Third,* vol 1 p.111

[22] John Watkins, *A Biographical memoir of his late royal highness Frederick Duke of York* (London, 1827) p.24

apartments at Kensington Palace and offered to allow Edward to move with him, but George rejected the offer and chose to stay at Saville House.[23] Edward was given his own household staff in November 1756[24] and this signalled the launch of Edward into society. Walpole soon joked that he was being seen so often with Lady Essex that he wondered if he should call her Princess Edward.[25] The Princess Dowager was appalled and told Edward to remember he was a prince and not act in so common a manner, but his grandfather told him cheerfully to ignore that instruction and go out and enjoy himself, which he did.[26]

His days of merriment ended sharply in the summer of 1758 when it was announced that Edward was to join the Royal Navy. At the time, England was involved in the Seven Years' War and the Fleet were off to France where they were to harry the French coast and to generally keep the French army busy, a move which it was hoped would prevent them attacking Germany.

Edward arrived in Portsmouth in July where he was placed into the care of Commodore Richard Howe, captain of the Essex. Howe, noted with some surprise that Edward arrived totally unprepared having been sent from home in just the clothes he wore. As a result, Howe had to go out and buy Edward a midshipman's uniform plus all the other things he would need from cutlery to linen.[27] On 27th July, Edward went on board the Essex where he lined up with the other midshipmen to welcome the captains on board. Howe recounted how one sailor watching from the forecastle said to his mate that the new boy was going to be in trouble because he had not taken his hat off when the captains came in. [28]

On 6th August, the fleet anchored off Cherbourg. The goal was to destroy the port and fortifications together with its ships and military supplies. Shells and mortars were launched against the town and the heavy nature of the firing was reported to have disconcerted the French cavalry. Edward got his first chance to see action by going aboard the Pallas and then some of the smaller bomb ketches to see how the actual firing was done.[29]

---

[23] Horace Walpole, *Memoirs of the Reign of King George the Second* (London, 1847) vol 2 p.207

[24] *London Evening Post*, 9th November 1756

[25] Horace Walpole to George Montagu, 27th May 1757. Like most of Edward's female companions over the years, Lady Essex was married. Pregnant with her second child at this time, she died in childbirth in July 1759.

[26] George Jesse, *Memoirs of the Life and Reign of George III* (London, 1902) vol 1 p415

[27] John Barrow, *The Life of Richard, Earl Howe* (London, 1838) p.58

[28] Barrow, op cit. p.59

[29] The fullest accounts of the battle are to be found in the anonymous account written by an

Under cover of the ships firing, the flat bottomed boats were launched and the army started to embark. Over two thousand men were landed safely and they made their way toward the hill. The greatest difficulty was experienced in landing the two cannon. Throughout the process, the French, whose troops were visible along the coast, did not fire a single shot. The next morning the army set off for Querqueville intending to attack Cherbourg from the rear. They met little resistance. Sir John Irwine said the French had behaved "shamefully" in abandoning the town rather than fighting like men. Commodore Howe took its formal surrender on August 8th. The British thereupon began their work of destruction. They blew up the harbour and set fire to the ships that were in it. They demolished the forts and batteries and all the iron cannons which they found. The brass guns were taken on board ready to go home as trophies of victory.[30] The French shells, shot and gunpowder were thrown into the sea. It was noted that Edward went ashore every day and took a great interest in all the various operations.

The behaviour of the British troops was, however, poor. Their own officers criticised the "brutality" and "dissolute" behaviour they showed as they went on a marauding spree. In an attempt to stem the violence, one soldier was hanged. Some French peasants, tired of not having their complaints taken seriously, took the law into their own hands and murdered some soldiers who were pillaging their homes and threatening their women. The British soldiers had uncovered large wine stores in the town and this played its part in bringing about a general collapse of discipline. The senior officers could only wait for the men to sober up. Edward played no part in this debauchery but he was horrified when he saw what the British army had done to the inhabitants. He decided to donate one hundred guineas to a relief fund to help those left homeless and hungry as a result. Back in England, Walpole – who never served in any battle – sneered that this was an "excess" of generosity and queried whether the French should replace their beacons with alms pots so that the soft hearted English could "give a Christmas box to your enemies."[31] Edward's gift was, however, generous and genuine. [32] In celebration of the victory, the English held a ball to which the French noblewomen were invited. Clearly in high spirits Edward announced that he was too young to know how a gentleman in France would behave at

---

officer entitled *A Journal of the Campaign on the Coast of France* (London, 1758), Barrow's *Life of Richard, Earl Howe* and in the *Report on the Manuscripts of Mrs Stopford-Sackville* (HMSO, 1904). The last source was written for Lord George Sackville who was an enemy of Howe and is thus very critical of the whole campaign.

[30] Horace Walpole wrote to Sir Horace Mann on 9th September 1758 to say that the cannons were on display in Hyde Park having been dragged across land from Portsmouth. They were later moved to the Tower of London

[31] ibid.

[32] In early twenty-first century money, it was worth over £18,000. It was about a fortieth of Edward's annual income at the time.

such an event so he would do what he would in England if he was keen to please. He then went around the room kissing each and every lady.[33]

On the 15th and 16th of August, the troops and equipment were embarked ready to sail to England. Edward stayed on shore with the last band of grenadiers and then came aboard with them, steering the boat back to the ship himself. On the 18th, the British departed Cherbourg and they reached Weymouth the next day. Edward went ashore on Sunday so he could go to church. Meantime, the fleet was reprovisioned and set sail again on the 24th August.

Commodore Howe's new plan was to attack St Malo. Whilst a detachment of grenadiers went to destroy vessels in St Brieuc, troops were embarked near to St Malo on 4th September as the ketches bombarded the town. Aside from one small boat overturning and drowning the eight soldiers aboard, the landing went smoothly. The next three days were spent on various reconnaissance missions. Edward went out on several such trips. On one occasion, a French cannon was aimed directly at him and the ball landed at his feet. A sergeant who observed the approaching missile leapt in front of the prince to save his life, a gesture for which Edward thanked him profusely and generously. On another occasion, Edward and Commodore Howe were prevented from returning to the ship by enemy soldiers and they were forced to hide and spend the night sleeping on straw and dirty sacks in an empty hovel.

The general agreement was that St Malo was too well defended for an attack to succeed and that fact, together with the poor weather, meant Howe decided the army would have to embark at St Cas instead. Whilst the fleet sailed round to St Cas on 7th September, the army advanced on foot only to find the woods full of French soldiers and armed peasants. Over a dozen British soldiers were killed. On the 8th September, the British crossed the river, wading waist high through the waters whilst under constant fire from the French. A similar number of casualties resulted. The next day, a battalion of French soldiers attacked the army as it marched and more than thirty were killed. Thirteen soldiers were taken prisoner but one escaped and made it back to the British camp where he described how the French had shot the other prisoners in cold blood. The British learnt that the French had at least three thousand men nearby and at daybreak next morning they heard the French beat to arms. Aware that their retreat was about to be cut off, they had no choice but to try and get to the coast as fast as possible. Forced to try and dodge the enemy, it took the army seven hours to cover three miles.

---

[33] Horace Walpole to Sir Horace Mann, 24th August 1758

On Monday 11th September, the fleet was in position and from six in the morning, the boats were ready to be launched to get the men back on board. At first things went well and the artillery and light horse divisions were embarked. By noon, French troops could be seen along the ridge overlooking the beach. The British began shelling them which frightened the horses but it was an uneven battle. The British had around 1,500 men left ashore and the enemy had an estimated 17,500. Amongst the British on the beach was Edward who literally had to run for his life to reach a boat and row to safety. For an hour, three companies of grenadiers fired into the enemy and their efforts, together with the firing from the fleet, caused significant casualties amongst the French. Then, the British ran out of ammunition. The commanding general urged the men to fix bayonets or take their swords and to engage in hand to hand combat. Shouting "Remember the honour of Old England depends upon us. Let us die or conquer!" he led the way forward only to be shot in the chest and then blown apart by a French cannon ball.

As the beaches descended into total confusion, Howe ordered the fleet to stop firing in case they hit British troops. Hundreds of the grenadiers were killed on the beaches and more drowned as they struggled to reach the boats that were valiantly trying to rescue them. Howe decided that in order to strengthen the resolve of the men, many of whom were understandably terrified, he would get in one of the boats himself and go out to try and rescue some of the men. Edward jumped into the boat with him but Howe ordered him back on board saying that the prince would be a target for the enemy and so put the lives of the other men in danger. Many were saved but over two hundred wounded were left on the beaches where the French either bayoneted them or beat their brains out with their guns. Nearly four hundred men were taken prisoner.[34] Casualties amongst the sailors were described as "very great" as well since many had been killed by the French as they attempted to reach the men on shore. Inevitably, there had been a massive loss of equipment in the retreat too.

By any reckoning, the affair at St Cas was a total disaster and one can only speculate on the effect that watching such a massacre had on the nineteen year old prince. Before the fleet had departed, the Duke of Newcastle had questioned whether George II was sure he wished to risk his grandson's life in a war but the King had said that danger was part of a sailor's life.[35] However, he had not expected Edward to be placed in such a position and his displeasure was quickly felt with all those involved in what

---

[34] A graphic account of the scene was written by an officer who was taken prisoner and published in the *Whitehall Evening Post* in two instalments on the 17th and 19th October 1758.
[35] Barrow op.cit. p.53

was widely seen as a foolhardy enterprise. Walpole wrote: "No shadow of an excuse can be offered for leaving them so exposed with no purpose or possible advantage in the heart of an enemy's country."[36] Although Edward was to continue in the navy, he was never allowed to go into a frontline position again. His requests to join the expedition to Quebec at the start of 1759 were firmly rejected by the King.[37]

Despite the failure of the expedition, Edward returned to a hero's welcome. He was cheered as he marched with the troops through the streets of Portsmouth and became the subject of a popular song:

Tis rumoured the French will soon visit our coast
And pour on this isle an invincible host,
We're prepared and will sing, however proudly they boast
Oh the bold blades of England,
and oh, old England's bold blades

Rise gallant Prince Edward, the god of the main
Invites thee to share in his watery reign,
Then grasp Britain's flag and its honour maintain
Oh the bold blades of England,
and oh, old England's bold blades. [38]

His fame caused him to be invited out. In January 1759, he was guest at the British Museum which was about to be opened to the public for the first time.[39] A week later, he went to see the Microcosm, a combined astronomical clock and organ created by Henry Bridges,[40] and a newly invented horseless carriage designed to carry people at up to six miles an hour along level roads.[41] He also found himself a new lady friend in the Duchess of Richmond[42] though one suspects this was not a very serious relationship. His brother George recounted around this time a conversation which he had with their youngest brother who was then aged nine. The child pointed out a

---

[36] Horace Walpole to Sir Horace Mann, 22nd September 1758

[37] Horace Walpole to Henry Seymour Conway, 19th January 1759

[38] anon. *The Apollo or the Muses' Choice being a Collection of the most celebrated new songs sung at Ranelagh, Vauxhall, Marylebone Gardens* (London, 1759) song 81 pp68-70

[39] *London Evening Post*, 11th January 1759

[40] *Public Advertiser*, 25th January 1759. For a full account of the clock, see, Anon *A Succinct Description of that Elaborate and Matchless Pile of Art called the Microcosm* (Newry 1763)

[41] Patent number GB714 by John Ladd

[42] Horace Walpole to George Montague, 26th April 1759. The Duchess of Richmond was sister in law of Lady Sarah Lennox, soon to be a girlfriend of Prince George

well known courtesan and described her as a woman who sold oranges, adding "not such oranges as you buy. I believe they are a sort that my brother Edward buys."[43] The courtesan in question was Kitty Fisher, a lady whom Edward was reported to have deeply offended. According to Kitty, Edward spent the night with her and departed leaving her a £50 note. Since her fee was a hundred guineas a time, she contemptuously placed his note between two slices of bread and ate it for breakfast, telling her servants that if he called again, she was not at home.[44]

Such pleasures could not last long when there was a war on and on June 14th 1759, Edward was promoted to the rank of Captain ready to sail again. He was to take charge of the Phoenix, a forty-four gun ship being built at Limehouse. Just over a week later, Edward went to the yard to launch the ship. The carving on the stern showed the British lion towering over a cowering France who was accompanied by Deceit.[45] Patriotism was running high and everyone was full of praise for the young prince. The only sour note was expressed by his jealous elder brother George who complained that he was being left "immured at home like a girl" whilst his younger brother was allowed to go and fight the enemy.[46]

A month later, Edward sailed from Plymouth to join the fleet off Brest. The objectives for 1759 were not to land but rather to maintain a blockade on the French to prevent them being able to carry out their plan of sending an invasion army into Scotland. For reasons which are unclear, Edward remained on the Ramillies until late in the autumn and did not take up his command on the Phoenix. It is possible that it was felt more important that he learn about tactics from Admiral Hawke than get involved in the control of a single vessel. The logs show that Edward made several visits to Barrington's squadron off Brest during this period.[47] The morale boost which his visits gave were described in a letter by an officer at Brest who wrote: "He has imparted if possible new vigour to our brave countrymen and I doubt not but his presence will, if an occasion should offer, additionally animate our fleet in the day of battle."[48]

The fact that this was not a combative mission meant that the officers

---

[43] Horace Walpole to George Montagu, 16th May 1759

[44] De Archenholtz, W. *A Picture of England* (London, 1797 – English edition) p.305

[45] *London Evening Post* 23rd June 1759. The account of the carving is taken from a report in the *Lloyd's Evening Post* of 27th June 1759.

[46] R. Sedgewick (ed.), *Letters from George III to Lord Bute* (London, 1939) p.27

47 D. Bonner-Smith (ed.), *The Barrington Papers* volume 1 (Navy Records Society, 1937) p.262. Notice of Christopher Bethell's appointment to the Phoenix appears in the *London Chronicle* 4th August 1759.

[48] *Universal Chronicle* 1st September 1759

had time to consider other subjects. That summer, Edward and his mathematics tutor Dr Blair, went to view a contraption invented by Christopher Irwin which was designed to assist sailors in measuring longitude. The device was essentially a chair which was stabilised to enable a reading to be made of the position of jupiter's satellites using a telescope. From these, it was possible to calculate the longitude and thus the exact position of the ship. The need to find an efficient method to do this was so great that Parliament had offered a reward as early as 1714. As an island nation, Great Britain was deeply dependent on her navy, both for her defence and for the protection of her shipping. Safe long distance travel required accurate navigation and that meant sailors needed to be able to identify their location. Dr Blair pronounced himself very satisfied with Irwin's chair, clapping his hands and crying, "this will do!"[49] Edward sat in the chair and tried it out too. Whether he was so impressed that he wanted another trial or was less convinced and thought he should test it again, Edward later returned for a second test of the apparatus. His response is unknown but the chair was sent on to his friend Howe who tried it on board his ship the Magnanime. He wrote on 11th August 1759 that in his opinion it was accurate to within three minutes of time.[50]

Not long after Edward's return, George II decided to show his very public support for him. On April 1st 1760, just two weeks after Edward's twenty-first birthday, the following proclamation was issued from Whitehall:

The King has been pleased to grant unto His Majesty's dearly beloved grandson Prince Edward Augustus and to the heirs male of His Royal Highness, the dignities of duke of the kingdom of Great Britain and of earl of the kingdom of Ireland by the names, styles and titles of Duke of York and of Albany in the said kingdom of Great Britain and of Earl of Ulster in the said kingdom of Ireland

George was not pleased. As Prince of Wales, he thought he should have been consulted, either by Edward asking him to support the application or by the King in asking his opinion.[51] Edward, meanwhile, was delighted and

---

[49] *Annual Register*, vol 2 (London, 1760) , p.114

[50] Barrow, op.cit., p.424. The marine or pensile chair failed to win general acceptance for three reasons, Firstly, although it worked very well in calm seas or good visibility, it did not function in fog or high wind. Secondly, the fact that the readings had to be related to tables meant that it was neither simple nor quick. Thirdly, the eclipses were only visible at most around sixty times a year. For a full discussion on various methods then under consideration, see the article by Astrophilus "On the Inventions for discovering Longitude" in *The Gentleman's Magazine* 22nd October 1761 pp437-439. It was suggested by Doug Cowan in *British Horology Times*, November 2001, pp4-5 that Astrophilus was James Bradley the British Astronomer Royal.

[51] Sedgewick op.cit. p.41. Curiously, Horace Walpole had referred to Edward as "my friend the Duke of York" in a letter to George Montagu dated 7th January 1760 indicating the private

set about ordering new robes and regalia as befitted his new station in life. Accounts kept by the Treasury and now held in the National Archives show that the total cost of his creation was £1,343 pounds, and 2s 6d.[52]

As Duke of York, Edward was entitled to a seat in the House of Lords. At the time, the Lords were about to try Lord Ferrers for murder. Edward decided that he did not wish to sit in judgment on a fellow peer so he watched the trial from the Prince of Wales' box.[53] Ferrers was convicted to be hanged and have his body delivered to the surgeons for dissection. Two weeks later on 9th May, Edward went to take his seat in the House. He was presented by the Dukes of Rutland and Devonshire and took the necessary oaths of loyalty to the King and Church of England. As a reminder of the country being at war, his summons referred to the "arduous and urgent affairs concerning us, the state and defence of our kingdom of Great Britain" and the first item of business was a letter from the King discussing the likelihood that "sudden emergencies may arise which may be of the utmost importance and be attended with the most pernicious consequences" asking for support "in all such measures as His Majesty shall judge necessary or proper to take in order to defeat any enterprises or designs of his enemies."[54]

Edward remained, however, a young man with a young man's interests. On June 17th, Edward was present at the fight between Bill "the Nailer" Stevens and Jack Slack for the championship of England. The fight took place at the Tennis Court in James Street with a prize of one hundred pounds being offered to the winner, about fourteen thousand pounds today. Slack had been champion since 1750 and was under the patronage of Edward's uncle the Duke of Cumberland who had long been associated with the sport. Edward may have been introduced to it by him or by his fencing master Angelo who regarded pugilism as another form of manly self defence. To add to the excitement, Edward decided to sponsor Stevens, at that time a relatively inexperienced light heavyweight. Stevens was twenty-four and Slack thirty-eight. The fight lasted almost half an hour with Slack having the best of the opening rounds. Stevens had a good defence though and endured the onslaught. As Slack tired, Stevens opened up with his right and his blows to Slack's head knocked him off balance. Slack fell and Stevens took the title. Edward's interest in Stevens was short lived, however, for in March 1761, Stevens appalled the boxing world by accepting a bribe from Slack to lose a fight against George Meggs. Edward never sponsored him

---

expectation that he would be so honoured.

[52] T 1/452/319-320

[53] Horace Walpole to George Montagu, 19th April 1760. Edward did attend the trial of Lord Byron for murder in April 1766. Byron – great uncle of the poet – was cleared of murder and found guilty of manslaughter only.

[54] House of Lords Journal, volume 31 p675

again.[55]

Despite a number of rumours that Edward was about to sail with the fleet in 1760 and several trips by him to Portsmouth complete with his baggage, he never left England. He started to take on more official duties such as welcoming ambassadors from overseas countries and became patron to the Magdalen Hospital, a rescue home for repentant prostitutes.[56] Although no reason was given at the time and his friend Walpole made no comment on this excessive changing of plans at short notice, the most likely reason was that the King's health was failing. It is normally said that George II died unexpectedly and it is true that his demise on 26th October 1760 was sudden, but he was almost eighty. Only a week before his death, the final decision had been made that Edward was not to sail and all his goods had been returned to London.[57] The general public may have been left in the dark about the King's health but it would seem that in private, Edward was being prepared for a change of role.

The King's death meant that Edward's brother George became King. His first act was to appoint Edward and Bute to the Privy Council. His next concern was to change the family's accommodation arrangements. George and Edward had been living together in Saville House, the house next door to their mother. George naturally moved to St James' Palace upon his accession. As heir to the throne, Edward was expected to have a fine establishment of his own and so a building grant of £16,000 was made to him together with a doubling of his personal allowance. Within the month, Edward had determined that he wished to live in Pall Mall and had purchased four houses there next door to Carlton House.[58] Demolition of these began in December 1760 and work began on a new house in 1761. The architect whom Edward had chosen was Matthew Brettingham who had designed the home of the Earl of Egremont in Piccadilly. His desire was for a house which would be plain but elegant with plenty of room for entertaining.[59] Plans and sketches of the property show that the finished house, completed in the late Palladian style, met these requirements. By royal standards, it was not ornate except for one room, the music room where oval mirrors appeared to hang suspended from a variety of musical instruments.[60] Edward was extremely keen on music. He played the cello and he loved to sing, frequently being known to perform at dinner parties

---

[55] Pierce Egan, *Boxiana* vol.1 (London, 1830) pp.63, 70-71. In another account of the fight, Stevens was accused of tripping Slack up, see Anon, *Pancratia,* (London 1812) p.54

[56] *Whitehall Evening Post* 26th January 1760

[57] *Public Ledger,* 17th October 1760

[58] His father, Frederick, had purchased Carlton House in 1732. Edwards, op.cit. p119

[59] *Public Ledger,* 31st December 1760 and *Lloyd's Evening Post,* 2nd January 1761.

[60] See plans and description in John Woolfe, *Vitruvius Britannicus* volume 4 (London, 1767)

with friends.[61] During the summer, he had paid the first of what would be several visits to the annual music festival at Salisbury where he had enjoyed a variety of church music in the cathedral as well as the oratorios of Saul and Jephta.[62] Edward's new house, therefore, was not just to be a place where he could perform his official duties but one which was to be his home, a place where he could enjoy his private interests too.

As heir to the throne, there was no question about Edward being allowed to continue in active naval service, though civilian life could be dangerous too. He was almost killed just three weeks after George's accession at what should have been a routine public engagement. Edward had gone to Woolwich to view another proposed improvement to the offensive capabilities of the navy. On this occasion, the item being demonstrated was a new form of cannon designed to fire balls of smoke toward the enemy and thus confuse them. The first balls were shot successfully and suitable clouds of smoke produced. The next caused the equipment to explode. Ex Commodore Howe was wounded in the face whilst Colonel Desaguliers had his arm broken. Lord Eglinton, who was standing near Edward, had his sword broken in two by the force of the explosion. Edward was fortunate to survive with just a bad cough caused by a lungful of smoke.[63]

With his options limited, Edward spent an increasing amount of time having fun. He attended operas and balls and went riding. As a highly eligible young man, there was no shortage of ladies willing to entertain him. An anecdote of this time suggests that he was not the confident casanova figure sometimes suggested after his death. Edward had been attracted to the two daughters of a local clergyman. He did his best to develop a friendship with the father and eventually managed to be invited to the house. He made a good impression and secured a further invitation and another. Soon, Edward was having regular meals with the vicar and his family. Eventually, he plucked up his courage and decided to ask the vicar if he might take one or both of his daughters out for a ride in his carriage. He said he was concerned that their being indoors so often was bad for their health. The vicar looked at him and thanked him warmly for his concern. He continued: "but look at them, a couple of hale fresh coloured hearty wenches. They need no airing, they are well enough, but there is their mother, poor woman, who has been in a declining way many years. If your Royal Highness would give her an airing now and then, it would be doing her a

---

[61] For example, see Horace Walpole to George Montagu, 14th January 1760

[62] *Public Ledger*, 8th October 1760. The newspaper noted that Mr Handel's composition of God Save the King was played in the cathedral to good reviews suggesting that although the anthem had been composed in 1745, it was not in regular use or known outside London.

[63] *Public Ledger*, 17th November 1760

great kindness indeed!"[64]

A few days after his twenty-second birthday, Edward was promoted to the rank of Rear Admiral. He also received the freedoms of London, York and Scarborough. Although clearly an honorary gesture, these freedoms were a sign of how the various places wished to welcome the new reign as well as their admiration for Edward himself. Each freedom was presented in a gold box engraved with a symbolic image. In the case of London's, for example, Edward was shown as an admiral maintaining a state of naval readiness whilst supporting freedom and trade. On Scarborough's box, he was standing against a cannon reviewing a battleship as Neptune rose from the depths to pay him homage. The Lord Mayor of London told Edward that the City was grateful to him for his choice of a naval career which was not only an act of service to king and country but an encouragement to others. Edward's reply was a promise that: "I shall always exert my best endeavours in that profession to which I belong, and which is so essentially connected with the reputation and independence of this commercial country."[65]

For the general public, much interest was aroused by having a handsome twenty-three year old bachelor for a King instead of an old German man. George III was the first British monarch to have been born and brought up in England since Queen Anne almost fifty years before. There was considerable speculation about whom he would marry. Would it be one of the ladies of the court or a foreign princess? Finally, an announcement was made on 8th July 1761. George was to marry Sophia-Charlotte (known simply as Charlotte) of Mecklenburg-Strelitz. It was, as was customary in royal circles, an arranged marriage. The couple had never met. The marriage would be followed by the coronation on 22nd September 1761.

Inevitably, there was a lot to do with a royal wedding and coronation to arrange and Edward was closely involved throughout. George III, in an effort to try to stop arguments about who should do what at the coronation, set up a committee to hear and assess the claims of different parties who believed they had a traditional right to a particular function. The committee was to be headed by "our most dearly beloved brother and councillor, Edward, Duke of York." After making the necessary decisions, Edward went north on a tour of Yorkshire where he did his best to visit all the noble families as well as make himself agreeable by attending various balls, theatrical events, the races, and reviewing militia. With kings always basing themselves in London, this gesture of Edward's was very well

---

[64] Paget Toynbee (ed.), *Correspondence of Thomas Gray* vol 2 p.726 (Oxford, 1939)
[65] Galt, op.cit. p.225

received and his tour was a public relations triumph. He returned to London to find most arrangements going well but that there had been serious problems with the scaffolding being prepared for the coronation. A carpenter had been killed at Westminster and whole sections had been removed as unsafe. On August 18th, the *St James' Chronicle* announced:

> There will soon be opened in Westminster, an office for insuring on very moderate terms the lives and limbs of all persons who shall take places in Coronation Row. The prices of insurance will differ as the seats are more or less dangerous...hazardous, double hazardous and treble hazardous.

In a further attempt to reasuure the public, it went on "A sufficient number of surgeons will attend." Ten days later, Edward himself went to view the scaffolding and to test it out. After all, if the King's brother was seen to be willing to stand on it, the hope was that people would be willing to take their places and the country would be saved the embarassment of such an important occasion being played out before empty stands. Edward also took part in the rehearsal for the coronation on 18th September.[66]

Before there could be a coronation, there had to be a queen. Charlotte arrived at Harwich on the 7th September 1761 and went to Colchester to rest after her journey. The following day, she was escorted to London where Edward welcomed her at the gate of St James' Palace at 3.15pm. He took her across the garden to where George was waiting to meet her and to introduce her to his mother. The royal family had a meal before the King and his bride went to the windows to wave to the crowds. At nine o'clock the wedding took place in the Chapel Royal. Edward accompanied Charlotte to the altar being heard to whisper in French to the nervous girl, "Courage, Princess, courage." Her concerns were probably exacerbated by what might be termed a wardrobe malfunction, if Walpole is to be believed. He commented that Charlotte's mantle of velvet and ermine was so heavy "that the spectators knew as much of her upper half as the King himself."[67] She clearly relaxed afterwards because she was reported to have stayed up into the early hours chatting with George and Edward in French and German and playing the harpsichord whilst they all sang. The next evening, there was a celebratory ball where the opening minuet was particularly special

---

[66] *Public Advertiser*, 19th September 1761

[67] Horace Walpole to Henry Conway 9th September, 1761. Walpole wrote to Sir Horace Mann the next day that the weight of the mantle had "dragged itself and almost the rest of her clothes halfway down her waist."

having been composed for the occasion by Edward.[68]

The coronation was naturally an elaborate affair. Edward was the senior prince and walked directly in front of the sword of state, the sceptre, orb and crown. [69] He had arrived for the event in a very grand coach which had been newly built. Reports suggest that as well as being the most sumptuously dressed, he had the most magnificent coach on the day.[70] The event was not, however, without incident. The champion, whose role was to enter the hall and promise to fight anyone who wished to challenge the right of the king to the title, lost control of his horse and rode in backwards presenting the royal party with a rump view. The Bishop of Rochester was so nervous that he almost dropped the crown. The Duke of Newcastle found himself unable to sit through the whole event and made a hasty departure to relieve himself only to be caught in the act by a lady in waiting because he had accidentally wandered into the Queen's private closet.[71]

George and Charlotte soon settled into a very happy married life. Both were naturally retiring individuals and they delighted in simple pleasures and early nights. Each Wednesday, the Queen arranged a concert for her husband, mother in law and the younger members of the royal family. Charlotte and Princess Augusta would play on the harpsichord, Edward the cello and Prince William the flute.[72]

For Edward though, this domesticity seemed rather stifling and he soon escaped to go on a tour of the south west where he was once again able to enjoy his passions for the theatre and dancing. The idea of a prince leaving the capital and going to meet people was something new and a source of great excitement. The welcome which he received at Bristol was typical and prefigured many royal visits that were to follow across the centuries. Edward arrived by coach at lunchtime with his equerry and was welcomed by the Mayor and Aldermen. There was a coach procession along the quay and through the city. The buildings and ships had all been decorated with flags and streamers and crowds of people lined the route. All the church bells rang and there was a twenty-one gun salute. When the procession reached the Mayor's House, there was a row of invalid ex-servicemen waiting to greet him. Edward spoke to them and no doubt waved at the crowds before going inside to meet with representatives of the local

---

[68] James Greig (ed.), *The Diaries of a Duchess*, (London, 1926) p.32. Other examples of Edward's compositions may be found in the British Library.

[69] *An Account of the Ceremonies observed at the Coronation* (London, 1761)

[70] *St James' Chronicle* 8th August 1761. The gold state coach which has been used by monarchs at coronations since from 1820 to 1953, had been ordered but was not completed on time.

[71] Toynbee op.cit. p.756

[72] Greig op cit. p.41

churches, council and merchant communities. Various army and naval officers were presented and Edward took refreshment. Late in the afternoon, he walked through cheering crowds to the Merchants Hall accompanied by the Mayor. It was a sumptuous meal with three courses of ninety dishes each followed by toasts to each member of the royal family. Around seven o'clock, Edward went to the Assembly Room where hundreds of people were gathered. He opened the dancing with the mayor's daughter and stayed until midnight when he returned to the Mayor's House for supper and fireworks. He spent the night there before leaving to visit the fort the next morning escorted by a battalion of the Gloucestershire Militia.[73]

Despite the fun of going out and meeting new people, Edward must have been frustrated. In February 1762 he was allowed to return to Portsmouth but only to watch the fleet departing. The extent of his official role was to escort the Queen's brother around the sights including the Tower of London zoo.[74] He continued to spend time with the Spencers at Althorp and with Walpole. At the end of January 1762, they went to see the big sensation of the day, Scratching Fanny. This was not a person but a ghost who was said to inhabit a house in Cock Lane and who communicated by making noises, two for no and one for yes. Sensationally, she had used her knocks and scratches to reveal that she had been poisoned by her husband, a man with whom the owner of the property happened to have an unresolved financial disagreement. Despite waiting until half one in the morning, Edward and his party saw and heard nothing and went away as sceptical as they had arrived.[75] The case of Scratching Fanny continued to attract attention, even engaging the attention of such luminaries as Oliver Goldsmith, Samuel Foote and Samuel Johnson. Goldsmith noted that the ghost never appeared to real men, just "ladies, or perhaps some men about as courageous as ladies"[76] and ridiculed the way the maid would announce "Miss Fanny is angry" if she thought people in the audience were disbelievers. The business was only ended when the householder was prosecuted in July.

Finally, however, Edward got his chance to depart from his rather frivolous life and return to the navy. With the Queen expecting and his brother William now an adult, there was less concern about the succession. Spain had joined the war on the side of France in January 1762 and had attacked Portugal, a long standing British ally. There was a requirement to defend her and also to prevent the French from sending money, men and

---

[73] *London Chronicle*, 7th January 1762
[74] *Public Advertiser*, 13th April 1762
[75] Horace Walpole to George Montagu, 2nd February 1762
[76] Oliver Goldsmith, *The Mystery Revealed* (London, 1762) p.25

ammunition to their territories in the West Indies, bases from which she could attack British held islands. At the end of June, Edward took command of the Blue Squadron, taking as his flagship the Princess Amelia, one of the largest warships in the navy with eighty guns and a crew of almost seven hundred men.[77] He joined the ship at Spithead on 23rd June and two days later the fleet departed toward the Bay of Biscay. A sailor on board the Royal George penned a poem about Edward to mark the occasion which said:

The gentle sports of youth no more
Allure him to the peaceful shore
For war and fame alone can please
To war, the hero moves,
through storms and wintry seas...
Unmoved he leads the rugged way
Despising peril and dismay
His country calls; to guard her laws
The avenging naval sword he draws.[78]

Over the course of the next two months, the squadron patrolled the coasts and investigated sightings of other ships. On 16th July, a Spanish enemy vessel from Buenos Ayres was captured. They carried out various manoeuvres such as getting into battle lines at speed and testing their cannons and small arms. One night, a fire broke out close to the magazine which could have had disastrous results had not Captain Howe stepped in quickly. He was able to ensure it was extinguished before Edward was even woken. The crew were probably more concerned about the state of supplies. Faulty casks meant that beer soaked out and huge quantities of butter and cheese had to be thrown overboard on July 31st. The next day, one sailor received two dozen lashes for "mutinous expressions and misbehaviour to the purser."[79]

The ship returned to Torbay at the end of August where it fired a twenty-one gun salute to celebrate the birth of the new prince, later to rule as George IV. On 27th August, Edward was ordered to return to London. In September, he was on hand to give an audience to the ambassadors from

---

[77] D. Bonner-Smith (ed.), *The Barrington* Papers volume 1 (Navy Records Society, 1937) pp. 372, 382, 389

[78] A. Miller, *Ode on the Duke of York's Second Departure from England* (London, 1763). His reference to wintry weather may have indicated that he anticipated a long voyage.

[79] ADM51/736, Barrow op.cit. p.69

Russia and Venice and to attend the baptism of Prince George.[80] Raised also to the rank of Vice Admiral of the Blue, Edward then returned to the fleet for another six weeks which were spent in the Canaries trying to intercept French and Spanish treasure ships.

Back in London for Christmas, Edward was involved in a round of diplomatic meetings, including giving an audience to the French ambassador. After seven years of war, all the combatants were tired and with depleted treasuries. France and Spain had been particularly badly affected. There was a desire for peace and it was the policy of Bute, the new Prime Minister, to obtain it. The terms which were agreed in February 1763 satisfied almost nobody being widely thought far too generous to the enemy. In order to get parliamentary approval of the treaty, Bute and the King had to resort to a widespread campaign which involved financial rewards, titles, and for those who were unwilling to accept either, loss of position. Edward had never liked Bute and he was vociferous in his opposition to the terms. Walpole was later to recall: "The Duke of York whom they would not silence by favours they obliged to go on an idle expedition to Italy."[81]

For the King, Edward's opposition was not only embarrassing, it was potentially dangerous. By aligning himself with Bute who was so unpopular that he could not leave his house with any degree of safety, the King was reducing his own popularity. When he and the Queen went to the Mansion House, they were received with a hostile silence. By contrast, Edward was invited to attend balls there and was highly regarded. When the town of Plymouth sought to honour Edward, Bute tried to dissuade them but had to admit defeat.[82] As the King sat cloistered at St James, Edward went out. He launched ships, gave generously to the poor, toured the Midlands, and entertained a whole host of overseas ambassadors. He was the most popular royal for a century. It was little wonder that Bute thought he would be much safer if Edward was overseas, out of sight and mind.

Ironically, the Prime Minister was unable to maintain power long enough to see his goal achieved. Bute fell in April and was replaced by Grenville. The King remained unhappy about the situation and was convinced that Grenville would be unable to retain a majority. He confided his concerns to Edward and together the two of them met with William Pitt at the recently acquired Buckingham House. Pitt was the most respected statesman of the period but he was unwilling to form a ministry unless the King agreed to stop his own interference. The meeting broke down after two hours but

---

[80] *London Gazette*, 31st August 1762, *The Gazeteer*, 9th September 1762
[81] Horace Walpole, *Memoirs of the Reign of King George the Third*, vol 1 (London, 1845) p.209
[82] Sedgewick, op.cit. p.123

Edward spent the rest of the day with the King discussing options and probably his forthcoming tour. The event showed the trust which the King then had in Edward despite their political differences.

Less than a month later, Edward boarded the Centurion to commence his journey. Although it was not unknown for wealthy sons of the aristocracy to carry out a "Grand Tour" of the continent with a view to improving their cultural understanding, no member of the royal family had ever done such. In fact, other than the trips made by George I and George II to Hanover, no senior royal had voluntarily left the kingdom on tour since Prince Charles' visit to Spain in 1623. For Edward, it was not only a chance to relax after the years of warfare, but a diplomatic mission. The King might not be able to leave the country and travel, but Edward had much more freedom. His itinerary was selected less for the opportunities to review great works of art than for the chance to visit allies and potential friends of Great Britain. Around the same time as he departed, the King arranged to send out new ambassadors to a number of European countries including Denmark, Spain, Flanders, Austria and France.[83] It was clear that it was hoped that the end of the Seven Years' War would herald a new era in international relations. Once again, Edward had been chosen for a role which would become very familiar to later generations of princes. He was to "fly the flag."[84]

Edward's first stop was Portugal, England's longest standing ally. He arrived on the 3rd October and stayed just over three weeks, his visit extended by poor weather preventing his departure. During this time he was entertained by the royal family and spent time with the British expatriate community.[85] From there he went to Gibraltar, an island of great strategic importance to the British. He spent two days visiting the troops stationed there and inspecting the fortifications. His next stop was Minorca where he did the same again. The capture of Minorca by the French had heralded the start of the Seven Years' War and it had only recently been returned to British control as part of the peace treaty. Edward spent six days there, no doubt doing his best to reassure the locals that Britain would not permit their invasion again. As Edward was to reveal later in his journey, he was expecting to be given command of the Mediterranean Fleet in the event of another war, which explained why he was so keen to view

---

[83] D. B. Horn, *British Diplomatic Representatives 1689-1789* (Camden Society, 1932)

[84] Aside from the newspapers which covered the tour in detail, the best accounts are to be found in Anon *The tour of His Royal Highness Edward Duke of York* (Dublin 1764) and *The Gentleman's Magazine* vol XXXIV (1764)

[85] The British Ambassador described his arrival as totally unexpected and said that he would do the best he could in the circumstances. SP 89/58 held at the National Archives.

harbours and defence capabilities.[86]

On 28th November, Edward arrived in Genoa, a city where he was to stay until mid February. There is no doubt that Edward enjoyed himself there. His original plan had been to stop for three weeks only. He became a regular figure at the theatre, the opera and at the assembly rooms. Joseph Denham described the excitement his visit caused in a series of letters to his friend Mrs Earle:

> The Duke was very gracious and merry. He took great pains to instruct the nobility in the country dances at which they were all very much at a loss and danced himself with five or six different ladies. It must be allowed he dances well and has a certain majesty in his deportment which distinguishes him. ...The Duke talked more or less with almost every woman in the place for he is a remarkable woman's man and can entertain five or six of then at a time very well with that sort of conversation which, on account of its facility, has acquired the name of small talk.[87]

At various stages during his stay, Edward's name was romantically linked to Lady Balbi, the Figlia sisters and the painter, Madame Durazzo. His energy at this time was extraordinary. Denham said: "I pity our poor Consul who is already half dead with fatigue and want of rest for the Duke never goes to bed till four or five in the morning and rises again in three or four hours - so that I fear this job will shorten the Consul's days." [88] As well as socialising and visiting the sights, Edward took daily cello lessons and also regular rides out into the countryside to get some privacy. As Denham had noted: "The people are always flocking after him whenever he walks the streets and pursue him from one end of the town to the other." When he finally left, Edward gave gifts and jewels to the princes and rulers of Genoa which were estimated to be worth almost two years of his annual income.[89] It was abundant proof that his visit was officially sanctioned by George III.

From Genoa, Edward went to meet the King and Queen of Sardinia. The King had been employed as a go-between in the negotiations for peace between Britain and France the year before. He spent two weeks in Turin visiting more fortifications and also receiving the Duke of Savoy and

---

[86] Mentioned by Edward when he was in Genoa, see note following.

[87] D/EARLE/3/2/3. All the letters are held at the National Maritime Museum in Liverpool.

[88] ibid. Edward rose early so that he could write up his diary.

[89] Anon *The tour of His Royal Highness Edward Duke of York* (Dublin 1764) p.20. The 40,000 ducats were worth around £20,000. Analysis of the Civil List for this period shows an 18% increase in expenditure on gifts, see E. A. Reitan, "The Civil List 1761-77" in the *Bulletin of the Institute of Historical Research* vol 47 no 116 November 1974 pp186-201

emissaries from Spain. After a brief stay in Milan where he received music lessons from the cellist Francesco Zappa, Edward moved on to Florence where he met the Great Chancellor of Russia. In Florence, Edward stayed with Sir Horace Mann, one of Walpole's long standing friends and correspondents. During April, Edward visited some smaller towns such as Pisa, Trattolino and Leghorn before entering Rome on the 14th.

The visit to Rome was highly significant. Relations with the papacy had been severed by Henry VIII over two hundred years before and Rome continued to deny the legitimacy of the Hanoverian succession. With Quebec part of British held Canada since the end of the Seven Years War, this denial created a potential problem. Britain wanted to see a united Canada and hoped Edward could convince the Pope to encourage the citizens of Quebec to stay loyal to King George. In turn, the Pope wanted reassurance that the British would respect the rights of the Canadian Catholics to practice their own religion rather than be forced to become Protestants. To add to the difficulties of dialogue, Rome provided a home to the Stuart claimant to the title Duke of York. In order to prevent any diplomatic embarrassment, the Stuart claimant was requested to leave town for the duration of the visit and Edward was received as the Earl of Ulster. Whilst there, Edward was honoured with gifts of fine wine which he had shipped back home to his brother and by some horse races specially arranged for him by the Pope. He also had his portrait painted. It was a mark of Edward's personal success that soon after this visit, the Pope decided to accept the right of George III to reign in Great Britain. Some of the officials at the Vatican, however, were less impressed. They had thought Edward was coming to admire the art. Abbé Winkelmann wrote that Edward had shown no interest in viewing any of the sights and thought him as such a disgrace to the rank of gentleman.[90]

After Rome, Edward moved on to Sienna and Bologna, attracting more ladies as he went. He spent almost two weeks in Parma being entertained by the royal family. Parma was strongly under the influence of France and Spain and every effort was being made to make it a cultural and educational centre. In addition to enjoying the operas and musical concerts there, Edward gave a dinner for the reigning Duke, the Prime Minister, and for his friends Lord Spencer and the actor David Garrick. The latter wrote that the Duke of Parma spoke excellent English and said he had asked Garrick to recite some Shakespearean speeches after dinner.[91] Edward moved on through Verona, where he declined to stay and see a bull fight, and Vicenza, where he only left his carriage to see Palladio's Olympic Theatre. He arrived

---

[90] Friedrich Forster (ed.), *Winkelmann's Briefe*, (Berlin 1824) vol 3 pp.39-40
[91] David Little (ed.), *Letters of David Garrick* (London, 1963) vol 2 p.421

in Venice on 26th May.

During a three week stay in Venice, Edward took the opportunity of attending more operas and concerts and masked balls. Garrick wrote in his letters home that the Venetians had spent a fortune in entertaining Edward, adding: "they would have overlaid him with ceremonies and their great wigs had not he broke from them sometimes to prevent suffocation."[92] To show their respect, they arranged a spectacular regatta for 4th June, a day they knew was widely celebrated across England as the King's birthday. In the course of this, they exhibited a display showing the whole of Europe at the feet of Great Britain. Garrick said: "I have seen such sights I had no conception of but in fairyland and have seen the visions of the Arabian Nights realised by the Venetian regatta."[93] Edward also took time during his stay to tour the arsenal and to watch how the galleys were built and equipped. He spent time with the British Consul Joseph Smith who had only recently sold much of his art collection, including a number of works by Canaletto, to George III. He left assuring the Doge, one of the few independent rulers within Italy, of the eternal friendship of Great Britain.

Edward's tour was almost at an end. To save money, and also probably because it seemed fun at the time, he decided to return home via France. The King was appalled but since he had not supplied a ship to bring Edward home, it is hard to see how George thought he was going to get back. The original plan had been that Edward would travel via Paris but the diplomatic situation had deteriorated in the year since he left England and as a result, he was not allowed to do so.[94] Instead, Edward and two friends disguised themselves as minor British lords, and rode across France from Nice to Calais using the back roads and small country inns.[95] It was the stuff of novels rather than the behaviour expected of George III's brother and whilst it generated criticism of his sense of propriety, it also added to his glamorous image.

Back home in England and now in his new Pall Mall residence, Edward faced a problem. What was he to do with the rest of his life? He was not needed in the navy. He had no landed estate to run. George suggested he could settle down, get married and raise a family but Edward laughingly reminded him of St Paul's comment in 1 Corinthians 7 that "they who marry do well but they who keep single do better."[96] Yet it was a serious question

---

[92] ibid. vol 1 p419

[93] ibid p.416

[94] SP 78/262

[95] *London Chronicle*, 1st September 1764

[96] Robert Huish, *The Public and Private Life of His Late Excellent and Most Gracious Majesty,*

and there was no precedent for it. Edward was the first adult Duke of York since the middle ages to have no real prospect of inheriting the throne.

Whatever he was to do, he needed money and his first concern was to augment his income. On November 1st, he summoned Prime Minister Grenville to him and asked him for a solution. He said that he was currently having to ask the King daily for money and he did not believe he should be in this position. He observed that he was hurt that the King had not made him Lord High Admiral or Bishop of Osnabrück, either of which would have furnished him with a role and his own income.[97] Whilst Grenville expressed his sympathy, his advice the next day to the King was to reject the application on grounds there was no money and that it would be unwise to allow Edward to be financially independent. Keeping him dependent would ensure the King could exert some control over him.[98] Ultimately the King chose to give Edward a further £3,000 a year, a sum which was a sign of good will but left Edward still inadequately funded. [99] His income was now £15,000 per annum which was clearly more than most of the population but less than half what his father had said he should have almost twenty years before.[100]

From January 1765 onwards, Edward decided to devote his time to politics. Previously, he had scarcely made an appearance in the House of Lords but now he was there almost every day. He sat through debates on road building, enclosures, encouraging the native cloth industry, the armed services and poor relief. He was there for issues as diverse as the provision of fire engines in Manchester and the development of Ramsgate Harbour. He attended every session which debated Britain's overseas territories. As a prince, he never spoke, it being expected that he should be above narrow party politics. The cause of this sudden dedication was probably the King's illness which created such a panic in the early part of the year. If the King were to die, who would rule as regent? The Queen and the Princess Dowager were both German. That left the King's uncle, "Butcher" Cumberland of Culloden, or Edward. By demonstrating his interest in such a diverse range

---

George the Third (London, 1821) p.321

[97] The King had given the bishopric which was worth £25,000 per annum to his infant son.

[98] W. J. Smith (ed.), *The Grenville Papers,* vol 2 (London, 1852)p.521

[99] J. Redington (ed.), *Calendar of Home Office Papers* 1760-65 (London, 1878) p.509. Earlier in the reign, the King had been very generous in impromptu gifts to Edward. One day, it was reported that he expressed his concern at why Edward was looking sad. Edward explained it was because his creditors kept calling and he had nothing to give them. The King gave him a thousand pound note. As time went by and he had a family of his own and greater understanding of state finances, the King became less giving. see J.H. Jesse, *George Selwyn and his Contemporaries* (London, 1882) p.195

[100] Aubrey Newman, op.cit. p.192. Frederick had recorded the income intention on 19th February 1749 in his memoranda book.

of subjects, Edward was staking his claim to be taken seriously as effective ruler should George die.

Following Edward's successful tour of Italy the previous year, the King – duly recovered – decided to send Edward to the continent again. In June 1765, therefore, Edward departed for Germany. His role this time was twofold. Firstly, he was to reassure the King's subjects in Hanover of his concern for them. Secondly, he was to try to improve relations with Prussia which had broken down since the ending of the Seven Years' War. Prussia had been Britain's ally in that conflict but Bute's decision to sign a unilateral peace treaty with France was regarded by Prussia as a betrayal. The King of Prussia was closely related to the British royal family and his support was important for any future European war when Hanover might be threatened.[101] A strong Prussia was also seen as important to maintaining the balance of power in Europe and to keeping France in check.

Edward's first stop on his journey was Holland where his cousin ruled as Prince of Orange. He spent a week at The Hague, finding time to romance a Mademoiselle de Rechteren in a picturesque mill.[102] He moved on to Amsterdam where he became the first member of the British royal family to attend an act of worship in a synagogue. Amsterdam had a large Jewish population which turned out in full to welcome him saying that they always prayed for rulers who protected them.[103]

He arrived in Hanover on 27th June where the crowds were even larger and more rapturous. Edward impressed them by leaving his coach and walking about. There was a certain irony to the situation. George I had proposed a separation of Great Britain and Hanover with the eldest son of Frederick inheriting the throne in England and his second son, inheriting the Electorate. Frederick had also written that he wanted George to give up Hanover to his brother when he came of age[104] There is no evidence that Edward was aware of this and that he was being asked to visit a land which by right, he should have ruled. He did know that he should have inherited Osnabrück but he maintained his dignity throughout the visit and said nothing.

On 9th July, Edward arrived in Berlin together with his brother in law,

---

[101] Frederick the Great was first cousin to Frederick, the father of George III and Edward, Duke of York

[102] Greig, op.cit., p.68

[103] *London Evening Post*, 29th June 1765

[104] See Aubrey Newman 'Leicester House Politics' op.cit p192. Frederick's memorandum is dated 12th September 1749.

the Prince of Brunswick. Ostensibly he was there to attend the wedding of the Princess Elizabeth of Brunswick to the Hereditary Prince of Prussia. This event passed off with all the ceremony expected and Edward was reported to have duly enjoyed the operas, balls and fireworks which marked the occasion. He remained a month longer, however, during which time high level negotiations took place. Frederick the Great agreed to re-open diplomatic links between the two countries which was seen as a major step forward and a personal triumph for Edward. Frederick even agreed to arrange demonstrations of Prussian military prowess for Edward. Following this, Edward, together with his sister Augusta and her husband, returned to England where Edward reported to the new government on all that had been discussed.[105]

In December 1765, Edward became the first Duke of York to set up a charity. In the autumn of the previous year, on his way back from visiting Marlborough at Blenheim, he had come across a troop of itinerant players. They were almost destitute and explained to him that they had been unable to attract paying audiences. Edward asked them to put on a play for him in a nearby barn. He let it be known that he would be attending, knowing that this news would ensure a large turnout. The performance took place to a packed house and the grateful players reported that they had taken more in one night than they had in the previous eight weeks.[106] The incident set Edward thinking about how actors managed when they were out of work. Following discussions with the management, the Covent Garden Theatrical Fund was set up. The idea was that actors would contribute a fixed amount and that the money raised would be used to support actors who were out of work or sick, and also their widows and orphan children. It was a revolutionary idea and became the model for many later insurance schemes.[107] Less than six months later, Edward set up a second charity for the "Preservation, Maintenance and Education of the Infants and Orphans of Soldiers."[108] He was rapidly earning himself a reputation for good works.

Edward returned to Parliament for the 1766 session and became extremely active. The big issue at the start of the year was the proposed

---

[105] *Lloyd's Evening Post*, 31st July 1765 and *London Chronicle*, 10th September 1765. Grenville's government had fallen whilst Edward was away and been replaced by Rockingham's which was keen to agree a fuller treaty with Prussia. Frederick was to reject the terms proposed in November 1765. See Peter Thomas, *George III King and Politicians, 1760-1770* (Manchester, 2002) p.127

[106] *London Chronicle*, 25th October 1764

[107] It is often said that Thomas Hull began the fund but for decades after, toasts were given at Fund dinners to Edward, Duke of York as their founder. See Henry Reeve, *The Greville Memoirs* (London, 1899 p. 210)

[108] *St James' Chronicle*, 6th May 1766

repeal of the Stamp Act. Edward opposed the repeal and tried to arrange a meeting between his brother and the Duke of Bedford, one of the leading members of the opposition. In a moment of almost janus like delusion, George replied that "I do not think it constitutional for the Crown personally to interfere in measures which it has thought proper to refer to the advice of Parliament." [109] He was, however, willing to spend many hours discussing the bill with Edward and letting him know his views. On 11th March, Edward voted with the opposition against the repeal arguing that it should be modified instead. The King was displeased but still allowed Edward to get involved in the discussions relating to his sister Caroline's marriage to the King of Denmark.[110]

Following the Stamp Act debates, Edward went to spend a few days with his friends the Delavels where the dramatist Samuel Foote boasted that he was the finest horseman in England. Edward said that he could ride his own horse, a very spirited animal. Foote mounted the animal and set off only to get thrown. Foote's leg was fractured in two places. Despite Edward summoning his own surgeon, the leg had to be amputated. Foote wrote on March 19th that Edward had stayed with him for three days after the operation and spoke of: "the singular humanity and generosity he behaved at the time of my dreadful calamity. He warmly expressed a desire of securing me from the only additional distress that can now befall me – poverty." [111] Foote said that a licence to maintain his own theatre would do just that so Edward asked his brother. Foote's new theatre opened in the Haymarket in May 1767.

Unusually, Edward chose to spend the summer of 1766 in England. He visited two health spas, firstly Bristol Hot Wells and then Tunbridge Wells. He also spent time with the King trying to persuade Pitt to return to government.[112] After Christmas with the Spencers at Althorp, Edward decided it was time for some entertainment. He had always enjoyed the theatre and as a child had liked acting. Encouraged by his friend Francis Delavel, he decided to put on a play. in a theatre set up in Petty France.[113] The play selected was *The Fair Pentitent* by Nicholas Rowe, one of the most popular works of the eighteenth century. Edward played Lothario which gave him a chance to enact two sword fights as well as make love to Calista, played by Lady Anne Stanhope. At one point, Lothario reminds Calista of

---

[109] Fortescue, op.cit. p.273

[110] John Fortescue (ed.), *The Correspondence of George III* volume 1 (London, 1927) p.349

[111] HMC, *The Manuscripts of the Duke of Leeds, the Bridgewater Trust, Reading Corporation, the Inner Temple* (London, 1888) p.77

[112] George Keppel, *Memoirs of the Marquis of Rockingham*, (London, 1852) pp.361-2

[113] Richard Edgeworth, *Memoirs*, (London, 1821) volume 1 p.119

their night of illicit passion and says:

> *Dost thou call it ruin*
> *To love as we have done; to melt, to languish*
> *To wish for somewhat exquisitely happy*
> *And be blessed even to that wish's height*
> *To die with joy and straight to live again*
> *Speechless to gaze and with tumultuous transport?*[114]

His performance was described as ardent and was no doubt much enjoyed by the audience who were aware of the rumoured romantic relationship between the two.[115] In order to prepare for the play, Edward commissioned a performance of the same with his friend Garrick in the role of Lothario. Garrick said he was too old but Edward refused to be gainsaid.[116]

The King did not approve of Edward's friendship with the Delavels nor of his acting. For Edward, it was simply a way to have fun. The King had still not given him a worthwhile role. Contemporaries commented on his restless search for entertainment. The Duchess of Northumberland said he regularly attended a concert, both theatres and a ball on the same evening.[117] Walpole described it as an "immoderate pursuit of pleasure."[118] Probably, Edward was lonely. Although his name had been linked with many women by the gossips, there is no evidence that he ever experienced any serious relationship. His childhood happiness had ended when he was just twelve. He loved his music and he enjoyed reading but that latter could not last much longer. Edward's sight had always been poor and by March 1766, he was almost blind. His urgent desire to go out and have fun may have simply been a reflection of his need to escape the darkness that was enveloping him.[119]

---

[114] Act 4 scene 1

[115] Lady Anne was married to Sir William Stanhope. Her brother, Francis Delavel, hoped that Edward would marry Anne when William died but William survived to 1772 by which time Edward was already dead. The strength of the relationship was probably just in Delavel's mind because a review of the guest list at events which Edward attended that year shows that Lady Anne was not regularly invited and their mutual friend Samuel Foote made no reference to it in any of his letters.

[116] *Letters of David Garrick* vol 2 p.549

[117] Greig, op.cit., p.80

[118] Horace Walpole, *Memoirs of the Reign of King George the Third* vol 1 p.74

[119] Horace Walpole to Sir Horace Mann 1st March 1766. Edward suffered from a particularly severe form of oculocutaneous albinism which resulted in a constant involuntary rolling of his eyes, photophobia and extreme short sightedness. The condition accounted for his disinterest in

The start of 1767 saw Edward back in the House of Lords. He attended debates on many subjects but his special interest was the American colonies. The King was also interested in this and he was concerned too about whether his government, which had a very small majority would survive. George's letters at this time include many references to the names and numbers of people he could rely upon to vote in the House as he desired. After Edward's voting against the repeal of the Stamp Act the year before, George was worried about his loyalty. In May, the tense situation between the brothers finally came to a head and in a very public way. The issue was the claim by the Massachusetts Assembly to have the right to issue pardons to offenders, something which had traditionally been a Crown prerogative. The King sent a note to his brother William before the debate on 22nd May saying that as he was the most "sedate" of the brothers, he should take the lead and ensure that Edward and Henry voted with the government. Since William was not at home, the note was delivered to Edward who was naturally upset at the implied criticism. He went to see the King and asked what the question was to be. The King admitted that he did not know but that he wanted his brothers to support the government regardless. Edward retorted that he hoped the question would be such as a man of honour could support because he had his reputation to consider and he was not willing to accept orders which contravened his conscience.

In the House of Lords, Edward sat through the debate listening carefully. He then did something sensational and quite unexpected for a senior prince. He rose to speak. Walpole, who admitted that he had not been there, sarcastically commented that: "if the administration can stand till routed by his eloquence, they will be immortal."[120] Thomas Gray was more positive and said that Edward's speech had so encouraged the opposition that the government only won by six votes. Both agreed that the King was furious. Gray said that Edward "has been rattled on both sides of his ears and forbid to appear there anymore."[121] Walpole said that Edward was in "great disgrace, has been thoroughly chid, was not spoken to at a great review on Monday in the face of all England." [122] Despite this, Edward continued to take his seat in the House of Lords until 25th June when the session was prorogued. In fact, Edward's speech had been a call to dissuade the house from dividing and when he failed, he departed so that he would not be seen to vote against the government.[123] He had acted in what he felt was a totally

---

sightseeing when abroad and made it impossible for him to pursue an ordinary naval career. With the exception of George III, all of Frederick and Augusta's sons were albinos but Edward was by far the worst affected.

[120] Horace Walpole to Sir Horace Mann, 24th May 1767

[121] Toynbee, op.cit. volume 3 p. 959. Gray's letter is dated May 28th.

[122] Horace Walpole to Sir Horace Mann, 30th May 1767

[123] Grenville Correspondence, op.cit. pp.224-227

honourable manner and one which was consistent with his loyalty to his brother and he was deeply hurt that George did not see it that way.

That summer, Edward departed for Germany again. He arrived in Brussels on 11th July and then went on to Spa. He crossed back to France a week later where he paid an official visit to King Louis XV. In the course of a month's long visit, he spent time at Chantilly, Paris, Montaubon and Bordeaux meeting leading French politicians and nobles. Walpole, whose friendship with Edward had largely ended due to political differences a few years before, reported that his visit to the French court had been very successful. He said that the French had been impressed by Edward's quick wit, his openness and his dignity. They were also fascinated by his white hair which they thought resembled feathers.[124] One aspect of the trip which did not go to plan related to the military review at Compiégne. The King and Queen of France invited Edward to attend and he did so spending an enjoyable day watching manoeuvres and reviewing the troops. The King asked Edward what he thought and Edward replied: "They certainly make a fine appearance and for the sake of Your Majesty and my brother, I hope never to see them anywhere else!"[125] Unfortunately for Edward, his brother had sent him a letter specifically forbidding him to attend the event but he did not receive this until several days afterwards.[126]

On 29th August, Edward attended a ball at the home of the Duc de Villars. He became very hot, tired and sweaty. Colonel St John suggested that he stay the night there or at least change his clothes, but Edward was keen to get to bed and simply wrapped himself up in his cloak and got in his carriage. The next day, Edward felt the signs of a cold coming on but he went to the theatre at Toulon anyway. He felt too poorly to sit through the entire performance and returned home. He was alternately extremely hot and shivering and said he felt very thirsty. His servants gave him plenty of water and managed to get him to sleep. He woke up feeling much better the next day but still rather feverish. He decided to head on to Monaco which was the next stop in his itinerary. Edward's view, and that of his staff, was that he would find better care in the palace there than in small country inns. On Thursday 3rd September, he arrived at Monaco still feeling unwell. His equerry described him as "indisposed with an indigestion attended with feverish symptoms" and noted that Edward had gone directly to bed and been unable to take supper with his host. He woke in the night feeling worse and a physician was summoned who gave him something to make him

---

[124] Horace Walpole, *Memoirs of the Reign of King George the Third* volume 3 (London, 1845) p.104.

[125] *Annual Register*, London 1767, p.210

[126] Horace Walpole to Sir Horace Mann, 27th September 1767

vomit. This improved things slightly and he was able to meet with the Prince. However, he shortly after retired to bed and never got up again. On Saturday, he complained of pains and heat in the chest and another physician was summoned from Nice. This time Edward was bled and St John reported on the Sunday that following a good night's sleep: "the fever is so much abated that we are flattered that it is probably got to its flight."[127]

Sadly this was not the case and Edward's health deteriorated. The accepted fever cure of the day was James' Powders[128] but it was found that nobody had packed any. Messengers were sent out to obtain them and some were located in Italy at the home of Captain Schultz. The first dose appeared to work well and a second likewise, but the third made Edward much worse. Colonel St John wrote on the 11th: "He has had great evacuations, is quiet and composed and though he does not speak often possesses his senses." He added that his health: "is still very precarious and I am sorry to say he is not by any means out of danger."[129] Over the next two days, it became clear that Edward was not going to survive.

Although weak, Edward took charge of the situation. He composed letters to the King and his mother. He arranged bank drafts to ensure that his servants were paid. He was afraid that if they had to wait until they returned to England, they would be left in difficulties. He made plans on how the news was to be broken to his mother and brothers. He told his servant Morrison who was ill with the same fever that he should take to his bed: "thy life is of much consequence, the preservation of it is of more importance than mine; you have a family, be careful of your health for their sakes."[130] Edward only made two requests for himself. The first was for a Protestant clergyman to be brought. Sadly none could be found even though his staff sent to the British fleet. The second was that the blisters applied to him in an attempt to reduce the fever be removed so that he could spend his last few hours free of pain.[131]

On 16th September, Commodore Spry arrived from Genoa. He found Edward already unconscious. The next morning at eleven o'clock, Edward passed away. He was just twenty-eight.[132] The cause of death was simply given as a fever. It may have been typhoid or it could have been influenza.

---

[127] SP 78/273 f.131a.

[128] A mixture of phosphate of lime and oxide of antimony. They had a high arsenic content.

[129] SP 78/273 f.134

[130] *Universal Magazine*, October 1767 p.214

[131] *Annual Register*, 1767 p.133

[132] *Calendar of Home Office Papers* 1760-1765 op.cit. p.186

There had been an epidemic of the latter that summer in Paris.[133] However, Edward's equerry reported on the 11th that he had developed spots and bowel problems, both symptoms of typhoid which would almost certainly have been caused by consumption of unclean water.

Edward's body was lain in state in the Silver Chamber of the Palace at Monaco before being taken on board the Montreal for its journey back to England. His will was proved in London in October 1767. Edward had left all his property bar his garter insignia to his brother William.[134] In accordance with royal family tradition of the time, neither his mother nor any of his brothers or sisters, attended his funeral. Edward was laid to rest in the Henry VII chapel at Westminster on 2nd November. The same day, Queen Charlotte gave birth to her fourth son who was named Edward in memory of the recently departed Duke of York. This Edward was later to achieve fame as the father of Queen Victoria.

Although Edward had only been Duke of York for seven years, he had changed perceptions of that role and of the royal family. He was the first prince to travel widely across England and Europe and to actively seek to meet people and learn about the issues that concerned them. Those who met him were often surprised as how well read and informed he was about all sorts of issues from scientific developments to trade.[135] His sudden death robbed George III of a valuable and independent adviser and a potential high level diplomat. That he did not achieve more in his short life was largely because George refused to give him a proper role. He did what he could, however, and his loss was felt by many.

---

[133] Mary Townshend to George Selwyn, 13th October 1767, quoted in Jesse, *George Selwyn and His Contemporaries* vol. 2 (1882) p.187

[134] Edward had made his will four years before on the day before he departed for his 1763-64 tour. A copy is held in the National Archives – PROB 11/933 image 178

[135] Bishop Newton said he was "surprised and delighted with the pertinence and propriety of the Duke's questions and discourse." Quoted in Watkins, op.cit. p.207

Frederick

1763-1827

Duke of York 1784-1827

He was true to his God, his King and his country.[1]

O f the fourteen Dukes of York, Frederick remains one of the most famous. He was Commander-in-Chief of the British Army throughout the Napoleonic War, brother of the Prince Regent and uncle of Queen Victoria. A statue of him overlooks The Mall and some have argued that the nursery rhyme "The Grand Old Duke of York" is about him, though this is questionable.[2]

His eventful life began in Buckingham Palace on the morning of August 16th 1763 as the second of George III's fifteen children. His first public appearance was just under a month later on 14th September when he was taken to St James' Palace for baptism and his mother decided to show him to the crowds from the balcony. Amongst his godparents was Edward, Duke of York, the King's brother.[3] Following this, he was withdrawn to the

---

[1] Princess Augusta, 6th February 1827, quoted in Joyce Hemlow (ed.) *The Journals and Letters of Fanny Burney* vol. 12 (London, 1984) p.683

[2] A very similar verse dates back to the Elizabethan period and the story told in the traditional nursery rhyme more closely fits James, Duke of York, at the Battle of the Dunes, than Frederick.

[3] John Watkins, *Memoirs of Her Most Excellent Majesty, Sophia-Charlotte, Queen of Great*

privacy of the royal nursery where he spent most of his time with the brother closest in age to him and who was to be so influential in his life, George, Prince of Wales. Inoculated at two, he began his lessons just after his third birthday when Mr Bulley started to attend for two hours a day to teach him to write.[4] Over the years, the study period increased and Frederick was taught French, German, Latin and Greek, classical history, geography, mathematics and religion, though he found time to enjoy cricket, boxing, fencing, and the high jump as well. The two princes studied some of the classics of English literature and a love of reading remained with Frederick for his entire life as was demonstrated by the size of his library when he died. The King was an austere man who delighted in plain food and simple pleasures and he tried to inculcate these virtues in his children. One year he gave George and Frederick a plot of land at Kew. They were required to sow wheat and to tend the crop, harvest it and then thresh it unaided, before taking it to the mill to see it ground, then carry it back again to the royal kitchens where they had to turn it into bread. The King's objective was to teach his sons the value of hard work, the effort that went into things they might otherwise take for granted, and to give them an understanding of how ordinary people lived.[5]

Frederick seems to have been a conscientious boy and was undoubtedly the apple of his father's eye. At the age of just six months, he was appointed Bishop of Osnabrück. The title caused confusion in England where people were accustomed to bishops being religious leaders and some wondered if the infant had demonstrated some precocious sanctity. In Germany, however, it was the title of a secular prince. At the age of ten, Frederick contemplated the expectations of the inhabitants saying it: "made me think how much I had to do to render their hopes effectual... I shall be obliged to labour hard. ... Though I cannot place myself as high as my brother because his kingdom is much greater than my bishopric, yet I must have as much care of it as my brother must have of his kingdom....I hope I shall gain both the love and esteem of the public which are my most ardent wishes."[6] As an adult, he was to have some success, Busche describing him in 1795 as "the best master and sovereign possible", adding "he gives more and receives less than any of his predecessors" and that his orders were "all calculated for the ease or good of the subject and not himself."[7] Osnabrück was, however, over-

---

Britain (London 1819) p.177.

[4] James Greig, *The Diaries of a Duchess*, (London 1926) pp.63-64. Frederick was the first Duke of York to be inoculated.

[5] John Watkins, *A Biographical Memoir of his late Royal Highness, Frederick Duke of York and Albany*, (London, 1827) pp.41-42, hereinafter cited as Watkins.

[6] Historical Manuscripts Commission, *The Manuscripts of the Duke of Leeds, The Bridgewater Trust, Reading Corporation, The Inner Temple* (London, 1888) p.49

[7] Earl of Malmesbury, *Diaries and Correspondence of James Harris, first Earl of Malmesbury,*

run by the French in 1803 and later became part of Hanover thus ceasing to be Frederick's concern although he retained a compensatory income from it.

On 30th December, 1780, the seventeen year old Frederick departed Buckingham House en route to Hanover. He was to spend the next six years of his life there during which he would spend time in Osnabrück, visit Prussia and Brunswick and study military theory and practice. His daily routine, as he described it to George, consisted of getting up at seven ready for breakfast with lessons in fortification, geometry and engineering following until eleven when he went for a ride. Dinner was at one and lasted two hours but then he was left to his own devices. He might go out hunting or sit in his room playing cards with friends or drive his sleigh or carriage. After supper, he would read for two or three hours before retiring.[8] Clearly missing home, he asked George to send him his cricketing equipment and seeds of various English vegetables as well as some fine clothes with which to impress the ladies, even though he thought less than ten per cent were "the least pretty."[9]

As the months went by, Frederick took the opportunity to explore the country, visiting mines and watching craftsmen at work as well as attending military reviews and watching manoeuvres alongside the famous warrior ruler, Frederick the Great of Prussia. His growing maturity was shown in his letters home. Those to his father were full of serious and considered comments on international politics, economic relations and the European military situation. Those to his brother, meantime, were more frivolous in keeping with those of George to him. A clear example is in his accounts of the military displays in Silesia in the autumn of 1785. His description of the event to George is just two sentences and concentrates on the appearance of the horses and uniforms whereas his account to his father, written the same day, runs to more than two pages analysing the equipment and performance of each regiment and is followed by an account of the state of Anglo-Prussian relations and the role of the British embassy. A few days later, Frederick sent home to the King a new type of firearm which he had seen demonstrated and which he believed the British army should test. [10] It was no wonder that his father came increasingly to value him and even to seek his assistance in improving relations with George.

It was while Frederick was in Germany that he got to meet two ladies who were to become the future wives of himself and his elder brother.

---

vol 3 (London 1844) pp.201-202

[8] CGPW vol. 1 pp.52, 100-101

[9] ibid. vol.1 pp.50-51, 58-59

[10] ibid. vol.1 p.188, LCKG vol.1 pp.189-191

Frederica of Prussia was of similar age to himself but Caroline of Brunswick, who was to marry George, was just thirteen. He only saw the latter for half an hour because, being a child, she was not allowed to dine with the adults, but he described her as beautiful and lively.[11] When he learnt George was to marry her, he said she was "a very fine girl and in every respect in my opinion a very proper match for you."[12]

During his six years in Germany, Frederick had several bouts of illness which Macalpine and Hunter later suggested were caused by porphyria, the disease they claimed accounted for the madness of King George. The diagnosis chiefly rests on the evidence of Dr Zimmerman who noted that Frederick experienced the same symptoms as his cousin Frederick the Great and brother Augustus. Although Zimmerman did not specify Frederick's symptoms, he spoke of the other two having dark red urine, general debility, insomnia, gastric cramps, mental disturbances and rashes.[13] Frederick's own letters home refer to occasional colds and stomach cramps and he had stomach problems again in 1793 when he was in the midst of battle, and in 1796. Aside from measles in 1789, the only rash he ever referenced was in 1802.[14] Throughout his life of more than sixty years, there is no record of him ever having any of the other symptoms. It is, therefore, far from certain that Frederick had porphyria. His cramps may have stemmed from indigestion caused by his diet which was extremely rich, high in fat and sugar, low in carbohydrate and fibre, and supplemented by generous amounts of alcohol.[15]

In August 1787, two years after being created Duke of York, Frederick returned to England. The King was absolutely delighted to have his favourite son home again and so was George, but they found him changed. One observer described him as having developed a certain inflexibility and haughty manner as a result of his years spent in a "despotic land."[16] Sir Gilbert Elliot claimed Frederick appeared "much more blackguard, dissolute and foolish" than his elder brother.[17] Wraxall agreed Frederick was less cultured than George but suggested he was more reliable: "The Duke's

---

[11] LCKG vol.5 p.676

[12] CGPW vol. 2 p.454

[13] Ida Macalpine and Richard Hunter, *George III and the Mad-Business,* (London, 1969) p.17. Also Ilza Veith, 'The Medical World of Frederick the Great' in *The Western Journal of Medicine,* September 1971 vol 115 part 3 pp.78-88

[14] LCKG vol.1 pp.162, 429, vol.2 p.496, vol.4 p.13

[15] Kate Colquhoun, *Taste,* (London, 2007) pp.242-250 See also Ian Kelly, *Beau Brummell* (London, 2005) pp.249-255..

[16] Anon, *Tour of their Royal Highnesses the Prince of Wales and Duke of York to York* (London 1789) p.30

[17] LCKG vol. 1 p.17

manners, shy and embarrassed, formed a contrast to the gracious and noble yet familiar address of the Prince of Wales; but the Duke, nevertheless, maintained even in these hours of relaxation, some control over himself, and was not commonly betrayed by intoxication into unbecoming disclosures." Given George's propensity for frequent "bacchanalian festivals" and for every kind of excess, a degree of self discipline was necessary.[18] Nonetheless, General Grant observed that the reunion with George caused problems: "The Prince has taught the Duke to drink in the most liberal and copious way and the Duke in return has been equally successful in teaching his brother to lose money at all sorts of play."[19] Lord Bulkeley said: "his conduct is as bad as possible. He plays very deep and loses and his conduct is mauvais ton."[20] This enjoyment of gambling was to cause immense problems for Frederick throughout his life. By 1793, Frederick had debts of fourteen thousand pounds.[21] On one occasion in 1822, he had the embarrassment of emerging from an official reception to find that his coach and horses had been seized by his creditors.[22] Another time, he and his wife returned to their country estate only to find there was no water or food because the bills were unpaid.[23]

On 22nd October 1788, the Prime Minister, William Pitt, received a note from the King's doctor reporting that he had "just left His Majesty in an agitation of spirits bordering on delirium."[24] Dr Baker had not communicated his fears to any other members of the royal family in the hope that he was mistaken, and that the fever was simply a result of the King having sat about in wet stockings. Frederick, who saw his father two days later, duly reported this verdict to George and made no reference to any delirium. However, the King's behaviour started to become more uncharacteristic. On the 29th, Frederick acknowledged that his father was agitated but said that he hoped a rest would suffice. On 4th November, at a dinner with his wife and children, the King started to rant about the Prince of Wales. Sensational rumours were later spread that the King had taken George by force and thrown him up against the wall, causing the Queen and Princesses to start screaming and Frederick to forcibly restrain his father

---

[18] Henry B Wheatley (ed.), *The Historical and the Posthumous Memoirs of Sir Nathaniel Wraxall*, vol. 5 (London, 1884) p.394

[19] CGPW vol 1. p.273. As early as 1782 Frederick was asking George to get his lottery tickets which suggests that George was privy to, and probably participant in, his gambling, ibid. p.91.

[20] Edward Parry, *Queen Caroline*, (London 1930) p.84

[21] LCKG vol.2 p.107

[22] Earl of Ilchester (ed), *The Journal of the Hon Henry Edward Fox*, (London, 1923) p.125

[23] Charles Greville, *A Journal of the Reigns of King George IV and King William IV*, vol 1 (London, 1875) p.22

[24] *Report from the Committee appointed to examine the physicians who have attended His Majesty during his illness*, (London, 1789) p.101

and lead him away.[25] Certainly, something dramatic happened for the gates at Windsor were locked immediately afterward. Elizabeth Harcourt, lady in waiting to the Queen, wrote in her diary of the 5th November that the King "had no longer the least command over himself" and reported that the Queen had said that he now foamed at the mouth.[26] Frederick had another chance to witness his father's confusion the next night when the King wandered into the room where he and George were sitting, together with some courtiers. As the room was ordinarily occupied by the Queen, the King was puzzled and wanted to know why they were there. He then started to declare his love for Frederick and his confidence in his friendship. When one of the courtiers gently suggested that the King might like to return to his room, he became violent and had to be taken away.[27]

Experiencing such sights must have deeply upset Frederick. Mental illness was associated with stigma and created fear in both the victim and those about him. Lady Harcourt had observed that the King had always been especially terrified of insanity.[28] Nonetheless, Frederick remained at Windsor for almost a month trying to support his mother who was hysterical with worry and his elder brother, whose sensitivity meant he was not to be relied upon in a crisis. On November 9th, the King lapsed into a coma and Frederick spent two hours beside his bed, no doubt in prayer. Eventually, the crisis passed but on the 12th, George's own physician, Dr Warren, declared that the King was insane. All the time, there had been fever, the hope had been expressed that the King's mental state was a reflection of that. With the fever gone and the King showing evidence of just as much confusion, the verdict was that he was mad, though some days he was worse than others. The King's equerry, Greville, noted that the King had spent time with Frederick on the 15th without becoming agitated and that on the 21st, he appeared to have another rational conversation with him, albeit it was in German which Greville did not understand. Yet on other days, the King was deeply confused, claiming he could see Hanover through Herschel's telescope and panicking because he felt sure a deluge was about to destroy them all.[29] Fanny Burney, who waited on the Queen at the time,

---

[25] Parry op.cit. p.85. George's comptroller, Captain Jack Payne, was believed to be the source of this and many other lurid stories at the time. Mr Fairly, who was in attendance on both the King and Queen only mentioned a verbal not physical attack on George, see C F Barrett (ed.) *Diary and Letters of Madame D'Arbley* vol 4 (London, 1842) pp.283-4

[26] Edward Harcourt (ed.), *The Harcourt Papers*, vol.4 (London, 1880) p.21

[27] Barrett op.cit pp.299-300. Fanny Burney was told of the incident by the Prince of Wales himself.

[28] Harcourt op.cit p.15

[29] F. McKno Bladon (ed.), *The Diaries of Colonel the Hon Robert Fulke Greville* (London 1930) pp.87, 94-96. The royal family generally conversed in German when they wanted privacy.

wrote: "all was ignorance, mystery and trembling expectation of evil." [30]

Over the next three weeks, more doctors were called and new treatments tried including warm baths, blisters and quinine but nothing seemed to work. On 27th November, a meeting was held in Frederick's apartment at Windsor where it was agreed to move the King to Kew. It was felt that being nearer to London would assist in obtaining more effective medical opinion; the difficulties of travelling to and from Windsor in the winter being viewed as obstructive. Kew also offered greater privacy. George tried to persuade their mother to stay at Windsor but she declined saying: "where the King is, there I shall be."[31] The move was made on the 29th. The King loved Windsor and refused to go at first, even attempting to smuggle letters out to the local military to ask them to come to his aid. Eventually, however, he was persuaded by a promise of being able to see the Queen when he got there.

Although the staff at Kew had been warned of their arrival, the palace was not suited to occupation at that season having no heating, no carpets and the windows held shut by sandbags.[32] The King's own room was observed to be tiny and have damp running down the walls.[33] The day after they arrived, a frost began which lasted until January 13th with further snows until April. Clearly, none of the advisors had been able to predict it would be the coldest winter on record, with an average temperature of -4C[34], and occasional drops as low as -17C, something which would hamper the King's recovery by denying him for weeks the prospect of any outdoor exercise.[35]

On the same day as the frost began, a meeting was held between Frederick, George and the doctors to review Mary Harcourt's research into treatments for the insane. She had found a doctor whom she believed would be able to help named Francis Willis. The princes decided to invite Dr Willis to Kew.[36] It was a move which was to have a profound effect on the lives of everyone.

Francis Willis was a man in his seventies who was both a clergyman and a physician. At his base in Lincolnshire, he had been treating the insane for

---

[30] Barrett op.cit. p.335

[31] Harcourt op.cit. p.75

[32] Barrett op.cit. pp.349. 352-353

[33] Harcourt op.cit. p.76. Lady Harcourt believed the poor conditions were a deliberate reflection of the Prince of Wales' own desire to be rid of his father, if not physically at least politically.

[34] J. M. Stratton, *Agricultural Records,* (London, 1978) p.89

[35] *Report from the Committee* op.cit. p.92. This temperature relates to 12th January 1789

[36] Harcourt op.cit. p.68

many years and he claimed a remarkable success rate, alleging that ninety per cent of those committed to his care within the first three months of their attack beginning were cured. Unlike the other physicians about the King, he was a specialist in the disorder, and as such, he was looked down upon because mental illness was seen as a field for quacks. He arrived with his own team of staff and introduced a new regime of care which included purgatives like calomel and what was euphemistically called, "strict constraint", i.e. the strait waistcoat, a device attributed to his invention.[37] His argument was that the insane needed managing and that meant indicating to them their dependence. It also served to prevent the patient from harming themselves or others, something felt necessary as there were several reports of the King attacking his pages or the medical staff. Greville, shuddered at the thought of the King being so treated and wrote, "I can but grieve and hope the best."[38] Additionally, Willis worked by exerting a control through the force of his own personality, rather like Rasputin did over a century later in Russia. Pinel described how "the utmost sweetness and affability is the usual expression of his countenance" but when looking at a patient, "his features present a new aspect such as commands the respect and attention even of lunatics. His looks appear to penetrate into their hearts and to read their thoughts as they are formed. Thus does he obtain an authority over his patients."[39]

Willis's new system involved secluding the King from any source of excitement, including family visits, though George was later to claim that the restriction on family visits was the work of the Queen.[40] Dr Willis told Parliament that visits would "disturb His Majesty by creating fresh ideas" but as the King improved, he sanctioned these arguing: "it comforts the patient to think that he is with his family and that they are affectionate to him. There would have been even more anxiety in his not seeing them, for the irritation occasioned by a patient seeing his friends or relations is entirely overbalanced by the softening him into tears which ever leads to amendment."[41] Frederick, however, was not permitted to see his father until 23rd February despite the King asking for him.[42]

---

[37] Alexander Morison, *Cases of Mental Disease with Practical Observations on the Medical Treatment* (London, 1828) p.24. Prior to Willis' arrival, the King had been bound by sheets, see Macalpine op.cit. p.42

[38] Bladon op.cit p.127

[39] D. Davis (trans) *Pinel's Treatise on Insanity* (Sheffield 1806) pp.49-50

[40] Lord John Russell (ed.), *Memorials and Correspondence of Charles James Fox*, vol.2 (London, 1853) p.314

[41] *Report from the Committee appointed to examine the physicians*, 1789 op.cit pp.75, 111-112

[42] He did see him from the window of the library on 5th February, see Bladon op.cit. p.208. His request to see Frederick was reported by Mary Harcourt who noted that Dr Warren opposed it,

Even before the King's removal to Kew, George had been keen to take over the government. As early as the 9th of November, George had started to plan who would be granted which position and by the 28th the Duchess of Devonshire reported offers were being made.[43] George at the time was twenty-six and entertained himself by his support of the Whig opposition who were led by Charles James Fox. Four years before, he had shocked Malmesbury by saying: "the King hates me...I cannot abandon Charles and my friends."[44] Faced with the prospect of being able to favour his friends before his father, George made it clear that if he was in charge, Pitt's ministry would come to an end. He was encouraged by his physician, Dr Warren, and he not only spread stories of the King's misfortune, but he implicitly encouraged others to do so. There were stories of the King running round naked, dancing with his doctors, harming himself and racing a horse. Perhaps most disrespectful were the jokes about the King being treated with guaiscum, best known as a treatment for venereal disease.[45] The stories were nonsense. The one about dancing stemmed simply from the King observing one day that he felt so much better that he could dance.

To his shame, Frederick supported George in this behaviour. He openly discussed with outsiders private conversations he had had with the King in a manner designed to discourage respect, calling him "ridiculous" and "childish."[46] The Duchess of Devonshire noted that he "joins him in all his political sentiments" and talked of his frequent meetings in support of George's goal of being declared Regent, though even she noted: "I find people think it is wrong in the Prince and Duke of York to canvas so much."[47] Frederick twice chose to speak in favour of the Regency Bill in the House of Lords on 15th December and 31st January. His attitude was that if the King was ill, his heir should take his place and not Parliament who had no authority to "counterfeit" the royal assent. He reminded the Lords darkly of "the boundless mischief" that had resulted in the Civil War when "this house was once annihilated, the monarchy overthrown and the liberties of the people subdued."[48] They were not convinced.

---

see Harcourt op.cit. p.51

[43] J. Campbell, *The Lives of the Lord Chancellors and Keepers of the Great Seal of England*, vol. 6 (London 1846) p.191. 'Georgiana, Duchess of Devonshire's Diary' in Walter Sichel, *Sheridan*, vol 2 Appendix 3 (New York, 1909) p.406

[44] Earl of Malmesbury, *Diaries and Correspondence of James Harris, first Earl of Malmesbury*, vol 2 (London, 1844) p.128

[45] ibid. 404, 406, 408, 424. For the uses of guaiscum see John Stephenson and James Churchill, *Medical Botany*, vol.1 (London, 1834) chapter XC.

[46] Countess of Minto (ed.), *Life and Letters of Sir Gilbert Elliot, first Earl of Minto*, vol 1. (London, 1871) pp.273, 277-278

[47] Sichel op.cit. pp.409, 416-419

[48] *House of Lords Journal*, vol 38 p.332

Meanwhile, the King remained at Kew. At times, he seemed to have some awareness of what was happening. He reportedly reflected at one point: "I have not so much power as I used to have."[49] Yet he remained confused and his frustration resulted in either violence or tears. On Christmas Day 1788, aware that it was a special day when an important birth was to be celebrated, the King took to his bed clutching his pillow to him convinced it was about to turn into his son, Octavius, who had died some years before. Since the King refused to be parted from it voluntarily or to give up the notion, the doctors simply placed him in his strait-waistcoat for the rest of the day.[50] Records indicate that on many occasions, the King was left tied up for more than fifteen hours at a time, a position that left him without the dignity of being able to maintain any sort of personal hygiene and inevitably in great discomfort. Some months later, the King was to observe to General Harcourt the impossibility of sleeping "with his arms pinioned behind him in a strait waistcoat and his legs tied to the bedposts."[51] He did, however, after his recovery recognise the value of it, telling the doubtful Greville that the strait waistcoat was "the best friend I ever had in my life."[52]

The prospect of the King getting better was not what George wanted to hear and Dr Warren continued to assure him and Frederick that the King was simply becoming more subdued and remained wholly irrational. Such was not the case and the increasing number of positive reports emerging from Kew unsettled George and his party. The Prime Minister, Pitt, had successfully delayed the Regency Bill by introducing a concept of limitations and deciding on the need for a committee to investigate precedents. The ploys worked and on the day that the Bill was due to have its final reading in the Lords, 25th February 1789, the King was pronounced well. Whether the timing was an act of divine providence as most people felt or a sign that Dr Willis was in the pocket of Mr Pitt, was another issue. The country rejoiced, firstly because their much loved King was recovered but also because they had been saved from the prospect of the immature and self absorbed George achieving power.

The damage done to Frederick's reputation as a result of his association with George was immense. On 8th November 1788, the *General Evening Post* had noted with approval that Frederick never left the King's chamber "but for the purpose of rest or refreshment." By contrast, on February 21st, *The*

---

[49] Sichel op.cit p.411

[50] Bladon op.cit. p.133

[51] 'Mrs Harcourt's Diary of the Court of George III' in *Miscellanies of the Philobiblon Society*, vol XIII (London, 1871-2) p.37

[52] N. Wraxall, *Posthumous Memoirs of His Own Time*, (London, 1836) p.363

Times claimed Frederick was insincere in his rejoicing at his father's recovery and spoke of his "late unfeeling conduct" adding: "It argues infinite wisdom in certain persons to have prevented the Duke of York from rushing into the King's apartment on Wednesday. The rashness, the Germanic severity and insensibility of this young man might have proved ruinous to the hopes and joys of a whole nation."[53] The public too had their opportunity of expressing their opinion on 10th March when a mob attacked a coach carrying Frederick and George. A man opened the door and Frederick was forced to hold his brother back with one arm whilst hitting the man over the head with the other. The coach with its flapping door and its occupants escaped at speed but it was a sobering moment.[54]

Within the court itself, feelings ran high. The Queen showed no signs of forgiving her two eldest sons. Mary Harcourt said that everyone was astonished by the way that the King, nonetheless, continued to dote on Frederick writing "the Duke of York has fast hold on his heart, he sees him with marked delight. Alas what a pity that such affection should be so unworthily placed and meet with such a return."[55] Earl Cornwallis wrote: "I could have forgiven his wildness to the greatest excess but the want of feeling that he showed for a father who doted on him and the meanness of becoming the contemptible runner of a party and of keeping a table for fellows that he ought to have been ashamed to speak to, only because they had abandoned every principle of honour and honesty and even decency, have made me lament that I ever was acquainted with him."[56] The King's view was that Frederick had simply been led astray by the malign influence of his elder brother and he expressed his hope that as they got older and took on more responsibilities, Frederick would recover his good sense.

Barely a month after the official celebrations to mark the King's recovery, Frederick found himself once again in the public eye. At the time, Frederick had command of the Coldstream Guards and a dispute arose between him and one of the officers therein, namely Lieutenant-Colonel Charles Lennox. The origins of the altercation were disputed. Lennox's aunt said it was a "party affair" that stemmed from Charles being continually impertinent about the Princes, but she blamed the Queen for sowing the seeds of the discord by deliberately allowing Charles to be promoted above all the Duke's officers in his own regiment without his knowledge and despite his lack of experience.[57] What is certain is that Lennox challenged

---

[53] In December 1789, Frederick successfully prosecuted the editor for libel.

[54] Minto op.cit pp.283-284

[55] Mrs Harcourt's Diary op.cit. p.46

[56] CGPW vol. 2 p.45

[57] Henry Fox (ed.), *The Life and Letters of Lady Sarah Lennox*, vol.2 (London, 1901) .70. Her letter was written three days after the incident.

Frederick to a duel and that he accepted. In the early hours of the 26th May 1789, the protagonists met at Wimbledon Common. The two seconds issued a statement of what happened next:

> The ground was measured at twelve paces and both parties were to fire at a signal agreed upon. The signal being given, Lieutenant-Colonel Lennox fired and the ball grazed His Royal Highness's curl. The Duke of York did not fire. Lieutenant-Colonel Lennox observed that His Royal Highness had not fired. Lord Rawdon said it was not the Duke's intention to fire; His Royal Highness had come out upon Lieutenant-Colonel Lennox's desire to give him satisfaction and had no animosity against him ....Lieutenant-Colonel Lennox said he could not possibly fire again at the Duke as His Royal Highness did not mean to fire at him. On this, both parties left the ground.[58]

Newspapers and cartoonists had a field day with the incident. *The Times* described the curl as an object of "national importance" and said it was "a very useful outwork in the defence of the citadel of the forehead."[59] Theophilus Swift claimed Lennox was "an illegitimate descendant of the Stuart family" which explained his poor character and propensity for treason. [60] The Queen blamed Frederick but the King made his view clear by promptly transferring Lennox, against his will, to the 35th Foot Regiment.[61]

In order to promote his policy of gradually distancing his eldest two sons, the King encouraged Frederick to find a wife, anticipating that settling down would cause him to spend less time with George. It was a scheme which pleased everyone. George, by his own admission, did not want to marry and he was keen for Frederick to take on the job of producing the next heir.[62] Frederick was already in love with a Prussian princess he had met some years before and the knowledge that his parents approved and he would get an increased allowance as a result, was just a bonus. As a result, in May 1791 Frederick departed for the continent to collect his bride. He married Princess Frederica in Berlin on 29th September and reported "every day I am more attached and more convinced that I never could enjoy any happiness without her. She is really the best girl that ever was formed."[63] The journey home was quite dramatic when the young couple had to pass

---

[58] Watkins op.cit. p.138

[59] *The Times*, 3rd June 1789

[60] Theophilus Swift, *Letter to the King*, (London, 1789) p.3. Lennox challenged him to a duel too in July.

[61] LCKG vol. 1 p.425. The move appeared in the *London Gazette* of 13th June 1789.

[62] George had married Maria Fitzherbert in December 1785. CGPW vol 2 p.175. See also Malmesbury op.cit. p.130

[63] CGPW vol.2 184

through France which was at the height of the terrors when no aristocrat could assume the safety of his head. The couple's coach was attacked in Lisle by an angry mob and Frederick and Frederica had to retreat to an hotel whilst their carriage was repaired and the customary coats of arms removed from the sides and the clothing of their attendants. Thus disguised, they were able to depart the next morning in safety.[64] They arrived back in England and remarried in front of the King and Queen at Buckingham Palace on 23rd November. Frederick decided to break with tradition and was the first royal groom to marry in military uniform.[65]

Frederica was twenty-four at the time and a very petite, fair haired lady who was said to be even tempered and laugh a lot. She was the daughter of the King of Prussia and Frederick's fourth cousin and she was to remain Duchess of York for thirty years, the longest holder of that title to date. For the first ten years of marriage, they were idyllically happy. Malmesbury noted that he had never seen such genuine passion between a royal couple and St Leger commented they were the most deeply in love couple he knew.[66] They appeared frequently at court where Frederica's dresses won admiration for their style and magnificence. They often attended the theatre and enjoyed socialising and music. Frederica was a keen singer and one of the most popular songs of the period was written about her, *The Singing Girl*.[67] They took their holidays at the seaside which boosted the development of coastal areas such as the Isle of Thanet.[68] They did not have any children and it is unknown if Frederica ever conceived. She clearly liked children because she sponsored hundreds of poor boys and girls providing them with an education and a trade as well as clothes and tools. Each Christmas Day, she and Frederick would convert their dining room at Oatlands into a German style fair with booths along the sides containing different games and displays. In the centre, was a giant Christmas tree – probably the first seen in England – garnished with cakes, oranges and gingerbread. Each child was allowed to choose a toy and to enjoy a feast with Frederick and his wife who participated fully in all the fun.[69] Just as Frederica supported her husband in every way she could, being as one

---

[64] Watkins op.cit. p.172, *London Chronicle,* November 19th, 1791

[65] LCKG vol. 1 p.570. For a full account of the wedding see *Monthly Chronicle,* October 1791, p.531

[66] Minto, Lady, *The Life and Letters of Sir Gilbert Elliot, First Earl of Minto* vol 1 (London 1874) p.395, CSPW vol.2 p.185

[67] *Morning Post,* 3rd December 1804

[68] Their first trip to Broadstairs was for the summer of 1797, see *The Times,* 27th July 1797. Frederick wrote to tell his father that daily bathing in the sea had much improved his health, see LCKG vol. 2 p.615

[69] *Morning Post,* 29th December 1803.

visitor noted "his prime minister and truest friend", so he supported her.[70] As *The Times*, commented: "to speak justly of the Duke of York, his conduct towards the Duchess is a pattern worthy of the imitation of all other married men."[71]

However, from around 1800, Frederica's health started to deteriorate. She spent large parts of the years 1801 through to 1804 in Bath taking the waters in an attempt to regain her health. Ever devoted, Frederick did his best to spend all his weekends with her but the difficulties of making such a long journey every week from London were great.[72] The war with France required Frederick's attention and over time the couple started to drift apart. The affection did not decline but with Frederica physically unable to perform her marital duties, Frederick took a mistress, albeit one who bore a marked resemblance to his wife. A regular visitor to Oatlands a decade later said that the home remained happy and "that nothing could equal the respect and attention" with which Frederick treated his wife at all times: "I have heard him myself express the highest opinion of her good sense and I believe he rarely failed to consult her opinion on most questions of importance to himself."[73] Frederica's health remained poor for the rest of her life but she made the effort to get to Windsor and London whenever she could so she could spend time with her husband. Otherwise, it was left to Frederick to travel to Oatlands each weekend where she immersed herself in her charitable activities and her animals. She kept kangaroos, ostriches, eagles, monkeys and over a hundred and fifty dogs.[74] The anti-slavery campaigner, William Wilberforce, gave her an antelope.[75] Although she was not a vegetarian, Frederica refused to eat animals which had been bred or lived on the royal estate, commenting: "I never eat my acquaintances."[76]

Yet, it was not to be Frederick's marriage which created a separation from George but the war with France which began on 1st February 1793. Less than three weeks later, Frederick was appointed to lead an expeditionary force to the Netherlands to try to drive out the French and five days afterwards he appeared at the Horse Guards to address the men. He said that he did not want to force anyone into going on what was likely to be a dangerous mission but when he asked for volunteers, the entire

---

[70] F. Max Muller, *Memoirs of Baron Stockmar*, vol.1 (London, 1873) p.50

[71] *The Times*, 10th November 1796

[72] *Caledonian Mercury,* 26th March 1801

[73] Thomas Raikes, *A Portion of the Journal* kept *by Thomas Raikes, Esq.* (London, 1856) vol. 1 p.147

[74] *Morning Post* 31st August 1810. The paper reported that five staff were employed solely to care for the dogs all of whom Frederica herself exercised every day in the park.

[75] Robert Wilberforce, *The Life of William Wilberforce*, (London, 1839) p.358

[76] Raikes op.cit. p.150

gathering stepped forward as one. They then proceeded to Greenwich and set sail. It was an evidently hurried expedition. It was reported that no medicine was packed and that the vessels selected were so small that a third of the men were obliged to constantly stay on deck at night so others had room to breathe freely. Even the officers had to sleep fully clothed on the floor seven to a cabin "closely wedged together."[77] Calvert, Frederick's aide-de-camp, reported that half the regiments were led by boys, and said that the recruits lacked training. Frederick was so alarmed by the situation that he left the 37th and 53rd behind having deemed them totally unfit for service.[78]

The first thing which struck Frederick and his men was that many of the Dutch did not seem delighted to see them. They were not sure they wanted to be liberated and thought the French might prove better masters.[79] This was to prove a problem throughout the campaign but Frederick was not to be disheartened and set off immediately on a tour of the defences during which he came personally under fire for the first time. Almost two months of negotiations followed for the campaign was to be the work of an Allied army. Frederick had just over forty thousand men in his command but only a seventh were British. Almost a third were Dutch and the rest were German, the majority being from Hanover.[80] Since Frederick had spent six years living in Germany and had made a good impression there, they were very happy to have him in charge. Frederick's knowledge of the language also aided communications between the allies which included the Austrians and Prussians. The Austrians particularly impressed the British, one officer recording:

Their martial appearance filled all with delight
By seven years close practice inured to the fight
Well fed, and fine fellows above six feet high
Bewhiskered each visage, be-sabred each thigh
The least of them seemed to be able to eat
Six French at a breakfast and think it a treat! [81]

On 8th May, Frederick was engaged in the action in the Forest of Raismes but his first major battle was at Famars on the 23rd. Corporal Brown of the

---

[77] Anon, *An Accurate and Impartial Narratiuve of the War by an Officer of the Guards*, vol.1 (London, 1796) p.5

[78] Harry Verney, *The Journals and Correspondence of General Sir Harry Calvert*, (London, 1853) p.67.

[79] Verney op.cit. pp.23-24, *Officer of the Guards* op.cit p.6

[80] Alfred Burne, *The Noble Duke of York*, (London, 1949) p.46

[81] *Officer of the Guards* p.37

Coldstream Guards reported seeing "in one place squadrons of cavalry charging each other in full career, in another the enemy flying and ours pursuing with the Hanoverian flying artillery displaying all the skill and dexterity peculiar to themselves."[82] Another eyewitness described how the two sides: "Like contending waves driven together by opposite currents they at first appeared one firm consolidated body, neither side yielding for a moment, but to gain new force; at length the Republicans lost ground and their opponents pursuing them, the most dreadful carnage instantly ensured. Every broad sword appeared flushed with reeking gore up to the very hilt." In a letter to his elder brother, Frederick admitted that he had been under a severe cannonade from the "most dastardly set of miscreants that exist on the face of the earth" but said that the success of the battle had exceeded all expectations.[83]

From Famars, Frederick went on to besiege Valenciennes. The siege lasted for almost two months and Frederick was frequently under fire. He insisted on inspecting the trenches in person and was witness to the effects of the enemy bombardment on his own men. Brown described the usual evening scene: "The darkness of the night made more dreadful by sudden death glaring in all his fiery terrors added to the tremendous thunder of artillery all around mixed with groans and cries of wounded and dying men...This morning a shell burst close to a Hanoverian soldier as he was asleep in the trenches; his body was blown all to atoms and never seen more, except one arm which was found in the trench.... a third regiment grenadier got up to look over the trench towards the enemy and turning to speak to someone behind him, a cannon ball took his head clean off."[84] Frederick's policy of using incendiary bombs proved effective and he showed imagination in his innovative plan to fire propaganda into the town in hollow shells.[85] On the 28th July, Valenciennes surrendered.

Frederick was next ordered to take Dunkirk though he nearly did not get there. As he was leading two thousand men in pursuit of the French, he approached Marquion only to find the village on fire. Undaunted, he rode through the flames at full gallop to join what was believed to be the Hanoverians. At the last moment, Count Langeron realised that the soldiers in front were actually French and he made a daring dive across to grab the bridle of Frederick's horse and thus prevented him from riding straight into

---

[82] Robert Brown, *An Impartial Journal of a Detachment from the Brigade of Foot Guards*, (London, 1795) p.21

[83] CGPW vol.2. pp.354, 358

[84] Brown op.cit. pp.37-40

[85] Burne op.cit. pp.57-58

a deadly ambush.[86]

The decision to besiege Dunkirk was one taken by the British government without any military consultation and it was maintained against the wishes of Frederick himself. Frederick by this point had just over twenty thousand men with him of whom just over a quarter were British. He was assured repeatedly by the government that they would have everything in readiness for him by the 20th August but he found this was not the case. The British fleet were nowhere to be seen but rather enemy gunboats were on patrol and they kept his troops under continual fire. Frederick drove the French land forces back into the town itself ready for the siege, had the trenches started and waited. A transport arrived with some gunners but no guns. The situation was not helped by the weather. Brown spoke of the camp being flooded and men being made ill with the damp and cold. He wrote: "we can hardly pass from one place to another without swimming."[87]

Eventually, some equipment was landed but at Ostend instead of Nieuport. Frederick pointed out angrily to his father that this was little use since he would need a vast number of boats to bring it to him and he had none, nor indeed horses for the task. Meantime, the French were able to bring up men and attack both the Dutch at Lannoi and General Freytag's column which was due to provide cover for Frederick's force. With them defeated and his flank exposed, Frederick had no option but to withdraw. A shortage of carts together with extremely bad weather meant that many items had to be abandoned. Carts overturned in the mud and were lost. Men and horses drowned in the evacuation. Frederick himself said that he had lost ten thousand men in three weeks.[88] He wrote to his father: "I find myself completely abandoned by everybody. I have therefore resolved to try if possible to save this country alone....I will do my best and that with such brave troops as I command: everything may be expected which a man can do."[89]

Over the next couple of weeks, more men died and the hospitals were filled to overflowing with men suffering from fevers and dysentery. It was a major disaster and the British government, quick to deflect attention from their own failings, were anxious to blame Frederick. Privately, he blamed the government and the Allies for changing their own plans which meant that there had been no reinforcements available to assist him but in public

---

[86] ibid. pp.63-64
[87] Brown op.cit. p.74
[88] *Officer of the Guards* op.cit. p.92
[89] LCKG vol.2 p.90

he said nothing and he urged his friends to do likewise. In a display of selfless patriotism which is almost without rival, he declared to the King: "however I feel myself hurt and grieved at what is passed, I never will make my complaints public nor shall anything which has befallen me be brought forwards to weaken the hands of your government and administration."[90] Meantime, the French, who guillotined their general for failing to annihilate the defenceless British, admitted that had the Royal Navy reached Dunkirk on time with supplies, the town would have fallen.[91]

The British army wintered at Tournai. Frederick was able to make a brief trip home to see his father and to remonstrate about the lack of essential supplies. As a result, in spring, the army received new tents, great coats and kettles.[92] His request for maps of the area was not met, however, because the government admitted they possessed none, though this did not stop them drawing up campaign plans.[93]

Back with the army, Frederick had to face some discipline problems. He had been warned about officers writing "nonsense almost equal to mutiny" some from jealousy because they were not invited to dine with him and others because they were upset that the reality of war was not as much fun as they had imagined it would be.[94] One said: "That we have plundered the whole country is unquestionable. That we are the most undisciplined, the most ignorant, the worst provided army that ever took the field is equally certain but we are not to blame for it."[95] Although low pay and limited rations were encouraging plunder, this was not an excuse for violence. A man of the 24th Foot was sentenced to a thousand lashes for murdering a man whilst two from the 14th were executed for breaking into a house and killing a mother and leaving her infant with life-threatening wounds. Frederick issued a statement explaining the sentences and stating that he hoped they would be an effective deterrent to others.[96]

On the 1794 campaign, the Emperor of Austria accompanied his own troops but this did not help relations with the British. On 17th April, the two armies took Vaux and Frederick settled down to spend the night there. The Austrians decided to celebrate by setting fire to the town forcing Frederick to flee to the fields outside. Unfortunately for him, he had no sooner settled

---

[90] ibid. p.101

[91] Burne op.cit. p.71

[92] Brown op.cit pp.99-101

[93] Richard Glover, *Peninsular Preparation*, (Cambridge, 1963) p.19

[94] Malmesbury vol.3 op.cit. p.19

[95] Robert Biddulph, *Lord Cardwell at the War Office*, London, 1904) p.75

[96] *Officer of the Guards*, op.cit. pp.99, 105-106

down under the stars when it started to rain heavily. Frederick had to depart again, this time to shelter in an old windmill. It was a minor event but indicative of the growing problems between the parties.

Victories at Beaumont and Willems followed and these encouraged Frederick and the Emperor to plan an attack on Lille. The plan called for Frederick to command the central of five columns and to take Roubaix on 17th May. This he did, taking Lannoi on the way. The Emperor then sent Frederick word ordering him to advance to Mouveaux. Calvert described Frederick's discomfort at this instruction because he had received no news of the other four columns but he obeyed with a "heavy heart."[97] By the next morning it was apparent that Frederick's column had been the only one to achieve its objective which meant that his troops were isolated in the midst of the enemy. With the French bearing down upon them from all sides, Frederick had no choice but to retreat. As they approached Lannoi, two squadrons of Austrian hussars raced through his lines scattering men and terrifying the horses so they became unmanageable. The report in the *London Chronicle* said:

> All attempts to keep the retreating soldiers in order were ineffectual – the cavalry pressed over the flying foot and general dismay resigned them to the sabre of a pursuing enemy... in this dilemma, to resist was found impracticable; and no measure was in the choice of the British leader but to cut his way, sword in hand, through the numerous bands of every description by which he was thus hemmed in. His whole force did not exceed 3,500 men and it is no exaggeration to reckon the enemy at 60,000.[98]

With the roads blocked, Frederick had to take his remaining men across the country, a necessity which meant abandoning guns which could not be drawn across the hedges and ditches. Overall, about a thousand men were lost that day, a hundred and fifty horses and eighteen cannon. Desperate, Frederick separated from his army and tried to ride to General Otto for help. Accompanied by an Austrian general, Calvert and one other officer only, he reached Watrelos which the day before had been in the hands of the Allies. They galloped into the town only to find it was now in French hands. The Austrian general was shot dead as he rode next to Frederick who promptly had to turn down a side road and flee for his life. The trio reached the Espierres Brook still being fired upon by the French. Frederick's horse refused to cross and he was forced to dismount and wade across. On the other side, they found Captain Murray with a dragoon and a led horse.

---

[97] Verney op.cit. p.215
[98] *London Chronicle*, 20th May 1794

Frederick took Murray's horse and continued his journey.[99]

Anger at the disaster boiled over. Calvert wrote: "my indignation is excited to a pitch I can hardly describe by the reflection of what we have suffered by the obstinacy, ignorance and pride of those who take the direction of the war.... our loss was occasioned by the obstinate folly of others. No mobbed fox was ever more put to it to make his escape than we were."[100] The other officer with them said:

More and more every moment we're led to despise
Our valiant, our good, and our faithful allies
And simple John Bull far too nobly behaves
To a tribe of such pilfering pitiful knaves

..going on to compare Frederick who had "the form of a hero and strength of roast beef" with the Austrian Emperor who was "of diminutive stature, eyes sunk in his head...with swarthy complexion and pitiful mien."[101]

The French, scenting total victory, issued a proclamation that in future no captives were to be taken but instead any British or Hanoverians were to be killed immediately. This occasioned one of Frederick's most famous and statesmanlike speeches. Responding that "mercy to the vanquished is the brightest gem in the soldier's character" he suggested that it was inconceivable that the French could behave in such an "atrocious" manner. He warned them that if they did "the French army alone will be answerable for the tenfold vengeance which will fall upon themselves, their wives, their children and their unfortunate country."[102] By contrast, any French prisoners of war were given food and medical treatment by the English.

The remainder of the summer was spent in retreat. The water was bad and typhoid decimated the ranks so that by November more than half of some regiments were hospital bound. The King wrote to Frederick saying that he did not blame him at all. His letter ended:

Keep up your spirits: remember that difficulties are the times that

---

[99] *Officer of the Guards*, op.cit. p.49. The anonymous author was the third man in the party. In a separate incident, Sergeant John Brabyn took Frederick upon his own horse when Frederick's own was shot under him. The King subsequently rewarded Brabyn with a sword and a commission in the New South Wales corps, see the *London Gazette*, 9th June 1795

[100] Verney op.cit. pp.217, 220

[101] *Officer of the Guards*, op.cit. p.60

[102] Gilbert Wakefield, *Remarks on the General Orders of the Duke of York to his Army on June 7th 1794*, (London, 1794) pp.2-4

show the energy of character and as the rest of Europe seem blind to the evils that await the unprosperous conclusion of this business, it is my duty and that of my country by the greatest exertion to attempt to save Europe and society itself.[103]

Nonetheless, demands for Frederick's recall grew and in the end, the King agreed, though not before he had told the Prime Minister that he thought the responsibility for the failures rested with the Admiralty and Government.[104]

In February 1795, the King placed the newly returned Frederick in charge of the entire British army.[105] It was an enormous responsibility. His own experiences had demonstrated the limitations of the existing forces and the problems of organisation which hampered the command in the field. Clearly, he could not alter the political system and give the responsibility for planning campaigns to the military instead of government officials hundreds of miles from the action, but he could do something to improve the calibre of the army itself. Over the next thirty two years, Frederick transformed the army, improving its efficiency and morale and turning it into a force capable of defeating the French and building an empire. His reforms took place over many years and were effected often in the face of considerable opposition, but he refused to lose sight of his goals. It was universally agreed that they only became effective due to his constant personal supervision. On the days when Frederick was in the office rather than on tours of inspection, he regularly worked from ten in the morning to eight at night demonstrating, as Colonel Crawford told the Commons: "a degree of laborious assiduity rarely to be met with in any man, and still more rarely perhaps in a man of his high birth."[106] His work covered many areas including education, medicine, training, tactics and discipline as well as a host of general welfare concerns.

The British army at the start of the war was an object of national derision. Ordinary men would never have contemplated the army as a career. The daily pay rate had not altered since 1660 which meant that a soldier typically earned only a quarter as much as, say, a carpenter's mate.[107] It followed that the only people who chose to join up tended to be those who were either trying to escape women they had got pregnant or the

---

[103] Ernest Taylor (ed.), *The Taylor Papers*, (London, 1913) p.49

[104] Wraxall op.cit. p.127

[105] The appointment seems to have been in the King's mind for almost a decade because as early as 1787, Frederick was describing how his father had given him responsibility for certain army appointments, see *Gentleman's Magazine*, September 1850 p.254

[106] *Hansard*, House of Commons Debates, 12th December 1803, vol.1. c.261

[107] Glover op.cit. pp.214, 221

law. As Wellington said, they were the "very scum of the earth."[108] Although some effort was made to increase pay during the war due to the necessity of attracting more recruits, the rates remained unattractively low and ranks were often filled up with convicts. It was not a promising foundation.

Nor was the officer class any better. The vast majority of men had bought their commissions as an investment, not because they had any real desire to actually serve or fight. Prices varied according to regiment but it generally cost the equivalent of three years pay to become an ensign, four to be a lieutenant, five to be a captain, six a major and seven a lieutenant colonel.[109] It was possible, therefore, for a father to buy his ten year old son a captaincy and the son to draw the income until he died perhaps sixty years later, sometimes without ever so much as visiting his regiment. At the time when Frederick took over, there were officers being paid who turned out to be infants or women or else extremely aged. The oldest in the army was said to be over ninety.[110] When Frederick insisted that officers actually served with their regiments unless they had a valid medical certificate to excuse them, opprobrium was heaped upon him. Beau Brummell, the dandy friend of George, Prince of Wales, resigned his commission in 1798 along with several of his fellow officers, simply because Frederick posted the regiment to Manchester which was, Brummell commented, totally unfashionable and far too far away from London or Brighton.[111]

Frederick began his new role by making an extensive tour of regiments so that he could assess just how bad the situation was which he had inherited. His reports to his father make grim reading. There were regiments without basic clothing or equipment, cavalrymen who could not ride, gross levels of absenteeism and an almost universal inability to execute even the simplest drill.[112] His orders to date had been ignored, most likely because his ineffectual predecessor had never pressed any home and many assumed that as a prince, Frederick would be happy to be a titular head. They were to be proved very wrong as the stream of orders which emanated from Horse Guards afterwards showed, each closely followed up by inspections.

Aware that under the current system, each officer largely did what he

---

[108] Philip Henry, *Earl Stanhope, Notes of Conversations with the Duke of Wellington*, (London, 1888) p.18

[109] For prices of commissions see *General Regulations and Orders in The Army*, 1811 p.32. For pay rates at the same point see Philip Haythornthwaite, *The Armies of Wellington*, (London, 1994) p.270.

[110] *Gentleman's Magazine*, January 1827, p.163

[111] Kelly op.cit. p.147

[112] For example, see LCKG vol. 2 pp.396-397

wished, Frederick enforced a standardisation of drill. Regulations had been issued in 1792 but had not been used. Frederick made them compulsory and organised summer training camps so that units could experience working together. This was essential to enable future commanders to be able to control men in battle. Aware of the shortage of training materials, Frederick commissioned works such as Fawcett's translation of De Rottenburg's *Regulations for the Exercise of Riflemen and Light Infantry*. The introduction to this stated that the work was being recommended because it contained:

..many excellent rules and observations, adapted to the usual modes of carrying on active service in the field, and much useful instruction to young officers, not familiarized by practice to the arduous duties to be performed in the face of an enterprising enemy....Officers of the army at large, and particularly those who may not have had the advantage of much personal experience in the field, may, by a studious attention to the various examples therein stated, and to the useful lesson given for their conduct, imbibe that decree of military skill and information, which will enable them to discharge their duty to the satisfaction of their superiors, and their own honour, on the most trying occasions.

Frederick's desire to increase the flexibility of the army was behind his efforts to establish specialist units of riflemen and light infantry. He also tried hard to persuade the government to improve the transportation available to the army but to no avail. The government maintained that it was cheaper for commanders overseas to hire local transport, quite disregarding the problems of availability or the willingness of the locals to hand over their carts.

As well as camps, Frederick established more formal training opportunities for officers. The idea for a college had existed before and been rejected by government as too expensive but in 1798 Frederick was pleased to welcome to England a refugee named Francis Jarry whom he knew as head of the famous military school in Berlin. When Jarry offered to take a house at High Wycombe and teach selected British officers, Frederick was only too pleased to agree. As Jarry spoke almost no English, other tutors were recruited to assist and in 1801 this became the Royal Military College. The original plan had been to permit the gifted sons of soldiers and NCOs to attend but the government rejected this on grounds that men tended to desert if given orders by those who had been their social inferiors and they simply could not afford to lose men.[113] The trainee officers were taught

---

[113] Glover op.cit. pp.198-201

methods of reconnaissance, fortifications, military drawings, how to estimate and plan resources, calculations of shot and either French and German if they were destined for the European war or oriental languages if destined for India. They were also taught riding, fencing, running and swimming so that they could fight on the ground or horseback and make a quick escape if necessary. In the spring of 1802, a junior branch for teenage cadets was formed at Great Marlow.

Concerned too about the welfare of the children of ordinary soldiers, in 1801 Frederick established the Royal Military Asylum at Chelsea. Opening in 1803, it provided a basic education but also skills such as tailoring, carpentry and shoemaking for boys or domestic work for girls. The asylum was designed for orphans and those whose fathers were serving abroad and whose mothers were either dead or unable to care for them. After the first couple of years, it averaged a thousand inmates with thirty per cent of beds being taken by girls. Following expansion at the end of the Napoleonic war, numbers reached fifteen hundred. Children stayed at the asylum on average for five years before being either apprenticed, discharged to friends or, in the case of boys, joining the army. The vast majority of the children were aged between five and fourteen but there were instances of both very young children and some older ones becoming resident as the war drew on.[114] In India, Frederick went further and provided schools for the children of all soldiers. These too taught reading, writing, arithmetic as well as providing classes in knitting and sewing for girls.[115]

In addition to this, Frederick sought to promote general education amongst the men. It would be almost a century before there was any national provision for basic universal education and hence most of the soldiers were unable to read or write. Even amongst the NCOs, literacy and numeracy were limited and this had an effect on their work. An Anglican clergyman named Andrew Bell had developed a system of teaching in Madras which Frederick had implemented at Chelsea. This aimed to teach reading through the learning of syllables, and mathematics through a carefully planned series of short and frequently repeated lessons.[116] A key feature of Bell's system was that the teachers taught the oldest or most able children who in turn taught the rest in small groups. This meant less teachers were needed and this economy was very attractive to the

---

[114] For an account of daily life in the asylum see *The Royal Military Chronicle*, vol. 3 (1811) pp.242-249. Data about the Asylum comes from www.achart.ca

[115] HMSO, *Report from His Majesty's Commissioners for inquiring into the System of Military Punishments in the Army* (London, 1836), p.292

[116] For more on Bell's theories see Andrew Bell, *The Madras School or Elements of Tuition*, (London, 1808). In 1811, they were used by the National Society which established Anglican schools across Great Britain.

authorities. In 1811, Frederick extended the scheme across the army as a whole and urged officers to allow their men time to attend lessons.[117] Yet, whilst this opportunity was welcomed by many, others were sceptical. Colonel Dillon complained in the House of Commons that if men were to believe they would be forced into learning to read and write, it would ruin recruiting prospects.[118] To ensure that soldiers were encouraged to maintain their skills, Frederick encouraged the formation of regimental libraries containing textbooks, newspapers, magazines and novels and to help keep costs fair, admission was based on four days pay for each rank.[119]

With regard commissions, Frederick introduced radical changes. He set a minimum age of sixteen before anyone could become an ensign and specific qualifying periods before anyone could be considered for a higher rank. A major, from 1809 for example, needed to have at least seven years experience of which at least two were as a captain. Commissions were still generally purchased but Frederick did insist that the buyer had a recommendation from a senior officer and he established a system of regular confidential reports on all officers to build personnel files. He also made efforts to raise deserving claimants from the ranks though this was not always successful. He was disappointed to receive a letter from one officer he had created in the guards begging to be returned to the ranks saying that since his promotion, none of his fellow officers had spoken to him and everyone had refused to follow his orders. Frederick did not reply directly but instead decided to pay an unannounced visit to the regiment so he could have a chat, quite publicly, with the man concerned. The other officers interpreted this just as Frederick intended and apparently were very supportive thereafter.[120] In his belief that poverty should not be a bar to promotion for an able officer, Frederick was following the ideas of his father. On one occasion, the King had been presented with a recommendation for a major's commission in a particular regiment. The King queried why another officer whom he felt more deserving was not being promoted and was advised that the said officer could not afford to buy the commission. The King responded that service was far more important and offered to pay the fee himself.[121]

Frederick's concern existed for all ranks and was shown in many different ways from his increasing the fuel allowance in bad weather to his insistence on uniforms which were more practical for the conditions in

---

[117] *Royal Military Chronicle*, vol. IV May 1812 p.3

[118] *Hansard*, House of Commons Debates, 6th March 1812, vol.21 c.1203

[119] *United Services Journal*, 1831 part 1 p.45

[120] Richard Holmes, *Redcoat*, (London, 2001) p.172

[121] Watkin op.cit. pp.31-32

which the regiment was located. His eye for details went so far as reducing the postage on letters to frontline soldiers to help families stay in touch. Every Tuesday afternoon excepting summer when he went on tours of inspection, he would hold receptions for officers with a view to him getting to know as many of them as he could. In 1795, the army was around 125,000 strong with some 6,500 officers but by 1810 those figures had increased by sixty per cent, so it was not an easy task.

In addition to official matters, Frederick also received thousands of letters every year from people with various concerns. Some wanted promotion, others expressed dissatisfaction at what they considered an injustice, some described their hardship since injury or the death of a husband or father, a few offered ideas for improvements. He had letters from officers asking his advice on how to handle difficult situations including one who queried what he should do with a man whom he believed was faking illness in order to avoid strenuous activities. Frederick recommended blistering: "this treatment if the man is really disordered may contribute to his cure and if he is an impostor will most probably deter him from repeating the imposition."[122] Frederick took a pride in reading them all and replying to every one, even if it came from the most lowly private. He let it be known that any suspicious deduction from pay would be investigated and he authorised pensions for the needy.

Anxious also to ensure the men's spiritual welfare and aware of how the horrors of war could create reactions of fear and doubt, Frederick insisted that chaplains accompany their regiments overseas. All but two were so horrified that they resigned on the spot so Frederick sought replacements. These proved hard to recruit since the pay was hardly more than an NCO but in 1807, Frederick secured Treasury agreement to more than double the pay rate, a sign of how seriously he took the matter.[123]

Another area which Frederick sought to reform related to discipline. At the time, the most usual punishment for misdemeanours in the army was flogging. Liberals thought this was barbaric but advocates of the system replied that it was more lenient than the firing squad. It was also not obvious what alternative existed. Solitary confinement would keep a man out of service for longer and involve other soldiers in guarding him. Restriction to barracks was normally impossible because of the lack of premises. Transportation to Australia was frowned upon because, as General Bentinck observed, men "consider their removal to that land of

---

[122] Glover op.cit.p.185
[123] Sir J. Fortescue, *History of the British Army*, vol.10 (London, 1913) pp.197-199

promise as a boon rather than as a punishment."[124] It was furthermore, extremely expensive. Frederick himself believed in flogging but not to the extremes which endangered life. In a circular dated 25th March 1812, Frederick instructed that "on no pretence whatever shall the award of a regimental court martial hereafter exceed three hundred lashes." He said he was "decided in his opinion that when officers are earnest and zealous in the discharge of their duty and competent to their respective stations, a frequent recurrence to punishment will not be necessary." He urged more attention to the prevention of crime and stressed the importance of officers knowing their men and setting a good example. He warned that his opinion of officers would rest on their ability to maintain "strict discipline without severity of punishment and ...an ardent and military spirit in a corps without licentiousness."[125] Although Frederick was popular for seeking to control a system which could allow sadists to flourish, he was not a liberal. He had been flogged himself as a child[126] and he had ordered floggings when on campaign. In 1826, he wrote:

> Our regiments are generally speaking composed of the lowest and most thoughtless part of the community who are induced to enlist from some monetary motive mostly originating from the desire to extricate themselves from some scrape...Such people can be restrained by nothing but the strong hand of power...In all those corps where these new fangled notions of carrying on discipline without flogging have prevailed, insubordination has shown itself to such a degree as to require the strictest and most severe discipline and punishment to recover the lost ground.[127]

Not content with issues of education, training and discipline, Frederick concerned himself with health issues. His battlefield experience had taught him the importance of having adequately trained and well resourced medical services but at the start of the war, there was a lack of both. Upon his return, several general hospitals were established for the care of army veterans at Gosport, Plymouth, Walmer and Chelsea, the last being named in his honour.[128] They were necessary because of the casualty level. Typhoid had been a major killer in 1794 and its ravages had left many men unable to serve. Others had lost limbs or suffered mutilation as captives. In 1801,

---

[124] *Report from His Majesty's Commissioners for inquiring into the System of Military Punishments in the Army* op.cit. p.292

[125] ibid. p.309

[126] The flogging was witnessed by his sister Princess Sophia, see Parry op.cit. p.37

[127] J. R. Dinwiddy, 'The early nineteenth-century campaign against flogging in the army' in *English Historical Review* (1982) pp.320, 329

[128] A Pupil at St Thomas's Hospital, *The Hospital Pupil's Guide through London*, (London, 1800) p.29

there was a major expedition to Egypt where thousands of men fell prey to opthalmia and dysentery. Another common problem was what later generations would term "shell shock." John Haslam of the Bethlehem Hospital, popularly known as Bedlam Lunatic Asylum, reported that they had men "pouring in from the Transport Board and the War Office."[129] The army was faced with sickness on a previously unknown level which severely affected its ability to function. At Walcheren in 1809, ninety per cent of men became ill, mostly with malaria. A tenth of the army died and almost a third had to be discharged from the service. It was a huge problem and it was made worse by the government's refusal to fund care. Four army hospitals were closed in 1806 to save money, something the *Caledonian Mercury* applauded saying they were "expensive and useless establishments" and praising ministers for recognising the "inutility and baneful effects of general hospitals in the military system."[130]

Frederick disagreed totally with this but his options were limited. At the York Hospital Chelsea, he encouraged surgeons to try new methods. The first reconstruction surgery was carried out there in 1814 on two patients who had lost their noses. Frederick took a keen interest in their cases and sent his carriage daily so that they could get some fresh air.[131] He supported George Guthrie's pioneering work on syphilis, gangrene and eye disease as well as his important study of amputation practices with regard compound fractures after the Battle of Toulouse.[132] When the York Hospital was threatened with closure at the end of the war, he supported Guthrie in establishing the Royal Westminster Opthalmic Hospital, only the second specialist institution of its kind.[133] Frederick also took time to visit the wounded at the hospital. Today, royal visits to hospitals are not unusual, but at the time this was extraordinary. A case which particularly interested him related to a private named Peter McMullin of the 27th Foot. During the battle of Waterloo, McMullin had been hit at least three times. Both arms had been blown off and he had suffered severe intestinal damage. His wife had also been on the battlefield where she had been employed moving casualties back to the dressing stations. She had been shot in the leg and crippled. Both were returned to the York Hospital where Peter's wife gave

---

[129] James Sharpe, *Report of the House of Commons Committee on Mad Houses in England, together with the minutes of evidence and an appendix of papers*, (London, 1815) p.103

[130] *Caledonian Mercury*, 21st July and 23rd August, 1806

[131] Frank McDowell, *The Source Book of Plastic Surgery*, (Baltimore, 1977) p.98. The surgeon Joseph Carpue wrote a paper detailing his methods in 1816, *Account of two successful Operations for Restoring a Lost Nose*.

[132] Guthrie's own account appears in *The Lancet*, vol. 2. (1852) pp.188-189. For a modern analysis see Piers Mitchell et.al. 'George Guthrie' clinical trial' in *Journal of Medical Biography*, vol. 17 no 3, (2009) pp.139-143

[133] Thomas Joseph Pettigrew, *Biographical Memoirs of the most celebrated physicians, surgeons*, vol.4 (London, 1839) pp. 302-313.

birth to their first child. They named her Frederica and Frederick himself stood godfather and made a contribution to try to help the young family get back on their feet.[134]

As with the army itself, Frederick believed in the necessity of education. Medicine was not a closely regulated profession and qualifications were not common even amongst established surgeons. Besides, traditional study did not prepare doctors for war. As John Bell wrote:

The situation of a Military Surgeon is more important than that of any other. While yet a young man he has the safety of thousands committed to him in the most perilous situations, in unhealthy climates, and in the midst of danger. He is to act alone and unassisted, in cases where decision and perfect knowledge are required; in wounds of the most desperate nature, more various than can be imagined, and to which all parts of the body are equally exposed; his duties, difficult at all times, are often to be performed amidst the hurry, confusion, cries, and horrors of battle.

One of Frederick's early instructions was that surgeons must have "a complete knowledge of pharmacy and the treatment of medical cases."[135] To further improve their knowledge, a chair of Military Surgery was established in Edinburgh in 1806. Its first holder was John Thomson whom Frederick invited to study European hospitals and methods of caring for the wounded and to share new ideas with the British army. Thomson's classes in military surgery numbered almost three hundred pupils.[136] There was no money to fund a similar position in London but at the York Hospital, Chelsea, Guthrie lectured on battlefield surgery and William Adams invited medical students and interested doctors to attend him twice a week to watch operations and discuss case histories.[137] Frederick encouraged army doctors to take advantage of these opportunities and promoted the idea of study leave.

Although medical advances were made and encouraged, there remained a shortage of suitable candidates willing to serve on the front line. In 1803, the Army Medical Office wrote to Dublin urging doctors to come forward promising them their fare, new clothes and pensions for their dependents. Presumably few responded because a fifty per cent pay rise was approved

---

[134] *The Morning Post*, 23rd November, 1815

[135] Albert Gore, *The Story of our Services*, (London, 1879) p.145

[136] Derek Doyle, 'John Thomson' in *Journal of the Royal College of Physicians*, Edinburgh, (2009) vol 39 p.190

[137] *Edinburgh Magazine*, March 1818 p.269

the following year. The requirement for medical staff grew during the war, partly because of the growth of the army and the spread of its activities around the world, but also because of two further innovations of Frederick's. In 1796, he insisted that all potential army recruits be subject to medical examination before acceptance and in 1798 he established inspectors for army hospitals. Concerned about the state of facilities, Frederick issued detailed regulations for hospitals which laid great stress on the need for cleanliness and the isolation of infectious cases.[138] These undoubtedly saved lives though it was often impossible to follow them, particularly in the makeshift battlefield hospitals which of necessity had to be created. An account of one at Villa Formosa described surgeons operating on doors balanced on barrels saying "to the right and left were arms and legs flung here and there without distinction and the ground was dyed with blood....outside of this place was an immense pit to receive the dead... The bodies which but a short time before possessed life and were animated by the finest feelings were now stretched naked and unnoticed except by the birds of prey, not indeed a hump of cold inanimate clay but a moving mass of corruption."[139]

Frederick's dedication to medical advance was most clearly seen in the summer of 1800 when he ordered a trial of a new process called vaccination, something which he had seen demonstrated only a year before when he became President of the Smallpox Hospital.[140] Two regiments were selected for the experiment, the Coldstream Guards in London and the 85th Foot in Colchester. The process was carried out by Dr Edward Jenner who had pioneered the method just four years earlier and his nephew.[141] Not only the men were vaccinated but also their wives and children. It was reported that scarcely any became ill as a result and that there was hardly any absence of men from their duty.[142]

The importance of Frederick's support for vaccination cannot be over emphasised, either with regard to army history or the general welfare of the population. Smallpox was a deadly disease. In the year when Jenner devised his method, almost a fifth of London deaths were attributed to the disease.[143] Fatality rates varied according to the age of the victim, the exact strain of the illness caught and the method of infection, but rarely dropped below a sixth. The cost to the country in tending the sick, caring for those

---

[138] Watkins op.cit. pp.316-321

[139] 'Recollections of a Subaltern' in *United Service Journal*, (1831) part 1 pp.452-453

[140] *The Times*, 27th February 1799. The hospital was situated at St Pancras, in the vicinity of the present King's Cross station. Frederick had been a Governor of the same since 1788.

[141] Neil Cantlie, *A History of the Army Medical Department* (Edinburgh, 1974) p.281

[142] *Chelmsford Chronicle*, 20th June 1800

[143] Charlotte Roberts and Margaret Cox, *Health and Disease in Britain* (London 2003) p.334

left disabled by the disease or orphaned, was enormous. Efforts to counter the problem had begun earlier in the eighteenth century with the introduction of inoculation or variolation. In that process, live matter was taken from the pustule of a smallpox sufferer and transferred to a healthy person via a lancet. With vaccination, matter was taken from a cowpox sufferer instead. Variolation would make the person ill for perhaps two weeks and could kill. Frederick's own brother, Octavius, had died at the age of four as a result of smallpox transmitted to him by inoculation.[144] During these two weeks, the person was infectious which resulted in even more people developing the disease. One opponent wrote to Frederick saying: "If a father or mother of a family choose to murder their own children, they have no right to murder their neighbours."[145] Vaccination did not have these effects. It was quicker, safer and cheaper. The only problem was that cowpox was a relatively rare disease so obtaining matter was not straightforward. The mass vaccination of soldiers and their families represented a significant challenge and caused doctors to experiment with methods of transporting lymph including dried pieces of thread and glass plates.[146] Yet an order from the King's son and that issued during wartime, concentrated the minds and directly encouraged innovation.

Delighted with the results of the 1800 trial, Frederick issued a recommendation to other officers "to use their best endeavours to cause the whole of the men in their respective regiments on whom there are no marks of their having had one or other of the disorders, to be immediately inoculated with the vaccine matter."[147] In July 1801 he sent Walker and Marshall to vaccinate the army in the Mediterranean. In 1803, Frederick issued the order:

> The inoculation of the cow pock is to be constantly practiced. Let every man who does not bear the mark of the small pox either by inoculation or otherwise be subject to the trial of the cow pock (if it has not already been done) after the manner described in Appendix no 5. The cow pock occasions no disturbance to the frame or confinement from duty and therefore may be performed either in barracks or quarters. When cow pock matter is wanted, applications may be made

---

[144] Derrick Baxby, 'A Death from Inoculated Smallpox in the English Royal Family' in *Medical History*, vol 28, (1984) pp.303-307. Frederick had been inoculated himself on 3rd March 1766 when he was two, William Henry Ireland *The Universal Chronologist* vol. 2 (London 1835) p.972. Approximately one person in fifty variolated died as a result, F. Fenner et al., *Smallpox and its Eradication*, (WHO, 1988) p.255

[145] Anon, *Letter to the Duke of York*, (London, 1808) pp.8, 14

[146] Andrea Rusnock, 'Catching Cowpox: The Early Spread of Smallpox Vaccination' in *Bulletin of the History of Medicine*, Vol. 83, No. 1, (Spring 2009), pp.17-36

[147] *Gentleman's Magazine* vol. 71 (April 1801) p318

for it to this office; but the respective surgeons are expected to use every precaution to keep up a supply of fluid matter."[148]

It is always difficult to assess the effect of a preventive measure for it is uncertain how many would have been affected without, nonetheless, the fact that of 176,067 soldiers treated during the Peninsular Wars 1811-1814, not one had smallpox, is a testimony to the importance of Frederick's decision.[149] Armies in the past had been decimated by the disease. An outbreak in camp could change the outcome of a campaign and cost the lives of maybe a third of the men with almost as many more left blind or maimed.[150] Frederick was not the first commander to attempt to protect his men – General Washington in America and Frederick the Great in Prussia had both variolated their troops, the former cutting his death rate by over eighty-per cent[151] – but he was the first to vaccinate. Napoleon was so impressed that he decided to follow suit in 1805.

Despite his evident talent for administration, Frederick yearned to be back on the front line and on 9th September 1799, Frederick departed with another expeditionary force to Holland. After the disappointments of the 1793-94 campaign, he was keen to restore his own military reputation as a commander. This time, due to a shortage of British soldiers available, he was to work with the Russians. This proved an altogether more difficult relationship as Frederick spoke no Russian and few of the Russian troops spoke any English. Frederick was chosen to lead the expedition because he had some experience of the area, because as a prince his authority was recognised by the Tsar in the way that an ordinary general would not have been and because the aim of the expedition was to restore his brother in law.[152]

Once again, the expedition was arranged in a hurry and as a result the troops were badly supplied. Only six days food was provided and very little ammunition. Two battalions did not have a coat between them and less than half the wagons promised by the government had been built at the time they embarked. As a result, wagons which Frederick had condemned as unfit for

---

[148] WO 3/152

[149] Cantle op.cit. p.508

[150] Peter Razzell, *The Conquest of Smallpox*, (Sussex, 1977) p.132. Anon, *Letter to the Duke of York*, (London, 1808) p.11

[151] Nicolau Barquet and Pere Domingo, 'Smallpox: The Triumph over the most terrible of the ministers of Death' in *Annals of Internal Medicine*, vol.27, no. 8 (October 1997), p.638. See also Eric Croddy and James Wirtz (ed.), *Weapons of Mass Destruction*, (Santa Barbara) p.311

[152] Frederica of Prussia's younger sister had married the Hereditary Prince, a man for whom Frederick had scant respect and whom he called "Young Hopeful", see Malmesbury vol.3 op.cit. p.18

purpose in 1793 were dusted off and sent out. No fuel was supplied so Frederick had to resort to burning Dutch ships to try and keep his men warm.[153]

Despite these obstacles, the allied army began well. On October 8th, *The Times* proclaimed:

> It has never yet fallen to our lot to relate a happier or a more important event. It is no less than the entire defeat of the French and Batavian armies, the forcing of their strong entrenchments in West Friesland and the capture of the town of Alkmaar.

Frederick attributed the victory to God and "those animated and persevering exertions which have been at all times characteristic and which on no occasion were ever more eminently displayed; nor has it fallen to the lot of any General to have such just cause of acknowledgment for distinguished support."[154]

After such an announcement, it came as a shock for those at home to read just a few days later that the army was in retreat. There were a variety of reasons, not least the weather. As one medical officer reported: "we had constant rains and the whole country was one continuous swamp being nearly flooded with water."[155] Dysentery set in and just four days after the battle of Alkmaar, Frederick's troops were reduced to twenty-seven thousand men, just over half his original total.[156] The rain affected supplies and by damaging crops prohibited the finding of food locally. Other problems included the Dutch inhabitants showing no inclination to support the invaders, divisions between the allies and a lack of military prospects. Frederick was faced with a dilemma. He could remove his men safely from their current position of danger by opening the dykes but that would endanger the lives and livelihoods of many thousands of inhabitants. Reluctantly, he made the decision to sue for peace. His motives, as he stated on 17th October were: "to prevent the further effusion of blood and to preserve this country from the terrible effects of an inundation as also from the destruction of the best of its ports involving the total ruin of the principal channels of its interior navigation and commerce."[157] Although his efforts were a reflection of his Christian principles and saved many lives, they were not appreciated at the time. Frederick was roundly criticised for

---

[153] Fortescue vol.4 part 2 op.cit. pp.449, 667

[154] *London Gazette,* 8th October, 1799

[155] William Ferguson, *Notes and Recollections of a Professional Life,* (London, 1846) p.186

[156] W. Mitchell, *The Campaign in Holland, 1799,* (London, 1861) p.57

[157] Anon, *The Dutch Expedition Vindicated,* (London, 1799) p.32

weakly surrendering to the enemy. Some years later *The Times* was sympathetic saying of Frederick that he had "obstacles to encounter which no human foresight could have foreseen and which no General could effectually surmount." [158] An officer who served said that the troops behaviour had been "beyond praise and its sufferings beyond pity; whatever men could do was done but conduct and bravery were never of less avail."[159]

Although the army occupied the bulk of Frederick's time, there were other events which affected him. On 15th May, 1800, Frederick was witness to an attempt on his father's life. The family had gone to the Drury Lane Theatre for a performance of *She Would and She Would Not*. As usual, when the royal family entered their box, the King stepped forward to acknowledge the crowd. As he did so, two gunshots were fired from an assailant standing just over thirty feet away. Amidst the uproar which followed, the King stood calm and erect in the royal box though he motioned for the Queen and his daughters to step back. He reassured the Queen "they are firing squibs, just squibs." The man who fired was wrestled to the ground and hauled over the rails into the orchestra pit and from there taken to the Music Room for interrogation. The rest of the royal family took their seats saving the Duchess of York who had fainted and was "so long in a state of insensibility that she was supposed to be dead." Fortunately, Princess Elizabeth had some smelling salts with her. Sheridan quickly composed a new verse for the national anthem which was sung with gusto several times along with Rule Britannia.

> *From every latent foe*
> *From the assassin's blow*
> *God shield the King!*
> *O'er him thine arm extend*
> *For Britain's sake defend*
> *Our Father, Prince and Friend*
> *God save the King!*

The play then began though Frederick missed most of it for he was with the would-be assassin, a man named James Hadfield. As soon as Frederick entered the room, Hadfield said: "God bless you. I know you. You are a good fellow – you are His Royal Highness, the Duke of York." Frederick was surprised to realise that he knew the man too because he had served him as an orderly during the 1793-1794 campaign in the Low Countries. Frederick particularly remembered his service with the 15th Light Dragoons at the

---

[158] *The Times*, 8th January, 1827
[159] *The Dutch Expedition Vindicated* op.cit. p.12

Battle of Famars. Frederick asked him, "then why attempt to kill my father?" Hadfield said that he was tired of life but he lacked courage to kill himself and that he had therefore devised the plan of attempting to kill the King, confident that this would result in him being put to death. Thus far, as Frederick was to observe at Hadfield's trial, he appeared perfectly calm and collected but this impression changed when Hadfield alleged that he was given the idea by God who wanted him to suffer like Jesus. Frederick ordered the man to be taken away and resumed his seat in the theatre. After the performance when the King and Queen had left, Frederick ordered a search of the theatre and two marks were found, one just fourteen inches above the King's head and the other in the roof of the box below.

Hadfield's trial took place a month later and it emerged that he had been discharged from the army for insanity. Captain Wilson of the 15th said his early service had been excellent: "If a man was to be selected for courage, dauntless and bravery, intrepid spirit, Hadfield was that man." Captain Magill, agreeing, said that the change had taken place following the Battle of Lille where Hadfield "received a wound in the forehead with a thrust of a sword, his cheek almost separated from his face with a sabre, his arm from the shoulder bared to the wrist, a wound at the back of his neck twice through the body and the top of his head scalped" and was left for dead in a ditch. The wounds had healed physically but left severe mental scars. The jury in response brought in a verdict of not guilty on grounds of insanity and Hadfield was led away to spend the rest of his life in an asylum.[160] Frederick sought afterwards to persuade his father to use the services of a bodyguard but to no avail. The King argued that employment of such would show a want of faith in his subjects.[161]

In the autumn of 1803, with the country threatened with invasion, George, Prince of Wales, decided to volunteer his services to the nation. He wrote to the Prime Minister, Mr Addington, saying that although he had no military experience, he had "long made the Service my particular study" and suggested that his example would excite "the loyal energies of the nation." He went on: "the claim which I have advanced is strictly constitutional and justified by precedent and that in the present situation of Europe to deny my exercising it is fatal to my own immediate honour and the future interest of the Crown." Adding that he had no wish to embarrass the Tory government, he declared: "no event in my future life can compensate me for the misfortune of not participating in the honours and dangers which await the brave men destined to oppose an invading enemy" and concluded that he

---

[160] For accounts of the assassination see *The Times*, 17th May 1800, *Bell's Weekly Messenger*, 18th May 1800, *Caledonian Mercury*, 19th May 1800. For the trial see *Caledonian Mercury*, 30th June 1800.

[161] *Memoirs of Her Most Excellent Majesty, Sophia-Charlotte* op.cit. p.455

was entitled to be more than a "mere colonel."[162]

That George was unsuited for military command was clear to everyone who knew him, though flatterers – mainly from the Whig party – rushed to support him. Moore claimed that: "I am sure the powder in His Royal Highness's hair is much more settled than anything in his head."[163] Nathaniel Wraxall said he was:

..a most fascinating and accomplished gentleman, but he wanted all the qualities of a wise or of a great prince : self-command, application, economy, activity, firmness, and above all, economical principles.... There was from head to foot a flaccidity of muscle and a rotundity of outline ...his person...had, something diffused over it indicative of repose or of sloth, rather than of energy or activity.[164]

George had received no military training other than some generalised drill as a schoolboy. He had been to camp with his regiment but he had ensconced himself in a magnificent tent with specially made furniture including an extra large bed with lilac chintz curtains and chairs worth a thousand pounds and spent most of his time partying and dining. As Colonel of the 10th Dragoons, he excused his officers early drill so they could recover from their hangovers and wrote covering notes for when they had syphilis.[165] His "china tenth" were said to be the "most impertinent, the best dressed, the worse moralled regiment in the British Army."[166] The idea of him enduring the horrors of war was laughable and unsurprisingly the Prime Minister did not hurry to respond. Mr Addington did, however, advise the King of George's offer and relayed back to George the answer he received which was negative. George then wrote to the King himself saying "the fear of sinking in the estimation of that gallant army which may be the support of your Majesty's crown and my best hope hereafter command me to persevere." He reminded his father that his younger brothers all outranked him and claimed "when I am debased, the cause of Royalty is wounded." He added dramatically, "Europe, the world and posterity must judge between

---

[162] *The Correspondence between His Majesty, the Prince of Wales, the Duke of York and Mr Addington,* (London, 1803) pp.1-4

[163] Spencer Walpole, *The life of the Right Honourable Spencer Perceval,* vol 2, (London, 1874) p.226

[164] Wheatley op.cit. pp.353, 363. George had been noted to be substantially overweight in 1788, see Harcourt op.cit. p.38

[165] *The Times,* 5th August and 31st August, 1793. Kelly op.cit. p.136

[166] Grace and Philip Wharton, *The Wits and Beaux of Society,* (London, 1867) p.403. For the history of the nickname, see Robert Liddell, *The Memoirs of the Tenth Royal Hussars,* (London, 1891) p.207

us."[167] The King replied saying that if the enemy landed, George could lead his regiment. A furious George wrote back: "I ought to be first and foremost" and complained of his humiliation at only being a Colonel of Dragoons.

Aware that the King was not about to move, George then decided to protest to Frederick, arguing that as a long standing Colonel, he was more entitled to promotion than others whom had been raised. He said he had no desire for "idle inactive rank" but that being told he could serve only with his regiment was "a degrading mockery." Frederick politely pointed out that given there was a war on, he was rather busy, and reminded George of the King's statement in 1795 that no Prince of Wales could expect to regard the army as a profession or to advance in it like other officers. As a loyal subject, Frederick intended to abide by the King's wishes. George was not mollified and hinted that "every part of this transaction may be publicly canvassed hereafter," a threat he was to carry out to the King's perpetual anger. He said that he was not aware of any such policy on the part of the King. Frederick promptly responded that it was George who had told him this at Carlton House in 1793 and there were witnesses. Confirming that he was unable to promote him in the army, he suggested George contact the government for a political role. George absolutely exploded at this and accused Frederick of "a palpable misconstruction...I defy the most skilful logician in torturing the English language to apply with fairness such a construction to any word or phrase of mine."[168] When George announced he was returning to Brighton ready to defend the coast with his 10th Dragoons, Frederick promptly removed his regiment inland.[169]

The row was important because it severely soured the relationship between the brothers. Almost six months later, George was still refusing to see Frederick when he called at Carlton House.[170] Although they were eventually reconciled, the warmth was lost. When in 1809, a spurned mistress of Frederick's threatened to publicly humiliate him, George notably failed to support his brother and said that he should have given in to her blackmail.[171] In family disputes, George invariably sided with his other brothers against Frederick. Charles Greville said that whenever Frederick told anecdotes, George's "bad temper, bad judgment, falseness and duplicity were equally conspicuous. I think it is not possible for any man to have a worse opinion of another."[172] They shared a love of horses and Brighton and

---

[167] *Correspondence* op.cit. pp.8-11

[168] ibid. pp.16-31

[169] Christopher Hibbert, *George IV*, (London, 1976) p.242

[170] CGPW vol. 4 p.493

[171] Duke of Buckingham and Chandos, *Memoirs of the Court and Cabinets of George III* vol. 4 (London, 1853) pp.325-326, 329

[172] Charles Greville, *A Journal of the Reigns of King George IV and King William IV* (London,

an interest in the arts but they were very different as people. George was a total hedonist given to absurd displays of histrionics whenever he feared he was not about to get his own way. His illegal union with Maria Fitzherbert only took place after he threatened to kill himself and duly daubed himself with blood to create a false stab wound.[173] George's bad treatment of his wife, Caroline of Brunswick, was legendary. Just a couple of days after his daughter was born, George again declared he was going to end his life and composed a will in which left "her who is called the Princess of Wales" just one shilling and made detailed plans to remove the newly born child permanently from her mother.[174] Frederick and his wife deeply disapproved and did their best to support both Caroline and the baby, further attracting George's ire. Even when George became Regent, and later still when he was king, he treated Frederick with contempt. On one occasion, Frederick had arranged for a particular regiment to travel to the West Indies to handle an issue of national security, but at the very last moment, George decided he would prefer to have them at Windsor and demanded that all arrangements were changed.[175] Toward the end of his life, Frederick was building a new home at St James which was well under way when George suddenly decided he did not like the plans and so insisted on a complete redesign, something which was at enormous expense to his brother whom he knew could not afford it.[176] Princess Lieven, who knew both men well wrote: "Their relations are strange. They are afraid of one another; they have no affection for one another, no esteem; and yet they are always making up to one another. The Duke of York attaches importance to the King's favour, the King to his brother's moral support."[177] It is probable that George's attitude stemmed from jealousy for Frederick was regularly cheered in the streets unlike himself.[178]

In addition to his work with the army, Frederick supported a number of charitable endeavours. These fall into two main groups; medical and educational, though he also had links to things such as the London Lifeboat Saturday Fund. On the medical side, he worked with the Royal Universal Dispensary which provided medicine and doctor's visits to the poor and the Laying In Hospital which provided maternity care for poor women. His wife

---

1875) vol.1 pp.73-74

[173] CGPW vol. 1 p.139. See also Hibbert op.cit. p.94

[174] CGPW vol. 3 pp.133-138

[175] Greville op.cit. p.74

[176] Howard Colvin, 'The Architects of Stafford House' in *Architectural History*, vol.1 (1958) pp.17-30

[177] Peter Quennell (ed.), *The Private Letters of Princess Lieven to Prince Metternich* (London, 1937) pp. 286, 333

[178] Earl of Ilchester (ed), *The Journal of the Hon Henry Edward Fox* , (London, 1923) p.38, Fulford op.cit p.75, Quennell op.cit. p.43, *The Times* 24th May, 1822

supported a Laying In charity for poor soldiers' wives. He was a prime mover behind the Royal Westminster Opthalmic Hospital and was particularly concerned with smallpox serving as a governor and then president of the London Smallpox Hospital. During this time, he paid regular visits to the premises and "enquired attentively into the cases of the patients" even going to speak to some of them, a move at the time which was startling. Frederick was heir to the throne and smallpox was both deadly and contagious. In doing this, he publicly demonstrated his faith in the effects of vaccination and inoculation and in its safety.[179] Cartoons by Gillray and others had spread fears that injecting matter taken from a cow would result in "new diseases of frightful and monstrous appearance" so this was vital.[180] In 1806, Frederick told the Royal Jennerian Society that vaccination was an unspeakable benefit to mankind and looked forward to it spreading across the globe to eliminate the scourge of the disease.[181]

With regard to education, he supported the National Society which established schools for the working classes. He was a founder of the Philological Society which was set up to provide an education for the sons of clergymen, naval officers or merchants who were in straitened circumstances and otherwise unable to supply such. A school was established in Mary Street which taught not just reading, writing and arithmetic but Latin, geography and French with classes in navigation for those destined for a career at sea.[182] Frederick was President from 1799 to 1827 of the Philanthropic Society which aimed to provide hope to destitute children who had often fallen into a life of crime. An institute was opened at Southwark which sought to inculcate Christian values and to prepare the children for apprenticeships. Keen to lead by example, Frederick took in an abandoned child but the efforts of him and his wife at reform failed and the boy proved apt to steal. In 1797, the child was apprenticed as a framework knitter.[183] Still keen to work in the area of rehabilitation, Frederick was co-founder with Edward Whitaker of the Refuge for Persons Discharged from Prisons. Aimed at adults, this too sought to encourage habits of thrift and industry and to give people skills which would enable them to obtain regular work, the Refuge actively trying to obtain positions for them so they could start again. Skills taught included baking, spinning, knitting, carpentry and horticulture. Its goal as stated in 1810 was to provide convicts with

---

[179] *The London Medical Repository Monthly Journal*, vol 12 (1819) p.171

[180] 'Report of the Royal College of Physicians of London on Vaccination, 8th July 1807' in *The Philosophical Magazine*, vol. XXVIII, (Summer 1807) p.322

[181] *The Morning Post*, 19th May, 1806. See also Watkins op.cit. p.487. The world was finally pronounced free of smallpox by the World Health Organisation in 1980.

[182] John Adolphus, *The Political State of the British Empire*, vol.3. (London, 1818) p.673. The school later became the St Marylebone Grammar School.

[183] Muriel Whitton, *Nipping Crime in the Bud*, (Hampshire, 2011) pp.75-76.

"employment and subsistence when all other doors are shut against them" so they could "once more enter the world with a retrieved character and with the prospect of becoming useful members of society."[184]

Naturally, not all of Frederick's time was taken up with work. As a young man, he was an enthusiastic tennis player and he enjoyed playing cricket in the summer. He took a keen interest in boxing. Fighting at that time was particularly brutal. On the 25th October 1808, for example, he attended an evening where there were three contests on the bill. Held outdoors in an extra large ring, one contestant was "most dreadfully disfigured having received not less than one hundred severe blows in the face but although so completely beaten he fought till blind before he yielded and even then felt desirous of trying another round." Another became "so weak that his knees gave way and he fell on his hands and actually pulled at the grass with passion."[185] Frederick gambled on the results of sporting events as well as on cards. He was said to be addicted to faro, Wraxall writing: "To the attractions of the other sex he was not insensible, but a rage for play absorbed every other passion in his bosom."[186] He maintained his own stables and won the Derby with Prince Leopold in 1816 and Moses in 1822. The former was a great surprise to everyone but the latter was recognised to be one of the greatest horses of his generation. One writer said "his fame flies as fast as he gallops."[187] After Frederick's death in 1827, Moses was sold for eleven hundred guineas, almost ninety thousand pounds in today's money.[188] An avid collector of all forms of militaria and keen marksman, Frederick derived enjoyment too from reading, an interest he shared with his wife. When he died, his library was found to contain more than forty-five thousand volumes, many of them relating to history. Frederick was especially interested in the Tudor dynasty but also in archaeology, constitutional studies and medieval warfare. His collection included a number of books on natural history and travel suggesting that he wished he had had opportunities to go on voyages of his own and see more of the world. Perhaps surprisingly given their vicious lampooning of him, Frederick also possessed a volume of Gillray's political cartoons.[189]

Shortly after two o'clock on the morning of Saturday 21st January 1809, Frederick and his wife were startled to be awoken by the sound of drummers from the Guards regiment beating to arms. They dressed hastily

---

[184] Anthony Highmore, *Pietas Londinensis*, (London, 1810) pp.264-7. The institution was renamed the Refuge for the Destitute. For the story of its foundation, see Watkins op.cit. p.323

[185] Anon, *Pancratia*, (London, 1812) pp.319-322

[186] Wheatley op.cit. p.394

[187] *New Sporting Magazine* vol. 5 (1833) p.251

[188] *The Times*, 6th February, 1827

[189] *The Times*, 5th May, 21st May and 13th July, 1827

and emerged to find the whole of St James' Palace in a panic. Servants were running everywhere, people were shouting and women screaming. The palace was on fire. They evacuated immediately and waited outside with the Dukes of Cumberland and Cambridge. The fire had begun near the King's back stairs and it spread rapidly through the Queen's private apartments, the Dutch Chapel and as far as the King's closet. Engines were kept at the Palace but these had proved ineffectual because of a lack of water. A well existed in the grounds but could not be accessed because the man who had dug it had been dismissed from his job and nobody else could find it beneath the snow that lay about everywhere. As a result, they tried to convey water from St James' Park by using a relay of engines but this failed to provide more than a trickle of water nearest the flames. Meantime, servants leapt from windows or tried to escape across the roof which had started to melt casting down "liquid torrents" of lead on the firemen below. One failed and suffocated in her room. Frederick ordered soldiers to assist with removing valuables from the palace, but much was lost. By morning it was clear that the entire east wing was destroyed.[190]

As if the fire was not a big enough blow to the royal family, on Friday 27th January a worse one fell. On that day, Colonel Gwyllym Wardle gave a sensational speech in the House of Commons accusing Frederick of corruption. He alleged that Captain Tonyn of the 48th Regiment of Foot had purchased his commission as Major through a lady named Mary Anne Clarke whom Frederick had set up as his mistress. He said that Lieutenant Colonel Brooke of the 56th and Major John Shawe had also purchased their commissions through her and that Frederick was aware of this, even putting Shawe on half pay when he failed to pay Mary Anne the full amount due. Wardle spoke of a Captain Maling who was promoted "without one hour's military service" and a Colonel French who had secured a levy on favourable terms thanks to Mary Anne and shared the profits with her. To further blacken the picture, Wardle then told of an officer who feared his health would not withstand a posting to the West Indies but who, lacking money for a bribe to Mary Anne, had been sent there by Frederick quite deliberately where he had died. Wardle added that another mistress named Mrs Carey was performing a similar service with an office in London itself selling army commissions and positions in both Church and State and he called on Parliament to establish an enquiry "to investigate the conduct of His Royal Highness the Duke of York in his capacity of Commander-in-Chief with regard to appointments, promotions, exchanges, the raising of new levies and the general state of the army."[191]

---

[190] *Morning Chronicle*, 23rd January 1809, *The Times* 23rd January 1809

[191] The speech and minutes of the subsequent enquiry were published in full in the newspapers of the time and in Hansard and as official publications, but references here are to the *Full and*

Given the seriousness of the allegations, the government had no choice but to agree and as a result a committee of the whole house met from February 1st to February 22nd to take evidence from more than thirty witnesses. Wardle clearly enjoyed his role of public defender and during the course of the inquiry added some further allegations, including one that Mary Anne's footman had been given a commission as a favour to her. Yet the evidence produced failed to support his case. Captain Maling was shown to have had almost three years service[192] and the application for Brooke's exchange predated Mary Anne's involvement, though she had charged for her alleged expedition of it.[193] Shawe had promised Mary Anne a thousand pounds for his promotion but had in fact only given her half this amount. He claimed that he did not owe her anything because she had not in fact secured his promotion and army records supported this, General Gordon being able to demonstrate almost two years worth of correspondence regarding Shawe and recommendations from Lieutenant General Henry Burrard. With regard the claim that Frederick had put Shawe on half pay in response to his failure to pay Mary Anne, Gordon revealed that it was usual for field officers who accepted a staff position overseas to be automatically put on half pay and he provided evidence in confirmation of this, including salary information from Shawe's fellow staff officers at the Cape of Good Hope.[194] Samuel Carter, who had worked for Mary Anne as a footman for almost a year was shown to have been recommended for a commission back in 1801 by Lieutenant Sutton.[195] Captain Tonyn had been recommended by his father General Tonyn in June 1803 and was created a Major in August 1804 along with more than fifty others as part of an augmentation of the army. At the time, Tonyn had over twenty years military service.[196] Colonel French had indeed applied for a levy which had been granted through the usual channels and the special terms he had sought had been refused by Frederick.[197] Wardle offered no evidence to support his allegation that Frederick had sought a loan from French and none relating to Mrs Carey. It emerged that a Mr Kennett had promised that if he was granted a particular role in Surinam "I shall be ready to advance to His Royal Highness any amount he may wish" but also that Frederick had immediately ceased contact with him.[198] In short, Frederick was exonerated from all claims of corruption.

Accurate Report of the Evidence Produced on Mr Wardle's Accusation (Dublin, 1809). See p. 6
[192] ibid. pp.46, 48.
[193] ibid. pp.10, 30.
[194] ibid. pp.170-173
[195] ibid. pp.178-179
[196] ibid. p.140
[197] ibid. p.129
[198] ibid. pp.222-224

In addition to facts and figures regarding appointments, the investigation produced plenty of salacious and sensational material which ensured that Frederick and Mary Anne were the talk of the entire country. There was, for example, his manservant who reported that for two years he had gone to her house at eight each morning with Frederick's clothes and the housekeeper who confirmed taking them messages when they were in bed together.[199] Mary Anne claimed she would pin a list of names of men for whom she sought a promotion to the bedpost and that Frederick would then take it down to read and act upon.[200] She also produced two of his letters which included paragraphs such as:

How can I sufficiently express to my sweetest, my darling love, the pleasure and delight of her excellent and pretty letter. A million and a million of thanks, my angel, for this kindness which my heart acknowledges in its love for you.

Oh my angel! Never was woman adored as you are. How long and tedious is the time since we parted and how I long for the day after tomorrow when I shall again clasp my darling in my arms.[201]

Another note which read, "I have received your note and Major Tonyn's business remains as it is" caused considerable controversy. Mary Anne alleged it was written by the Duke and Wardle said this indicated Frederick was aware of her involvement in promotions. In his only utterance on the proceedings, Frederick responded: "I have no knowledge of the thing and believe it is a forgery."[202] The committee set about interviewing people to try and obtain the truth. Two officials from the General Post Office claimed the handwriting of the note matched the letters. Mr Beresford, an MP, detected "a very material difference" between the handwriting. General Gordon said that Frederick always signed his notes and this document was unsigned which made him suspicious of its authenticity. General Brownrigg said: "I don't think it is very like the Duke's handwriting." Colonel Hamilton said that the formation of the "t"s differed. Mr Dickie of Coutts Bank noted the size of writing was different. Mr Nisbett of the Bank of England said: "I perceive throughout the whole a neatness in almost every letter of the note which is not to be found in the two letters and the whole of the writing in the note appears to be of a smaller character that that of the letters in general. Besides this I think I perceive a stiffness in several of the letters of the note which I do not discern in the two letters." His colleague at the

---

[199] ibid. pp.40, 206
[200] ibid. pp.96, 289
[201] ibid. p.153
[202] ibid. p.249

Bank, Mr Bliss, said that he had thought they were by the same hand until he saw Mary Anne's letters. At this point, Mr Town, an artist who had given Mary Anne lessons, volunteered that she had boasted to him of her ability to "forge" Frederick's handwriting. Mary Anne did not disagree and admitted she was able to produce a very near likeness but said that she only did it for her own amusement. She happily added that she could copy the Speaker's writing too. Further revelations showed that the note had appeared just after Tonyn had asked for his money back. Apparently he had lost faith in Mary Anne's ability to procure his promotion and the note had been sent to him as reassurance. It all seemed just a little too convenient for the committee's liking.[203]

Another supposedly damning piece of evidence to be given and which turned out to be questionable came from a Miss Taylor. She claimed that she had regularly dined with Frederick and Mary Anne and that on one occasion, Frederick had asked Mary Anne for her opinion on Colonel French. When she replied "not very well", Frederick had said "French must mind what he is about else I will soon cut him up and his levy too."[204] She was, however, totally unable to remember when this conversation took place, if anyone else was there, or the context of it, adding that she had not even remembered the discussion until Mary Anne helpfully reminded her just before the hearing.[205] The butler meantime commented: "I never saw her in company with the Duke of York" which was in accordance with the statement of one of the footmen. [206] The housekeeper disagreed and said that Miss Taylor did indeed dine with Frederick and Mary Anne regularly. To add to the suspicion that the testimony was false, it was noted that both Miss Taylor and the housekeeper were related to Mary Anne although the exact details remained a mystery since the mothers of the ladies seemed uncertain as to the identities of the fathers.[207]

The committee were forced to conclude that whilst there was plenty of evidence to show that Mary Anne had told people she was able to obtain commissions and that she had accepted money on this basis, and moreover she had continued to trade in positions following her separation from Frederick in 1806, there was no evidence that Frederick himself had known anything about it. Indeed, every witness called testified that Mary Anne had

---

[203] ibid. pp. 231, 247, 251-252, 261, 267, 269, 271, 275. The note was addressed to George Farquhar which was a name Mary Anne claimed Frederick used for her. That a playwright of this name had written a play *The Recruiting Officer* in 1706 was deemed an allusion to her role.
[204] ibid. p.106
[205] ibid. pp.303-304
[206] ibid. p.123, 203
[207] ibid. pp.106, 206-207, 297-298, 306. Miss Taylor's brother had married Mary Anne's sister whilst the housekeeper – who used a variety of names – appeared to be her half sister.

sworn them to secrecy saying that they must take care not to let Frederick know or she would be lost. The day after the hearings ended, Frederick submitted his own statement asking that if there remained any doubt about his innocence, he would be happy to attend to give evidence himself:

> I observe with the deepest concern that in the course of the inquiry my name has been coupled with transactions of the most criminal and disgraceful nature and I must ever regret that a connection should ever have existed which has thus exposed my character and honour to public animadversion. With respect to any alleged offences connected with the discharge of my official duties, I do in the most solemn manner, upon my honour as a Prince, distinctly assert my entire innocence, not only by denying all corrupt participation in any of the infamous transactions or any connivance at their existence, but also the slightest knowledge or suspicion that they existed at all.[208]

Yet severe damage had been done to his reputation. People were shocked by the openness with which he had conducted the relationship, even securing Mary Anne a cottage near Oatlands where she had come face to face with the furious Duchess[209] and by his evident lack of judgment in getting involved with a woman like her in the first place. Mary Anne was shown throughout the inquiry to be an habitual liar, a prostitute, and a woman prone to threatening others. She admitted telling a number of people that if she did not receive money she would: "be compelled to publish the Duke of York's letters to enable me to pay my creditors which he refused to pay."[210] Princes often took mistresses but they were expected to show more taste and discretion. It was also evident that he had discussed military affairs with her, and even if she had been devoid of influence, this was not considered appropriate. As the Commons debated what to do next, Frederick resigned his position as Commander-in-Chief. It was an act of "manly indignation" as one paper put it, an acceptance that trying to alter public opinion now was like trying to "change the course of the Thames". He was "most falsely accused, most maliciously traduced and most scandalously persecuted" but to many, he was the fool and the villain.[211]

Meantime Mary Anne remained the heroine of the hour to the general public and she was treated with remarkable generosity by the committee who could and should have jailed her for perjury. Wardle was honoured for his public spirit in London and one writer summed up the mood by claiming:

---

[208] ibid. p.309
[209] ibid. p.92. See also Watkins op.cit. p.448
[210] ibid. p.20
[211] *The Satirist*, April 1809, pp.365-371

"Colonel Wardle has done more towards bringing down the goliath of corruption than all the rest of the parliamentary phalanx put together."[212] Some were more cynical, regarding it as simply the revenge of the Whigs who had hated Frederick since he opposed the military aspirations of their hero, the Prince of Wales, and who wanted to attack the government over the poor performance in the war. Just two days before Wardle's speech, Parliament had debated the disastrous Spanish campaign and recent retreat with heavy losses from Corunna.[213] Mr Yorke suggested it was "a conspiracy of the most atrocious and diabolical kind ... founded on the jacobinical spirit." [214]

Those who suspected the motives of Frederick's opponents were soon to find their suspicions confirmed. Later that same year, it emerged that Wardle had offered to furnish a house for Mary Anne in return for her story and that he had bribed others for information too. It was further revealed that he had worked with Major Dodd, the private secretary of Edward, Duke of Kent.[215] Mary Anne told Lord Folkestone, one of her paramours, that Wardle was "an agent of the Duke of Kent."[216] Relations between the royal brothers had not been good since Frederick had blamed Edward for the 1803 mutiny in Gibraltar to say nothing of his criticism of Edward's love life,[217] but the suggestion that he had been involved in the plot prompted the Duke of Kent to issue a statement denying that his secretary was acting on his behalf.[218] Further investigation showed that Wardle's own military ambitions had been frustrated by Frederick's reforms which gave him cause for a grudge.[219] A jury on 3rd July convicted Wardle of masterminding the plot and he in turn had Mary Anne charged with perjury on 10th December, though he failed to obtain a conviction. For Frederick, the squabbles between the protagonists were of little interest even though they resulted in his return to his army role, for he had more important things to worry about. In November 1810, his sister Amelia had died after a long illness and his father had gone mad with grief prompting the creation of elder brother George as Prince Regent on 5th February 1811.

---

[212] Elizabeth Taylor, *The Authentic Memoirs of Mrs Clarke* (London 1809) p.197

[213] Rachel Leighton (ed.) *Correspondence of Charlotte Grenville, Lady Williams Wynn* (London, 1920) p.142. See also *A Plain Statement of the Conduct of the Ministry and the Opposition* (London, 1808) which highighted the attacks made on Frederick by the Whigs since the demise of William Pitt, pp. 15-21, 43

[214] *The Times*, 28th January 1809

[215] Mary Anne Clarke, *The Rival Princes*, (London, 1810) pp.31-32, 42-43, 103-107, 114-118

[216] Herbert Maxwell (ed), *The Creevey Papers* vol.1 (London 1904) pp.113-115

[217] Mollie Gillen *The Prince and his Lady* (Toronto, 1970) pp.160-161, CGPW vol.4 p.81

[218] Watkins op.cit. pp.463-464

[219] Richard Holmes, *Redcoat* (London, 2001) p.82

Many people as they become older have to face the reality that a once dependable parent has now become a dependent and Frederick was clearly distressed by what was happening. His father with whom he had been very close was now incapable of maintaining a rational conversation. The King would talk too fast on a wide variety of subjects and it was impossible to understand him or reply. Even more disturbing, as a result of his illness, the King started to use coarse and obscene language, sometimes about his wife. After a lifetime in the army, Frederick was no prude but it was upsetting to see his ordinarily dignified and deeply religious father behaving in manner which was demeaning and out of character. The King became confused about simple things and hallucinated, seeing people who were not there and panicking about events that were not happening. As if that was not enough, the King whose eyesight had been poor for some time, went blind. He could no longer see Frederick when he visited or his family in the garden outside. He could not read or write. He could not move about freely but instead had to grope his way across the room. It followed that he could no longer feed himself or carry out basic hygiene tasks unaided. The King knew he was being watched by servants employed by his doctors but he did not know who or where they were and protocol meant they could not initiate communication unless he was at risk of harming himself or them. By 1817, his hearing was deteriorating. The extent of his deafness varied according to the medication he was taking but meant that Frederick now faced the problem of how to communicate with his father who could neither see nor often hear him. He could hold his hand but only if the King was having a good day and was not under restraint.

As early as September 1811, Frederick was expressing his concerns to George that the doctors did not agree about how to treat their father.[220] He noted how the medicine given to him seemed to be making him worse and commented on the fact that symptoms of insanity appeared immediately after administration of the stipulated dosages.[221] He was deeply worried about whether the right decisions were being made and, being anxious to do all he could to help, he started to offer financial support to doctors seeking to increase understanding of mental health. None of their work was published in the King's lifetime and Frederick probably felt guilty that the had not been able to help his father more but the encouragement he gave to the development of psychiatry would be of benefit to thousands of people over the decades that followed.

Frederick's earliest interest was centred around the theories of Dr William Heberden. He had treated the King in 1804 when there had been

---

[220] CGPW vol 8 p.151
[221] ibid. pp.160,197

signs of mental disturbance for two months.[222] Heberden had subsequently been appointed the King's personal physician in 1809, the year before the final madness began. He made no claim to be a specialist in mental health but the King had elicited a promise from him when he was ill that no matter what happened, Heberden would stay with him. As a man of principle, Heberden felt that it was therefore incumbent upon him to do his best. Amongst his wide reading on the subject, he read Philippe Pinel's *Treatise on Insanity* which advocated gentleness and patience on the part of nursing staff and soothing warm baths. Heberden said that the insane needed "firmness combined with mildness and aided by a judicious application of medicines and a modest interchange of exercise and rest, of occupation and amusement, of company and retirement." He said that remedies should not be "confined to drugs and potions but calculated to afford consolation and refreshment by giving a new direction to the mind." He even contemplated something which was totally novel at the time, namely "if little can be done to cure it perhaps more can be done than is commonly supposed to prevent it." [223] Heberden's theories were the antithesis of Dr Willis who continued to believe that the King should be treated in solitary confinement to a diet of emetics and purgatives with restraint used whenever he objected, which meant most of the time. Heberden protested vehemently going so far as to say that: "I am of the opinion that the present medical treatment and management applied to His Majesty's case are fundamentally and practically wrong."[224] Dr Heberden tried to improve things by reading a newspaper to the King and talking to him but Dr Willis complained to the Queen that they "impeded the recovery" and she promptly banned such practices.[225] Aware that he was not a doctor and conscious of the fact that Dr Willis' father had been successful in 1789, Frederick sided with his mother at the time but the doubts lingered and encouraged him to seek more answers.

Heberden's work was built upon by Alexander Morison whom Frederick chose to appoint as one of his own physicians as a means of funding his research and facilitating his entry into places. Morison had begun his medical career working alongside Alexander Crichton who wrote in 1798 *An Inquiry into the Nature and Origin of Mental Derangement* which argued

---

[222] From 14th February to 25th April 1804. The physicians had advised Parliament at the time that the King was not insane arguing that he remained competent to reign but that he required a rest from public business.

[223] Dr William Heberden 'Some remarks on Nervous Disorders' read at the College of Physicians and printed in *The London Medical Gazette* vol 20 (London 1837) pp.424-429

[224] Jane and Robert Cantu 'The Psychiatric Efforts of William Heberden jr' in *Institute of the History of Medicine Bulletin,* (1967) vol.41 part 2 p.136. The Dr Willis involved was the son of Dr Francis Willis.

[225] Duke of Buckingham and Chandos, *Memoirs of the Court and Cabinets of George the Third,* vol. IV, (London, 1855) p.476

the necessity of looking at factors such as lifestyle or upbringing as a means of understanding insanity. This was revolutionary at the time and formed the foundation for much of Morison's later work. Previously there had been a tendency to treat all forms of mental illness as the same and to utilise the same methods on every patient, namely bleeding, purging and restraint. Morison argued that different types of mania required different treatments such as dark rooms for the excitable and light ones for the depressive. Having decided to specialise, Morison went to France to visit Esquirol and Pinel, two of the leading exponents of what was termed moral treatment at the time. His accounts of the visit are held in the library of the Royal College of Physicians at Edinburgh. He noted that the strait waistcoat was hardly ever used there but that the idea of keeping the insane in cold rooms as Willis had used for the King at Kew remained current. In 1823, Frederick encouraged Morison to commence the first ever series of public lectures on mental diseases, an idea which proved so successful that they became an annual event. In 1826, Morison published these lectures for the first time and two years later, the influential *Cases of Mental Disease with Practical Observations on the Medical Treatment*. In this, he acknowledged the dearth of material and invited other practitioners to augment knowledge for the good of all patients by making public their own work. He spoke of the many dissections which he had attended or studied and noted the lack of physical manifestations in the brain of insanity. This was important for many earlier practitioners had based their idea of treatments on the theory that madness was caused by excess fluid in the brain. The King had been blooded for this reason, and given blisters and mercury. Although Morison conceded restraint may be necessary in cases of violence, he believed that the vast majority of cases could be treated by establishing a regular routine which diverted and exercised the mind. He advocated training nurses to care for the insane rather than trust them to keepers who often used them as a vehicle for their own violent tendencies. By providing for the first time detailed case histories, Morison was able to show clinical results of different medical treatments. Other books of the time only spoke in generalised terms but Morison laid bare both his successes and failures so that others could learn from them.

In addition to this patronage, Frederick visited asylums to see the methods employed elsewhere. In 1817 he and his wife visited the famous Bethlehem Hospital and pronounced himself impressed by the light airy rooms and the high standard of cleanliness.[226] His visits were calculated to heighten awareness of mental illness and the need to develop an effective treatment for those affected.

---

[226] Bethlehem Hospital had only recently moved into what is today the Imperial War Museum. Initially the windows were not glazed in order to keep the temperature down and avoid exciting the patients but full windows were installed shortly before Frederick's visit.

By now the King was over seventy and the prognosis was not good. Over the past fifty years, there has been considerable speculation about the cause of the King's problems. Doctors Macalpine and Hunter argued that he suffered from variegate porphyria. Peters and Beveridge argued it was bipolar disorder and manic depression.[227] An analysis of a hair sample in 2005 showed very high levels of lead, mercury and arsenic which suggested the possibility that the medications being prescribed were actually the cause of much of his ill health, something Frederick himself had pointed out at the time.[228] High levels of mercury have been associated with Alzheimer's disease and arsenic with cataracts, confusion and behavioural changes.[229] The truth of the case is unlikely ever to be known and is, in any case, irrelevant here except in so far as allegations of a hereditary disease may be said to have affected Frederick himself. Doctors at the time believed the King was insane and this was what they told Frederick which is why he interested himself in the subject. Until 1818, the King was in the care of his wife but following the death of Queen Charlotte, Frederick was appointed his custos or guardian. After a heated debate, Parliament voted to allow Frederick the same ten thousand pounds which the Queen had received toward her expenses as a result of the King's care. Frederick was highly embarrassed by the publicity. He had not asked for the money and indeed said that he did not want it. As a loyal son, he did not need to be paid to care for his father. However, his brother, George, insisted that he took the money arguing that if Frederick were to accept the responsibility without payment, it would set a bad precedent and encourage Parliament to burden the family with other expenses.[230]

Frederick's period of care for his father did not last long but he did make some important changes. Previously, Dr Willis had been adamant that the King should be subject to complete seclusion, a situation which had caused the unhappy and isolated King to conclude in September 1811 that all his sons must be dead so he must content himself with talking to their ghosts.[231] Frederick now refused to be debarred from seeing his father and advised Dr Willis that he would be attending Windsor regularly. He not only visited but encouraged his father in developing his musical interests again. He insisted

---

[227] T. J. Peters and A. Beveridge, 'The Blindness, Deafness and Madness of King George III' in the *Journal of the Royal College of Physicians of Edinburgh* (2010) vol 40 pp.81-85

[228] T. M. Cox, M. J. Warren et. al 'King George III and porphyria: an elemental hypothesis' in *The Lancet* 23rd July 2005 pp.332-335

[229] Joachim Mutter, Johannes Naumann et al 'Alzheimer Disease: Mercury as a pathogenetic factor' in *Neuroendocrinology Letters* vol 25 (October 2004) pp.331-339, Lai-Chu See, Chien-Jen Chan et al.'Dose response relationship between ingested arsenic and cataracts among residents in Southwestern Taiwan' in *Journal of Environmental Science and Health*, vol. 42 part 2 (2007) pp.1843-1851

[230] Anthony Aspinall (ed.), *Letters of King George IV*, vol. 2 (Cambridge, 1938) pp.265-267

[231] Macalpine op.cit. p.160

on the rooms being heated, on the King being given warmer clothes and commenced a detailed investigation into his diet to assess its nutritional value. He ordered that wherever possible medicine be incorporated within the King's food to avoid distress caused by trying to force him to take it. When he was unable to be there in person, he required daily reports from the physicians.[232] From Windsor, he sent occasional reports to his brother, commenting in one that the King was very thin but seemed quite happy in himself, playing on the harpsichord which had been used by Handel and singing.[233] Yet, the King, now over eighty, was in decline and on 29th January 1820, he passed away. Frederick told his friend the Princess Lieven that on his deathbed, his father had reached out and said "Frederick give me your hand". The Princess said that it must be of some comfort that his father had been lucid at the end, but Frederick replied sadly, "Oh no, he mistook me for somebody who is dead." [234]

As if the situation with his father was not difficult enough, Frederick also faced the problem of his wife's seriously declining health. Illness had forced her to spend most her time at Oatlands for some years and by April 1820 she was unable to walk and had to be carried from room to room.[235] Her last appearance in London was in November 1819.[236] Toward the end, unhappy at the way her illness was making her look, she tried to avoid seeing Frederick but he went to be with her anyway. He would sit with her and talk to her even when she reached the stage that she was unable to recognise him. He was with her to the very end. She passed away on 6th August 1820, bequeathing him a farewell letter expressing her love which Frederick carried about with him ever afterwards, although he was unable to read it without breaking down. [237] Princess Lieven commented that Frederick could not expect any help or support from his family at this difficult time and so it proved. Less than ten days later, George told Frederick to marry again claiming this was his duty as heir to the throne. Ordinarily, Frederick was quick to obey the demands of his sovereign but on this occasion he blankly refused.[238] He never lived at Oatlands again.

Just days after the funeral, the trial began in Parliament of Caroline, George's estranged wife. Frederick had every reason to not attend but he did so because he believed it was his duty. It was that same sense of

---

232 Ernest Taylor (ed.), *The Taylor Papers*, (London, 1913) p.180

233 CKGV vol 2 p.298

234 Quennell op.cit. p.11

235 *The Ladies Monthly Museum,*1st May 1820

236 *The Times*, 19th November, 1819

237 ibid pp.58-60

238 Maxwell op.cit. vol 2 (London, 1904) pp.27-28

responsibility which caused him to make his most famous speech in Parliament on 25th April 1825. The issue under debate was offering emancipation to Roman Catholics and Frederick presented a petition against this on behalf of the Dean and Canons of Windsor. He said that whilst he approved of toleration, allowing Catholics to have a say in the government of the Church of England was wrong. He attributed his father's "severe illness and ten years of misery" to upset over the issue and claimed that emancipation was inconsistent with the coronation oath which declared:

> I will, to the utmost of my power, maintain the laws of God, the true profession of the Gospel, and the Protestant reformed religion established by law; and I will preserve unto the bishops and clergy of this realm and to the churches committed to their charge all such rights and privileges as by law do or shall appertain to them or any of them.

Referring to his own Protestant beliefs, Frederick added: "I have been brought up from my early years in these principles and from the time when I began to reason for myself I have entertained them from conviction and in every situation in which I may be placed I will maintain them, so help me God."[239] Given that Frederick was heir to the throne and his brother George, now king, was sickly, the impact of the speech was especially strong and the motion was defeated.

Reaction to the speech was quick and generally extremely positive. Frederick received votes of thanks from communities across Great Britain and was cheered whenever he left his house. Typical were the inhabitants of Chester who sent him an enormous cheese saying that his address had given "unmixed satisfaction to the country...and has obtained for your Royal Highness the full confidence and gratitude of the nation... that the Protestant ascendancy in this empire shall be maintained inviolate and that no dependents on a foreign prelate shall share with the Protestant people of England in that supremacy belonging only to the Sovereign who reigns over this free and united empire."[240] Wynn spoke of placards across London reading "Damn the King. The Duke of York for ever!"[241]

In the summer of 1826, Frederick's health deteriorated sharply. He was suffering from heart disease which was made manifest in hydrothorax or

---

[239] *The Times,* 25th May 1825
[240] *The Times,* 4th June, 1827
[241] Buckingham op.cit. p.241

dropsy and the doctors advised that they could do little for him.[242] Frederick told the Bishop of London that he had faced death in various shapes and was now doomed to view its approach in slow and lingering form. He said that although he would regret resigning his existence: "God's will be done. I am not afraid of dying; I trust I have done my duty; I have endeavoured to do so. I know that my faults have been many but God is merciful; His ways are inscrutable; I bow with submission to his will." Endeavouring to be positive, he said that he rejoiced that being housebound was giving him time for serious reflection and prayer and said he hoped he would be able to use the time wisely.[243] In the end, he endured almost six months of excruciating pain without complaint and he succeeded in working on his official military papers until the day before he lost the ability to talk. He then passed into unconsciousness and died on the evening of January 5th, 1827. His brother had him laid beside his father at Windsor in recognition of the close bond which had always existed between them.

Following Frederick's death a monument to him was erected in the Mall, but whilst few doubted that his services had merited such a tribute, there were detractors for Frederick had died deeply in debt. *Bell's Life* suggested it would be: "far greater honour to the Duke of York to subscribe money to pay his debts than to erect a statue."[244] His executors were criticised for allowing his property to be sold too cheaply and George was condemned for not stepping in to help. It was believed that he had promised his dying brother that he would ensure the debts were paid and his decision to claim over one hundred and fifty thousand pounds worth of Frederick's jewels as Crown property, meant that there was nothing left for the tradesmen, many of whom faced penury as a result.[245] One upset veteran wrote to the *Morning Post:*

> If there be no funds for the liquidation of the just claims of the unfortunate creditors, I am convinced that there is not a soldier in the kingdom from the humblest drummer to those of the most elevated rank who would not contribute his mite towards putting an end to the circulation of statements calculated to awaken prejudices...this being of infinitely more importance to his memory than all that the most talented sculptor could effect.[246]

---

[242] William MacMichael, *Some Remarks on Dropsy with a narrative of the Last Illness of H.R.H. the Duke of York,* (London, 1835) p.16

[243] Herbert Taylor, *The Last Illness and Decease of the Duke of York,* (London, 1827) pp.27, 30, 38. His uncle Frederick had died of the same illness.

[244] *Bell's Life,* 26th August, 1832

[245] *Morning Chronicle,* 16th August, 1832, *The True Sun,* 17th August, 1832

[246] *Morning Post,* 28th August, 1832

His debts were over two hundred thousand pounds, of which almost half related to the interest on previous loans. His assets were just seventy-five thousand.[247] The home he had been building was taken back by the government even though it owed him money. It was, as *The Times* observed, very sad that the maladministration of those in the royal household should cause a "foul stigma to attach to the memory of an illustrious member of the Royal Family."[248]

Yet, the tributes which poured in when Frederick died were genuine and they came from the lowest to the highest members of society. There were soldiers who remembered him giving to them when they were in need, destitute wives and widows who remembered his refusal to see them turned away from Oatlands because Frederick said he was a soldier too and the Duchess but "a soldier's wife" and the sick who owed their lives to his support of various medical institutions. George spoke of "his assiduous attention to the welfare of the soldier, his unremitting exertions to inculcate the two principles of order and discipline, his discernment in bringing merit to the notice of the Crown and the just impartiality with which he upheld the honour of the service."[249] *Bell's Life* called him "a man who was decidedly of more use to his country in point of public service (for our army owes to him its present high character) than all his brothers put together" whilst the *True Sun* said: "He recognised the extraordinary fact that a soldier was worth something as a human being as well as a thing to stick caps on and be shot at.[250]

Following his death, a number of people came forward claiming to be his children or mothers of such although Frederick had never acknowledged any such offspring. The most famous alleged son of his was Captain Hesse of the 18th Light Dragoons. Gronow, who claimed to be a close friend of Hesse and therefore party to the secret, said Frederick fathered him when he was in Germany and hinted that it was Hesse's relationship to Frederick which enabled him to become intimate with Princesses Caroline and Charlotte of Wales. Hesse was in fact equerry to the Princess of Wales, a role which naturally necessitated him travelling with her and being privy to her affairs.[251] Gronow said that Hesse was seventeen when he became a cornet

---

[247] Anon, *Debts of His Royal Highness the Duke of York*, (London, 1832) pp.44-45. Although estimates of Frederick's income varied, the combination of money from Osnabrück, the Civil List and the army totalled around forty thousand pounds which would be around two and a half million today.

[248] *The Times*, 31st May, 1836

[249] *Gentleman's Magazine*, January 1827, p.170

[250] *Debts* op.cit. pp.9,14

[251] Rees Gronow, *Reminiscences and recollections of Captain Gronow, being anecdotes of the camp, court, clubs & society 1810-1860*, London 1872, pp..217-219. Like many such scandal

which would have meant a birth in 1791 and conception in 1790 or early 1791 – times when Frederick was in England – though Hesse's own army record shows he was born in 1786.[252] The *Brighton Gazette* commented when Frederick died that he had left a son and daughter and that the latter had children "whose likeness to their grandfather is most remarkable."[253] This was a reference to the two Vandiests, the son who worked in the Treasury and the daughter who had twin girls of four at the time and a further daughter of two. The fact that they were known as Fitzalban when younger could support this but the date of birth of the son shows he was either conceived when Frederick was serving overseas or born after an unusually long gestation.[254] The lack of children was a sadness to Frederick on both a personal and dynastic level. He was, however, fond of his niece Princess Victoria for whom he arranged puppet shows and purchased a donkey, a creature with which she had fallen in love on her visits to Ramsgate.[255]

Frederick's greatest contribution to the country was undoubtedly his work as Commander-In-Chief, a position he held for over thirty years. Without him, Britain would probably have lost the war with France. Yet his contribution to medicine should not be overlooked. He encouraged research into mental illness and he served as President of the London Smallpox Hospital for many years. His work in the rehabilitation of offenders was also ahead of its time. As a man, he was by his own admission, flawed. He tried to behave responsibly and there is no doubt that he loved his wife, but he was a compulsive gambler and he was unfaithful. A man of very firm opinions, those who disagreed with him labelled him as stubborn whilst those who supported his views regarded him as a staunch champion of all that was right. Yet, above all, he believed in doing his duty whether that was to his king through maintenance of the army or to God through his efforts to care for those in need. He was, as Sir Walter Scott summed up when he died "a prince and a great man."[256]

---

mongers, Gronow did not dare publish his story while either party was alive.

[252] He was gazetted cornet on 1st December 1808.

[253] Quoted in *Notes and Queries* vol CLIV (Jan 1928) p.29

[254] For more on the Vandiests see Anthony Camp, *Royal Mistresses and Bastards*, (London, 2007) pp.232-234

[255] Roger Fulford, *Royal Dukes*, (London, 1933) p.76. The Princess spent the summers of 1823, 1825, 1827, 1830, 1835 and 1836 in Ramsgate and 1829 in Broadstairs.

[256] Watkins op.cit. p.586

George

1865-1936

Duke of York 1892-1901

"I am only a very ordinary sort of fellow."[1]

An announcement was issued from Marlborough House on June 3rd 1865 at 2.30am:

> "Her Royal Highness the Princess of Wales was safely delivered of a Prince at 1.18a.m. Her Royal Highness and the infant prince are doing perfectly well."

Thus read the news of the birth of Prince George of Wales, a child never expected to be king but who would one day rule Great Britain as King George V.

George was the second child of Queen Victoria's eldest son and his Danish wife Alexandra. The couple had been married for five years and had just the one son who had been named Albert but was known as Eddy by the family. Three more daughters were to follow and a short lived son completed the family in 1871. George was christened at St George's Chapel, Windsor,

---

[1] Response of King George V to the celebrations of his Silver Jubilee, quoted in David Sinclair, *Two Georges: The Making of the Modern Monarchy*, (London, 1988) p.1

on 7th July. The Queen handed him to the Archbishop herself and confirmed that his name was to be George Frederick Ernest Albert. Amongst his eight godparents were the Queen of Denmark, the King of Hanover, the Duke and Duchess of Cambridge and the Duke of Saxe-Coburg-Gotha, an international gathering which reflected the way in which Victoria's family were connected with the crowned heads of much of Europe.

His childhood was spent at Sandringham and Marlborough House with occasional visits to see his grandmother at Windsor, Osborne or Buckingham Palace. On one of these occasions, the boisterous George created horror at a dinner party by crawling under the table and taking all his clothes off and then running round the table.[2] Queen Victoria found the incident quite amusing but decided that she should step in to ensure he received some discipline since his parents were clearly lacking in initiative. Thus when he was six, Queen Victoria chose to appoint the curate of Whippingham on the Isle of Wight as his tutor. John Dalton was to remain tutor to George and his brother Eddy until 1883 though he was to continue his friendship with them beyond this. Dalton did his best to give them a basic education but his task was made difficult by the fact that Eddy had learning difficulties which were neither understood nor treatable at the time and George was more interested in practical tasks than academics.[3] Both boys enjoyed the outdoor life of fishing, riding, skating, swimming and shooting. As they grew older, they took up tennis and cricket.

On 14th and 15th May 1877 when George was eleven, he sat his examinations at the Royal Naval College, Greenwich. His father had determined that he should have a naval career, something which George seems to have welcomed. As a result, five months later, George joined HMS Britannia at Dartmouth as a naval cadet. His brother Eddy joined at the same time, not because it was ever intended that he should have such a career but because it was felt advisable to keep the boys together. The Britannia maintained one hundred and sixty cadets at any given time, each of which spent two years on board. George and Eddy were required to follow the same course of instruction as their fellows with just the provision of a private cabin as a mark of favour. They learnt not just about seamanship and how to read charts and use instruments, but also Latin, French, drawing and sewing. At first, George was bullied, partly because he was

---

[2] *The Illustrated London News*, 10th July 1893 pp.15-16

[3] Eddy had been born some two months premature and was only just over five pounds in weight. There is a wealth of medical evidence now to associate premature low birth males with problems such as dyscalculia, attention deficit disorder, physical disabilities and psychological disturbances. Eddy was known to be an abnormally slow learner, unable to concentrate or comprehend mathematics, to have a hearing impediment and some behavioural issues. He may also have been dyslexic.

young and small, but mostly because he was royal and a number of the other cadets wanted to be able to boast that they had given a prince a bloody nose. As a junior cadet, he was required to run errands and do the shopping for the older boys and he complained that they often neglected to give him the money afterwards, which meant his pocket money allowance of one shilling a week soon ran out.[4]

Following almost two years at Dartmouth, George and his brother joined HMS Bacchante for an extended tour of the Empire. The ship was new and some three hundred feet long with a regular crew of some four hundred men. She was designed as a steamer but also carried sail. Although not intended to be used in an offensive situation, she carried torpedoes, sixteen guns and four fixed machine guns for defence.

After seeing the new ship on 6th August, the princes went on a trip to Denmark with their mother to visit relations. They returned and their last public engagement before sailing was a trip to the local prison where George recorded: "We heard some startling yarns as to former and present occupants of this establishment."[5]

On 25th September 1879, they set sail for Gibraltar. In theory they were to be treated as any other naval cadet and to some extent they were. They studied to be midshipmen and sat various examinations throughout their trip in practical seamanship, algebra, Euclid, trigonometry, astronomy, mechanics, hydrostatics, theoretical navigation and principals of steam. It was recorded that George did particularly well in seamanship.[6] They got involved in climbing the rigging and firing weapons and took their turns in keeping watch. George's diary refers to "scraping masts and booms and refitting upper yards."[7]

George appeared to enjoy naval life more than his brother. He took part in a number of cricket matches during the tour and was the regular cox of the officers' whaler in the various regattas that took place. He attended cricket practice on board and expressed his concern that so many balls got hit overboard that it was costing him quite a lot of money to replace them.[8] It would seem George was more enthusiastic than capable at cricket for he was only ever picked for the second eleven and the boys' diaries, which are

---

[4] Kenneth Rose, *King George V* (London, 1983) p.7

[5] John Dalton (ed.), *The Cruise of HMS Bacchante 1879-82*, vol.1. (London, 1886) p.3

[6] ibid. vol 2 p.782

[7] Fritz Cunliffe-Owen, 'Britain's Future King' in *The Junior Munsey* vol. x no 6 (September 1901) p.888

[8] ibid. vol 1 p.259

normally detailed on the results of matches, never actually mention his score anywhere. The boys also played polo once in Buenos Ayres and a fair amount of lawn tennis. [9] On board, they played quoits and took their turn in the gym. George was also said to have been given boxing lessons by a shipmate who went on to become a renowned lightweight fighter.[10]

Early one morning, George was woken by one of his fellow midshipmen who told him it was his turn to go on watch. George did his best to pretend to be asleep then finally swore and hit out giving the midshipman a black eye. The man departed and did the watch himself. Next day, the incident was discussed in the gunroom and it was agreed that George needed to be taught a lesson. An impromptu unofficial court-martial was held and it was agreed that George should be spanked. Four midshipmen held him face down on the table whilst the injured man duly carried out the punishment. George was most unhappy at this indignity and departed with a variety of oaths and threats, yet having had time to consider, he went and apologised to the midshipman whom he had forced to do double duty.[11]

Yet, the princes' time on board was not quite the same as that of their fellows. They had brought their tutor with them, the Reverend John Dalton, who was serving as chaplain. They had additional lessons with him daily in French, Bible study, economics and history. The princes were required to keep their own journals of the trip which were later edited by Dalton, at the Prince of Wales' request, and published. These show that alongside the chance to read novels by Charles Kingsley[12] and Charles Dickens, they were required to consume a vast quantity of volumes on the history and culture of all the places they were to visit. Other cadets and midshipmen might be on board all day, but the princes generally went ashore each afternoon for some suitably improving and educational excursion. They also had to carry out a number of royal duties when abroad, such as making speeches and attending official receptions. The journals do, however, act as a reminder that they were still boys. George was just fourteen at the start of the trip and Eddy fifteen. They took delight in the various pets they had on board and had great fun experimenting with the microphone and trying to record different sounds.[13] In Japan, George was pleased when a museum allowed him to dress up as a warrior knight in authentic clothes.[14] Further

---

[9] ibid. vol.1 p.291

[10] Cunliffe-Owen op.cit. p.884

[11] ibid. pp.886-7

[12] The princes had known Kingsley well for he was a frequent visitor to their parents at Sandringham and they both wrote letters to him, see *The Illustrated London News*, 10th July 1893 p.18

[13] ibid. vol 1 p.6

[14] ibid. vol 2 p.100

excitement was caused when the captain took delivery of a new invention shipped out from England called an electric light. The effects of this were most impressive to those on the Bacchante and people ashore but the captain was disappointed to find that the apparatus "occupied the whole space under the poop and would require at least a dozen hands to lift it."[15]

After some naval exercises at Gibraltar, they went to Minorca where they were able to visit a linen manufactory and go shooting, the first of many hunting stops on the journey. The next stop was Sicily where they saw the ancient sculptures and observed the smoke ascending from the recently erupted Mount Etna. After that, it was across the Atlantic toward the West Indies. On Christmas Day 1879 they arrived in Barbados. George described how the people welcomed them:

..flourishing cotton Manchester-made pocket-handkerchiefs flag fashion, with likenesses of us both woven in colours on them, and one or two triumphantly produced framed photographs of us taken at Dartmouth, which they waved about, bobbing and kissing their hands, all one huge grin of delight.[16]

An old lady threw an ancient guinea labelled 'souvenir of Barbados' into their carriage as they drove through the crowds which George had mounted on his watch chain and wore for years afterward.

From Barbados they went to Trinidad where both Eddy and George were raised to the rank of midshipmen. The crew put on a minstrel show to celebrate their achievement and the locals came to the house where they were staying to perform impromptu dances. Concerned that some of them had been waiting hours to see them, George decided to take some cake out to the children, a kindly gesture which was very well received. After a trip to view a sugar plantation and lesson on production processes and the importance of that to the local economy, they went on to Jamaica and Bermuda. They then sailed back to England where they spent the summer with their parents.

In September 1880, following the regatta at Cowes, the Bacchante set sail again, this time heading toward the Mediterranean. As they studied and fished and practised firing torpedoes, they resumed their journal and that demonstrates the pleasure they took in the voyage:

There is a white whale following us, turning and rolling in the waves

---

[15] ibid. vol 1 p.36
[16] ibid. vol 1 p.51

in the wake of the ship. Three pretty little birds with black spots on white breasts, something like starlings, settled in the mizzen rigging; they were quite exhausted and very tame. We chopped up some raw mutton in thin strips to look like worms, and put it here and there on the poop; after eyeing it wistfully for a short time they hopped down and devoured it eagerly, and then went off into the cutter at the davits to sleep and woke an hour or so afterwards chirping merrily. An old cat we have on board improved the occasion and came prowling out along the deck; but the birds had recovered their strength and made light of her attentions.[17]

At Madeira, they dined with Prince Louis of Battenberg whose ship, the Inconstant, was to meet up with the Bacchante on several occasions during its tour.[18]

On 29th November, they crossed the equator where the naval tradition of King Neptune coming to mark the passage was enacted. The princes gave a very long account of the ceremony in their journal. One of the midshipmen played Neptune "uncommonly well" sitting on a makeshift throne over the engine room hatchway. A tank of sea water about five feet deep had been created with a ladder up to it on which a barber's chair was placed. As recruits were led out blindfold and sat in the chair, they were successively tipped over backwards into the water. George recorded:

Everything went off with the utmost good humour, and it was most refreshing having the steam hose played over us as the temperature, both of the air and water, was 78°. We all had great fun in slushing and squirting each other with these, turning a hose now on one officer or man, and now on another, as we ran about, in more or less light attire, all over the deck and climbed up in the rigging.[19]

On 21st December, the Bacchante arrived at Montevideo. The Christmas Day service was celebrated on deck with George noting that "Hark the Herald Angels" sounded especially good in the open air despite the wind. The princes had spent some time in the weeks before writing out Christmas cards so that every man on board received their own hand written greeting from them, not a small feat with over four hundred men on board.

They travelled to Argentina for New Year where they played polo with

---

[17] ibid. vol 1 p.242

[18] Prince Louis was the father of Earl Mountbatten of Burma and grandfather of Prince Philip, the Duke of Edinburgh.

[19] Dalton op.cit. vol 1 p.257

Prince Louis and went to shoot wildfowl. By the time of Eddy's seventeenth birthday on January 8th 1881, they were said to be "as red as boiled lobsters" from the wind and the sun.[20] From there, they sailed to the Falkland Islands but the weather was very poor. The princes commented that some of the officers had said the journey was "the worst knocking about they had ever had."[21] Their description of the entry to Stanley read:

> The hills are rounded, bleak, bare, and brownish, like Newmarket Heath; the cliffs are white, though not of chalk, something like the Isle of Thanet, but more desolate looking, though on some we can see the herds of cattle grazing...The few houses that form the town look like an Irish village snugly nestling on the hill-side in the distance....the thermometer at noon is 45°.... All sorts of birds - albatross, gulls, divers, and a great many others swarming round the ship. From where we lie the hill-sides sloping down to the harbour seem all of monotonous brown grass.[22]

The bad weather had delayed their arrival which meant they were able to spend less than two days there and the planned visit to the penguins had to be cancelled, much to the disappointment of both princes. Fog and severe winds accompanied them as they crossed the Atlantic again, this time going toward South Africa. Their journal noted that for days they saw neither land or other vessels which gave them "a strange weird feeling when we looked south, and fancied there was no more land down there, over the liquid hills and valleys of rolling water, but only the icy homes of birds and sprites. As we seemed to be sailing along on 'the sloping edge of the globe,' we could imagine that if we went far enough down there we should slip off the edge into space."[23]

En route to South Africa, the Bacchante carried out a number of intense training exercises from firing weapons to practicing landing parties and having the crew practice skirmishing and drilling in full military kit. This led the princes to wonder if they might be about to go into action, the British being in conflict with the Boers at the time. Sadly for them, they were to be disappointed. Their six weeks in South Africa were spent visiting schools and museums and an ostrich farm, and climbing Table Mountain. The only shooting they did was of rabbits and pheasants. A disgruntled George noted that they were anchored in so desolate a spot that the Dutch did not even know they were there: "We are patiently awaiting orders as to what is to be

---

[20] ibid. vol 1 p.298
[21] ibid. vol 1 p.308
[22] ibid. vol 1 p.305
[23] ibid. vol 1 p.317

done next. We have been no use in any way here yet to anybody but the beef contractor." It was he felt "a very hollow, make-believe affair."[24]

Although the frustration was understandable, the need to safeguard the lives of the second and third in line to the throne was not lost on those in charge. The British were doing very badly in the war. It was while they were at Cape Town that news was received of the bloody defeats at Laing's Neck and Majuba Hill where hundreds of British troops had been annihilated. This news naturally upset all on board but especially the princes whose background meant they had a greater familiarity with the regiments involved. It also put them in a difficult situation. Should they be seen to mourn or should they continue with their programme of activities? Eventually they decided that regardless of their own mood, they must make the effort to carry on to avoid disappointing all those about them who had put so much effort into arranging special events.

On 10th April 1881, they set sail for Australia. Again they faced rough seas, George noting that they had to lash their chairs to the table and eat their food with just one hand, the other being needed to hold on to the plate. They were to stay in Australia from 17th May to 20th August and it was to make a lasting impression on them. No country which they visited absorbs more space in their journal or more praise. They totally fell in love with the place and were impressed with everything. Melbourne in particular seemed to them to be a modern paradise. They said its public transport system was better than London's, the drains were first class, there was more work, the climate was the best in the world, prices were cheaper, people were healthier, some three quarters of skilled working men by middle-age owned their own homes and "the existence of miles and miles of streets, made up of dens of squalid tenements, hardly fit for an animal to dwell in, such as we have passed over in the railway when going out of London, are impossible here."[25]

The tour began in Albany, Western Australia, where a policeman took George off quail shooting and taught him how to imitate the bird sounds so that he could attract more game. They took a journey into the bush to study the fauna and went on a kangaroo hunt. They killed two and sent the pads back to their mother. One of the animals was then minced and served up for their tea which they described as "excellent."[26] On Queen Victoria's birthday, they went to the telegram office to send her a greeting and they were extremely pleased to get a reply back. An afternoon of games was

---

[24] ibid. vol 1 p.319
[25] ibid. vol 1 p.524.
[26] ibid. vol 1 pp.454-456

arranged to celebrate including three legged, piggy back and sack races, a tug of war and an Aunt Sally.

From Albany they went by P&O steamer to Adelaide where they played tennis and toured the botanical gardens. Judging by the number of entries in the journals about plants and George's later enthusiasm for horticultural shows, he had a keen interest in this subject. They opened the National Art Gallery and attended the races and theatre. They went on a couple more kangaroo hunts and also tried hare coursing. They visited various schools, colleges and hospitals, planted trees and attended official receptions at Government House. On 14th June, they went to a copper mine at Moonta where they were interested to find many of the miners were Cornishmen. As an example of the relative informality of the tour, the princes recounted an incident which occurred on their way to visit the school at Angaston. A group of well-wishers came out, one of them carrying quite a large banner. Whether the man was unused to riding or had not sufficiently rehearsed his greeting was uncertain, but it was not long before the horse threw him, the man going one way and the banner the other. The princes hurried across to pick him up and decided they had best put him in the carriage and take him home, depositing him "a little stunned and bruised" in the care of his no doubt rather astounded wife.[27]

They went by train to Melbourne where they attended more official functions and carried out a similar programme of visits to schools, libraries and factories. They laid the foundation stone of Melbourne Cricket Club and took away matching silver trowels as souvenirs. They also turned a fountain on named in honour of their mother and went to the mint where they were able to try their hands at making coins. Amongst the sights shown to them was the outlaw Ned Kelly's home made steel armour which they tried on and declared "very heavy and clumsy."[28] Ned had been executed in the city only eight months before. What excited them more was their trip to the Band of Hope Gold Mine when they had to don miners clothes and descend over four hundred feet in a tiny cage just big enough for three. They emerged, lit candle in hand, to a crowd of miners gathered to sing the National Anthem which echoed resoundingly and strangely along the passages. Both princes then went off to see the men at work and to try swinging the picks themselves to knock away some quartz. When they returned to the surface they found a photographer waiting to get an image of them in their workmen's clothes, an image that was turned into a print and widely circulated.

---

[27] ibid. vol 1 p.476
[28] *The Argus*, 6th April 1901

At Melbourne, they should have rejoined the Bacchante but the severity of the damage incurred in the voyage across from South Africa meant they had to transfer on 8th July to the Inconstant. Three days later, their journal recorded a very curious incident:

> At 4 A.M. the Flying Dutchman crossed our bows. A strange red light as of a phantom ship all aglow, in the midst of which light the masts, spars, and sails of a brig 200 yards distant stood out in strong relief as she came up on the port bow. The look-out man on the forecastle reported her as close on the port bow, where also the officer of the watch from the bridge clearly saw her, as did also the quarterdeck midshipman, who was sent forward at once to the forecastle; but on arriving there no vestige nor any sign whatever of any material ship was to be seen either near or right away to the horizon, the night being clear and the sea calm. Thirteen persons altogether saw her, but whether it was Van Diemen or the Flying Dutchman or who else must remain unknown.[29]

They noted that the two ships sailing on their starboard signalled that they saw her too. Maritime tradition regarded a sighting of the Flying Dutchman as a portent of doom and the journal adds that: "10.45 A.M. the ordinary seaman who had this morning reported the Flying Dutchman fell from the foretopmast crosstrees on to the topgallant forecastle and was smashed to atoms." A few days later, the Admiral was also taken ill which meant the scheduled one week stay in Sydney stretched to a month which in turn prevented their planned visit to New Zealand.

In Sydney they saw steam driven tramcars which they thought a "great nuisance" to the horses and they visited the university, the races and factories making pots and railway carriages. A special boomerang throwing exhibition was put on for them which they found fascinating. They went to Botany Bay for a picnic where Eddy was said to have earned his lunch for as he was walking along with his tutor:

> ..a marauding dog which had pilfered a plump turkey dashed past hotly pursued by the waiter whose inattention had given the animal his opportunity; whereupon Prince Edward joined in the chase and outpacing the waiter, made a cut with his stick at the thief. The dog opened his mouth to howl and amid the hearty laughter of the Prince and his companion, the waiter retrieved the bird.[30]

---

[29] ibid. vol 1 p.551
[30] *Maitland Mercury* 13th August 1881 p.5

The next stop on the tour was Brisbane where a public holiday was declared and they carried out yet more engagements. As they prepared to depart on August 20th, they wrote in their journal that they had enjoyed themselves more in Australia than anywhere else. They said: "After England, Australia will always occupy the warmest corner of our hearts." They added: "The enthusiasm of the people (which means of course their attachment to Great Britain not to us personally) is most hearty and thorough." They concluded that the Australians were showing: "an amount of energy and of activity in all branches of commerce, education, government and everything that makes a people great which have never before been surpassed in the whole course of English history."[31]

The Australian press followed every move the princes made though they seemed confused by the name of the elder, referring to him variously as Prince Albert, Prince Victor and Prince Edward. In Victoria, George was described as the "more vivacious" of the two, his brother being a "pleasant, quiet and unassuming young gentleman."[32] In Brisbane, George was a "careless sailor boy with a fine wholesome love of fun and possibly, if the restraints of his position did not forbid it, a taste for mischief also." Eddy, who had to make all the speeches, was said to be tall but to "display some nervousness when playing his part in the ceremonies to which the affectionate loyalty of the colonist subject him." [33] In short, the tour had been a triumph all round and was the more remarkable because so much of it had been unplanned or arranged at very short notice due to the unscheduled work on the Bacchante.

From Australia, they went to Fiji where they saw native dances and spear drill. They played cricket and examined the local canoes and were a trifle bemused by Chief Thakombau who told them how he had killed his first person when he was just six. He described how his father would sail home with the bodies of infants tied to the yard arm of his boat which they would then eat and he "relished exceedingly well." He had given up cannibalism upon his conversion to Christianity but as the princes noted in their diaries, the echo of the drums conjured up some nightmarish images and they were pleased when they could start their journey to Japan.[34]

The voyage from Fiji to Yokohama took six weeks and gave the princes a chance to have a rest and to resume their studies. It was a pleasant trip for them except for one incident which befell their parting gift from the people

---

[31] Dalton op.cit. vol 1 pp.481,624, 626

[32] *Kilmore Free Press*, 9th June 1881 p.4

[33] *The Brisbane Courier*, 16th August 1881 p.3

[34] Dalton op.cit. vol 1 pp.657, 673

of Sydney:

> Today, unfortunately, the little kangaroo, who had become a general
> favourite with every one on board on account of his perfect gentleness
> and tameness, and who used to go bounding all over the quarter deck
> and aft, as well as forward to play with the men during the dinner
> and supper hours, and who had learnt to find his way down the ladder
> on to the main deck and call in at the several messes for
> contributions, and then to finish up with the captains cabin for
> sponge-cake and bananas, jumped overboard. He had got in the habit
> of sitting outside on the glacis aft, and on the billboard of the sheet-
> anchor forward, for coolness during the close weather we have had,
> and it was from there, where he was last seen, that he is supposed to
> have lost his balance and slipped into the water. We are all the more
> sorry, as we had hoped to have taken him home to Sandringham for
> sisters. He was never frightened at anything.[35]

The visit to Japan was a formal affair where they spent much time with
the Mikado and Prince Higashi Fushimi, the latter of whom they knew from
England. They spent a lot of time visiting temples and touring Tokyo and
Kobe by rickshaw. They tried making pottery teapots and playing a
Japanese sport akin to polo. Although they enjoyed the activities, they were
less keen on the food noting the frequency of raw fish and seaweed on the
menu and admitting their favourite was the "plain boiled rice which was
very nice." In Tokyo, they both got tattoos with George having a dragon put
on his arm.[36] There had been rumours that he had had a tattoo in Barbados
which had sent his mother into a complete panic for she had heard he had
ordered an anchor to be tattooed on his nose. She wrote to him instantly
bewailing that he would become a figure of ridicule and wondering what his
grandmother might say. George was able to reassure her that his tattoo was
not on his face but his arm and that neither his parents nor Queen Victoria
should be in the least alarmed.[37]

From Japan they went to China for a fortnight's hunting. They then went
to Hong Kong, Singapore and Ceylon. In Singapore they were visited by the
Queen of Siam who presented them with gifts for their father and Queen
Victoria. She was the wife of King Chulalongkorn who had been educated by

---

[35] ibid. vol 2 p.16. They had also been given two wallabies which Eddy decided to present as a
gift to the Empress in Japan, something which George seems to have regretted for he describes
them as "great pets" and spoke fondly of how they would hop about and go into the cabins
where they would "sit themselves down on a chair by the side of anyone reading there and look
over his shoulder in the most ludicrously wistful way at the book." p.31

[36] ibid. vol 2 p.46, 53

[37] Denis Judd, *The Life and Times of George V* (London, 1973) pp. 28-29

the Englishwoman Anna Leonowens.[38] In Colombo, they were able to see elephants being rounded up for sale, an event George found particularly interesting for he stayed hours longer than his brother despite his position of standing out in the pouring rain and he only left most reluctantly in order to comply with his official programme of events. He wrote:

> At last we heard that the small herd were within a hundred yards of the gate, and we could see the tree-tops waving through the movements of the elephants, and we could hear the shouting of the beaters who were close upon them. We see the smoke of a fire, coming up from the centre of the valley, which has been lighted behind a cow elephant who has her calf with her, about a fortnight old, and who is very wild. She kept charging the beaters again and again, desperate about her calf, and after having wounded three beaters, ultimately had to be shot. We went down near to where the beaters were, and saw the herd of seven elephants pass about sixty yards from us in the open. After the cow was wounded, the other five bolted into the kraal about half-past one... Four tame elephants then enter the kraal, and proceed to crash down the trees and undergrowth by leaning their foreheads against the larger trees and twisting their trunks round the foliage. Up several of these people had climbed to the jeopardy of their lives and in their eagerness to see the end.... The wild elephants were in a great state of perturbation, rushing from one side of the kraal to the other, going down into the hollows to throw water and mud over their backs : spurting each other with water seemed to be a favourite occupation; and it was most amusing, as well as touching, to see the little calves do this to the tame elephants when near them, once or twice, as if to appease them and make friends.[39]

After George left, some of the elephants escaped but the rest were tied and tamed so they could be sent to work building roads and clearing jungle.

From Ceylon they sailed through the Suez Canal to Egypt where they spent almost a month taking a cruise down the Nile and visiting the pyramids and ancient temples. They admitted to carving their initials on the south west corner of the platform of the Great Pyramid next to someone called A.E. who had been there in 1868. From there, they moved on to Palestine and two weeks of exploring Biblical locations. They attended the celebration of the Passover in the home of the Chief Rabbi in Jerusalem and followed the pilgrim procession on Palm Sunday to the Church of the Holy

---

[38] The King was to visit England in 1897, George being sent to meet him on behalf of the Queen.

[39] Dalton op.cit. vol 2 pp.332-336

Sepulchre and on down the Via Dolorosa. On Good Friday, they were camped in the Shepherds' Fields at Bethlehem where they expressed their dismay that armed guards were found necessary "in the very grotto itself to prevent squabbles and worse between two branches of the Catholic Church over the birth-place of the Prince of Peace."[40] They celebrated Easter in a tent beside the Dead Sea before riding out to visit the caves of the Essenes. The experience of travelling around the Holy Land clearly made a deep impression on them and enhanced their understanding of the life of Jesus. In years to come, George was to be a patron of the Palestine Exploration Fund attending public lectures on the continued excavations in the area.[41] Yet, they expressed their doubts about the authenticity of some of the sites they were shown and were disappointed by others describing Galilee as a "hotbed for malaria" and the River Jordan as a "muddy, turbid and narrow stream."

On 7th May 1882, the Bacchante left Damascus for Athens. The King of Greece was their uncle, being brother to Alexandra. George missed much of the trip because he was ill with a fever on board but he recovered in time to go to the Acropolis and to spend time playing with his cousins, including meeting the newborn Prince Andrew.[42] After further stops at Corfu, Palermo and Gibraltar, they reached home on 5th August 1882. During the course of their time on Bacchante, they had travelled almost 55,000 miles of which just over half had been under sail and the rest under steam. It had been nearly two years since they had seen their parents and they were delighted to see them waiting on the docks at Portsmouth. The princes were then escorted to Osborne to see Queen Victoria so they could tell her all about their trip.

On 8th August 1882, they were confirmed by Archbishop Tait in Whittingham Church. His address impressed him so much that they asked for a copy of it for their journal. The Archbishop told them:

> Experience has already taught you that the life of a true Englishman cannot be a life of mere pleasure; it must be above all things a life of duty. Duty first, pleasure afterwards... God grant that you, sirs, may show to the world what Christian princes ought to be. A great field

---

[40] ibid. vol 2 p.622

[41] For example, *The Times* 8th May 1894

[42] Andrew later married the daughter of Prince Louis of Battenberg. The couple had one son Prince Philip, who married Princess Elizabeth of England. The current Duke of York is named after him.

lies before you.[43]

In accordance with previously laid plans, the lives of the two princes diverged soon after the voyage. Eddy was to pursue an army career as part of his preparation to become king, and George to stay in the Royal Navy. As a mark of his growing up, George was instituted as a Knight of the Most Noble Order of the Garter in 1884.

In 1883, George was sent to North America on board HMS Canada. Following receipt of a first in Seamanship, he became a Sub-Lieutenant on his nineteenth birthday. On one occasion, he was ordered by the Captain to show an important American visitor round the Canada. The vessel was taking on coal at the time and George enthusiastically got down to show the visitor exactly how the system worked, getting his clothes and face covered in black dust in the process. Afterwards, the visitor thanked the Captain for the tour and commented on what a good job his guide had done. He then laughed and said: "I guess on a day like this when you're coaling, you keep your prince wrapped up in cotton wool."[44] He clearly had no idea about the identity of his guide and that was the way George liked it. On other occasions, more care was taken of the young prince. When George went seine fishing off the coast of Newfoundland and returned to the ship absolutely soaked through having spent the day hauling nets and sorting fish, the Captain sent him straight off to bed with a dose of medicine whilst his shipmates returned straight to normal routine.[45]

On 8th October 1885, following more examinations,[46] George was made a Lieutenant and from January to August 1886 he served on HMS Thunderer. He then spent almost two years on HMS Dreadnought before two six months stints on HMS Alexandra and HMS Northumberland respectively. During this time, he visited the King of Greece, the Sultan at Constantinople and Egypt as well as returning home for Queen Victoria's Golden Jubilee and making a visit to Ireland with his brother. In July 1889 he was given command of Torpedo Boat number 79 and it was while he was engaged in manoeuvres at Portsmouth that his commanding officer told him that his father had arrived and wanted to take him to Goodwood. George responded that: "I have received orders to take my torpedo boat to Spithead, sir, and I must obey orders" and off he went leaving the commander to

---

[43] Dalton op.cit. vol 2 pp.800-802

[44] Graham Brooks, *The Dukes of York*, (London, 1927) p.240

[45] *Chums*, 30th August 1893

[46] George scored 82.5% in practical navigation but just 7.2% in mechanics, see Rose op.cit. p.17. He also scored a first in gunnery, see *Windsor Magazine*, June 1899 p.3

explain to the Prince of Wales why his son was not going to see him.[47]

George's abilities earned him high praise from *The Times* in August 1889. Reporting how he had steamed to the rescue of another torpedo boat in heavy seas and towed her to safety, they said it was a "very smart piece of seamanship" on his part. They reminded readers that torpedo boats were "wet and comfortless craft" which soaked the crew in good weather and created "hideous discomfort" on rough days.[48] The Admiralty also admired his feat of "skill, judgment and nerve" which is why he was given command of HMS Thrush in May 1890. It was on that ship that he returned to Canada and the West Indies on a tour of duty which included Bermuda and Jamaica where he was deputed to open the Industrial Exhibition on the Queen's behalf at Kingston.[49] As captain of the Thrush, George was required to lead the weekly prayers and he aroused widespread laughter by the frequency with which he got the words wrong in the confession, proclaiming "we have done those things which we ought to have done and we have left undone those things which we ought not to have done" when, of course, they should have been confessing "we have left undone those things which we ought to have done and we have done those things which we ought not to have done."[50]

In August 1891, he was raised to the rank of Commander and left the Thrush. He did not get to spend much time in this new role – just sixty-six days in total – due to circumstances beyond his control. In November 1891, George was taken ill with typhoid fever and it took many weeks for him to recover his strength.[51] No sooner was he convalescent than his brother – who had been with George throughout his illness - succumbed to the influenza epidemic which was then raging across Western Europe. To everyone's shock and horror, Eddy died on 14th January 1892. George was with him to the end and was understandably overwhelmed. Not only had he lost a brother whom he loved and with whom he had been extremely close, but this event meant he was now destined to become king. As second in line to the throne, he would have to give up his beloved career in the navy. His life, which had previously gone along quite smoothly, had changed overnight.

Four months later on May 24th 1892, the following announcement was made:

---

[47] Brooks op.cit. p.243

[48] *The Times* 7th August 1889 and 26th August 1889

[49] *The Times* 11th February 1891

[50] Cunliffe-Owen op.cit. pp.887-888.

[51] It was believed he had contracted it on a visit to Dublin to see Eddy.

The Queen has been pleased to direct Letters Patent to be passed under the Great Seal of the United Kingdom of Great Britain and Ireland, to bear this day's date, granting unto Her Majesty's Grandson, His Royal Highness Prince George Frederick Ernest Albert of Wales, K.G., and the heirs male of his body lawfully begotten, the dignities of Baron Killarney, Earl of Inverness, and Duke of York.[52]

There seems little doubt that George did not wish to surrender his naval career. It also seems probable that he had no great desire to play an active public role, though he did his duty. Excepting the year of the Queen's Diamond Jubilee, George averaged just thirty-five engagements a year as Duke of York. That included around five state banquets, two or three occasions when he represented Queen Victoria at events such as an overseas wedding or funeral, a trip to Trooping the Colour, an occasional meeting with an ambassador and normally just the single review of troops. The other engagements consisted of trips to open buildings and to attend exhibitions and half a dozen or so fund raising dinners. Even allowing for the transport limitations of the time, he was not overworked. Dukes of York two hundred years before him had been busier. The bulk of his charitable activities were sea related and involved his support of organisations such as the Royal National Lifeboat Institution, Trinity House, Missions to Seamen, the British and Foreign Sailors' Society, the Royal Humane Society and the Royal Navy Fund. George admitted at a presentation to cadets in 1899 that "although my active service is, I fear, practically over, I am just as devoted to my profession now as I was when I first joined it and I shall always continue to take the greatest possible interest in all that concerns the sea, ships and sailors."[53]

Away from his nautical concerns, George was active in his support of the Royal Agricultural Society. He served as president 1897 to 1898 and did his best to attend the monthly meetings. He went to shows across the country and acted as judge on occasions. At Sandringham, George bred Norfolk red poll cattle and Berkshire pigs, and he often won prizes for these. He also kept pigeons and bred horses, earning several prizes for his hackney horses.[54] One of the fixtures in his diary was his attendance at the annual Thoroughbred and Hunter Improvement Society Show in London.

The third main area of interest to him was health. His mother had been extremely active in encouraging the care of the sick, the Queen Alexandra Nurses bearing testimony to that to this day. George opened various

---

[52] *London Gazette* 25th May 1892

[53] *The Times,* 20th July 1899

[54] *The Times,* 12th March 1895, 7th June 1897

hospital wards as part of his duties and visited sick veterans from conflicts such as the Boer War and Benin.[55] A long standing supporter of the London Eye Hospital which he opened in 1892, in June 1899 he opened Moorfields.[56] He visited the training college for teachers and hosted fund raising events for the Oral Instruction of the Deaf and Dumb, speaking with enthusiasm about how lip-reading enabled the deaf to integrate into society in a way in which sign language did not.[57] His interest in that cause stemmed from the fact that both his mother and brother had hearing problems. George was also patron of the National Society for the Employment of Epileptics, visiting their establishments and spearheading a fund raising campaign for them. In 2003 George was to be portrayed as having a very negative attitude to epilepsy in the BBC film *The Lost Prince* but this was not the case. His understanding of the condition was exhibited at Windsor in July 1899 when a woman had a fit whilst listening to the Guards band. George, who had been standing on the private terrace above, saw this and rushed down to her aid ensuring she was treated correctly and even having her taken inside to be checked over by the Queen's physician before she went home.[58] His knowledge of the condition must have been extremely helpful to him in understanding the problems faced by his own youngest son when he was found to be an epileptic.[59]

Other causes in which he became involved included the National Society for the Prevention of Cruelty to Children which were then concerned about the practice of killing infants for insurance money[60] and the Honourable Society of Cymmrodorion whose goal was to promote the Welsh culture and language.[61]

Being in direct line to the throne, it was deemed necessary that George marry. Queen Victoria selected the bride, Princess Victoria Mary of Teck, a lady generally known as Princess May. She had been engaged to George's brother Eddy and the couple were five weeks away from their wedding when he died. Although it was not a great love match at the outset as George himself admitted, there was considerable respect and friendship and that did turn to love. George was to remain faithful to his wife and to write to her before their first wedding anniversary: "I do love you darling girl with all my

---

[55] *The Times*, 1st April 1897, 26th February 1900

[56] *The Times*, 16th December 1892, 28th June 1899

[57] *The Times*, 6th March 1897 and 18th March 1897.

[58] *The Times*, 10th July 1899

[59] Prince John also had learning difficulties like George's brother, though it appears they may have been more serious.

[60] *The Times*, 7th February 1893

[61] *The Times*, 18th March 1896

heart and am simply devoted to you...I adore you sweet May."[62] Despite her name, May was regarded as an English princess having been born at Kensington Palace and lived most of her life in England. She was to bear George five sons and one daughter.

Except for maybe a couple of trips a year to a major city, George's domestic engagements never took him beyond London or Portsmouth. As a result, he was not well known. In October 1894, George and his wife went to visit Leeds. For whatever reason, the trip was something of a shambles. The carriage which had been due to meet the royal couple at the rail station, did not turn up. After waiting about for almost an hour, it was decided that another carriage should be used. George and May rode through the crowded streets which had been bedecked with flags in almost total silence because nobody recognised them. When they reached the Town Hall and were announced, an evidently poor man in shabby clothes, ran past the police and jumped up on the carriage. George, no doubt surprised, nonetheless politely held out his hand. This was an extraordinary thing to do for at this time, royalty never physically greeted the working classes, and it demonstrated a great deal about George's attitude to people. However, at this point, two of the lancers accompanying the royal party, charged in. One struck the man's hand with his sword whilst the other knocked him down whereupon he was trampled by the horses. [63]

This was not the only unfortunate event to occur at one of his visits. At Brighton in 1896, the fire service were stood upon a triumphal arch erected over the procession route which started to sway alarmingly. Some of the men were able to jump to safety before the structure collapsed but the rest had to be rescued by their colleagues. Fortunately, the fire engines were drawn up nearby.[64] In 1898, the crowds were so large at the launch of HMS Albion that a number of working men and their families decided to take up a position on a wooden gangway close to the ship from which they could get a good view of proceedings. This was despite warnings to keep away which were posted on the gangway and were voiced by the police, who sadly lacked numbers to enforce the ban. As the ship went down into the water, the resultant wave swept over the gangway destroying it and all those upon it. Thirty eight people drowned, almost half being children, the youngest victim being just three months old.[65]

---

[62] Dennis Judd, *The Life and Times of George V*, (London, 1973) p.51

[63] *The Times* 6th October 1894, *Leeds Mercury* 6th October 1894. The man had a long history of mental illness being described as simple minded but harmless.

[64] *The Times*, 10th April 1896

[65] *The Times*, 22nd June 1898

In August 1897, George and his wife went on a tour of Ireland. He had been there several times before his marriage including an official Jubilee tour in 1887 and an unofficial one in 1889 when his torpedo boat was active off its coast.[66] During the tour he opened a horticultural show and an exhibition of Irish linen and he received the Order of St Patrick. He also went to Belfast where he toured the Harland and Wolff shipyard. It was a difficult tour for political reasons and George refused to meet with Orangemen least it antagonise nationalists. As it was, the visit was a great success and Ireland was to report a great increase in tourism as a result.[67] George paid another visit in April 1899.

Perhaps tired from the exertions of the overseas tour and the rush of engagements during the Diamond Jubilee as people came from across the globe to celebrate Queen Victoria's long reign, George decided he wanted some time away. In the summer of 1898, he returned to naval life becoming Captain of HMS Crescent, a new ship which he was required to take through its commissioning and initial manoeuvres. George decided to commission Mr West to record life on board in a twenty minute film, or "animated photograph" as it was then called. The movie, which consisted of small film fragments interspersed by magic lantern slides, showed a sailor dancing the hornpipe on the forecastle, field gun drill, the midshipmen carrying out their physical training exercises with cutlasses, the crew parading before the Captain, torpedoes being fired and activities on the various parts of the ship. George had the film shown to the whole crew at Portsmouth. The screen was erected on the jetty with the crew watching from on board or on the jetty whilst he and the other officers watched from the bridge. The film was then taken to show to Queen Victoria at Osborne where it was exhibited on a screen hung across the doorway of the drawing room. Admiral Michael Culme-Seymour declared it the finest show he had ever seen. The film represents the first real footage of George as a sailor and shows his interest in the new medium, something which had been kindled by his attending a demonstration of the cinematoscope at Marlborough House in June 1896.[68] Years later, he was to be the first monarch ever to speak on radio when he opened the British Empire Exhibition in 1924.[69]

The significance of George's encouragement of moving pictures should not be underestimated. The cinematoscope had received its first demonstration in January 1896 with some brief films of a rough sea at

---

[66] *Belfast Newsletter*, 15th August 1889

[67] *The Times*, 23rd August 1898

[68] Rose op.cit. p.36. For an account of the film and reaction to it, including stills taken from it, see the feature 'Our Sailor Prince' in *Windsor Magazine*, June 1899 pp.3-11.

[69] George also began the annual Christmas broadcast in 1932.

Dover, the university boat race and the Derby. This was a month before Robert Paul had demonstrated the theatograph and the Lumières their cinématograph with their famous shots of a train pulling into a station and factory workers leaving work.[70] All three inventions enabled images to be projected rather than simply shown in individual booths like Edison's Kinetoscope. This was essential to the development of cinema. Alfred West, a maritime photographer who had invented the instantaneous shutter to enable the capture of moving objects, was inspired and began experimenting with film himself, recording the firing of torpedoes in 1897. It was these few seconds of film which George saw and which so impressed him that he commissioned the movie about HMS Crescent. Royal patronage enabled West to exhibit the film more widely and to develop his work. He produced a series of films called Our Navy which sought to promote pride in the work of the Royal Navy. Later, he moved on to record life in the army. Not only were these amongst the earliest documentary films produced, they were invaluable in raising the perspective of the armed services and in encouraging recruitment in the Boer War and First World War.[71] They were also important technically for capturing images at sea required the development of a stabilised camera and equipment capable of withstanding the elements.

Another new invention which George was to encourage was the flying machine. On July 31st 1894, Hiram Maxim had achieved self-powered free flight in his steam powered flying machine, the first man to do so. He had flown over three hundred yards at a height of around four feet off the ground. His aeroplane was almost one hundred feet across, weighed eight thousand pounds and covered in balloon fabric coated in boiled oil. It had five wings either side and carried a crew of three. A year later, George went to see the machine at Baldwyn's Park near Dartford. He reported in his diary that he watched it make a run and then decided to go for a ride himself. He reported that "it did lift off the ground part of the time."[72] Whether this was an act of bravery or foolhardiness is open to question. Even the inventor recognised the danger involved saying: "I do not consider it safe to attempt free flight directly from a railway track with a great number of very large trees in every direction; the slightest hesitancy in manipulating the rudder or the least mistake might prove disastrous."[73] He did, however, foresee the future potential of the aircraft adding that with

---

[70] The Lumière demonstration in London took place on the same day as Paul's. They had demonstrated their invention in Paris previously.

[71] Alfred West's unpublished autobiography *Sea Salts and Celluloid* (1936) is available on www.ournavy.org.uk. Although the film of the Crescent has not survived, the 1897 torpedo explosions which George saw, can still be seen on the website.

[72] Quoted in John Halperin, *Eminent Georgians*, (New York, 1998) p.22

[73] Hiram Maxim, 'A New Flying Machine' in *The Century* vol 49 no 3 (January 1895) p.455

Seven Centuries of Service

George 1892-1901

investment "aerial navigation would soon be so perfected that flying machines would be as common as torpedo boats and the whole system of modern warfare would be completely changed."[74]

Amongst other events of note from George's public life were his attendance at the opening of the Forth Bridge in 1890 and Tower Bridge in 1894.[75] He accompanied Queen Victoria to lay the foundation stone of the Victoria and Albert Museum in 1899 and his father to the opening of the Blackwall Tunnel in 1897.[76] Amongst overseas events, he was a guest at the wedding of Tsar Nicholas II. The Tsar was his cousin and he had got to know him well as a boy when holidaying in Denmark.[77] Nicholas had attended George's wedding and visited England on a number of occasions before and after his accession. After he was killed by the Bolsheviks in 1917, George wrote in his diary that "I was devoted to Nicky who was the kindest of men and a thorough gentleman; loved his country and people."[78]

In 1898, George presented a Union Jack to the leaders of the George Newnes Antarctic Expedition. Led by the Norwegian, Carsten Borchgrevink, the men left England in August 1898, arriving in the southern ice field on December 30th. On March 1st, Borchgrevink hoisted the flag on Victoria Land and the men prepared to spend the next nine months in Antarctica, the first men ever to winter in its harsh conditions. During the course of their stay, they studied wildlife, made meteorological observations and witnessed the birth of an iceberg, an event which nearly cost them their lives. In thanksgiving for George's support – which had been given despite the British government's lack of interest – Borchgrevink chose to name an island he discovered in the area, Duke of York Island. This was declared a site of great geological interest due to it being particularly rich in minerals, though Borchgrevink's claim to have found gold there was later disproved, the material being tested as iron pyrite. The men camped on the new island where they pioneered the use of dogs to pull their sledges.[79]

Away from his official duties, George continued to have a passion for shooting. He had been elected President of the Royal Society for the Prevention of Cruelty to Animals (RSPCA) in 1894 but he defined this as meaning pets and livestock rather than wildlife.[80] He spent weeks every

[74] ibid. p.456
[75] The Times, 2nd July 1894
[76] The Times, 18th May 1899, 22nd May 1897
[77] Nicholas' mother Dagmar was sister of George's mother, Alexandra.
[78] Quoted in Rose op.cit p.216
[79] The Times, 26th June 1900. Antarctica continues to have areas named after George and his wife.
[80] The Times, 12th April 1894

year away on shooting trips, sometimes donating part of the game to the charity hospitals of which he was a patron.[81] George was a very good shot and capable of killing a thousand birds in a day.[82] He spent a lot of time fishing too. His chief indoor recreation was stamp collecting, something which had been reported as early as 1889.[83] Indeed, in 1897, he spent three whole days at the London Philatelic Exhibition and he was said to spend several afternoons each week working on his collection.[84]

When in London, he was sometimes to be found visiting art galleries, generally when they had an exhibition on of sea related works, such as that of Wyllie's seascapes in 1896[85] or P&O cruises in 1893.[86] He rarely went to any sporting events, though he did see the Oxford and Cambridge University Boat Race in 1894 and sometimes went to see the cricket at Lord's with his father. He liked to go to the theatre and his taste was for burlesque musical comedies, swashbucklers and sentimental melodramas such as *Don Juan, Little Jack Sheppard, The Princess and the Butterfly, Black Ey'd Susan, The Runaway Girl,* and the *Prodigal Father*. He saw the most famous performers of the day such as Sarah Bernhardt, William Terriss, Henry Irving and Ellen Terry. He did attend a few operas such as *La Bohème,* and *Pagliacci* but on those occasions, he had his mother with him suggesting that they were more her taste than his. There is only one report of him going to see a Shakespeare play. For the most part though, he preferred to remain at Sandringham.

His relationship with his father was close throughout his life. The two of them frequently went to the theatre together and went yachting at Cowes. They also went off on many shooting expeditions, to the races and regularly attended lectures at the Royal Geographical Society. His father was to say that "We are more like brothers than father and son."[87] George himself described him as "my best friend and the best of fathers" adding that he had never had a row with him in his life.[88]

In January 1901, Queen Victoria died at Osborne. George was present

---

[81] For example to the London Eye Hospital in January 1895 and the London Skin Hospital in October 1893.

[82] Rose op.cit. pp.87, 100

[83] *The Friendly Companion,* 1st January 1889. p.26. He was said to have become interested whilst serving on HMS Alexandra, his uncle, the Duke of Edinburgh, being a keen collector.

[84] *The Times,* 22nd July 1897

[85] *The Times,* 13th April 1896

[86] *The Times,* 7th February 1893

[87] Christopher Hibbert, *Edward VII: The Last Victorian King,* (London, 1976) p.219

[88] George's comments were made in his diary entry recording the death of his father and are quoted in Rose op.cit. p.74

and recalled in his diary how she had "called each of us by name and we took leave of her and kissed her hand. It was terribly distressing....I shall never forget the scene in her room with all of us sobbing and heartbroken around her bed."[89] He did, however, miss his grandmother's funeral because by then he had contracted German measles.[90]

Two months later, on March 16th 1901, George and his wife departed on what was to be the longest royal tour since Edward, Duke of York, had gone to the Mediterranean in 1763. Their journey took them first to Gibraltar and then on to Malta where there was a spectacular water carnival with vessels disguised at different animals including a swan, elephant, crocodile and whale as well as fantasy creatures such as dragons and sea serpents, all breathing smoke and issuing fireworks. Going on down the Suez Canal, they had the first of two encounters with troop ships taking men home from their service abroad. The band of HMS Ophir struck up 'Auld Lang Syne' and 'Home Sweet Home' and George saluted as they passed. They reached Colombo on 12th April where they stayed just a few days. En route to Singapore they encountered such a severe tropical storm that even the royal compartments were soaked. Petty Officer Harry Price wrote it was "as if the sea had been taken up to the clouds and then dropped in a lump....In fact it was just the same as if a fire hose was being played full in the face."[91]

A few days later came the ceremony of crossing the line. Neptune politely sprinkled Mary with water from a goblet. George, meanwhile, happily got in the barber's chair and was duly pushed head over heels into the tank of water where he received a "severe ducking." It was noted that throughout the voyage, George was happy to join in with the ship's entertainments, be they sports or musical shows. He also impressed the crew by showing no signs of seasickness no matter what the weather threw at them, unlike his wife who kept to her cabin as soon as the wind got up.

On 6th May, they reached Melbourne where the serious business of the tour began. George was to spend almost two months in Australia and one in New Zealand carrying out a range of engagements, the most important of which was the opening on 9th May of the first federal parliament of the newly created Commonwealth of Australia. This was naturally a very formal event but one which showed how the world was changing. After George declared the Parliament open, the trumpets sounded, the guns fired a salute, and a button was pressed to transmit the news to England. A

---

[89] Halperin, op.cit, p.23

[90] *The Times,* 1st February 1901

[91] Harry Price's illustrated log was shown to George during the tour and published by his son in 1980.

cablegram from the King, received whilst George had been speaking, was then read before the band launched into the Hallelujah Chorus and Rule Britannia.[92]

Although the tour went very well, the Australian newspapers did express their concern about George's appearance. In Melbourne, he was described as "grave of demeanour, reflective, not given to much speech" and marked by "an almost oppressive sense of his responsibilities in life." They recalled how on his last visit, he had been "the jolliest little fellow they had ever come across" and anxiously quizzed his staff to discover if he still had a sense of humour, being relieved to learn that apparently he did though it was not evident.[93] In Brisbane, they bluntly commented: "the years have not dealt too kindly with our illustrious visitor" and said he was "looking even beyond his age."[94]

Following Australia, the Ophir travelled to Mauritius, giving George and his wife a few days break. As at Brisbane, Mauritius had an outbreak of plague which meant that the royal party had to travel with minimal attendants and the programme of events was curtailed. The next stop was South Africa where the Boer War was still being fought. George's role was to encourage and support the troops and to award medals. He also laid the foundation stone of St George's Cathedral, Cape Town. A long voyage toward Canada followed with just a brief stop at St Vincent for provisions.

They arrived in Quebec on 15th September amid a severe gale. The wind dropped by evening so the official welcome took place as planned. Unfortunately, one of the tugs in the display caught fire and the fireworks on board exploded sending flames and sparks in all directions. Fortunately nobody was fatally hurt and George and Mary were able to board the train which was to take them across Canada in a month long trip which included Montreal, Ottawa, Winnipeg, Calgary, Vancouver, Toronto, Niagara and Halifax. They attended a range of functions, presented a lot of medals and George found time for some shooting, killing a moose and sending its head back to the Ophir as a trophy. One of their more interesting excursions was on a raft at Chaudiére Falls which took them to an Indian canoe which carried them to see war races. They then boarded an electric tram to take them to a lumberman's shanty where they were treated to a meal of pork and beans, described as the staple fare of such a worker, before witnessing a demonstration of tree felling and dancing.[95] At Calgary in a Great Pow-

---

[92] *The Age,* 10th May 1901, *The Argus,* 11th May 1901
[93] *The Argus,* 6th April 1901
[94] *The Brisbane Courier,* 21st May 1901
[95] Joseph Pope, *The Tour of their Royal Highnesses the Duke and Duchess of Cornwall and*

Wow, George met with two thousand representatives of native Indian tribes who wished to express their sorrow at the loss of their "Great Mother" Queen Victoria. In a speech redolent of native rhythms, George assured them:

> The Indian is a true man. His words are true words and he never breaks faith and he knows that it is the same with the Great King. His promises last as long as the sun shall shine and the waters flow. ...I wish to assure you that His Majesty, your Great Father, has as much love for you of the setting sun as of his children of the rising sun....We have come a long way, many thousands of miles across the deep waters and vast prairies to see you....With the help of the Great Spirit, may peace, prosperity, contentment and happiness be your lot and rest among you always.[96]

The royal couple travelled through the Rockies in a special train and went to Niagara Falls where George, in an unusual moment of romanticism, hired a singer to perform Ave Maria as they watched the waters. The only hitch in the arrangements was at Halifax where six thousand children gathered to serenade the royal couple but the train steamed straight past them without stopping.[97]

A final stop was made at St John where George accepted a Newfoundland dog and cart as a gift for his eldest son. Then it was back to England. George and Mary had not wanted to go on such an extended tour, not least because of the separation from their children, but it had been a great success both politically and personally. George recorded in his diary that he had been away for 231 days during which he had laid 21 foundation stones, received 544 addresses, presented 4,239 medals, reviewed 62,000 troops and shaken hands with around 25,000 people.

The tour had been filmed by the same company who had recorded life on HMS Crescent three years before. The result was a programme that lasted over an hour and consisted of footage of Maori war dances, Canadian log chopping competitions, Niagara Falls, the review of troops at Sydney and a panorama taken from the moving train as it travelled through the Rockies, all interspersed with lantern slides. It was a celebration of empire and demonstrated the warmth in which the royal family were held. On 9th November, the day that the film was shown to the King at Sandringham, George was created Prince of Wales, his father saying it was in

York, (Ottawa, 1903) p. 60
[96] ibid. pp.78-81
[97] ibid. pp.123, 142

"appreciation of the admirable manner in which you carried out the arduous duties in the Colonies."[98]

Less than nine years later, on 6th May 1910, George became King. He was to reign for twenty-five years and become one of the most popular monarchs of the twentieth century. Just as his son was to play an important role as a steadying figurehead through the grim days of World War Two, so George was to steer the country through the unimaginable horrors of the First World War. The world he left in 1936 was very different to that into which he had been born in 1865.

As Duke of York, George was honoured and respected but he was not idolised in the way that some of his predecessors, such as James, had been. Few people outside his immediate circle knew him or ever saw him. Nonetheless, he was the first Duke to travel beyond the confines of Europe, the first to travel by train or car,[99] the first to fly, the first to appear on film and the first to act as pallbearer to a British Prime Minister,[100] an event which demonstrated how the balance of power had changed since the creation of the first Duke in 1375. For a man who was essentially a home lover, he took a keen interest in technology and his encouragement of that, together with his patronage of charities aimed at improving the lot of the working man, showed him to be a true Victorian. For this reason, he was a successful Duke of York for he represented all that was best about his era. The exposure which he gained as Duke of York to the rich cultural and economic variety of the empire, contributed to his success as King and the subsequent development of the Commonwealth.

---

[98] West op.cit. pp.31-32

[99] George attended a demonstration of motor cars at the Imperial Institute in 1896, see *The Times*, 1st July 1896

[100] George was a pallbearer at the funeral of William Gladstone, see *The Times*, 30th May 1898.

Albert

1895-1952

Duke of York 1920-1936

A wonderfully hard working Englishman.[1]

Few things are better known about Queen Victoria than her intense mourning following the death of her beloved husband, Prince Albert. The day on which he died, 14th December, was commemorated within the royal family as a day of sorrow. However, in 1895, the Queen made the following entry in her diary:

> This terrible anniversary returned for the thirty-fourth time. When I went to my dressing room, found telegrams from Georgie and Sir J Williams saying that dear May had been safely delivered of a son at three this morning. Georgie's first feeling was regret that this dear child should be born on such a sad day. I have a feeling it may be a blessing for the dear little boy and may be looked upon as a gift from God.[2]

The boy in question was predictably named Albert after his illustrious

---

[1] Louis Greig, long term companion of the Duke, quoted in Geordie Greig, *The KingMaker*, (London, 1999) p.116

[2] *Queen Victoria's Journal* – Princess Beatrice copies – vol. 102 p.150

great-grandfather and he would go on to reign as King George VI. His parents, at the time of his birth, were Duke and Duchess of York but would later become King George V and Queen Mary. He was their second child, the first son being eighteen months older and called David, a boy known successively as Prince of Wales, Edward VIII and Duke of Windsor.[3] Four more children were to follow.

Like all royal children, Albert had a privileged upbringing. He had nursemaids and footmen to wait upon him and he had the sort of clothes and food and home that most of the population could only dream about. Despite this, his childhood was not trouble free. Albert was an unhealthy child prone to extremes of mood. His tutors complained about his bad behaviour and his mother's lady in waiting commented on his spells of either silence or naughtiness.[4] It was considered that part of the problem stemmed from his genu valgum, popularly known as knock knee. Contemporary medical opinion was divided about whether genu valgum existed as a condition in its own right or was just a form of rickets, something already known to be associated with malnutrition and therefore not to be expected in a prince.[5] In an attempt to cure the problem, Albert was given splints. Despite the opinion of one modern biographer that wearing these "humiliating and inhibiting objects" constituted a "drastic" and "inhuman treatment", the use of splints to correct genu valgum was extremely common and there were numerous designs of splint on the market.[6] The principle was always the same, to gradually straighten the limbs through use of a key to exert pressure on the prominent internal condyle. The splints would be worn both day and night until the process was complete and then for a steadily reducing time each day for a period of around three months in order to maintain the improvement and prevent the child from developing any posture or motor problems. The first splints used were unsuccessful so Albert's father had his own physician specially design a new set which were used from February 1904.[7] These did their job and

---

[3] David was one of his middle names but his first name was Edward and he was to take the throne as Edward VIII. He was known as David because it was almost certain, his father being heir to the throne, that he would one day be Prince of Wales and David was the patron saint of Wales.

[4] Jennifer Ellis (ed.) *Thatched With Gold – the memoirs of Mabell, Countess of Airlie*, (London, 1962) p.113. Sarah Bradford, *George VI*, (London, 1989) pp.40-41

[5] See William MacEwen, *Osteotomy*, (London, 1880)and Newton Shaffer, 'A Lecture on Knock Knee and Bow Legs' in the *American Journal of Obstetrics and Diseases of Women and Children*, vol 14. (July 1881) pp.755-773. George V said it was hereditary but this was not generally believed at the time, see John Chiene, 'The treatment of knock-knee' in *Edinburgh Medical Journal*, vol 24 no 10 (1879) p.880. For further discussion on the hereditary nature of rickets amongst the Stuarts, see the chapter on Charles, Duke of York.

[6] Bradford op.cit. pp.38-40

[7] John Wheeler-Bennett, *King George VI – His life and reign* (London, 1958) p.28

Albert's sporting prowess as an adult showed his debt to the treatment.

His other major health problem was not to be so readily cured. From an early age, Albert displayed signs of a serious speech defect. Lady Airlie, who joined the royal household, when Albert was just past his sixth birthday, noted from the first that he was "intensely sensitive over his stammer." [8] Initially, there was little concern for such a situation was not unusual in children of that age and it was known that over three quarters grew out of it.[9] Besides, it was noted that the defect disappeared when he was relaxed and with people whom he knew.[10] This fact suggested there was no physical problem but rather that it stemmed from nervousness, something which those about him would have assumed was within Albert's own ability to control if he was only to exert some self discipline and be a man. His tutors and parents would therefore have seen it as their duty to encourage him to get his words out in a way which some have regarded as insensitive. For example, his elder brother was later to reflect that being required to learn poems in French, German and English and recite them before their parents was "a nightmare" but at the time it was believed that reciting poetry was helpful in effecting a cure because it assisted breath control and rhythm.[11] Indeed, not requiring a child to speak aloud before others was held to be one of the causes of stammering because it encouraged shyness.[12]

As Albert's problem persisted into adolescence, concern would have grown, especially as the majority of contemporary authorities were convinced that speech defects were the result of masturbation.[13] If the royal family were worried about the prospect of Albert being publicly associated with having rickets, that was nothing compared to him being linked with what was euphemistically termed "secret vice" or "self abuse." Baden-Powell had given the defeat of such activities as being the chief goal of the

---

[8] Ellis op.cit. p.113

[9] Kate Watkins, 'Structural and Functional Abnormalities of the motor system' in *Brain,* vol 131 January 2008 p.50 says that one in twenty children stammer at some point in their lives but just one in a hundred adults. The same pattern was recognised in the nineteenth century, see James Hunt, *Stammering and Stuttering,* (London, 1870) p.255. For studies of percentages recovering, see Gavin Andrews et. al. 'Stuttering: A Review of Research Findings and Theories circa 1982' in *Journal of Speech and Hearing Disorders,* vol. 48 (August 1983) p.228

[10] Ellis op.cit. p.114

[11] H.R.H. The Duke of Windsor, *A King's Story,* (London, 1951) p.47. For attitudes to recitation see Henry Monro, *On Stammering and Its Treatment,* (London, 1850) p.16, Hunt op. cit. p.278

[12] William Abbots, *Stammering, Stuttering, and other speech affections* (London, 1894) p.30

[13] Algernon De Bale, *Exhausted Brain and Nervous Exhaustion,* (London, 1879) p.56, Edward Conradi, 'Psychology and Pathology of Speech Development in the Child' in *The Pedagogical Seminary* vol 11 (1904) p.355, Alfred Appelt, *The Real Cause of Stammering,* (London 1911) p.133. This view persisted until the end of the 1920s in the works of Tamm, Liebmann, Gutzmann and Steckel.

formation of the Boy Scouts whilst Stanley Hall's influential work had attributed an immense range of physical and moral ailments to the practice arguing that it was fundamentally unpatriotic because it weakened the race.[14] Advice was consequently sought and efforts made to help Albert but to no avail. His speech problems lasted well into adulthood. That they made him miserable and affected his life is evident from a story he himself told about when he was a teenager at Dartmouth Naval College and the day he was asked what was half of a half. Unable to get the word "quarter" out, he just blushed and wished the floor would swallow him up whilst his classmates laughed and his tutor concluded he was profoundly stupid.[15]

Yet, Albert's young life was not all sad or dominated by health concerns. He had outings to see the cricket at Lord's and to London Zoo. He went to the Tower of London to view the Crown Jewels which he was to see in use at the coronations of his grandfather and father. He learnt to ride which proved the start of an abiding passion for horses. He played golf and together with his elder brother, used to race his bicycle down the hill to watch the trains come in. During the Boer War, which began when he was four and ended three years later, he marked troop movements on maps and practiced drill with his father's piper. He also had a vegetable garden where he grew sprouts, radishes, peas, potatoes and cabbages.[16] Like other royal children, he was taught at home so he had a very cloistered existence but it was not devoid of affection. As was customary for upper class homes of the time, the children were brought up by nurses and governesses just seeing their parents after tea for an hour a day. Their mother would read to them or lead the singing as they engaged themselves in useful activities such as making scarves for troops.[17] Their mother's lady-in-waiting later wrote that Mary disliked babies and lacked any understanding of a child's mind even though she tried her best.[18] She wrote in 1907: "I do so hope our children will turn out common sense people which is so important in this world. We have taken no end of trouble with their education and they have very nice people around them."[19] Albert also spent time visiting his grandparents who had become King Edward VII and Queen Alexandra when Albert was five. Life at court was much more opulent than at Sandringham as well as more exotic. At the time of the 1901 census, over a hundred household staff from

---

[14] Michael Rosenthal, *The Character Factory*, (London, 1986) p.188, G Stanley Hall, *Adolescence*, Vol 1 (London, 1904) pp.438-443

[15] Taylor Darbyshire, *The Duke of York*, (London, 1929) p.86

[16] W. E. Shewell-Cooper, *The Royal Gardeners King George VI and his Queen*, (London, 1952) p.2. Unlike the children of George III, Albert and his siblings were only expected to do the light work. The staff did the digging.

[17] Windsor op.cit. pp.33, 38, 49

[18] Ellis op.cit. pp.112-113

[19] James Pope-Hennessy, *Queen Mary*, (London, 1959) p.394

India, Germany, France and across the United Kingdom were employed to care for just eleven members of the royal family.[20]

As was usual for the period, discipline was left to father and in his memoirs, the Duke of Windsor spoke of the dread of a summons to the study.[21] His comments have been seized upon by critics keen to seek for signs of family dysfunction or trying to claim that Albert's speech defect was induced by his father being a bully. The Duke of Windsor was certainly negative describing his father as "a very repressive influence" and suggesting that he made their mother's life a misery with his temper and unreasonable behaviour.[22] Although he was in the home unlike later historians, it must be remembered that the Duke's opinions were expressed late in life after he had spent years harbouring a deep seated hatred of his father who had failed to appreciate his beloved Wallis Simpson. Lady Airlie, also a member of the royal household and who saw at first hand how parents and children interacted wrote: "Prince George was fond of his sons but his manner to them alternated between an awkward jocularity of the kind that makes a sensitive child squirm from self consciousness and a severity bordering on harshness."[23] To some extent, their father's comment to Lord Derby was responsible for much of the talk. He was supposed to have said: "I was frightened of my father and I am damned well going to see to it that my children are frightened of me."[24] However, to a Victorian, this was a perfectly normal ambition and entirely in line with Christian doctrine. Although as the century progressed there was a move toward a sentimentalised view of children as naturally innocent, the prevailing one remained that all were born with original sin and in need of loving correction by a father whose responsibility was to represent the authority of God within the home. As God was to be regarded with awe and fear, so was the father.[25] This was particularly true in the royal family where formality was the order of the day. This was demonstrated on Albert's fifth birthday when his father wrote to advise him: "try and be obedient and do at once what you are told as you will find it will come much easier to you the sooner you begin. I always tried to do this when I was your age and found it made me much happier."[26] The Duke of Windsor concluded: "The difficulty I

---

[20] RG13/1169/89/1. The census shows that the Battenbergs were also in residence including daughter Alice who would subsequently be the mother of Prince Philip and nine month old baby Louis, later Earl Mountbatten of Burma.

[21] Windsor op.cit. p.35

[22] James Pope-Hennessy, *A Lonely Business* (London, 1981) pp.214-215

[23] Ellis op.cit. p.112

[24] Quoted in Bradford op.cit. p.30

[25] Article IX of the Church of England. Romans 13:1-4, Colossians 3:18-20, Proverbs 13:24, 22:15, 23:13-14, 29:15, 2 Corinthians 7:1

[26] Bradford op.cit. p.29

believe was in large measure implicit in our circumstances. Kings and Queens are only secondarily fathers and mothers." [27] As to Albert's own attitude, he was asked once which parent he liked most and he summed it up briefly: "Well, Mother I think, but Daddy spoils us most."[28] It was hardly the response of a cowed child.

In 1909, when he was thirteen, Albert joined the Royal Naval College at Osborne as a cadet to start what was intended to be his lifelong career as a sailor. Things did not go too well for him. He was small for his age and his speech defect caused unwelcome attention. Aside from dancing lessons, he had hardly ever met any boys of his own age and now he was in a dormitory with strangers and subject to the much harsher conditions of hard iron beds, plain food and ice cold early morning baths. Most of his fellow cadets had been to school before and so were used to fraternising with one another. They were also brighter than him and therefore found the work easier. Whether Albert was naturally backward or the victim of poor teaching was uncertain. His elder brother did not fare much better but he predictably chose to blame his tutor.[29] However, their tutor at home, Mr Hansell, was an experienced educator who had served as a master at Ludgrove and Rossall schools and he was supported by a team of experts.[30] The fact that Albert could not divide by two when he was seven and a half boded ill and faced with Albert continually coming at the bottom of class despite a range of new teachers at Osborne and later at Dartmouth, his father was forced to hire a specialist mathematics instructor to provide extra coaching. [31] Part of the problem was Albert's attitude. From Osborne, Captain Christian reported: "I am sure the boy has determination and grit in him but he finds it difficult to apply it to work, though with games it comes out strongly." Mr Watt said he had a "mercurial temperament...I don't think he regards a rebuke any more seriously than his work."[32] Albert's father was not amused and sent a letter to his son saying that the reports were not at all satisfactory because they said: "you don't seem to take your work seriously nor do you appear to be very keen about it. My dear boy, this will not do."[33]

Notwithstanding his poor results, in January 1911 Albert moved on to the Royal Naval College at Dartmouth for a further two years training. His time there was seriously interrupted by events beyond his control. Within a

---

[27] Windsor op.cit. p.182

[28] Major J. T Gorman, *George VI King and Emperor*, (London, 1937) p.1

[29] Windsor op.cit. p.28

[30] Darbyshire op.cit. pp.16-18

[31] Wheeler-Bennett op.cit. p.25, 49

[32] ibid. p.45

[33] Bradford op.cit. p.58

month of his arrival, he succumbed to an epidemic of measles which affected two thirds of the cadets and caused the death of two. Illness caused him to miss almost the entire first term and his second saw him removed so that he could participate in the events surrounding his father's coronation. When he was born, Albert was fourth in line to the throne but following the death of his great-grandmother Queen Victoria when he was five and his grandfather Edward VII when he was fourteen, he was now second in line. His elder brother, with whom he had shared most of his early life, was increasingly to pursue a separate path for he was soon to be Prince of Wales. Albert was later to comment to Mrs Baldwin that he had started to feel very jealous at this point of the growing differences between them.[34]

From Dartmouth, Albert joined the naval training ship, Cumberland, for a six month tour of the West Indies and North America. It was a chance for all the cadets to put the theories they had been taught into practice. Despite living in the same conditions as his fellows, the fact that he was a prince meant that he did have some unique experiences. He was driven round Tenerife in an open carriage for the crowds and called upon to open Kingston Yacht Club. For Albert, the attention was unwelcome and he persuaded a cadet who looked like him to go and wave at the crowds whenever he could. Often, however, this was impossible because he was required to speak and it was this which made public appearances so painful to him. At the end of the voyage, his Captain recorded that Albert's conduct had been very good and he had special language skills owing to his fluency in German and French adding: "Promises well. Takes charge well and assumes responsibility. Nervous of speech."[35]

Upon his return, Albert was promoted to the rank of Midshipman and posted to HMS Collingwood which he joined on 15th September 1913. It was to be his ship for the coming three years although he was to only spend eighteen months on board. His service began with a trip to the Mediterranean where he was able to visit his cousin, King Constantine of Greece.[36] Whilst there, he celebrated his eighteenth birthday and he did so by taking up smoking, the practice which was ultimately to be so significant a factor in his early death from lung cancer. Six months later, Archduke Franz Ferdinand was assassinated and at the end of July 1914 the British Fleet was put on war stations. A week afterwards, the First World War began, an event which was to dramatically change the lives of everyone in the country. Albert's father wrote in his diary: "Please God that it will soon

---

[34] ibid. p.62

[35] ADM/196/118/129

[36] King Constantine I was to be uncle of Prince Philip, Duke of Edinburgh and Princess Marina who married the Duke of Kent. His grandchildren include Queen Sophia of Spain and ex-King Constantine.

be over and that He will protect dear Bertie's life." [37]

In the event, Albert was to see relatively little of the war. Nineteen days after war was declared, he was taken ill with severe stomach pains. He was given morphine and taken ashore where appendicitis was diagnosed and an operation performed in Aberdeen. He was sent home to his parents to recover but he failed to make the anticipated progress. Toward the end of November, Albert was transferred to a desk job at the Admiralty in London. His role was to update the location of ships on maps so that senior officers could make tactical decisions. At first, Albert was very keen on taking the job. He was aware of the pressure being put on young men to serve, especially after Mons and Ypres, and he wanted to be seen to be playing his part. The fact that the King's son had been taken ill at the start of the war and that almost three months after a routine operation he was still classed as unfit, had resulted in some suggestions being made that he was being deliberately protected and kept out of action. Albert wrote to his father saying: "now people cannot say that I am not doing anything."[38] However, he did not enjoy the role and was delighted when in February 1915 he was told he could return to his ship.

Within three months of going back to HMS Collingwood, Albert was taken ill again with stomach pains. This was the same problem which he had experienced in August 1914 and in November 1914 which raised questions about the original diagnosis of appendicitis. After two months on board with recurrent illness, he was diagnosed with a weakening of the muscular wall of the stomach and transferred ashore again for a period of rest. He was to spend almost a year at home with his parents travelling between London, Sandringham and Balmoral. He did pay a brief visit to the trenches in France with his elder brother and he played host to the Crown Prince of Serbia, but it was a period of frustrating inactivity for him. On 26th April 1916, Albert was finally assessed as fit to return to duty and he went back to the Collingwood. This time he managed to spend four months on board before being discharged to private medical treatment on 2nd September 1916.[39] It was during this period that Albert was finally to see action at the Battle of Jutland on May 31st.

Although the army had been engaged in daily conflict with the enemy since the war began, the navy had barely had any combative contact with the Germans for their role had been seen as primarily defensive. They were seeking to safeguard shipping and supplies by keeping the German fleet out

---

[37] Bradford op.cit. p.78
[38] Bradford op.cit. p.80
[39] ADM/196/118/129

of British waters. When the Germans decided to change their tactics and go on the offensive, the British were ready. Captain Ley of the Collingwood noted that the first reports of enemy movement were received at 3.15pm though it was to be another three hours before the first flashes of enemy guns were seen.[40] Owing to poor weather and the smoke of battle, visibility was only four miles. Albert's own account of the battle reveals that he was in the sick bay with food poisoning when news of the enemy approach was first received but he got up and took his place in gun turret A. He chose to sit on top of the turret so he could see better and was startled by the firing, later claiming that he descended very rapidly "like a shot rabbit."[41] The Collingwood began firing just before 6.30pm but most of the action was in the distance. They saw HMS Defence blown up behind them with the loss of over nine hundred lives and a shell hit HMS Colossus in front of them. The Germans decided to launch a torpedo attack to cover their retreat and Albert was part of the gun crew which opened fire in response. One vessel, eight thousand yards away, was hit and set on fire. Meantime, two torpedoes passed by Collingwood, one very close astern and the other just thirty yards ahead. Yet by just after half past seven, it was all over and Albert made cocoa for everyone.[42] In a letter to the Prince of Wales, he wrote about his reaction to his first experience of being under fire: "When I was on top of the turret I never felt any fear of shells or anything else. It seems curious but all sense of danger and everything else goes except the one longing of dealing death in every possible way to the enemy."[43]

On 15th September, Albert was one of eighty-one personnel officially commended for their services in the battle.[44] From Russia, he was awarded the Order of St Vladimir fourth class.[45] His father created him a Knight of the Garter on his first birthday after the battle, his twenty-first. His own Captain's report read: "All ranks and ratings performed their duties to my complete satisfaction. There was a complete absence of excitement in all departments and I am convinced that had Collingwood suffered damage, the behaviour of officers and men would have proved to be entirely in accordance with the best traditions of His Majesty's Navy."

Following the battle, Albert was diagnosed with a duodenal ulcer and he left his ship for good at the start of September. A period of rest and controlled diet followed and Albert was able to take a naval desk job from

---

[40] The Captain's account appears in HMSO, *Battle of Jutland 30th May to 1st June 1916: Official Despatches,* (London, 1920) pp.95-98

[41] Wheeler-Bennett op.cit. pp.94-95

[42] Darbyshire op.cit. p.47

[43] Bradford op.cit. p.89

[44] *London Gazette,* 15th September 1916

[45] *London Gazette,* 5th June 1917

November 1916 to May 1917 in Portsmouth. His commanding officer wrote when he left that he "was of much assistance in my office and I found him very zealous and hard working." [46] Albert departed to join HMS Malaya as a Lieutenant but just five weeks after his arrival, he was ill yet again. By August, he was back ashore.

By now, Albert was desperate. He had experienced stomach problems for three years. The attacks tended to follow the same pattern in that he would experience severe pain a few hours after eating accompanied by nausea. This would last for a few days and then he would be well again for maybe three or four days when the cycle began again. As a result of the bouts of illness, he had lost weight noticeably to the point where his colleagues described him as "wasting away."[47] The treatment he had been given consisted of pain killers such as morphine plus a restricted diet based around milk products and minced food. From 1915, he was having nightly enemas. On 22nd September 1917, Albert asked his father to agree to him having surgery in the hope that this would finally resolve his problems and allow him to lead a normal life again. The operation took place on 29th November 1917 and was successful, though it left him with a permanent weakness.[48]

There has been some criticism about the length of time it took to diagnose Albert's problem and to resolve it but the doctors were working in line with current medical practice.[49] Until the advent of radiography, it was considered impossible to accurately diagnose an ulcer in a living patient and it was not until just before the First World War that X-ray technology was properly understood.[50] At St Thomas' in London, for example, one of the capital's leading hospitals, it was not until 1912 that equipment was installed which enabled stomach images to be taken in an environment that

---

[46] ADM/196/118/129

[47] Bradford op.cit. p.80

[48] Albert was still wearing an abdominal support belt fifteen years later. Logue op.cit. p.96.

[49] It is uncertain if they were aware of the family history of stomach problems which existed amongst the Hanoverians as well as some descendants of Queen Victoria. In the 1960s, these were to be identified as the result of porphyria, see T. M. Cox, M. J. Warren et. al 'King George III and porphyria: an elemental hypothesis' in *The Lancet,* 23rd July 2005 pp.332-335. It may be doubted whether all of those identified as porphyriacs by Macalpine and Hunter were so. In some cases, the individuals may simply have suffered the repercussions of a bad diet exacerbated by high levels of lead ingestion. There is no evidence that Albert was a porphyriac but research has shown that duodenal ulcers are six times more common in people with porphyria and twice as likely to be chronic, see D. Adjarov et.al. 'Porphyria cutanea tarda and peptic ulcer' in *Clinical and Experimental Dermatology,* vol 18 part 1 (January 1993) pp.32-35

[50] Even with radiography, diagnosis was not completely certain, see Charles Pannett, 'Discussion on the Treatment of Duodenal Ulcer' in *Proceedings of the Royal Society of Medicine,* vol 19 (6th January 1926) pp.49-50

offered the patient proper protection.[51] What caused duodenal ulcers was unknown at the time and would not be discovered until 1939 when Freedberg uncovered helicobacter pylori. This ignorance of the pathology of the disease encouraged caution on the part of doctors: besides, it was known that rest and a plain diet would resolve eighty per cent of ulcers.[52] For either the royal or naval doctors to have prescribed otherwise to Albert would have been irresponsible. Surgery was only ever recommended for chronic cases of "repeated attacks sustained often over a period of years" and even then it was not straightforward.[53] Should the surgeon perform a gastro-enterestomy or a resection? The former, pioneered in 1893, was the most common but proved successful in only about sixty per cent of cases.[54] It required the ulcer to have grown to a reasonable size which meant that it was impossible to carry out in the earlier stages of the disease.[55] The resection was more difficult and generally only used where there was evidence of further damage to the stomach itself and it was a more experimental procedure, although early results suggested a higher success rate. In either case, at least one in twenty patients who underwent an operation for duodenal ulcer, died.[56] It is small wonder that the surgeons about Albert were nervous. Added to their concern was the fact that Albert's ulcer had been haemorrhaging as is evident from the treatment prescribed. This was not unusual and was unlikely to be fatal but it did indicate that surgery would ultimately be needed, although that could not take place until Albert was stronger.[57] Blood transfusions, taken for granted today, were still in their infancy and it was not until 1916, a year before Albert's operation, that a process had been perfected to store blood safely for use by surgeons. To have operated without blood available would have been risky. It is reasonable to conclude therefore that the doctors about Albert did a good job given the extent of medical knowledge at the time and the availability of resources.[58]

Despite the surgery, it was felt unwise for Albert to return to sea. A land based role would keep him closer to hospitals in the event of complications

---

[51] A D Reid, 'History of the X-ray department at St Thomas's Hospital' in *Proceedings of the Royal Society of Medicine*, 16th January 1914 pp. 23-25

[52] Charles Pannett, 'Debatable Aspects of the Surgery of Gastro-Duodenal Ulceration' in *British Medical Journal*, 14th April 1928 p.624.

[53] B. G. A. Moynihan, *Duodenal Ulcer*, (Philadelphia, 1912) p.159

[54] Pannett *Proceedings* op.cit. p.46

[55] Moynihan op.cit. pp.161-162

[56] Pannett *BMJ* op.cit. p.624

[57] J. B. McGee, 'Duodenal Ulcer' in *Cleveland Medical Journal*, vol XVII no 1 (January 1918) pp.337-338

[58] Today such ulcers are more usually treated with antibiotics but that discovery was made more than twenty years after Albert's case.

and would enable him to regain his strength. At Albert's own suggestion, he was transferred to the Royal Naval Air Service from 1st January 1918 and he took up the position of Officer Commanding Boys at Cranwell in Lincolnshire. He was still there on 1st April 1918 when the RNAS became part of the newly formed Royal Air Force. Although Albert had not seen his move as being permanent, writing to his old tutor in November 1917: "what I want is a useful and permanent job which will keep me busy for at least a year till I am fit for sea again" he was never to return to the Royal Navy.[59]

Albert was not to stay at Cranwell long being transferred to St Leonard's on 2nd August. From there on 23rd October he went to France to serve at the headquarters of Major-General Trenchard. He was still there when the Armistice came into being at 11am on the 11th November 1918. Less than two weeks later he represented his father by riding alongside King Albert of Belgium as he entered Brussels in a procession to celebrate liberation. On 28th November, he was reunited with his elder brother and father for a similar procession in Paris. His brother wrote that the crowds cheered themselves hoarse.[60] Albert was to spend two weeks with his father visiting battlefields and meeting servicemen and hospital staff. The sights he saw shocked him deeply.

He returned to England where he commenced flying lessons at Waddon near Croydon. It was not easy for him. By his own admission, he did not enjoy it. He had described his first flight at Cranwell when he was a passenger as "a curious sensation and one which takes a lot of getting used to" adding "I would much sooner be on the ground."[61] He had been declared psychologically unfit to fly by the RAF Director of Medical Services, Lieutenant-Colonel James Birley which meant he could not fly solo.[62] As a result, Albert did the bare minimum to achieve his wings which he did on 31st July. The next day he was granted a permanent commission as Squadron Leader which effectively marked the end of Albert's military career.

The question arose of what he should do next. The initial response was simple. He took advantage of a scheme to enable those young men who had sacrificed educational opportunities to fight for their country and spent a year at Trinity College, Cambridge studying history, economics and the constitution. Albert described this as "everything that will be useful for the

---

[59] Greig op.cit. p.110

[60] Rupert Godfrey, *Letters from a Prince*, (London, 1998) p.137

[61] Greig op.cit. p.95

[62] ibid. p.153

time to come."[63] Whilst there, he was able to spend time with Louis Mountbatten and to learn to ride a motor bike. Further signifying his return to civilian life, on 5th June 1920, his father created him Duke of York. His elder brother suggested that Albert had been very keen to obtain this honour saying "his rather pompous nature makes him want to be one."[64] Albert wrote to his father: "Thank you again ever so much for having made me Duke of York. I am very proud to bear the name that you did for many years and I hope I shall live up to it in every way." The King replied "I feel this splendid old title will be safe in your hands and that you will never do anything which could in any way tarnish it."[65]

Like many returning servicemen after the Great War, Albert was looking for love. He found his ideal match in Elizabeth Bowes-Lyon, daughter of the Earl of Strathmore. At first she was not keen being fully aware of the changes that would be necessary to her life if she married the King's son, but eventually she decided that she would take him on and Elizabeth and Albert married at Westminster Abbey on 16th April 1923. Albert wore his Royal Air Force uniform, thus becoming the first royal groom to marry in such attire, and the wedding set a location trend which has continued to today with other royal weddings including Princess Elizabeth and Prince Philip in 1947, Prince Andrew and Sarah Ferguson in 1986 and Prince William and Catherine Middleton in 2011.[66] George V wrote to Albert on his wedding day to congratulate him on finding "such a charming and simply delightful wife as Elizabeth" and public opinion was to second this opinion.[67]

Their first home was White Lodge at Richmond which proved completely unsatisfactory as the electricity was unsafe, both toilets and heating were in short supply and the drains had failed. It was for this reason that their first child, a daughter who would go on to reign as Queen Elizabeth II, was born in Bruton Street which was the London home of Albert's in-laws. Their second child, Margaret, was born four years later at Glamis Castle which was the country home of Albert's in-laws.

A month after the birth of their first child, the family moved into 145 Piccadilly, a property advertised in *The Times* as:

Important mansion at Hyde Park Corner overlooking Green Park and

---

[63] ibid. p.156

[64] Godfrey op.cit. p.379

[65] *Majesty Magazine* vol 3 no 11 March 1983 p.15

[66] The Abbey had been used for the wedding of Albert's sister in 1922 at which Elizabeth Bowes-Lyon served as bridesmaid.

[67] *Majesty Magazine*, vol 9 no 8 December 1988 p51

Hyde Park. To be let on lease for sixty years...The Mansion contains spacious and well lighted accommodation including ball room, study, library, about fifteen bed and dressing rooms, conservatory, kitchen, and offices, passenger lift &c.[68]

This house was to remain their London home until the Abdication and was to offer them considerable privacy, not least because Albert's office was in a separate building at 11 Grosvenor Crescent. Bombed during the war, this property was later leased by the film director Alexander Korda who owned the houses either side.[69]

In 1931, George V gave them the Royal Lodge at Windsor as a country retreat. It was here that Albert discovered a love of gardening and a particular passion for rhododendrons. He planted a considerable number of them as part of his landscaping plans but he was also keen on lilies for their fragrance near the house. A sprig of myrtle from Elizabeth's wedding bouquet was planted and grew into a tree from which another cutting was taken for their eldest daughter's marriage. [70]

Elizabeth was to prove a great support to Albert in his public work as well as developing her own interests. Since the war, Albert had become involved in a number of charities which were associated with helping injured RAF personnel or assisting their dependents.[71] He was also active with Safety First, an organisation later to be known as the Royal Society for the Prevention of Accidents (ROSPA). Albert served as President of the London Safety First Council from 1923 and became Patron when it expanded to become a national organisation in 1926. Part of its work related to industrial safety and it was this element which had originally attracted Albert's interest. However, its focus shifted increasingly to road safety. Throughout the 1920s, the number of cars on the road rose sharply and so did the volume of accidents. At the society's first national congress it was revealed that in the period 1919-24, two hundred thousand more people had been injured on the roads than had been wounded in the Great War. On average, three hundred and sixteen people were hurt every day with more than ten killed. There was almost one accident per year for every two vehicles on the road. [72] Anxious to try and use his position to help to spread the road safety message, Albert took part in two short educational films, one

---

[68] *The Times*, 12th May 1925

[69] The house was bombed on 7th October 1940, see incident report 552 at National Archives CD131.2. Korda took the property over in 1947, see *The Times*, 25th March 1947

[70] Shewell-Cooper op.cit. pp.46-52. The house is today the home of the current Duke of York.

[71] He was Chairman of the Flying Services Fund administered by the Royal Aero Club and President of the RAF Memorial Fund.

[72] *The Times*, 14th April 1926

silent and another made a few years later when sound had been introduced.[73]

Another area of interest for him related to sports. Albert was a keen sportsman enjoying golf, squash, running and riding. He was particularly keen on tennis and played twice at Wimbledon. In 1920, he won the RAF Doubles Cup and in 1926 he competed in the main championship, again in the doubles. His partner on both occasions was Louis Greig. In 1926, he faced the team of Gore and Ropers Barrett who had won the title back in 1909. Both of them were in their fifties but despite this, they defeated Albert and Greig 1-6, 3-6, 2-6. The five times Wimbledon Ladies Champion Suzanne Lenglen watched the match and reported: "The Duke has a really good forehand drive which would trouble the best of players but he is too much inclined to go out for the winning shot every time." Albert himself commented to the referee on leaving the court that the standard was just too good for him.[74]

Yet the defeat did not diminish his enjoyment of the game nor his desire to encourage others to take up a sport. In July 1925, Albert launched the Playing Fields Association which had an objective of providing facilities that everyone could enjoy. The launch was attended by the Olympic champion runner Harold Abrahams and by the politicians Lady Astor and Ramsay MacDonald. Albert told them that children needed to play games to "absorb that spirit of sportsmanship which must continue to remain one of our national characteristics if we are to maintain our proud position in the world of tomorrow." MacDonald supported him saying that fitness was only part of the goal and that without sport "the human mind and human character might be very faulty and too failing to bear its national responsibilities."[75] Albert continued an active supporter of the Association approving a generous grant to it from the King George V Jubilee Fund of which he was Chairman and taking part in many fund raising activities for it.[76] In 1928, he told them how his staff had been surprised to receive a knock on the door of his Piccadilly home from two small boys who had demanded to see the Duke. Albert had met them and the boys told him how London County Council was taking away their cricket pitch. They asked him quite bluntly what he intended to do about it. Albert replied that he would do his best and although he could not save that pitch, he was able to secure them an alternative.[77]

---

[73] Darbyshire op.cit. p.252, *The Times,* 8th March, 1933.

[74] *Majesty Magazine,* vol 1 no 8 (1980) p.37

[75] *The Times,* 9th July 1925

[76] *The Times,* 5th November 1935. The Trust promoted youth work through established organisations such as the Boy Scouts and Girl Guides and also the erection of sports centres.

[77] Darbyshire op.cit. p.136

The cause with which Albert was to be most associated in the public eye was the Industrial Welfare Society. This had evolved from the work which the Reverend Robert Hyde had done with boys engaged in munitions work during the war. Hyde had asked the Archbishop of Canterbury to speak to the King about having a royal patron and the King had proposed Albert. The work would involve him not just in making speeches and attending fund raising events but in visiting factories. Albert said that he would be pleased to do the latter provided there was "no fuss, no publicity and no red carpet."[78] From 1919 until 1936 when he became King, Albert averaged visits to ten factories a year across the United Kingdom as well as finding time to visit other industrial sites on his overseas tours. Amongst the companies he visited were McVitie and Price biscuits, Greenwich Inlaid Linoleum, Courtauld Silk Works, Sanderson wallpaper manufactory, Raleigh Cycle Works, Josiah Wedgwood and Sons pottery, Beckton Gas Works, Rutland Steel Works, Tompkinson and Adams carpet factory at Kidderminster, Austin Motors in Birmingham, Garnett's woollen mill at Bradford, Bromborough margarine works, Lea Mills beachwear factory in Matlock, Carreras Cigarettes in London, and Crockett and Jones shoe factory in Northampton. His personal touch was shown on a visit to a glue works in Glasgow where the manager advised him not to go into one area because of the smell. Albert retorted: "Why not? People work there don't they? What's good enough for them is good enough for me." On many of his trips, he was invited to try his hand at one or other of the processes. He went down one mine and insisted on trying to hew some coal with a pick. He emerged so covered in coal dust that the band at the top who had been awaiting his return failed to recognise him and so missed their cue to play the National Anthem.[79]

Albert's interest in people was genuine but the motivations of the Industrial Welfare Society were not simply philanthropic. The King had stated that one of the duties of his sons was "to bring the Monarchy, in response to new conditions, ever nearer to the people."[80] This was seen as important due to the prevailing political conditions. Albert's great-uncle had been murdered by revolutionaries in 1913 and his Russian cousins had been deposed and murdered by the Bolsheviks. There was a fear that class warfare would break out in Britain and this would destabilise the entire country and create economic ruin. Albert's own speeches show that he considered support of the Society a patriotic duty. In 1920, he said:

The saving and brightening of the worker's life should be and must

---

[78] Robert Hyde, *Industry was my Parish,* (London, 1968) p.78
[79] Gorman op.cit. pp.27-28
[80] Windsor op.cit. p.207

eventually be an industrial issue and when the community realises that the country is richest which nourishes the greatest number of happy people a big step will have been taken towards the contentment and prosperity of the nation.[81]

In 1922, he appealed to wartime memories by claiming that welfare was an issue of good comradeship:

I feel sure that no one can fail to realise the obligation as well as the desirability of taking every step calculated to nurture, conserve and harmonise our priceless human forces so that not only will our fellow citizens of the workshops be more healthy and happy but we shall be able to out distance in competition every other nation.[82]

In 1924, he said the work was based on "great moral principles" and in 1935 he drew parallels between modern welfare and pre-industrial paternalism.[83] In his final address, made just hours before he became King, Albert said: "The Society has done much to remove from industry many of those hardships, anxieties and insecurities which once threatened to disturb industrial peace and prosperity."

The work of the Society covered the provision of information and advice to employers about a wide variety of staff related issues from interview practices to pensions. They encouraged the establishment of canteen facilities and recreational opportunities and promoted safer working practices. At first, they were regarded with suspicion by employers and workers alike. Employers resented what they regarded as interference in how they ran their businesses and workers feared that concentration on issues such as refreshment breaks was just a means of deflecting attention from their main concern which was wages. Albert's support helped to alleviate these concerns but membership of the Society remained extremely small. In 1928, there were over a quarter of a million workshops and factories in Great Britain but just eight hundred member companies of the Industrial Welfare Society.[84] In 1923, the Society was forced to close all its regional offices due to lack of funds and debts hampered their work until they received a large bequest a decade later.[85] Moreover, the members they had were mostly from the eight per cent of industrial employers who had

---

[81] Wheeler-Bennett op.cit. p.167

[82] *The Times,* 29th November 1922

[83] *The Times,* 8th November 1924, 21st November 1935

[84] *The Times* 28th January 1928

[85] Hyde op.cit. p.94

more than a hundred staff.[86] They covered a variety of industries such as cement works, shipbuilding, steel works, confectioners, textiles, mining and printers as well as some well known retailers including Boots the chemist, Burton the tailors and the Lyons restaurant chain.[87]

Despite the fact that they were not representative as an organisation and many of their goals were unrealistic, Albert's dedicated public support over the years gave them an influence far beyond their strength. A lot of the improvements in workers lives such as reduced hours, guaranteed breaks, pensions, sick pay, would require state intervention. Nonetheless, the Society continued to pursue its work despite the appalling economic situation. In the 1920s, unemployment averaged ten per cent across the country, though the rate in the north and Wales was twice as high as it was in London and the south east. Following the crash of 1929, the 1930s saw unemployment rise sharply with an average of thirty per cent in Wales and more than a quarter in Scotland and the north. [88] Faced with such a recession, it was hardly surprising that employers were reluctant to invest in things like canteens and social clubs.

Albert was directly responsible for the introduction of what was to become the most famous aspect of the Society's work. In 1921, a party of apprentice lads from the Briton Ferry Steelworks were brought to London by their Welfare Officer. He asked the Society if it could arrange for them to play football with lads from other companies or schools. Arrangements were duly made and Albert went to watch the game played against Westminster School together with Alexander Grant, the chairman of McVitie's. Enjoying the match, Albert commented that it was good to see working class boys mixing with public school boys in such a friendly way. Grant agreed and said that he would willingly contribute to any similar scheme in the future. Albert gave the matter some thought and decided that a camp would be the best option. A year before, the London Boys Brigade had offered to rent their campsite at New Romney in Kent to any member firms of the Society and now the Society decided it would use the premises itself. Invitations were despatched to one hundred public schools and to one hundred factories to send two boys each, aged sixteen to nineteen, whom they thought would enjoy a week's camp beside the sea. The first camp was held in 1921 and was such a success that it was held annually until 1939, excepting for 1930.

---

[86] Eric Hopkins, *The Rise and Decline of the English Working Classes 1918-1990*, (London, 1991) p.19

[87] See a list of member companies in *The Times*, 8th December 1925

[88] W. R. Garside, *British Unemployment 1919-39*, (Cambridge, 1990) p.10. See also Hopkins op.cit. p.29-30 for data on patterns of unemployment by duration, age, skill level and location.

The aim of the camps was to break down class barriers which is why the boys were divided into twenty groups each of which comprised ten workers and ten scholars. During the week they had the opportunity to swim, dress up and perform shows, take part in organised events such as cross country runs and to sing songs beside the campfire. Albert attended the camp each year and was filmed by Pathé leading the singing of *Under the Spreading Chestnut Tree*. A number of games were arranged but these were deliberately of the informal type such as sack races, tugs of war, pillow fights. It was felt that traditional sports such as cricket would give the public school boys an unfair advantage, partly because they were better practiced but also because they tended to be taller, heavier and healthier than their working class counterparts. In the evenings, they had magic lantern shows, conjurers and gramophone music and the occasional guest speaker. The organisers wanted camp to remain fun rather than overtly educational but were happy to welcome people such as Herbert Ponting who had been the photographer for Robert Scott's famous Terra Nova polar expedition of 1910-13. Albert said that by bringing the boys together at an impressionable age, camp was "playing a part in oiling the wheels of industry with good fellowship and understanding."[89]

Throughout the 1920s, Albert carried out around seventy public engagements a year. Many of these involved the unveiling of war memorials or opening of hospital wings which had been established in memory of those who had been killed in the war. He attended a variety of sporting events and took a key role in the annual Hendon Air Pageant giving his name to a Challenge Cup. Initially the competition for this was between RAF stations and involved a message carrying relay of three different planes but in later years it became an individual event.[90]

Albert also took a keen interest in airships inviting Captain Hugo Eckener in 1930 to come and tell him about his round the world tour in the Graf Zeppelin which had taken place eight months before. Albert's enthusiasm for the giant airship almost got him into trouble because he invited it to carry out a low flypast over the Cup Final at Wembley on the Saturday following which he was due to attend. The Graf duly did this about a quarter of an hour into the match which was recognised to be a spectacular sight but totally distracting for those present and had the effect of plunging the pitch into almost complete darkness.[91] Eckener had taken the opportunity of trying to persuade Albert to support his scheme for a

---

[89] Accounts of camp each year appear in *The Times* and further details can be found in Robert Hyde, *The Camp Book*, (London, 1930)
[90] *Flight*, 29th June 1922, 3rd July 1931
[91] *The Brisbane Courier*, 30th April 1930

regular international airship service. Discussion of such a service had existed since 1921 with Great Britain keen to establish a regular service to Australia, India, Egypt and South Africa. The chief obstacle was cost. Such a service was reckoned to need at least twelve airships which would cost £150,000 each with a further £111,000 per annum in running costs. Setting up an airship station was estimated at £266,000 with ongoing running costs of £120,000 per annum.[92] In current values, that required an investment of about seventy million pounds which was clearly beyond private enterprise. Eckener had no interest in the British Empire but was keen on a transatlantic service to America and was about to launch a regular service between Spain, Brazil and America.[93] Britain had in 1924 launched its own Imperial Airship Programme and by 1930 had built two of the only four rigid airships to exist in the world. Eckener, during his visit, had the chance to observe their progress. The R100 had been successfully launched but the R101 was in process of being re-designed.

Less than six months after Albert met Eckener, R101 took off on its maiden flight to India. Eight hours later it was forced to make an emergency landing in France whereupon it caught fire and killed forty-eight of the fifty-four people on board. The dead were taken to Westminster Hall to lie in state before their funeral at St Paul's Cathedral. The BBC broadcast the service and then closed down for the day as the nation went into mourning.[94] Albert attended the funeral along with Eckener. The disaster effectively ended all dreams of British airships including Albert's own.

In addition to his duties in Great Britain, Albert was called upon on several occasions to represent the King abroad. Mostly, these were family events such as the wedding of Alexander of Serbia to Marie of Romania. In December 1924, Albert and his wife departed on a tour of Africa that would last almost five months. They visited Kenya, Uganda and the Sudan. The trip involved various official receptions and provided opportunities to meet with service personnel but the trip was also designed to be an extended holiday, a boost for the health of the royal couple both of whom had been ill. A keen shot like his father, Albert relished the opportunity to go hunting and his wife joined him. She shot two zebra, a gazelle, an oryx and a rhinoceros as well as buffalo and recorded in her diary: "I enjoyed it so much and became very bloodthirsty."[95] Albert wrote to his father: "In the evening I

---

[92] For a summary of the various schemes and their costs see *Flight,* 25th August 1921 p.576

[93] Douglas Botting, *Dr Eckener's Dream Machine* (London, 2002) p.218

[94] *The Times,* 10th October 1930. Forty-six were killed instantly and two died of injuries shortly after.

[95] William Shawcross, *Queen Elizabeth the Queen Mother,* (London, 2009) pp.226-232

shot a very good elephant whose tusks weighed 90lbs each. It was very lucky as there are not very many big ones left. I got a smaller one two days later...I went out and shot a white rhino with a horn 33" long which is quite good."[96] He also shot a lioness. Attitudes to big game hunting have changed over the years and most people today would probably agree with Prince William who described participants as "extremely ignorant, selfish and utterly wrong."[97] Albert can only be judged in the context of his own era but he was not unaware of concern because he had opened the RSPCA conference just nine months before where one speaker had criticised the trade in rare animals as demonstrative of "callous indifference to the sanctity of human life which characterised so many commercial concerns when the raw material was drawn from Nature's own treasure store and the end in view was profit."[98]

Not long after his return from Africa, Australia requested that the King send a representative to open their new Parliament building in Canberra. The Prince of Wales had travelled extensively and the King decided it was time that Albert have his opportunity. His decision was not met with universal approval. That Albert was dutiful and dedicated to the imperial cause was not in doubt, however, he remained painfully shy. Those about him attributed the problem to his speech defect. One friend recalled the hours that he would spend before any public appearance practising his speech often followed by even more hours afterwards as he shut himself away in depression convinced he had been a failure.[99] Robert Hyde of the Industrial Welfare Society who attended hundreds of engagements with him recalled: "He was conscious that as a public figure he lacked the personality associated with his father King George V as well as the spontaneous charm and ease of his eldest brother. His faulty speech too caused him anxiety amounting at times almost to mental torture."[100] By Albert's own admission, he just struggled through but he was not happy. It was not that he did not try to overcome the problem. In 1919, he asked to be brought back to England so he could start work with a speech therapist who seemed to be making some progress. In 1920, Lord Crawford wrote of Albert: "He has a really bad stammer but by dint of careful training he has almost mastered this infirmity, and apart from halting pauses between his words, he gets along much better than the average."[101] Albert's father was similarly optimistic writing to him the same year: "Your Italian friend is doing you

---

[96] Wheeler-Bennett op.cit. p.205
[97] BBC News 19th June 2012
[98] *The Times* 24th June 1924
[99] Darbyshire op.cit. p.87
[100] Hyde op.cit. pp.100-101
[101] Bradford op.cit. p.125

good which is a great thing. If you could only stick to it and persevere now, he will very likely cure you entirely."[102] Yet, the hopes were to prove short lived and Albert's halting performance at the opening of the British Empire Exhibition in 1925 which was broadcast on radio and newsreel across the country, just highlighted the extent of the problem. It was deemed essential to try and find another speech therapist to see if some improvement could be made before Albert set off on his trip.

On 19th October 1926, Albert had his first appointment with the Australian Lionel Logue who reported:

> Well built with good shoulders but waist line very flabby....top lung development good. Has never used diaphragm or lower lung – this has resulted through non control of solar plexus in nervous tension with consequent episodes of bad speech, depression. Contracts teeth and mouth and mechanically closes throat.[103]

More than eighty appointments were to follow as Albert endeavoured to follow Logue's advice which involved a series of breathing exercises followed by enunciation practice of the vowels and when those were mastered, of the consonants and tongue twisters. Logue's recipe for success was not new. As early as 1828, Henry McCormac had prescribed exactly the same routine of breathing exercises followed by practice of the vowels then consonants. McCormac had claimed that over ninety per cent of speech defects were caused by "the patient endeavouring to utter words or any other manifestation of voice when the air in the lungs is exhausted and they are in a state of collapse or nearly so."[104] Since this had been written almost a century before and numerous other experts had argued since on the same lines, it must be wondered why Albert had not been cured before. In 1902, for example, *Medical News* had reported: "in a majority of cases the speech difficulty can be traced fundamentally to the management of the breath and the results obtained by training a patient to manage his voice by means of diaphragmatic action are marvellous."[105] Albert's first official biographer, Taylor Darbyshire, suggested that the reason Logue succeeded where others had failed was because he convinced Albert that the problem was physical rather than mental, something which cheered him up and gave him confidence that he could work to overcome it just as he had worked to

---

[102] Wheeler-Bennett op.cit. p.135

[103] Mark Logue and Peter Conradi, *The King's Speech*, (London, 2010) p.67

[104] Henry McCormac, *A Treatise on the Cause and Cure of Hesitation of Speech*, (London, 1828) p.15. For his treatment recommendations see pp.84-87.

[105] *Medical News*, vol 80 June 14th 1902 p.1148

improve his tennis and golf.[106] Whether Logue believed this himself is less certain for he was reported as having observed privately that he believed the defect had been caused by the way Albert had been treated in childhood.[107]

The allegation that Albert's problems were the result of a tyrannical father has been repeated often in various books, magazines, films and documentaries. John Gore, for example, who knew George V wrote: "His manner of chaffing them or interrogating them added to the shyness and tied the tongues of those by nature the most diffident."[108] Such a serious charge needs examining both in light of contemporary understanding of the issue and more modern medical opinion.

The first problem is identification of the nature of his speech defect. Lady Airlie, Lord Crawford and Lord Mountbatten all said he stammered whereas Lieutenant Lambert and Wing Commander Townson said he stuttered.[109] Marion Crawford, governess to the Princesses Elizabeth and Margaret noted that Albert had in 1932 "a slight impediment in his speech that was not so much of a stutter in the ordinary sense as a slight nervous constriction in the throat."[110] None of these witnesses were experts and the two terms were used interchangeably by many as they are today but contemporary therapists distinguished between the two. Stammering was seen as habitual and characterised by the inability to properly and distinctly enunciate some or many speech sounds. As such it affected the person at all times and was more likely to have a physical cause, either with the larynx or even perhaps the hearing. Stuttering was manifested most usually through the repetition of a letter or syllable at the start of a word but could also be a convulsive contraction of the various muscles of the respiratory, vocal or articulating apparatus which resulted in an extended pause before a word. As stutterers were often able to talk normally at home with family or close friends, the problem was seen as primarily the result of nerves.[111] Albert himself seems to have felt this was the case saying in a letter to his father: "twenty four years of talking in the wrong way cannot be cured in a month... now that I know the right way to breathe my fear of talking will vanish." [112]

---

[106] Darbyshire op.cit. p.87

[107] Logue op.cit. p.67

[108] John Gore, *King George V, a Personal Memoir* (London 1941) p. 370

[109] Bradford op.cit. pp.39, 74, 96, 125. *Majesty Magazine* vol 1 no 7 Nov 1980 p.41

[110] Marion Crawford, *The Little Princesses,* (London, 1950) p.7

[111] James Hunt, *Stammering and Stuttering,* (London, 1870) pp.9-12

[112] Bradford op.cit. pp.161-162

Just as treatment varied according to whether stammering or stuttering was diagnosed, so the causes were seen to differ. A link between stuttering and German measles was noted and Albert did indeed contract this just after his fifth birthday which was around the time his speech defect began.[113] Monro in 1850 speculated that stammering was caused by a defect in the part of the brain which controlled speech and commented that this was often hereditary.[114] Although it had been suggested as early as 1809 that language was a function of a specific part of the brain, it was not until 1861 that Broca proved that severe speech problems were the result of lesions on the left frontal lobes.[115] Since there was no means at the time to check for such during a patient's lifetime, this discovery did not materially affect views on speech defects until, in 1912, Ballard recalled that Broca had also observed that the damaged lobe was opposite to the dominant hand for most people. Ballard conducted a study which showed that over a sixth of naturally left handed people who had been forced to use the right stammered.[116] Albert had started using his left hand as a child and he had been taught to use the right as was common at the time. Teachers generally believed that using the left was just a case of bad habit or education and not a natural trait, and hence like other bad habits it should be corrected. In the first official biography of Albert to be written after his death, it was confidently claimed that forcing Albert to use his right hand had been the cause of his speech defect.[117] As the link between speech problems and handedness was not made until he was past childhood, neither his father nor tutors could be blamed for this. Subsequent studies of handedness and speech disorders have produced conflicting evidence. Bryngelson in the 1930s thought forcing a change of hands could cause brain damage and hence speech problems but saw it as only affecting those with an hereditary tendency to the problem.[118] A large study in the 1960s after the official biography, found no link at all, whilst a smaller one in the 1980s did.[119]

---

[113] Edward Conradi, 'Psychology and Pathology of Speech Development in the Child' in *The Pedagogical Seminary* vol 11 (1904) p.357. Albert and his elder brother were ill at the time Queen Victoria died, see Windsor op.cit. p.23

[114] Henry Monro, *On Stammering and Its Treatment*, (London, 1850) p.27

[115] N. F Dronkers et al. 'Paul Broca's historic cases' in *Brain*, vol. 130 no 5 (May, 2007) p.1432. For the earlier study see E Gall and G Spurzheim, *Recherches sur le système nerveux*, (Paris, 1809)

[116] P. Ballard, 'Sinistrality and speech' in *Journal of Experimental Pediatrics* vol.1 no 4 (1912) p.309

[117] Wheeler-Bennett op.cit. p.27

[118] Bryng Bryngelson and Thomas Clark, 'Left handedness and Stuttering' in *Journal of Heredity*, vol. 24, October 1933 pp.387-390

[119] Andrews op.cit. p.231 quotes twenty-two studies of handedness and speech disorders and notes that thirteen found no link at all. One study which did was Norman Geschwind and Peter Behan, 'Left handedness: Association with immune disease, migraine and developmental learning disorder' in *Proceedings of the National Academy of Science USA* vol 79 (August 1982) pp.5097-5100

Even where a link with lateralisation is found, it does not follow that there is any causality for the propensity to left handedness could be caused by the same cerebral patterns as the speech defect.

Today, the idea that chronic stammering or stuttering could be caused by a poor relationship with anyone would be seen as being as ridiculous as the theory prevalent when Albert was a boy that it was the outcome of masturbation. Modern MRI technology has enabled detailed studies to be made of the brains of sufferers and these have found structural white matter abnormalities, although the exact cause of these remains unknown. It is even possible that the abnormalities are as a result of rather than cause of speech defects.[120]

In the 1980s, it was discovered that for neurological reasons, stammerers lacked central processing capacity for concurrent attention demanding tasks which affected their performance generally.[121] Albert was recognised to be less than intellectually able by all his teachers and a study in 1912 found that that stammerers were on average six months behind educationally.[122] It was noted that speech training such as that which Albert underwent could have a dramatic effect on reducing hesitations because it reduced processing load.

Most recently, researchers investigating the often recorded fact that some defects have a familial link, have identified specific genes that feature in a number of sufferers.[123] It is known that Albert's grandfather, Edward VII, stammered and his youngest brother John was an epileptic so a genetic link is quite possible and even probable.[124] It may be concluded therefore that Albert's speech defect did have a physical cause but that it had nothing to do with his diaphragm, childhood or handedness.

Filled with confidence after his lessons from Logue and excited at the prospect of all that lay ahead, Albert wrote to his father: "This is the first

---

[120] Kate Watkins, 'Structural and Functional Abnormalities of the motor system' in *Brain*, vol 131 January 2008, pp.50-59

[121] The theory appears in Andrews op.cit. pp.238-240. For a later study which came to the same conclusion see Hans- Georg Bosshardt, 'Cognitive processing load as a determinant of stuttering' in *Clinical Linguistics and Phonetics*, vol 20 no 5 (July 2006) pp.371-385

[122] E Conradi, 'Speech defects and intellectual progress' in *Journal of Educational Psychology* vol 3 (1912) pp.35-38

[123] C. Kang et al. 'Mutations in the lysosomal enzyme-targeting pathway and persistent stuttering' in *New England Journal of Medicine*, vol 362 (2010) pp.677-85

[124] Christopher Hibbert, *Edward VII*, (London, 1976) pp.6-7. R. Ottman, 'Genetic epidemiology of epilepsy' in *Epidemiologic Reviews* vol 19 (1997) pp. 120-128. For an overview of research relating to genetics and prenatal brain damage see Andrews op.cit. pp.228-229

time you have sent me on a mission concerning the Empire, and I can assure you that I will do my very best to make it the success we all hope for."[125] The royal couple departed in January 1927 after a farewell party which was attended by Fred Astaire and his sister Adele. They were good friends with Albert and his wife and had been amongst the first outsiders to see the baby Princess Elizabeth the year before. They sent flowers to the ship and Albert replied saying he would miss them and hoped to see them soon: "London is never the same when you are not there."[126]

After stops in Jamaica and Fiji, Albert and Elizabeth arrived in New Zealand on 22nd February 1927. Albert visited a number of industrial sites and had the opportunity to drive a train named the Passchendale which had been purchased in memory of New Zealanders who had died in the Great War. Elizabeth was taken ill with tonsillitis so Albert had to carry out half of the tour on his own but he was relaxed by the friendly welcome and seemed to enjoy proceedings. In Australia the crowds were even larger and Albert was amused to see a general, otherwise very staid, climb a tree in his enthusiasm to spot Elizabeth.

A large number of the engagements on the tour related to the war with Albert being able to publicly thank the thousands of Australians who had fought on behalf of the Empire and to unveil various memorial plaques and buildings. He was present in Melbourne for the Anzac Day march which that year was led by thirty-two winners of the Victoria Cross followed by a number of wounded ex-servicemen, some being wheeled on their hospital beds, others on crutches or being led by carers. Australian forces followed marching ten abreast and then the New Zealanders. Toward the end came the Boer War veterans and some of the British and Imperial expatriate community including some of the "Old Contemptibles". The procession of almost thirty thousand men took an hour and a half to pass through and was believed to represent the largest ever gathering of Victoria Cross winners. Speaking of the war, Albert told the crowds:

> That great feat of arms and the heroic deeds of all who shared in it will be remembered as long as the Empire lasts. They gave their all for King and Empire and their sacrifice will remain for ever a shining example of what human will and endurance can accomplish...Therefore I would beg you to regard this day not so much as one of mourning for the dead as one of earnest resolve on the part of us, the living, to emulate their example. Let us try to live more worthily of those who made the last great sacrifice for us and to do the

---

[125] Shawcross op.cit. p.266
[126] Fred Astaire, *Steps in Time*, (London, 1960) pp.143-146. Fred had first met Albert in 1923.

utmost that lies in our power to maintain and hand down to the children who come after us those traditions of loyalty, fortitude and devotion to duty which animated those gallant men and on the preservation of which the whole welfare and security of the Empire depend.[127]

Afterwards he met some of the veterans including John Jackson, the youngest winner of the VC who had gone four times into No Man's Land at Armentieres to bring casualties back despite heavy fire and having his own arm blown off below the elbow. He was eighteen at the time. He met Albert Jacka, the first Australian to win the VC who had single handedly killed seven Turks at Gallipoli and captured three others, calmly telling those who found him the next day, "Well I got the beggars, sir." He met Henry Dalziel who had been wounded thirty-two times during the war including having his trigger finger blown off and his skull smashed at Hamel where he won his VC for attacking a German machine gun post and bringing back much needed ammunition despite constant bombardment. Other VCs whom Albert met that day included William Currey who volunteered to focus fire on himself by walking alone into No Man's Land so that his comrades could withdraw safely, an action which resulted in his being gassed and Arthur Sullivan, the most recent recipient of the VC, who had earned his fighting the Bolsheviks in Russia in 1919 when serving with the British Army.[128]

From Melbourne, he went to Adelaide and Canberra and then to Pinjarra to visit the Fairbridge Farm School. This had been set up in 1913 and was a project which enjoyed financial support from the British government. Its objective was to take children who had no future in England to Australia where they would have fresh air and learn how to cultivate land so that they could go forth and settle parts of Australia which were yet undeveloped. At the time that Albert and his wife visited, the school had around two hundred and forty children who occupied thirteen cottages. Albert commented that he had never seen happier or healthier children.

The tour involved Albert making more speeches and carrying out more engagements that he had ever done before but it was universally agreed to have been a great success. Part of the reason for this was that Albert allowed his own personality to show through. For example, at Lawson, Albert saw crowds on the platform waiting for the chance to catch a glimpse of the royal couple. As the train slowed to take on water, he slipped out and

---

[127] *The Register*, 26th April 1927

[128] Details of their bravery can be found in their citations which appear in the *London Gazette* on 9th September 1916, 23rd July 1915, 17th August 1918, 13th December 1918 and 29th September 1919 respectively

ran to join the crowds who failed to identify him. When the train finally stopped and Elizabeth lent out to wave at the crowds, she was able to see Albert in their midst joining in the cheers. On other occasions, he showed no compunction in altering the programme at short notice or demanding that barriers be moved so that those who had waited for hours to see them could have their opportunity. At Greymouth in New Zealand, he had the local theatre opened so that all the children who had gathered to perform a welcome drill outdoors and who had consequently been soaked by a sudden downpour could have the chance to dry off. He and his wife then spent an hour chatting to them. At Newcastle in New South Wales he insisted on driving about with the car roof down despite the rain saying that if the crowds could get wet, so would he. They were little things but they made him and Elizabeth very popular.[129]

Upon his return to the UK, Albert settled down to family life. An account of his regular routine when in London appeared in 1929. It noted that he worked on his correspondence and speeches from ten to twelve before going for a walk with his wife whilst lunch was prepared. In the afternoon he might have an engagement or else spend time in one of his sporting activities. He and Elizabeth would then go to the nursery to spend time with their daughter who was by then three years old. After tea and the ritual of settling the little princess down, they would either go out to dinner and the theatre or else dine at home with Albert then spending the evening doing a crossword or some embroidery or reading a thriller.[130]

Although not as socially glamorous as the Prince of Wales, the Yorks were very much a couple of their time. They enjoyed jazz with Elizabeth delighting in dancing and teaching others the Charleston.[131] When they travelled overseas they took with them a selection of Harold Lloyd films, the quintessential clean cut American comedian who personified the go-getting approach to the American dream.[132] Albert was also keen on cartoons, particularly Walt Disney's Mickey Mouse and Silly Symphonies.[133] He enjoyed all aspects of cinema from the mechanics of projection to the actual making of films. He bought his own camera so he could make home movies of the children as well as record some of his visits. In 1929, he was thrilled to have the opportunity to visit British International Pictures at Elstree

---

[129] A very full official account of the tour was written by the journalist Taylor Darbyshire who was present throughout.

[130] Darbyshire op.cit. pp.246-248. Marion Crawford reported that Albert had made a dozen petit-point seat covers for Royal Lodge though he got bored doing the backgrounds and asked her to finish them. Crawford op.cit. p.36

[131] Taylor Darbyshire, *The Royal Tour of the Duke and Duchess of York*, (London, 1927) p.42

[132] Shawcross op.cit. p.268

[133] Gorman op.cit. p.25

where he was able to see four films in production. It was a time of transition in the film industry as was shown by the fact that he was invited to tour both the silent film stages where three films were being made and the new sound stage.[134] On the silent stage he found Betty Balfour, the biggest British star of the 1920s who had made her name as a comedienne in the Squibs series of films. She was at work on *The Vagabond Queen,* a comedy about mistaken identities. The sound stage was being used by a young director named Alfred Hitchcock for a film called *Blackmail* which starred the blonde Czech actress Anny Ondra. Owing to her accent, she was simply miming the words whilst Joan Barry spoke them into a microphone to the side.[135] A silent version of the same film had already been filmed by the same crew and released to popular acclaim. The sound version was advertised as "the first full length all talkie film made in Great Britain" and was keenly awaited, even though there were less than a hundred cinemas equipped for sound across the country. Albert went into the recording booth to watch the new process whilst his wife sat in the camera booth with Hitchcock. Albert's interest in sound had been evident some years before when he obtained some phonofilm shorts which used De Forest's patented sound on film system and he was interested to see how the technology had advanced.[136]

Albert's domestic idyll and routine of royal engagements was interrupted in 1936 by the death of his father. George V's health had been failing for some time but his passing was still a shock. The family dynamics changed as Albert's elder brother became King Edward VIII and it was very soon evident that there were going to be problems. Edward seemed unwilling to behave in the manner which people expected of a king. He did not attend church, although he was Defender of the Faith. He either declined to read official papers or sent them back with wine or food stains. He started talking to representatives of other governments about policy matters, thereby undermining the foundations of parliamentary democracy. He publicly demonstrated his sense of priorities when he chose to drive over to collect his girlfriend rather than carry out a long standing engagement at Aberdeen Infirmary where considerable time and effort had been spent on preparations. Instead, he sent Albert to deputise for him.[137] Despite supposedly being in mourning, he maintained his party loving lifestyle and throughout it all his constant companion was a married woman named Wallis Simpson. Edward's argument was that his private life was his own affair but he neglected the fact that he was a public figure with

---

[134] *The Times,* 14th May 1929.

[135] Patricia Warren, *Elstree – the British Hollywood,* (London, 1988) pp.41-45. The character of Chief Inspector was played by different actors in the silent and screen versions.

[136] Shawcross op.cit. p.268

[137] Anne Sebba, *That Woman,* (London, 2011) pp.144-145

responsibilities.

In October, Albert was told by the new King's Private Secretary that Wallis was about to obtain a divorce and it was believed that Edward would then marry her. This created consternation. Wallis had already been divorced once and there was no possibility that the Church would agree to marry her and the King because it was against Christian teaching.[138] For the King to live in sin would have been a scandal. As if the moral situation was not bad enough, there was considerable concern about Wallis' perceived Nazi sympathies. She was under surveillance by MI6 and the Prime Minister was aware of her contacts.[139] He authorised the Foreign Office to with-hold documents from the King because he feared he could not be trusted either, not necessarily because he shared her beliefs although Baldwin was unsure about that, but because it was known that Edward let her read confidential documents. The situation was set for a confrontation and this happened when Edward confirmed to the Prime Minister his intention of marrying Wallis. Baldwin advised that the country would not accept it and neither would the dominions. Edward said that he would rather abdicate than live without her.

At first, the royal family thought that Edward would bow to reason and give her up and do his duty. His mother later wrote: "It seemed inconceivable to those who had made such sacrifices during the war that you, as their King, refused a lesser sacrifice."[140] Albert said: "If the worst happens and I have to take over, you can be assured that I will do my best to clear up the inevitable mess, if the whole fabric does not crumble under the shock and strain of it all." However, he made it clear that he had no wish for his brother to leave. When it became obvious that Edward really was going to abdicate, Albert was horrified. His wife said: "the agony of it all has been beyond words" whilst he admitted to feeling like "the proverbial sheep being led to the slaughter." [141]

On 10th December 1936, Edward signed the Instrument of Abdication in front of his three brothers. The following day at 13:52, Albert became King and Emperor adopting the name of George VI in honour of his father. Officially his response was:

I declare to you my adherence to the strict principles of constitutional government and my resolve to work before all else for the welfare of

---

[138] Mark 10:12, Luke 16:18, I Corinthians 7:10-11.

[139] Sebba op.cit. pp.125-126, Charles Higham, *Wallis*, (London, 1989) p.218

[140] Bradford op.cit. p.235

[141] ibid. pp.240, 242, 258

the British Commonwealth of Nations. With my wife and helpmeet by my side, I take up the heavy task which lies before me.[142]

Privately, he went to see his mother, Queen Mary, and by his own admission "broke down and sobbed like a child."[143] He was the sixth Duke of York to become King and undoubtedly the most reluctant. His life had been transformed with barely a month's warning and the enormous adjustments required of him and his family were to have far-reaching effects. Yet Albert was just the man for the job. As his elder brother admitted, Albert was very like his father and the country wanted a king who was devoted to his family and to duty. [144] George V had once said "Bertie has more guts than the rest of his brothers put together" and history was to prove that to be the case.[145]

---

[142] *Belfast Gazette*, 11th December 1936

[143] Wheeler-Bennett op.cit. p.286

[144] Windsor op.cit. pp.241, 259

[145] Ellis op.cit. p.202

Andrew

1960-

Duke of York 1986-

Intelligent, charming at will...a warrior prince.[1]

On 14th August 2011, the *Sunday Mirror* ran a headline "Prince Andrew frolics on yacht with mystery woman as Britain is gripped with economic misery and riots." Other members of the royal family were on holiday at the same time, together with around seven million Britons[2] but the newspaper chose to highlight just the Duke of York and to contrast his relaxed smile with the pain on the faces of those whose homes or businesses had been destroyed in the riots. It was a vivid example of the way in which the current Duke has had to endure media coverage which differs sharply from that faced by his predecessors or even other members of the royal family. No newspaper, for example, has ever published an image of a starving child next to one of a laughing Princess Anne with a view to drawing similar negative conclusions about her attitude to world poverty. In a statement talking about press coverage of someone else just a fortnight earlier, the lawyer Louis Charalambous spoke of the "regular witch hunts and character

---

[1] Donald Edgar, *Prince Andrew*, (London, 1980) p.130

[2] Office of National Statistics, Visits and Spending by UK residents abroad and overseas residents in the UK - monthly series derived from the International Passenger Survey (IPS).

assassination conducted by the worst elements of the British tabloid media."[3] It could be argued that Prince Andrew has been a victim of such treatment. Certainly the decline of deference in the late twentieth century has been a factor in this but the press coverage has also highlighted the very real question of what should be the role of the Duke of York today?

Prince Andrew was born at 3.30pm in Buckingham Palace on 19th February, 1960, the first child born to a reigning monarch since Queen Victoria gave birth to Princess Beatrice on 14th April, 1857. A healthy seven pounds and three ounces, it was reported that he and his mother, Queen Elizabeth II were doing well and that his father, Prince Philip, was delighted. Gun salutes were fired in Hyde Park, at Windsor and at Cardiff to celebrate the event. Across the Commonwealth, gifts and messages of congratulation were prepared, the most unusual of which was a live baby crocodile from Gambia which had to be transported in a bathtub on board the Royal Yacht Britannia.[4]

Just under two months after his birth, he was baptised in the Music Room by the Archbishop of Canterbury, Geoffrey Fisher, using water brought specially for the occasion from the River Jordan, the river in which Jesus Christ Himself had been baptised. His names were given as Andrew Albert Christian Edward, the first two names being those of his grandfathers Andrew of Greece and Albert of York and the second two being the names of their grandparents.[5] For his baptism he wore the family heirloom gown of Honiton lace made in 1841 and the ceremony took place using the lily font designed by Queen Victoria's husband, Prince Albert.[6] The gold ewer used to hold the water was older still dating back to the time of the Stuarts, almost three centuries before. He had five godparents including the Duke of Gloucester and Princess Alexandra.[7] The private ceremony was emblematic in its tradition of the new arrival's role in history and a sign of the formality which would play a major role in his adult life.

---

[3] Louis Charalambous was speaking on behalf of Christopher Jefferies on 28th July 2011

[4] Graham and Heather Fisher, *The Queen's Travels* (London, 1987) p.76, *History Today*, vol. 60 (August 2010) p71

[5] Prince Andrew of Greece (d.1944) was the father of Prince Philip and the grandson of Christian IX of Denmark. Prince Albert was the father of the Queen who had assumed the name of George VI when he came to the throne in 1936 and his grandfather was Edward VII. In accordance with the edict of the Privy Council just before his birth, the new prince was to have no surname and neither would his children, see *The Times*, 9th February, 1960. If he had a son, his grandchildren would be Mountbatten-Windsor

[6] The font is generally on display at the Tower of London. Just under eighteen inches high, it shows a lily supported by cherubs, a lion and a unicorn. The lily is a traditional Christian symbol of purity.

[7] Henry, Duke of Gloucester, died in 1974 and was the Queen's uncle. Princess Alexandra is the Queen's cousin, sister to the current Duke of Kent and Prince Michael.

As a toddler, Prince Andrew was described as "naturally fearless and not at all shy."[8] As he grew older, he was seen as rather boisterous. He played tricks on people like hiding the cutlery or moving the antenna so that the Queen could not watch her racing programme. He poured bubble bath into the pool and tied the shoelaces of the sentries together. On one occasion, he went too far and hit one of the horses on the leg, whereupon a groom picked him up and tossed him into the dung heap and shovelled manure over him. The young prince ran back threatening to tell his mother and was no doubt disappointed to find the Queen sided with the groom.[9] In some ways, his childhood was much like that of other children of the period. He watched *Play School* and *Blue Peter* and enjoyed the repeats of *Champion the Wonder Horse* though he hid behind the sofa when the daleks came on in *Doctor Who*. His toys were mostly handed down from his elder brother and sister and were quite traditional including teddy bears, rabbits, pedal cars and footballs.

Yet, it was not an entirely normal life. He was almost nine before he went to school because his early lessons had been taken in Buckingham Palace with a few companions such as his cousin David Linley. When he did start at Heatherdown, he became the subject of a kidnap threat from the Irish Republican Army who hoped to capture and hold him in return for the release of some of their jailed members. Other schoolboys were not constantly accompanied by a private detective and other schools did not have armed police on every gate. As he grew up, he had experiences which were not usual such as receiving tennis lessons from Dan Maskell at Wimbledon, cricket lessons from Len Muncer at Lords, skating lessons at Richmond and tuition in advanced driving techniques from World Champion Graham Hill. Not only were his tutors above the average but security considerations meant that he was taught either alone or with his brother or cousin. He was allowed to join the Cub Scouts but even with this, the rest of the troop had to come to him as he was not permitted out to play in case of terrorist attack. As if proof were needed that the threat was real, in 1974 his sister became the object of a kidnap attempt in The Mall.

In 1973, His Royal Highness moved on to Gordonstoun School in Scotland. Its relatively remote location meant that Prince Andrew was allowed a bit more freedom. Unlike his elder brother, he enjoyed life there immensely and he earned places in the rugby, cricket and hockey teams as well as the school yacht crew. One of the school's most deeply cherished beliefs was that education should be to create character and not just academics, and it fostered this through its stress on outdoor activities and

---

[8] Lisa Sheridan, *A Day With Prince Andrew*, (London, 1962) p.3
[9] *Majesty Magazine*, vol 14 no 8 Aug 1992 p.16

service. The prince served with the school's coastguard patrol, regularly taking his turn on night watch and going out in the lifeboat. He also worked through to the gold standard in the Duke of Edinburgh's Award scheme, something which involved him carrying out volunteer work for a year in the community. He joined the Air Cadet Corps too and at sixteen became the first Royal to earn his wings as a glider pilot. Away from these activities, Prince Andrew continued his studies achieving six O-levels and three A-levels which he sat under a false name so that there could be no accusations of favouritism. His best subjects were English, French and History though he took Economics and Political Studies through to A-level. He had been taught French from a young age but became particularly proficient after a three week school exchange trip to Toulouse where he not only studied the language but took the opportunity to go and see the new Concorde which was being built.[10]

Toward the end of his time at Gordonstoun, Prince Andrew went to Canada where his mother was due to open the Montreal Olympics and where his sister, Princess Anne, was going to compete in the equestrian events. During the visit, the Canadian Prime Minister Pierre Trudeau, suggested that the Queen might like to send her son to a school there, an idea to which Prince Andrew enthusiastically gave his agreement. As a result, he joined Lakefield School ninety miles north of Toronto. It was a small school, less than two hundred and fifty boys, and like Gordonstoun, it placed a lot of emphasis on physical activity. Prince Andrew learnt to play ice hockey, how to handle a kayak, went rock climbing and windsurfing but the greatest enjoyment for him was the chance to explore the Canadian countryside. He toured the national parks such as Banff and at the end of term, flew up to Beechey Island to see the grave and storehouses of Sir John Franklin, the British explorer who had died in 1846 whilst seeking the fabled north-west passage. He went on to Grise Fjord, known as the place which never thaws, to see the native inuit demonstrate how to build a kayak and to tour a fish factory. He then journeyed on to Cape Columbia, an arctic wilderness with soaring glaciers just four hundred miles from the north pole which is home to some of the rarest birds on the planet as well as whales and polar bears. Whilst there, he helped create a stone monument to mark his visit and the fact that he was the first member of the royal family to travel so far north.[11] He returned to Yellowknife on the Great Slave Lake to meet up with four boys from Lakefield and two of the teachers. They flew up to Point Lake on the Coppermine River from which they started the three hundred mile canoe trip to Kugluktuk on the shores of the Arctic Ocean. During the journey they camped out at night, saw bears and wolves, and

---

[10] His Royal Highness was to be at Filton for the final flight of Concorde on 26th November 2003 too

[11] Graham and Heather Fisher, *Prince Andrew the Warrior Prince*, (London, 1982) pp.125-128

lived off fish they caught and dehydrated food. It was a hard journey through dangerous rapids such as the Rocky Defile and they capsized several times. By the time he made it back to school he was still suffering from calloused hands and bites but the Head Girl reported: "He came back more thoughtful, much more considerate and responsible."[12] Prince Andrew enjoyed it so much that he repeated the experience in 1983, 1987 and 2011.

The reception he got in Canada was a foretaste of things to come for the next decade. Everywhere he went, he was greeted by hundreds if not thousands of young girls, almost all of whom were ready to give him their number and more besides. As his elder brother Prince Charles remarked, Andrew was the one "with the Robert Redford looks." Teenage magazines ran features on him with special pull out posters and advice to girls on how to attract one of the world's most eligible bachelors. One journalist termed it Andymania and compared it to Beatlemania with girls regularly screaming themselves senseless and fainting whenever he appeared. There were suggestions that HRH stood for His Royal Heart-Throb and one newspaper called him "Six feet of sex appeal."[13] The object of this adoration was not entirely unhappy about his virile image and possibly encouraged it when he told one interviewer who was interested in why he was a teetotaller, "my only vice is women!"[14]

After leaving school, his mother decided that it was time that Prince Andrew got to see a little of what the future held by taking him on tour. Aside from a brief visit made to Northern Ireland two years before as part of the Silver Jubilee, the Prince had not been involved in any other official visits. In 1979, the Queen and Prince Philip were off to Africa for the Commonwealth Heads of Government Conference. The tour encompassed four countries, Malawi, Botswana, Tanzania and Zambia and gave Prince Andrew a chance to explore native cultures, learn about copper mining, visit a hospital and try his hand at driving the largest truck in the world which had wheels more than ten feet in diameter. As he was spared most of the ceremonial duties, he took the chance to go on a safari and visit some national parks where he saw rhino, hippopotamus, zebra, elephant, impala, leopards, crocodiles, lions and antelopes. As part of his commitment to the World Wildlife Fund which he had joined in Canada, he attended a Save the Rhino meeting in Zambia. His performance on the tour was well received and he only made one mistake which was when he got distracted by a group of young ladies and left his father waiting to start a speech.[15]

---

[12] Andrew Morton and Mick Seamark, *Andrew, the Playboy Prince,* (London, 1983) p.54
[13] ibid. pp.9-12, 45
[14] *My Guy,* 19th February 1983 p.8
[15] *Woman,* 20th October 1979 pp.9-10

In September 1979, Prince Andrew joined the Royal Navy. It was to be his career for the next twenty-two years and to provide him with a wide range of skills. He said that he chose the navy because "I've always wanted to fly and I've always wanted to go to sea so the two mix...it's the way to go."[16] Initially, he learnt to fly the Gazelle helicopter before moving on to the Sea King and then the Lynx. In 1980, he went to Lympstone where he completed the demanding Royal Marine Commando course to earn a coveted Green Beret. This involved a nine mile speed march carrying a full 31lb kit, an extreme assault course complete with a rope climb up a thirty feet tall vertical wall, again carrying full kit and an overnight self-navigated thirty mile march across Dartmoor with even heavier kit. There was also an endurance course which involved crawling through tunnels and wading waist high through icy water before starting a four mile run which was followed by a shooting challenge. All of the required elements were subject to strict time limits and required a very high level of fitness. His own commanding officer admitted it was ten days of hell but said that Prince Andrew had passed all parts with flying colours. He subsequently undertook further survival training which involved being abandoned for ten days in the New Forest having to forage for food or scavenge in bins. A fellow midshipman said: "he proved himself to be quite tough. It was as though he had something to prove – that he could do anything just as well as the next man."[17] Fortunately other aspects of his training were rather more enjoyable. During a brief period of leave whilst on a three week exercise on HMS Hermes, he was able to visit Disneyland. As a member of the royal family, protocol required him to be escorted by the British consul but there were concerns that he might be recognised in such a public place. As a result, the two of them had to don staff overalls and the disguise was so successful that several people found themselves being directed toward various parts of the park by the second in line to the throne.[18]

On 28th October 1981, His Royal Highness joined 820 squadron at Royal Naval Air Station, Culdrose. This was considered to be the leading frontline helicopter squadron but there was no expectation at the time that they would ever be going to war; yet just six months later they were to embark for the Falkland Islands which had been invaded by the Argentineans.

The British task force departed Portsmouth on 5th April 1982 led by HMS Invincible with Prince Andrew aboard and a number of journalists. The ship carried 801 squadron of eight sea harriers led by 'Sharkey' Ward and 820 squadron of twelve Sea King helicopters led by Ralph Wykes-Snead.

---

[16] Interview on TV-AM 13th November 1983
[17] Morton and Seamark op.cit. p.74
[18] ibid. pp.72-73

Initially, there was no certainty that there would be a conflict as hope remained that a political resolution would be found. However, the Argentineans declined to leave and so the British government ordered a forcible repossession of the Falkland Islands on 20th April. By this date, His Royal Highness had already been busy, taking part in preparatory exercises and in the regular patrols which went on twenty four hours every day. Although trained in anti-submarine warfare, the squadron had received no instruction in how to evade enemy aircraft or the capabilities of the exocet missiles and this was part of its training on the way south.[19] The prince's cabin was located directly beneath the flight deck used by the Sea Harrier jump jets which further added to the difficulty of obtaining sufficient sleep. Nonetheless, his commanding officer said: "I think the Prince relishes his time at sea. It's probably the only place he can be left alone. He gets no favours and would be annoyed if he did."[20]

As they neared the Falklands, the reality of the situation became more obvious. Pilots were working shifts to ensure a minimum of two aircraft were always airborne and sleeping fully clothed in case of an emergency. They carried morphine filled hypodermics in case of injury, pistols and ammunition in case of contact with the enemy, and protective masks against gas and explosions, the flare of which could melt flesh and maim for life. In his helicopter, Prince Andrew was required to search for enemy aircraft, ships and submarines and to fire at the latter if any were located. The flying conditions were atrocious with "waves as high as tower blocks, freezing fog and howling gales" and the danger was shown on 23rd April when three helicopters were lost, one from HMS Hermes and two from HMS Antrim.[21] Amidst the worsening storm with driving rain and lightning, Prince Andrew set off to try and rescue the crews. After some hours, he found one of those from the Sea King on HMS Hermes but the body of the other man on board was not recovered. It must have been a sobering moment for the twenty-two year old prince who had completed his training just six months before but as the campaign continued, he was to gain considerably more experience of this sort of work.[22]

On 1st May, HMS Invincible came under fire itself for the first time. It was inevitable that it would do so, not only because of its strategic importance but because it contained the Queen's son. The Argentineans had openly expressed their aim of destroying the ship and Prince Andrew with it

---

[19] Interview with Ralph Wykes-Snead, 1999, Imperial War Museum catalogue reference 17596

[20] Morton and Seamark op.cit. p.92

[21] ibid. p.106

[22] Belying perhaps his background, it was noted that Prince Andrew always made a special point of extending his sympathies to those senior officers who faced the grim task of writing to the families of those lost.

because they thought it would destroy British morale. They called it their "priority target." The attack lasted nine hours and Prince Andrew reflected: "To be told to lie down on deck of a ship is the most lonely feeling I know, waiting for either the bang...or the all clear."

Three days later, Prince Andrew witnessed an exocet missile destroy HMS Sheffield. He described it as the worst experience of the war and said that for ten minutes "I really didn't know which way to turn and what to do. I was very frightened." His training then came to the fore as he carried out his search and rescue duties amidst the flames. The next day he flew over the still-burning vessel in search of survivors and said: "It was a dreadful sight. It's something I never thought I would see – a British warship devastated." One of the reasons for his concern—aside from simple humanity—was that by this stage His Royal Highness had started the extremely dangerous job of decoy flying; the task he had been performing at the time the Sheffield was hit.[23] This required him to hover at the rear of a vessel so that if an exocet missile were launched, it would lock on to him. He would then lead the missile off course before making a rapid ascent so that the missile would explode safely in the sea. The theory was the exocets could not travel above around thirty feet but Prince Andrew was aware that the one which had hit the Sheffield had been above that. During the war, His Royal Highness was to spend many hours on decoy duty and he later told reporters about another risk of the process which was that he could be caught in friendly fire by a British missile being launched at the exocet. He said that on three occasions during the conflict a British Sea Wolf missile had locked on to his helicopter: "It really makes the hair stand up on the back of your neck. It is not much fun at all having one of those fellows pick you out as a target."[24]

By the middle of May, Prince Andrew was engaged in the task of taking soldiers and members of the SAS from one ship to another as Britain prepared for the invasion. The weather remained very poor and a Sea King from another squadron was lost at the cost of twenty-two lives. On 21st May, the day troops were landed at San Carlos, he was airborne in shifts from dawn to dusk as part of the watch to protect the ships and men. At this stage, the conflict was at its worst with seemingly every day news of another loss. On 25th May, the fleet came under a particular onslaught from the Argentineans. Prince Andrew described the scene:

I was airborne when the Atlantic Conveyor was hit. We saw the odd 4.5 inch shell come pretty close to us and I saw Invincible fire her

---

[23] *The Montreal Gazette*, 19th June, 1982
[24] Interview on BBC News, 18th June, 1982

missiles. Normally I would say it looked very spectacular but from where I was it was very frightening. I think the moment really sticks in my mind. It was horrific and terrible and something I will never forget. It was probably my most frightening moment of the war.

For hours afterwards, he was involved in scouring the seas for survivors in conditions which were challenging to say the least. The Commander of 801 Squadron, who had been on board Invincible when the attack began, described the impact as missiles were fired: "it was like an explosion on deck. The force behind each launch was mind boggling...The sky was full of smoke trails from chaff rockets and missiles. Exocet decoy helicopters had launched from both carriers and all ships were manoeuvring at high speed."[25] One of those rescued from the stricken vessel by Prince Andrew described how he had been one of twenty-six men clinging to a tiny life raft "like sardines one on top of another. The weather was dreadful. It was very cold and the waves were about twenty feet high." Hypothermia had already struck by the time they were found and winched to safety. He said of Prince Andrew: "he was very cool, just like the rest of the helicopter crew. He and the rest of the crew did a great job." He added that he had tried to thank them afterwards but the Prince had said he was just doing his job like everyone else.[26] Commander Ward, however, was also impressed describing him as "an excellent pilot and a very promising officer."[27]

For Prince Andrew, the hours of anti-submarine and surveillance patrol flying continued as the troops proceeded to wrest control of the Falklands in a series of bloody battles across very harsh terrain. On 14th June, the Argentineans surrendered and the British flag was raised again over Port Stanley. His Royal Highness was on board at the time the news broke and he observed "When the end came there was no cheering and shouting, no celebrating. We could not really believe that was the end of it. Everyone just looked at each other and said: 'its over then.'" Four days later, Prince Andrew, together with his Commanding Officer and that of 801 Squadron, flew to the Islands themselves to inspect the scene. He was to comment later on the "mess and the grime" and the long lines of captive Argentinean soldiers and the "looks on their faces of dejection and of relief that it was all over."[28] Commander Ward recalled:

Wherever we walked we found countless rounds of unspent ammunition littering our path...The occupying forces had not had the

---

[25] Commander 'Sharkey' Ward, *Sea Harrier over the Falklands*, (London, 2005) p.281
[26] *Sydney Morning Herald*, 20th June 1982
[27] Ward op.cit p.143
[28] *Woman's Hour*, broadcast 1st October 1985

common decency to dig themselves latrines and had used all the open spaces in and around the town as one large toilet...Handguns of all descriptions from machine pistols to shotguns were piled in disorganised heaps. There were also the bodies of dead Argentine soldiers lying about at random...Their faces were waxen images of their former selves with lifeless eyes, skin tinged a yellowish brown and lips a stronger slate blue. ...Each corpse represented the threat of a booby trap; perhaps a grenade placed under the armpit with the safety pin withdrawn. There were many such nasties left behind.[29]

Yet for Prince Andrew, there was one moment of relief amidst the gloom when he was able to make a telephone call home to his mother at Buckingham Palace. He chatted with the Queen for fifteen minutes and emerged with a message from her of admiration for all involved.

Following the victory, most of the ships who had been part of the Task Force, set sail for home. Invincible remained for another two months to keep watch against any further enemy activity and to support the troops who remained and were left with the hazardous work of defusing mines. Prince Andrew himself only narrowly escaped being blown up when he was engaged in ferrying troops and had to land barely a yard from a minefield.[30] Nonetheless, there were times when he was able to relax. He took responsibility for on board entertainments, arranging movies and bingo evenings and taking his turn as a disc jockey. On one occasion, he had some leave and he decided to go fishing. Whilst there and on his own, he was approached by a shepherd and his dogs. The shepherd asked if he had any dogs at home and His Royal Highness replied that he had corgis. The shepherd, who had clearly not recognised whom he addressed, remarked that corgis were no good for working with sheep. He then indicated that if the young man would care to give him a hand in unloading his lorry full of peat, he would be happy to give him a cup of tea. Prince Andrew put his fishing gear away and duly helped the old shepherd in his work. As they sat in the kitchen afterwards, the shepherd asked him about his home. Prince Andrew said that he had two, one in England and one in Scotland. "My God," exclaimed the shepherd, "you must have bloody rich parents!"[31]

In September 1982, Prince Andrew made it home for a hero's welcome and emotional reunion with his parents. Reflecting on the conflict afterwards he said: "You don't go to an active war zone and not come back a changed person...I went away a boy and came back a man...There were

---

[29] Ward op.cit. pp.330-331
[30] *Daily Mail*, 10th August 1982.
[31] *The Times*, 20th March, 1986

some sharp edges and war takes the sharp edges off very very quickly because you begin to understand who you are and you put yourself into a lot of danger."[32] He told the journalist Andrew Morton who had sailed on Invincible: "If I had the choice I would not want to go through it all again. ...its been one hell of an experience. I am sure I have changed somewhat since the Falklands. I guess I had to after seeing what I have seen and feeling what I have felt. ..I have to pick up where I left off. It may not be easy. I have learnt things about myself that I never would have learnt anywhere else....during those moments when there was fear I overcame it with the simple maxim that I must think positive. I told myself 'I am going to survive this.'"[33]

Following the conflict, His Royal Highness decided to take his then girlfriend, Koo Stark, on holiday. His aunt, Princess Margaret, offered them the use of her home on Mustique but sadly the Press discovered the plan and descended on the island forcing Prince Andrew and Koo to flee. His angry younger brother, Prince Edward said: "He'd been at war. He wanted to get away from everything and relax. They hounded him to such an extent that he had to stop the holiday. He came back from that holiday more drawn, more tired, than he had from three months at war and I think to treat someone who's just come back from serving their country like that is absolutely despicable."[34] The relationship, however, continued and it was through Koo that His Royal Highness developed his interest in photography. In 1985, he published a volume of images he had taken in aid of the recently created Prince Andrew Charitable Trust.[35] The book included pictures taken whilst he was serving overseas, a series highlighting the spectacular scenery of Canada, the results of his experiments in macro-photography and the highly creative images used for the Ilford calendar. In his introduction, the Prince said that he hoped his book would not only raise money for charity but encourage other amateurs to "have a go" and experiment more. He added: "The great pleasure in taking photographs is that of giving pleasure to other people by being able to give them the photograph you have taken and showing how good they can look. But I also like to take common sights from a different viewpoint or with something funny on top of them."[36]

By the time that the book was published, His Royal Highness was serving on HMS Brazen where he was flying the only Lynx helicopter. He

---

[32] *Frost over the world* interview, 16th May 2008

[33] Morton and Seamark op.cit. p.132

[34] *Woman*, 9th March, 1983

[35] Charity registration number 290140. For Koo's encouragement of his hobby see HRH The Prince Andrew, *Photographs,* (London, 1985) p.8

[36] *The Times*, 27th September, 1985

remained there until March 1986 when he returned to shore for further training. After this, he joined 702 squadron as an instructor in helicopter warfare techniques and weapons advisor but 1986 was a memorable year for him in another way too for on 23rd July, before some five hundred million television viewers and just minutes after being created Duke of York, Prince Andrew married Sarah Ferguson at Westminster Abbey.[37] The marriage produced two daughters but collapsed in 1992 following a string of scandals and bad publicity relating to Sarah's relationships with other men, her frequent holidays and her want of self control with regard to money. A mountain of debt was accumulated, paid off, and then accumulated again. Over the years, Sarah's lifestyle has spawned a number of books and innumerable column inches in the media but throughout, Prince Andrew has stayed loyal to her, maintaining his marriage vow to love her till death do them part, and his Christian duty of forgiveness. This loyalty has come at a considerable cost to his personal reputation but the Prince has always put integrity before public opinion. The couple remain close, though the relationship has clearly changed. At his fiftieth birthday, he referred to Sarah as being effectively his third child.[38]

The Duke's naval responsibilities meant that he had little time for royal duties and he suggested the experience of trying to be a prince and a pilot was turning him into a "conscious schizophrenic."[39] He carried out tours of Canada in 1985, 1987 and 1989, America and Australia in 1988, Papua New Guinea in 1991, Russia and Malta in 1998 and New Zealand in 1999. A wet day in spring 1987 saw him becoming involved in a special television event called *It's a Royal Knockout* or the *Grand Charity Tournament*. The BBC had shown *It's A Knockout* from 1966 to 1983 when it regularly attracted fifteen million viewers.[40] The format was simple. Teams from various towns competed in around half a dozen games plus a repeating exercise called a marathon, all of which were designed to be fun. The *Grand Charity Tournament* did not alter the format in the slightest. It simply had four teams of celebrities captained by different members of the royal family, each attempting to raise money for a particular charity.

The idea for the event came from Tim Hastie-Smith and was originally conceived as a money-making venture for the Duke of Edinburgh's Award

---

[37] Sarah was his sixth cousin once removed and he had known her from childhood. She was fourth cousin to Diana, Princess of Wales.

[38] *The Mail on Sunday,* 28th February, 2010

[39] Interview with David Frost, 6th November 1983

[40] An international version *Jeux Sans Frontieres* was created les than twenty years after the continent had been torn apart by the Second World War. In the days before cheap international flights, it was a valuable means of encouraging young Europeans to meet together in a spirit of fellowship and fun.

Scheme. His friend, Prince Edward, became the producer and he played the leading part in recruiting the various competitors. A variety of stars were involved representing the worlds of music, sport and film. Prince Andrew's team included the pentathlete Judy Simpson, the racing driver Nigel Mansell, the high jumper Sharon McPeake, the footballer Gary Lineker and the skier Steve Podborski. Representing the arts were the actresses Fiona Fullerton and Margot Kidder, the *James Bond* star George Lazenby, Michael Palin from *Monty Python,* Griff Rhys Jones, movie star John Travolta and finally the television presenter Anneka Rice. Stars in other teams included Tom Jones and Cliff Richard, Kiri te Kanawa and Chris de Burgh, Jackie Stewart and Barry McGuigan. All of these gave their time for free, most considering it an honour to be involved, although it was noted that jaws did start to drop when they saw super fit members of the Royal Corps of Signals demonstrate the games and collapse exhausted. One competitor from Prince Edward's team said: "their resultant apoplexy and florid countenances made us all feel we'd been embroiled in some kind of premature euthanasia for charity!"[41]

The royal captains – Princess Anne, Prince Edward and the Duke and Duchess of York, did not take part in the games themselves. Their role was to motivate their teams and encourage the crowd to support their chosen charity. Their cousin, the Duke of Gloucester served as one of the judges. The good cause espoused by the Duke of York was the World Wildlife Fund.

The games on the day were typical of *It's A Knockout.* Men dressed up and clamboured across rafts with a rose between their teeth to rescue damsels on a balcony. Trios turned giant capstans to draw cannons up a field, Gary Lineker losing half his costume in the process. Other competitors dressed up as giant vegetables and raced around the field to try to avoid the cooking pot. Meantime blindfolded giants tried to knock over suits of armour and jesters sought to make their way across a revolving pole suspended over icy cold water whilst being bombarded by plastic hams. Backstage, Prince Andrew's team tucked into hamburgers and chips, ordered by him after he tasted the ones John Travolta had smuggled into the event.

Over the years, the royal involvement in this innocent fun has been criticised by some as being undignified. The episode reflects the difficulty for the modern royal who is on the one hand told to get more involved with the common people and at the same time told to keep their distance to preserve the mystique of royalty. It is perhaps a reflection of the changing times that when in 2011, Prince William and his wife captained dragon boat teams for a race in Canada which was televised across the globe, nobody criticised

---

[41] HRH The Prince Edward, *Knockout – The Grand Charity Tournament,* (London, 1987) p.38

them or suggested that this was inappropriate behaviour for the future king. The Duke of York's involvement in the event left the World Wildlife Fund almost a quarter of a million pounds better off, a substantial sum, and one which had significant repercussions for endangered species. Money was used to safeguard elephants and black rhinos in Zambia, to carry out a detailed ecological study of the Serengeti National Park and to find new ways of fishing in Malawi which did less damage to the environment whilst protecting and enhancing the income of the fishermen.

Such charity events were a rarity as the Duke remained a serving naval officer. In May 1988, he left 702 Squadron and joined HMS Edinburgh as Officer of the Watch to earn his Watchkeeping and General Navigation Certificates. He spent a year at sea in the Far East and Australia during which he took time off to represent the Queen at Australia's bicentennial celebrations. He returned to the UK to spend two years as Flight Commander on HMS Campbeltown, part of the NATO standing force in the Atlantic. His Captain said he was the "eyes of the ship" and praised the way in which he carried out his responsibilities which included searching for hostile vessels and engaging them if necessary plus carrying out life saving missions: "it takes some considerable skill to land a helicopter on the deck of a moving ship in a force seven gale."[42]

In 1992, he commenced a course at the Army Staff College in Camberley and it was while he was on leave from this that he found himself at the centre of a serious incident when fire broke out in the private chapel at Windsor Castle. It was late morning and His Royal Highness was the only member of the royal family present, though he was working in a different part of the building. Hearing the fire alarm, he immediately went to investigate and quickly aware of the risks, he started to organise the evacuation of people and artworks. The Duke served as part of a human chain which hand carried goods out of the Waterloo Chamber in less than half an hour before moving on to the next room. He described himself as being intensely shocked by the speed at which the fire spread but his quick reactions, honed by years of military service, saved many of the nation's treasures. As thirty fire engines and over two hundred firemen fought the blaze, which was visible from miles away for more than nine hours, the Duke also maintained telephone contact with the Queen until she was able to arrive. He described her as "absolutely devastated" and BBC cameras caught an unusual shot of him with his arm around his mother comforting her as Brunswick Tower burnt.

Following his course at Camberley, the Duke took command of HMS

---

[42] *Majesty Magazine,* vol 12 no 2 Feb 1991 pp.42-43

Cottesmore in April 1993, a vessel designed to locate and destroy mines and which carried a normal company of six officers and thirty-nine ratings. Although most of the time was spent in training exercises to prepare for war, he was at the helm when the vessel took part in a more relaxed search to try to locate the wreck of the Blessing of Burntisland which had sunk in 1633. Keen to resume his flying career, he moved on to become Senior Pilot of 815 Royal Naval Air Squadron, the largest of its type in Great Britain, a position he held until the end of 1996. In January 1997, he left both the sea and the air to take up a position within the Ministry of Defence as a Staff Officer in the Directorate of Naval Operations. His responsibilities included determining the operational requirements for aviators on frigates and destroyers and then preparing reports justifying the cost. After two years he was promoted to the rank of Commander and joined the Diplomacy Section where he was involved in planning and organising bilateral naval talks and in international affairs. It was in this position that he ended his naval career in 2001 after twenty-two years service.

Since his departure from the Royal Navy, the Duke has carried out on average more than five hundred engagements every year making him one of the hardest working members of the royal family. In 2009-2010 he undertook a record 757 engagements, more than any other royal has managed before or since. For the most part, he receives no publicity for these except in a negative sense. As his father once observed, the media are only interested in scandal not good works.[43] The British Press nicknamed him Airmiles Andy because his travel costs were higher than his siblings even though this was inevitable given that over half his engagements were carried out overseas compared to less than a quarter of theirs.[44] His areas of work can be broadly separated into engagements related to his support of the Queen as Head of State, his charitable work, his commitment to armed forces across the Commonwealth, his support of Yorkshire interests and his promotion of British trade and industry.

It is in his role of supporting the Queen that the Duke is seen most by the public. He appears at the Royal British Legion Festival of Remembrance each year and lays a wreath on behalf of the Royal Navy at the Cenotaph. He generally attends one or more of the official garden parties held each year by the Queen to reward those who have made a contribution to their community and he plays his part in the visits of overseas heads of state, often welcoming them to the country and escorting them to events. On occasion he represents the Queen directly such as opening the Parliament in

[43] Interview in *Woman's Own*, 15th June 1986

[44] Data on engagements is tabulated by Tim O'Donovan and appears in *The Times* newspaper each year. His data is calculated by calendar year, the Duke's office by financial year.

Bermuda in 2005, convening the General Assembly of the Church of Scotland in 2007 and attending the funeral of Prince Rainier of Monaco. In 2012, he visited India as part of the Diamond Jubilee celebrations.

Sometimes, His Royal Highness is required to travel on behalf of the Queen and the entire royal family at short notice to visit a disaster zone. This is one of the most challenging areas of royal duties requiring a balance of compassion for the survivors as well as technical understanding of the difficulties faced by rescue workers. Prince Andrew has been sent in this role to a number of places. In March 1987, he was sent to Zeebrugge to meet the survivors of the Herald of Free Enterprise, a ferry which had capsized only moments after leaving port killing almost two hundred people. The disaster was attributed to the ferry departing with its bow doors open but it was the speed of the sinking – less than two minutes - which shocked everyone. Prince Andrew spoke to those involved in the rescue efforts and obtained firsthand accounts of what had happened. He expressed his surprise at the number who had escaped and at their mood: "The British have a way of retaining their sense of humour at the most impossible times." One magazine described it as his "finest hour... for the first time the Duke has established himself as a significant national figure...representing us all in such tragic times."[45]

On 22nd December 1988, he was sent to Lockerbie, a small Scottish town which had been decimated by a Pan-Am aircraft which had been blown up mid-air by a terrorist and crashed down upon some houses leaving a crater more than one hundred and fifty feet long. Almost three hundred people had been killed and at the time His Royal Highness visited, dead bodies were still strewn across gardens. He spent time talking to the bereaved and the emergency services, to those who had lost their homes and the people involved in the task of sifting through the wreckage and trying to identify the charred remains.

Owing to his naval duties, the Duke carried out few similar visits over the next few years but in 2002 he visited three disaster zones. He went to Peru to see the site of the Moquegua earthquake, to Belize where a hurricane had caused considerable damage and was also sent to Australia where bush fires had wreaked havoc across New South Wales. In 2005, he travelled to Bangkok to offer official thanks to all of those involved in assisting victims of the Boxing Day Tsunami in which one hundred and fifty-five Britons lost their lives. He met with doctors and nurses, police and rescue services, those who had the painstaking task of trying to identify bodies and also the Consul staff who had worked around the clock to keep

---

[45] *Majesty Magazine*, vol 8 no 1 May 1987 p.13

families informed about the whereabouts of loved ones and to arrange emergency shelter and returns home for those who lost everything. A year later, he went to see the aftermath of Hurricane Katrina in New Orleans and in 2008 he went to China where a huge earthquake in Sichuan province had killed around seventy thousand people, injured nearly four hundred thousand and rendered millions homeless. At home, in 2005, he visited the Metropolitan Police and the London Fire service in the wake of terrorist attacks on London.

His experience in the Royal Navy has given the Duke a greater comprehension of the rescue process than many would have and he understands the impact of terrorism only too well for his great-uncle, Lord Louis Mountbatten, was blown up by the IRA in 1979.[46] Yet it is not easy to be brought face to face over and over with such tragedy. As the Duke commented: "You never get accustomed to seeing people suffering these problems."[47] The importance of this sort of visit cannot be over estimated. Everyone likes to be thanked and it is appropriate that in times of emergency when people come together across national and racial boundaries in order to help total strangers, this service is recognised at the highest level. Yet it is not always easy to strike the right note. At Lockerbie, His Royal Highness commented that the houses lost could be rebuilt but the lives lost could not be replaced. It was a completely true comment but it was seen as unfeeling by those who had just lost their homes.[48] However, his position has also enabled him to intervene to secure a rapid improvement in conditions. In 1997, he went to Montserrat where the Soufriere Hills volcano had erupted. Although his visit was made some months afterwards, there were still more than one hundred people living in emergency accommodation and the Duke was shown how they survived with just one toilet between them and two showers, neither of which had a door. Far from praising the efforts of officials, the Duke told the Governor that the conditions were "appalling" and that the situation must be rectified immediately.[49]

Like other members of the royal family, His Royal Highness is patron of a number of charities though inevitably, he spends more time with some than with others. It would be impractical, for example, to visit the Falklands

---

[46] The attack was responsible for the death of one of his cousins too and serious injuries to another. At the time that the news broke, Prince Andrew was with his mother at Balmoral, both Prince Philip and Prince Charles being away. Prince Andrew escorted the Queen to the funeral whilst his father and elder brother walked behind the hearse. In 1983, Prince Andrew opened the Mountbatten Centre in Portsmouth as a memorial to his great-uncle.

[47] *Hello*, no 115, 11th August 1990 p.67

[48] *The Times*, 23rd December 1988

[49] *Majesty Magazine*, vol 18 no 3 March 1997 p.25

Conservation Trust as often as he does the Royal National Orthopaedic Hospital or the English National Ballet or the London Contemporary Dance Trust. The charities and voluntary organisations which he has chosen to support fall into four principal areas – heritage, sport, young people and health.

The health charities relate principally to sensory deprivation. He has associations with a number of organisations across the Commonwealth which work with the deaf. The Duke has an understanding of the difficulties caused by deafness because his father's mother, who lived at Buckingham Palace until her death shortly before His Royal Highness' tenth birthday, was profoundly deaf from infancy. Despite this, she carried out public duties and served as a nurse during the second world war, later winning an award for her bravery in sheltering Jews during the Nazi occupation of Greece.[50] He is also Patron of Fight for Sight which funds research into various vision problems including glaucoma, cataracts, macular degeneration and diabetes. Across the world, one person goes blind every five seconds but it is estimated that over three quarters of sight loss could be prevented or treated. Amongst work carried out by the charity has been the establishment of the UK Corneal Transplant Service which carries out thousands of operations a year and which has saved the sight of individuals aged from a few days old to over a hundred years. Research into the effects of oxygen deprivation has resulted in new care regimes which have safeguarded the sight of hundreds of premature babies and it is anticipated that the pioneering study into the use of human retinal stem cells to repair glaucoma damage will have a dramatic effect in reducing sight loss due to that disease in years to come.[51] As the Duke himself observed, the work of the charity is vital in "helping reduce the incidence of these diseases along with the consequent suffering. It also offers hope to thousands of others." His support of these causes stems from his own awareness as a pilot of the importance of good vision and the risk to hearing which comes from working with aircraft. However, he is also following a family tradition. The eleventh Duke of York was involved in the foundation of the Royal Westminster Ophthalmic Hospital and in encouraging the development of new techniques to treat those blinded during the Napoleonic Wars. Godson of the tenth Duke who was almost blinded in his twenties by severe oculocutaneous albinism, he was himself subsequently blinded by cataracts. The twelfth Duke was an active supporter both of Moorfields Eye Hospital which he

---

[50] In 1994, Prince Philip collected the award from the Holocaust Museum Yad Vashem in Israel on her behalf. His mother was the sister of Lord Louis Mountbatten and became a nun in 1949.

[51] Astrid Limb et al., 'Human Müller Glia with Stem Cell Characteristics Differentiate into Retinal Ganglion Cell (RGC) Precursors In Vitro and Partially Restore RGC Function In Vivo Following Transplantation' in *Stem Cells Translational Medicine*, vol 1 no 3 (March 2012) pp.188-199

opened and of organisations to support lipreading, his own mother, Queen Alexandra, being deaf.

With regard to heritage, the Duke is a particularly active Patron for the SS Great Britain Trust which aims to safeguard this pioneering vessel, designed by Isambard Kingdom Brunel and launched by Prince Albert in 1843.[52] He is also much involved with the National Maritime Museum at Greenwich and with smaller groups such as the Alderney Maritime Trust, attending exhibitions, assisting fund raising efforts and meeting with workers. He supports the Army Museums Ogilby Trust and visits regimental museums across the world, believing that they play an important role in promoting understanding of the work carried out by British troops in defence of freedom. The Duke is keenly aware that it is our heritage which is one of the chief reasons that people come to the UK and this underlies his involvement in ALVA, the Association of Leading Visitor Attractions. Tourism is a significant industry accounting for one in eight jobs in Wales, one in ten in Scotland, one in twelve in England and one in twenty in Northern Ireland.[53] On 12th August 2010, the Prime Minister, David Cameron, said: "It's fundamental to the rebuilding and rebalancing of our economy. It's one of the best and fastest ways of generating the jobs we need so badly in this country."

The Duke's commitment to causes involving young people has existed for many years. In a speech at the Mansion House in 1986 he criticised "the amount of gratuitous violence purveyed on television in the name of entertainment" plus "the increasing availability of drugs and the misuse of alcohol" which combine "to cause acts of criminal ferocity" and an atmosphere of "moral pollution." Appealing for more investment in activities to offer an alternative focus to young people, he added: "We are told in the Services, the single greatest factor is the man or woman. We must not lose sight of that, machines can't and won't do everything." [54]

His speech was made in aid of the Outward Bound Trust, the charity which accounts for on average seventeen engagements per year in his calendar, more than any other cause, and of which he has been Chairman of the Trustees since 1999. In September 2012 he abseiled 785' down the Shard in London to raise funds for them earning almost £150,000. The Trust was begun by Kurt Hahn, the founder of Gordonstoun School, and

---

[52] *The Times*, 20th July, 1843. The newspaper report expressed reservations about the design and suggested it was "infinitely below" necessary specification. Despite this, the ship remained in use for almost a century and served in the Crimean War and the First World War.

[53] Deloitte and Oxford Economics, *The economic contribution of the Visitor Economy*, (2010) p.45.

[54] *The Times*, 10th June 1986

Lawrence Holt in 1941 to teach merchant seamen the physical and mental endurance skills they would require for the dangerous convoy work they were about to undertake. It turned its attention to young people after the war and more than a million have attended one of its courses since then. The objective is to take people outside their comfort zone and into the wild where, through a process of planned activities, they develop leadership skills and a greater understanding of others and of the world around them. There is a focus on environmental concerns and compassion, on self discipline and the need to take on challenges, working through problems until the goal is achieved. Community projects are also encouraged both for the benefit they give to the wider world and to the individual participants. As His Royal Highness commented in 2002: "Learning through service, or through international work, can lead to a changed, more realistic, more committed and more prepared adult view of the world." Two thirds of those attending the courses receive financial assistance because their families lack economic resources and there is a conscious effort on the part of the Trust to target those who have behavioural difficulties such as either being a bully or a victim of this and those with learning problems. A study in 2011 found that 93% of teachers reported that students returned from an Outward Bound course with improved confidence and greater self esteem which translated into better relationships at school and at home. 83% of teachers stated that attitudes to learning were improved with better academic results generally following.[55]

Other organisations supported by the Duke share the same goals. These include the British Schools Exploring Society which aims to send young people on challenging expeditions into the wild where they carry out scientific research relating to the natural world and biodiversity, and Round Square. The Jubilee Sailing Trust and the Tall Ships Youth Trust endeavour to encourage teamwork and enhance physical and mental health with a view to promoting good citizenship by enabling those who would not ordinarily have the opportunity to go to sea and experience life on a traditional vessel. The Jubilee Sailing Trust has the particular objective of reaching out to the disabled to improve their sense of confidence in what they can do by demonstrating the importance of their strengths rather than their weaknesses. Using two specially adapted tall ships which have features such as a speaking compass for the blind and hearing loops, it aims to have half the crew places taken by those with particular needs.

Although a firm believer himself in the benefits of activity for all young people, whether they come from a supportive background or have special needs, the Duke has not neglected charities that have tried to reach out to

---

[55] Outward Bound Social Impact Report (2011) pp.13, 27

children in other ways. He is Patron of the SickKids Foundation in Canada and he consciously endeavours to make time to visit hospitals and promote awareness of the charity on his trips there. In 1999, he launched the NSPCC Full Stop campaign which aimed to eradicate the abuse of children within a generation. It was a cause very close to the Duke's heart. He told *Hello* magazine that he had reviewed the statistics and "as a father of two young children, I simply could not sit back and do nothing." The Duke served as Chairman for ten years carrying out numerous engagements in support of its fund raising target and its goal of education and in meeting those involved in running its helpline. The objective was to teach children that abuse was wrong and that they were never responsible for it, with the hope being that by increasing their awareness, they would avoid either becoming or tolerating abusers in the future when it was their turn to be parents. It was suggested to the Duke that such a goal was unrealistic and he agreed that abuse could not be eradicated totally for there would always be a small minority of "highly disturbed and irrational individuals" who would wish to get involved but much of it could be prevented and anyway, it was important to try: "If you are faced with a wall, you don't push the top of the wall, you try to undermine its foundations....If you attack the bottom of the wall, eventually the whole structure will crumble."[56]

Another aspect of his work in this field involves the encouragement of young people to develop their potential in a way which is likely to lead to a career. The Duke is a keen patron of Young Engineers and in 1994 chose to introduce the magnificent rose bowl award which bears his name and which is awarded each year to the student who has made the most creative use of technology.[57] Projects that have won include a domestic remote control and security interface system, a device to measure the intensity of foetal contractions, a multimedia router, an ultrasonic ranging device to guide firefighters through dense smoke and a GPS system to assist those engaged in adventure activities to keep track of each other's locations. Whenever possible, the Duke has attended the exhibition of projects in person so he can select the winner and he also visits school engineering clubs to see what they are working upon and encourage their progress. Many of those who have won his award, which is now one of the most prestigious electronic design prizes, have gone on to patent their designs and to develop a career in this field. Speaking of why he chose to get involved in this organisation, His Royal Highness said: "Engineering is so important to the prosperity of the nation and it is essential that more young people are attracted into the profession." In a similar vein, the Duke is patron of BusinessDynamics which runs courses in schools and with young offenders to open their eyes to

---

[56] *Hello*, no 581 October 12th 1999 pp.63, 65

[57] The bowl was made by Mappin and Webb at the Duke's personal direction and expense.

the possibilities of a career in business and also to improve their employability by helping them learn skills such as teamwork, how to make presentations, the basics of cash flow and problem solving.

The need for this varied and proactive type of approach to child development was highlighted in the 2009 report by the New Economics Foundation and Action for Children which predicted that the cost of dealing with the problems which resulted from family breakdown, drug abuse, mental ill health, poor diet and domestic violence could exceed four trillion pounds in the UK alone over the next twenty years. It proposed a greater investment in preventative measures on behalf of government and charitable organisations to create:

..a future where all children feel loved, are free from poverty, have supportive relationships with other children and adults, feel happy and safe, and are free to imagine and explore as they journey through their local neighbourhoods. A future where all children feel valued; where they give their ideas, time, passions and their creativity to everyone they meet and to all that they do.[58]

The final charitable area in which the Duke is particularly active relates to sport. He has been a keen golfer for many years and has raised thousands of pounds for charity by playing in pro-celebrity tournaments. He explained his passion for the sport in 1992:

It provides a test of patience, application, perseverance and character for players at all levels and is played in virtually every corner of the world. It is a fully international game which is on offer to anyone from whatever walk of life who is physically able to try his or her skill at the game...It is a social game but it also has the ability to afford solitude when you only require to play a few holes on your own in order to refresh the mind and to escape the madding crowd. One of the many advantages of golf is that it is essentially a game of skill and timing and players need not depend on any special physique to succeed. It is a game of equal opportunities.[59]

In 2004, he established the Duke of York Sports Foundation which grants scholarships allowing gifted young players to combine professional tuition with a high quality education. His Royal Highness said he had been "determined to provide a scholarship programme of my own. It's vital we

[58] New Economics Foundation and Action for Children, *Backing the Future: Why investing in children is good for us all"*, (London, 2009) pp.6-7

[59] Lewine Mair, *One hundred years of Women's Golf*, (London, 1992) p.9

encourage our young sportsmen and women to achieve academic excellence as well as sporting excellence."[60] In 2001, he launched the Duke of York Young Champions Trophy which is held in September each year on one of the UK's top links courses and which attracts competitors from over thirty different countries. Previous competitors in this have included Rory McIlroy and Anna Nordqvist and the event has become sufficiently prestigious that results count toward the world amateur golf rankings. In his address at the start of the 2011 event, the Duke said: "it is through this sort of competition that future great golfers both professional and amateur will be identified and encouraged. There are so many talented young sports people and I am determined to assist with their endeavours."

In 2010, His Royal Highness launched another new initiative called On Course. He wrote:

As a serving member of the Royal Navy for 22 years, and with continuing close links with a number of Regiments as well as the Royal Navy and Royal Air Force, I know of the extraordinary work that our armed forces do to protect the security of our nation and of the sacrifices that they are called upon to face and make in the course of their service. Technical advances have meant that many of those seriously injured in the course of serving us are no longer bound to wheelchairs. On Course has been created to offer these injured men and women of our armed forces the opportunity to partake in golf - one of the few sports in which disabled people can compete with their able counterparts.

On Course will assist injured individuals to play golf by providing adaptive golf days, access to golf professionals, to personally tailor individual coaching and by the provision of golf equipment. As important, On Course will also help with employment in the golf industry as well, and will offer individuals the opportunity to learn the skills required to work in the golfing industry, such as Green keeping and Golf Management, through courses and apprenticeships. And, it will offer the opportunity to compete in specially created competitions, including a biennial Ryder Cup style tournament against their USA equivalents.[61]

Although a very new charity, it has already started to find work for disabled ex-service personnel and it has provoked technological advances in

---

[60] *Golf Monthly,* October 2007 p.71

[61] www.oncoursefoundation.com

prosthetic limbs due to the need to provide greater swivel in the ankles.[62] The Queen featured its work in her Christmas Broadcast of 2010. One twenty-six year old soldier who lost both legs in an explosion whilst in Helmand Province said: "I was completely lost and devastated when I realised that my military career had to come to my end. Through the On Course foundation I have found a new lease of life with a clear sense of direction. Now I am about to embark on a very different but equally rewarding career."[63]

Like other members of the royal family, the Duke is an active supporter of the armed services, carrying out around thirty such engagements each year. He has visited troops on exercises in Oman, Belize, Germany, New Zealand, Canada and Brunei. He has visited frontline troops in Iraq in 2005 and 2007 and in Afghanistan in 2008, 2009 and 2010. Many of these visits have been to regiments of which he is Colonel-in-Chief. These include the Royal Irish Regiment which was created in 1993 with the amalgamation of the Ulster Defence Regiment and the Royal Irish Rangers. With its experienced Air Assault Battalion, this Regiment has served across the world in some of the most dangerous and hostile conditions. Since 2006, he has been Royal Colonel of the Royal Highland Fusiliers, 2nd Battalion, an infantry regiment who have twice served in Helmand. He is Colonel-in-Chief of two reconnaissance regiments, the 9th/12th Royal Lancers in Great Britain and the Queen's York Rangers in Canada. These carry out the vital work of collecting information about the enemy through covert operations and open patrols. Some of their work is dismounted and some of it is carried out using armoured vehicles such as the Scimitar. They use the most technologically advanced equipment in the world to do this, much of it designed and manufactured in the United Kingdom.

As Duke of York, it is perhaps natural that His Royal Highness should be associated with the Yorkshire Regiment. Spread across Germany, Cyprus and England, it includes two light infantry battalions which are trained to engage with the enemy as well as to use modern surveillance techniques, plus an armoured battalion equipped with Warrior tanks. On 6th March 2012, five men from the regiment were killed by a Taliban roadside bomb in Afghanistan, one of the largest losses of life in a single incident. Ten days later, the Duke took the salute of the regiment and met with men and their families. Meeting the bereaved, the injured and the young soldiers who are at once nervous and excited about their first tour of duty, is a routine but challenging part of his work. In June 2011, he travelled to Ireland on a similar mission and he has also made private visits to soldiers from his

---

[62] Interview with the Duke of York on BBC Television, 17th July 2010.
[63] *Lancashire Telegraph*, 29th June 2011

regiments in hospital or at Headley Court rehabilitation centre. He has described himself as constantly impressed by the determination and resilience of those who have endured horrific injuries and it is certain that they have appreciated his visits, not least because, unlike most Royal colonels, he has been to war and understands the pressures involved. He said: "They have to live in some very very harsh country conditions. What they do and how they do it from my experience of having been to see them do it is quite outstanding...These guys are doing a job they've been asked to do under some horrendous circumstances and I find them absolutely amazing."[64]

His other military appointments include the Royal New Zealand Army Logistics Regiment and the Princess Louise Fusiliers of Nova Scotia which have both lost men in Afghanistan, the Royal Highland Fusiliers of Canada and the Small Arms School Corps. Given his own twenty-two years service, the Duke retains a naval role being Commodore-in-Chief of the Fleet Air Arm and Admiral of the Sea Cadets, regularly visiting different units and their training ships. He is also Honorary Air Commodore of RAF Lossiemouth, one of the busiest bases in the United Kingdom which is home to both Tornado jets and Sea King search and rescue helicopters.

A further aspect of his work with the armed services is in reminding the living of the sacrifices made in the past. In 2001, he travelled to Korea to see the site of the Battle of Imjin River and to lay a wreath in memory of those members of the Gloucestershire Regiment who died there in the ferocious fighting. In 2007, he went to Tobruk, site of a major battle in the Second World War where hundreds of British and Australian troops lost their lives. 2012 saw him at Kohima in India, site of what Earl Mountbatten called "one of the greatest battles in history" where feats of "naked unparalleled heroism" took place. His visit to Murmansk in 2005 was particularly appreciated. Between 1941 and 1945, around three thousand British sailors were killed as they made what Churchill called "the worst journey in the world." Their role was to take supplies to Russia, travelling through almost total darkness in temperatures which were so cold that waves crashed on deck as ice and any skin which touched the surface of the ship was immediately flayed. A sixth of ships involved in these Arctic convoys were lost to U-boats. Although the heroism of the crews is taught in all Russian schools and veterans have received medals from the Russian government, they have felt slighted by the British so the public tribute paid to them by the Queen's own son was regarded as particularly important. In these acts of respect he is maintaining a tradition he began in 1979 when he went with his parents to pay his respects to the men who served in the King's Own

---

[64] Interview with ITN, 14th February, 2010

African Rifles, a unit which had casualty rates of a fifth in the First World War.

The Duke is a firm believer in the importance of memorials, both as a reminder of the sacrifices made for the freedom we have today but also as a focus for those who mourn, be they family or members of the armed services themselves. He is very aware of the mental scars left by war. In 2002, it was revealed that the number of suicides amongst Falklands veterans had exceeded the number killed during the war.[65] That same year, he travelled to the Falklands where he laid wreaths to remember those lost on both sides. He described it as being "emotionally healing" for himself and said that he now felt it was time to look forward.[66] Admitting "I don't wake up at night screaming. It affects people in different ways" he spoke of the importance of being able to talk about things with friends who were there rather than outside counsellors wherever possible.[67] In 2011, he praised the National Arboretum for providing just this sort of focus and meeting point for people in the UK which he said was particularly important given that many monuments were miles away overseas and hard to reach.

Away from his charity and military work, His Royal Highness is the first Duke of York to have made a conscious commitment to the area represented by his title. He visits the county on average five times a year undertaking four or more engagements on each trip encompassing a wide variety of organisations. For example in 2006 he visited O2 in Leeds to see not only the company but how telecommunications were benefiting the city economy. He visited the Get Sorted Academy, a music charity in Rotherham aiming to provide lessons to those who might otherwise not have the chance and organising workshops to boost confidence and channel self expression. He went to see the Archbishop of York to discuss the restoration of York Minster, a campaign which the Duke had actively supported for some time, and the work of the church in communities across the county. He visited the Yorkshire Air Ambulance in Halifax which typically flies over a thousand missions a year to learn about the challenges it faced in its work. He spent time at the Springboard Business Centre in Stokesley which had been set up to provide serviced office space to start up technology companies plus conferencing facilities for hire. He went to St Williams College in York and attended a meeting with business leaders in Sheffield. He visited the legal firm DLA Piper and the recently opened test and research facilities of Castings Technology International. He toured the Ryedale Folk Museum

---

[65] Mary Spencer, 'Suicide Claiming more British Falkland veterans than fighting did' in *Canadian Medical Association Journal*, vol. 166 no 11 (28th May 2002) p.1453

[66] *The Times*, 11th November, 2002

[67] *Majesty Magazine*, vol. 24 no 1 January 2003 p.49. The same view was expressed by Ralph Wykes-Snead in his interview for the Imperial War Museum, op.cit.

which had won an award in 2003 for Heritage Education for its hands on approach to teaching history and which was playing a major role in building conservation. His final visit was to Asian Trades Link in Bradford, an organisation supporting start up businesses, training, apprenticeships, job fairs and also encouraging networking and community relations.[68]

In 1997, he founded the Duke of York's Community Initiative to foster the development of local schemes to meet local needs.[69] Over the years it has given awards to over two hundred groups in recognition of the work which they do. These cover a wide variety of projects including a charity working with the homeless in Leeds, a group helping children with special needs in York and another supporting the elderly in Batley, day nurseries in Hull, Harrogate Hospital Radio, a group promoting environmental improvement in Conisbrough, people trying to restore and support places such as the Abbeydale Picture House and Middleton Railway and those seeking to encourage enjoyment of all that the county has to offer, such as the Crookstone Adventure Trust or Scuba Diving for All in Ripon or Barwick in Bloom. The Initiative aims to recognise those schemes which have achieved a high standard with regard both the work they do and the way they are organised, and to assist other groups in attaining this level. To this end, support is offered in areas such as financial management and social sustainability through workshops and mentoring programmes. The Duke makes an effort to distribute awards in person and takes a keen interest in all the various schemes. He clearly enjoys spending time in the county commenting: "There is something about Yorkshire that makes people know they are somewhere special."[70]

The Duke is, however, best known for his involvement in business affairs. In 2001, when he completed his naval service, he was invited by Peter Mandelson, to take on the role of supporting the development of UK trade and investment at home and overseas.[71] This ambassadorial position was totally unpaid, though expenses were covered which was only fair given that visits were carried out at the behest of the government. The previous holder was the Duke of Kent who had carried out the duties alongside his other charitable and military commitments and they did not appear onerous. In 2000, the Duke of Kent undertook fifty-five trade related engagements of which forty-five were overseas. Prince Andrew, immediately, infused new energy into the role and in his first year on the job carried out one hundred and seventy seven trade related engagements.

---

[68] In 2006, the Duke visited the county on 19th April, 17th May and 22nd September.
[69] Charity registration 1119460
[70] *Yorkshire Post*, 15th June, 2005
[71] *Daily Mail*, 31st March 2011

By 2009-10, he was carrying out five hundred and fifty trade-related engagements and making contact with three thousand companies a year.[72] As he said: "If I'm asked to do something then I'll go and do it to the best of my ability if I have the capability to do it."[73]

There were a number of reasons why the Duke was selected for the role. In the first place, he had made an excellent impression on his previous overseas tours. The Canadian Minister Gerald Merrithew said: "Prince Andrew is a great ambassador for Britain and an asset to the royal family. He should be used more, he's got great charisma."[74] The editor of the *Sunday Express*, Sir John Junor wrote: "He is a one off. A fizzer with clearly an enormous potential for leadership. We are out of our minds if we make him spend most of the rest of his life walking around, hands behind his back, opening church bazaars." [75] Secondly, he had diplomatic experience and an understanding of government processes through his years working at the Ministry of Defence. Thirdly, as a member of the royal family, he had the ability to open doors and garner important publicity for business in a way that the most experienced entrepreneur or official could never do. Reviewing the role in 2010, he said that the royal family had: "a greater ability to be able to help people not only here in the UK but also globally and I believe very, very strongly that we have a sense of duty and a sense of responsibility. I've taken on the business community in this country as a champion for them and I believe its very important that they should get the best advantages and the best opportunities because our competitors in other nations will do exactly the same thing and if we don't get out there and help them, there aren't very many other people who will."[76] Fourthly, there was his own sense of dedication and his enthusiasm. He made no pretence to be an economic expert at the start but he worked hard to increase his understanding of different industries and business processes. He told Sky News that "the real people who are actually making the UK what it is are the people who are doing business" which meant that it was his patriotic duty to support it.[77] The fact that he was also willing to do the work for nothing, must also have been seen as an advantage in government circles.

Although the extent of the role has grown over the years – the increased demand itself a testament to how business has perceived the benefit to be gained from his involvement – the nature of the role has not. The Duke

---

[72] Annual Report, 2009-2010 p.4

[73] Interview with ITN 14th February, 2010

[74] *Majesty Magazine,* vol 6 no 5 September 1985 p.23

[75] *Majesty Magazine,* vol 4 no 7 November 1983 p.19

[76] Interview with David Frost in *Frost over the World,* 16th May 2008

[77] *Sky News,* 5th Feb 2008

himself listed the responsibilities as follows:

- strengthening bilateral relations with heads of state and heads of governments;
- visiting businesses large and small in their own environment, listening to their views and representing these back to the UK Government
- receiving business leaders and co-ordinating campaigns to win business in overseas markets
- hosting business events and receiving inward visiting leaders and business delegations at Buckingham Palace[78]

Or as he put it in a speech to the Confederation of Indian Industry in Calcutta:

In my role as the United Kingdom's Special Representative for International Trade and Investment I seek to help UK business grow and succeed in an increasingly competitive and global economy. In this role I also encourage overseas companies who are possibly, or should be, planning to invest overseas to base themselves in the UK which gives you the best access to the largest market in the world, the European Union.

A key part of the role revolves around his own communication skills. At the World Economic Forum in Davos in 2008, he told CNN: "I've built up a network of contacts both in business and in government. I've also built a large international relationship field and Her Majesty's government have been saying to me please continue to build those relationships and to work them because we need to know what people are thinking. My role is to make sure that those flows of communication are as good if not better today than they have been in the past....There is a danger that if we don't consider the international community and the fact that we are an international trader that we risk perhaps poorly co-ordinated economic actions."

In practical terms, the job involves not just meeting people and introducing them to one another, but visiting companies across the globe, talking to ministers, and supporting British expatriates working overseas. Over five and a half million Britons work in the countries visited by the Duke.[79] There is also a considerable amount of time spent behind the scenes in report writing, research and speech writing, the Duke taking care of the

---

[78] Annual Review, 2008-2009 p.1

[79] See Catherine Drew and Danny Sriskandarajah, *Brits Abroad: Mapping the scale and nature of British emigration,* (London, 2006)

latter in person. Although His Royal Highness has no role in actual contract negotiations, he does make a very real contribution to business growth. There is no doubt that the decision by Saudi Arabia to purchase Hawk trainer jets in May 2012, a contract worth almost two billion pounds, was helped by the Duke's promotion of the British supplier. The deal safeguarded more than two hundred jobs and will hopefully lead to the creation of new jobs in the future.[80] In a similar vein, the Duke was responsible for persuading AirAsia to spend over £2.6 billion in buying Rolls Royce engines and Airbus jetliners, a decision which was a significant boost to UK manufacturing.[81] Abacus Lighting, based in Nottingham and specialists in outdoor and stadium illumination, have directly attributed their growth in China to the Duke's inspiration, ideas and contacts which generated new business opportunities which they were able to capitalise upon due to the calibre of their own product and service.[82] Union Electric Steel Limited said that the Duke's positive promotion of their work had helped them win a large order in Mexico.[83] Benoy, attributed the winning of contracts in the Middle East worth more than five billion pounds, to his assistance, contracts which naturally have created jobs for British people. The Chief Executive of Serco said: "As a result of the Duke of York's very significant help we have won a four hundred million pound contract to operate the new Dubai Metro. His ability to skilfully establish and develop strong relationships in this important market has been very helpful." Jobs have also been created in the UK by overseas companies choosing to invest here following the Duke's encouragement for them to do so. This has particularly been the case with financial services but has also affected manufacturing. His visits to Thailand were influential in persuading Sahaviriya Steel Industries to purchase and reopen steelworks on Teeside creating a thousand new jobs and safeguarding seven hundred more.[84] Every day too, millions of people around the globe access music on Youtube without realising the Duke's key role in ensuring its availability through his assistance to Audio Network.[85]

Although the Duke's involvement has covered a whole range of industries, he has made a special focus in some areas. His own military links have given him a deep interest and understanding of the defence industry. Over the years he has visited most of the major defence companies including Thales, BAe, Northrop Grumman, EADS, Lockheed Martin and

---

[80] BBC News, 23rd May 2012

[81] Annual Review, 2009-2010 p.7, *Daily Mail,* 20th June, 2009.

[82] Reports on the Duke's visits to Abacus appear on the company's website www.abacuslighting.com

[83] *The Journal,* 21st October 2011

[84] *Northern Echo,* 5th March, 2012

[85] *Annual Review* 2010-2011 p.9

Goodrich Sensors. The defence industry is worth thirty-five billion pounds a year to the UK economy and employs three hundred thousand people, a tenth of British manufacturing.[86] He has been actively involved in motor sports, both the establishment of British teams and supporting the engineering behind them. This is an industry in which the UK leads the world and it is worth more than five hundred million pounds a year to the national economy, employing thousands of people.[87] In 2010 he opened the new Silverstone Circuit and had a ride with ex F1 World Champion, Damon Hill, describing it as "an extraordinary experience. I likened it to sitting in the back seat of a tornado at low level."[88]

Education has been another area of focus. Often overlooked in favour of more traditional industries, education is worth almost thirty billion pounds a year to the UK economy.[89] The Duke has visited countless British schools and universities overseas from Uruguay to the Philippines. He claimed on a visit to Wellington College in November 2010 that a British education was the best in the world and the number of students in places such as China, India, Singapore and Malaysia who select to take UK degrees indicates that he is not alone in this opinion. For example, by this date, more than eighty British universities offered Malaysian students the chance to study for a British qualification in Malaysia whilst a further twelve thousand Malaysians travelled to study in the UK itself. Education has been a growth industry, even during the recession. Vietnam now has a British owned university and in October 2010 the Duke launched his own scholarship programme there to promote business development.[90] Amongst the many international projects he has encouraged has been the neuroscience research collaboration between the University of Warwick and Nanyang Technological University, the Clinical Research Unit in Vietnam sponsored by the University of Oxford and the Wellcome Institute and the creation of the world's largest telescope by scientists at Jodrell Bank.

A key interest of the Duke's over recent years has been the promotion of renewable energy, a subject with which he first became associated in 2007 and about which he is very well informed. In 2010 he visited the Sustainable Energy Research Group at the University of Southampton and he has inspected projects around the world which aim to develop new energy technologies and to reduce emissions. He attended a series of meetings at

---

[86] *The Telegraph,* 7th January, 2011

[87] BBC News, 28th June, 2011.

[88] *Reuters News,* 29th April, 2010. Damon Hill was son of Graham Hill who had previously tutored the Duke.

[89] Pamela Lenton, Global Value: The Value of UK Education and Training Exports, (2007) p.4

[90] This offers four students each year a chance to earn a BA in Marketing Management or International Business Management awarded by Staffordshire University

the University of Strathclyde in 2011 and spent a day on the Orkneys reviewing wave and tidal energy projects plus another similar day in Northern Ireland. He is currently involved with the promotion of coastal wind farms. In a speech to the World Future Energy Summit, the Duke said: "We are at a crossroads of evolution; ....We live in an increasingly global society and as citizens of the world, it is important that we all work together to ensure we can stabilise emissions in order that the health of our planet remains capable of sustaining our life form otherwise it will mean the extinction of the human species rather than the end of the world."[91]

Although his elder brother receives considerably more publicity for his pronouncements on environmental subjects, the Duke has not been deficient. In 2007 he visited Brazil for a series of business meetings covering oil, meat, medical care, education, investment and financial services. He also went on a tour to see the effects of deforestation and he was so appalled that he went to lobby the Prime Minister in person about the subject and to ask him to fund creation of a highly sophisticated satellite based camera to monitor and expose illegal logging in the Amazon basin and congo. This was duly agreed with the work being carried out in Great Britain. Professor Richard Holdaway, director of Space Science and Technology at Rutherford Appleton Laboratory, said: "It was definitely the Duke of York who opened doors. Without his very very strong support this wouldn't have happened."[92]

From 2002 to 2011, he made on average twenty-two overseas trips per year, though not all were related to his trade role. Some were to troops serving overseas or to visit disaster zones. His schedule at times verged on the ridiculous. On one occasion, he flew in from America after a five day trip, and the same day departed for a three day trip to Bulgaria.[93] In another week, he had twenty four engagements spread across Cornwall, Northern Ireland, London, the Isle of Man, Canada and Dorset.[94] In January 2011, he carried out twenty-nine trade engagements in two days in a day that left barely half an hour free.

His international role has often been misunderstood, particularly by the media. A typical example of this came in *The People* who announced late in 2004 that the "fun loving" Duke was enjoying a "hectic five weeks of freebies at the taxpayers expense" the purpose of which were "lavish dinners in Moscow followed by a luxury alpine trip to Switzerland and Italy before

---

[91] 21st January, 2008

[92] *The Guardian*, 27th April 2009

[93] 17th October, 2001

[94] Week commencing 14th October 2008. On four of the days, engagements extended from morning to evening.

escaping winter bound Britain for a sun-kissed twelve day tour of the Far East."[95] In fact, the engagements in Switzerland and Italy were carried out on a single day and involved opening a UK trade fair and attending an Emissions Trading Seminar. The trip to the Far East was so that he could visit members of the Royal Gurkha Regiment, open new facilities for the Outward Bound charity, attend an official event in support of the London 2012 Olympics bid, tour the Centre for Renewable Energy in Manila and meet researchers in malaria at the University of Sarawak who were working as part of an international effort to reduce deaths. Although malaria is not a killer in the UK, it is responsible for the deaths of around 725,000 people across the Commonwealth every year, over half being infants and more than a third adults.[96] The three day trip to Russia had a combined humanitarian and business focus. The Duke visited TNK-BP, one of the largest oil companies in the world and responsible for a quarter of the oil produced by BP. It was an example of international co-operation uniting British technology with Russian resources and a chance to meet expatriate British workers as well as to encourage future investment. He went on to deliver donations collected by British industry for the Taganka Children's Project which aimed to support families with disabled children and spent some hours in the Moscow hospital visiting seriously injured children who had been taken there following the Beslan school massacre. A few weeks before, armed Chechnyan rebels had taken over a thousand prisoners at Beslan in North Ossetia, of which more than seven hundred and seventy were children. Security forces had gone in to try to break the siege and in the battle which followed, more than three hundred people had been killed – over half of them children – and many more had been badly injured. The Duke was there to meet those affected and to talk to the medical staff, in particular seeking to discover what more Great Britain could do to help. It was a harrowing experience and an aide described the Duke as "deeply shocked."[97] To have the media dismiss the visit as if it was a fun filled holiday would have been deeply depressing to most people but the Duke is stoical about this sort of thing. In an interview to celebrate his fiftieth birthday, he told Sky News: "If you live in that goldfish bowl and you are a public figure then to a certain extent you've got to expect somebody to throw stones and then you've just got to live with it."

Yet, the figures speak for themselves. As Special Representative, the Duke visited seventy-two different countries but his efforts were

---

[95] *The People*, 14th November, 2004

[96] See Christopher Murray et al.,'Global malaria mortality between 1980 and 2010: a systemic analysis' in *The Lancet,* vol 379 issue 9814 (4th February 2012) pp.413-431. World deaths average 1.3 million per annum. Work on malaria is partly funded by the Wellcome Trust in London.

[97] *The Sun*, 23rd October, 2004

concentrated in Asia, the Middle East and Eastern Europe. Over the decade, he made nine visits to China, four to India, five to Malaysia, three to Mongolia, seven to Singapore and four each to Thailand and Vietnam. In the same period, exports to the countries he visited from the UK rose by 237% compared to an increase of 68% in countries not visited. Similarly, imports from those countries rose by 210% compared to 19% of those not visited. In the Middle East, he visited Algeria twice, Egypt four times, Jordan and Oman three times, Kuwait six times, Qatar nine times, Saudi Arabia nine times, Bahrain twelve times and the United Arab Emirates on fifteen occasions. Exports from the UK to those countries rose by 142% compared to a decline of 30% to other countries in the region who were not visited. Imports from countries visited increased by 329% whereas those not visited rose by just 31%. In Eastern Europe he visited Azerbaijan seven times, Kazakhstan four times, Russia five times, Turkmenistan twice and Ukraine on three occasions. Exports to these countries rose by 381% compared to 134% in non-visited countries. Imports rose by 277% compared to a 242% increase in the other countries in the sector. Although these spectacular results and the benefit to the UK economy which followed cannot be attributed to the Duke's efforts alone, it suggests that the impact of sending a royal representative to these areas in a focussed manner is extremely beneficial.[98] It is also worth noting that the twenty-seven billion pounds increase in exports is some seven thousand times the cost of the Duke's expenses.[99]

Looking at the situation in the UK, there is a similar pattern. Of all the UK based manufacturing companies visited by the Duke in 2006, but excluding the large multinationals, ninety-four per cent increased their turnover in the year following and this by an average of a third. Eighty per cent of companies found it necessary to take on more staff, resulting in five hundred and ninety five jobs being created. Half of the companies who had never exported before achieved that goal within a year of the visit with a third more becoming exporters a year later. Overall, exports in the first year increased by twenty per cent which compares to a national decline of ten per

---

[98] Data concerning the Duke's visits appears in the Court Circular. The trade figures are taken from the Office of National Statistics table of imports and exports based on SITC Code.

[99] *The Telegraph*, 7th March 2011 reported that in ten years as Special Representative, the Duke's travel expenses had amounted to four million pounds with an extra ten million pounds spent on security. The UKTI website publishes its accounts online and these show that in 2011 alone, it spent almost three million on travel and subsistence. The Foreign Secretary, William Hague, spent £275,000 on private jets on a single three day overseas trip in February 2011 which was more than three quarters the amount that the Duke spent in the entire year when he carried out ten overseas tours, see *Daily Mirror*, 18th March 2011. Concerns have also been expressed about ministers using RAF jets to take them to party conferences or to visit their constituencies, see *The Telegraph*, 12th April, 2006.

cent.[100] The worst recession in almost eighty years began in 2008 and this inevitably had an impact, though it hit different companies and different industries at different times. Five years after the Duke's visit, three companies had closed and one had been sold and was trading under new ownership, yet forty-four per cent of companies were still increasing their number of employees and seventy per cent were still growing. One company had grown almost fourfold and another ninefold.[101] Again, it is impossible to determine what the results would have been without a royal visit, but the rate of growth is substantially above the normal. From 2006 to 2010, the manufacturing sector as a whole saw average turnover decline by nineteen per cent and overall employment by twenty four per cent.[102]

As part of his work at home and abroad, the Duke receives regular visits from government ministers and members of the Shadow Cabinet and attends briefings with government departments, particularly those related to defence, trade, energy and education. He also attends seminars at RUSI. Although these connections are vital for his activities, they can be dangerous. The royal family is completely separate from the political system and it must remain so. His Royal Highness once described the role of the Queen as being: "almost a responsibility for all the people of the United Kingdom, regardless of race, colour or creed, and an understanding that you have an individual connection with each and every one."[103] The Duke, in support of British trade, has been asked to visit a number of countries and meet various people who have subsequently fallen from grace. A notable example of this was his meeting with the Libyan leader, Colonel Gaddafi on 21st November, 2008. This visit was arranged following the "deal in the desert" made by the Colonel and the British Prime Minister, Tony Blair. At the time, the belief was that Libya would be a valuable ally in the war against terrorism and to this end, Blair agreed to lift the arms embargo and to promote trade between the two countries. Prince Andrew was sent to facilitate this economic link and within three years, one hundred and fifty British firms were operating in Libya. However, by 2011 the political situation had changed and the British government, now led by David Cameron, was actively supporting rebel insurgents in their campaign to topple Colonel Gaddafi who was now seen as an evil dictator running an oppressive regime. The Duke, who had met the Colonel at the previous government's request, found himself being criticised for having friendly

---

[100] Office of National Statistics table of exports based on SITC Code.

[101] Data was calculated using accounts lodged and publicly available at Companies House. The names of companies visited appeared in the Court Circular.

[102] Office of National Statistics Annual Business Surveys

[103] *Time Magazine*, 9th April, 2006. As Queen of sixteen different countries, Her Majesty has the same responsibilities for people from Australia to Canada

relations with what was now regarded as an enemy power. [104]

In the spring of 2011, the Duke became the centre of a media furore when it was revealed that he was a friend of the American financier Jeffrey Epstein. This in itself was not news because articles had referenced the relationship more than a decade earlier, however, at the time the Duke met Epstein, he was just known for his business career. By 2011, Epstein was a convicted paedophile who had served time for encouraging under-age girls into prostitution. There was no suggestion whatsoever that the Duke had been involved in these activities but it was a massive embarrassment to someone who not only spent much of his time representing the country abroad but who had also been the figurehead of the NSPCC Full Stop campaign and devoted much of his life to encouraging young people. For the Duke as a devout Christian, he had maintained his friendship with Epstein because he believed in forgiving the sinner whilst continuing to hate the sin, but he did admit that the meeting had been "unwise" because it was subject to misinterpretation.

The media called for the Duke to be stripped of his trade role and in the summer they trumpeted that he had responded to their demands and stepped down when they read his official press release: "I have decided that the label I gave myself when I began this role of Special Representative has served its purpose and is no longer necessary to the work." Yet they had failed to read the document in full where he said that he was simply widening his role to reflect evolving economic needs and "I will of course continue to work internationally promoting the UK in key markets." To this end he would be encouraging science and engineering "because they are a key part of the innovation and entrepreneurship that is required to create the ideas, opportunities and resources for our young people and businesses to thrive and prosper", promoting training and apprenticeships, supporting the development of high tech and high value manufacturing, increasing the recognition of innovation and business excellence, ensuring SMEs are aware of the opportunities that exist to develop their businesses internationally and making certain that UK businesses can derive the utmost benefit of the Olympics.[105] Current projects include helping British companies obtain a share of the work involved in rebuilding the transport infrastructure of St Petersburg and the export of British medical expertise to the developing world.

Reflecting his interest in science and technology, the Duke has also been active recently in the promotion of graphene, a product developed at the

---

[104] *The Telegraph*, 28th February, 2011
[105] *Annual Review* 2010-11 pp.3-4

University of Manchester and which earned those responsible the Nobel Prize for Physics in 2010. The Duke visited the University in 2011 and 2012 and highlighted graphene's potential for technological change across many industries and the opportunity it presented for boosting the economy of the area and the UK as a whole.[106] In December 2012, the government responded with a multi-million pound investment toward commercialising graphene and researching its application.

Since the furore died down, the Duke has continued his work. He remains totally dedicated to his promotion of this country and to the good causes with which he is associated. He is also committed to the principal of openness, maintaining a website which details his work and publishing an Annual Report, something which makes him virtually unique within the royal family. His enthusiasm for his chosen subject is undimmed and his constant refrain when visiting firms is "what are the messages I need to take away?" and "what else can I do? What else is required?"[107] An example of this came in his visit to Byotrol where he was shown an innovative cleansing gel which retained its efficacy even when dry and was believed to protect against MRSA. The Duke agreed that it had huge potential in the National Health Service to save lives and to reduce the costs and distress caused by infection, and immediately volunteered to ensure the firm were connected to the appropriate people.[108]

In all his roles, be that supporting the Queen or industry or serving as patron of a charity or Colonel-in-Chief of a regiment, the Duke has showed dedication. He has not always got things right as he himself observed in a speech to the Gordonstoun Association: "I will not disguise or make excuses for the fact that I did not do as well as I might have done"[109] The media have chosen to concentrate on every flaw and to ignore every achievement but as President Theodore Roosevelt once wrote:

> It is not the critic who counts: not the man who points out how the strong man stumbles or where the doer of deeds could have done better. The credit belongs to the man who is actually in the arena, whose face is marred by dust and sweat and blood, who strives valiantly, who errs and comes up short again and again, ... who spends himself for a worthy cause....[110]

---

[106] *Manchester Evening News,* 17th October 2011 and 16th February, 2012

[107] *Wall Street Journal,* 11th October 2011

[108] *Manchester Evening News,* 17th October 2011

[109] *Majesty Magazine,* vol 5 no 2 June 1984 p.9

[110] Speech at the Sorbonne, 23rd April, 1910

Or as Bishop Magee more succinctly put it: "The man who makes no mistakes does not usually make anything."

The Duke is content to leave people to say what they like for he has his duty to perform and he intends to carry on doing that as long as he draws breath. He is very like his father in many ways; he has little time for pomposity or political correctness and is impatient of red tape. He has incredible energy and enthusiasm for life and he enjoys a joke. Like both his parents, he has a deep rooted sense of public service and a great care for people. He commented upon the Queen's Diamond Jubilee that he had learnt compassion and responsibility from his mother and duty and discipline from his father.[111] Unless he has a son, Prince Andrew will be the last Duke of York for some years but his record stands proudly with those of his illustrious predecessors and there is no doubt that the country is in his debt.

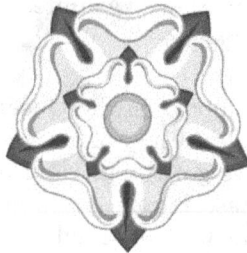

---

[111] Interview with Alan Titchmarsh in *Elizabeth: Queen, Wife, Mother*, ITV, 1st June, 2012

www.ingramcontent.com/pod-product-compliance
Lightning Source LLC
Chambersburg PA
CBHW070858140426
R18135300001B/R181353PG42812CBX00002B/3